Research on Social Movements

The student mobilizations of the 1960s were followed by various protest movements and increasing interest in the systematic analyses of such phenomena. These studies and the debates associated with them, however, are typically restricted to national perspectives to the neglect of important and relevant work done elsewhere. This book offers an international survey of the state-of-the-art of social movement research. It is composed of country-specific reports on theoretical and methodological questions, relevant empirical findings, and institutional aspects of research. The volume addresses on-going controversies, including the debates on the resource mobilization and new social movements approaches, and it offers a general assessment of the strengths and weaknesses of this field of study. Each report is accompanied by an annotated bibliography.

Dieter Rucht is a fellow at the Social Science Research Center Berlin. He has co-authored several books published by Campus Verlag. He co-edited (together with Roland Roth) a book on New Social Movements in the Federal Republic of Germany, 1987.

Dieter Rucht (Editor)

Research on Social Movements

The State of the Art in Western Europe and the USA

Campus Verlag · Frankfurt am Main
Westview Press · Boulder, Colorado

Published in 1991 in the United States by WESTVIEW PRESS
Frederick A. Praeger, Publisher
5500 Central Avenue
Boulder, Colorado

Library of Congress Cataloging-in-Publication Data

Research on social movements / edited by Dieter Rucht.
p.cm.
ISBN 0-8133-1163-2
1. Social movements--Research. I. Rucht, Dieter.
HN29. R43 1990
303,48'4' 072--dc20 90-12777
CIP

Die Deutsche Bibliothek – CIP-Einheitsaufnahme

Research on social movements: the state of the art in Western Europe and the USA/Dieter Rucht (ed.). - Frankfurt am Main : Campus Verlag; Boulder, Colo.: Westview Press, 1991
ISBN 3-593-34298-7 (Campus Verlag)
ISBN 0-8133-1163-2 (Westview Press)
NE: Rucht, Dieter (Hrsg.)

Printed in West Germany

Table of Contents

List of Contributors

Jenny Chapman:
Department of Government, University of Strathclyde

Mario Diani:
Università Commerciale Luigi Bocconi, Milan

Peter Gundelach:
Department of Political Science, University of Aarhus

Ron Eyerman:
Department of Sociology, University of Lund

Andrew Jamison:
Research Policy Institute, University of Lund

Bert Klandermans:
Department of Social Psychology, Free University of Amsterdam

Herbert Kitschelt:
Department of Political Science, Duke University, Durham

Hanspeter Kriesi:
Department of Political Science, University of Geneva

Philip D. Lowe:
Bartlett School of Architecture, University College London

Margit Mayer:
Department of Political Science, Free University of Berlin

Alberto Melucci:
Department of Sociology, University of Trento

James Mitchell:
Department of Government, University of Strathclyde

Friedhelm Neidhardt:
Science Center Berlin for Social Research

Anton Pelinka:
Institute for Political Science, University of Innsbruck

Philip van Praag, Jr.:
Department of Political and Social Sciences, University of Amsterdam

Wolfgang Rüdig:
Department of Government, University of Strathclyde

Dieter Rucht:
Social Science Research Center Berlin

Sidney Tarrow:
Department of Political Science, Cornell University

Alain Touraine:
Maison des Sciences de l'Homme, Paris

Mayer N. Zald:
Department of Sociology, University of Michigan

Preface

Dieter Rucht

From the mid-sixties onward, many advanced Western countries experienced waves of various protest activities and social movements. Among the most significant were the student movement, the women's movement, the antinuclear and environmental movement and the peace movement. Despite the diversity of issues around which these movements were organized, their followers shared certain common concerns. Chief among these were their quest for more political participation and autonomy, their critique of centralized and bureaucratized apparatuses, and their skepticism about a one-sided concept of progress which stressed economic growth while ignoring its negative side effects.

Social scientists, many of them sympathetic to these movements, soon began to analyze the growing protest activities. There is by now a large body of literature providing both new concepts and paradigms and a wealth of empirical findings. In the US particularly, conventional ideas about collective behavior have been challenged; the focus of interest shifted definitively from this broader field to that of social movements. During the 1970s a new approach, the so-called resource mobilization theory, took shape. In contrast to earlier mainstream perceptions of social movements, this approach stressed the rational and organized character of social movement activities. And in contrast to earlier assumptions, the followers of social movements were no longer perceived as consisting mainly of disparate and alienated masses. Also, the once constitutive, conceptual boundary between conventional and unconventional behavior became blurred and protest tended to be acknowledged as a rather normal phenomenon of social and political life. Concepts of rational choice and the sociology of organizations were established. As a consequence, social scientists perceived protest movements as similar or equal to conventional interest groups and voluntary associations, although there was always an element of radical grassroots organization which did not fit the model of pressure group politics.

In Western Europe, the development of the study of social movements can hardly be described in terms of a major paradigmatic change. In line with its highly diverse cultural and scientific traditions, the study of social movements in various countries also followed very different courses and patterns. If one contrasts the situation in the USA with that in Europe, however, some features that are common to most heterogenous European approaches become apparent, in particular the search for the relationship between social movements and broader social change as a central point of reference. But this aspect is by no means new; it was already prevalent in the 19th century. Connected to this is a more recent trend in Europe: the ideal that all these aforementioned heterogenous movements are part of an overarching, though internally subdivided, phenomenon which has become known as »new social movements«. Although many observers stress the differences between and within the various movements, or emphasize the parallels to earlier movements, some analysts promote the idea that the new social movements herald a new societal type. In their most speculative forms, these concepts of new social movements theorize that these groupings will assume the central role that the labor movement and the liberal-bourgeois movement had in earlier societies.

As usual, behind such a crude sketch of a field of study we can expect a highly differentiated and complex world which can hardly be comprehensively surveyed by one person from a specific country. With particular regard to such social phenonema as movements which seem to be ubiquitous, but hard to grasp, it is difficult to keep informed about the state of knowledge and ongoing research. In that case, even specialists usually have only a selective knowledge of the field. In comparison to subdisciplines of, say, medicine or physics, which are well coordinated on the national and international levels and have their own established institutes, journals and congresses, the field of social movements is underdeveloped. This is due not only to a lack of organizational resources and coordination, but also to the specificities of the research object: its vague contours, its multi-facetted nature, and its dependency on temporal and spatial circumstances. Moreover, language barriers come into play. To be sure, within a given country those people working on social movements for a longer period of time usually have knowledge of the each other's work or even meet from time to time. But there may be fascinating studies written in Dutch or Italian unknown to a

French or English scholar. And from the standpoint of an American researcher, it may be still more difficult to have a close look at the debates in this broad range of Western European countries.

It was precisely the perception of a need for improved exchange and understanding of past and present research on social movements in various countries which was the driving motive for producing this volume. Some social scientists in Western Europe felt that need in the early 1980s when they launched a series of meetings of an autonomous study group on »new social movements«. This group was loosely affiliated with the *European Group for Organizational Studies*. Together with my German colleagues Wilfried Nelles and Dirk Gerdes I had the chance to organize the third workshop of that study group in the Summer of 1985 in Bonn. Becoming aware of how ignorant we were with regard to discussions and research in many countries which were or were not represented at the meeting, we came up with the idea to edit a volume designed to reduce this gap. The core of this volume was to be a collection of overviews of social movement research from various countries. But from the idea to its realization there was a long way.

The design for this book had taken shape already by the end of 1985. Though we decided to organize the book around these country reports, we did not want it to be limited to that aspect. In particular, we were also interested in a more general debate and assessment beyond national boundaries and particular schools of thought.

As for the selection of countries, it was clear that the integration of Third World regions would be beyond the scope of this book and our organizational capacities.[1] On the other hand, it was evident that by no means should one neglect the USA, the country where – certainly in quantitative and probably also in qualitative terms – the most significant research on social movements has been carried out. (This also explains why this country report occupies much more space than any other.) With respect to European countries, we made a deliberate choice to focus on the Western part of the continent. Of course, in the light of the dramatic changes in Eastern Europe since Summer 1989, we would have preferred not to exclude these countries. Meanwhile, as we learned, the interest in movements in Eastern European

---

1 For a recent work on one Third World area, see Susan Eckstain (ed.). *Power and Popular Protest. Latin American Social Movements.* Berkeley: University of California Press 1989.

countries has exploded.[2] With regard to Western Europe, it was obvious that a selection had to be made. Although such a choice is arbitrary, and we admittedly had no hard criteria, a pragmatic selection was made along two lines: first, to integrate countries which, to our knowlege, are important both in terms of movement activities and corresponding studies; second, to include countries where we had or could establish contact with colleagues able to provide overview of the situation in their home countries. By and large, but with one major exception, our plans were realized. Regrettably, despite the long production phase, the report on France finally had to be dropped. The respective manuscript did not fulfill the requirements for this book, and it was too late to look for another author.

Several first drafts for the volume were written as early as 1986. For various reasons, however, some other drafts came in with a considerable delay. In two cases the original planned authorship was not held to; fortunately other authors took over the tasks. Moreover, Dirk Gerdes, who meanwhile has changed his professional field and became overburdened with other engagements, withdrew from the project.

Because this volume's first contribution, authored by Bert Klandermans, can be easily read as an introduction to the field and I share most of his observations and statements, I felt no need as an editor to write a separate introduction. Hence at this point I can limit my task to presenting only the outline of the book and to thank those who have contributed to it.

Apart from *Bert Klandermans*' introductory chapter, which presents an overview of recent European and American approaches to the study of social movements, the book consists of two parts. The first is devoted to the state of the art in nine selected countries. These include the USA (authored by *Margit Mayer*), Great Britain (*Wolfgang Rüdig, James Mitchell, Jenny Chapman*, and *Philip D. Lowe*), Italy (*Mario Diani* and *Alberto Melucci*), West Germany (*Dieter Rucht*), Switzerland (*Hanspeter Kriesi*), Austria (*Anton Pelinka*), Sweden (*Ron Eyerman* and *Andrew Jamison*), Denmark (*Peter Gundelach*) and The Netherlands (*Philip van Praag, Jr.*) As a service to those readers who might not be interested in all aspects of all selected countries, the authors of this part of the volume were urged to organize their chapters along a common framework, i.e. to refer to (1) theories, (2) meth-

2 For a collection of essays on Eastern movements before the »revolutionary« years, see Louis Kriesberg, Bronislaw Misztal with Janusz Mucha (eds.), *Social Movements as a Factor of Change in the Contemporary World.* Vol. 10 Research in Social Movements, Conflicts and Change, Greenwich, Conn.: JAI Press 1988.

ods, (3) empirical findings, (4) institutional aspects of research, (5) debates and, (6) to present an annotated bibliography. Although some of the authors found it difficult, most of them have followed these guidelines closely.

The second part of the volume is not devoted to specific countries. Here the intention was rather to discuss relevant approaches under various perspectives. In some sense, the first four essays in this part can be grouped together. For both the USA and Europe one outstanding approach – resource mobilization theory and new social movement theory, respectively – was selected as an object of discussion. On the one hand, *Herbert Kitschelt* presents his critique of the resource mobilization approach; *Mayer N. Zald*, a prominent promoter of this approach, responds to that critique. On the other hand, *Dieter Rucht* criticizes Touraine's version of (new) social movement theory and the related method. *Alain Touraine* shortly replies to that critique. A further contribution authored by *Sidney Tarrow* discusses European and American approaches in a more integrative perspective. Although this essay is relatively close to the concern of Klandermans' article, it puts special emphasis on comparative research as a useful method for studying social movements. In the concluding chapter, *Friedhelm Neidhardt* and *Dieter Rucht* present a comprehensive assessments of the state of the art with regard both to various country reports and general trends in the field. Here, the emphasis lies on advances and unsolved questions of social movement research.

As usual, a book like this one cannot be published without the collaboration and assistance of many people. First of all, I owe thanks to the contributors and in particular to their patience with me. I am also grateful to Dirk Gerdes who, as already mentioned, was originally supposed to co-edit this book. He was engaged not only in the state of planning, but also, in commenting on some of the early drafts. Third, a number of people gave me valuable assistance, among them Richard Rogers and Bruce Spear who, as native American English speakers, revised most of the manuscripts, Prinzessin zu Löwenstein and Katrin Haacke, who were helpful in organizational and technical matters, and Thomas Eller, who contributed to standardizing most of the manuscripts. Finally, I wish to thank the institution to which I am affiliated. The Wissenschaftszentrum Berlin für Sozialforschung, and especially the research unit »Öffentlichkeit und soziale Bewegung,« headed by Friedhelm Neidhardt, provided generous financial and organizational support for publication.

Berlin, June 1990 Dieter Rucht

Part I
Basic Approaches

New Social Movements and Resource Mobilization: The European and the American Approach Revisited

Bert Klandermans

Several years ago I wrote an article titled »New social movements and resource mobilization: The European and the American approach« (Klandermans 1986). This article emanated from my amazement over the fact that the social movement literature took such different directions on the two continents. The movements were the same: student movements, environmentalist movements, women's movements, and peace movements developed on both sides of the Atlantic Ocean. In Europe they were successors to large prewar movements such as the suffrage movement, the workers' movement, and more in general, socialism, communism and fascism. In the U.S. the civil rights movement was their most important predecessor. The theoretical approaches that developed, however, differed widely: While in the U.S. resource mobilization theory shifted attention from deprivation to the availability of resources to explain the rise of social movements, in Europe the »new social movement approach« came forward, which focused on the growth of new protest potentials resulting from the development of new grievances within the highly industrialized societies.

Characteristic of the poor communication between social scientists in these two parts of the world, it would take until the 80s before scholars in Europe became aware of resource mobilization theory, and it took even longer before the U.S. got to know the new social movement approach. I found this regrettable, not only from the point of view of the exchange of scientific knowledge, but more importantly because each of these approaches showed but one side of the coin. Taken separately, each of them offered an inadequate explanation for the rise of the movements of the 60s.

Five years have gone by since I wrote that article, years in which the landscape of social movement literature has changed considerably. Meetings between scholars from Europe and the U.S. were organized. Out of these meetings anthologies were published encompassing contributions from both sides (Katzenstein and Mueller 1987; Klandermans, Kriesi and Tarrow 1988; Dalton and Kuechler 1990). Consequently, the awareness of each others work grew rapidly. In the U.S. there is an increasing interest in the »new social movement« approach as witnessed by, indeed, critical discussions (Gamson 1990; McAdam, McCarthy and Zald 1988; Rochon 1988; Walsh 1988) or by the recent publication by an American publisher of Melucci's work (1989). In Europe new social movements were studied with resource mobilization's frame of reference (Huberts 1988; Klandermans and Oegema 1987; Van Noort 1988; Opp 1986, 1988) and scholars from a »new social movement« background started to include concepts of the resource mobilization approach in their analyses (Kriesi, 1989; Roth and Rucht 1987; Rucht 1989; Roth 1989). Equally important was the emergence of new themes stimulated by critical discussions of either approach to social movements: the social construction of protest and the embeddedness of social movement organizations in multi-organizational fields. As a consequence models of mobilization and participation became more dynamic, underscoring the necessity of lontitudinal research.

Time to revisit the original argument and to discuss the new themes that have emerged. Although I have provided detailed descriptions of resource mobilization and the new social movement approach in two earlier publications (Klandermans, 1986; Klandermans and Tarrow 1988), it is worthwhile for our present discussion to reiterate the distinguishing features of the two approaches since much of what I argued at that time in comparing the two is still valid. From there I will proceed with a discussion of the new directions the social movement field took. But I will set out by briefly summarizing the major characteristics of the four movements that served as points of reference for both approaches.

Social movements in Europe and the U.S.

In describing the four movements that wrote recent history I will confine myself for Europe to The Netherlands and West Germany, because recent survey studies are available about these countries.[1] The same movements developed in other European countries. They were similar in many respects to the movements in the Netherlands and West Germany, although there were differences as well (cf. Brand 1985; Cerny 1982; Kaltefleiter and Pfaltzgraff 1984; Kriesi 1985; Rochon 1988).

The dynamics of the four movements are remarkably similar in the three countries. The student movement grew up in all three countries in the mid-1960s. By the end of the decade, the women's movement and the environmental movement had arisen, and early in the 1980s the new peace movement appeared. The student movement is the only one of the four that no longer exists as such, but the women's movement and the peace movement has declined almost everywhere in its original form. The environmental movement is still very much alive.

The interrelations among different types of movements are equally striking. In the U.S. the student movement was preceded by the civil rights movement, which greatly influenced both it and the women's movement. The environmental movement was partly a result of the growth and radicalization of already existing organizations; the women's and the peace movements were revivals of movements that had earlier periods of mobilization that left important organizational legacies.

The student movement and (in the United States) the civil rights movement were the starting point for the others, not only because many members of these earlier movements joined later on the other movements, but also because the earlier movements invented new forms of action that the later movements employed. The women's movement and the environmental movement contributed greatly to the peace movement, as their overlapping activities and membership make clear.

West Germany was the first to experience the formation of a political party rooted in these movements: the »Grünen« (the Greens), a rainbow coalition of environmentalists, feminists, pacifists and other anti-establish-

---

1 This section is based on the following publications: *For the Netherlands*: Janssen & Voestermans 1978; Van der Loo, Snel & Van Steenbergen 1984; Briët, Klandermans & Kroon 1987; Klandermans & Oegema 1987a & b; Rochon 1988; Van Noort 1988. *For West Germany*: Brand 1985; Brand, Büsser & Rucht 1986; Ferree 1987; Mushaben 1983a & b; Roth and Rucht 1987; Rudig 1983; Rucht 1984a & b; Wasmuht 1989. *For the U.S.*: Barkan 1979; Benford 1984; Brand 1985; Ferree, 1987; Gitlin 1980; Heirich 1971; Lo 1982; Mitchell 1979, 1984; Oberschall 1978; Perrow 1979; Rochon 1988; Rucht 1984b; Rudig 1983; Wasmuht 1984.

ment groups. In the Netherlands, the movements aimed initially much more to influence political parties, while in the U.S. they tried to set up lobbies that would be as effective as possible. Recently however, Green parties were founded successfully in many European countries.

The *student movement* was a fundamentally antiauthorian movement aimed at achieving university reforms that would give students more power. But this was never its sole aim; it was also a movement against developments in our postindustrial age. It opposed the war in Vietnam, the university as a factory of knowledge, and the University's connections with business. Though it rapidly produced radical forms of action, its leaders also became skilled at using the media and other conventional resources to mobilize allies, and parts of this movement soon merged with older protest traditions.

In the U.S. the student movement brought the action techniques of the civil rights movement to the campus and also invented new ones (sit-ins, teach-ins, happenings, occupations of university buildings). More generally, it contributed a great deal to the »esthetification of protest« by surrounding its protest meetings with all sorts of artistic expressions and demonstrating that American students were shrewd users of the media – at least until the media got tired of them (Gitlin 1980; Oberschall 1980). From the U.S., the movement crossed the Atlantic to Europe. There the student movement was more successful than in the U.S. in achieving its demands for university reforms. Although European students stressed activities on the campus, the movement spread beyond the campuses more rapidly than it had across the Atlantic. Coordinating organizations played a key part in the student movement for a certain length of time. In the U.S. this was SDS (Students for a Democratic Society), in West Germany SDS (German Socialist Student Union), and in The Netherlands SVB (Student Union Movement). But in all three countries, internal ideological conflicts, cooptation and, in the U.S., government infiltration, as we now know, soon put an end to the movement as such.

The *environmental movement* in all three countries embraces groups ranging from conservative or at least moderate conservation organizations to radical organizations that are not averse to direct confrontations with the government. Parts of the movement have been in existence for quite some time, but have taken advantage of the growing public interest to become bolder and gain more members. And the movement not only accomodates several organizations. And the movement not only accomodates several organizations, it teems with single-issue initiatives: against the construction of a particular road, a runway or a pipeline, against large-scale urban development projects, soil or water pollution.

Antinuclear energy protests have been quite prominent in all the countries. In the U.S., antinuclear protests were initially highly legalistic involving court cases, appeals, and referenda. Success could be measured not in actual victories but in terms of delay: the construction of nuclear plants would be deferred so long that they became uneconomical and new information would cast doubt upon their safety. After the Three Mile Island disaster, utility companies throughout the country encountered financial trouble and state legislatures began to refuse licencies for the construction of new plants.

Radical tactics were frequently used by some elements of the ecological movement. Encouraged by the successful occupation of the construction site of a nuclear power plant in West Germany, the American movement occasionally used occupations as well. But it was in West Germany (and France) that the strategy of occupation was most commonly used. Protest against nuclear energy soon became more radical in The Netherlands too, where it focused on the issue of waste disposal.

But occupations and blockades of construction sites or plants ultimately proved to be a dead end in all the countries, for governments could muster much more physical power than the activists. Nevertheless, the movement succeeded in delaying or even preventing the construction of nuclear power sites in The Netherlands and Germany.

There are also important differences between the countries. In the U.S. we see a strong environmentalist lobby, with national organizations that make much use of direct mail campaigns for the mobilization of resources. The organization made particularly successful use of this when it looked like the Reagan administration was threatening all that had been gained in the field of environmental protection. The movement has a powerful lobby in the Netherlands as well. Environmental organizations have found their way far inside government machinery. Good relations with government agencies are a resource which is regularly tapped. The West German environmental movement, initially took a strong anti-established stand. It was nowhere near as institutionalized as it is in the U.S. and The Netherlands. Wherever a certain degree of institutionalization took place (for instance, in the founding of the Green political party) the danger of further institutionalization was a point of violent dispute. Recently, however, Rucht observed signals of institutionalization in the German environmental movement as well (1987).

The *women's movement*. Ferree (1987) distinguished between radical feminists, who take the oppression of women to be the root and image of all oppression, socialist feminists, who attempt to combine feminist insights with socialist programs, and liberal feminists, who stress self-determination and individual rights. All these elements are present in all three countries but in different proportions.

In the U.S., where the new wave of the women's movement begun earlier, liberal feminists constitute the mainstream, and the key organization is the National Organization for Women (NOW). It is »autonomous« in the sense that it is not dependent on a party, but much of its effort has gone into supporting political candidates. Neither West Germany nor the Netherlands has a similar coordinating organization, and their women's movements are divided between autonomous and party-connected, socialist and radical feminist organizations. In West Germany the term »feminist« refers only to the radical element of the women's movement.

The greater part of the women's movement in West Germany is autonomous, anti-hierarchical and highly decentralized. To a much greater extent than in the U.S., the West German movement works outside the system. Consequently it has only a weak grasp of politics. The Dutch movement occupies an intermediate position in this respect. On the one hand, its autonomous wing is well represented; on the other hand, thanks to their ties with political parties, important segments of the movement are capable of and willing to work within the system.

Despite the differences, the three movements still use many similar action forms. The American movement has been taken as an example in many respects by the movement in Europe. Consciousness-raising groups, women's networks, shelters, rape crisis centers are some of the practical measures Europeans have adopted from the American movement. Lobbying and electoral campaigns have become more important than the radically expressive forms of action which have, in any case, always been exaggerated in the media. A major outcome of the women's movement has been the prominence women have attained in related movements. The women of Greenham Common and the charismatic Petra Kelly were only the most visible examples of this development.

The *peace movement* had several of the same predecessors in all three countries: the ban-the-bomb movement and the anti-Vietnam War movement. More specific to West Germany were protests against German rearmament, and to the U.S. was test ban movement. The new peace movement that arose in the late 1970s and early 1980s now concentrates all its energies on nuclear disarmament.

We may speak of grass roots movements in all three countries, each movement exhibiting greater or lesser levels of institutionalization. These movements are, for the most part, unstructured, decentralized, extra-parliamentary, with strong internal organizations, rather than unified bureaucratic structures. The Dutch movement deviates somewhat from this pattern, but only in part. It has a centralized organization, though a modest one; the movement's real strength lies in the organization at the base.

The NATO decision to locate cruise missiles in Western Europe considerably accelerated the growth of all three European movements, and this growth manifested itself in the unprecendented demonstrations between 1981 and 1983. The American peace movement expanded around the same time but was aimed more at a general reduction of armaments and was reinforced by the simultaneous fear of involvement in Nicaragua, an issue with far less resonance in Europe. The Reagan administration's bellicose rhetoric stimulated the movement's rebirth in all four countries. The movements did not achieve directly their goals: forcing back the nuclear arms race. They have been very successful, however, in an indirect way by putting nuclear armament on the political agenda.

This was only a very brief survey of the four movements that have determined the political picture in highly industrialized western societies in the past two decades to such a large extent. Of course it does not pretend to be complete. It necessarily overlooks many differences which exist between the movements upon closer inspection. And movements that coloured the socio-political landscape on a more limited scale were left out. The object was to show that, despite national differences, the developments on both continents show remarkable similarities. The more remarkable are the differences between the leading approaches in the literature in the U.S. and Europe to explain this wave of protest: »resource mobilization« and the »new social movement« approach.

A. Resource mobilization and new social movements

Resource mobilization and new social movement approaches represent rather different appraisals of contemporary social movements. A brief review of the two will underscore this differences and point to weaknesses the two approaches share.

Resource mobilization theory departed from the traditional social movement approach, according to which social movements are explained by the existence of grievances in a society. Resource mobilization theorists argued that grievances are ubiquitous in every society and that as a consequence, grievances alone cannot be sufficient conditions for the rise of social movements. The availability of resources and opportunities for collective action were considered more important than grievances in triggering social movement formation (Zald and McCarthy 1987; Jenkins 1983).

The resource mobilization approach has been most fruitful in analyzing mobilization processes and in emphasizing the role of existing organizations and networks in laying the groundwork for social movement formation (Oberschall 1973). Existing organizations and networks not only increase the chance that persons will be confronted with a mobilization attempt (Bolton 1972; Snow, Zurcher and Ekland-Olson 1980; Granovetter 1983; Klandermans and Oegema 1987a), but also make »bloc recruitment« (Oberschall 1973) possible. Pinard (1983) showed that an increase in relative deprivation only leads to more protest if a collectivity has a certain degree of organization.

Three key elements of the approach can serve to describe it in more detail.

Costs and benefits of participation. The costs and benefits of participation play an important role in the analysis of mobilization processes (Oberschall 1973, 1980; Klandermans 1984). This component of resource mobilization theory leans heavily on Olsen's (1968) logic of collective action, and particularly on his distinction between collective and selective incentives. Incentives differ in the way they are related to participation; since collective incentives are characterized by jointness of supply, obtaining collective incentives is not contingent upon participation, while obtaining selective incentives is contingent upon participation. This core argument of Olson's theory is that rational individuals will not participate in collective action unless selective incentives encourage them to do so.

Olson's theory is attractive because it offers an explanation for the fact that people *do not* take part in collective action, despite their interest in the collective goals. This explanation is consistent with the initial assumption that grievances are not sufficient condition for the rise of a social movement.

In building on Olson's theory, resource mobilization introduced a different problem: Olson can indeed explain why individuals *do not* participate in collective action; but why they sometimes *do* participate, even in the absence of selective incentives, remained a vexing problem.

Various solutions have been suggested to this problem. Fireman and Gamson (1979) asserted that individuals participate because they realize that the collective good would never be achieved if everyone reasoned like Olson's rational individual did. Oberschall (1980) explained that, given the multiplicative relationship between the value of the collective goal and its possible realization, for some people the goal is so valuable that even a slight chance of success is enough to motivate participation. Klandermans and Oegema (1987a) showed that this was indeed true for participation in one of the large peace demonstrations in The Netherlands. Carden (1978) pointed to the ideological incentives people receive by working for a cause they believe to be just. Fireman and Gamson (1979) presented an alternative approach in which it is not selective incentives but group solidarity, group interests and personal interests in the collective goods, along with the perceived urgency of collective action, that motivate people to participate.

The introduction of costs and benefits of participation made possible a more sophisticated approach to the study of recruitement into social movements. Collective (or purposive) incentives were distinguished from selective incentives, and selective incentives were in turn divided into social and non-social incentives (Wilson 1973; Oberschall 1980; Klandermans 1984). Olson's thesis that collective incentives make no difference is no longer taken seriously except by a minority of social movements students; instead, in recent work the two types of incentives are seen as reinforcing or compensating for another. A distinction is made between willingness to participate in different forms of action, in moderate and militant action (Klandermans 1984), and low and high risk activities (McAdam 1986), because of a divergent cost-benefit ratio. Certain categories of incentives turned out to appeal more to one social group than to another. Middle and upper class groups were more receptive to purposive incentives and lower class groups to selective incentives (Wilson 1973).

Organization. According to the resource mobilization approach, organization is an important resource for a social movement. Organization decreases the costs of participation (Morris 1984); it is important in the recruitment of participants (Oberschall 1973, 1980); and, in the opinion of most students, it increases the chances of success (Gamson 1975; but see Piven and Cloward 1979 for a different view). Resource mobilization's emphasis on organization as a resource was a departure from the traditional approach, which deemed a low level of organization characteristic of social movements, Gerlach and Hine (1970) observe in this connection that the impression of disorganization could easily be evoked by the specific organization form of social movements: a network of groups and organizations without centralized decision making and leadership. But formalized organizations can occur alongside loosely related groups and cells even in one and the same movement.

Expectations of success. Expectations of success play an important role with respect to the collective incentives of participation (Oberschall 1980; Pinard 1983; Klandermans 1984; Oliver, Marwell and Teixeira 1985). This factor is related to several others noted in the literature: political opportunity structure (Eisinger 1973; McAdam 1982; Tarrow 1983), the influence of sympathetic third parties (Pinard 1971; Jenkins and Perrow 1977) and alliances (Tilly 1979). A favorable political opportunity structure, the presence of third parties and allies, and the discovery of a new tactics considerably increase the chances that a social movement will succeed.

New social movements

In contrast to the resource mobilization orientation, the new social movement approach seeks an explanation for the rise of the social movements of the past two decades in the appearance of new grievances and aspirations. It stresses that the new movements differ from old movements (generally characterized as the labor movement) in values, action forms and, constituency (Melucci 1980; Brand 1982, 1987; Van der Loo et al. 1984). Though individual proponents of new social movement theory may offering differing interpretations, they agree that the following characteristics typify new social movements:

Values. New social movements do not accept the premises of a society based on economics growth. They have broken with the traditional values of capitalistic society and seek a different relationship to nature, to one's own body, to the opposite sex, to work, and to consumption.

Action forms. New social movements make extensive use of unconventional forms of action. They take a dissociative attitude toward society, as indicated by their antagonism toward politics. They prefer small-scale, decentralized organizations, they are anti-hierarchical, and they favor direct democracy.

Constituency. Two population groups are particularly predisposed to participate in new social movements. The first group includes people who are paying the costs of problems resulting from modernization, primarily those people who have been marginalized by societal developments. This group cannot be defined by social class or rank, because the problems it confronts are not limited to particular social strata. The second group consists of those who, because of more general shifts in values and needs, have become particularly senstive to problems resulting from modernization. Members of this group are found primarily among the new middle class and among the well-educated young people working in the civil service. Brand et al. (1986) state that new social movements recruit primarily from the latter category. To a great extent the values and needs of these people determine the dynamics of the new social movements.

The new social movement literature seeks to answer the question of where these new values, action forms, and constituencies come from. The answer has been sought in various sources, but all explanations link the new developments to industrialization and economic growth. Brand (1982) classifies them in theories focusing either on rising demands or on need defense. The former seek an explanation in new values, needs and wishes rooted in the modernization process that clash with the traditional system; the latter seek it in the negative consequences of modernization for the individual.

New aspirations. One group of authors, drawing on Inglehart's theory about post-material values, ascribes the rise of new social movements to changed values. Inglehart (1977) described a »silent revolution« in Europe: a dramatic change from materialist to post-materialist values. Post-war youth, assured of the satisfaction of material needs, developed non-material needs such as self-actualization and participation. Other observers discerned changes in other values as well: conventional middle-class values appeared to be eroding, the traditional work ethic was declining, and attitudes towards work and career were changing (see Brand, 1982 for research on West-Germany; Oudijk, 1983 for research on the Netherlands). Adherents of these new values were coming into conflict with a political and social system that is essentially materialist.

Another group of authors describe new social movements as a reaction to the welfare state. The welfare state has created new entitlement needs with respect to government services, they argue (Klages, 1980; de Geest, 1984). Increased prosperity has caused the demand for scarce goods to grow. Many of these are positional goods (pleasant living surroundings, a car, good education). When used extensively, they become an obstruction to the satisfaction of other needs (traffic jams, suburbs, the devaluation of degrees). The general result is increased competition, which in turn produces to more grievances (F. Hirsch, 1980).

Satisfaction of needs endangered. Some of those who seek to explain the rise of new social movements attribute the phenomenon not to an »explosion of aspirations« (Klages, 1980), but to increased strain related to industrialization and bureaucratization. These two processes, it is argued, have resulted in a *loss of identity*, leading to the loss of traditional ties and loyalties. As a consequence people become receptive to new utopias and new commitments. Young people are supposed to be particularly vulnerable to this (Horn, 1973; Berger et al., 1975; Löwenthal, 1979; Narr, 1979).

Industrialization had many negative consequences for the satisfaction of important needs (Raschke, 1980). Self-destructive aspects of western society (e.g., the exhaustion of resources, conflicts between industrialized countries, rising economic, social, psychological and ecological costs of production) together with a decreased problem-solving capacity have generated tremendous social problems. Having been accustomed to new services, people then become dissatisfied with the level at which services are performed (Hirschman, 1982). These dissatisfactions provide the breeding ground for new social movements.

Yet other theorists consider the intervention of the state and capitalistic economy into new reaches of life as the chief explanation for the rise of new social movements (Habermas, 1973; J. Hirsch, 1980; Melucci, 1980; 1981). The state took upon itself the responsibility for the satisfaction of needs which the market economy could no longer meet. The restructuring of the capitalistic economy in the wake of recession led to the exclusion of a growing number of unemployed or otherwise disqualified persons. More and more, the state was given the task of alleviating the consequences of this process of restructuring. Thus led a network of regulatory, ministering, supervisory, and controlling institutions developed and increased the danger of loss of legitimacy.

The significance of new social movements, as Melucci argues, must be determined against the background of these changes. The new social movements fight for the »reappropriation of time, of space, and of relationships in the individual's daily experience« (1980, p. 219).

B. Critical appraisal and new directions

The preceding description of resource mobilization theory and the new social movement approach – brief though it is – provides the basis for a recapitulation of the critical comparison of the two approaches I made at the time. In comparing the two approaches, I realized that in many ways each was the opposite of the other. The weakness of one appeared to be the other's strenght. For instance, critics of resource mobilization theory have charged that it focused too much on organizations and resources, neglecting the structural preconditions of movements. Melucci (1980) formulated this criticism succinctly: resource mobilization theory focused too much on the »how« of social movements and too little on the »why«. The problem characterizes for the new social movement approach. Its one-sided focus on structural origins of strain neglects the »how« of mobilization. While resource mobilization seems to argue that »demand« (grievances) will appear if there is some »supply« of social movement organizations, the new social movement approach seems to argue that social movements materializes automatically if some demand (grievances) exist. Resource mobilization helps to describe how participants in social movements are mobilized. The new social movement approach defines the structural conditions that generate deprivations and aspirations that make people susceptible to the appeals of social movements. Thus the two approaches complement each other.

More importantly for my present topic neither of the two explains what makes people define their situation in such a way that participation in a social movement seems resasonable. The new social movement approach indeed tried to discover the origins of the »demand« for social movements during the last decades, but it failed to see that structural change – however unpleasant – does not automatically generate social movements. Resource mobilization theory, meantime, investigated the »supply« of social movements, but overlooked the fact that the presence of social movements does not by itself produce grievances and convince people that movement participation is effective. Neither approach took into account the significance of the process of grievance interpretation, and the fact that collective action is socially constructed (but see Melucci 1989), nor the important role social movement organizations play in this regard.

In the five years since I first compared the two approaches, cumulative criticism has stimulated a rapidly growing interest in the themes these approaches neglected. Consequently, theorists in the field of social movement mobilization and participation have discovered new areas of research, which they have only recently begun to explore: the social construction of protest and the ways in which social movement organizations are embedded in multi-organizational fields.

C. The social construction of protest

Neither the resource mobilization approach nor the new social movement approach demonstrated much awareness of the fact that social problems are not objectively given. After all, many situations that could be considered a social problem never do become an issue, even though they may be no less troublesome than situations that do become a rallying point. Further, a social problem does not generate *inevitably* a social movement. Resource mobilization theory recognized this fact insofar as it postulated that resources play a significant role in the generation of social movements. Nevertheless, the resource mobilization approach left several important questions unanswered, for it assumed a direct relationship between objective circumstances and individual behavior – that is, it did not take into account mediating processes through which people attribute meaning to events and interpret situations. Scholars of social movements have become increasingly aware of two principles: (1) what determines the individual's behavior is not so much reality per se as reality as the individual perceives and interprets it; and (2) social movement organizations themselves play an important role in generating and diffusing meanings and interpretations. These principles hold true not only in the case of grievances but also in relation to resources, political opportunities, and outcomes of colletive action.

In the past five years, scholars have proposed a number of concepts for analyzing both the ways in which people attribute meaning and define situations and the way in which social movement organizations help create such meanings. These concepts include: the sponsorship of ideological packages (Gamson 1988, 1991) consensus mobilization (Klandermans 1984, 1988, 1991), frame alignment (Snow and Benford 1988, 1991), and collective identity (Melucci 1988, 1989). To suggest the kinds of issues these new areas of research raise, I will discuss each concept briefly. All four concepts refer to the development of a shared definition of the situation within a group, but each refers to a different part of this process.

The *sponsorship of ideological packages* as discussed by Gamson concerns public discourse (1988). At any particular moment in a given society, one political theme will be represented by several ideological packages. In addition, each political theme generates a set of packages and counterpackages. An ideological package is constructed around a few core ideas and symbols – for example »belief in progress,« a core idea that Gamson observed in his search for ideological packages concerning nuclear energy. Specific ideological packages are diffused throughout a society particularly by the mass media. Gamson, more emphatically than any other scholar, stresses the importance of the mass media for the mobilization of social movements. Because the mass media play such a central role in modern societies, social movements are increasingly involved in a symbolic struggle over meaning and interpretations (1989). Gamson believes that unless we examine media discourse and investigate how this discourse changes over time, we will not be able to understand the formation and activation of the mobilization potential of social movements.

Social movement organizations themselves contribute to the public discourse. As sponsors of specific ideological packages and as organizers of collective action in support of those packages they influence the discussion in the media. Of course, they do not have the media all to themselves. They must compete with sponsors of other packages: representatives of the »official« position, opponents, and competitive organizations, who also want a voice in the public debate. The media, that is, are by no means a passive conduit. Research in the U.S., for instance, has revealed that the media give more attention to official positions than those of challengers, and challengers bear the burden of proving the official stand is wrong.

Attempts to disseminate the views of a social actor throughout various sectors of the population are what I have called *consensus mobilization* (Klandermans, 1984, 1988). We must distinguish consensus *mobilization* from consensus *formation*: the former is a deliberate attempt by a social actor to create consensus among a subset of the population; the latter concerns the unplanned convergence of meaning in social networks and subcultures. Consensus mobilization is necessary for every mobilization campaign and at every stage of a campaign. But the nature of consensus mobilization differs, according to which stage the mobilization process is in. We can identify four steps in the process of mobilization: the formation of mobilization potential, the formation and activation of recruitment networks, the arousal of the motivation to participate, and the removal of barriers to participation (Klandermans & Oegema 1987).

In forming mobilization potential, movement organizations must win attitudinal and ideological support. In the forming and activating of recruitment networks, they must increase the probability that people who »belong« to their mobilization potential will be reached. In arousing the motivation to participate, they must favorably influence the decision of people who are reached by a mobilization attempt. In removing barriers, they must increase the probability that people who are motivated will eventually participate. Klandermans and Oegema (1987) have applied this conceptualization of the mobilization process to a concrete situation in their research on the Dutch peace movement.

We must mention one further distinction: between consensus mobilization in the context of the formation of mobilization potential in a society and consensus mobilization in the context of action mobilization. The first refers to the generation of a set of individuals with a predisposition to participate in a social movement; the second, to the legitimation of concrete goals and means of action.

Given this distinction, one can infer that the two forms of consensus mobilization have different time frames: the formation of mobilization potential is a long-term problem; action mobilization a short-term matter. The target audiences differ as well. The formation of mobilization potential means the creation of commitment; in this case, the audience is very broad, usually a social category of people who share some characteristic related to the movement's cause. Action mobilization means the activation of commitment; thus it restricts itself to people who already »belong« to the mobilization potential of a movement organization. The two different processes involve different requirements for communication channels: the formation of mobilization potential requires channels with a relative high impact, but can usually employ long-term strategies; action mobilization on the other hand, is bound to short-term strategies but can confine itself primarily to limited forms of persuasion. And they involve different arguments as well: legitimating the existence of the movement versus legitimating its strategy.

Like Gamson (1989), Klandermans (1989) stressed that social movement organizations are not the only sources of information in a society and often not even the most credible source of information. In almost every mobilization campaign social movement organizations must compete with other sometimes opposing sources of information.

Frame alignment brings us one step closer to the individual participant. Snow and his colleagues (1986, 1988, 1991) try to describe how the cognitive frame of individual participants and the ideological frame of a movement organization are brought together. Social movements frame – that is, assign meaning to and interpret – relevant events and conditions in ways that are intended to mobilize potential adherents and constituents, garner bystander support, and demobilize antagonists. In mobilization campaigns, movement organizations try to connect the interpretations of individuals with those of movement organizations so that they are congruent or complementary. Snow et al. break down the process of frame alignment into four distinct activities that a movement will find more or less relevant, depending on the degree of similarity between the two frames of reference. These four are (1) frame bridging, which involves the linkage of two or more ideologically congruent but structurally unconnected frames regarding a particular issue or problems; (2) frame amplification, which refers to the clarification and invigoration of an interpretive frame that bears on a particular issue, problem or set of events; (3) frame extension, which involves the expansion of the boundaries of a movement's primary framework so as to encompass interests or points of view that are incidental to its primary objectives but of considerable salience to potential adherents; and (4) frame transformation, which refers to the redefinition of activities, events, and biographies that are already meaningful from the standpoint of some primary framework, such that they are now seen by the participants to be quite something else (1988, p. 215). Clearly, going from frame bridging to frame transformation the four activities are progressively complex. Consequently, the more of those activities a movement organization must engage in, the complicated its task will be.

In elaborating the notion of frame alignment Snow and his colleagues have tried to formulate answers to the question of What are the key determinants of the differential success of movement framing efforts? Which characteristics of an organization and its frame of reference contribute to its ability to persuade?

With his concept of *collective identity,* Melucci (1989) localizes the process of the construction of meaning completely within the groups of participants that constitute a social movement. In his view the formation of a collective identity is the central task of a social movement. A movement that has developed a collective identity has defined itself as a group, and it has also defined its view of the social environment, the participants' shared goals, and their shared opinions about the possibilities and constraints of collective action. Groups can be more or less successful in developing a collective identity. If a group fails to develop a collective identity, it cannot accomplish any collective action. According to Melucci, the formation of a collective identity is not only instrumental for successful collective action; it is a goal in itself. if a movement succeeds in creating a new collective identity, the participants will integrate this new identity in their everyday lives. And group experimenting with new lifestyles, are themselves a challenge to the dominant culture.

Melucci objects to the other three concepts I have described here because he feels they take for granted what they must explain: the existence of collective actors. The sponsorship of ideological packages, the mobilization of consensus, and frame alignment presuppose the existence of a collective identity.

D. Multi-organizational fields

Social movements are related to structural factors: on this point proponents of the »resource mobilization« approach and proponents of the »new social movement« approach agree, even though the former focus on factors that generate resources while the latter concentrate on factors that generate grievances. In the forgoing discussion I criticized both approaches for neglecting the processes and mechanisms that transforms these structural factors into collective action. These processes – conceived of as the social construction of protest – do not proceed in a vacuum but in interaction among social actors, between social actors and individuals, and between individuals. All these interactions occur within the context of the movement organization's multi-organizational field – that is, the set of organizations in the organization's environment (Curtis and Zurcher 1973). It is there that grievances are interpreted, means and opportunities are defined, opponents are appointed, strategies are chosen and justified, and outcomes are evaluated. Interpretations and evaluations are as a rule controversial; each of the various actors may challenge the interpretations of the others. As a social movement organization competes to influence public opinion or the opinion of its constituency, its multi-organizational field determines its relative significance as an individual actor.

In exploring and analyzing the social construction of protest, scholars became increasingly interested in networks of groups and organizations which serve as carriers of the cognitive processes involved in these constructions (Fernandez and MacAdam 1989; Klandermans, Kriesi and Tarrow 1988; Melucci 1989; Roth 1987; Tarrow 1989). As a result, a much more dynamic model appeared in the social movement literature: movement groups and organizations are now seen as elements in changing configurations. Cooperation, opposition, and competition for resources and opportunities within the multi-organisational field shape episodes of protest. Elsewhere (Klandermans 1990) I have proposed that we employ the concept of a multi-organizational field – introduced by Curtis and Zurcher in 1973 – as the conceptual frame for this process. I will summarize here the characteristics of the concept (see Klandermans 1989 and 1991 for a more extensive discussion).

Until recently social movement literature focused primarily on the *support* a social movement organization receives from sectors of the multi-organizational field. Resource mobilization made this support one of its core tenets, initially by pointing to the significance of external support (Jenkins and Perrow 1977), later on by stressing the importance of indigenous organizations (McAdam 1982; Morris 1984; Jenkins and Eckert 1986). Generally, the literature contains surprisingly little about the fact that multi-organizational fields need not necessarily be supportive (although Curtis and Zurcher (1973) do note that the opponents of the anti-pornography movement also constitute a multi-organizational field). In fact, some part of the multi-organizational field of a movement organization always consists of opponents.

In other words, the multi-organizational field of a social movement organization has both supporting and opposing sectors. We can describe these two sectors as (1) a social movement organization's alliance system, consisting of groups and organizations that support the organization, and (2) its conflict system consisting of representatives and allies of the challenged political systems, including countermovement organizations (Kriesi, 1981).

The boundaries between the two systems remain vague and may change in the course of events. Specific organizations that try to remain aloof from the controversy may be forced to take sides. Parts of the political system (political parties, elites, governmental institutions) can coalesce with social movement organizations and join the alliance system. Coalitions can fall apart, and previous allies can become part of the conflict system.

Alliance systems serve to support social movement organizations by *providing* resources and *creating* political opportunities; conflict systems *drain* resources and restrict opportunities.

Different social movement organizations have different but overlapping conflict and alliance systems. The greatest overlap will exist among organizations from the same social movement industry (organizations from the women's movement, from the environmental movement, etc.). But movement organizations from different social movement industries will also have overlapping conflict and alliance systems. Many activists from the peace movement, for example, were also involved in the women's movement or the environmental movement (Kriesi 1987). The cleavage between a social movement organization's alliance and conflict system may coincide with other cleavages, such as those created by social class, ethnic divisions, or Left/Right affiliation.

The specific make-up of the multi-organizational field will vary over time and with the particular movement, and situation. The proportion of the multi-organizational field engagned in one of the two systems expands or contracts according to cycles of protest. At the peaks of protest, almost every organization will be enmeshed in one system or the other; in the valleys most organizations will not belong to either. Walsh (1981), for example, showed that in the communities surrounding Three Mile Island, after the reactor accident there, various social movement organizations developed, each with different alliance systems, depending on existing differences in the multi-organizational field. The Dutch squatter's movement was an example of a movement that experienced dramatical changes over time in its multi-organizational field. This movement initially received substantial sympathy and support from the general population and the political parties, but when its confrontations with the authorities became increasingly violent, the movement rapidly lost public support. Indeed, it began to arouse strong opposition (Van Noort 1988).

By situating social movement organizations within multi-organizational fields consisting of sectors that may be supportive, antagonistic, or simply indifferent, we gain a much more dynamic picture of social movements than that implicit in the earlier approaches, which analyzed the social movement as a self-contained phenomenon. In this new picture, the career of a social movement organization is determined by the dynamics of the multi-organizational field. Such factors as the relationship between a social movement organization and its opponents, the presence of countermovements, the formation of coalitions, the relationship with sympathetic and opposed political parties, and the relationship with the mass media, all shape the fields of tension in which social movement organizations develop, change, and decline. These multi-organizational fields are continually changing. Coalitions fall apart; controversies are resolved; organizations that were once competitors decide to join forces; countermovements come into being; new organizations appear on the scene; existing organizations radicalize; and so on. In his study of the Italian protest cycle of the 1960s, Tarrow (1989) mapped the kinds of transformations social movement sectors undergo. Precisely by making his unit of analysis the totality of protests in a specific period rather than an individual movement, Tarrow was able to demonstrate that it is not so much individual organizations as configurations of collaborating, competing and opposing organizations which determine the protest cycle.

The concept of a multi-organizational field provides us with a new way of looking at the mobilization of individual citizens. We can no longer analyze mobilization and participation within the simple frame of a social movement organization that approaches separate individuals. Individuals (like organizations) occupy positions within multi-organizational fields, and depending on their place in these complex fields, they become more or less involved in events. They may, for example, find themselves at the intersection of different organizations, if they are involved in organizations that are in conflict with each other. Or they may become caught in the crossfire of opposing opinions. One piquant illustration of the complications mobilization campaigns within multi-organizational fields can create appears in Jane Mansbridge's book *Why we lost the ERA* (1986). Describing the struggle of the pre- and anti ERA forces for the minds of the American citizens, Mansbridge reveals that, in its defence of the ERA the women's movement helped to create the caricature that the countermovement effectively exploited in its countercampaign. Gamson, in describing how competing and opposing organizations determined the public discourse on nuclear power in the United States (1968), showed that accidents at nuclear power plants became a prominent element in the debate only with the emergence of movement organizations that made this problem an issue. Our own research on the Dutch peace movement demonstrated how supporters of the peace movement who used to vote for one of the two political parties in office increasingly found themselves under pressure from both sides (Klandermans et al. 1988).

E. Conclusion

During the seventies and early eighties new social movements entered the political arena in Europe and the U.S. Students of social movements on both continents while studying these new waves of protest developed different theoretical approaches: resource mobilization in the U.S. and the new social movement approach in Europe. In an earlier review (Klandermans 1986) I compared these two approaches critically and arrived at the conclusion that they could very well compensate each other. Resource mobilization – focusing on factors that generate resources – and the new social movement approach – concentrating on factors that generate grievances – each provided parts of a larger frame on explanations of the movements of the seventies and the eighties. None of the two, however, paid attention to the significance of social construction. Rather than generated in a mechanical way by the availability of resources or the existence of grievances, protest is socially constructed, argue an increasing number of scholars. Their critical appraisal of the existing approaches led social movement research into new directions. As specimen of these new directions the concepts of the social construction of protest and the multi-organizational field were discussed in this chapter.

By developing the concepts of the social construction of protest and the multi-organizational field students of social movements have attempted to link the macro level of structural change with the micro level of individual participation in collective action. We can see these concepts as representing the structural and cognitive aspects of mobilization into social movements.

Both concepts require comparative and longitudinal research. Comparative research is needed to distinguish constellations within multi-organizational fields and to investigate their impact on mobilization and participation. One might usefully attempt comparisons between movements, between countries, and, on a more restricted scale, between multi-organizational fields both within one community and between several communities. Longitudinal research is needed to study the fluctuations within multi-organizational fields and the influence of such fluctuations on mobilization and partizipation. For this research too we can divise projects of varying scope: from an investigation of the changes in the multi-organizational field of a movement organization within a single community to an exploration of multi-organizational fields on the international level.

Bibliography

Barkan, S.E. (1979): Strategic, Tactical and Organizational Dilemmas of the Protest Movement against Nuclear Power, *Social Problems* 271: 19-37.

Benford, R.B. (1984): *The interorganizational Dynamics of the Austin Peace Movement.* Thesis: Univ. of Texas.

Berger, P.L.; Berger, B.; Kellner, H. (1975): *Das Unbehagen in der Modernität.* Frankfurt/New York: Campus.

Bolton, Ch. D. (1972): Alienation and Action: A study of Peace Group Members, *American Journal of Sociology* 77: 537-561.

Brand, K.W. (1982): *Neue soziale Bewegungen, Entstehung, Funktion und Perspektive neuer Protestpotentiale, eine Zwischenbilanz.* Opladen: Westdeutscher Verlag.

Brand, K.W. (1985): *Neue soziale Bewegungen in West Europa und den USA. Ein internationaler Vergleich,* New York/Frankfurt: Campus.

Brand, K.W. (1987): Kontinuität und Diskontinuität in den neuen sozialen Bewegungen, in: R. Roth, A. Rucht (eds.), *Neue soziale Bewegungen in der Bundesrepublik Deutschland.* Frankfurt/New York: Campus.

Brand, K.W.; Büsser, D.; Rucht, D. (1986): *Aufbruch in eine andere Gesellschaft. Neue soziale Bewegungen in der Bundesrepublik.* Frankfurt/New York: Campus.

Briët, M.; Klandermans, P.G.; Kroon, F. (1987): How Women Become Involved in the Women's Movement, in: M. Katzenstein, C. Mueller (eds.). *The Womens' Movements of the United States and Western Europe: Consciousness, Political Opportunity and Public Policy,* Philadelphia, Pa.: Temple Univ. Press.

Cerny, P.G. (ed.) (1982): *Social Movements and Protest in France.* New York: St. Martin's Press.

Carden, M.L. (1978): The Proliferation of a Social Movement: Ideology and Individual Incentives in the Contemporary Feminist Movement, in: L. Kriesberg (ed.). *Research in Social Movements, Conflict and Change,* Vol. I. Greenwich, Conn.: JAI Press.

Curtis, R.L.; Zurcher L.A. (1973): Stable Resources of Protest Movements: The Multi-organizational Field, *Social Forces* 52: 53-61.

Dalton, R.J.; Kuechler, M. (eds.) (1990): *Challenging the Political Order.* Oxford: Polity Press.

Eisinger, P.K. (1973): The Conditions of Protest Behavior in American Cities, *American Political Science Review* 67: 11-28.

Fernandez, R.; McAdam, D. (1989): Multiorganizational Fields and Recruitment to Social Movements, in: P.G. Klandermans (ed.). *Organizing for Change: Social Movement Organizations Across Cultures.* Greenwich, Conn: JAI-Press.

Ferree, M.M. (1987): Feminist Politics in the U.S. and West Germany, in: M. Katzenstein and C. Mueller (eds.). *The Womens' Movements of the United States and Western Europe: Consciousness, Political Opportunity and Public Policy.* Philadelphia, Pa: Temple Univ. Press.

Fireman, B.; Gamson, W.A. (1979): Utilitarism Logic in the Resource Mobilization Perspective, in: M.N. Zald, J.D. McCarthy (eds.). *The Dynamics of Social Movements.* Cambridge, Mass.: Winthrop Publishers.

Gamson, W.A. (1975): *The Strategy of Social Protest.* Homewood, Ill.: The Dorsey Press.

– (1988): Political Discourse and Collective Action, in: P.G. Klandermans, H. Kriesi, B. Tarrow (eds.). *From Structure to Action: Comparing Movement Participation Across Cultures.* Greenwich: Conn., JAI-Press.

– (1989): Challenging Groups Since 1945, in: W.A. Gamson. *The Strategy of Social Protest. 2nd edition.*

– (1991): The Social Psychology of Collective Action, in: A. Morris, C. Mueller (eds.). *Frontiers in Social Movement Theory.* New Haven, Conn.: Yale Univ. Press.

Gerlach, L.P. and Hine, V.C. (1970): *People, Power, Change: Movements of Social Transformation*, Indianapolis: Bobbs-Merill.

De Geest, A. (1984): Nieuwe sociale bewegingen en de verzorgingsstaat, *Tijdschrift voor sociologie* 5: 239-267.

Gitlin, T. (1980): *The Whole World is Watching.* Berkeley, Calif.: Univ. of Calif. Press.

Granovetter, M. (1983): The Strength of Weak Ties: A Network Theory Revisited, in: R. Collins (ed.). *Sociological Theory 1983.* San Francisco, Calif.: Jossey-Bass Publ.

Habermas, J. (1973): *Legitimationsprobleme im Spätkapitalismus.* Frankfurt: Suhrkamp.

Heirich, M. (1971): *The Spiral of Conflict. Berkeley 1964.* Columbia: Columbia Univ. Press.

Hirsch, F. (1980): *Die sozialen Grenzen des Wachstums. Eine ökonomische Analyse der Wachstumskrise.* Hamburg: Reinbek.

Hirsch, J. (1980): *Der Sicherheitsstaat.* Das »Modell Deutschland«, seine Krise und die neuen sozialen Bewegungen. Frankfurt: Europäische Verlagsanstalt.

Huberts, Leo W. (1988): *De politieke invloed van protest en pressie: Besluitvormingsprocessen over Rijkswegen.* Leiden: DSWO-Press.

Inglehart, R. (1977): *The Silent Revolution: Changing Values and Political Styles among Western Publics.* Princeton, N.J.: Princeton University Press.

Janssen, J.; Voestermans, P. (1978): *De vergruisde universiteit: een cultuur-psychologisch onderzoek naar voorbije en aktuele ontwikkelingen in de Nijmeegse studentenwereld.* Dissertatie. Meppel: Krips Repro.

Jenkins, J.C. (1983): Resource Mobilization Theory and the Study of Social Movements, *Annual Review of Sociology* 9: 527-553.

Jenkins, J.C.; Eckert, C.M. (1986): Channeling Black Insurgency, *American Sociological Review* 51: 812-830.

Jenkins, J.C.; Perrow, C. (1977): Insurgency of the Powerless Farm Worker Movements 1946-1972, *American Sociological Review* 42: 249-268.

Kaltefleiter, W.; Pfalzgraff, R.L. (1984): *The Peace Movement in Europe and the United States.* London: Croom Helm.

Katzenstein, M.; Mueller, C. (eds.) (1987): *The Womens' Movements of the United States and Western Europe: Consciousness. Political Opportunity and Public Policy*. Philadelphia, Penn.: Temple Univ. Press.

Klages, H. (1980): *Überlasteter Staat – verdrossene Bürger?* Zu den Dissonanzen der Wohlfahrtsgesellschaft. Frankfurt: Campus.

Klandermans, P.G. (1984): Mobilization and Participation: Social Psychological Expansions of Resource Mobilization Theory, *American Sociological Review* 49: 583-600.

– (1986): New Social Movements and Resource Mobilization: The European and the American Approach, *International Journal of Mass Emergencies and Disasters*: 4 (2): 13-39.

– (1988): The Formation and Mobilization of Consensus, in: P.G. Klandermans, H. Kriesi, S. Tarrow (eds.). *International Social Movement Research*, vol. 1, *From Structure to Action: Comparing Movement Participation Across Cultures*. Greenwich, Conn.: JAI-Press.

– (1989). (ed.). *Organizing for Change: Social Movement Organizations in Europe and the United States*. Greenwich, Conn.: JAI-Press.

– (1991): The Social Construction of Protest and Multiorganizational Fields, in: A. Morris, C. Mueller (eds.). *Frontiers in Social Movement Theory*. New Haven, Conn.: Yale University Press.

Klandermans, P.G.; Kriesi, H.; Tarrow, S. (eds.) (1988): *From Structure to Action: Comparing Movement Participation Across Cultures*. Greenwich, Conn.: JAI-Press-

Klandermans, P.G.; Oegema, D. (1987a): Potentials, networks, motivations and barriers: steps toward participation in social movements, *American Sociological Review* 5: 519-531.

– (1987b): Campaigning for a Nuclear Freeze and Local Government in The Netherlands, in: R.G. Braungart (ed.). *Research in Political Sociology*, vol. 3, Greenwich, CT.: JAI-Press.

Klandermans, P.G. (ed.). (1988): *Tekenen voor de vrede. Portret van een campagne*. Assen: Van Gorcum.

Kriesi, H. (1985): *Bewegungen in der Schweizer Politik. Fallstudien zu politischen Mobilisierungsprozessen in der Schweiz*. Frankfurt: Campus.

– (1987): The Alliance Structure of the Dutch Peace Movement, Paper presented at the workshop New Social Movements and the Political System, ECPR Joint Session, Amsterdam, April 11-15, 1987.

– (1989): The Political Opportunity Structure of the Dutch Peace Movement. *West European Politics* 12: 296-312.

Lo, C.Y.H. (1982): Counter-Movements and Conservative Movements in the Contemporary U.S., in: R.H. Turner, J.F. Short (eds.). *Annual Review of Sociology*. Palo Alto, Calif.: Annual Reviews.

Löwenthal, R. (1979): *Gesellschaftswandel und Kulturkrise. Zukunftsprobleme der westlichen Demokratien*. Frankfurt: Fischer.

Mansbridge, J.L. (1986): *Why We Lost the ERA*. Chicago, Ill.: The Univ. of Chicago Press.

McAdam, D. (1982): *Political Process and the Development of Black Insurgency*. Chicago, Ill.: The Univ. of Chicago Press.

– (1983): Tactical Innovation and the Pace of Insurgency, *American Sociological Review* 48: 735-754.
– (1986): Recruitment to High-Risk Activism: The Case of Freedom Summer. *American Journal of Sociology* 92: 64-90.
McAdam, D.; McCarthy, J.D.; Zald, M.N. (1988): Social Movements, in: N.J. Smelser (ed.). *Handbook of Sociology*, Beverly Hills, Calif.: Sage.
Melucci, A. (1980): The New Social Movements: A Theoretical Approach, *Social Science Information* 19: 199-226.
– (1981): Ten Hypotheses for the Analysis of New Movements, in: D. Pinto (ed.). *Contemporary Italian Sociology*. Cambridge, Mass.: Cambridge Univ. Press. 173-194.
– (1988): Getting Involved: Identity and Mobilization in Social movements, in: P.G. Klandermans, H. Kriesi, S. Tarrow (eds.). *From Structure to Action: Comparing Movement Participation Across Cultures*. Greenwich, Conn.: JAI-Press.
– (1989): *Nomads of the Present. Social Movements and Individual Needs in Contemporary Society*. London: Hutchinson Radius.
Mitchell, R.C. (1979): National Environmental Lobbies and the Apparent Illogic of Collective Action, in: C.S. Russell (ed.). *Collective Decision Making: Applications from Public Choise Theory*. Baltimore, Md.: The Johns Hopkins Univ. Press.
– (1984): Moving Forward vs. Moving Backwards: Motivation for Collective Action. Paper presented at the 79th Annual Meeting of the American Sociological Association. San Antonio, Tex., August 1984.
Morris, A. (1984): *The Origins of the Civil Rights Movement: Black Communities Organizing for Change*. New York: Free Press.
Mushaben, J.M. (1983): Innocence Lost: Environmental images and Political Experiences among West German ›Greens‹. Paper presented at the Annual Meeting of the International society for Political Psychology, Oxford, U.K., July 10-22, 1983.
– (1983): Cycles of Peace Protest in West Germany: Experiences from Three Decades. Paper presented at the Annual Meeting of the American Sociological Association, Detroit, Aug. 31-Sept. 4, 1983.
Narr, W.D. (1979): Hin zu einer ? gesellschaftsbedingter Reflexe, in: Habermas, J. (ed.). *Stichworte zur geistigen Situation der Zeit. 2. Band*. Frankfurt: Suhrkamp.
Oberschall, A. (1973): *Social Conflict and Social Movements*. Englewood Cliffs, N.J.: Prentice Hall.
– (1978): Theories of Social Conflict, *Annual Review of Sociology* 4: 291-315.
– (1980): Loosely Structured Collective conflicts: A theory and an application, in: L. Kriesberg (ed.). *Research in Social Movements. Conflict and Change*. Vol. 3. Greenwich, Conn.; JAI Press.
Oliver, P.; Marwell, G.; Teixeira, R. (1985): A Theory of the Critical Mass. I. Group Heterogeneity, Interdependence and the Production of Collective Goods, *American Journal of Sociology* 91: 522-556.
Olson, M. (1965): *The Logic of Collective Action. Public Goods and the Theory of Groups*. Cambridge, Mass.: Harvard Univ. Press.
Opp, K.-D. (1986): Soft Incentives and Collective Action: Participation in the Anti-Nuclear Movement. *British Journal of Political Science* 16: 87-112.

– (1988): Grievances and Participation in Social Movements. *American Sociological Review* 53: 853-864.

Oudijk, C. (1983): *Sociale atlas van de vrouw*. Sociale en culturele studies 3, Sociaal Cultureel Planbureau. Den Haag: Staatsuitgeverij.

Perrow, Ch. (1979): The Sixties Observed, in: M.N. Zald, J.D. McCarthy (eds.). *The Dynamics of Social Movements, Ressource Mobilisation. Social Control, and Tactics*. Cambridge, Mass.: Winthrop Publ.

Pinard, M. (1971): *The Rise of a Third Party*. Englewood Cliffs, N.J.: Prentice Hall.

– (1983): From Deprivation to Mobilization. Paper presented at the Annual Meeting of the ASA, Detroit, August.

Piven, F.F.; Cloward, R.A. (1979): *Poor People's Movements: Why They Succeed. How They Fail*. New York: Vintage Books.

Raschke, J. (1980): Politik und Wertwandel in den westlichen Demokratien, in: *Aus Politik und Zeitgeschichte* (B. 36/38): 23-45.

Rochon, T.R. (1988): *Mobilizing for Peace. The Antinuclear Movements in Western Europe*. Princeton, N.Y.: Princeton Univ. Press.

Roth, R. (1987): Kommunikationsstrukturen und Vernetzungen in neuen sozialen Bewegungen, in: R. Roth, D. Rucht (eds.). *Neue soziale Bewegungen in der Bundesrepublik Deutschland*. Frankfurt: Campus.

– (1989): Fordismus und neue soziale Bewegungen, in: U.C. Wasmuht (ed.). *Alternativen zur alten Politik? Neue soziale Bewegungen in der Diskussion*. Darmstadt: Wissenschaftliche Buchgesellschaft.

Roth, R.; Rucht, D. (eds.) (1987): *Neue soziale Bewegungen in der Bundesrepublik Deutschland*. Frankfurt: Campus.

Rucht, D. (1984): Zur Organisation der neuen sozialen Bewegungen, in: J.W. Falter, C. Fenner, M.T. Greven (eds.). *Politische Willensbildung und Interessenvermittlung*. Opladen: Westdeutscher Verlag.

– (1984): Comparative New Social Movements, Organizations and Strategies in a Cross-Sectional and a Cross-National View. Paper presented at the Conference of European Group of Organizational Sociologists on New Social Movements, Aarhus, Denmark, August.

– (1987): Von der Bewegung zur Institution. Organisationsstrukturen der Oekologiebewegung, in: R. Roth, D. Rucht (eds.). *Neue soziale Bewegungen in der Bundesrepublik Deutschland*. Frankfurt: Campus.

Rudig, W. (1983): Clustered Nuclear Siting Anti-Nuclear Opposition. Paper presented at the Sixth Annual Scientific Meeting of the International Society of Political Psychology. Oxford, St. Catherine's College, July 1983.

Snow, D.A.; Benford, R.D. (1988): Ideology, Frame Resonance, and Participant Mobilization, in: B. Klandermans, H. Kriesi, S. Tarrow (eds.). *From Structure to Action: Comparing Movement Participation Across Cultures*. Greenwich, Conn.: JAI-Press.

– (1991): Master Frames and the Cycle of Protest, in: A. Morris, C. Mueller (eds.). *Frontiers in Social Movement Theory*. New Haven, Conn.: Yale University Press.

Snow, D.A.; Rochford, E.B. Jr.; Wordan, S.K.; Benford R.D. (1986): Frame Alignment Processes, Micro-mobilization and Movement Participation. *American Sociological Review* 51: 464-481.

Snow, D.A.; Zurcher Jr., L.A.; Ekland-Olson, S. (1980): Social Networks and Social Movements: A Micro-Structural Approach to differential Recruitment, *American Sociological Review* 45: 787-801.

Tarrow, S. (1983): Resource Mobilization and Cycles of Protest: Theoretial Reflections and Comparative Illustrations. Paper presented at the Annual Meeting of the American Sociological Association, Detroit, August 1983.

– (1989): *Democracy and Disorder: Protest and Politics in Italy. 1965-1975*. Oxford: Oxford U. Press.

Tilly, Ch. (1979): Repertoires of Contention in American and Britain, 1750-1830, in: M.N. Zald, J.D. McCarthy (eds.). *The Dynamics of Social Movements*. Cambridge, Mass.: Winthrop Publ.

Van der Loo, H.; Snel E.; Van Steenbergen, B. (1984): *Een Wenkend Perspectief? Nieuwe Sociale Bewegingen en Culturele Veranderingen*. Amersfoort: De Horstink.

Van Noort, W.J. (1988): *Bevlogen bewegingen. Een vergelijking van de antikernenergie-, kraak- en milieubeweging*. Amsterdam: SUA.

Walsh, E.J. (1981): Resource Mobilization and Citizen Protest in Communities around Three Miles Island, *Social Problems* 29: 1-21.

– (1988): New Dimensions of Social Movements: The High-Level Waste-Siting Controversy, *Sociological Forum* 3: 586-605.

Wasmuht, U.C. (1984): A Sociological Survey of American Peace Movements. *Alternatives* 9: 581-591.

– (1989): *Alternativen zur alten Politik? Neue soziale Bewegungen in der Diskussion*. Darmstadt: Wissenschaftliche Buchgesellschaft.

Wilson, J.Q. (1973): *Political Organizations*. New York: Basic Books.

Zald, M.N.; McCarthy, J.D. (1987): *Social Movements in an Organizational Society. Selected Essays*. New Brunswick: Transaction Books.

Part II
The State of the Art in Selected Countries

Social Movement Research and Social Movement Practice: The U.S. Pattern

Margit Mayer

The analysis of social movements in the United States reflects the development and state of the movements themselves. Social movements here have been extremely heterogeneous, fragmented and scattered, yet at the same time have tended to be oriented towards participation in the American Dream. From a European perspective, their differences in terms of history and praxis, and in terms of analytical approaches developed to understand them, appear quite striking and call for explanation.

Social movement research in Europe has been preoccupied with and shaped by the challenge to older conceptual forms by the novel and distinctive features of various contemporary social movements. The »progress of capitalism« is no longer questioned by working class movements but rather by new actors and new demands and in non-conventional forms which explode traditional definitions of »the political«. Even the New Left of the 1960s, while itself raising problems of identity, hierarchy, and autonomy, still adhered to the classical critique and vision of transforming society by way of the proletarian revolution. But such movements as the ecology, women's, anti-nuclear, and various alternative and counter-cultural movements escape these categories and challenge them.

While European scholars were initially slow to advance interpretations more in line with the emerging new cleavages and conflicts, researchers in all disciplines now share the concern with the fundamentally new qualities of contemporary social movements. To be sure, the analyses being developed (see other contributions in this book) suggest rather remarkable divergence in European scholarship, but there is widespread agreement – across disciplinary boundaries – about the need to more adequately comprehend what appears as a qualitative shift in the practice and meaning of social movement activity.

The field in the United States is shaped by neither a comparably drastic shift nor by similarly concentrated new efforts. Social movement research in the United States has a far different conceptual basis, history, and trajectory. Contemporary literature on social movements, collective behavior, and protest is a motley and disparate field shared by sociologists, social historians, social psychologists, and political scientists. Even within the same discipline, versions of social movement theories are being developed without taking account of each other. For example, political science segments the field into surveys of mass attitudes, organizational case studies, and aggregate data analyses, which are not related to each other nor systematically related to a specific approach. Within sociology and social psychology, it has been particularly difficult to detach the study of social protest from collective behavior in general, and thus from »non-institutional phenomena« like crowds or from innerdirected movements like cults. The study of »social movements« thus looks at a far greater variety of behaviors than is usually the case in European research.

This, in part, reflects the fact that »non-conventional« and extra-institutional politics and non-working class actors appear as nothing »new« on the American terrain. While the concept of »new« in Europe clearly denotes a break with the »old« working class movement, U.S. history does not know *one* but countless social movements. The term ›social movement‹ here embraces a multitude of social protest and reform movements including religious cults, sects, millenarian and nationalist movements, ethnic groups, uprisings and political violence of all kinds. This does not mean that class relations were marginal for social conflict, but they may be seen as overdetermined by demographic, ethnic, political and sociocultural variables in ways that shaped a very specific social movement pattern. Modern social movements appear to reproduce this pattern in their themes, action repertoires and openness to participants.

Though there was not a comparably obvious shift in social movement activity and interpretation, this overview will focus on theoretical and empirical work pertaining to *contemporary American* social movements such as peace, ecology, anti-nuke, neighborhood and women's movements. It will concentrate on studies done by *American* scholars, even though some European new social movement research has recently also entered the debates and the published literature,[1] but is not yet received to the degree that it spawned original work.

The phenomenon of social movements in the U.S. has given rise to theoretical approaches that are rather different from those developed in Europe.[2] We have already mentioned the most widely used approaches. However, at least five different tendencies can be distinguished:

- the *»classical« traditions of collective behavior and breakdown theories*, which attempt to explain, in historically general terms, why and how people protest.
- Apparently equally time- and place-unspecific, general mechanisms of social movements are elaborated in the *resource mobilization approach*, which developed as a critique of the classical traditions. This approach, though rather heterogeneous in itself, is currently the dominant paradigm in standard social science.
- *Class analytical approaches*, which originated within urban sociology, developed from the traditional hierarchy of contradictions (capital-labor) to an analysis of contemporary class society, in which the new social movements are no longer secondary phenomena, but correspond to the crisis of the fordist mode of accumulation.
- A *populist-traditionalist interpretation*, which focusses primarily on the explosive expansion of »citizen action« of the 1970s in a more or less uncritical partisan way.
- *Integrative perspectives*, which emphasize *cultural* and *symbolic* dimensions and the construction of meaning, thereby making it possible to also capture those current social movements or aspects of movements, which are not about participation in the American mainstream, either economically or politically, but rather challenge the validity and hegemony of the dominant power structures and cultural systems. This type of analysis has not (yet) developed into an approach, but various descriptive attempts are made to capture such phenomena.

---

1 Compare the articles by Touraine, Melucci, and Offe in *Social Research* 52 (4) 1985; various issues of *Social Science Information*; Klandermans/Kriesi/Tarrow, 1988; Dalton/Küchler, 1990.

2 For comparisons between European new social movement perspectives and U.S. approaches to the study of social movements see Klandermans/Tarrow, 1988, 3-10; Tarrow, 1986; for a comparison with new social movements in West Germany, Kitschelt, 1985b.

Before I describe these trends in detail, I will establish the distinguishing features of social action in the United States in order to provide a better grounding for the assessment of the specificity of research on social movements in the United States. The U.S. case illustrates very clearly how a specific political culture and a national style of politics influence not only social movements, but also social scientific research about them.

I. Distinctive Patterns of American Social Movements and American Social Movement Research

The origins of American society allowed for far-reaching experiences of egalitarian and liberal forms of social and political organization. To be sure, the rich public-communal sphere in which civic voluntarism could flourish[3] always existed on the basis of the exclusion of certain parts of the population. Native Americans were pushed aside and decimated, Blacks were imported as slaves and their labor appropriated, and women did not enjoy citizenship rights either. Nonetheless, the salience of this civic sphere exerted a powerful influence on the cultural dispositions and on the organization of the political system of the USA. Because civil society is so richly organized, one does not see the same clear-cut and deep line between civil society and the state that we see in Europe. In fact, not only is the formal organization of the American state weak by design, the founders consciously setting powers against each other to insure their diminution, there is also a tradition of disobedience to established authority at the heart of Amerian political culture. Civil disobedience, which the founding myths and the liberal theories of consent have legitimated, is a tradition on par with anti-statist, decentralist tendencies of self-government. Both have encouraged radical movements and colored them with libertarian hues, and have informed uprisings against authority throughout American history. At the same time, the fragmented and unobtrusive state also encouraged the appearance of a multitude of special movements and interest groups (whereas in Europe the condition of strong states led to the formation of political parties). Emerging out of the heterogeneity of living conditions and the segmentation of American society, voluntary associations and culturally/morally oriented protest movements

3 Cf. Hartz, 1955; Lipset, 1963; Mayer, 1977; Kilian, 1979.

complemented the formal political party system. The open, fluid and decentral American political system usually prevented a polarization between movements and political establishment. This also meant that a challenging group's identity would not come automatically as in Europe where groups excluded from the democratic state and faced with its intransigence would a priori be defined as »preexisting solidary groups« for having established themselves outside of (and hence against) established forms of processing interests. Instead, the collective identities of the movements have to be created in the process of mobilization. As I will explore in more detail later, this process is also reflected in the assumptions and categories of American research on social movements.

On the one hand, the open and flexible nature of the American political system has always facilitated responses, if selective, to publicized grievances and may be seen as intensifying the tendency towards »single issues« and the conversion of movement groups into pressure groups which frequently succeeded in gaining access to the political arena. On the other, the heterogeneous and segmented social patterns which underlie the high degree of civic voluntarism, self-reliant public participation and self-regulative communitarianism, also imply pronounced sectoral unevenness and sharp economic disparities, a still incomplete representation of the working class, and a lack of welfare state policies which might mitigate these disparities. As a consequence, social movements to this day tend not only to raise the particular issue their members feel aggrieved about, they also implicitly raise, or are soon forced to confront, an »unfinished« class and race agenda.

As long as problems of economic inequality and working class representation remain so uniquely unresolved, as is the case in the U.S., *new* social movements which challenge the concepts of industrial growth and progress, and focus on environmental or identity problems, are unlikely to become dominant in the American landscape. This does not mean that certain themes of the so-called »life chance movements« (as Kitschelt has called them, 1985b) do not resonate within contemporary American social movements. Claims to the right to difference, challenges to hierarchical forms of organization, and the rejection of a growth model which tends to destroy the preconditions of life, were even first articulated within American contexts.[4]

4 Within the 60s movements, parts of the women's movement prefigured the decentralized, segmented networks of autonomous groups with their conscious lack of formal organization and hierarchy, their emphasis on participation by everyone, and their sharing in a common culture. The early civil rights movement prefigured the spontaneous style

This is no contradiction. The comparatively advanced state of economic and social structures, combined with the strong disposition for voluntarist political participation, and the long tradition of grassroots movements around special issues, allowed the early appearance and the leading role of American social movements compared to others.

But these new social movements are again and again forced to confront the very material needs of social groups who experience class or ethnic or racial discrimination in acute form. Their agenda, therefore, is forced to include more or less »traditional« demands for distributive policies, political rights and equality.

As opposed to this situation, the new social movements which began to dominate the European terrain, do not protest against the *failure* of state and society to provide for economic growth and material prosperity, but rather, against the *price* of that growth. Furthermore, they strongly reject traditional political agents such as parties, interest groups, or bureaucracies to solve the problem. American social movements, on the other hand, have both an unfinished class agenda to confront *and* are forerunners in terms of articulating such »post-materialist« values as direct participation, rejection of representation, insisting on the right to have difference recognized, and defining the personal as political.

Not unlike the career of earlier social movements in American history, the contemporary movements are then characterized by, first, an uncomplicated emergence. Secondly, they are marked by a relatively accelerated proliferation thanks to the existing tradition and resources for voluntary associations and interest groups and the favorable opportunity structure which the American political systems provides. Finally, they are subject to an equally quick dispersal into disparate and often rapidly declining movements. In the course of this career, individual political entrepreneurs often play a crucial role; they seize upon new issues to advance their own political fortunes. Especially during the last two decades, promotional groups and liberal philanthropic elites have taken on a prominent role for the development of a variety of reform movements. This so-called »advocacy explosion« has stimulated the growth of certain kinds of professional »movements« which press

---

of new social movements by introducing the sit-ins. It also shared the expressiveness of the new social movements in that activists attempted to rid themselves of racism. Further back in American history, there is even a tradition of the anti-technology theme, to which the new ecology movement could refer – not coincidental in a society with such rapid capitalist expansion.

for various social reforms (cf. Berry, 1984, 16ff; Jenkins, 1986). The diffuse qualities of the American administrative structure make it easy for the state to respond to the movements with concessions and inclusion. But they also allow ample opportunity for subverting and eroding the new provisions later in the course of implementation (cf. Friedland/Alford, 1975).

Indeed, large segments of the 60s and other movements are easily absorbed either directly into the Democratic Party or the lower echelons of the administrative structure, or their demands are included in the policy-making process. Many of the 60s political activists, especially in the minority communities, are now in positions of power (so that activists working with them today seem more liberal than radical, see Atkins, 1987, 19). Many of the movement demands have also been absorbed economically, into new markets and sectors »unideological« enough to make a profit[5] (cf. Case/Taylor, 1979).

The differences with European democracies are noteworthy. For example in the FRG, a relatively closed political system and a repressive state response caused cohesive anti-system mobilization by »producing« something like a shared structural position for movement participants. In contrast, the American movements operated in a far less ideologically polarized climate and, as a consequence, confronted the *problems* of the favorable response of established culture and political system much earlier than their European counterparts. These significant differences between the U.S. and Europe have led to frequent misunderstandings and serious errors in the making of cross-cultural generalizations. Since all the western advanced industrial countries have witnessed a rise in citizen groups activity or even displayed similar forms of action, identities have been assumed where there were none; categories developed within very different settings have been used indiscriminately. For example, the wave of new citizens initiatives which arose in Germany in the early 70s, massively challenged for the first time in post-war Germany the closed (established parties') definition of politics. In contrast, grassroots citizen action in the U.S., which also expanded during the 1970s, did so in the peculiarly American manner. Grassroots community groups organized around such issues as energy costs, housing, public health (measures

5 Media coverage and the willingness of the publishing industry to publish radical authors is an example. While such publicity helped movements initially, it also, as it later turned out, prevented the movements from building their own infrastructure, whereas many European movements had to create their own publishing houses, organizational networks and communication media. See also Tarrow, 1983a, 46-7.

to control smoking, e.g.), the nuclear freeze *and* conservative movements such as anti-abortion[6], and organized lobby organizations, frequently even on the national level.[7] A representative example would be IPAC (Illinois Public Action Campaign): »IPAC has offices in 6 Illinois cities, an annual budget of $ 1.4 million, canvasses 7,000 homes a day and lobbies full-time in the state legislature.« (Holcomb, 1986, 127-8)[8] Such professionally-run, policy-oriented social movement organizations both occupy different places in the political/cultural system than their German counterparts and involve very different mobilizational and motivational strategies.

The fundamental structures of the American political system and history have impacted not only on the quality and patterns of American social movements. They have also directed the interests of researchers in certain directions and led to the selection of specific situations as problems. The fact that the American situation has produced a *permanent* coexistence of social movements side by side with established institutions of the political system has led analysts to conclude that the existence of mobilization potentials has been continuous as well. They appear as self-evident, i.e. their relationship to causes lying deeper in the contradictions of capital or the forces of history need not to be explored. The American situation has also produced a pervasive pattern of *self-limiting* movements which focus on single issues, achievable success and individual self-reform. Movements claiming to become part of the American mainstream, by demanding equal opportunities or integration into established institutions, tend to flourish as do those which struggle for (partial) autonomization of various subcultures. However, movements

6 These were usually organized according to the pragmatic Alinsky model of community organization (cf. Lancourt, 1979; Mayer, 1982; Miller, 1980).

7 Cf. for example John Herbers, »Grassroots Groups go National.« New York Times Magazine, Sept. 4, 1983, 23; Jane E. Brody, »The Growing Militancy of the Nation's Non-Smokers,« New York Times, Jan. 15, 1984. Cf. also Burdett A. Loomis, »A New Era: Groups and the Grass Roots,« in: Allan J. Cigler/Burdett A. Loomis, eds., Interest Group Politics. Washington, D.C.: Congressional Quarterly, 1983.

8 Other similar statewide citizen groups are: Mass Fair Share or the Campaign for Economic Democracy (CED) in Massachusetts and California respectively. While the literature of 1968 still presents CED as alive and growing (»15,000 members in 20 local chapters...« Holcom, 128), it has in fact been closed down by its erstwhile founder Tom Hayden and replaced with a new organization »less critical of business and ... more supportive of the private entrepreneur as a source of economic growth, jobs and innovation.« Hayden as quoted in Jon Wiener, »Tom Hayden's New Workout,« *The Nation*, Nov. 29, 1986, 603. Hayden admits in retrospect that »1982 was the end (of CED, MM).«

demanding radical societal change have remained marginal in American history. Given the tension within American liberal ideology, and the permanent conflict between ideals and institutions in American politics – which »naturally« produces regular periods of »creedal passion« (Huntington, 1981) –, social movements have not needed to define themselves *outside of* the hegemonic American dicourse. In fact, Jeffersonian democracy, communitarian self- reliance and decentral participatory forms of politics are constitutive parts of Americanism. And, while not always compatible with the principles of a free market economy, they were clearly values which even movements such as the students' (cf. SDS' Port Huron Statement) or the anti-nuclear direct action movement (cf. Livermore Action Group) could claim.

In this context, it is no surprise that American social movement analysts persistently reach similar conclusions. Again and again they find that insurgencies that restrict their goals to single issues and leave the existing structure of authority uncontested, are more likely to secure tangible gains. Or they find that when the values and beliefs a movement seeks to promote are of low hierarchical salience within the larger belief system, the mobilizing potential is weakened (or the task of consciousness raising becomes more central; Snow/Benford 1986). The peculiarity and restrictedness of such findings to the American context is rarely acknowledged nor is the fact that the long and legitimate tradition of pluralist interest group participation and coexistence of voluntary associations and extra-parliamentarian activity alongside established institutions has led to various assumptions among scholars, which might be questioned in other contexts. While extremely heterogeneous in itself, the American scholarly community deals with the phenomenon of social movements in an extremely self-referential way. It can afford to do so, of course, since ample exchange and debate is possible within a huge English-speaking market; the need to gather and to analyze data on a cross-national level, which most European scholars have to account for, does not exist.

American researchers generally assume that in the course of their career social movements acquire formal organization and centralized control; that they are aided by professional advocacy groups and propelled forward by »organizers«. The most exhaustively studied movements, such as the farmworker movements (Jenkins, 1985, 13), the urban movements (Fainstein/Fainstein, 1974, 202-6), the women's movement (Freeman, 1983, 27), the neighborhood movement (Oliver, 1982), or the statistical analysis of 53 different protest movements in American history (Gamson, 1975, 89/99), all confirm[9] that the formal movement organization increases »combat readiness« and provides more flexible tactical repertoire, hence sustained mobilization, that social movements with professional or full-time organizers are »advantaged«. However, social movement analysts who look outside of the U.S. stumble over the fact that »the traits of professional movement entrepreneurs are hard to discern among the grassroots militants« of Italy, for example. (Tarrow, 1983a, 50-1)

The assumptions gained on the basis of the dominant type of American social movement restricts the usefulness of American-developed categories when applied abroad. But even within the United States one has to wonder how the experience and success of contemporary groups, such as direct action oriented anti-nuke groups (e.g. Livermore Action or Clamshell Alliance), are even possible if it has been »shown« that clear rules and centralized resource management are major pluses in »maximizing general combat readiness.« (Gamson, 1975, 89-110) This does not seem to be much of a problem insofar as such movements appear to be »invisible« in the American public sphere: local movements which do not achieve media recognition tend to be confined, literally, in space and time and never acquire the successful social and/or lobby influence which capture the attention of the researchers. Less marginal movement behavior, which could not so easily be overlooked yet did not conform to the familiar pattern, had to be »fitted« into the conceptual apparatus. For example, confronted with the ghetto riots of the sixties analysts found themselves at pains to invent adequate categories outside the classical paradigm which would have described the participants as irrational and alienated individuals. By exchanging »social movement organizations« with »ecological units«, and labelling the spontaneous riots as »situational assembling«, the researchers managed to remain within the familiar framework of the resource mobilization approach (Snyder/Kelly, 1979, 222; McPhail/Miller, 1973).

While the general assumptions about formal organization and the role of the »organizers« tends to lead to the exclusion of newer phenomena from view, the American experience also continues to confirm and reproduce these peculiar qualities. On the one hand, direct action movements (such as

9 Studies of the civil rights movement, however, began to show something different. See Morris, 1984.

anti-nuclear weapons) do transform into institutional politics (such as the Freeze). On the other hand, the all-pervasive entrepreneurial ideology and practice shapes not only voluntary associations but also social movements. Commodification of everyday life takes place at a speed and scope far greater than decommodifying effects of social movements. Even the so-called new, »post-acquisitive« and »non-negotiable« values turn out to be quite marketable and useful for the innovation of capital (»New Age capitalism«). Social movements which started out as radical critiques of state policies (e.g. nuclear policies) have opened up to the solar and soft technology market.

Given the pervasiveness of these trends, the dominance of the resource mobilization approach among the various interpretations makes sense: it locates the »business« of social movement »industries« in the acquisition of resources, while neglecting concrete goals and motives of the participants. Since the belief systems of most movements of the 60s and 70s were extensions of the basic liberal concepts which dominate American public philosophy, the analysis could take ideology for granted, for the motivating force of the movements simply did not require explanation. Instead, the methods of organization and mobilization captured the attention of researchers.

The fact that many social movements in the U.S. have been quick to adopt strategies of sales and advertising firms and instrumental ways of fundraising has resulted in much research – under the heading of »aggregation techniques for recruitment attempts« – on the new forms of »mobilizing resources« such as mass mailing, newspaper advertising, telephone canvassing and high-tech campaign techniques. But their effects of transforming (or splitting) the movement milieu go less well-researched. The »careers« or »cycles« of movements are only just becoming a research topic, as a few authors are beginning to systematically study their effects on policy outputs and the political system. But the currently observable disintegration of the movements themselves, which, among other things, appears to be one result of the successful adoption of professionalization strategies, is not the subject of any empirical research. There exist today, on most movement issues, both national umbrella organizations which (re)present the demands of the movements with pressure group politics in the respective legislative and administrative arenas, and so-called grass-roots organizations, which tend to limit themselves to local struggles over particular grievances. Corresponding to this organizational split one finds a separation of communitarian expressivity (outside of established institutions) and political instrumentalism (interest group politics).[10] But even the local grass-roots movements may develop professional ways of working, hire staff, »market« their issue, or groom cooperative relationships with the police and with the local state.

Overall, the social movements in the U.S. are more entrepreneurial, more competitive, and less ideological than elsewhere. And the research upon them, rather than inquiring into the significance of this specific quality, itself reflects it in the kinds of questions asked, the problems perceived, the language and the methods used. The language and the categories of inquiry may, however, impede the disentangling of various components and agendas of new social movements such as separating their sublimated class agenda from a potential life chance component or distinguishing a possibly relevant new actor from the more familiar ones. The focus of existing research is (tacitly) on the *dominant* types of American social movements: U.S. research studies the housewives around Three Miles Island or Love Canal, and less the incipient revival of anti-nuclear and ecological movements. It focusses on low-risk, safe forms of action much more than on other forms of activism. Interaction between researchers and social movements more often pertains to IPAC[11] or the Bicentennial Peace Campaign[12] than to marginal social movement organizations such as »No Business As Usual«. Most researchers have a penchant for examining collective action via data sources that reveal the visible and public side of social movements, reflecting how American social science in general has been more positivist, relying on survey data and official statistics, as the emphasis is on *measuring* rather than on exploring the significance or the signifying work of social movements.[13]

---

10 Cf. on this split for the peace movement: Mayer, 1984; for the civil rights movement: McAdam, 1983.

11 See p. 44.

12 A typical entrepreneurial movement organization »with hired organizers, 60 chapters nationally, $ 1 million raised annually ...« Gamson, at International Workshop on Participation in Social Movements: Transformation of Structure into Action, Free University, Amsterdam 1986.

13 For an exception see the frame alignment approach as developed by Snow/Benford, 1988.

II. Theoretical Approaches

A. The classical perspective

Dominant until the early 1970s, the so-called »classical« approaches studied a plethora of social phenomena under the heading of »collective behavior and social movements«: fads, crowds, panics, sects, riots and social movements all appeared as reactions to rapid social and economic change and to concomitant disorganization. These societal strains were seen as generating dislocation and anomie (Smelser) or frustration and anger (Gurr). The researchers were politically preoccupied with preventing a rise of fascist and authoritarian movements. In order to explain these, different variants were elaborated: the collective behavior approach[14] with its roots in the Chicago School[15], the mass society approach,[16] and the relative deprivation approach[17]. They all share the basic assumption that individual deprivations, breakdowns of the social order, and homogenizing ideologies are important preconditions for the emergence of social movements. They do not define particular macro-structural strains (generating specific types of mobilization). Rather, any incompatibility, tension, or breakdown in the system may

---

14 Turner/Killian, 1957; 1972; Blumer, 1951; Smelser, 1962. Collective behavior is seen to arise under some form of structural or cultural breakdown that leads to noninstitutionalized efforts aimed at reconstituting ruptured social structures. Smelser, however, moved away from the emphasis on process and toward a social structural conception of movements as response to strain. For a summary of collective behavior work see Marx/Wood, 1975; Zurcher/Snow, 1981; Turner, 1981.

15 Cf. Hadley Cantril, The Psychology of Social Movements, New York, 1967 (4th ed.); Ralph E. Turner, ed., Robert E. Park on Social Control and Collective Behavior: Selected Papers. Chicago: University of Chicago Press, 1867.

16 Due to the characteristics of mass societies (detachment, isolation, lack of strong networks of secondary groups), movements are seen to spread as numerous individuals become detached and susceptible to proselytization and suggestibility. Cf. W. Kornhauser, The Politics of Mass Society. New York: Free Press, 1959; Hannah Arendt, The Origins of Totalitarianism, New York: HBJ, 1951; Lipset, 1963.

17 Here, the movement participants are not seen as alienated rebels without a cause (as likely to participate in radical movements as in reactionary ones, as in the mass society approach). Theorists focus on macro changes and subsequent psychological changes in individuals (frustration – anger – aggression), but have not elaborated the process by which the relatively deprived come to act collectively. See Gurr, 1970; 1973; James Davies, 1962; 1963. For a critical review of this perspective see Gurney/Tierney, 1982.

generate collective action: fascist or communist movements, escapist/ regressive or emancipatory/progressive movements: the category of social movements used here includes all forms of collective behavior which occurs outside of the established institutions. As opposed to institutional-conventional action, non-institutional collective behavior is seen as not guided by existing social norms, but as formed to meet the unstructured situations of a breakdown of social control or of normative integration.

This non-institutional collective behavior follows a life-cycle which moves from spontaneous crowd action to the formation of publics and social movements. Structures which do emerge in the process and their consequences receive little attention. If growth of movements occurs, it is understood to be the result of crude processes of communication such as contagion, rumor, circular reaction and diffusion, for which homogenizing ideologies play an important role.

Hence, classical theorists have focussed particularly on the *micro* level of social-psychological analysis: while the collective behavior approach would emphasize the role of emergent norms and values in the generation of social movements, and the mass society approach would stress feelings of »alienation and anxiety« engendered by »social atomization« (Kornhauser 1959, 32), and while relative deprivation theory took its name from the psychological state thought to trigger protest, they all explained the origins of social movements by reference to the same dynamics that accounted for individual participation in movement activities.[18] Hence, answers to micro questions of individual participation *and* answers to macro questions of movement emergence are sought in the characteristic psychological profile of the participant and the presumed psychological functions associated with participation.

While not all theorists in this tradition deem collective behavior to be an irrational response of atomized individuals to change, they all stress psychological reactions to breakdown, crude modes of communication, volatile goals and the transitory nature of social movements. Movements are seen as a likely consequence of the momentary imbalance when a society is not capable of realizing the values and expectations it nurtures in its members, and to which it normally appeals for the legitimation of the social order. American society in particular is known for the extent to which its hegemonic dis-

18 Only Turner/Killian, 1956/1972/1986 have long been critical of explaining movements on the basis of individual states of mind.

course nurtures far-reaching democratic expectations (cf. Huntington, 1981). But most researchers in this tradition share a certain distaste, sometimes subtle, sometimes not, for these movements and their participants.

Since the common premise underlying the classical models is an approximation to the pluralist ideal of an open polity (see Smelser, Bell, Parsons; and Jenkins, 1985, xii,3, for a summary), the viability of social movements as vehicles for social change has to be contested. As spontaneous, essentially expressive autbursts, they are not accorded the capacity to influence, in the long run, societal development or institutional/policy outcomes in the way parties, interest organizations, and elites do. Hence, political processes and actual political change do not need to enter the scope of analysis. Hence there *is* no significant interaction between the social movements studied by the sociologists and the political system.[19]

This long prevailing view within traditional American sociology also explains the lack of overlap and exchange between different disciplines in the study of social movements. While sociologists assumed that collective mobilization had little impact on institutional outcomes, for most political scientists social movements are »nascent groups« which do not become interesting until they have »crossed the treshold into organizational life.«[20] Social movement research within the two disciplines therefore developed in relative isolation from each other. Political scientists focussed on those movements which eventually »mature« into interest groups with a well-defined membership, stable funding, a permanent staff, and a knowledge of how to operate within the political process. Since these organized groups have long been perceived as fundamental components of the American political process,[21] they have obviously been looking at very different phenomena than the classical sociological approaches.

---

19 This still holds true for analysts sympathetic to the movements. Cf. Gusfield, 1970; Gerlach/Hine, 1970.

20 Theodore Lowi, The Politics of Disorder: New York, Basic Books, 1971, 54. Research in the 1980s has begun to rediscover the centrality of politics to the analysis of origins, dynamics, and outcomes of social movements. See Tarrow, 1988.

21 See above, first chapter. Cf. also The Federalist # 10; Tocqueville, Democracy in America; David Truman, The Governmental Process in America. New York: Knopf, 1958.

B. The Resource Mobilization Perspective

Some of the inadequacies of the classical tradition became obvious in the 1960s when high mobilization was created by the civil rights, anti-war, women's and black movements. These massive social movements stimulated a shift in theoretical assumptions and analytic emphases, which eventually became formalized in the resource mobilization theory. The movement actors whom social scientists then witnessed hardly conformed to the image of the anomic, irrational and deviant behavior which traditional social psychological conceptions were holding. Clearly, they enjoyed wide societal and also academic support, and the dynamic of these movements could neither be explained by reference to deprivations nor individual fear reactions. Thus, a renaissance in the study of social movements was triggered by a critical rethinking of the dominant theories in the field. (McCarthy/Zald, 1973, 1977; Shorter/Tilly, 1974; Gamson, 1975; Useem, 1975; Oberschall, 1973)

In order to arrive at meaningful explanations of (and interventions into) the observable movements, the focus and level of analysis were shifted from social-psychological to more macro political and structural accounts of movement dynamics. Against the presumed irrationality of movement actors and against the denial of their role in social change in the traditional theories was now set a concept of social movements as forms of rational interest politics.

Because the long-standing discontent of Blacks, women, Native Americans or other deprived minorities did not afford much analytical leverage for explaining the widespread mobilization of the 60s and early 70s, resource mobilization theorists largely dismissed grievances as explanatory variables. For them, the ubiquity and constancy of mobilizing grievances can be assumed.[22] In a similar vein, these authors thought that the role of ideology could be downplayed since the belief systems of most movements of the 60s and 70s were recognized as extensions of the basic liberal concepts which dominate American public discourse. Whereas in the classical tradition »ideology« (usually understood as irrational »generalized beliefs«) played a crucial role in the transformation of discontent into action, with the resource mobilization approach ideological orientations and motivations are taken for granted. Instead of objective tensions, deprivations, and belief systems, the *variability of resources* becomes the most important factor in explaining

---

22 Jenkins/Perrow, 1977, 250-1; McCarthy/Zald, 1977, 1214-5; Oberschall, 1973, 194-5.

emergence and development of insurgency. Aided by newly available or improved resources, deprived groups can be mobilized into collective political behavior.[23]

Under these conditions, social movements are no longer *apart* from mainstream political parties, lobbies and interest groups, but rather, they share space with them as legitimate players. A fundamental continuity between institutionalized and movement politics was thus posited: »In place of the old duality of extremist politics and pluralist politics, there is simply politics ... Rebellion, in this view, is simply politics by other means.« (Gamson, 1975, 138-142) The political scientists, too, began to see »protest as a political resource« (thus the title of the 1968 article by Lipsky), a resource which could be exchanged for »policy goods« (Piven/Cloward; Lipsky; Eisinger; Jenkins/Perrow). This view fundamentally changes the relationship between protesters and their adressees; it is now understood as a bargaining process between rational actors on both sides. Protest leaders were seen as using the threat of disruption as a resource, administrators were seen as using the tools of their office to set the terms of the agenda, and intermediate actors would weigh in on one side or the other depending on how the agenda was structured (Lipsky, 1968, 1145-6). »Rational actors« employing strategic and instrumental reasoning were entering every field: historical research on crowd behavior emphasized the rational aspects of the recruitment to crowds (Rude, 1960, 1964); American analysts of the 60s riots found at least »crude rationality« (Spilerman, 1972; Aldrich/Berk, 1972).

The resource mobilization approach was initially elaborated by scholars directly affected by the 60s movements and the New Left. They knew from direct experience that these movements involved highly educated activists and enjoyed the support of many academic social scientists. This explains why academic reflections explicitly adressed the innovations in the organization and mobilization processes and why, often, the standpoint of analysis approximated that of the movement organizer concerned with the imperatives of mobilization. While one strand of researchers emphasized such mobilization processes as grassroots participation, decentralized structures, and

23 While resources were conceived of differently by different authors – for McCarthy/Zald they consist of money, facilities, labor and legitimacy, for Tilly of land, capital, and technical expertise, and Freeman distinguishes between tangible assets (such as the just mentioned) and intangible, human assets such as organizing and legal skills, labor of supporters etc. – all of them assume an economy of social struggle in which a movement's success depends upon the amount of assets a social movement organization has.

goals such as direct personal involvement and the creation of new identities and solidarities[24], the majority of resource mobilization theorists concluded that such new orientations would result in a loss of strategic effectiveness.

With increasing elaboration, the dominant approach began to split into two competing perspectives, with one maintaining the organizational focus and the other developing a political process emphasis. The first (sometimes called the »organizational-entrepreneurial«, Morris/Herring, 1987, 161ff) focusses on how burgeoning social movement organizations (SMO)[25] seek to mobilize and routinize – frequently by tapping elite sources of support – the flow of resources to insure movement survival. Grievances are here not only structurally given, they are seen as being more and more *»manufactured«* by the mobilizing efforts of movement »entrepreneurs«. These movement »entrepreneurs« and the SMOs are seen as the catalysts which transform the discontents and demands into purposive movements. The SMOs have full-time, paid staffs, cultivate conscience constituencies, and concentrate on manipulating the mass media so as to influence public opinion and to generate elite responses and policy changes. While such movements have in fact frequently occurred in the American setting, they were hypostasized by this perspective as it defined the 60s movements as historically unique, in that the majority were professional movement organizations, when in fact the strongest empirical support for this theory came from studies of the public interest »movement« (cf. Berry, 1977; also P. Wood, 1982), from studies of movements of deprived groups such as welfare recipients or the farm workers (which provided fertile ground for cadre entrepreneurship, cf. Jenkins/Perrow, 1977; Bailis, 1974), and from studies of right-wing and conservative social movements (cf. Lo 1982; Liebman/Wirthnow, 1983; McCarthy 1987).

In this perspective, the economization of politics, which is generally inherent in the resource mobilization approach, is taken farthest. Influenced by the insights of Mancur Olson (1968), Oberschall proposed that social movements could best be seen as managers of the resources afforded by given groups. He described forms of cost-benefit analysis by collective actors

24 Cf. Breines, 1982, who writes that SDS adopted a »leaderless,« decentralized model of democratic structure in order to maximize the values of direct participation and communal involvement, and to avoid the dangers of oligarchy and cooptation.

25 »A complex or formal organization which identifies its goals with the preferences of a social movement ... and attempts to implement those goals.« McCarthy/Zald, 1977, 1218.

(1973, 168-70). Extending the economic metaphor, McCarthy/Zald defined a »social movement industry« (1977, 1219) as the set of movement organizations oriented toward a similar social change goal, making clear that the fate of a particular organization depends not only on its internal organization and resources, but also on »market conditions« such as the behavior of competing groups and the entrepreneurship of leaders. They defined the »social movement sector« (1977, 1220) as the sum of all social movement industries in the society, which as such competes with other sectors of society for resources in a (capitalist free) enterprise market.[26] In this sense, McCarthy/Zald do not at all oppose the pluralist view of politics which locates political action in an open market place of groups and ideas without biased structural rigidities. Rather, this strand of resource mobilization theory maintains the myth of free enterprise in ideas, as SMOs are seen as competing with non-movement organizations for the allegiance and resources of the population. Social movement behavior is viewed as the consequence of competition between various SMOs as they calculate and execute actions that give themselves notoriety and expand their membership in the same way a corporation would engage in advertising campaigns to increase sales and profits (McCarthy/Zald, 1977, 1229).

The other resource mobilization perspective gives primacy to *indigenous protest mobilization* while also acknowledging the importance of reactive external support from movement patrons and also paying attention to the presence/absence of a supportive political opportunity structure. Based on empirical work, particularly about the early civil rights movement, authors here argue that two sets of macro-structural factors facilitate the generation of social insurgency: a) the level of organization within an aggrieved population, i.e. the degree of structural »readiness«, and b) the political realities confronting members and challengers, i.e. the structure of political opportunities. (Tilly, 1978; McAdam, 1982; Morris, 1984; Jenkins, 1985 – some of these authors even reject the resource mobilization label.)

---

26 In 1985, Garner/Zald redefined the SMS as the configuration of social movements, the structure of antagonistic, competing, and/or cooperating movements, which in turn is part of a larger structure of action that may include parties, state bureaucracies, media, pressure groups, churches etc. They claim that this new definition is both more inclusive and less economistic, as it not only includes action generated by SMOs. (Garner/Zald, 1985, 120)

Specific studies of the interplay between opportunity structures and collective mobilization have focussed on the relationships between the repressiveness or openness of a political system and the development and strategies of social movements (Eisinger, 1973; Kitschelt, 1986). But while the conditions for the responsiveness of the political system (as distinct from the conditions of mobilization) appear to have been the province of political scientists, who display a greater interest in analyzing the distribution of power in society and the differential policy responses to citizen participation, political science has lagged behind sociology with regard to developing the theoretical frameworks to analyze the development of protest movements and to studying the impact and outcomes of such movements (cf. Garrow, 1985).

Underlying both approaches is an elitist model of politics, in which both the regular channels for interest realization and the resources for political action are unevenly distributed. Hence, resources for deprived or excluded groups have to come from outside their own sphere – either from reform-oriented factions of the elite (McCarthy/Zald, 1973, 18; 1977, 1221) or from intermediary agencies in the political environment (Tarrow, 1983a, 24). Hence, movements in this model do not correspond to either the short-term riot nor to totalitarian mass movements. Instead, the model assumes that, in the course of their career, social movements generate the attributes of formal organization and centralization. They are defined as well organized SMOs striving to maximize their power through skillful use of resources, balanced cost-benefit calculations, and the crucial role of the »organizer«. According to Gamson, McCarthy/Zald, Freeman, or Jenkins, a social movement is »successful« when – due to hierarchical formal organization, professional full-time organizers, and the successful mobilization of outside support – it gains strategic effectiveness and combat readiness.

On this basis, further derivations of the resource mobilization approach have been developed in recent years, which seek to balance some of the weaknesses and problems of the paradigm:

1. Integration of structural/organizational with social-psychological factors (frame alignment).
2. Political system/impacts on political system.
3. Integration of resource mobilization approach with macro sociological approaches.

1. Various authors have articulated the necessity of (re)integrating social-psychological factors, which were displaced by the emphasis on instrumental, purposive rationality of the resource mobilization approach (Ferree/ Miller, 1985; Jenkins, 1983: 527, 649; McAdam, 1984; Snow et al., 1985). In particular, some of the qualities of the *new* social movements led to a rediscovery of earlier social-psychological work, e.g. that of Orin Klapp (1979) and of Turner (1969), who had already predicted the themes and key concepts of the contemporary social movements (cf. Perrow, 1979). Also, certain approaches had not been available at the time the resource mobilization approach was developed, such as cognitive social psychologies, and critical and hermeneutic approaches to culture were now seen as relevant to the ongoing social movements which engaged the attention of concerned social scientists.

Snow et al. (1986) and Snow/Benford (1988) have shown how Goffman's frame analysis can be tied to participation processes in social movements. They developed the so-called frame alignment approach which links individual and SMO interpretive orientations in such a way that individual interests, values, beliefs and SMO activities, goals, and ideology are congruent. This expansion of the resource mobilization approach to include *interpretive* resources, meanings and other ideational elements, no longer neglects the process of grievance interpretation. The authors focus on the manner in which grievances are interpreted and on the diffusion of those interpretations. Because they see social movements not only as carriers and transmitters of ideas, but as actively engaged in the production of meaning for participants and antagonists, as part of the »politics of signification« (Snow/ Benford, 1988), they look not only at the factors that facilitate or impede the actualization of latent structural potential, but simultaneously at the structural *and* cognitive/interactional factors. Hence, they do not have a static view of participation, but a processual and dynamic one. This allows them to avoid generalizations, as if there were just one or two overarching microstructural or social-psychological processes that explain participation in *all* movements regardless of variation in objectives, organizational structure, and constituency.

They find that occurrence, intensity, and duration of protest cycles are not just a function of available resources, opportunity structures and regime responses, but are also due to the presence/absence of a potent innovative master frame, i.e. to the way these variables are framed and to the degree with which they resonate with the targets of mobilization.[27]

Because the assertion of the social-psychological level in social movement research reifies the micro/macro distinction as distinct levels of analysis, others (e.g. McAdam, 1988; Klandermans et al., 1988) have called for intermediate theoretical »bridges« to join empirical work at both levels of analysis. McAdam proposes to study the relationship between macro political factors and individual decisions to participate as mediated through the conceptual »bridge« of the *micromobilization context*. Mediating between opportunity and action are people and the subjective meanings they attach to their situation. The micromobilization context is that small group setting in which processes of collective attribution are combined with rudimentary forms of organization to produce mobilization for collective action, for example pre-existing political groups or friendship networks. Because these settings supply established structures of solidary incentives (defined as »the myriad interpersonal rewards that attend to ongoing participation in a group«), it is not necessary to provide selective incentives. Rather, an intense ideological identification with the values of the campaign acts to »push« the individual in the direction of participation, while the integration into supportive networks acts as the structural »pull« encouraging the individual to make good on her/his belief.

Even though the resource mobilization approach as such dismisses the ideological content of movements as irrelevant, recently efforts have been made to expand it in the direction of accounting for ideological factors, too. Downey's (1986) ethnographic study of organizational dilemmas of the Clamshell Alliance is an interesting attempt. He extends theory from symbolic anthropology to integrate the analysis of ideology into the resource mobilization approach without sacrificing the latter's emphasis on rational calculation.

---

27 Since they can inquire into the relationship between types of frame alignment and types of movement, they find distinctions between low demand, professional movements (»that are difficult to distinguish from conventional interest groups«), which use »frame bridging;« reactive movements and segmentally organized movements, which use »value amplification;« and movements with »world-transforming goals« and those that are »greedy« in terms of time, energy, and orientation, which use »frame transformation.«

2. Other authors, political scientists in particular, have undertaken efforts to remedy the systematic lack of the resource mobilization approach concerning the relationship between social movements and the *political system*, because of which the relations between protests and reform could not be posed as a researchable problem.

Tarrow (1988a) expanded the resource mobilization approach on the assumption that acts of disruption affect not only the personnel and dimensions of the organizations involved, but also engage the attention of elites and the mass public. He adopted from Eisinger the concept of political opportunity structure and enlarged it to include other aspects of the political structure which seemed useful to understanding the success of social movements. The unfolding of a process of policy innovation in the political system, which addresses the protesters' stated needs, is his evidence for successful goal achievement of a social movement and the basis for detecting waves of policy innovation coinciding with waves of social protest. (For a systematic definition of the concepts ›political opportunity structure‹ and ›cycles of protest‹ see Tarrow, 1989).

While Tarrow applies this cyclical concept to non-American contexts (Italy, 1966-1975), other authors have studied the relation between cycles of protest and cycles of reform for the U.S.. Browning et al. (1984) have studied minority mobilization and urban political change. Piven and Cloward (1977) pointed to the effects of imminent changes in electoral coalitions on the national administration, which facilitated the protest movements of the 1930s and the civil rights movement.

Piven and Cloward seized much of the debate during the dissolution of the 60s movements. This was not because of the fact that they included the interplay of movements and the political system in their analysis, but rather, because of the way in which they interpreted its impact. Their research led them to insist on the principal incapacity of movements to protect themselves from cooptation. Hence, protest is successful only as long as it challenges the state, formal organizations are seen as diluting the collective energy of the poor because they divert social movement energies into routine politics.[28] They regard leadership, the professional organizers and movement

---

28 »Insurgency is always short-lived. Once it subsides and the people leave the streets, most of the organizations which it temporarily threw up and which elites helped to nurture simply fade away. As for the few organizations which survive, it is because they become *more* useful to those who control the resources on which they depend than to the lower-class groups which the organizations claim to represent.« (p. xi)

entrepreneurs, which loom so large in the organizational-entrepreneurial variant, as inducing failure, since they tend to direct a group's efforts towards institutionalization rather than towards radical change. Underlying this apparent contradiction within the resource mobilization approach is the fact that Piven and Cloward were looking at a different social movement: Blacks faced more repression and intransigence, historically and during this period, hence did not accept so easily the existing procedures of conflict resolution.

3. Another American tendency proposes to connect the insights of resource mobilization theory to a version of the European-imported »identity-approach« in order to capture the new quality of the movements of the 70s and 80s. On the basis of the »inadequacy of class analysis« with respect to these new movements proliferating in the West (Cohen, 1983, 97), a marriage of the (American) resource mobilization – and (what is taken to be the European) identity-oriented paradigm, facilitated by Habermas' theory of communicative action, has been called for (Cohen, 1985, 705).

The contribution of resource mobilization theory would be the emphasis on the plurality of associations and organizations created by movement actors. The contribution of Touraine, the exemplary European author, would be his emphasis on the dual character of movements[29] and their contestation over alternative institutional potentials of cultural developments (1985, 715). This argument, however, takes place more on the level of ideological debates *about* social movements rather than being grounded in actual social movement research. As a consequence, the synthetic result of this marriage has more to do with normative prescriptions about how social movements ought to be than with an analysis of the character of actually existing new social movements. Their newness is described in the following manner:

> »... the movements meet and discuss in such odd places as churches, town meetings, clubs ... and ... create complex networks and economic self-help organizations. ... These movements are radical without being revolutionary. They are creating public spaces alongside a political system that has become too rigid or too cynical.« (Cohen, 1983, 106-7; Arato/Cohen, 1984, 271)

Movement activity in the U.S., even in the mentioned »odd« places, has *always* complemented regular political activity, there is nothing radical or new about it. Thus, the »anti-institutional bias« of American movements is not to be seen in the context of »the degeneration of institutionalized public

29 that they involve a double reference both to cultural orientations *and* to social relations.

spaces,« but rather in the long-standing American tradition appreciated since Tocqueville.[30] Pointing to the decline in vigor of the representative process and to the growth of corporate manipulation (Arato/Cohen, 267-8) does not explain much about the conflict structure underlying the emergence and the demands of the new social movements. The movements they refer to in particular, i.e. the peace and anti-nuclear movement, are refuting the expansion of powers of an unaccountable, militarized security state, while Arato/Cohen assume as a »crucial norm« of the new social movements a societal democratization which involves pushing back but not eliminating the state (Arato/Cohen, 1984, 277).

This type of new social movement debate, as carried on in Telos (and Telos-sponsored conferences), consists basically of advice freely offered by »sympathetic theoreticians« (Cohen, 1983, 111) who feel strongly about dissociating themselves from the »eschatological, revolutionary ideologies of the historical Left and part of the New Left« in order to identify the »democratizing and emancipatory« versus the »authoritarian and regressive« dimensions of the movements (Telos conference, New York, Dec. 1984; cf. also Luke, 1986). This betrays the effort to import Habermas' postulates of what movements must do in order to become carriers of societal evolution, but fails to account for the relevant features or dynamics of actually existing social movements.

***

Though an integration of *resource mobilization* and *classical* perspectives has repeatedly been recommended and attempted (see McAdam/McCarthy/Zald, 1988), the competition between the »schools« seems too intense to allow such integration. According to Morris/Herring, who interviewed proponents of both perspectives, the adherents of the classical perspective think of it as the more comprehensive theory which should integrate the other; but resource mobilization adherents so strongly reject the premise of a break in social structure as 19th century heritage that integration seems highly unlikely (Morris/Herring, 1987, 188).

Even though the research field appears to be structured mainly by these two theories and their struggle for dominance (which has clearly been won

30 For a contemporary reference to the typicality of such movements and such meeting places, see Bellah et al., 1986.

by the resource mobilization approach), there are also other perspectives which researchers have worked with.

C. The Class-Analytical Perspective

Within the realm of urban sociology developed an approach which did not discard class analysis so whole-heartedly. Various authors have attempted to relate the transformation in the local political system, including the growing role of neighborhood movements, to larger transformations in the class structure of society and to read them as exemplary cases of new class coalitions. Mollenkopf's work on community organizations and city politics (1980, 1984), Hill's work on the crisis of industrial cities (1978, 1980, 1984) and Katznelson's study *City Trenches* (1981) are but a few examples of this approach, which was also widely debated in the International Journal of Urban and Regional Research. Earlier work of Castells (1976, 1978, 1979) also moved within the parameters defined here, but he has since come to criticize them for theoretically downgrading the new movements by viewing them as secondary and mediated contradictions in the sphere of reproduction. Castells has attempted to transcend this limitation of the class-analytical approach by drawing up a cross-cultural, comprehensive theory of urban movements (1983), which – he claims – systematically includes cultural and ideological factors besides macrostructural factors. Reflecting the European puzzle of having a working class actor replaced by movements in other spheres, Castells argues that the arena of history has moved away from the factory floor into the neighborhood, where people threaten ongoing systems by their demands, not for control of the means of production, but for control of collective consumption, the right to build a common culture, and the capacity to mutually determine their fate as citizens.

In my opinion, these different factors are, however, not successfully integrated into a comprehensive explanation of urban movements. For example, Castells describes the 60s black power revolts in American cities as results of the threat of urban renewal and the presence of bad services, but does *not* link them to the civil rights movements which preceded them, nor to the »rising expectations« induced by the War on Poverty, nor to the general turmoil of the period, where student and anti-war movement provided a context in which this cycle of protest emerged. His analysis is still basically characterized by the familiar structuralist pattern of collective consumption, economic restructuring, and state organization, to which he simply, and in rather ahistorical fashion, *adds on* the new movements' features like ethnic, cultural, and other solidaric bonds.

Other work probing in the direction of locating the movements within economic and political restructuring processes that have their origin in the crisis of the current system of capital accumulation (cf. Aglietta, Hirsch, Jessop) hold some promise of actually explaining the emergence of new actors, new demands, and new forms of action on the basis of a comprehensive theory of the transition from one societal pattern to another, say from fordism to post-fordism (cf. Smith/Feagin, 1987; Clarke/Mayer, 1986). Work on the implications of this type of urban restructuring for social movements is, however, still in its infancy.

D. The Populist Perspective

Resource mobilization was triggered by – and remained tied to – the 60s movements: the bulk of the literature deals with the civil rights, women's, student and anti-war movements of the decade. Only some of the later variants, the frame alignment approach for example, have included the new peace, ecological, anti-nuclear and new urban movements in their analysis. Where they looked at newer mobilizations, researchers frequently saw themselves forced to return to some of the theories the resource mobilization approach had set out to displace (hence the revival of the relative deprivation approach, cf. Walsh, 1981).

The class analytical direction has remained restricted to the urban field, where theorizing efforts about *new* social movements are still contradictory and limited. American social scientists generally tend to dismiss the new movements as simply another wave of short-lived, marginal, and inconsequential mobilization. The same bias that was prevalent in the original class-analytical perspective, which focussed on the traditional hierarchy of societal contradictions, also still marks social scientists on the Left, who have a hard time even acknowledging the political relevance of contemporary direct action movements. Even the publication of an excellent account of the »Culture of Direct Action« (Epstein, 1985) in a left journal did not seem legitimate without pointing out that this movement »could help revitalize a *larger, left-wing* protest movement in the United States.« (33; emphasis MM)

The exceptions to this general neglect or awkward deprioritizing tend to place new social movements in the U.S. in a populist tradition, which blurs the specificity and newness of their claims and dynamics. These are primarily descriptive, but partisan studies that focus on the explosive expansion of »citizen action« and on how community-organized initiatives consolidate and revive a very American tradition. (Especially Boyte, 1980, 1984; cf. also Boyte/Riesman, 1986; Boyte/Booth/Max, 1986). In these analyses, societal or structural conditions are hardly present, instead, one gets broad, occasionally romanticizing descriptions of community struggles, which often refer back to Alinsky's community organization approach (cf. Alinsky, 1969, 1971; Lancourt, 1979; Kahn, 1970; Miller, 1981; Fisher, 1984) or try to ground current struggles in the American tradition of popular revolt (Adamson/Borgos, 1986; Bouchier, 1987) and of pacifism (Cooney/ Michalowski, 1977; Wittner, 1969; Lynd, 1966). Community researchers in the U.S. in particular, find it easy to define »the neighborhood« with all its grassroots organizations in populist opposition to »the state« and all other megastructures.

A specific variant within this category is the ecological neighborhood literature, which – closely connected to respective lobby organizations – attempts to spread a certain concept of »neighborhood power«: »a working tool in bringing political and economic power down to a human and working scale« (cf. Kotler, 1969; Morris/Hess, 1975; D. Morris, 1982; Cunningham/Kotler, 1983).

The latest variant within this approach is the neo-communitarian debate, which comes from such proselytizers of a »green movement« as Capra/ Stretnak (1984) or Mark Satin (1978), and has also entered the academic field in the form of a ›Conference Group on Transformational Politics‹ within the APSA.

Some of the monographs and case studies in this tradition do introduce more analytic criteria and typlogies (pertaining to issue, form or background of the movement) to better describe the phenomenon, but they do not transcend it in the direction of a more theoretically grounded analysis (Perlman, 1976, 1979; Fainstein/Fainstein, 1974; Delgado, 1986; Milbrath, 1984). Boggs (1986) does interpret the populist movements in some U.S. cities as part of the »new social movements« that are »situated within the unfolding contradictions of a rapidly changing industrial order« (3). But even this comparative study remains theoretically limited by the bias of this approach; the author is so concerned with the movements' apparent »failure to confront the issue of power« that the book is primarily a struggle for a political translation of the new movements.

E. Integrative Perspectives

All approaches presented so far look at social movements as phenomena taking place in the public arena as defined by the dominant pattern of politics. The new movements, however, have a side to them which is either not expressed and measurable in public spaces and through institutional change, or striving towards a different definition of »public«. The construction of new gender relations, the development of new cultural patterns, the refusal, often, to even participate in the given polity or to challenge it for benefits, frequently do not enter the public arena or imply the generation of an own version of a public arena. This redefinition of participation in the public sphere, though difficult to mesure, may however have an impact on the general public (cf. Katzenstein, 1988).

Gusfield (1981) has offered a non-linear model of social movements, where a movement connotes »a change in the meaning of objects and events rather than the occurrence of associations« (322). While this feature is not at all restricted to movements that »rebel against the prevailing social structure,« it directs our attention to dimensions of movements which seem to have taken on particular significance for the »new« life chance movements.

Thus, Kitschelt (1985) argues that social movements have to be seen as contingent not only on the structural preconditions in a social formation, and on their practical actions, but also on the cultural representations of claims by the social actors involved. In comparing life chance movements in the U.S. and Germany, he finds that their demands concern collective, intangible, and indivisible claims (which the established procedures of pluralist bargaining are ill-equipped to process). He suggests viewing them as fragmented, sectorally confined conflicts that aim at incrementally limiting the expansion of commodity relations and administrative control. Though disjointed, these processes of social conflict may eventually result in profound, systemic transformations since they pose severe constraints on the internal logic of markets and administrations.

While also stressing the level of cultural representations, Foss/Larkin (1986), echoing the interpretation of Piven and Cloward, go a step further. In an attempt to account for the lack of political opposition in contemporary

USA, they interpret the 1970s as a recoil from the political dissidence of the 60s »whereby some of the cultural dissidence was incorporated, shorn of oppositional content, into a drive to expand the domestic market.« The book attempts to ground this reading in a transhistorical interpretation (roaming throughout history from the English Revolution of 1649 via Iran in 1977, all the way to the »social movement to come«), which defines social movements as the actual periods of overt open conflict »where rebellion against the prevailing social structure« takes place (71). These social movements are »exciting, unique experiences« comparable to so-called peak experiences in the life of an individual (142).

While the terminology is that of a class-analytical approach, Foss/Larkin focus on the construction of meaning and identities through participation in conflict: »As social movement members participate in unalienated learning, engage in self-governance, and struggle against their subjugation, they participate in mass therapy, helping each other overcome the crippling effects of their socialization to positions of subordination.« (106)

Less interested in the historical specificity of either the movements or of reform and policy innovation, but primarily interested in the ongoing process of reinterpretation of social reality which the authors see as taking place in all social movements, and which, according to their definition, interferes with the reproduction of »hegemonic ideology« (72), they draw generalizations which however mirror the historical reality of the first world's 60s.[31] As opposed to most of the essays in Sayres et al. (1984), which offer the same interpretation of the 60s movements, but do not claim transhistorical truth, the dynamics gleaned from the 60s and 70s are here generalized: The very process of engaging in social movements »liberates new human potentialities, which, in the following period of social quiescence, are alienated from their possessors and incorporated into new forms of alienation.« (106; cf. 155)

---

31 For example, Foss/Larkin write that in periods of social quiescence members of »subordinated social categories« accept their subordination, and problems of alienation and stratification are seen as »personal.« During periods of social movement, however, they are reinterpreted as political. »During social movement periods,« they write, »a subjectivation of the social structure takes place, whereby the institutionalization is redefined as ›interest‹.« (90) While this was a recurrent phenomenon, practiced particularly by the American Left, movement protagonists in other places have not needed to subjectivize structures in this manner. – This is not the only place where this ›transhistorical‹ study mirrors the experience of the American 60s movements.

III. Methodological Orientations

Since the classical tradition included such a plethora of social phenomena in the category of social movements, no typological unanimity could emerge. The field consisted primarily of, a) synthetic literature reviews and typologies, and b) case studies of noteworthy, sometimes extreme forms of collective behavior. Besides such accumulation and classification of cases, few systematic studies and even fewer comparative analyses were undertaken.

The 60s added various new dimensions to the study of social protest. First of all, more thorough case studies of pedestrian forms of collective behavior were undertaken (e.g. Lipsky, 1968; Gerlach/Hine, 1970), which allowed to draw out some analytical conclusions. Secondly, quantitative research began to spread in the form of, a) approaches using survey data (for example on black attitudes: Sears, 1969), b) ecological analyses of the correlates of mass disturbances (best exemplified by Gurr, 1970, or Spilerman, 1970), and c) historical reconstruction of collective action (Shorter/Tilly, 1974; Snyder/Tilly, 1972; Tilly/Tilly/Tilly, 1975; Tilly, 1978). With growing sophistication, trend analysis was later added which uses multiple regression, interspliced by cross-sectional analysis, on trend data from survey research archives.

As Tarrow (1983a) pointed out, however, much of this quantitative research is of uncertain relevance to the study of social movements, since the aggregate data merely record incidents of collective action without implying any necessary organizational or group presence in such behavior. An additional problem is that frequently the records come from courts, police departments or other governmental agencies, and therefore tend to »cover the rebel's tracks« (Tilly). Similarly, it is problematic to draw conclusions from global survey data (on the development of »issue publics«) about the mobilizing potential of social movements (Watts, 1987). Attitudinal data that are won with methods focussing on the individual necessarily remain distant from a research object consisting of mobilized networks and collectivities. But quantifiability, even if it explains little or nothing, affords the authentic look of »real« simulated science. It is therefore no accident that Gurr's work for ›Why Men Rebel‹ was well supported (see IV) and was well received.[32]

---

32 It won the Woodrow Wilson Foundation Award from the Political Science profession, and a rave review in the New York Times by Lewis Coser, president for 1974-5 of the American Sociological Association. (Foss/Larkin, 116).

Quantitative research on violence up until the late 70s was dominated by (primarily bivariate) cross-tabular analyses (e.g. Gamson, 1975; Shorter/Tilly, 1971) and therefore often ignored relevant variables such as exogenous determinants of social change. Snyder/Kelly (1979) charged that the omission of determinants in models that estimate the effect of collective action on outcome will result in over- or understatement of the relationship between collective action and social change. (228)

Generally, resource mobilization theorists prefer in-depth process analysis of particular movements to quantitative analyses. Most of the work guided by this perspective reconstructs a mobilization process in great detail and presents it in the form of a case study or narrative on the developments of movements in a given setting. But the intention is to arrive at generalizable statements, which would serve to explain and predict such radically different movements as Common Cause and Moral Majority.

If Gamson's work is a methodological exception within the bulk of the resource mobilization literature, it still represents the basic substantive thrust. He collected information on an unbiased sample of *all* relevant collectivities in the U.S. from 1800 to 1945. His procedure was to read a variety of historical accounts to generate a list of protest groups, to sample from that list, to exclude groups which did not meet his operational definition of a challenging group, and to use the accounts for information on group characteristics (such as size, goals, organization, involvement in violence etc.) and on the outcome of the political challenge.

Tarrow's project gathered a large sample of systematic information from public records (using a single newspaper) and coded the articles on protest events. Similarly, Jenkins used research assistants to conduct a content analysis of New York Times entries, after »identifying relevant headings in the index under which movement actions are reported.« They then scanned for movement actions, content coding these for type of action, type of acting unit, and major issues.

Other resource mobilization theorists showed that the use of such secondary sources does not provide data on most resources and not at regular enough intervals, and suggested therefore reliance on internally generated data sources of the groups studied (and on newspapers, which Jenkins and Tarrow already used). This strategy, pursued by Snyder and Kelly, requires »samples of convenience,« i.e. choosing groups for which the appropriate information exists over a long time span.

These difficulties (as well as the problem that arises from the fact that the New York Times also de-emphasizes populist politics, civil disobedience etc. and thus corresponds to the blind eye of the resource mobilization approach) are avoided in analyses based on primary data such as Morris' (1984), who collected it from archives and in-depth interviews with grass-roots leadership in the civil rights movement. They are also avoided by studies using questionnaire survey data from demonstrators, as Ladd et al. (1983)[33] used, or by the method applied by Snow et al., who gathered data on the U.S. peace movement by extensive ethnographic participation in local and regional peace movement activities. In order to explore the signifying work of social movements, their approach required that the researchers be involved in ongoing encounters with movement members. So they conducted formal and informal interviews with local participants, and local and national activists, and also analyzed movement-generated documents and periodicals.

Though not dealing with an ongoing movement, McAdam also managed, in a different way, to access information exhaustively. For his case study of the 1964 Mississippi Freedom summer project (1988), he analyzed archival data (the 1068 completed application forms of participants, rejects, and withdrawals) to assess the relative importance of various factors in recruitment to activism. He coded them, and thus was able to find that the motivations for participation did not differ significantly for withdrawals and participants, but that integration into a variety of micromobilization contexts did differ.[34]

There is also some interaction between researchers in the way that data sets are being exchanged. (E.g. McAdam's on civil rights/black movements 1953-1976; Charles Perrow's New York Times-derived data series for the women's movement [1947-1972] and anti-war movement [1953-1970.])

---

33 This survey data from participants in a national anti-nuclear demonstration was complemented with a thematic review of the anti-nuclear literature.

34 In assessing the importance of three different micromobilization contexts, he looked at them separately in terms of how well they differentiate Freedom summer participants from withdrawals. The effects of all three were measured simultaneously by means of a logit regression equation predicting participation, computed an »interpersonal contact score« for each participant, and found a strong positive relation between participation and the weighted sum of an applicant's interpersonal ties. From this he could conclude that both the nature and the greater number of interpersonal ties enjoyed by the participants had a significant effect on their decision to go to Mississippi. – He also conducted some 80 in-depth interviews as a follow-up study.

Many of the scholars within the resource mobilization approach are not »merely detached observers,« as Harrington put it in the Foreword to Freeman (1983), since they »come from« the movements they analyze. While they are more sympathetic to the movements than scholars in the collective behavior tradition, presumably even representing the »theoretical consciousness of the participant observer« (Harrington), this has not meant a high degree of interaction between researchers and social movements. Nor has it meant that the researchers would inquire into the meanings, values, and consciousness of movement participants. The emphasis being on phenomena that can be *measured* and subjected to variable analysis, emergent trends of new cleavages and forms of resistance have rarely entered the horizon of mainstream social movement research.

IV. Empirical Findings

As can be gathered from the divergence of theoretical and methodological approaches being used in the U.S., it is not possible to compose the findings of empirical research on social movements into a comprehensive, homogeneous picture. Since empirical research follows and reflects the divisions amongst the paradigms and the separations between »materialist« and »life chance« movements, we are faced with a rich diversity of findings. But there are virtually no connecting links established between the different nuclei of movements existing (black/poor people vs. peace/environmental etc.) in the U.S. and between the different types of movements (professional, routinized vs. direct action).

Therefore, in putting together the findings, we do not end up with a representative image at all, but with a rather spotty and unbalanced one which is heavily weighted on the side of routinized movements – due to the preponderance of the resource mobilization approach.

Furthermore, not many researchers deal with fundamentalism and the new right as a social movement. Left-liberal scholars refuse to grant such phenomena the status of social movements; work on religion does not usually incorporate a social movement perspective. However, such movements as the anti-ERA, anti-abortion, or PTL (television ministery) do also raise issues about identity as citizens or as women in a rapidly changing society. While feminist researchers are looking at these relationships (Petchesky,

1981; Mueller/Dimieri, 1982; Conover/Gray, 1983; Luker, 1984; Stacey, 1987; Stacey/Gerard, 1989), the social movement perspectives under review here have been interested in classical resource mobilization type questions such as internal organization, environment and degree of unity among conservative movements (Zurcher/Kirkpatrick, 1976; U. Useem, 1980; Mottl, 1980; Lo, 1982; Zald/McCarthy 1987).

This overview therefore focusses on the empirical findings of work done within the resource mobilization approach, and summarizes those findings with regard to the dimensions of the formation, the mobilization process, the status of organization, and the outcomes of the movements.

Formation. Whether using a multi-factored approach or exclusively emphasizing organizational resources, both tendencies within the resource mobilization approach find that social movements form because necessary resources have become available, opportunities for collective action have improved, and organizing facilities and cadres have become available (the latter point being particularly stressed by the entrepreneurial theory). As most of the researchers studied the dominant type of American social movement, their presuppositions of resourceful, well-organized groups for the formation of movements was invariably confirmed.

One has to turn to more scattered and less systematic literature if one wants to find out about the formation of less or differently resourceful movements and those that form even though the opportunities for action seem scarce. These findings are as polarized as the partisan standpoints of the activist/journalist/intellectual who wrote them and preclude any generalizing statements.

It does seem, however, that besides the citizen action groups which formed after the oil crisis of 1974/75 (when the commitment to nuclear power was made, Price, 1982, 9) to prevent nuclear plants, which used legal and political tactics and lobbying, and which were often successful in achieving stricter safety regulations, also small local groups mobilized, which did not have the resources for extended local action against the powerful nuclear industry (often supported by the government). Either for lack of other resources or encouraged by the presence of groups such as Quakers, people would turn to direct action and come to reject the organizational structures required for »normal« strategies. Similarly, the traditional environmentalists became victims of their own success with the passage of the air- and water-quality acts in the 1970s and the formation of the Environmental Protection Agency. Their task shifted to seeing that the laws were properly carried out.[35] As a reaction, new ecologists emerged who are, again, more confrontational, and who use civil disobedience and direct action as their strategies.

Most movements in the U.S. today consist of these two parts: whether the women's movement, the environmental movement, or the anti-nuclear movement, they all have their bureaucratic and professional NOW, Friends of the Earth, or Freeze besides respective local grassroots wings. Mainstream research ignores these differences while tacitly focussing on the formally organized, frequently national (umbrella) organizations, leaving the more radical or the more direct-action oriented parts of the movements, which work outside of and against established power stuctures, to activism-journalism.

Mobilization. There is less unanimity amongst resource mobilization researchers with regards to the process of mobilization than with respect to the formation of social movements. While McCarthy/Zald or Oberschall found that the 60s and 70s movements were mobilized primarily through the professional SMO and through external sponsorship and institutional resources (all of which certainly did increase during the 1960s and did play significant roles in the rise of such movements as the welfare rights, farm workers, or the older wing of the women's movement[36]), others have argued that these features hardly explain the mobilization of generalized political turmoil in the 60s. Their studies would show that most of the movements were *not* composed of professional SMOs and did not rely on external resources for their crucial victories. Thus, Morris (1984) could demonstrate that indigenous Black leaders and resources generated the civil rights movement and independently forced the Southern power structure to accede to their de-

35 »The environmentalists are now entrenched. They're professionals. They're not in it for a cause – they're in it because it's a ›public interest,‹ highfalutin *job*. You've got a new group of professionals, bureaucratic professionals ...« is how Sale (1987) quotes a former staff member at Friends of the Earth. (25)

36 Also the environmental, consumer rights, and public interest »movements« of the 1970s fit the professional SMO model well (cf. McFarland, 1976), and professional SMOs such as Mobilization for Youth (Helfgot, 1981) or the Community Action Program (Greenstone/Peterson, 1977) did function as social control devices. (McCarthy/Zald, 1973: 26).

mands. Underlying the major campaigns, he and also McAdam (1982; 1988) found a complex network of »local movement centers« rather than the handful of charismatic leaders celebrated in standard histories. Still others found that changing cultural values and elite actions were responsible for the mobilization of students, as in SDS (Students for a Democratic Society) and the anti-war movement (cf. Freeman, 1983).

Role of organization. Resource mobilization-guided empirical research has produced rather divergent findings on the role of organization and structure for the success of movements, also. The ›mainstream‹ found that centralized and bureaucratically organized movements were more efficient (Gamson, 1975, 89-109; McCarthy/Zald, 1973; 1977), while others – not leaving the framework of efficiency – have found that decentralized, informal movements were more likely to succeed (Gerlach/Hine, 1970; Breines, 1982; Piven/Cloward, 1977).

These contradictory assessments are echoed in research on the anti-nuclear power movement, where Barkan (1979) and Vogel (1980) have argued that its direct action form is a liability, and that the process of consulting numerous affinity groups has hindered strategic effectiveness. In a less evaluative effort, Freeman (1979) has explained that the two wings of the women's movement developed different structures because of the political experiences and values inherited from the initial organizers: conventional reform politics vs. direct participation and personal transformation. Others have appreciated the organizational structure of direct action, affinity groups, and consensus process – not only because they *were* effective for the anti-nuclear power movement (Dwyer, 1983), but also because there are other relevant criteria besides effectiveness. Sturgeon (1986) has pointed to the consensus process as constituting both a rejection of liberal democratic politics and a practical method of learning an alternative form of citizenship. »In its rejection of hierarchy and representation, consensus process refuses the expertise of intellectuals, vanguard parties, and abstract political actors.« This reading of the specific organizational structure employed by some new social movements uses very different criteria of »success« as it adheres more closely to the self-definition of the movement actors who self-consciously discuss the role of leadership, recognizing the various appearances of power even within localized relationships. This type of organizational structure cannot be captured by the categories of the dominant resource mobilization approach.

Outcomes. As opposed to classical social movement theory, where movements were seen as passing through a *standard* evolutionary life cycle (culminating either in collapse or in institutionalization), resource mobilization researchers have found that the outcomes of movements are shaped by the larger political environment (such as the stance of political elites, the support or opposition of established interest organizations and other movements, and governing coalitions and structures of regimes), but most of them could measure only the tangible gains or took »formal access« as a measure of success. This, however, in the U.S. does not necessarily imply any tangible policy gains (cf. I, p. 43/44). Depending on what criteria for success authors have used, and on whether the goals of the movement and the political context are included in the consideration or not, rather different results are reached (cf. the debates between Gamson and Goldstein and Piven/ Cloward). Most resource mobilization researchers agree, however, that polity access does create a qualitative increment in the »returns« to collective action and that it shelters the movement against repression (Tilly, 1978, 125-33). Only in exceptional cases is repression seen as a factor which qualitatively impacts on the development of a movement: Morris, in his historical case study, discovered such effects of the campaign of legal repression mounted by southern states against the NAACP (National Association for the Advancement of Colored People) on civil rights strategies. By outlawing the NAACP and subpoenaing membership lists for reprisals, the states forced the activists to form *new community organizations* which later became local movement centers. This also compelled the activists to abandon their faith in the NAACP's legalistic strategies, paving the way for *direct action.*

Except in monographs of particular movements, this focus on processes of qualitative transformation occurring *within* a movement is rather rare. Downey's (1986) study of the Clamshell Alliance is another exception. He showed that the Clamshell's anti-nuclear »ideology« established an egalitarian identity which structured not only the initial selection of strategies *but also* later efforts to modify them. This discussion of the participants' critique of nuclear power explores »ideology« both as a cultural/political practice *and* a vision of an egalitarian future.

The attempts to *generalize* findings on the politics of American social movements neglect such substantive changes in favor of an apparent common denominator. Jenkins (1983, 548) summarizes these finding by pointing out that the rules governing routine political processes shape not only the composition of the social movement sector, but also its links to the established political system. Because of the way the American polity functions, social movements in the U.S. are more likely to be independent of partisan alliances and adopt single issue strategies rather than linking their programs to electoral campaigns and broader ideological definitions.

This general definition is, however, too narrow to capture the variety of existing social movements in the U.S. For example, while the issue in the case of the anti-nuclear direct action movement presumably is the »single« issue of eliminating nuclear power, the movement simultaneously has both broader ideological contents and an altogether different attitude towards power.

Tentative findings on new social movements

Empirical findings on the type of social movements which Europeans have come to call »new social movements« are extremely thin in the U.S. While there are obviously empirical findings on the recent American women's movement (besides Freeman 1975, see also Katzenstein/Mueller, 1987 and Ferree/Hess, 1985) and the environmental movement (O'Brian, 1983; Milbrath, 1984; Gale, 1986), these movements are rarely interpreted as »new social movements«. The few scholars who address the question of their historical specificity prefer to engage either in philosophical speculation or in setting up postulates of what movements must do in order to qualify for the label. Empirical investigation of the historically specific nature of post-60s mobilization is undertaken by activism-journalism or insiders.

Thus, Paul Loeb's (1986) profiles of the new peace movement activists reveals data on the unlikely constituency of the movement (an amalgam of priests and atheists, communists and Republicans, members of Congress and welfare recipients), which is confirmed by studies of some other authors who are self-described »academics with political commitments and activists with theoretical concerns« (Sturgeon, 1986, 6). Epstein has found the direct action movement at Livermore to include »hippies and Montclair housewives« (1985:47), pagans and Christians: a constituency across classes, occupations, and religious backgrounds. Reasons why the unlikely coalition of such different political positions has not paralyzed the movement are found in the strong contingent of people influenced by the 60s and previous activism (anti-war, civil rights, feminism, disarmament) and in the flexibility which the organizational form of direct action allows.

Engaged descriptions, such as Rudolph/Ridley (1986) who report on the state of activism at Seabrook, Shoreham, and Shearon Harris, or Cabasso/ Moon (1985) who document the 1983 action at Livermore from within the anti-nuclear movement, seem to corroborate those tentative findings on the composition and political strategies of the movement. In terms of strategies, everything from »village politics« (emphasizing local and environmental issues) to building coalitions (to put steady pressure on politicians) is used. This flexibility allows for a variety of forms and intensities of participation.

But this variety is *also* due to the fact that many authors describe the respective movement by *issue* rather than modelling a new type of collective action, in which the form of the action is the message, a symbolic challenge. Hence, they include lobbying groups, legal advocacy organizations, and electorally-oriented groups along with the newer variants of movements (e.g. Gale, 1986, and Gale/Dunlap, forthcoming, for the environmental movement; Lewis, 1972; Wasserman, 1979; Mitchell, 1981; Price, 1982; Gyorgy and friends, 1979 for the anti-nuclear movement). Other authors (Sturgeon, 1986; Epstein, 1988) have found that the direct action movement has created a model of political action, in which affinity groups are both fluid and flexible, that participation in direct action is both prefiguration and opposition, and that it implies a view of social change that is not necessarily oriented towards seizing »state power« or entering the interest group system.

Whereas the resource mobilization approach takes beliefs and motivations for granted and dismisses the ideological content of the movements, all writers who have looked at the anti-nuclear and environmental direct action movements could not but find that such ideological features as social anarchism, radical feminism, anti-militarism and non-violence are very salient to comprehending the dynamics of these movements (cf. Sale, 1986; Downey, 1986; Day, 1983). While their exploration of the role of »ideology« in the direct action movement focusses on the substantive dimensions of consensus or feminist process as they keep shaping both the ethical practice and the vision of the participants, Ladd et al. (1983) are interested in confirming the mere presence of ideology, of a certain worldview, *as a motivating factor*. They used questionaire survey data from demonstrators at a national rally to examine ideological diversity in the movement. Though a national rally is not the same as confrontational direct action, their finding of a consensus of belief among the demonstrators regarding the values underlying their rationale for participation confirms the wide reach and the internal tension of

American ideology, since the values they found both challenge and incorporate larger dominant beliefs of U.S. society.

To sum up: the mainstream of American social movement research has not devoted much investigation to the changing areas of resistance (and domination) in the context of the crises and adjustments advanced capitalism is undergoing. Journalistic or partisan reporting on some of the contemporary movements reveals more about such areas, since the self-identities of the movement actors (woman, gay, lesbian, punk, black person, pagan, hippie etc.) point to these areas. However, we are left with a confusing, and not at all systeamtically researched picture, since the actors who experience the system's contradictory requirements as conflictual issues do not remain in this role/identity all the time. While the actors at Seabrook or Livermore have been described as building »communities of resistance« where they explore new cultural models, new forms of citizenship, and alternative viewpoints, what seems to characterize these networks more than anything else is their instability, the fact that they emerge sporadically in response to specific issues, and otherwise remain submerged. This kind of dispersed, instable collective actor has apparantly been too difficult for the mainstream of American social movement research to access.

V. Institutional Aspects

Research on social movements within the different discplines developed in relative isolation from each other until the mid-70s. Freeman, in putting together her anthology (which took shape by 1979), still had to battle the scattered state of work being done in different professions. A first national symposium (organized by Zald and McCarthy at Vanderbilt in 1977) created the rudiments of a network of social movement scholars, which then became institutionalized into the Section on Collective Behavior and Social Movements (CBSM) in the American Sociological Association. Both collective behavior and resource mobilization scholars here managed to establish their bastion, from which they set the parameters for debate, control institutional resources and grants, and officially sanction[37] and informally validate the

37 For example by presenting awards for »the best book or article in the field of collective behavior and social movements«. In 1988 it went to John Lofland's *Protest*.

work which conforms to the scientific assumptions and the discourse of this mainstream.

The American Political Science Association similarly provides space and support to the study of social movements. While it does not have an organized committee on social movements, its yearly conference over the last few years has seen sections on »Interests, Groups, and Social Movements«[38], »Political Organizations and Parties«[39], »Religion and Politics«[40], and a roundtable on studying political movements and groups.[41] Since 1987, panels have started to address *new* social movements under the heading of »Social movements in advanced democracies«. And of course there has always been room for the study of minority politics: their focus on political power in urban areas has occasionally included some social movement developments. Recently, panels on »justice« (universal or gender specific?) have also included papers e.g. on the »Challenge of contemporary social movements to the ideal of universal citizenship« (1987).

The CBSM section within the ASA, while »almost dead in the early 1970s«, is now a lively growth area in the discipline (*Critical Mass Bulletin* 13/2, July 1988, 2[42]). It regularly has panels and roundtables at the annual ASA meetings, and has also sponsored occasional workshops funded by discipline grants (e.g. the 1988 Workshop on Frontiers in Social Movement Theory organized by Carol Mueller and Aldon Morris). At the 1988 convention, the 7 refereed roundtables ranged from micro models of activism to an analysis of the 1985 Soccer Riot in Beijing.[43] This variegated presence of

38 Social movements are here defined as »less formally institutionalized social groupings« (PS, summer 1986, 700). Panels within this section in 1986 dealt with interest group politics and social movements, Native Americans, Group mobilization in local politics, Groups and coalition building in contemporary American politics.

39 At the 1986 meeting, one of 12 panels within this organized section addressed the nexus of parties and interest groups.

40 Two of 14 panels dealt with social movement-relevant issues: Political Religiosity – Trends and Prospects for the New Christian Right; Religion and Politics in Western Europe – the Peace Movements.

41 which focussed on participant observation and other techniques.

42 »Critical Mass Bulletin« is the newsletter of the section on CBSM, now in its 14th year. It keeps members up to date with recent publications and meetings of interest.

43 Other panels at the convention (not sponsored by the section on CBSM) dealt more specifically with movements in the U.S.: »The Sociology of the Women's Movement in America« organized by Rose Brewer, »Political Activists and Local Structures of Movements« organized by Clarence Lo. In 1989, the section panel was organized around Cognitive, Emotional, and Structural Factors in Collective Behavior, and the roundtables

social movement-related topics and approaches does not, however, mean that dialogue and exchange are growing. What the *New York Times* observed on the occasion of the 1988 ASA convention, also holds true for the development of social movement research: »Such things as feminism – or what are called »gender studies« – homosexual practices, studies of the peace movement, and the sociology of ethnic groups and minorities have turned a profession once dominated by two or three major areas into a scholarly buffet table groaning under the weight of diversity.«[44] Additionally, over the last few years the section on Sociology of Peace and War has put more and more papers dealing with the peace movement on its panels. In both associations, work on social movements is often tied up with either the sociology of religion or political religiosity.

While the political scientist Walker at the Roundtable on social protest movements at the 1985 APSA meeting (which, for the first time, provided for cross-disciplinary exchange of views) still bemoaned the fact that over the past 20 years the study of social movements belonged more to sociology than political science, that political science has produced far fewer young scholars interested in such subjects than has sociology, and that the discipline has suffered from too heavy a focus on institutions and on traditional political action (Garrow, 1985). Meanwhile young political scientists have made some inroads into the arena by organizing »unaffiliated groups« such as the Conference Group on Political Economy (which would include the topic of social movements in discussing issues of ideology and class in the welfare state) or the Conference Group on German Politics (which reports on new social movements and the impacts of new social movements on political culture). Since 1986, a Conference Group on Transformational Politics holds meetings at the APSA conventions for scholars interested in »green« and »post-socialist« politics of the American kind.[45]

---

had expanded to 9 different topics ranging from »A Case Study of a Southern California Flying Saucer Cult« to »The Victim-Activist Role in the Anti-Drunk Driving Movement«. Additionally, social movements were »present« in other panels such as »The Fate of the Sixties Generation« (to assess McAdam, 1988 and Whalen/Flacks, 1988), »Social Movements of the 1960s«, »Issues of Gender in the Analysis of Social Movements«, »Issues on Social Movements I and II« and in the context of the section on Racial and Ethnic Minorities.

44 Richard Bernstein, »Sociology is branching out, but will the field be splintered?« *New York Times*, August 30, 1988.

45 Panels have dealt with post-liberal politics and its critics, new directions in environmental politics and policy, feminists and eco-feminist perspectives, intentional commu-

Besides the publications associated with the disciplines' associations, various journals (such as *Social Research*) and book series (such as the Research Annual *Research in Social Movements, Conflicts and Change* edited by Kriesberg and its supplement *International Social Movement Research* edited by Klandermans) are particularly open to movement topics.

Collaborative research with Western European new social movement scholars has been promoted by the Council for European Studies, which allowed for an international workshop on participation in social movements, where resource mobilization scholars could expose their work to some challenges of the Europeans' new social movement approach and vice versa.[46] It also supported a workshop on women's movements in Western Europe and the U.S. held at Cornell University in 1983.[47] Grants from the American and West German National Science Foundations supported a Joint US/FRG Seminar on New Social Movements at Florida State University in 1987.[48]

The funding sources for the varied research projects on social movements consist primarily of the big academic foundations: National Science Foundation[49], National Endowment for the Humanities, and National Institute of Mental Health[50] and secondarily of university grants and smaller foundation support.

Scholars who are less interested in quantifiability than in exploring the significance of new societal cleavages and new social movements, while still marginal and having – at this point – less success in securing financial support, also organize local study groups and workshops. While still having to struggle to receive exposure in the pertinent journals and forums, they have

---

nities, and the transformational movement »as a social movement.« One panel is also devoted to books considered important such as (in 1988) Charlene Spretnak's *The Spiritual Dimensions of Green Politics*. The group has recently petitioned to become an organized section within the APSA.

46 The results have been edited by Klandermans/Kriesi/Tarrow, 1988.

47 The results have been edited by Katzenstein/Mueller, 1987.

48 The result of this seminar is Dalton/Küchler, eds. (1990).

49 The NSF gave grants to the Cornell project of Tarrow; to the 1977 Conference at Vanderbilt, out of which Zald/McCarthy, *The Dynamics of Social Movements*, came; to Tilly for a study of social change and collective action in France and Britain; to Dalton for a study of environmental movements in Western Europe; also Downs', McAdam's and Jenkins' studies were funded by NSF.

50 The latter additionally funded Jenkins' and Perrow's farm workers project and Jenkins' new study of philanthropic elites and the social movements of the 60s and 70s.

begun to challenge the mainstream assumptions within the professional organizations.

VI. Debates and Controversies

As has become obvious from the preceding chapters, American social movement research is characterized by the controversial paradigms of the collective behavior and resource mobilization approach, by extensive controversies within particular paradigms (especially within the resource mobilization paradigm), and by propositions which challenge these established paradigms. We will survey these in turn.

1. The controversial issues between the traditional and the resource mobilization approaches have been mentioned in this overview, as they played important roles in shaping the concepts, assumptions, and methodological orientations of the perspectives developed later. The main critical points have been that basic concepts such as »structural strain« have been so broad as to be meaningless; the concrete definition of key categories such as »relative deprivation« has been vague; and essential hypotheses such as that social movements are a function of deep-seated frustrations, deprivations, or of status inconsistency, have empirically failed to explain the movements of the 1960s if not others.[51]

The response of collective behavior theorists to the challenge of the resource mobilization approach was either to claim that the new perspective was not as distinctive as its proponents argued, or that it rested on too narrow a theoretical framework (Turner, 1982; Gusfield, 1982; Zurcher/Snow, 1981). The main source of contention in this debate has been the conception of social movements: while the traditional definitions see social movements as extensions of elementary forms of collective behavior, comprising movements of personal change as well as those focussed on institutional changes, the resource mobilization definition sees them as extensions of institutionalized actions, and as limited to those of institutional change. Some recent ef-

51 Cf. for the critical literature: Oberschall, 1973; J. Wilson, 1973; Useem, 1975; Marx/Wood, 1975: 375-383; McAdam, 1982: 11-35; Jenkins, 1983; Morris/Herring, 1987.

forts have tried to mediate this dualism (e.g. McAdam/McCarthy/Zald, 1988), but it remains doubtful whether any such integrative attempts would not burst the framework of either one of the approaches (Morris/Herring, 1987). Resource mobilization theorists, aware of the bias of their model in favor of institutional change movements (rational actions oriented toward clearly defined, fixed goals with centralized organizational control over resources and clearly demarcated outcomes that can be evaluated in terms of tangible gains), have gone in various directions in order to account for *other* types of movements, too. Some have expanded and refined the resource mobilization approach to include the study of micro-mobilization contexts (McAdam, 1986; Gamson/Firemen/ Rytina, 1982), applied it to micro-level processes (Granovetter, 1978), or to the organizational aspects of personal change movements (Lofland, 1977; 1979). Others found it necessary to transcend it in order to adequately deal with movements of cultural change, with the link between macro- and micro-processes, and with questions of causality. Within this trend, some authors (e.g. Foss/Larkin) have again posited the *disjunctive* nature of social movements with »normal« society (where the resource mobilization perspective had emphasized the continuity to counter the traditional view of social movement as deviant, but thereby trivialized them). Other authors within this trend have made the beliefs, consciousness, and signifying work of social movement participants into priority topics of research again, focussing on how participants redefine their understanding of the social order as they engage in praxis, and how they develop new repertoires of behavior in line with their new interpretations (e.g. Snow et al.). While some of these efforts point to continuities with earlier work, none of them can be qualified as systematic integration of classical approaches with resource mobilization perspectives.

2. The debates internal to the resource mobilization perspective have implicitly been dealt with in my discussion of the emergence of the different variations of the approach (see II). Much of the discussion focussed on Gamson's (1975) analysis of *success/failure* of movement organizations. His measures of success included a) the provision of tangible benefits that meet the goals established by movement organizations and b) the formal acceptance of the movement organization by its main antagonist as a valid representative of a legitimate set of interests. He distinguished four possible movement outcomes: full success, cooptation (acceptance but no benefits), preemption (benefits but no acceptance), and failure. He found that success-

ful movement organizations were bureaucratic, pursued narrow goals, employed selective incentives, and used unruly methods; that coopted movement organizations had larger memberships and formalized structures; and that preempted organizations were typically small and centrally controlled.

These measures and findings were challenged by Goldstone (1980), who reanalyzed Gamson's data and found that organizational and strategic considerations were irrelevant once controls were introduced for the goals and the political context. Hence, »non-displacement« movements were found to consistently succeed in the American polity.

While Gamson (1980) claimed that Goldstone's conclusions were based on an erroneous reading of several cases and a narrowing of the meaning of success, other critics charged that Gamson's model employed too narrow a concept of success, as it deals with tangible forms of benefits only and relatively weak measures of changes in power relations (Jenkins, 1983, based on Turner/Killian, 1972). Turner and Killian have already pointed out that intangible gains, while less measurable, can be highly significant, and that formal acceptance is an extremely weak measure of – only one form of – change in social power. U.S. history is rich with examples of how formal access does not imply tangible policy gains.

The most provocative challenge to Gamson's model has been Piven and Cloward's (1977) charge that formalized organizations divert energies from mass defiance and provide political elites with a forum for propagating symbolic reassurances. This finding, based on empirical evidence of the policy impacts of the urban riots of the 1960s, has been challenged by other research of different »poor people's movements,« which have made effective use of formalized organizations such as the farm workers union (Jenkins, 1985) and the welfare rights movement between 1967 and 1970 (West, 1981, 292-303). Tarrow (1982) and Jenkins (1983) among others have refined the definition of conditions for success by including electoral shifts linked to changes in governmental coalitions as a factor.

Except for the Piven/Cloward interpretation, the resource mobilization approach favored the view that grassroots orientation and leaderless structures were rather a liability to the movements, to the 60s movements in particular, whose loss of strategic effectiveness is ascribed to this factor. This prevailing view has been challenged by some less orthodox New Left participants (cf. the essays in Sayres et al., 1984). Since the beginning of the 1980s, when »trashing the 60s has become a strategic feature of the current struggle for hegemony« (ibid, 8), politically engaged authors have set out to salvage the multi-level, complex experience of those movements. Many contributions to the recent panels and discussions on the sixties movements (e.g. at the 1989 ASA convention) are not only concerned with refuting the academic social movement interpretations, but especially with intervening in the general debunking of the sixties in the media.

3. While many authors have attempted to overcome specific weaknesses and limitations of the resource mobilization approach, its assumptions, underlying framework, and methodology have so far not been systematically criticized. Both its lack of explanatory power with respect to the post-60s mobilization and its structural indifference towards history make such a critique necessary, however.

As the preceding chapters have revealed, this indifference has implications for the questions asked and the findings arrived at within the resource mobilization paradigm. Since the approach is indifferent towards the type of insurgency, the kind of praxis, the substance of ideology, and the idea of society envisioned by the movements, it lumps social movements together with routine and sporadic collective action as well as with interest group organizations. The focus on SMOs and their task of mobilizing resources is not only due to the particular historical movements researchers were studying (primarily »non-displacement« movements, which neither challenge the monopoly of coercive force of the state nor the hegemonic cultural code), but to the methodological individualism with which they view society: not as forms of social organization possessed of classes, ownership relations, and specific logics of production and reproduction, but as a static arrangement of (relatively homogenous) elites and (undifferentiated) non-elites, of political insiders vs. excluded groups. The excluded groups »*strive to scramble aboard*« (Jenkins, 1985, 227), and all the resource mobilization approach is concerned with the conditions under which this striving is achieved. Both assumption *and* finding is that if the group is well organized, it can get its share in the basically pluralistic society. The goal is assumed to be *tangible gains* for movement participants – more so than reform or change or society; more so than rejection of the hegemonic definition of growth and efficacy. »Victories generally begin with policy successes and culminate in distributional goals.« (Jenkins, 1985, 21) Gaining legitimized new modes of action is seen as goal achievement and acceptance (Tarrow, 1983a, 21) and interpreted as a refutation of Michels – not as the beginning of new questions about the dynamics and crisis of a particular mode of societal reproduction.

The success measurement, as undertaken by the resource mobilization perspectives, is problematic to the extent that they ignore the concrete, historical context, the substantive praxis, and are not concerned with the manifold relationships between social movements and the state. Where state responses are included in the analysis (Tarrow e.g. is explicitly interested in the political system), the concern is primarily with *positive* »elite responses,« i.e. with policy success. What is ignored, but crucially important for the development of social movements, are the formal and informal social control and repression processes the state may bring to bear on the movements,[52] and, even prior to that, the effects of structured socio-economic relations such as unemployment or economic dependence. (Empirical research over time, if it includes such variables, can easily demonstrate how such factors as rising unemployment rates have transformed certain movements from expressly radical into pragmatic ones). Thus, the needs and demands of participants change in the course of a movement and in the interaction with the state. Already in the translation process from movement goals to policy language, and by segmenting demands into ressort-specific issues, transformation occurs. Similarly, social control effects of external patronage from ostensible movement supporters, such as foundations, can be expected. (Jenkins/Eckert, 1986, have begun to test such hypostasized effects.)

Even though all conflicts show that »policy success« is never a matter of direct, uncompromised adoption, there has been very little work done on the institutionalization of movement goals into the formal policy process. Just as the establishment of the Environmental Protection Agency had effects on the environmental movement, so the expansion of the Civil Rights Division in the Justice Department and the creation of the Equal Rights Commission affected the civil rights movement: the ground and tactics of contention had to shift once agencies had been mandated to pursue goals similar to the movement goals, once channels of access were opened up on the basis on which policy claims could be made. Shifting tactics from organizing demonstrations to bureaucratic bargaining and the concomitant organizational adaptation have consequences for the relation between SMO and constituencies. (Cf. e.g. work on the success of neighborhood mobilizations such as Katz/Mayer, 1985.)

---

52 Where repression and social control are not ignored, the emphasis is on the *direct* repression of movement participants by authorities (Marx, 1979). Freeman has pointed to the fact that the state as »solid opponent« can unify a group and heal its splits (1979, 187).

Not just the impact on movements, but also the effect on the political system as a whole have gone relatively unresearched. On the one hand, studies of urban politics have shown that the establishment of new channels may well function as an additional means to process and regulate policy claims. On the other hand, a hypothesis might be that the institutionalized social movement industry could weaken the role of political parties in a way similar to the explosion of interest organizations. Resource mobilization theorists, unconcerned with what social movement research may tell us about the political culture or social structure of a specific society,[53] have not inquired into the relationship of movements to political parties' agendas. Political coalitions are occasionally seen to play a role – as supportive opportunity structures (e.g. the liberal coalition in power in the 1960s), but changing relationships with regard to conservative parties have not caught the interest of any researcher. The response of conservative parties may vary from repressive or marginalizing stands to *affinities*. The phenomenon of increasing affinities between the positions of populist neighborhood, citizen or middle class movements and the agenda of conservative leadership has gone unresearched except in the case of feminist developments.

Many of these limitations and problems can be related back to the underlying socio-theoretical framework, which is all but exclusive to the resource mobilization theorists. The view of society as an unstructured ensemble of groups more or less well-organized; the view of ruling classes as a relatively homogeneous elite (cf. Tarrow, 1983b, 6); the view of the state either as structurally permeable (Gamson, 1975) or as institutionally biased against insurgency (Jenkins, 1985), all act together to produce the image of a static social arrangement, which continually adapts due to its permeability and openness (in the pluralist view), or is only exceptionally perturbed (in the social-democratic view) when realignments and political turmoil force the state to be a »facilitative agency for the institutionalization of genuine social reforms« (Jenkins, 1985, 228). This basically static view prevents an understanding of social movements as both reflecting and resisting a particular historical mode of societal organization. It prevents an inquiry into qualitative changes of movements as well as an understanding of social movements in their relation to processes of socio-historical restructuring.

The social-democratic view, which emphasizes the intrinsic restrictiveness of political systems, due to which *all* social movements are seen as

---

53 For an exception see the comparative work of Kitschelt, 1986.

posing a threat to institutional arrangements (because they »raise the spectre of restructuring the polity membership,« McAdam, 1982, 26; Jenkins, 1985, 226), preempts an interpretation of the historical process, in which the polity *has* opened up to specific groups and/or to particular demands, as it processes various historically evolving contradictory relationships – and these openings all but produced »a general collapse of state power«!

Therefore, to address the question of the significance of »policy success« for the reproduction of the system as a whole is of critical importance to the study of social movements. Just as the gains of the working class movement significantly transformed the previous mode of regulation by introducing new bargaining structures (New Deal), and as the opening of the welfare state to Blacks has shifted the terrain for their struggle, so the increase in citizen participation on various levels of government in different arenas, or other neo-corporatist structures which some movements have been evolving, need to be researched; for their transformative impact on the post-war Keynesian mode of regulation redefines the conditions for their own development. This is why research has to ask: which social groups have been included, in which historical conjuncture, during which phase of capitalist development?

So far, one has to turn to historical studies of American politics such as Davis (1986) for information on how the continually shifting balance of forces between different classes and groups, and the political processing of those shifts, has impacted on social movements.

4. The fact that most existing approaches examine social movements, with history providing only a backdrop, probably also accounts for the conspicuous lack of research on the new areas of domination and resistance.

Contemporary movements, which to varying degrees are bearers of both traditional and new elements, cannot be fully analyzed in terms of the concepts of prior developments. With forms of protest in mind that are primilary characterized by new elements (e.g. the anti-nuclear direct action movement), one is particularly struck by the inadequacy of existing approaches to capture, even in descriptive terms, the essential features of these movements – much like social scientists of the 60s must have felt about relative deprivation theories or collective behavior conceptualizations.

The aspects of the movements which cannot be analyzed by the traditional concepts are those whose symbolic challenges are not easily adapted to existing channels of political representation. While the existing approaches assume that the goal of insurgency is the interjection of the interests of the excluded group into the centers of economic and political power, strands of the new movements are not about inclusion into the polity, nor about distributional gains. Rather, their theme involves an oppositional attitude towards the process and the politics of modernization.

Where they defend spaces, for the creation of new identities and solidarities as they do in occupations, these movements »reclaim private space as common space, collectively redefining ownership« and public responsibility (Sturgeon, 1986); where they practice civil disobedience, it is a practice of direct participation (instead of representation) to register the collective desires against the nuclear state and corporations; where they engage in consciousness raising, as the women's movement has done, they reconceptualize the legitimacy of existing norms and practice around the sexual use of power. These actions do not so much oppose the dominant culture as they expose its contradictions: the women's, ecology, or direct action movements do not reject the values of liberal democracy such as equality or solidarity, but by giving a different substance to their claims, they expose how the selective enforcement of existing values of the liberal democracy creates conflict and reproduces exploitation (of nature, of women, of »non-citizens«, of minorities).

These new aspects of the movements force us to enlarge our definition of social movements – and not only in terms of the social ties and networks linking people together in their everyday lives, which underlie many apparently spontaneous protests. Tarrow (1983b, 4) has pointed to these support bases, distinguishing their role from formal protest organizations, as a largely uncharted area of social movement research. But beyond that, the features and goals of the new social movements can be – and have to be – related to the logic and crisis of the historically specific mode and structure of accumulation and reproduction, which these movements reflect and resist at the same time. European scholars such as Melucci (1988) and Touraine (1981) have placed new social movements in a context of social theory which allows to analyze why they concentrate on specific issues and affect the sphere of cultural needs as well as carry with them a new theme which questions the very process of modernization. More than being merely »identity-centered«, these frameworks offer theories of societal change to which, because they focus on the role of new social movements within societal transformation, U.S. social movement research might well want to open up to.

Annotated Bibliography

Adamson, M.; Borgos, S. (1984): *This Mighty Dream. Social protest movements in the United States.* Boston Routledge & Kegan Paul.

Aglietta, M. (1979): *A theory of capitalist regulation: The U.S. experience.* London: New Left Books.

Alario, M. (1989): »The state crisis and new social movements: the emergence of a political paradigm«, Conference of the American Sociology Association, 1989.

Aldrich, H.E.; Berk, R. (1972): »Patterns of vandalism during civil disorders as an indicator of selection of targets«, *American Sociological Revue* 37 (10):533-47.

Alger, C.F.; Mendlovitz, S. (1984): »Grassroots activism in the US: global implications?« *Alternatives.* 1984.

Alinsky, S. (1869): *Reveille for Radicals.* New York: Vintage.

– (1971): *Rules for Radicals.* New York: Vintage.

Aron, S.; Torpey, J. (1986): »Alles für einen guten Zweck. Politische Organisationen in den USA sammeln an der Haustür«, *links* 190.

Aronowitz, S. (1988): »Postmodernism and politics«, in: A. Ross (ed.), *Universal abandon? The politics of postmodernism.* Minneapolis: University of Minnesota Press.

Atkins, N. (1987): »Activism among the yuppoisie«, *Village Voice*, 24 (2), 17ff.

Barkan, S.E. (1987): »Strategic, tactical and organizational dilemmas of the protest movement against nuclear power«, *Social Problems* 27: 19-37.
Argues that the process of consulting numerous affinity groups has significantly hindered strategic effectiveness of the anti-nuclear power movement.

Berry, J.M. (1984): *The interest group society.* Boston: Little Brown & Company.

Blumer, H. (1951): »Collective behavior«, in: A. McClung Lee (ed.). *New Outline of the Principles of Sociology.* New York: Barnes & Noble.

– (1957): »Collective behavior«, in: J.B. Gittler (ed.). *Review of Sociology: Analysis of a Decade.* New York: Wiley.

Boggs, C. (1983): »The new populism and the limits of structural reforms«. *Theory and Society* 12 (3): 343-63.
A critical study of populism in U.S. local electoral efforts focussing on Santa Monica.

– (1986): *Social movements and political power.* Philadelphia: Temple University Press.
This book analyzes the dynamics of modern popular movements – feminism, antimilitarism, environmentalism and others – in Western Europe and the U.S. Explores above all their political trajectories. Concerning the U.S., the new social movements are represented by the radical activists who were able to win local elections in cities like Santa Monica.

Borgos, S. (1984): »The ACORN squatters campaign«, *Social Policy* 15 (1): 17-26.
The history of a squatters movement in Philadelphia is recounted. ACORN has succeeded in creating friendly terrain for its efforts locally despite an unfavorable larger political context.

Bouchier, D. (1986): »The Sociologist as Anti-Partisan: A Dilemma of Knowledge and Academic Power,« *Research in Social Movements, Conflict and Change* 9: 1-24.
Discusses ethical problems of research into groups which are secretive or hostile to the researcher's interest.

– (1987): *Radical citizenship: The new American activism.* New York: Schocken Books.
This study of grassroots politics in the 1970s and 1980s envisions a citizen movement which would be powerful and popular enough to transform the definition of political freedom in America.

Boyte, H.C. (1980): *The backyard revolution: Understanding the new citizen movement.* Philadelphia: Temple University Press.

– (1984): *Community is possible: repairing America's roots.* New York: Harper & Row.

Boyte, H.C.; Riessman, F. (eds.) (1986): *The new populism.* Philadelphia: Temple University Press.

Boyte, H.; Booth, H.; Max, S. (1986): *Citizen action and the new American populism.* Philadelphia: Temple University Press.

Breines, W. (1982): *Community and organization in the New Left. 1962-1968: The Great Refusal.* New York: Praeger.

Browning, R.P.; Marshall, D.R.; Tabb, D.H. (1984): *Protest ist not enough. The struggle of blacks and hispanics for equality in urban politics.* Berkeley: University of California Press.
This comparative study of »reformed« California cities shows that the political composition of the governing coalition explains a good deal of the variance in municipal posts opened up to minorities.

Burstein, P. (1985): *Discrimination, jobs and politics: the struggle for equal employment opportunity in the U.S. since the New Deal.* Chicago: University of Chicago Press.

Cabasso, J.; Moon, S. (1985): *Risking peace: why we sat in the road.* Berkeley: Open Books.
This book documents the 1983 anti-nuclear action at Livermore from within the movement.

Capra, F.; Spretnak, Ch. (1984): *Green politics. The global promise.* New York: Dutton.

Carden, M.L. (1978): »The proliferation of a social movement: ideology and individual incentives in the contemporary feminist movement«, *Research in Social Movements, Conflict and Change* 1: 179-96.

Case, J.; Taylor, R. (eds.) (1979): *Coops, communes and collectives. Experiments in social change in the 1960s and 1970s.* New York: Pantheon.

Castells, M. (1977): *The urban question.* London: Arnold.

– (1978): *City, class and power.* London: Macmillan.

– (1983): *The city and the grassroots. A cross-cultural theory of urban social movements.* Berkely: University of California Press.
This major attempt to move beyond Castells' earlier work covers both historical and recent cases of urban social movements, among others the American inner cities in the 1960s.

Clarke, S.; Mayer, M. (1986): »Responding to grassroots discontent: Germany and the United States«, *International Journal of Urban and Regional Research* 10 (3): 401-416.

Clayborn, C. (1981): *In struggle: SNCC and the black awakening of the 1960s.* Cambridge: Harvard University Press.
This book offers a balanced discussion of the internal life of the student civil rights movement.

Cohen, J. (1982): »Between crisis management and social movements«, *Telos* 12 (2): 21-40.

– (1983): »Rethinking social movements«, *Berkeley Journal of Sociology* 28: 97-113.
– (1985): »Strategy or identity: new theoretical paradigms and contemporary social movements«, *Social Research* 52 (4): 663-716.
Cohen, J.; Arato, A. (1984): »Social movements, civil society, and the problem of sovereignty«, *Praxis International* 4 (3): 226-283.
Collin, S. (1986): *The Rainbow Challenge.* New York: Monthly Review Press.
Conover, P.J.; Gray, V. (1983): *Feminism and the new right: conflict over the American family.* New York: Praeger.
Cooney, R.; Michalowski, H. (1977): *The power of the people.* Culver City: Peace Press.
This volume is a pictorial encyclopedia of the struggles of U.S. women and men working for peace and justice through nonviolent action.
Costain, A.J.; Costain, W.D. (1983): »The Women's Lobby: Impact of a movement on Congress«, in: A.J. Cigler, B.A. Loomis (eds.), *Interest group politics.* Washington, D.C.: Congressional Quarterly Inc.
Curtis, R.L.; Zurcher, L. (1973): »Stable resources of protest movements: the multiorganizational field«, *Social Forces* 52: 53-61.
– (1974): »Social movements«, *Social Problems* 21: 356-70.
These authors argue that personal change movements tend to adopt decentralized structures and exclusive membership rules while institutional change movements are typically centralized and inclusive.
Dalton, R. (ed.). (1988): *Citizen politics: Public opinion and political parties in the United States, the United Kingdom. France, and West Germany.* Boston: Chatham House.
Dalton, R.; Küchler, M. (eds.) (1990): *Challenging the political order.* Cambridge: Polity Press.
This book presents the results of the joint seminar on new social movements organized by W. Bürklin and R. Dalton at Florida State University, April 1987. It concentrates on the theoretical origins of the new social movements and their impact on the political process.
Davies, J.C. (1983): *Human nature in politics: The dynamics of political behavior.* New York: John Wiley.
One of the chief proponents of the relative deprivation approach, Davies attributed social movement activism to the perception that one's membership group is in a disadvantageous position relative to some other group.
Davis, M. (1986): *Prisoners of the American Dream: Politics and economy in the history of the U.S. working class.* London: Verso.
Day, S.H. Jr. (1983): »The nuclear resistance«, *The Progressive* 47 (4): 22-30.
Delgado, G. (1986): *Organizing the movement: the roots and growth of ACORN.* Philadelphia: Temple University Press.
This book is a first rate organizational movement history of the Association of Community Organizations for Reform Now.
Donati, P.R. (1984): »Organization between movement and institution«, *Social Science Information* 23 (4/5): 837-859.
Downes, B.T. (1968): »Social and political characteristics of riot cities: a comparative study«, *Social Science Quarterly* 49: 504-20.

Downey, G.L. (1986): »Ideology and the Clamshell identity: Organizational dilemmas in the anti-nuclear power movement«, *Social Problems* 33 (5): 357-373.
This ethnographic study examines the role of ideology in the development of organizational dilemmas in the Clamshell Alliance.

Dwyer, L.E. (1983): »Structure and strategy in the anti-nuclear movement«, in: J. Freeman (ed.), *Social Movements of the 60s and 70s*. New York: Longman.

Eisenstein, Z. (1980): *The radical future of liberal feminism*. New York: Longman.

– (1982): »The sexual politics of the new right«, in: N.O. Keohane et al. (eds.), *Feminist theory*. Chicago: University of Chicago Press.

– (1984): *Feminism and sexual equality*. New York: Monthly Review Press.

Eisenstein, Z. (ed.). (1979): *Capitalist patriarchy and the case for socialist feminism*. New York: Monthly Review Press.

Eisinger, P.K. (1973): »The conditions of protest behavior in American cities«, *American Political Science Review* 67 (1): 11-28.
This influential study of organized protests in the 1960s (in 42 U.S. cities) finds that protest occurred more frequently in cities in which the opportunity structure had begun to open up. It was the first to operationalize the concept of ›political opportunity structure‹ after Lipsky (1968) implicitly developed it.

Epstein, B. (1985): »The culture of direct action: Livermore Action Group and the peace movement«, *Socialist Review* 15 (4/5): 31-61.

– (1988): »The politics of prefigurative community: the non-violent direct action movement«, in: M. Davis; M. Sprinker (eds.), *Reshaping the U.S. Left: Popular struggles in the 1980s*. London, New York: Verso.

Evans, R.R. (1969): *Readings in collective behavior*. Chicago: Rand McNally.

Evans, R.R. (ed.). (1973): *Social movements: A reader and source book*. Chicago: Rand McNally.

Evans, S.J. (1979): *Personal politics: The roots of women's liberation in the civil rights movement and the New Left*. New York: Knopf.
This study locates the roots of the women's movement in the informal networks of women who had come to know one another in the context of civil rights and New Left organizing.

Evans, S.; Boyte, H.C. (1985): *Free spaces: The sources of democratic change in America*. New York: Harper and Row.

Fainstein, N.; Fainstein, S. (1974): *Urban political movements*. Englewood Cliffs: Prentice Hall.

Ferree, M.M.; Hess, B.B. (1985): *Controversy and coalition: The new feminist movement*. Boston: Twayne Publishers.
The authors explain the emergence of the women's movement similar to Freeman, but add that other events of the 1960s, expecially Kennedy's Commission on the Status of Women, were necessary for a movement to develop. They describe how rapidly the movement grew in the 1970s while facing problems associated with diversity and show that in the 1980s differences still exist which they trace to 3 intellectual traditions: moral reform, liberalism, socialism.

Ferree, M.M.; Miller, F.D. (1985): »Mobilization and meaning: Toward an integration of social psychological and resource perspectives on social movements«, *Sociological Inquiry* 55: 38-51.

Fireman, B.; Gamson, W.A. (1979): »Utilitarian logic in the resource mobilization perspective«, in: M.N. Zald; J. McCarthy (eds.), *The dynamics of social movements.* Cambridge, Ma.: Winthrop.

This essay attempts to add a consideration of solidarity, collective identity, consciousness, and ideology to the resource mobilization perspective. The approach is to instrumentalize »solidarity and principle« from the standpoint of movement organizers' task of mobilizing participants.

Fisher, R. (1984): *Let the people decide: Neighborhood organizing in America.* Boston: Twayne Publ.

In documenting the history of the various forms of neighborhood organizing in the U.S., this study accounts for recent multi-faceted populist organizing.

– (1984): »Neighborhood organizing: Lessons from the past«, *Social Policy* 15 (1): 9-16.

Fisher, R.; King, J.M. (1987): »Two approaches to the role of ideology in community organizing«, *Radical America* 21 (1): 31-46.

Fitzsimmons, M.; Gottlieb, R. (1988): »A new environmental politics«, in: M. Davis; M. Sprinker (eds.), *Reshaping the U.S. Left. Popular struggles in the 1980s.* London: Verso.

Freeman, J. (1973): »The origins of the women's liberation moement«, *American Journal of Sociology* 78: 792.811.

– (1975): *The politics of women's liberation.* New York: Lognman.

This book was, for a decade or more, *the* study of how the U.S. women's movement came about. It argues that changes in women's family and work positions combined with women's political activities in other social movements set the stage for a new women's movement.

– (1979): »Resource mobilization and strategy: A model for analyzing social movement organization actions«, in: M.N. Zald; J.M. McCarthy (eds.), *The dynamics of social movements.* Cambridge, Ma.: Winthrop.

Freeman, J. (ed.) (1983): *Social movements of the sixties and seventies.* New York: Longman.

In analyzing movements largely from the left (the 60s: civil rights, SDS, women's) and those from the right as well as the left as well as »unclassifiable on a lift-right spectrum« (the 70s), this book raises questions of immediate interest to movement participants: it is concerned with mobilization, organization, strategy and social control – not with collective behavior, sources of discontent, motives for participation or ideology.

Freudenberg, N. (1984): *»Not in our backyards!« Community action for health and the environment.* New York: Monthly Review Press.

This book pulls together the diverse strands of a movement that had its nationally visible beginnings in 1978 when residents of Love Canal found out they were living atop a massive dump of toxic chemials. Drawing on experience from around the country, it gives a complex picture of the movement's origins, its lessons, its potential.

Friedland, W.; Alford, R. (1975): »Political participation and public policy«, *Annual Review of Sociology* 1: 429-479.

Gale, R.P. (1986): »Social movements and the state. The environmental movement, countermovement, and government agencies«, *Sociological Perspectives* 29 (2): 202-240.

Gale, R.P.; Dunlap, R.E. *The American environmental movement* (forthcoming).

Gamson, W.A. (1975): *The strategy of social protest.* Homewood, III: Dorsey.
This is an elementary analysis of the »success and failure« of 53 randomly selected movement organizations active in the U.S. between 1800 and 1945. By combining case study with time-series analysis, G. revealed the importance of political alliances and state action in the success or failure of challenging groups.

– (1980): »Understanding the careers of challenging groups«, *American Journal of Sociology* 85: 1043-60.

– »Organizing the poor: A review essay [on Piven and Cloward's Poor people's movements]«, *Theory and Society* 13 (4): 567-585.

– (1989): *The strategy of social protest* (revised edition), Belmont, Ca.: Wadsworth Press.
This revised edition includes a new chapter on »challenging groups since 1945« and an appendix with the Goldstone-Gamson exchange from the *American Journal of Sociology* and other published work analyzing the data set used in *Strategy.*

Gamson, W.; Fireman, B. (1979): »Utilitarian logic in the resource mobilization perspective«, in: M.N. Zald; J.M. McCarthy (eds.). *The dynamics of social movements.* Cambridge, Ma.: Winthrop.

Gamson, W.; Fireman, B.; Rytina, S. (1982): *Encounters with unjust authority.* Homewood, III.: Dorsey.
This book is an attempt to not ignore micro-level processes while using the resource mobilization model. The authors argue for a »threshold« model of resources. Beyond this threshold, additional resources make little difference.

Garner, R.; Zald, M.N. (1981): »Social movement sectors and systemic constraint: Toward a structural analysis of social movements«, Center for Research on Social Organization, Unviversity of Michigan, CRSO Working Paper N. 238, Ann Arbor, Mich.

– (1985): »The political economy of social movement sectors«, in: G.D. Suttles; M.N. Zald (eds.), *The challenge of social control: Citizenship and institution building in modern society.* Norwood, J.J.: ABLEX.
This article explicitly contrasts the structural features constraining the social movement sector in Western Europe and the United States.

Garrow, D.J. (1985): »Social protest movements: what sociology can teach us«, *Political Science* 18 (4): 814-816.

Gelb, J.; Palley, M.L. (1982): *Women and public policies.* Princeton, N.J.: Princeton University Press.
By focussing on incremental, single issue reforms that built on institutionalized conceptions of social justice, this book argues that the moderate wing of the women's movement has successfully brought about policy successes in the form of legislation and administrative reforms.

Gerlach, L.; Hine, V. (1970): *People, power, challenge: Movements of social transformation.* Indianapolis: Bobbs-Merrill.
This book examines a particular form of movement organizations: one that is characterized by what the authors call »multicephalous« structures. Their argument is that decen-

tralized, multicellular organizations, whose units possess partial autonomy, carry out the tasks of social movements best.

Gitlin, T. (1987): *The sixties: Years of hope, days of rage.* New York: Bantam Books.
Gitlin traces the growth of dissent from the affluent postwar years through the Fifties to the optimistic early days of the Sixties by focussing on the transformation of the young civil rights and ban-the-bomb movements. It brings alive the political activism of the Sixties.

Goldstein, R. (1978): *Political repression in modern America.* Cambridge, Ma.: Schenckman.
The thesis illustrated in this book is that the history of U.S. politics is studded with challenges that made a significant beginning only to be destroyed by political repression.

Goldstone, J.A. (1980): »The weakness of organization: A new look at Gamson's *The strategy of social protest*«, *American Journal of Sociology* 88 (5): 1017-1042.
This reanalysis of Gamson's data found that the incidence of success »seems to depend heavily on the incidence of broad political and/or economic crises in the society at large.« (p. 1029, 1038).

Gowan, S.; Lakey, G.; Moyer, W.; Taylor, R. (1986): *Moving toward a new society.* Philadelphia: New Society Publ.
»Handbook« for social change activists with a vision of a new democratic, decentralized and caring social order and a nonviolent strategy.

Granovetter, M. (1973): »The strength of weak ties«, *American Journal of Sociology* 18: 1360-1380.

– (1978): »Threshold models and collective behavior«, *American Journal of Sociology* 83: 1420-43.

Gurney, J.N.; Tierney, K.T. (1982): »Relative deprivation and social movements: A critical look at 20 years of theory and research«, *Sociological Quarterly* 23: 33-47.

Gurr, T.R. (1968): »A causal model of civil strife: A comparative analysis using new indices«, *American Political Science Review* 62: 1104-1124.

– (1979): *Why men rebel.* Princeton, N.J.: Princeton University Press.
This aggregate data study provides maps of protest and collective violence, while it highlights the kinds of events which alarm authorities.

– (1980): »On the outcomes of violent conflict«, in: T.R. Gurr (ed.), *Handbook of Political Conflict.* New York: Free Press.
This piece is among the first to seriously adress the outcomes of social movements.

Gurr, T.R.; Duvall, R. (1973): »Civil conflict in the 1960s. A reciprocal system with parameter estimates«, *Comparative Political Studies* 6: 135-169.
This article explains variance in collective action largely by political variables.

Gusfield, J.R. (1962): »Mass society and extremist politics«, *American Sociological Review* 27: 19-30.

– (1963): *Symbolic crusade. Status politics and the American Temperance movement.* Urbana: University of Illinois Press.
Carefully examining threatened elites and middle strata, this work emphasizes that temperance was a symbol of identification with a group's lifestyle, desired character traits, and notions about success in life. The conflict between dry and wet was a conflict between two cultures: protestant middle classes vs. that of the immigrant workers.

– (1968): »The study of social movements«, in: *Encyclopedia of the Social Sciences* 14: 443-52, New York: Macmillan.
This classical explanation of why movements form emphasizes sudden increases in short-term grievances created by »structural strains« of rapid social change.
– (1970): *Protests, reform, and revolt: A reader in social movements.* New York: Wiley.
– (1978): »Historical problematics and sociological movement« in *Research in the Sociology of Knowledge, Science and Art* 1: 121-148.
This piece reviews the major empirical monographs on social movements up to this time.
– (1981): »Social movements and social change. Perspective of linearity and fluidity«, *Research in Social Movements, Conflict and Change* 3: 317-339.
Here G. points out that the resource mobilization approach tends to neglect movements which rely on a cultural »quickening« of social change rather than organized protest and which never enter formal political arenas.

Gyorgy, Anna & friends (1979): *No nukes: Everyone's guide to nuclear power.* Boston: South End Press.

Handler, J. (1978): *Social movements and the legal system.* New York: Academic.

Hartz, L. (1955): *The liberal tradition in America.* New York: Harcourt, Brace & World.

Hayes, L. (1983): »Separatism and disobedience: the Seneca peace encampment«, *Radical America* 17 (4): 55-64.

Helfgot, J.H. (1981): *Professional reforming: Mobilization for Youth and the failure of social science.* Lexington, Ma.: Lexington Books.

Hertz, S.H. (1981): *The welfare mothers movement: A decade of change for poor women?* Washington, D.C.: University Press of America.

Hill, R.C. (1978): »Fiscal collapse and political struggle in decaying central cities in the U.S.«, in: W.K. Tabb; L. Sawers (eds.): *Marxism and the metropolis.* New York/Oxford: University Press.
– (1984): »Fiscal crisis, austerity politics, and alternative urban politics«, in: W.K. Tabb, L. Sawers (eds.). *Marxism and the metropolis.* New York/Oxford: University Press.

Himmelstein, J.L. (1989): *To the Right: The transformation of American conservatism.* Berkeley: University of California Press.
Examines how conservatism evolved into a viable political alternative that came to dominate contemporary American politics.

Hirsch, J. (1983): »The fordist security state and new social movements«, *Kapitalistate* (10/11), 75-87.
– (1988): »The crisis of fordism, transformations of the ›Keynesian‹ state, and new social movements«, in: *Research on Social Movements, Conflict and Change* 10: 43-56.

Holcomb, J. (1986): »State and local politics during the Reagan era: Citizen group responses«, in: M. Gittell (ed.), *State politics and the New Federalism.* New York: Longman.

Huntington, S.P. (1981): *American politics: The promise of disharmony.* Cambridge: Harvard University Press.

Inglehart, R. (1981): »Post-materialism in an environment of insecurity«, *American Political Science Review* 75 (4): 880-900.

Jenkins, J.C. (1979): »What is to be done? Movement or organization?« *Contemporary Sociology* 8: 527-53.

This article is a critique of Piven and Cloward (1977), especially of their conclusion that nothing succeeds like disruption, and of their skeptical view of organization.

– (1981): »Sociopolitical movements«, in: S.J. Long (ed.). *The handbook of political behavior* vol. 4. New York: Plenum Press.

– (1982a): »The transformation of a constituency into a movement«, in: J. Freeman (ed.). *Social movements of the 1960s and 1970s.* New York: Longman.

– (1982b): »Resource mobilization theory and the movements of the 1960s«, paper presented at the Annual Meeting of the ASA, San Francisco.

– (1983): »Resource mobilization theory and the study of social movements«, *American Review of Sociology* 9: 527-53.

– (1985): *The politics of insurgency. The farm workers movement in the 1960s.* New York: Columbia University Press.

This study treats the UFW experience as a model for insurgency among powerless, excluded groups. In this case, they created a sustained basis for organizing efforts by building a membership association led by professional organizers.

– (1986): »Nonprofit organizations and policy advocacy«, in W. Powell (ed.). *Handbook of Nonprofit Organization.* New Haven: Yale University Press.

– (1989): *Patrons of social reform: Private foundations and the social movements of the 1960s and 1970s.* New York: Russell Sage.

This book traces the growth and shifts in philanthropic foundation support for social movement activity.

Jenkins, J.C.; Perrow, C. (1977): »Insurgency of the powerless: Farm workers movements (1946-1972)«, *American Sociological Review* 42: 249-268.

A paired comparison of the farm worker organizations of the 1940s and 1960s, which shows that what varies most between the two periods was the attitudes of support organizations (especially liberal groups and organized labor) and governmental actions.

Jenkins, J.C.; Eckert, C.M. (1986): »Channeling black insurgence: Elite patronage and professional SMOs in the development of the black movement«, *American Sociological Review* 51 (6): 812-829.

This piece critically evaluates the theory of patronage and professional SMOs advanced by McCarthy/Zald (1973, 1975, 1977) and the social control theory advanced by their critics (McAdam 1982; Haines 1984) in interpreting the development of black insurgency.

Kaplowitz, S.A.; Fisher, B.J. (1985): »Revealing the logic of free-riding and contributions to the nuclear Freeze movement«, *Research in Social Movements, Conflict and Change* 8: 47-64.

The authors conducted a field experiment in which they created an organization and sent out a mass mailing to solicit contributions for the Freeze, varying the content of the appeal according to their experimental design.

Katsiaficas, G. (1987): *The imagination of the New Left: A global analysis of 1968.* Boston: South End Press.

K. flays the defects of mainstream sociology for its failure to understand the rationality of revolutionary movements. His own preference is for a holistic, value engaged critical sociology.

Katz, A.H. (1981): »Self-help and mutual aid: An emerging social movement?« *Annual Review of Sociology* 7: 129-155.

Katz, S.; Mayer, M. (1985): »Gimme shelter: Self-help housing struggles within and against the state in New York City and West Berlin«, *International Journal of Urban and Regional Research* 9 (1): 15-46.

Katzenstein, M.F.; Mueller, C.M. (eds.). (1987): *The women's movements of the United States and Western Europe: Consciousness, political opportunity, and public policy.* Philadelphia: Temple University Press.

Katznelson, I. (1981): *City Trenches: Urban politics and the patterning of class in the United States.* Chicago: University of Chicago Press.

Kazis, M.; Grossman, R. (1984): »The future of the environmental movement«, in: F. Riessman (ed.). *Beyond Reagan.* New York: Harper & Row.

Kerbo, H.R. (1982): »Movements of ›crisis‹ and movements of ›affluence‹. A critique of deprivation and resource mobilization theories«, *Journal of Conflict Resolution* 26 (4): 645-663.

One of the authors who do feel that the approaches compared complement each other, Kerbo claims that movements in industrial society can be explained mostly in terms of relative deprivation, while movements in contemporary societies require resource mobilization approaches.

Killian, M. (1979): *Die Genesis des Amerikanismus.* Frankfurt: Campus.

Killian, L.M. (1964): »Social movements,« in: R.E.L. Faris (ed.). *Handbook of modern sociology.* Chicago: Rand McNally.

King, C.W. (1956): *Social movements in the United States.* New York: Random House.

Kitschelt, H. (1985a): »Zur Dynamik neuer sozialer Bewegungen in den USA. Strategien gesellschaftlichen Wandels und ›American Exceptionalism‹«, in: K.W. Brand (ed.), *Neue soziale Bewegungen in Westeuropa und den USA.* Frankfurt: Campus.

– (1985b): »New social movements in West Germany and the United States«, in: M. Zeitlin (ed.). *Political Power and Social Theory,* vol. 5.

Kitschelt asks to what extent existing (macrostructural, Durkheimian, and utilitarian) perspectives can explain the new life chance movements.

– (1986): »Political opportunity structures and political protest: Anti-nuclear movements in four democracies«, *British Journal of Political Science* 16 (1): 57-85.

Klandermans, B. (1984): »Mobilization and participation: Social-psychological expansions of resource mobilization theory«, *American Sociological Review* 49: 583-600.

Klandermans, B.; Kriesi, H.; Tarrow, S. (eds.). (1988): *From structure to action: Social movement participation across cultures.* International Social Movement Research, vol. 1. Greenwich, Conn.; JAI Press.

This volume is the result of the activities in the RPG on Participation in social movements sponsored by the Council for European Studies.

Klandermans, B. (ed.). (1989): *Organizing for Change: Social movement organizations in Europe and the United States.* International Social Movement Research, vol. 2. Greenwich, Conn.: JAI Press.

This anthology brings together papers that examine the organizational characteristics of social movement organizations.

Klandermans, B.; Oegema, D. (1987): »Potentials, networks, motivations, and barriers: Steps toward participation in social movements«, *American Sociology Review* 52 (4): 519-531.

Klandermans, B.; Tarrow, S. (1988): »Mobilization into social movements: Synthesizing European and American approaches«, in: Klandermans, B.; Kriesi, H.; Tarrow, S. (eds.), *From structure to action* (Vol. 1 of International Social Movement Research). Greenwich, Conn.: JAI Press.

Klapp, O. (1969): *The collective search for identity*. New York: HR&W.

Klatsch, R. (1987): *Women of the New Right*. Philadelphia: Temple University Press.

Klein, E. (1984): *Gender politics: From consciousness to mass politics*. Cambridge: Harvard University Press.

Klein develops a society-focused theory of social learning in her account of the emergence of the women's movement. She charts a strong correlation between the beginnings of feminist activism and changing patterns of divorce, fertility, and work-participation rates.

Knopp, L. (1987): »Social theory, social movements and public policy: Recent accomplishments of the gay and lesbian movements in Minneapolis, Minnesota«, *International Journal of Urban and Regional Research* 11 (2): 243-261.

Kotler, M. (1969): *Neighborhood Government: The local foundations of political life*. New York: Bobbs-Merrill.

Kriesberg, L. (ed.) (1978-1988): *Research in social movements, conflicts and change*. vol. 1-10. Greenwich, Conn.: JAI Press.

Kriesberg, L. (1988): »Peace movements and government peace efforts«, in: Kriesberg, L.; Misztal, B. (eds.), *Research in social movements, conflicts and change*. vol. 10. Greenwich, Conn.: JAI Press.

Ladd, A.E.; Hood, T.C.; Van Liers, K. (1983): »Ideological themes in the anti-nuclear movement: Consensus and diversity«, *Sociological Inquiry* 53 (2-3): 252-272.

Questionaire survey data from demonstrators at a national anti-nuclear rally are used to examine ideological consensus and diversity evident in the national protest over nuclear power.

Lancourt, J.E. (1979): *Confront or concede: The Alinsky Citizens Action Organizations*. Lexington, Ma.: D.C. Heath.

This study concludes that Alinsky style groups are efforts to bring previously excluded groups into the existing political system, rather than to fundamentally alter the system.

Langdon, St. (ed.) (1979): *Citizen participation in America*. Lexington, Ma.: Lexington Books.

Lawson, R. (1984): »The rent strike in New York City, 1904-1980: The evolution of a social movement strategy«, *Journal of Urban History* 10: 235-258.

Lewis, R.S. (1972): *The nuclear power rebellion*. New York: The Viking Press.

Liebman, R.C.; Wirthnow, R. (1983): *New Christian Right: Mobilization and legitimation*. New York: Aldine.

The authors demonstrate the utility of resource mobilization concepts for right wing movements.

Lipset, S.M. (1979): *The first new nation: The U.S. in historical and comparative perspective, 2nd ed.* N.Y.: W.W. Norton.

Lipset, S.M.; Raab, E. (1978): *The politics of unreason: Right-wing extremism in America. 1790-1977.* Chicago: University of Chicago Press.
Using survey and historical data, Lipset/Raab have here documented the social bases of the important right-wing extremist groups in the U.S. up to 1972.

Lipsky, M. (1968): »Protest as a political resource«, *American Political Science Review* 62 (4): 1144-1158.
This article became important in the debate because it does not perceive the relation between protest organizations and the targets of protest as a contrast between blind, collective rage and quiet pragmatic response, but rather as bargaining between rational actors.

Lipsky, M.; Olson, D. (1976): »The processing of racial crisis in America«, *Politics and Society* 6: 79-103.

Lo, C. (1982): »Countermovements and conservative movements in the contemporary United States«, *Annual Review of Sociology* 8: 107-134.

Lofland, J. (1977): *Doomsday cult: A study of conversion, proselytization, and maintenance of faith.* New York: Irvington (2nd ed.).
This book studies the intricacies of the worldview of millenarian Protestantism through field work and in-depth interviews.

– (1979): »White-hot mobilization: Strategies of a millenarian movement«, in: M.N. Zald; J.M. McCarthy (eds.). *The dynamics of social movements.* Cambridge, Ma.: Winthrop.

– (1985): *Protest: Studies of collective behavior and social movements.* New Brunswick, N.J.: Transaction Books.
Lofland introduces a sociology of emotions and culture into the movement literature by arguing that collective action can also elate members and produce »crowd joys«. The articles deal with the Unification Church and other cult organizations, some theorize on contemporary religious movements.

Lofland, J.; Jamison, M. (1984): »Social movement locals: Model member structures«, *Sociological Analysis* 45 (2): 115-129.

Loeb, P. (1986): *Hope in hard times: America's peace movement in the Reagan era.* Lexington, Ma.: D.C. Heath.

Loomis, B.A. (1983): »A new era: Groups and the grass roots«, in: A.J. Cigler; B.A. Loomis (eds.). *Interest group politics.* Washington, D.C., Congressional Quarterly.

Luke, T. (1986): »Class contradictions and social cleavages in informationalizing post-industrial societies: On the rise of new social movements«, paper presented at the annual meeting of the American Science Association, August 28-31, 1986.

Luker, K. (1984): *Abortion and the politics of motherhood.* Berkeley: University of California Press.
This study of women in the anti-abortion and pro-choice movements links the movements to structural shifts in family composition and career patterns. Both pro-choice and anti-abortion women come to their politics through calculations of self-interest.

Lynd, S. (1966): *Non-violence in America: A documentary history.* Indianapolis: Bobbs-Merrill.

Majka, Th. (1980): »Poor people's movements and farm labor insurgency«, *Contemporary Crises* 4: 283-308.

Mansbridge, J. (1986): *Why we lost the ERA*. Chicago: University of Chicago Press.

Marwell, G.; Oliver, P. (1984): »Collective action theory and social movement research«, *Research in Social Movements, Conflicts and Change* 7: 1-27.

Marx, G.T. (1979): »External efforts to damage or facilitate social movements: Some patterns, explanations, outcomes, and complications«, in: M.N. Zald; J.D. McCarthy (eds.). *The daynamics of social movements*. Cambridge, Ma.: Winthrop.

This article analyzes the techniques used by government agents to suppress and control social movements in the 60s. Because in many ways the movements were successful, the effectiveness of the police tactics is called into question.

Marx, G.T.; Useem, M. (1971): »Majority involvement in minority movements: Civil rights, abolition, untouchability«, *Journal of Social Issues* 27 (1): 81-104.

Marx, G.T.; Wood, J.L. (1976): »Strands of theory and research on collective behavior«, *Annual Review of Sociology* 1: 368-428.

This is still the best survey of the literature in the collective behavior approach, and also the first place where the outcomes of protest for the political system were systematically reviewed and analyzed.

Mayer, M. (1977): »The formation of the American nation-state«, *Kapitalistate* 6 (Fall): 39-90.

– (1982): »The profile of contemporary neighborhood movements«, in: G.-M. Hellstern; F. Spreer; H. Wollmann (eds.). *Applied urban research*. Bonn: BfLR.

– (1984): »Friedensbewegung in den USA: Protestbewegung in zwei Teilen«, *Vorgänge* 23 (4): 36-43.

– (1987): »Restructuring and popular opposition in West German cities«, in: M.P. Smith; J. Feagin (eds.). *The capitalist city*. London: Basil Blackwell.

McAdam, D. (1982): *Political process and the development of black insurgency, 1930-1970*. Chicago: University of Chicago Press.

This study develops a process model of mobilization in which the indigenous organizational strength and the political opportunities for articulation and protest are key variables.

– (1986): »Recruitment to high risk activism: The case of Freedom Summer«, *American Journal of Sociology* 92 (1): 64-90.

– (1988): »Micromobilization contexts and recruitment to activism«, in: *International Social Movement Research* 1: 125-154.

– (1988): *Freedom Summer*. New York, Oxford University Press.

McAdam interviewed 348 of the 566 volunteers in the movement. He explores the varied motives that compelled these students to make the journey south and examines the intents, expectations, and the long-term effects.

McAdam, D.; McCarthy, J.; Zald, M.N. (1988): »Social movements«, in: N.J. Smelser (ed.). *Handbook of Sociology*. Newbury Park: Sage.

McAllister, P. (ed.). (1982): *Reweaving the web of life: Feminism and nonviolence*. Philadelphia: New Society Publ.

McCarthy, J. (1987): »Pro-life and pro-choice mobilization: Infrastructure deficits and new technologies«, in: M. Zald; J. McCarthy (eds.). *Social movements in organizational so-*

ciety: Resource mobilization, conflict and institutionalization. New Brunswick, N.J.: Transaction Books.
This article clarifies the infrastructural concept and explains the more successful mobilization of the pro-life movement vis-a-vis its pro-choice adversary.

McCarthy, J.; Zald, M.N. (1973): *The trends of social movements in America: Professionalization and resource mobilization.* Morristown, N.J.: General Learning Press.

– (1977): »Resource mobilization and social movements: A partial theory«, *American Journal of Sociology* 82 (6): 1212-1241.
Both works apply the rational actor model to the behavior of individuals in movements and to the strategy of movement organizations. They explore the interplay between social opportunity structure, resources for collective action, and the behavior of social movement organizations.

McFarland, A.S. (1978): »Third forces in American politics: The case of Common Cause«, in: J. Fishell (ed.), *Parties and elections in an anti-party age.* Bloomington, University of Indiana Press.

McLaughlin, B. (ed.) (1969): *Studies in social movements: A social psychological perspective.* New York: Free Press.

McPhail, C.; Miller, D.L. (1973): »The assembling process: a theoretical and empirical investigation«, *American Sociological Review*, 38: 721-735.

McPhail, C.; Wohlstein, R. (1983): »Individual and collective behaviors within gatherings, demonstrations and riots«, *Annual Review of Sociology*, 9: 579-600.

Mendlowitz, S.H.; Walker, R.B.J. (eds.) (1987): *Towards a just world peace: Perspectives from social movements.* Toronto: Butterworths.
This anthology brings together various articles on the peace movement world wide, including a study by Alger and Mendlovitz on local peace and justice activists.

Milbrath, L. (1984): *Environmentalists: Vanguard for a new society.* Binghampton: SUNY Press.
This a cross-cultural study of environmental values among citizens and government leaders.

Miller, A.S. (1987): »Saul Alinsky: America's radical reactionary«, *Radical America* 21 (1): 11-20.

Miller, J. (1987): *»Democracy is in the streets«: From Port Huron to the siege of Chicago.* New York: Simon and Schuster.

Miller, M. (1979): *The »ideology« of the community organization movement.* San Francisco: Organize Training Center.

– (1984): »Community organization U.S.A.: The view from the movement«, *International Journal of Urban and Regional Research* 5 (4): 565-572.

Mitchell, R.C. (1979): »National environment lobbies and the apparent illogic of collective action«, in: C.S. Russell (ed.), *Collective decision-making: Applications from public choice theory.* Baltimore: Johns Hopkins University Press.
This is an important critique of Olson; it stresses the importance of ideology in people's affiliations with environmental groups.

– (1981): »From elite quarrel to mass movement«, *Society* 18 (5): 76-84.
This overview of the evolution of the U.S. anti-nuclear power movement describes its three major phases; particular attention is given to the radical, decentralized character of

the alliances and their commitment to nonviolence strategies and consensus decision-making.

Mollenkopf, J. (1980): »Neighborhood political development and the politics of urban growth«, in: R. Hollister; Ph. Clay (eds.), *Neighborhood Policy*. Cambridge, Ma.: MIT Press.

– (1983): *The Contested City*. Princeton, N.J., Princeton University Press.

Moore, H.A.; Whitt, H.P. (1986): »Multiple dimensions of the Moral Majority platform: Shifting interest group coalitions«, *The Sociological Quarterly* 27 (3): 423-439.

Morris, A. (1981): »Black southern student sit-in movement: An analysis of internal organization«, *American Sociological Review* 46 (6): 744-767.

This piece argues that the Southern sit-in movement of 1960 grew out of existing institutions and organizational forms. The spread of the sit-ins followed the networks of these pre-existing institutional relationships.

(1984): *The origins of the Civil Rights movement: Black communities organizing for change*. New York: McMillan Inc.

The book documents the organizing role of black churches in the early stages of the civil rights movement. As it emphasizes rationality, resources, networks of solidarity, continuity between unruly challengers and institutionalized politics, and the central role of movements in generating social change, it stands squarely in the center of the resource mobilization perspective.

Morris, A.; Herring, C. (1987): »Theory and research in social movements: a critical review«, in: S.P. Long (ed.). *Annual Review of Political Science* vol. 2. Norwood, N.J.: Ablex Publ. Corp.

Morris, D. (1982): *Self-reliant cities*. San Francisco: Sierra Club.

Mottl, Tahi (1980): »The analysis of counter-movements«, *Social Problems*, 27 (6): 620-635.

Mueller, C.M.; Dimieri, T. (1982): »The structure of belief systems among contending ERA activists«, *Social Forces* 60: 657-675.

Nichols, E. (1987): »The anti-nuclear movement«, *Berkeley Journal of Sociology* 33: 167-192.

Oberschall, A. (1973): *Social conflict and social movements*. Englewood Cliffs, NJ: Prentice Hall.

– (1978a): »Theories of social conflict«, *Annual Review of Sociology* 4: 291-315.

– (1978b): »The decline of the 1960s social movements«, *Research in Social Movements, Conflict and Change* 1: 257-289.

– (1980): »Loosely structured collective conflicts: A theory and an application«, *Research in Social Movements, Conflicts and Change* 3: 45-88.

O'Brian, J. (1983): »Environmentalism as a mass movement: Historical notes«, *Radical America* 17 (2/3): 7-27.

Oliver, P. (1980): »Rewards and punishments as selective incentives for collective action: theoretical investigations«, *American Journal of Sociology* 84: 1356-1375.

– (1983): »The mobilization of paid and volunteer activists in the neighborhood movement«, *Research in Social Movements, Conflicts and Change* 5: 133-170.

– (1984): »If you don't do it, nobody will: Active and token contributors to local collective action«, *American Sociological Review* 49: 601.610.

– (1985): »Bringing the crowd back in: The non-organizational elements in social movements«, ASA paper.

Olson, M. (1971): *The logic of collective action: Public goods and the theory of groups.* Cambridge, Ma.: Harvard University Press.
He developed a model of individual involvements in collective action for the sake of private maximization. Although evidence has been assembled challenging Olson's dictum, Gamson (1975) made a strong case that »selective incentives« (plus something else) are found in most groups. Olson's economic reasoning lies at the heart of McCarthy/Zald's resource mobilization approach.

Ortiz, R.D. (1982): »Land and nationhood: The American Indian struggle for self-determination and survival«, *Socialist Review* 12 (5): 105-120.

Ovryn Rivera, R.J. (1987): *A question of conscience: The emergence and development of the Sanctuary movement in the United States.* Ph.D. dissertation, City University of New York.

Perlman, J. (1976): »Grassrooting the system«, *Social Policy* 7: 4-20.

– (1979): »Grassroots empowerment and government response«, *Social Policy* 10 (2).

– (1979): »Grassroots participation from neighborhood to nation«, in: S. Langdon (ed.), *Citizen participation in America.* Lexington, Ma.: Lexington Books.

Perrow, Ch. (1979): »The sixties observed«, in: M.N. Zald; J. McCarthy (eds.); *The dynamics of social movements.* Cambridge, Ma.: Winthrop Publ.
Presenting a series of competing explanations of the rise and decline of social movements, he evaluates the various positions with a data set from the New York Times. He finds that none of the perspectives does an adequate job of accounting for all the movements: the strengths and weaknesses of each are specified.

Petchesky, R. (1981): »Antiabortion, antifeminism, and the rise of the New Right«, *Feminist Studies* 7: 206-246.
This article analyzes the link between antifeminism and right-wing politics. It claims that the New Right seeks to destroy liberal democracy and is using women's issues as a lever for the return of patriarchy and militarism.

Piven, F.F.; Cloward, R.A. (1977): *Poor people's movements: Why they succeed, how they fail.* New York: Pantheon.
The argument is made that poor people's movements derive their gains solely from mass defiance; hence, building permanent membership organizations is inherently counterproductive. The evidence supporting this thesis comes from four different cases of social protest, among them the urban riots of the 1960s.

Powell, W. (ed.) (1987): *Handbook of nonprofit organizations.* New Haven; Yale University Press.

Price, J. (1982): *The antinuclear movement.* Boston; G.K. Hall & Co. Revised edition 1989, Boston: Twayne Publ.

Roach, J.K.; Roach, J.L. (1980): »Turmoil in command of politics: organizing the poor«, *Sociological Quarterly* 21: 259-270.

Roberts, R.E.; Kloss, R.M. (1974): *Social movements: Between the balcony and the barricade.* St. Louis; C.C. Mosby.

Rudolph, R.; Ridley, S. (1986): »Chernobyl's challenge to anti-nuclear activism«, *Radical America* 20 (2/3): 7-21.

Rush, G.B.; Denisoff, R.S. (eds.) (1971): *Social and political movements*. New York; Appleton-Century-Crofts.

Ryan, B. (1989): »Ideological purity and feminism: The U.S. women's movement from 1966 to 1975,« *Gender and Society*, 3/2 (6); 239-257.

Sabatier, P. (1975): »Social movements and regulatory agencies«, *Policy Science* 6 (3): 301-342.

Sale, K. (1973): *SDS*. New York: Random House.

– (1986): »The forest for the trees: Can today's environmentalists tell the difference?« *Mother Jones* 11: 25ff.

Saltzman Chafetz, J.; Dworkin, A.G. (1986): *Female revolt: Women's movements in world and historical perspective*. Totowa, NJ.: Rowman & Allanheld.

Satin, M. (1978): *New Age Politics. The alternative to marxism and liberalism*. Vancouver, British Columbia: Whitecap.

Sayres, S.; Stephanson, A.; Aronowitz, S.; Jameson, F. (eds.). (1984): *Sixties without apology*. Minneapolis: University of Minnesota Press.

This anthology contains a number of insightful essays covering political and cultural questions related to the New Left.

Scaminaci III, J.; Dunlap, R.E. (1986): »No Nukes! A comparison of participants in two national antinuclear demonstrations«, *Sociological Inquiry* 56 (2): 272-282.

Two sets of demonstrators (mail questionaire survey) are found to be young, well-educated and politically liberal, and to reject several dominant U.S. values.

Schnaiberg, A. (1983): »Redistributive goals versus distributive politics: Social equity limits in environmental and appropriate technology movements«, *Sociological Inquiry* 53 (2/3): 200-219.

Schwartz, M. (1976): *Radical protest and social structure*. New York: Academic Press.

Smelser, N.J. (1982): *The theory of collective behavior*. New York: Free Press.

Smelser defined collective behavior as »mobilization on the basis of a belief which redefines social action« (p. 8) and organized the entire theoretical structure around the nature of generalized beliefs, i.e. ideology.

Smith, D.H.; Pillemer, K. (1983): »Self-help groups as social movement organizations: Social structure and social change«, *Research in Social Movements, Conflicts and Change* 5: 203-233.

Smith, L. (1980): »Labor and the No Nukes movement«, *Socialist Review* 10: 135-150.

Snow, D.A.; Zurcher Jr., L.; Ekland-Olson, S. (1980): »Social networks and social movements: A micro-structural approach to differential recruitment«, *American Sociological Review* 45 (5): 787-801.

The authors apply the resource mobilization model to micro-structures of recruitment in personal change movements.

Snow, D.A.; Benford, R.D. (1988): »Ideology, frame resonance and participant mobilization«, *International Social Movement Research* 1: 197-217.

Snow, D.A.; Rochford Jr. E.B.; Worden, S.K.; Benford, R.D. (1986): »Frame alignment processes, micromobilization, and movement participation«, *American Sociological Review* 51 (4): 464-481.

Both articles examine the framing efforts in which movements engage (frame alignment processes) so as to mobilize and activate participants. The second article considers in particular the conditions that affect or constrain framing efforts.

Snyder, D.; Kelly, W.R. (1979): »Strategies for investigating violence and social change: Illustrations from analyses of racial disorders and implications for mobilization research«, in: M.N. Zald; J. McCarthy (eds.) *The dynamics of social movements*. Cambridge, Ma.: Winthrop.

The authors argue for the incorporation of an investigation of the *consequences* of social movements into the mainstream of research and develop an analytic model for such incorporation.

Spilerman, S. (1970): »The causes of racial disturbances: A comparison of alternative explanations«, *American Sociological Review* 35: 627-643.

– (1971): »The causes of racial disturbances: Tests of an explanation,« *American Sociological Review* 36: 427-442.

– (1972): »Strategic considerations in analyzing the distribution of racial disturbances«, *American Sociological Review* 37: 520-532.

– »Structural characteristics of cities and the severity of racial disorders«, *American Sociological Review* 41 (5): 771-793.

Spretnak, C. (ed.) (1982): *The politics of women's spirituality: Essays on the rise of spiritual power within the feminist movement*. New York: Doubleday.

Spretnak, C. (1987): *The spiritual dimension of Green politics*. Santa Fe, N.M.: Bear & C. Publ.

Stacey, J. (1983): »The new conservative feminism«, *Feminist Studies* 9: 559-583.

– (1987): »Sexism by a subtler name? Postindustrial conditions and postfeminist consciousness in the Silicon Valley«, *Socialist Review* 17 (6): 7-28.

Stacey, J.; Gerard, S.E. (1989): »›We are not doormats‹: The influence of feminism on contemporary evangelicals in the United States«, ASA paper.

Steedly, H.R.; Poley, J.W. (1980): »The success of protest groups: Multivariate analyses«, *Social Science Research* 8: 1-15.

Steffy, J.M. (1986): »A survey of the San Francisco peace movement«, *International Journal of World Peace* 3 (3): 65-83.

The accomplishments and pitfalls of the 400 groups that comprise the San Francisco area peace movement are discussed, based on interviews with representative leaders of the movement and telephone surveys of peace organizations.

Sturgeon, N.A. (1986): »Direct theory and political action: The American direct action movement«, Qualifying essay, University of California at Santa Cruz.

– (1990): »Collective theorizing in the U.S. nonviolent direct action movement: Oppositional structures and practices«, forthcoming in M. Mayer (ed.). *New Social Movements in Europe and the United States*. London: Unwin Hyman.

Swank, D.H.; Hicks, A. (1984): »Militancy, need and relief. The Piven and Cloward AFDC caseload thesis revisited«, *Research in Social Movements, Conflicts and Change* 6: 1-29.

Tarrow, S. (1983a): *Struggling to reform: Social movements and policy change during cycles of protest*. Ithaca, N.Y., Cornell University (Western Societies Program, Occasional Papers No. 15).

– (1983b): »Resource mobilization and cycles of protest: Theoretical reflections and comparative illustrations«, ASA paper.
– »National politics and collective action: Recent theory and research in Western Europe and the United States«, *Annual Review of Sociology* 14: 421-440.
– (1989): *Democracy and disorder. Protest and politics in Italy, 1965-1975.* Oxford; Clarendon Press.
Tilly, Ch.; Tilly, L.; Tilly, R. (1975): *The rebellious century, 1830-1930.* Cambridge, Ma.: Harvard University Press.
This book analyzes the modernization of collective action.
Tilly, Ch. (1978): *From mobilization to revolution.* Reading, Ma.: Addison-Wesley Publ. Co.
This book explains variance in collective action largely by political variables.
Tilly, Ch.; Tilly, L. (1981): *Collective action and class conflict.* Beverly Hills: Sage.
Tilly, Ch. (1985): »Models and realities of popular collective action«. *Social Research* 52 (4).
In this essay, Tilly turns to *contemporary* movements, which do not (as opposed to the older ones he studied) address the economy or the state for inclusion or increased benefits, and do not involve actors defining themselves in class or national terms.
– (1988): »Social movements, old and new«, *Research in Social Movements. Conflicts and Change* 10: xxx
Touraine, A. (1981): *The voice and the eye.* New York: Cambridge University Press.
– (1985): »An introduction to the study of social movements«, *Social Research* 52 (4).
Turner, R.H. (1964): »Collective behavior«, in: R.E.L. Faris (ed.), *Handbook of Modern Sociology.* Chicago: Rand McNally.
– (1969): »The theme of contemporary social movements«, *The British Journal of Sociology* 20: 390.405.
Turner contends that within each historical era there are typically »one or two movements that color the preoccupations and social change effected during that era« (392).
– (1981): »Collective behavior and resource mobilization as approaches to social movements: Issues and continuities«, *Research in Social Movements, Conflicts and Change* 4: 1-24.
Turner, R.H.; Killian, L.M. (1957): *Collective behavior.* Englewood Cliffs, N.J.: Prentice Hall. 2nd ed. 1972; 3rd ed. 1986.
Useem, B. (1980): »Solidarity model, breakdown model, and the Boston anti-busing movement«, *American Sociological Review* 45: 357-369.
This article argues that participation in the anti-busing movement in Boston was not related to measures of social disorganization but rather to prior organization: individuals' feelings of attachment to the neighborhood and active participation in politics and personal networks in the community.
Useem, B.; Zald, M.N. (1982): »From pressure group to social movement: Organizational dilemmas of the effort to promote nuclear power«, *Social Problems* 30 (2): 144-156.
While social movement theorists usually focus on the efforts of groups to gain the right to routinely influence government policy, this article looks at the opposite process, in which groups lose this right. The development of the pronuclear movement in the U.S. is

examined as a case study of a pressure group that lost power and mobilized a social movement to restore it.

Useem, M. (1975): *Protest movements in America.* Indianapolis: Bobbs-Merrill.

Vellela, T. (1988): *New voices: Student political activism in the '80s and '90s.* Boston: South End Press.

Based on travel, research and interviewing, this book brings together different strands of activism that make up the current multi-issue student movement (divestment, Central America, CIA, gay and lesbian rights, racism etc.)

Vogel, D. (1978): *Lobbying the corporation.* New York: Basic Books.

– (1981): »The public interest movement and the American reform tradition«, *Political Science Quarterly* 95: 607-627.

Vogel, S. (1980): »The limits of protest: A critique of the anti-nuclear movement«, *Socialist Review* 10: 125-134.

Walsh, E.J. (1978): »Mobilization theory vis-a-vis a mobilization process: The case of the United Farm Workers Movement«, *Research in Social Movements, Conflicts and Change* 1: 155-177.

– (1981): »Resource mobilization and citizen protest in communication around Three Mile Island«, *Social Problems* 29 (1): 1-21.

– (1986): »The role of target vulnerability in high-technolgoy protest movements: The nuclear establishment at Three Mile Island«, *Sociological Forum* 1 (2): 199-218.

– (1988): *Democracy in the shadows. Citizen mobilization in the wake of the accident at Three Mile Island.* New York: Greenwood Press.

The book (and in part also the latter articles) covers the political struggle surrounding the Three Mile Island nuclear accident in 1979. Walsh documents the dynamics of the conflict between local communities and national nuclear elites in the wake of the desaster. His findings confirm the importance of grievances for causing a social movement.

– (1988): »New dimensions of social movements: The high-level waste-siting controversy«, *Sociological Forum*, Fall: 586-605.

Walsh, E.J.; Warland, R.H. (1983): »Social movement involvement in the wake of a nuclear accident: activists and free-riders in the Three Mile area«, *American Sociological Review* 48: 764-781.

Von Eschen, D.; Kirk, J.; Pinard, M. (1971): »The organizational substructure of disorderly politics«, *Social Forces* 49: 529-544.

Wasserman, H. (1979): *Energy war: Notes from the front.* Westport, Conn.: L. Hill.

West, G. (1981): *The national welfare rights movement.* New York: Praeger.

Whalen, J.; Flacks, R. (1989): *Beyond the barricades: The sixties generation grows up.* Philadelphia: Temple University Press.

A longitudinal study of 18 of the 25 who were on trial for the burning of a bank in Santa Barbara during the early stage of the student movement. Results challenge the media-promulgated picture that the sixties rebels have sold out or »settled down«.

Wilkinson, P. (1971): *Social movements.* London: Pall Mall.

Wilson, J.Q. (1961): »The strategy of protest: Problems of negro civic action«, *Journal of Conflict Resolution* 5: 291-303.

Wilson, J.D. (1973a): *Introduction to social movements.* New York; Basic Books.

– (1973b): *Political Organizations.* New York: Basic Books.
– (1983): »Corporatism and the professionalism of reform«. *Journal of Political and Military Sociology* 11: 53-68.
Wittner, C. (1969): *Rebels against war. The American peace movement. 1941-1960.* New York: Columbia University Press.
Wood, J.L.; Jackson, M. (1982) *Social movements. Development, participation, and dynamics.* Belmont, Ca.: Wadsworth Publ. Co.
The authors borrow eclectically from a variety of approaches arguing that each is suited to explanations of different facets of movements: »structural theories« explain movement origins, »psychological theories« explain the motivational level of composition and participation etc. The array of perspectives is complemented with 7 empirical articles on specific movements.
Wood, P. (1982): »The environmental movement: Its crystallization, development and impact«, in: J.L. Wood; M. Jackson (eds.). *Social Movements: Development, participation, and dynamics.* Belmont: Wadsworth.
Yates, G.G. (1975): *What women want. The ideas of the movement.* Cambridge, Ma.: Harvard University Press.
Zald, M.N. (1980): »Issues in the theory of social movements«, *Current Perspectives in Social Theory* 1: 61-72.
– (1985a): *The future of social movements in America: The transformation of ends and means.* Center for Research on Social Organization. Working Paper Series No. 328. University of Michigan, Ann Arbor.
– (1985b): »Political change, citizenship rights, and the welfare state«, *Annals of the American Academy of Political and Social Science* 479: 48-66.
– (1988): »The trajectory of social movements in America«, *Research in Social Movements, Conflicts and Change* 10: 19-41.
Zald, M.N.; Ash, R. (1966): »Social movement organizations«, *Social Forces,* 44: 327-341.
Zald, M.N.; McCarthy, J.D. (eds.). (1979): *The dynamics of social movements.* Cambridge, Ma.: Winthrop Publishers.
This book came out of a conference held in 1977 to facilitate interchange between scholars working with the resource mobilization approach. It contains commissioned papers on specific movements and theoretical papers that both criticized and synthesized the resource mobilization perspective and extended it into new areas.
Zald, M.N.; McCarthy, J.D. (1980): »Social movement industries: Competition and cooperation among movement organizations«, *Research in Social Movements, Conflicts and Change* 3: 1-20.
Since social movements are generally characterized by multiple social movement organizations, a multi-organizational model allowing the coexistence of diverse types is more appropriate in gauging the organization of a single movement.
Zald, M.N.; McCarthy, J.D. (eds.). (1987): *Social movements in an organizational society.* New Brunswick, N.J.: Transaction Books.
This book is a collection of 14 of their theoretical and empirical contributions to the resource mobilization perspective, all but 3 have been published elsewhere. The first section provides a theoretical overview, the second focusses on the infrastructure of social movements, the third on processes of organizational change (including the new classic

Zald/Ash Garner article on the growth, decay, and change of SMOs, the fourth on movements within organizations, the fifth on countermovements, and the sixth is on »social movements and the future«.

Zald, M.N.; McCarthy, J.D. (1987): »Religious groups as crucibles of social movements«, in: M.N. Zald; J.D. McCarthy (eds.). *Social movements in an organizational society.*

Zald, M.N.; Useem, B. (1987): »Movement and countermovement«, in: M.N. Zald; J.D. McCarthy (eds.). *Social movements in an organizational society.*

Zaroulis, N.; Sullivan, G. (1985): *Who spoke up? American protests against the war in Vietnam 1963-1975.* New York: Holt, Rinehart & Winston.
This book is a comprehensive history of the anti-Vietnam War movement in the United States.

Zurcher, L.A.; Curtis, R.L. (1973): »A comparative analysis of propositions describing social movement organization«, *The Sociological Quarterly* 14: 175-188.
Data from a study on two anti-pornography crusades and the social movement organizations which created and directed them are used to assess 9 propositions formulated by Zald/Ash (1966) concerning the structure and dynamics of social movement organizations.

Zurcher, L.A.: Kirkpatrick, R.G. (1976): *Citizens for decency: Antipornography crusades as status defense.* Austin: University of Texas Press.
This book (a case study inspired by Gusfield's concept of status symbolism) definitively analyzed the campaigns against antipornography.

Zurcher, L.A.; Snow, D.A. (1981): »Collective behavior: Social movements«, in: M. Rosenberg; R.H. Turner (eds.), *Social Psychology, Sociological Perspectives.* New York: Basic Books.

Social Movements and the Social Sciences in Britain*

Wolfgang Rüdig, James Mitchell, Jenny Chapman and Philip D. Lowe

Introduction

The most striking aspect of the voluminous and empirically rich literature on social movements in Britain is the fragmentation and particularism of the work done. While such research elsewhere has been set in an established framework of social movement theory, in Britain disparate accounts have rarely been integrated into a more generalised theory, but more often have been cast in context of other debates, with little or no reference to the social movement literature. The reasons for this may partly lie in the atheoretical inclination of much of British social sciences but also, undoubtedly, academic research has faithfully reflected the political fragmentation of social movements themselves. In consequence this chapter is mainly based on the study of particular social movements and attempts to elicit from such work common themes and arguments which might provide the foundations for a more generalised theory of social movements in Britain. Before looking at the body of work covering new religious movements, urban social movements, nationalist movements, the feminist movement, the peace movement and the environmental movement, we shall consider those few British contributions to the more general debate on social movements.

---

* We gratefully acknowledge the assistance of Lynn Bennie, Laura Gurevitz and Dr. David Judge in compiling this article.

I. The Development of Social Movement Theory in Britain

There has been no major attempt to construct a specifically British theory of social movements; hardly any monographs by British authors address the sociology of social movements as their major aim; and contributions to general social movement theory are few and far between. Apart from historical and anthropological studies, mainly of movements outside of Britain (see, for example Worsley, 1957; Hobsbawm, 1959), the first signs of a British interest in the theoretical analysis of social movements only emerged in the 1970s. W.C. Runicman (1966) may be regarded as the only other forerunner in this field; he may not have mentioned social movements and was largely concerned with attitudes and voting behavior but in discussing relative deprivation his work was closely related to the main theoretical development in US social movement research.

In the early 1970s, a number of works began to consider social movements in a wider and more theoretical context. Paul Wilkinson (1971), a political scientist, presented the first broadly-based review of the literature on social movements in Britain. Wilkinson's main contribution consisted of providing an exhaustive typology, identifying ten main types of social movements.

While other political scientists remained largely oblivious to social movement theory, British sociologists did not notably enter the breach, despite the publication in 1972 of a sociological volume exclusively devoted to the topic. In his slim book, *The Sociology of Social Movements*, J.A. Banks reviewed a major part of the American literature, but also proceeded to develop a more advanced research plan. Banks concentrated on a critique of the functionalist view of social movements as manifestations of social malfunctioning and historical epiphonemena. Instead, he proposed to see social movements as »self-conscious and successful attempts to introduce innovations into a social system« (Banks, 1972, 17), and discussed the terms of such an innovative role with reference to self-help movements, »›cause‹ pressure-group movements«, and revolutionary movements. For Banks, social movements were characterised by their ability to affect social change; and the role of the co-operative movement was highlighted as an example. Movements not consciously pursuing a socially innovative role, such as millenarian movements, were excluded from the category of social movements. His review was intended »to alert sociologists to the possibilities and the promise which research in this field can offer« (Banks, 1972, 56). But his call went largely unheeded by British sociologists. A number of further research papers appeared during the 1970s, but they hardly constituted a mainstream activity in the social sciences.

One of the more interesting contributions came from Ruth Levitas (1977) who criticised Banks' »voluntaristic« view of social movements as social innovators. She argued that the success of a social movement had to be seen in the context of a process of social interaction in which the aims of a social movement were defined and changed. Success of social movements, she argued, »may be due less to achieving what was originally desired than to desiring what was eventually achieved« (Levitas, 1977, 50). The co-operative movement cited by Banks as a successful innovative movement only attained that position because it moderated and adapted its aims »to those which appeared feasible« (Levitas, 1977, 56). Levitas instead proposed an interactionist view which characterised a social movement as »a dialectical process whereby a problem is defined simultaneously with a solution being constructed and attempts being made to implement its solution« (Levitas, 1977, 62).

Other authors of the 1970s included Angus Stewart (1977) who sketched the skeleton of a radical theory of movements emerging as a result of political crises carried by those sections of society which are marginal to the centres of power, and David Bouchier (1977; 1978) who was centrally concerned with the ideology of social movements.

From the point of view of political science, the most innovative contribution of the 1970s came from Martin Kolinsky and William Paterson (1976). In the introduction to their edited volume *Social and Political Movements in Western Europe*, they discussed various theoretical approaches to the study of social movements and proposed a combination of sociological and political science approaches, trying to mobilize the major sociological authors (Heberle, Smelser, Zald and Ash) for an analysis of the relations between social movements and political parties and the interaction of movements and political systems. Empirically, the other contributions to the volume did not live up to the promise of the introduction and, unfortunately, few authors have drawn inspiration of the conceptual innovation provided by Kolinsky and Paterson.

Also in the 1980s, we cannot find any great interest in the development of the general theory of social movements. More work was published on social movements in Britain, but many of these contributions were actually authored by researchers working outside the country (Kent 1982; Eyerman 1984; Turner 1986; Mullins 1987).

One exception was Keith Webb who was one of the first British authors sensitized to the US debate between relative deprivation and resource mobilization approaches. He developed an ambitious empirical research programme and proposed the integration of the two as the basis for a comparative analysis of protest movements throughout Europe (Webb, 1982; Webb *et al.*, 1981; 1983).

As to ›grand theory‹, social movements figured briefly in Anthony Giddens' highly influential *The Constitution of Society.* Organisations and Social Movements were distinguished from associations according to Giddens' criteria of reflexively and self-reflexively regulated systems (Giddens, 1984, 199-206). Rather than creating a new conception of social movements, the emphasis was clearly on the integration of social movements into a broader theoretical concept. In doing so, Giddens drew inspiration from a variety of authors writing on social movements, amongst them Banks, Blumer, Cohn and Touraine. His recent textbook focussed particularly on Tilly, Smelser and Touraine (Giddens, 1989, 624-630). It is thus fair to say that Giddens makes no special effort to develop a separate theory of social movements, but merely reflects on the contribution of – mostly non-British – social movement theorists in the framework of his own theoretical enterprise in which social movements play a fairly marginal role.

Another British social theorist who combines an interest in contintental theory and social movements is John Keane (1984a,b; 1988a,b), who translated and edited Claus Offe's work and is also one of the editors of Melucci's *Nomads of the Present* (1989). It was in an article on the British peace movement published in an Australian journal that Keane first applied the civil society concept to the study of a social movement, arguing that the »decisive significance and political potential of the movement lies in its militant defence of a civil society against the state« (Keane, 1984b, 6). The idea of new social movements as defenders of civil society against the state has played and important role in the European discussion, and Keane's work has found some recognition in the international social movement literature (cf. Melucci 1989; Schmalz-Bruns 1989).

In Britain, the term »new social movement« did not emerge from any indigenous discussion as a generic concept. Bottomore (1979, 41) actually referred to »new social movements – among them the student movement, various national and ethnic movements, and the women's movement« but clearly it is used as a merely incidental combination of words rather than a new generic term. Some British authors with neo-marxist inclinations picked up the terms at the end of the 1980s (Lash and Urry, 1987; Jessop *et al.*, 1988), but this did not lead to a body of new theory which specifically addressed the ›new social movements‹.

It is only with Alan Scott's recent book *Ideology and the New Social Movements* that a more systematic attempt is made by a British author to analyse the theoretical literature on new social movements. Scott provides critiques of Castell, Touraine and Habermas and argues that sociological middle-range theories in combination with political science approaches are the way forward in social movement analysis (Scott, 1990).

Overall, British contributions to a general theory of social movements have been few and far between. But such a review captures only a small part of the British contribution to the social movement literature. It is in the work on individual movements that most of the strengths of British social movement research can be found. However, in terms of explicit theoretical contributions, there is also relatively little to uncover. A notable feature of much of British writing is the frequent but perfunctory use of the term *social movement* without exploration of its potential connotations or efforts to set it into relevant theoretical or conceptual contexts. Typically it is undefined and is often used quite promiscuously, covering a range of phenomena as diverse as Thatcherism (Jessop *et al.*, 1988, 18, 61) and the commune movement (Rigby, 1974).

Despite these limitations, a broad range of authors analysing individual social movements have made more or less systematic efforts to use social movement approaches.

One major area of social movement research in British sociology is the analysis of new religious movements (cf. Barker, 1989; Wallis and Bruce, 1989). Research in this area boomed in the 1970s and 1980s, based on a strong tradition of historical and anthropological work on millenarian movements and other religious movements in the 1950s and 1960s (Cohen, 1957; Worsley, 1957; Wilson 1961; 1967). Most of the early theoretical work was, however, largely self-contained and did not link up with the general social movement literature. This relative isolation was only slowly overcome in the 1970s and 1980s when sociologists of religion developed broader interests in social movement behavior going beyond religious manifestations. It is particularly in the works of James Beckford (1975a,b,), Roy Wallis (1976; 1979; 1984) and Steve Bruce (1988) that American social movement theory has been reflected upon. Overall, however, the contribution of social movement theory to the analysis of new religious movements has been quite marginal. Sociologists of religions made some forays into the study of protest generally (cf. Wallis and Bruce, 1989) but these instances have remained rather isolated. There has certainly been very little cross-fertilisation between sociologists of religion and political sociologists studying social movements.

One area where the debate of one particular social movement theory has been central is the study of *urban social movements*. Until the late 1970s, the study of urban protest in Britain had been dominated by traditional institutional approaches. The role of citizens in local politics was mainly analysed in terms of public participation, voluntary organisations or pressure group activity. Alternative conceptions of local politics emerged to challenge these approaches in the 1970s, and their main theoretical inspiration was the work of the Spanish sociologist and Althusser-pupil Manuel Castells. His work became available in English in the late 1970s (Castells, 1977; 1978) and quickly reached prominence. The most important British contributor to the advance of his views in Britain has been C.G. Pickvance who had drawn attention to his work as early as in 1975 (Pickvance 1975; 1976; 1977). Castells' approach was further picked up by authors such as Peter Saunders (1979) and Patrick Dunleavy (1980) who looked for radical approaches to the study of urban politics.

Pickvance, Dunleavy, and Saunders drew attention to Castells' work, but they were also highly critical of some elements of his approach to urban protest. All authors reviewed the British evidence on urban protest and confronted it with Castells' work, only to find that Castells' theory of urban social movements had severe limitations. In the 1980s, Castells' approach to the study of urban social movements – which had changed quite substantially with his new book published in 1983 – was subjected to increasingly heavy criticism, in particular by Pickvance (1985), Lowe (1986) and Saunders (1986). Despite this criticism levelled at Castells, British authors did not come up with any comprehensive alternative framework. Pickvance's article on the comparative study of urban social movements which also included reference to the American resource mobilization literature is perhaps the most advanced statement of a possible alternative framework. Apart from Pickvance (1985), only Elliott and McCrone (1982) referred to the general social movement literature as a possible inspiration for further empirical work on urban protest movements. No such work has appeared yet. In terms of empirical work, no study has ever been carried out in Britain using Castells' analytical framework.

References to the concept of social movement are somewhat more rare in the literature on other British movements. As far as nationalist movements are concerned, a-theoretical, descriptive accounts and the study of voting behaviour using traditional political science approaches predominate (cf. Denver, 1985). One of the main theoretical inspirations again came from abroad in the form of Michael Hechter's (1975) book *Internal Colonialism* which did not make any explicit use of social movement concepts but which could be reformulated in terms of the relative deprivation approach. The only major study of nationalist movements referring to social movement theory is Jack Brand's *The National Movement in Scotland.* Taking Smelser's framework as a heuristic starting point, Brand (1978) explained the rise of Scottish nationalism as a combination of a general dissatisfaction with established party politics and increasing interest in Scottish affairs transcending party politics. In the 1980s, academic interest in nationalist movements declined in Britain. Overall, the analysis of nationalist movements in Britain has totally dominated by historians and political scientists who, with the exception of Brand, showed no interest in social movement concepts.

The situation was slightly better in the study of the femist movement. Already in 1964, J.A. and Olive Banks tried to provide a comprehensive framework for the study of feminism as a social movement. Feminism clearly constituted a genuine movement and could not just be reduced to a form of pressure group activity. Deploring the absence of sociological studies of feminist movements, they discussed a number of hypotheses and routes of inquiry.

Unfortunately, the assessment of 1964 has hardly been overtaken today. Despite a huge feminist literature which has sprung up in Britain, there are very few studies which use social movement approaches to analyse feminism. Academic books usually refer to feminism as a social movement (e.g. Lovenduski, 1986; Randall, 1987), but then fail to use concept analytically.

The major attempt to analyse feminism as a social movement has come from Olive Banks, a co-author of the 1964 article referred to above. In her book *Faces of Feminism: A Study of Feminism as a Social Movement*, Banks provided a comprehensive comparative analysis of the historical development of the feminist movement in Britain and the USA. However, despite its title, the reference to ›feminism as a social movement‹ remained a-theoretical. There is no single reference to social movement theory in the book (not even to Banks and Banks 1964), and any conception of »feminism as a social movement« actually remained implicit. Banks' book was certainly full of valuable insights, and a social movement perspective could probably be »reconstructed« from her analysis. But her book did not constitute an explicit contribution to the theory of social movements.

Research into the women's movement in Britain has been dominated by historically-descriptive approaches. Apart from Banks and Banks (1964), few authors make direct reference to social movement theory: David Bouchier (1978) analysed the ideology of feminist movements; Jan Pahl (1979) looked at women's centres, mainly in the context of »social problems as social movements.« Brown and Hosking (1986) referred to a range of social movement approaches in their analysis of women's centres. The analysis of feminism in social movement terms has thus been a very isolated affair, and despite the ubiquitous use of the term ›social movement‹ in the British literature, one has to turn to American authors (e.g. Gelb, 1989) to find an analysis of the British feminist movement couched in terms of social movement theory.

The absence of social movement approaches is even more noticeable turning to the British literature on the environmental movement. The pressure group approach has dominated the study of many social movements in Britain. The environmental movement provides a prominent example. Case studies of individual groups and conflict using this traditional political science approach were notable in the 1970s (cf. Lowe and Rüdig, 1986 for a bibliography). Lowe and Goyder (1983) are virtually alone in making some reference to other approaches including a »social movement perspective« linking the environmental movement to broader social processes including changes of values and social structure. Their book, nevertheless, stressed the organisational and pressure group perspectives of environmental groups in Britain. Atkinson (1988) discussed a wide variety of social movement theories but did not carry out his analysis of English environmentalism specifically within a theoretical framework set by social movement theory.

British work on environmentalism has largely been dominated by geographes, planners, environmental studies specialists, and political scientists, and therefore the absence of social movement approaches is not entirely surprising. Stephen Cotgrove has been the only British sociologist who developed a strong interest in the analysis of the environmental movement. The main inspiration for his study of *Friends of the Earth* and the *Conservation Society* was, however, the value change approach proposed by Inglehart, and references to the social movement literature were very limited (Cotgrove 1982).

The absence of the employment of the social movement approach is also a reflection of the failure of a strong radical ecology movement developing in Britain (cf. Rüdig and Lowe, 1986). The protest movement against nuclear energy, for example, was always rather subdued and was virtually ignored by British social scientists as an object of study. While Ward (1982) looked at the anti-nuclear lobby in terms of pressure group activity, it was only in the framework of a wide-ranging internationally comparative analysis of the anti-movement that social movement theory was employed in a central position to account for Britain's failure to develop a stronger protest movement against nuclear energy (Rüdig, 1986; 1990a).

Perhaps the most important individual social movement in post-war Britain has been the peace movement, and one would thus expect a theoretically more inspired literature (in terms a social movement approaches) to have emerged in this area. Perhaps the internationally best known and most widely cited book on a social movement emanating from Britain was concerned with the peace movement, Frank Parkin's *Middle Class Radicalism: The Social Bases of the British Campaign for Nuclear Disarmament.* But while the results of this study still have a major influence today, its explicit theoretical contribution to the social movement literature has been very limited. Parkin's main theoretical reference points were theories of political alienation. Apart from one brief reference to Heberle, there is no discussion of social movement approaches in the book (Parkin 1968).

Interest in the peace movement only picked up in the early 1980s, but further publications (e.g. Taylor and Pritchard, 1980; Taylor and Young, 1987; Taylor, 1988; Hinton, 1989) provided more empirical material on the peace movement but added little to a social-scientific analysis. This is partly a reflection of the predominance of peace researchers and historians in this literature while political scientists and sociologists – with few exceptions (Keane 1984b) – seemed strangely uninterested in this movement. This changed only in the later 1980s with the publication of a series of books and papers by sociologists John Mattausch (1986; 1987; 1989), Graham Day and David Robbins (1987) as well as political scientist Paul Byrne (1988).

Among these authors, it is the political scientist who showed the strongest interest in social movement approaches. Byrne (1988) started his book reporting the findings of a major survey of members of the *Campaign for Nuclear Disarmament* (CND) with a theoretical chapter looking at a variety of social movement theories which could inform his study. While this is the first British publications on the peace movement containing such a discussion, the author made only very limited use of the concepts discussed in the remainder of the book. In effect, Byrne used the discussion of social movement theory merely to introduce a few terms, such as *social movement organization*; the influence of the approaches discussed on the design and analysis of the study remained negligible.

Day and Robbins (1987) based their discussion of a survey of Welsh CND activists on a broad background of mainly neo-marxist writings, stressing the concept of ›new politics‹. Castells and Touraine were mentioned but the authors did not couch their analysis in terms of social movements. Mattausch (1989) ignored the social movement literature completely, opting instead for a categorisation of factors responsible for individuals joining CND based on Wittgenstein's ›family resemblance‹ concept. Also as far as the peace movement is concerned, the social movement framework thus remained marginal in the analysis of Britain's major post-war social movement.

There are many other forms of collective behaviour in Britain which could have been analysed in terms of social movement approaches. Only very few were. Worth mentioning is here particularly Andrew Rigby's (1974) study of the commune movement between 1969 and 1971 and Elliott and McCrone's study of *bourgeois social movements* in the 1970s (Elliot et al., 1982; Elliott and McCrone, 1987). Rigby essentially drew on Blumer's work while Elliott and McCrone's main theoretical inspiration was the work of Charles Tilly.

Overall, it is fair to say that social movement approaches have played a marginal role in British movement research. Occasionally, such as in the case of urban social movements and new religious movements, major theoretical debates developed focussing on the concept of social movements. In other areas, approaches such as pressure group analysis annd atheoretical-descriptive approaches were clearly dominant.

In the absence of a significant theoretical inspiration by British authors, those interesting in applying social movement theory generally had to turn to foreign social theoretists for inspiration. While works such as Wilkinson (1971) and Banks (1972) were widely quoted, the main influences have either come from the long-standing American debate on social movements or the new continental European approaches on ›new social movements‹ whose first manifestations emerged in the late 1970s. By necessity, the theoretical element of British work on social movement had thus to be eclectic, and very often, the British use of social movement theory lagged behind the theoretical development by a decade or more. A brief look at the references to foreign theorists of social movements illustrate this well.

The ›collective action‹ approaches influenced by structural-functionalism, most prominently represented by Neil Smelser, provided one of the most popular and enduring reference points. Bryan Wilson describes Neil Smelser's work as the »most interesting sociological theory of collective action« though he went on to say that he did not find it possible to use it (Wilson 1973, 3). Brand (1978) adopted Smelser's stages of movement behaviour as a heuristic device, representing the core of his application of social movement theory.

Even more popular than Smelser have been the various theories of status inconsistencies as well as relative deprivation which were popular in the USA during the 1960s and early 1970s. Status inconsistency theories have been particularly popular amongst sociologists of religion (Wallis, 1977; Cliff, 1979). Bruce (1988) made this body of the literature his main reference point in his study of the American New Right.

Relative deprivation was the main theoretical reference point for other work on nationalist movements. The American studies by Schwarz (1972) and Brooks (1973) using relative deprivation theory for an explanation of Scottish Nationalism were widely discussed (cf. Webb and Hall, 1978; Brand, 1978; Mughan and McAllister, 1981). In the late 1980s, British studies of urban riots drew on relative deprivation as the main explanation (Benyon and Solomos, 1987).

The resource mobilization perspective, however, was picked up relatively late in Britain, and many of its numerous facets are still completely unexplored by British social scientists. Authors such as James Beckford (1975a,b) and Jack Brand (1978) were very critical of relative deprivation theories in their writing of the 1970, and one could classify the explanations they developed out of a criticism of relative deprivation concepts as a manifestation of a resource mobilisation approach. Similarly, Pickvance's criticism of Castells led him to conclusions which come very close to the resource mobilization concept (Pickvance, 1975; 1976; 1977). None of these authors made, however, any reference to the body of resource mobilisation theory which was already available in the USA at the time.

It is only much later, effectively in the early 1980s, that resource mobilization theory is recognized explicitly as a separate approach in the British literature. Keith Webb was probably the first to do so in 1981; other articles in the 1980s, in particular Pickvance (1985), now made explicit reference to this approach and discussed its promise and limitations.

What is interesting in the British case is that Webb and Pickvance right away promoted an integration of resource mobilization and other approaches. Webb explicitly sought to combine relative deprivation and resource mobilization approaches, and also Pickvance (1985) moved into a direction where features of relative deprivation and resource mobilisation theories were combined with continental Eureopean approaches. Brown and Hosking (1986) also argued for a wide integration of several approaches, in particular resource mobilization and social-psychological concepts.

This is a point which is essential in Rüdig's work (1986; 1990a) who argued for a combination of relative deprivation and resource mobilisation theory in the comparative study of anti-nuclear movements. Rüdig and Lowe (1986) suggested that social movement approaches may be used for the international comparison of the development of green parties; and Rüdig (1990b) and Rüdig and Lowe (forthcoming) combined social movement theories with political science approaches on the emergence of new cleavages and their transformation into party and non-party political action in their comparative study of Green parties.

The influence of the »new social movements« approach has been far more limited in the analysis of individual movements. Apart from the study of urban social movements, other continental authors such as Melucci, Offe, Habermas, and Touraine did not make a major impact amongst those engaged in empirical analysis of social movements. Rüdig and Love (1984) dismissed the empirical usefullness of Touraine's approach to the analysis of anti-nuclear movements; Rüdig (1986; 1988; 1990a) argued that the structuralist analysis of new social movements made it largely unsuitable for the explanation of international differences.

II. Methodology

Given the paucity of systematic social movement research in Britain, there has been very little discussion of the methodological problems involved. Rootes' (1981) critique of the Political Action study of protest potentials; Franklin's (1986) exposition of the methodological problems of empirical work on public protest in a comparative perspective; Lowe and Rüdig's (1986) review of a variety of approaches taken in international research on environmental movements; and Mattausch's (1987; 1989) detailed critiques of survey work on CND activists appear to be the only explicit contributions to a debate on methodological questions. Scott's (1990) critique of ›grand theory‹ approaches to the study of new social movements also has important methodological implications but, generally, these questions have not been aired very prominently.

Traditional case study approaches are the most common form of empirical inquiry in British social science and also dominate the work on social movements. The studies on urban protest movements, nationalist movements, feminist movements and environmental movements all have been totally dominated by the case study approach. And even in areas where some important survey work has been carried out, the case study approach figures prominently.

It is particularly in two areas that some more sustained efforts to apply quantitative methodologies have been made. In the case of the new religious movements, a number of relatively small surveys were carried out. In the biggest survey, Roy Wallis (1979) distributed 2030 questionnaires to participants at a London rally of the *Nationwide Festival of Light* and 1106 (54 %) were returned. Other studies have had to rely on much smaller samples. Beckford (1975a), in his study of Jehova's Witnesses, managed to distribute a brief questionnaire among members and received analysable information on 180 members. Wallis (1976) obtained 37 questionnaire responses from scientologists. Despite the small size of the samples, the success in acquiring enough access to the field to carry out these surveys is quite remarkable. The analysis of new religious movements does suffer from special access problems as many of these groups are rather suspicious of if not hostile to independent research by social scientists. Given the secretive nature of some of these groups, researchers had to rely on qualitative methods to gather information for most of the time.

The movement which has been subjected to most survey work is the peace movement. The quantitative data on members and activists of CND is unrivalled in the study of social movements in Britain and extends back to the 1960s. Parkin's (1968) study of CND involved collecting the names and addresses of young supporters on the annual Easter march of 1965, of whom 445 (81 %) returned usable questionnaires. In addition, a sample of adult

CND members – names and addresses supplied by CND – was also sent a questionnaire resulting in 358 usable responses (61 % response rate).

A systematic evaluation of former CND activists was carried out by Richard Taylor and Colin Pritchard (1980). They appealed to people who had been peace movement activists between 1958 and 1965 through the media to help them in their inquiry. Questionnaires were sent to everyone who came forward with his name and address. A total of 403 usable questionnaires were received.

The most wide-ranging surveys of CND members were carried out by Paul Nias (1983) at Bradford University's Peace Studies Institute and have remained unpublished. According to Mattausch (1989), Nias conducted two major surveys in 1982; a national CND membership survey (postal questionnaire, random sample of 413, 299 responses, 72 %) and a survey of CND marchers in a national demonstration (marchers interviewed by students, 768 responses). A survey of members of the campaign for European Nuclear Disarmament (END) was also carried out.

A further unpublished survey was conducted by Nigel West (also at Bradford) amongst people travelling by coach to a national CND rally in 1985; 241 responses were elicited on six coaches (cf. Mattausch 1989, 178). Paul Byrne (1988) conducted a survey of members of national CND in 1985; 1011 questionnaires were sent out and 620 (61 %) usable replies were received. Mattausch (1989) carried out 62 intensive semi-structured interviews with members of two local CND groups in two Scottish locations.

As to the environmental movement, surveys of members of environmental groups have also been quite a common feature. Some groups, such as the *Conservation Society* (ConSoc) and *Friends of the Earth* (FOE) are known to have conducted some internal membership surveys but none has been published. Internal surveys of members of the National Trust, the Royal Society for the Protection of Birds, and the Council for the Protection of rural England were also carried out in the 1970s (see Lowe and Goyder, 1983, pp. 10-11).

Stephen Cotgrove and Andrew Duff conducted a survey of members of ConSoc, FOE and the *World Wildlife Fund* (WWF). Names were randomly selected from national membership lists: 567 ConSoc and FOE members were sent postal questionnaires in 1978, eliciting 441 usuable responses (79 %). 500 WWF members were mailed a questionnaire in 1980, 313 responses were received (63 %) (Cotgrove 1982).

A membership survey of conservation groups was carried out by Chris Bull. Three County Nature Conservation Trusts – Bedfordshire and Huntingdonshire, North Wales and Yorkshire – were selected; all members of the Bedfordshire and Huntingdonshire Trust (1800, 661 responses, 36 %) and a random sample of members of the North Wales (757, 332 responses, 45 %) and Yorkshire Trusts (1007, 552 responses, 55 %) were sent questionnaires in 1980 and 1981 (Bull 1986).

Another important area of quantitative work carried out in Britain are surveys of environmental groups (rather than members). A range of surveys of local amenity societies have been carried out, the most comprehensive survey was undertaken by Anthony Barker in 1974: a questionnaire was sent to 1,135 amenity societies registered with the Civic Trust, 635 usuable responses were received (Barker/Civic Trust, 1976; Barker and Keating, 1977).

Lowe and Goyder (1983) carried out a survey of 77 environmental groups (81 were approached, 4 declined to participate), using structured interviews with leading group representatives, in 1979-80.

While the peace and environmental movement has been the subject of fairly extensive survey research, no quantitative work at all has been carried out on urban protest, and the nationalist and feminist movements. There is thus no reliable information on the members of these movements.

The range of methodologies employed in Britain is thus fairly limited. The ›action research‹ approach has never been adopted for the study of a social movement, and more advanced methodologies, such as the aggregate analysis of protest events, have not been employed.

III. Results

The empirical material available on social movements in Britain, both in terms of case studies and survey work, is quite extensive, and it is not feasible to report all the results of these studies in such a short article. However, it is possible to isolate two major ›themes‹ of social movement research in Britain which have attained particular importance: the social background of social movement activists or members of social movement organisations; and, second, the relations of social movements to the political system and their role in policy making.

The theme of the social background of movement members has been prominent following Frank Parkin's pathbraking study of CND. Parkin concluded that CND membership was not so much a matter of instrumental considerations but could best be explained as a symbolic confirmation of a more general moral and political outlook. Secondly, the social basis of CND was not just »middle class« but a very distinct part of the middle class, namely those who were highly educated and were engaged in welfare and creative professions rather than in business or industry (Parkin, 1968).

Taylor and Pritchard (1980), in their follow-up study, found a similar dominance of public sector professions. The new CND members of the 1980s had a similar background: most were young, well educated, middle class and employed in the public sector with the caring professions dominant (Nias, 1985). Also Byrne's results confirmed Parkin's, Taylor and Pritchard's and Nias' findings in that respect. Most CND members of the mid-1980s came from the educated middle classes, occupations in the public sector, particularly education dominated (Byrne 1988).

The theme of the recruitment from a very special section of the middle class was also highlighted by Cotgrove and Duff (1980; 1981). Their sample of ›new‹ environmental movements showed that also they came from the »non-productive service sector«, they were teachers, social workers, artists rather than managers, bank clerks or accountants. Cotgrove and Duff speculated on the reasons for this very special part of the middle classes to become involved in environmental action. Environmental values could be acquired at an early stage of the socialization process and influence the choice of occupation. Alternatively, environmentalism could be seen as »an expression of the interests of those whose class locates them at the periphery of the institutions and processes of industrial capitalist society« (Cotgrove and Duff, 1980, 340-341).

The theme of the special background of social movement activists is picked up by later studies. Bull in his study of conservation groups found that also the membership of conservation trusts consisted mainly of people with an occupational background in the »service/welfare/creative sector«. This was contrary to Cotgrove's findings on the WWF and his assertion that conservationists could not be expected to be located in »non-market occupations« because they did not express any fundamental challenge to the economic system (Cotgrove 1982, 137-138). Perhaps the sharp distinction between radical environmentalists and nature conservationists, Bull argued, is not as appropriate and significant as Cotgrove (and others) suggested.

Earlier work on the peace movement and Cotgrove's and Duff's findings provided the background for Mattausch's study of CND members in which he concentrated on the issues of their occupational background. He found a similar predonderance of caring, education and other public sector professons in his small sample, confirming the findings of all previous surveys, and proceeded to elicit the special factors leading these individuals to join CND. However, his ›family resemblance‹ methodology led to few generalisable results, and Mattausch mainly proceeded to explore the heterogeneity of individual motivations. If there is one core result from his study it is the following:

> »... it is not simply the case that welfare professionals choose this area of employment because they reject the values of industrial capitalism. This study suggests that state apprenticeships and/or vocational practices, that is to say *the welfare state itself* encourages the identification with, the assimilation of, the distinctive ethic which finds expression in disarmament campaigning.« (Mattausch, 1989, 146-147).

The data on the social background of members of other social movements are far more sketchy or non-existent. There seems to be a potential overlap between peace/environmental movements and the ›new religious movements‹, particularly the ›world-rejecting‹ one appealing to younger generations in the 1970s and 1980s. They are said to be young, well-educated, with a prosperous middle-class background and a dominant interest in fine arts and the humanities (Beckford and Levasseur, 1986, 39-40). However, these findings do not appear to be based on any hard survey data from British groups. There are no data whatsoever on members of feminist and nationalist movements.

What role do social movements in Britain play in decision making? This question has been extensively discussed in various case studies and also in survey work. The main results of this work indicates that the British state either integrates social movements quite well, either directly in the policy making process or through political parties, and gives them some limited influence in exchange for the co-operation; or it shuts them out completely, denying them any opportunity to influence policy-making.

The first method of integration by accommodating groups within the process of public policy making has been extensively analysed in the case of the conservation and environmental movements. Case studies and surveys (Barker and Keating, 1977; Lowe and Goyder, 1983; Lowe and Rüdig, 1986) have demonstrated the high level of integration achieved. This is one factor for the absence of a stronger radical ecological movement in Britain.

The second framework of political integration is party politics. Labour and the Liberals have become a haven for various social movements in the 1980s. The commitment of CND members to the Labour Party is particularly well established. All surveys show that around two-thirds of CND members support the Labour Party (e.g. Parkin, 1968; Byrne, 1988). Parts of the more radical end of the environmental and anti-nuclear movement established themselves within Labour and the Liberals. At the urban level, the link between Labour and various urban protest movements is particularly strong. Parts of the feminist movement, anti-racism and gay liberation movements have been firmly associated with the ›urban left‹ which established itself in London in the early 1980s, particularly around the now-abolished Greater London Council (cf. Boddy and Fudge, 1984; Lansley *et al.*, 1989). It was in that context that a coalition of various ›new‹ social movements seemed to emerge and that some British authors suddenly took the concept of ›new social movements‹ more seriously (cf. Lash and Urry, 1987; Jessop *et al.*, 1988).

Why have these two forms of integration played such a dominent role? Any challenging group in the British system which fails to be recognized as a relevant group by policy makers has very few options open to it. It can campaign to be recognized and to be integrated into formal government consultation by demonstrating its expertise, its moderation and responsible attitude. In doing so, groups have to become very specialised and segmented, concentrating on ›single issues‹ rather than challenging the entire basis of government policy. Any groups failing to conform to this model is excluded and has enormous difficulties to mobilize resources.

In his study of urban protest, Saunders' (1979) confirmed this view: while there were very many grievances which could be taken up by urban social movements, there were very few ways in which these demands could be effectively expressed. Potential carriers, such as the Labour Party or tenants associations, were so well integrated into the local political system that they shunned taking up radical causes. Any attempt to organize radical protest outside the established procedures had no impact.

For a group with radical aims, the alternatives are very limited. The centralisation of British government means that there are very few countervailing influences which any challenging group can mobilise. One of these very few opportunities consists of changing Labour Party policy, for example through campaigning in trade unions. Since 1979, the challenge of radical Labour councils to central government provided one such opportunity to find a niche in the system. However, any social movement wanting to use such an opportunity has to make certain compromises. In particular, there are two forces within Labour which limit any social movement involvement: on the one hand, the more radical sections firmly believe in the predominance of the labour movement as *the* social movement with other ›new‹ social movements being seen as a coalition partner reinforcing, but not challenging, that dominance. On the other hand, the Labour leadership's striving to present itself as a moderate, responsible and respectable party limits the operational basis of any social movement activity within the Party.

This brief sketch of the political opportunity structure for social movement in Britain at the same time serves as a good starting point for any explanantion of the weakness of social movement research. On the one hand, many social movements effectively operate as pressure groups within established policy making systems, and therefore they fit the established analytical framework of pressure groups. On the other hand, groups which present a more radical challenge have few opportunities to mobilize; association with Labour politics aligns them with ›old‹ social movements or marginalises them as Labour strives to become respectable. Objectively, the chances for any ›new‹ social movements to emerge as an independent entity are thus very slim. Where such movements emerge and refuse any association with the interests dominating British society, they remain marginalised. More frequently, grievances which do not find a ›respectable‹ expression in terms of an integrated interest group appear to find their expression in unorganized, spontaneous collective actions such as inner-city riots or football hooliganism.

Wyn Grant captures this relationship well with his distinction between insider and outsider pressure groups (Grant, 1978; 1989; 1990). This distinction in itself demonstrates the influence of British patterns of policy making on the research agenda. The British system has only very few access points but at the same time manages conflict well enough so that outsider groups remain marginal. In this context, the attraction of the social movement concept is rather limited: groups either manage to get ›inside‹ and while they may still openly campaign for their causes (Grant distinguishes between low and high-profile insider groups), their activity conforms to established patterns of interest group behaviour; or groups remain outside, retaining some movement characteristics as long as they are struggling to get ›inside‹ (Grant distinguishes between potential insiders and outsiders which do not have the political skills or the ideological inclination to become insiders) or remaining outside but ineffective. From that point of view, the social movement characteristic would only apply to marginal outsider groups – which do not constitute a very attractive research focus. It is perfectly possible to apply social movement concepts also to high-profile insider pressure groups, and Wilkinson (1971), Banks (1972) and Grant (1989) are quite happy to classify such pressure groups as social movements. The activities these pressure groups engage in with their ›insider‹ status makes them far more amenable to the pressure group concept, leaving social movement theories on the sidelines.

IV. Institutional Aspects of Social Movement Research

There is no individual centre of research which specialises in social movements in Britain. Most of the research is carried out by individual academics who are spread around Britain's universities, often scattered across different disciplines. There are no networks or other organisations which bring together researchers engaged in the study of individual movements. As the approaches to the study of social movements are segmented, so is the research community. In each segment, social movement researchers are usually not numerous enough to constitute an organisation of their own. Interest in social movements is thus incorporated in more broadly-based networks on women in politics, urban politics, youth culture etc. Essentially, social movement research in Britain is institutionally marginalised with no community of researchers stretching across disciplines.

V. Conclusions

Research on social movements has not been a particularly fashionable enterprise in Britain in the last two decades. However, the empirical material on social movements in Britain is rich and compares favourably with countries such as Germany where the theory of new social movements may have flourished but empirical inquiry into these movements has been dogged by a mixture of scientific disinterest and a refusal by the movements to give access to researchers, particularly for any type of survey research.

As far as the theory of social movements is concerned, the British contribution to the debate is rather limited, however. Banks (1972) and Wilkinson (1971) remain the only monographs which have been written and published in Britain to give an overview of social movement theory. While these individual contributions are well regarded, it has to be stated that their overall impact on the research scene in Britain and abroad has been rather limited. The sociology of new religious movements has produced a number of theoretical concepts which have had an impact on the international research effort on these movements. The British critique of Castell's theories of urban social movements may have led to some valuable insights. But progress in these individual fields was not translated into any major British contribution to the field of social movement theory generally.

Ultimately, the state of social movement research in Britain reflects the development of social movements themselves. It is noticeable that there are very few publications which address contemporary public protest in Britain generally. Marsh (1977) reported his results on protest potentials in a pathfinding study, but little has followed in terms of broadly based studies of actual protest behaviour. Murphy (1985), Spear (1987) and Rootes (1984, 1989) review the general development of social movements and social movement research in Britain but, in all cases, the initiative or the inspiration for these articles in the form of theories of ›new politics‹ and ›new social movements‹ came from abroad.

The so-called »new social movements« do not have a common political identity in Britain. Some authors dispute that the concept of new social movements is applicable to the British case at all (Scott, 1990; Rothgang, 1990). The fragmentation, integration and exclusion of various movements has helped to make the pressure group approach dominant. The »system« has »proved capable of absorbing new issues and new groups« (Jordan and Richardson, 1987, 285), and as long as the system is doing that, British social scientists studying British social movements will have little motivation to turn to social movement approaches.

Annotated Bibliography

Atkinson, A. (1988): *Environmentalism: A Study of the Ideology and Practice of Radical Environmental Initiatives in Modern Britain.* Unpublished Ph.D. thesis, London School of Economics.

Banks, J.A. (1972): *The Sociology of Social Movements.* London: Macmillan.
Main contribution of British sociology to the theoretical literature.

Banks, J.A. and Banks, O. (1964): »Feminism and social change – A case study of a social movement«, G.K. Zollschan, W. Hirsch (eds.). *Explorations of Social Change.* London: Routledge & Kegan Paul, 547-569.

Banks, O. (1981): *Faces of Feminism: A Study of Feminism as a Social Movement.* Oxford: Martin Robertson.
Main empirical study of the historical development of the feminist movement in Britain and the USA.

Barker, A./Civic Trust (1976): *The Local Amenity Movement.* London: Civic Trust.

Barker, A. and Keating, M. (1977): »Public spirits: Amenity societies and others«, in: Crouch 1977, 202-221.

Barker, E. (1989): *New Religious Movements: A Practical Introduction.* London: Her Majesty's Stationary Office.
Useful overview of the evidence on ›new religious movements‹, written for a non-academic readership.

Backford, J.A. (1975a): *The Trumpet of Prophecy: A Sociological Study of Jehova's Witnesses.* Oxford: Basil Blackwell.
Important study of Jehova's witnesses, using social movement theories for the construction of a model explaining the process of joining a religious movement.

– (1975b): »Organization, ideology and recruitment: The structure of the Watch Tower Movement«, *Sociological Review* 23: 893-909.

Beckford, J.A. and Levasseur, M (1986): »New religious movements in Western Europe«, in: J.A. Beckford (ed.). *New Religious Movements and Rapid Social Change.* London: Sage, 29-54.

Benyon, J. and Solomos, J. (eds.) (1987): *The Roots of Urban Unrest.* Oxford: Pergamon Press.
Studies of urban riots and unrest in Britain in the 1980s.

Boddy, M. and Fudge, C. (eds.) (1984): *Local Socialism? Labour Councils and New Left Alternatives.* London: Macmillan.

Bottomore, T. (1979): *Political Sociology.* London: Hutchinson.

Bouchier, D. (1977): »Radical ideologies and the sociology of knowledge: A model for comparative analysis«, *Sociology* 11, 25-46.

– (1978): *Idealism and Revolution: New Ideologies of Liberation in Britain and the United States.* London: Edward Arnold.
Study of the ideology of the student and feminist movements in Britain and the USA.

Brand, J. (1978): *The National Movement in Scotland.* London: Routledge & Kegan Paul.
Main study on the Scottish nationalist movement, using social movement theory, in particular Smelser, as a heuristic framework.

Brooks, R. (1973): *Scottish Nationalism: Relative Deprivation and Social Mobility*. Unpublished Ph.D. thesis, Michigan State University.

Brown, M.H. and Hosking, D.M. (1986). »Distributed leadership and successful organization in social movements«, *Human Relations*, 39, 65-79.

Bruce, S. (1988): *The Rise and Fall of the New Christian Right: Conservative Protestant Politics in America 1976-1988*. Oxford: Clarendon Press.

Bull, C.J. (1986): *Popular Support for Wildlife Conservation: An Analysis of the Membership and Organisation of Country Nature Conservation Trust*. Unpublished Ph.D. thesis, University College London.

Byrne, P. (1988): *The Campaign for Nuclear Disarmament*. London: Croom Helm/Routledge.
Comprehensive survey of CND members of the 1980s.

Castells, M. (1977): *The Urban Question*. London: Edward Arnold.

– (1978): *City, Class and Power*. London: Macmillan.

– (1983): *The City and the Grassroots*. London: Edward Arnold.

Cliff, D. (1979): »Religion, morality and the middle class«, in: R. King, and N. Nugent (eds.). *Respectable Rebels: Middle Class Campaigns in Britain in the 1970s*. London: Hodder and Stoughton, 127-152.

Cohen, N. (1957): *The Pursuit of the Millenium: Revolutionary Messianism in Medieval and Reformation Europa and its Bearing on Modern Totalitarian Movements*. London: Secker and Warburg.

Cotgrove, S. (1982): *Catastrophe or Cornucopia: The Environment, Politics and the Future*. Chichester: Wiley.
Major study of the new environmentalism based on a comparison of the background and values of members of environmental movements with trade unionists, businessmen and the general public.

Cotgrove S. and Duff, A. (1980): »Environmentalism, middle class radicalism and politics«, *Sociological Review*, 28, 333-351.

– (1981): »Environmentalism, values and social change«, *British Journal of Sociology*, 32, 92-110.

Creighton, C. and Shaw, M. (eds.) (1987): *The Sociology of War and Peace*. London: Macmillan.

Crouch, C. (ed.) (1977): *Participation in Politics*. London: Croom Helm.

Day, G. and Robbins, D. (1987): »Activists for peace: The social basis of a local peace movement«, in: C. Creighton, Shaw, M. 1987, 218-236.

Denver, D. (1985): »Scotland«, in: I. Crewe and D. Denver (eds.). *Electoral Change in Western Democracies: Patterns and Sources of Electoral Volatility*. London: Croom Helm, 151-172.

Dunleavy, P. (1980): *Urban Political Analysis*. London: Macmillan.

Elliott, B. and McCrone, D. (1982): *The City: Patterns of Domination and Conflict*. London: Macmillan.

– (1987): »Class, culture and morality: Sociological analysis and neo-conservatism«, *Sociological Review*,, 35, 485-515.

Elliott, B.; Bechhofer, F.; McCrone, D.; and Black, S. (1982): »Bourgeois social movements in Britain: repertoires and responses«, *Sociological Review*, 30, 71-96.

One of very few sociological studies of a British social movement, employing Tilly's concept of repertoires as a key analytical concept.
Eyerman, R. (1984): »Social movements and social theory«, *Sociology*, 18, 71-82.
Franklin, M.N. (1986): »Some problems of method in research on political protest«, Paper presented at the *ECPR Joint Sessions*, Gothenburg, April.
Study of the methodological implications of a major comparative study of social movements employing Webb's approach combining relative deprivation and resource mobilisation approaches.
Gelb, J. (1989): *Feminism and Politics: A Comparative Perspective*. Berkeley, CA.: University of California Press.
Giddens, A. (1984): *The Constitution of Society: Outline of the Theory of Structuration*. Cambridge: Polity Press.
– (1989): *Sociology*. Cambridge: Polity Press.
Grant, W. (1978): *Insider Groups, Outsider Groups and Interest Group Strategies in Britain*. Working Paper 19, Coventry: Department of Politics, University of Warwick.
– (1989): *Pressure Groups, Politics and Democracy in Britain*. Hemel Hempstead: Philip Allen.
– (1990): »Insider and outsider pressure groups«, *Social Studies Review* 5, 3 (1): 107-111.
Hechter, M. (1975): *Internal Colonialism: The Celtic Fringe in British National Development, 1536-1966*. London: Routledge & Kegan Paul.
Hinton, J. (1989): *Protests and Visions: Peace Politics in 20th Century Britain*. London: Hutchinson Radius.
Hobsbawm, E. (1959): *Primitive Rebels: Studies in Archaic Forms of Social Movement in the 19th and 20th Centuries*. Manchester: Manchester University Press.
Important early text analyzing pre-industrial forms of collective action.
Jessop, B.; Bonnett, K.; Bromley, S. and Ling, T. (1988): *Thatcherism: A Tale of Two Nations*. Cambridge: Polity Press.
Jordan, A.G. and Richardson, J.J. (1987): *Government and Pressure Groups in Britain*. Oxford: Clarendon Press.
Keane, J. (1984a): *Public Life and Late Capitalism: Towards a Socialist Theory of Democracy*. Cambridge: Cambridge University Press.
– (1984b): »Civil society and the peace movement in Britain«, *Thesis Eleven*, 8 (1): 5-22.
– (1988a): *Democracy and Civil Society*. London: Verso.
– (ed.) (1988b): *Civil Society and the State: New European Perspectives*. London: Verso.
Kent, S.A. (1982): »Relative deprivation and resource mobilization: a study of early Quakerism«, *British Journal of Sociology*, 33, 529-544.
Kolinsky, M. and Paterson, W.E. (1976): »Introduction«, in: M. Kolinsky, W.E. Paterson (eds.). *Social and Political Movements in Western Europe*. London: Croom Helm, 9-33.
Important conceptual text, proposing a combination of sociological and political science approaches for the explanation of the relationship between social movements and political systems.
Lansley, S.; Goss, S. and Wolmar, C. (1989): *Councils in Conflict: The Rise and Fall of the Municipal Left*. London: Macmillan.
Lash, S. and Urry, J. (1987): *The End of Organized Capitalism*. Cambridge: Polity Press.

Levitas, R.A. (1977): »Some problems of aim-centred models of social movements«, *Sociology*, 11, 47-63.
Lovenduski, J. (1986): *Women and European Politics: Contemporary Feminism and Public Policy*. Brighton: Wheatsheaf.
Lowe, P. and Goyder, J. (1983): *Environmental Groups in Politics*. London: George Allen & Unwin.
Survey of environmental groups, demonstrating their high levels of integration in the British policy making system.
Lowe, P. and Rüdig, W. (1986): »Political ecology and the social sciences: The state of the art«, *British Journal of Political Science*, 16, 513-550.
Lowe, S. (1986): *Urban Social Movements: The City After Castells*. London: Macmillan.
Comprehensive critique of the literature on urban social movements and their applicability to the analysis of urban protest in Britain.
Marsh, A. (1977): *Protest and Political Consciousness*. Beverly Hills, CA.: Sage.
Mattausch, J. (1986): »The political situation of the British Campaign for Nuclear Disarmament«, Unpublished paper.
– (1987): »The Sociology of CND«, in: C. Creighton and M. Shaw 1987, 199-217.
– (1989): *A Commitment to Campaign: A Sociological Study of CND*. Manchester: Manchester University Press.
Study of CND members, trying to explore the range of factors accounting for individuals to join local CND groups.
Melucci, A. (1989): *Nomads of the Present: Social Movements and Individual Needs in Contemporary Society*. London: Hutchinson Radius.
Mughan, A. and McAllister, I. (1981): »The mobilization of the ethnic vote: a thesis with some Scottish and Welsh evidence«, *Ethnic and Racial Studies*, 4, 189-204.
Mullins, P. (1987): »Community and urban movements«, *Sociological Review*, 35, 347-369.
Murphy, D. (1985): »Von Aldermaston nach Greenham Common: Politischer Protest und neue soziale Bewegungen in Grossbritannien«, in: K.W. Brand (ed.), *Neue soziale Bewegungen in Westeuropa und den USA: Ein internationaler Vergleich*. Frankfurt: Campus, 140-199.
Nias, P. 81983): *The Poverty of Peace Protest*. Unpublished M.A. thesis, Bradford University Postgraduate School in Peace Studies (quoted after Mattausch 1989).
Pahl, J. (1979): »Refugees for battered women: social provision or social movement?« *Journal of Voluntary Action Research*, 8, 25-35.
Parkin, F. (1968): *Middle Class Radicalism: The Social Bases of the British Campaign for Nuclear Disarmamament*. Manchester: Manchester University Press.
Highly influential early study of CND activists, focussing on the ›expressive‹ rather than instrumental motivation to join peace movement activities.
Pickvance, C.G. (1975): »On the study of urban social movements«, *Sociological Review*, 23, 29-49.
– (ed.) (1976): *Urban Sociology: Critical Essays*. London: Tavistock.
Important collection of French and British essays on the study of urban social movements.
– (1977): »From ›social base‹ to ›social force‹: Some analytical issues in the study of urban protest«, in: Harloe, M. (ed.), *Captive Cities*. London: Wiley, 175-186.

– (1985): »The rise and fall of urban social movements and the role of comparative analysis«, *Environment and Planning D: Society and Space*, 3, 31-53.
Most advanced theoretical model for the comparative study of urban protest movements, combining various social movement approaches.

Randall, V. (1987): *Women and Politics: An International Perspective.* 2nd ed. London: Macmillan.

Rigby, A. (1974): *Alternative Realities: A Study of Communes and Their Members.* London: Routledge & Kegan Paul.
Study of the commune movement between 1969 and 1971, based on intensive interviews on the motivation to join communes.

Rootes, C.A. (1981): »On the future of protest politics in Western democracies – a critique of Barnes, Kaase et al., *Political Action*«, *European Journal of Political Research*, 9, 421-432.

– (1984): »Protest, social movements, revolution? An overview«, *Social Alternatives*, 4, (1): 4-8.

– (1989): »The New Politics and the New Middle Class in Britain«, Paper presented at the *ECPR Joint Sessions*, Paris.

Rothgang, H. (1990): *Die Friedens- und Umweltbewegung in Grossbritannien: Eine empirische Untersuchung im Hinblick auf das Konzept der ›Neuen Sozialen Bewegungen‹.* Opladen: Deutscher Universitäts-Verlag.

Rüdig, W. (1986a): *Energy, Public Protest and Green Parties: A Comparative Analysis.* Unpublished Ph.D. thesis, University of Manchester.

– (1988): »Peace and ecology movements in Western Europe«, *West European Politics*, 11, 26-39.

– (1990a): *Anti-Nuclear Movements: A World Survey of Opposition to Nuclear Energy.* Harlow: Longman.
Comparative study of protest movements against nuclear energy, employing a combination of relative deprivation and resource mobilisation approaches.

– (1990b): *Explaining Green Party Development: Reflections on a Theoretical Framework.* Strathclyde Papers in Government and Politics No. 71. Glasgow: Department of Government, University of Strathclyde.

Rüdig, W. and Lowe, P.D. (1984): »The unfulfilled prophecy: Touraine and the anti-nuclear movement«, *Modern & Contemporary France*, 20, 19-23.

– (1986): »The withered ›greening‹ of British politics: A study of the Ecology Party«, *Political Studies*, 34, 262-284.

– (forthcoming): *The Green Wave: A Comparative Analysis of Ecological Parties.* Cambridge: Polity Press.

Runciman, W.G. (1966): *Relative Deprivation and Social Justice: A Study of Attitudes to Social Inequality in Twentieth-Century England.* London: Routledge & Kegan Paul.
Main British contribution to relative deprivation theory.

Saunders, P. (1979): *Urban Politics: A Sociological Interpretation.* London: Hutchinson.
Detailed discussion of Castells' concept of urban social movement and urban protest in Britain.

– (1986): *Social Theory and the Urban Question.* 2nd ed. London: Hutchinson.

Schmalz-Bruns, R. (1989): »›Civil-society‹ – neue Perspektiven der Demokratisierung«, *Forschungsjournal Neue Soziale Bewegungen*, 2, (3-4): 20-34.

Schwarz, J.E. (1972): »The Scottish National Party: Non-violent separatism and theories of violence«, in: K. Feierabend, R.L. Feierabend and T.R. Gurr (eds.). *Anger, Violence and Politics. Theories and Research.* Englewood Cliffs, N.J.: Prentice-Hall, 325-341.

Scott, A. (1990): *Ideology and the New Social Movements.* London: Unwin Hyman.

Discussion of continental approaches to the study of ›new social movements‹ and the development of middle-range theories combining sociological and political science approaches.

Smelser, N. (1962): *Theory of Collective Behaviour.* London: Routledge & Kegan Paul.

Spear, R. (1987): »Overview of UK Research on new social movements«, Unpublished Paper.

Stewart, A. (1977): »Political movements and political participation«, in: Crouch 1977, 19-37.

Taylor, R. (1988): *Against the Bomb: The British Peace Movement 1958-1965.* Oxford: Clarendon Press.

Main historical study of the first phase of the development of the post-war British peace movement.

Taylor, R. and Pritchard, C. (1980): *The Protest Makers: The British Nuclear Disarmament Movement of 1958-1965, Twenty Years On.* Oxford: Pergamon Press.

Taylor, R. and Young, N. (eds.) (1987): *Campaigns for Peace: British Peace Movements in the Twentieth Century.* Manchester: Manchester University Press.

Turner, B.S. (1986): *Citizenship and Democracy: The Debate over Reformism.* London: Allen & Unwin.

Wallis, R. (1976): *The Road to Total Freedom: A Sociological Analysis of Scientology.* London: Heinemann.

– (1977): »A critique of the theory of moral crusades as status defence«, *Scottish Journal of Sociology*, 1, 195-203.

– (1979): *Salvation and Protest: Studies of Social and Religious Movements.* London: Frances Pinter.

Collection of articles on a variety of religious and non-religious movements including two case studies of two non-conservative tax protest groups of the early 1970s.

– (1984): *The Elementary Forms of the New Religious Life.* London: Routledge & Kegan Paul.

Wallis, R. and Bruce, S. (1989): »Religion: the British contribution«, *British Journal of Sociology*, 40, 493-520.

Ward, H. (1982): »The anti-nuclear lobby: An unequal struggle?«, in: D. Marsh (ed.). *Pressure Politics: Interest Groups in Britain.* London: Junction Books, 182-211.

Webb, K. (1982): »Resource mobilization and protest groups«, Unpublished paper.

Webb, K. and Hall, E. (1978): *Explanation of the Rise of Political Nationalism in Scotland.* Glasgow: Centre for the Study of Public Policy, University of Strathclyde.

Webb, K. *et al.* (1981): »Social change and conflict interactions: groups and system response«, Unpublished paper.

– (1983): »Etiology and outcomes of protest: New European perspectives«, *American Behavioral Scientist*, 26, 311-331.

Ambitious theoretical model for the comparative analysis of social movements in a variety of settings in Western Europe.
Wilkinson, P. (1971): *Social Movement.* London: Pall Mall.
Broad overview of social movements of various types and the approaches employed to study them.
Wilson, B.R. (1961): *Sects and Society: A Sociological Study of Three Religious Groups in Britain.* London: Heinemann.
– (ed.) (1967): *Patterns of Sectarianism: Organisation and Ideology in Social and Religious Movements.* London: Heinemann.
– (1970b): *Religious Sects: A Sociological Study.* London: Weidenfeld and Nicolson.
– (1973): *Magic and the Millenium: A Sociological Study of Religious Movements of Protest among Tribal and Third-World Peoples.* London: Heinemann.
Worsley, P. (1957): *The Trumpet Shall Sound: A Study of ›Cargo‹ Cults in Melanesia.* London: MacGibbon & Kee.
Important anthropological study of millenarian movements.

The Growth of an Autonomous Research Field: Social Movement Studies in Italy

Mario Diani and Alberto Melucci

I. Theoretical Contributions to the Study of Collective Action

The theoretical and practical difficulties encountered by Italian sociologists in developing an approach to social movements were not unlike those faced elsewhere by others engaged in related themes[1].

They had to free themselves conceptually from the categories used in intellectual fields in many ways similar to their own: in particular, the theory of collective behavior and crowd psychology as well as the study of political activism. At the same time they had to define, in conceptual and practical terms, a new and specific area of study, including the setting up of a network of communication among the various sociologists working in the field, to permit the circulation and comparison of theories, methods and results.

Almost twenty years after the earliest attempts in this direction it can safely be said that both goals have, to a large extent, been achieved. On the theoretical and conceptual level not only have the need for, and the value of, the new categories been widely recognized, but a number of original attempts in this direction have already been made. Meanwhile, the bulk of research and analysis, as well as exchange between researchers, has increased

---

1 Although we are both responsible for this chapter as a whole, we like to recall that Mario Diani wrote section two, three and four, Alberto Melucci sections one and five. An earlier version of our contribution was published under the title »Searching for autonomy: The sociology of social movements in Italy« in *Social Science Information,* Vol. 27, n. 3, 1988. We are grateful to SAGE Publications and to the editors of SSI for granting permission to reprint. We are also grateful to Brian D. Olsen for his translation.

significantly testifying to an increasing interest in the field within the scientific community. Our intention here is to try to document the development on both levels.

Interest in social movements never was entirely autonomous within the Italian sociological tradition but found itself frequently placed amongst historico-comparative analyses of mass phenomena and collective action. The intellectual influence of Antonio Gramsci or Gaetano Mosca can be discerned in the work of many contemporary authors, especially in the field of political studies.

It was only in the sixties therefore, alongside rapid changes in society, that research on collective action in Italy took its first uncertain steps towards autonomy. It is in this period that we see the earliest attempts to treat the subject with something like a fresh conceptual outlook while nevertheless remaining within already existing theoretical frameworks. Such attempts were certainly attentive to developments in the international arena, and above all, in Anglo-American sociology. A look at these early works may help us to understand more clearly the significance of the problems outlined above.

In his approach to collective action, Franco Ferrarotti takes as his starting point the social consequences of the process of rapid modernization that swept Italy from the mid-fifties on. In particular, Ferrarotti concentrates on the growing cultural and social isolation of those groups which remain marginal to this process (the urban proletariat, the rural dwellers etc.), and subsequently, on the collective responses to this condition. There is, meanwhile, an evident interest in collective violence and the various forms of popular religious beliefs: an interest which was to emerge later throughout his work (1976, 1977, 1981). Though in some ways similar to those analysts who see the deprived areas of society as the primary source of potentially active subjects, Ferrarotti differs, however, in placing greater emphasis on the autonomy of the actors involved and in giving significance to conduct only apparently reducible to mere deviance and/or culturally marginal status.

Francesco Alberoni, on the other hand, is more specifically concerned with social movements as such within the framework of a wider interest in collective phenomena in mass society (1966). In his introduction to the Italian edition of a well known work by Smelser (1968a), he takes the opportunity to present a more fully worked-out formulation of *collective behavior theory* at the same time keeping his distance and suggesting a possible way of going beyond it. The publication in the same year of *Statu Nascenti*

(1968a) represents a further step forward in a body of theoretical work which is constantly being enriched right up to the most recent formulations (1981).

With regard to sociology, the conceptual reference points of Alberoni's analysis are essentially two-fold. The first of these is a different reading of the classics placing a special emphasis on the divide between two social conditions: one, where the predominant characteristic is the ordinary, the institutional, the *normal*; the other dominated by the drive towards overturning established norms and systems and the construction of a new social order, the predominant characteristic being the *exceptional*. Here we find explicit reference to the basic dichotomies of Durkheim (solidarity vs. collective effervescence), Weber (bureaucracy or tradition vs. charisma) and Marx (alienation vs. class consciousness). Alberoni places his examination of *collective movement* in this perspective, relating the concept to a social condition outside the norm, in contrast to the idea of *institution*.

His second important reference point is collective behaviour theory where he criticizes what he sees as the unwarranted tendency to treat as one what are, in reality, quite distinct phenomena. Alberoni points out the specific nature of collective movements and makes a distinction between *aggregation* and *group* phenomena. The first class covers behavior where the participation of individuals in a collective phenomenon is wholly atomized and does not presuppose any solidarity among the individuals involved, e.g. pop cults, crazes, fashions, etc. The second class refers to behavior where membership involves the development of a specific sense of solidarity.

The study of movements must, therefore, be understood as the study of groups that question a determined existing aspect of society, encouraging the formation of a new social order. Within the process: »old institutions« ⇒ »movement« ⇒ »new institutions«, attention is drawn to the transitional phase known as the *nascent state*. This represents an experience of liberation and rebirth, in which the normal divide between reality and contingency is overcome and the foundations of a new order are laid. In some ways one can speak here of a *liminal* stage between the old and the new and in this sense its presence can be discerned in all types of social formation, from the most complex to the most simple (the couple). From this it follows that analysis of collective movements cannot be limited only to such restricted phenomena as the anti-establishment mobilization in the West in the sixties and seventies. On the contrary, the same conceptual apparatus can be applied to a much broader range of cases. Thus, Alberoni turns his attention to such widely differing processes as political and messianic movements, broad cultural developments, as well as falling in love (1979) where the couple is analyzed as a »two-member collective movement«. Movement is in effect the »historical process beginning with the nascent state and ending with the reconstruction of the daily routine situation« (1981: 347), whatever the underlying social sub-system.

Perhaps Alberoni's most specific contribution can be seen in his treatment of the process of development of a movement. Although he relies strongly on *relative deprivation theory*, when identifying potential participants in collective action the successive stages of his argument display an original formulation. Adopting a conceptual framework borrowed from psychoanalysis, Alberoni first of all observes how the whole social dynamic may be interpreted through an elaboration of the ambivalence between impulses of eros and aggression. In a stable social situation, these impulses are directed, respectively, towards institutional and persecution objects. Progressive change and transformation, however, weaken the normative framework in which a balanced handling of the two types of impulses is possible. It thereafter becomes increasingly difficult to sustain the former objects of one's love (the existing institutions), inducing a depressive state that Alberoni defines as »the subjective threshold beyond which, given the existing social structure and the past channeling of eros and violence, the continual shifting of eros impulses from one object to another leads the subject to self-destruction« (1981: 141). In other cases there is a greater emphasis on the persecution aspect. In any case, an overall restructuring of the social sphere as well as the identification of new objects of love and aggression becomes inevitable. This phase corresponds to the experience of the *statu nascenti* (»nascent state«).

As we have seen, Alberoni's analysis assumes an extremely broad perspective, drawing on sources differing widely in type and historical origin. The same attention to comparative treatment can be found in Lanternari's anthropological analysis (1974) of Third World religious movements. Within a Marxist framework, he interprets millenarian, messianic and prophetic movements as the first and most powerful expression of desire for liberation by a people in the process of emancipation. Though quite distinct from the line of study we are presently concerned with, this work deserves mention for the richness of the material presented and for the stimulus it offers to comparative analysis.

The contribution of Pizzorno (1978a, 1978b, 1983a), and in particular his notion of *collective identity*, has meanwhile exercised a significant influence on our specific field of inquiry, despite his concentration on Italian and European worker's movements as his major empirical source. His theoretical analysis, which began with the study of political participation (1966) and has maintained close links with Anglo-American political science (1983b, 1986), is part of the debate sparked off by Olson's famous proposition (1965). In a critique of *free rider* theory, Pizzorno stresses that the logic of group action cannot be reduced to the sum of individual actions, but must be considered as the result of a combination of different elements (organization, leadership, membership, etc.). In practice it is the actual belonging to a network of relations that enables the individual to assess the effects of his action and evaluate the costs and benefits of his decision to mobilize. The introduction here of the category of *collective identity* is fundamental. The individual's decision to commit himself to collective action, that is to say, to invest resources in activity whose outcome is often unsure and remote, is in fact closely connected to his ability to evaluate the effects of such action. The individual involved must recognize the existence of a market in which his resources might have value. But this depends precisely on his participation in a system of relationships and the relative sense of belonging. According to Pizzorno, the single member of the group relocates his individual rationale within a different, wider and more complex one that corresponds to the norms of the collective identity. Recently, Pizzorno (1987) has taken the point up again providing a review of the main contemporary approaches to social movements in the light of the problem of incentives and of the relationship between collective and individual identity.

The persisting lack of a closely defined approach to the sociology of social movements (aside from the attempts mentioned above), as well as the wide diffusion of the phenomenon and its impact on Italian society in the seventies, has encouraged scholars from »neighboring« areas to make positive and constructive intrusions into the field. It would obviously be impossible to give a complete account here to the many and various contributions made to the question. We will therefore limit ourselves to a few essential examples: systematic interpretations, action theory, political science approaches, collective psychology and the study of deviant behaviour.

The relationship between systematic crisis and the emergence of new collectives has attracted the attention of analysts from different fields such as Ardigò (1980) and Rusconi (1984). The first counts social movements amongst the fundamental elements in the scenario that we are witnessing following the breakdown of the welfare state. The second places them rather within the framework of an analysis of the changed nature of conflict in highly complex society. Meanwhile, in the development of action theory, we should mention Ceri (1979, 1986) as well as a large group of analysts of workers' action (La Valle, 1982; Cella, 1979; Romagnoli, 1976; Regalia 1984; Pizzorno et al., 1978).

Concentrating on trade unions and worker's action, these writers provide a useful conceptual framework in which to consider the »collective« aspects of union activity and industrial relations. Going beyond the level of organization and negotiation they bring out very clearly the logic of the »collective subject«: the process of mobilization and leader/grass-roots relations.

Under the same heading come the contributions made to the debate on the concept of both individual and collective identity (Sciolla, 1983; Crespi et al., 1983).

Others (Tarozzi, 1982; Tarozzi and Bongiovanni, 1984) investigate the relation between emerging movements and other forms of solidarity-based collective action such as voluntary service drawing on both identity theory and Ardigò's systemic interpretation. In particular, what emerges with respect to the new movements is their orientation towards members' needs (not only material, but above all, the need for identity). The development of new forms of action would tend to free increasing areas of »life worlds«[2] from the influence of systemic apparatuses of social control: self-management of services, promotion of alternative business activities, and the creation of new solidarity structures/groupings. The central question posed by the analysis is whether such groups would find it possible to escape the existing tradition of choice between integration in the dominant system and marginalization. More empirical analysis of the same phenomena are provided by Pasquinelli (1989a and b) and Ranci (1985).

The relation between social movements and the political system is at the centre of other studies (Goio, 1981; Ergas, 1981, 1982a, 1986a). In particular, the work of the latter contains wide empirical references to the Italian situation in the seventies. In Ergas's view, the response of the state and the political system in developing welfare structures was primarily designed to neutralize the movements' conflictual content, progressively reducing their capacity for action. On the other hand, the political elite proves largely impregnable to any effort towards internal reform or to change in the channels

2 The concept of »life worlds« is to be taken as Schutz's and Habermas' *Lebenswelt*, firstly adopted in Italy by Ardigó.

through which political demand is mediated. The movements must therefore find breathing room for action between the political system and civil society. From a more theoretical and comparative perspective, Fabbrini (1988) puts special emphasis on the emergence of »new social movements« as one major outcome of the crisis of traditional politics and welfare models of interest representation.

By contrast, Mucchi Faina (1983; see also Crespi and Mucchi Faina, 1988) proposes a broad study of »crowd psychology« in a socio-psychological context covering the whole tradition from its origins to the most recent developments.

From the seventies on, Melucci has contributed consistently to this field of study (Melucci 1974, 1976, 1977, 1982, 1984a, 1987). Via a succession of adjustments, his work has progressed in two main directions: defining the concept of collective action and studying contemporary movements. His writing in English, right up to the most recent work (Melucci 1980, 1981a, 1981b, 1984b, 1985, 1986, 1988, 1989 – and also 1982 and 1984a in Italian), has concentrated on this second aspect. In his work on »new movements«, Melucci has tried to achieve a synthesis between a European »structuralist« approach and the American resource mobilization approach (see section 2, below for empirical details).

On the purely theoretical level Melucci insists on the need to use analytical concepts rather than empirical generalizations in defining collective phenomena. He proposes a concept of »social movement« which involves three analytical dimensions: conflict, solidarity, and breaking the system's limits of compatibility. These three categories serve to distinguish movements from other forms of collective action (those regulated by competition, deviant behaviour, aggregative behaviour, etc.).

The field of collective action is seen as a set of systems rather than as a single homogeneous entity. The participants play many different games at the same time, depending on their internal relationships and environmental circumstances, and it is the task of analysis to reveal this plurality. The empirical behavior of a group is not considered as a »datum«, but as a »product«; it is the result of a variety of systems, orientations and meanings. Melucci is particularly interested, here, in the relation between movements and political systems and has applied his theoretical model to research on contemporary movements using an experimental method (described in section 3) to shed light on the plurality of action systems that movements present within them.

II. Principal Areas of Empirical Research

The major reference point for empirical research on social movements in Italy since the sixties is the Milan metropolitan area. This is perhaps partly explained by the fact that the only research centres devoted predominantly to this theme are situated in Milan; but in any case Milan represented, and at least in part still represents, the most fertile ground for the development of the new forms of collective action (due to the inclusion of the area in a very advanced pattern of post-industrial society and to its tradition of political and social participation).

The only relevant analysis of protest behavior in Italy on a national scale is by an American scholar – although very familiar to Italian society and politics – Sydney Tarrow. Following some preliminary contributions (see for instance Tarrow, 1984, 1986, 1989a; della Porta and Tarrow, 1986; Stefanizzi and Tarrow, 1989), his recent volume on the cycle of protest in 1966-1973 (Tarrow 1989b) provides an impressive account of the protest events which developed in that phase. Relying mostly, though not exclusively, on newspaper articles for data and information, the book assigns a special relevance to the relationship between unconventional protest behavior and most institutionalized patterns of political participation between cycles of protest and cycles of reform[3].

We present the principal findings of Italian empirical research by listing the various types of mobilization according to their respective issues. To begin with, however, we think it useful to take a brief look at work done on the general analysis of the intermediate levels of action that lies between the structural determinants and the events: leadership, forms of organization, processes of mobilization, and the role of ideology (Grazioli and Lodi, 1984; Diani and Donati, 1984, Donati and Mormino, 1984). Using data gathered by Melucci (1984a) in the Milan area in the course of his research, these authors highlight certain distinctive features of the most recent social movements: inclusive participation, characterized by variable and non-binding personal

---

3 Although this chapter is devoted to Italian authors, we included Tarrow's contribution in this field because of the constant involvement of Italian co-researchers in his work (see the above references). As far as we know, the only other non-Italian books on Italian movements are by Judith Adler Hellman (1987), who analyzed the Feminist movement and its relationship to leftist parties and unions in several Italien cities, and by Bob Lumley, who investigated protest cultures in Italy between 1968 and 1979 (Lumley, 1990).

investment, foreign to the idea of total commitment; a style of leadership free of personal or charismatic tendencies based instead on role-rotation and the legitimaziation of leaders primarily on the grounds of specific technical and/or cultural skills; and a diffuse organizational structure, i.e., one founded on multiple networks of largely non-formalized relations activated only when necessary rather than by a bureaucratic party-type structure. Donati (1984) goes on to criticize the tendency to identify the organizational patterns of the movements with the various organizations active within them. Any analysis of the latter must take into account the overall relations amongst the social movement organizations (SMOs), informal groupings and single individuals committed to action. Sassoon (1984a, 1984b) has pointed out the symbolic dimension of collective action, making reference to anthropology and Baudrillard's analysis. The recourse by militants to all-inclusive, comprehensive ideologies is by now considered a left-over from the past, albeit recent and still alive; the approach favoured today is that of the symbolic challenge. The antagonistic nature of social movements is to be seen, above all, in the production of symbolic codes and alternative rituals. The ability of the State to take over such codes means that a movement must be equipped with a strong creative potential: »no longer endless struggle, but endless invention« (Sassoon, 1984a: 406).

This range of contributions brings out, besides the specific characteristics of the »new movements«, the importance of the intermediate level between structure and action. It is in this space that the networks are activated towards mobilization; analysis of this level also provides a bridge between the American and the European approaches.

A. Youth Mobilization

When one turns to *youth mobilization* during the sixties and seventies, truly sociological studies are hard to find in Italy. With the exception of one book by Statera (1975), most authors choose to concentrate on the political aspects. Nevertheless, a few examples of this approach merit our attention including works by Beccalli (1977, 1981); Manconi (1983); Lerner et al. (1978), which look above all at the changes brought about by the so-called »1977 Movement«. Bobbio (1988), on the other hand, has reconstructed the history of the organization of the new-left group, »Lotta Continua«, combining his scientific skills with his own experience as ex-leader.

The crisis of the Leninist model and the emergence of a dialect between political commitment and the private life lie at the base of more properly scientific analyses. Both the research of Lodi and Grazioli (1984) in Milan and that of Altieri et al. (1983) in Bologna concentrate on new forms of action which began to emerge around the instrumental poverty (both in terms of political goals and individual fulfilment) of action and its richness of expression and between the apparent disintegration of the movement, at least of its centralized organization, and the multiplicity of hidden initiatives (counterculture, innovation, alternative professionalization). Rather than a wave of non-commitment, it would seem more appropriate to talk of a co-existence within the movement of numerous *visible* forms of commitment consisting mostly of short term campaigns together with broader systems of relations (*latency*) which also involve individuals on the emotional and everyday-life levels. The study of the Bologna movement similarly highlights its polymorphic and fragmented nature. This heterogeneity to some extent reflects certain fundamental aspects of the ex-militant's existence: the constant tension within the subject between the search for stability and the desire to experiment, the definition of needs impossible to satisfy within the existing institutions, and the emerging perception of time as a scarce resource in relation to which the actor's strategy must be worked out (working and non-working time).

The striking cultural and symbolic connotations of the various juvenile groups has been recorded in a study of street gangs (mods, rockers, etc.) in the Milan metropolitan area (Caioli et al., 1986), and in an article by the Evangelisti (1984). Lodi's analysis (1984, 1990) of the Italian pacifist movement concentrates on the cyclic character of mobilization. Diverse cultural and political components converge periodically in common episodes of activity only to disperse again without stable organized structures beyond purely formal coordination. Other articles on pacifist activity in Italy have been produced by Isernia (1983) and Ruzza (1989).

B. Women's Movement

The most substantial research and documentation on the *women's movement* is undoubtedly that carried out by researchers backed by the Feltrinelli Foundation. Data on women's action was gathered both in Milan and in other parts of Lombardy to compare the situation in the metropolis with that in the outlying areas (Calabró and Grasso, 1985). Three phases of collective activity were identified: the feminist movement, the women's movement and widespread feminism. The first phase, prior to 1976, covers practice linked to the intellectual inheritance of the previous years revolving around group membership and a critique of male-dominated society. The second marks the increasing presence of women in other areas of collective action (politics, trade unions) and the growth of mobilization aimed at eliminating discrimination against women in society. The third phase corresponds to the development of life-styles and activities, often remote from collective practice, but informed by a feminist perspective, Some of the issues taken into consideration are the role of groups which, significant in the smaller centers where loosely-structured groups prevail; the relationship, between political action and feminine identity (individual and group), a relationship that becomes increasingly difficult to maintain after 1976; the role of writing and talking as specifically female forms of expression; the comparison between different generations of militant feminists, at first homogeneous, later increasingly divergent in terms of personal history, social background and political experience, right up to the present situation which almost suggests the presence of more than one movement.

The variety of experience within the movements is emphasized by Bianchi and Mormino (1984), again using Milan as their point of reference. The groups are classified according to the type of resources predominantly employed (emotional and relational vs. technical/cultural and political experience) as well as group attitude, either inward-looking (private/individual orientation) or outward-looking (public/collective action). Ergas's analyses of the feminist movement (1982b, 1986a, 1986b) consider, besides the problem of female identity, the more general nexus of movements and the political system.

Recently, Crespi and Mucchi Faina (1988) have coordinated an ambitious research project on the Italian women's movement. Through an extension of Moscovici's framework, it aims at providing a reconstruction of how minorities may exert their influence on society by analyzing the Italian women's mobilizations for free abortion.

Finally, drawing upon Tarrow's dataset, Stefanizzi (1988) compares the styles of political participation adopted by the women's and the ecology movement in their early phases.

C. Environmentalist Action

The growth of »green lists« and ecology groups in Italy has been followed by a similar rise of interest among students of social movements. A reader edited by Biorcio and Lodi (1988) provides a comprehensive perspective on various aspects of collective action on ecological issues. A wide spectrum of topics is covered, ranging from the organizational structure of the main ecology SMOs to the social background and ideological beliefs of both green lists' activists and voters (see also Biorcio, 1987 on this point). Ceri (1987a,1987b) is concerned with the theoretical analysis of environmentalist action, as well as with evaluating the impact of the Chernobyl accident on the Italian political system. Diani (1988a, 1990) investigates the network structure of the environmental movement, paying special attention to the patterns of relationship between the main currents of the movement as well as between the movement as a whole and its social *milieu.* His conceptualization of differences in approaches to environmentalist action draws largely upon an earlier paper by Barone (1984), which distinguishes the various components according to two variables: the emphasis placed on an overall transformation of social relations (political/social ecology) rather than mere nature conservation (protectionism), and the decision to adopt direct forms of action rather than intervention through the political system. Along the same lines, Diani and Lodi (1988) identify different kinds of participants in the different currents of the environmental movement. A special accent on the different ways of conceptualizing the environmental issues by the various components of the ecology movement is also adopted by Farro (1990). Finally, Donati (1989) presents an original investigation of the relationships between consumer behavior and protest behavior with reference to the growth and development of the environmental question in Italy.

D. Religious Movements

Studies devoted to *religious movements* in Italy are plentiful, but for the most part they treat the phenomenon in a classical »sociology of religion« perspective rather than in terms of collective action with the exception of work by Alberoni (1981). Rich in interest, nevertheless, are the studies by Cuminetti (1983); Pace (1983) and Ferrarotti et al. (1978) on Catholicism, Macioti (1980) on Transcendental Meditation, and Bartolomei and Fiore

(1981) on the Hare Krishna movement. An attempt to locate the new religious groups within the framework of a sociology of collective action has been made by Diani (1984, 1986). The articulation of the neo-orientalist area is examined pointing out both the relations with the counter-cultural movements of the seventies and their subsequent distancing from them. The heterogeneity of demand within the area and the wide social range of actors involved may be seen as a sign of the gradual abandonment of a marginal perspective in favour of a broader culturally innovative function.

E. Ethno-Nationalist Movements

Though never so intense as in other countries, the mobilization of Italian cultural minorities has played, and continues to play, a significant role. As with religious phenomena, here again studies of the linguistic problem or the various »national questions« tend to be more numerous than those concerned with nationalist collective action. Canciani (1980) provides an excellent overall picture of these works that is rich in empirical documentation. Other analyses, more explicitly focused on collective action, present a more theoretical/comparative standpoint (Biagi, 1982; Pistoi, 1983; Melucci and Diani, 1983). Pistoi is also the author of an empirical study of the role of the military and police in repressing irredentism, with reference to the case of Northern Ireland (1980). Della Porta and Mattina (1985) propose an analysis of the Basque seperatist movement.

F. Political Violence

Political violence and terrorism had profound effects on Italian society during the seventies and as such have encouraged widespread discussion though more often from a political than a sociological standpoint. Notable exceptions are works by Statera (1979, 1983), Manconi and Dini (1981) and Vasale (1980) on terrorist ideology, and in particular, research conducted by the Cattaneo Insitute of Bologna (Della Porta, 1988, 1990; Della Porta and Pasquino, 1983, 1986; Manconi, 1988; see also section 5 below). Della Porta in particular adopts the categories of *resource mobilization theory* and action theory to produce a detailed account of the role played by the internal dynamics within terrorist organizations in the escalation of violent practices.

Recently, increased attention has been paid to the *radical right*, the first results of which are documented in a book by Ferraresi (1984). Also worthy to mention, although not devoted to the Italian situation, is the analysis of the American neo-conservative movement performed by Fabbrini (1986).

III. Methodology

During the seventies, research on social movements in Italy took a predominantly traditional form. The majority of scholars adopted a two-pronged approach consisting, on the one hand, of classical survey techniques (questionnaires, in-depth interviews) and, on the other, detailed analysis of the groups' or organizations' literatures. Both methods can reveal important limitations, however, when they give undue weight to the participants' ideological statements without relating the actual patterns of action. However, other well known techniques were often applied in this field, such as participant observation, in the case of youth subcultures (Caioli et al., 1986), and group interviews, for women's organizations (Calabri and Grasso, 1985) and for youth centers (Altieri et al., 1983).

Recently, therefore, more thought and greater care has been given to the search for more suitable techniques for this area of research. As already mentioned, an original methodological contribution has been made by Melucci (1984c) in the study on »new forms of collective action« in the Milan area.

Following extensive preliminary field work, during which researchers obtained information concerning groups in four areas of movement (youth, women, environmentalist, »new consciousness«) by means of in-depth interviews and participant observation, as well as from informants, four groups were selected. These groups represented in each area the point of convergence of those dimensions of collective action that preliminary observation revealed as significant. The four groups were invited to take part in an experimental programme involving video-recorded sessions; the stimuli provided by the researchers, together with video feedback, fed a process of self-reflection in the group concerning its action and collective identity. The groups agreed to participate under a contractual relationship with the researchers based on an exchange of information: the researchers would provide their services to aid the process of self-examination while the groups would provide information regarding their activity. The groups remained fully responsible for the process of self-examination and the researcher's feedback related to the phenomenological level alone – the *how* of the action. The *why* question was only faced after the experimental phase, working on the video-recorded material and comparing it with information obtained from other sources, as well as from discussion sessions with representatives of the various groups.

The experimental situation is expected to yield information about action and not about opinions: the groups provide the opportunity to analyse the action »in action«. The researchers do not expect a mimetic-reproduction of real action (the illusory target of much action-research methodology and sociological intervention). They seek, rather, in an explicitly artificial setting (provided by role playing, simulation games and focused interaction), to understand the formal logic of the action which can be compared with information obtained from other more traditional sources. By inter-relating the orientations observed in the experimental situation and comparing them with information about the more extensive networks, it is possible to obtain a useful map of the problems around which the actors establish their collective identity and the ways in which they actively confront them.

There are numerous other examples of innovative research methods which have been used in recent times, but a comprehensive account of these would be impossible. Instead we will limit ourselves to a few projects with which we were acquainted with the exception of the already cited work by Sidney Tarrow (1989) who makes massive use of event analysis.

Firstly, we should recall the work done by Della Porta (1987, 1988, 1990) on militants in left-wing terrorist groups using a life-history technique. Della Porta has investigated the part played by parental relations and those with friends and associates in influencing the subject's decision to join a terrorist group. Passerini (1988) has also made an extensive and creative use of life bibliographies in her account of the '68 movement. Recent and sophisticated techniques of discourse analysis have been picked up by Crespi, Mucchi Faina and associates (1988) in their analysis of local branches of pro-abortion movements. They allowed for a better comprehension of the multiplicity of frames which social movement groups adopt to describe their action. With a different methodological approach, Diani (1988, 1990) has attempted to apply the techniques of *network analysis* to environmentalist action in Milan. Networks linking the various groups with one other and with the outside world are examined on four different relational levels: cooperation on specific initiatives; exchange of information; exchange of organizational resources; channels created by activists through overlapping membership.

IV. Institutional Aspects

Research on social movements, though presently occupying fairly large numbers of academics, is still largely lacking in institutional support. No specific disciplinary field, for instance, is recognized by the Italian Association of Sociology. As regards university departments, the only research group offically constituted and still active is LAMS (Collective Action and Social Movement Research Workshop) directed by Alberto Melucci of the Department of Sociology at the University of Milan. Besides the activities mentioned above, LAMS coordinates a number of basic research programmes, guiding final-degree dissertations and promoting the systematic collection of data on the subject. Under this heading came the publication of a bibliography of Italian and international works during the period 1975-1985 (Donati and Diani, 1985).

Turning to private research bodies, the Feltrinelli Foundation of Milan is one of the few, if not the only one, to pay consistent attention to the phenomenon of social movements, and in particular, to youth and feminist action. The Foundation addresses itself, on the one hand, to collecting documentation and testimonies, and on the other, to the promoting of communication and encounters between academics. Thus, it organized the international seminar on »Social Movements and the Political System«, held in Milan in June 1983, the results of which were published in Melucci (1986). Since 1979 the Foundation has also housed the Centre for Historical Studies on the Women's Liberation Movement in Italy. The Foundation is also hosting a recently constituted Research Workshop on Green Politics and Policies.

During the seventies and eighties local government, and in particular, the respective cultural and social affairs offices, have taken a particular interest in the problems of collective action. Although this interest has been primarily in terms of deviant activity, these bodies have at times supported research and analysis with a broader-based theoretical perspective. Especially relevant here is the work on terrorism and political violence commissioned by the Bologna City Council from the Cattaneo Institute and directed by Raimondo Catanzaro.

The Institute has so far also promoted a number of conferences, the results of which are brought together in Della Porta and Pasquino (1983); Della Porta (1984); Pasquino (1984); Catanzaro (1990a; 1990b).

Finally, we would like to call attention to the role played by the International Sociological Institute of Gorizia (ISIG). Although not specifically concerned with social movements, the scholars active at the Institute deserve mention for their substantial contributions to the development of the sociology of disasters and mass emergencies in Italy (see for instance Cattarinussi et al., 1981; Dynes et al., 1987).

V. Concluding Remarks

The conceptual autonomy and professional growth of sociology of social movements in Italy has certainly consolidated in the last decade and Italian contributions have now taken their place in international debate. In spite of some persisting shortfalls (noted in part by other observers, e.g. De Marchi 1986), the present situation nevertheless allows a number of positive conclusions. First, the findings of Italian sociology confirm what is emerging from the international literature, e.g., that contemporary forms of collective action are multiple and varied and affect different levels and areas of the social system. This finding, which is difficult to refute empirically, leads to certain further considerations. Whilst in the past analysis of conflict might have coincided with analysis of the social conditions of a group, today it is becoming increasingly necessary to begin with the conflictual issues at the systemic level and explain how the specific social groups come to be actively involved. Again, the multiplicity and variety of actors reveal a much greater plurality of meanings and orientations within empirical movements than in the past. Finally, these contemporaneous phenomena unite together in the present the »geological strata« of social life and the various movements become the empirical bearers of problems, conflicts and forms of struggle which correspond to the different stages of a system's historical development.

The main outstanding problems for theory and research on social movements, especially in Italy, remain the necessity to improve analytical capability and to escape from global philosphical or ideological positions. In the second place there is the need to analyze in greater detail the systemic processes at the base of conflict, but also, to give a thorough account of the actors and forms of action in a comparative perspective. There then emerges the importance of developing a multipolar analytical perspective which is not constrained by the internal logic of the actors themselves, but which reconstructs the networks of relations, in particular between movements and the political system. Finally, we cannot begin to think about autonomous analysis without the development of adequate research methods. Analysis of structural variables, motivation and events provides the necessary basis for research on collective action, but the action itself, its formation and evolution, must also become an object of investigation.

Annotated Bibliography

Adler-Hellman, Judith (1987): *Journeys among Women*, New York, Oxford: University Press.

Alberoni, F. (1966): »Sociologia del comportamento collettivo«, in: AA.VV. *Questioni di Sociologia*. Brescia: La Scuola.

– (1968a): »Smelser ed il problema del comportamento collettivo«, Introduction to N.J. Smelser, *Il comportamento collettivo*. Florence: Vallecchi.

– (1968b): *Statu nascenti. Studi sui processi collettivi*. Bologna: Il Mulino.
Drawing upon the Weberian tradition the book focuses on that particular »state« of the social structure when creativity can appear in human action. Conversion, falling in love and collective movements are analyzed as examples of innovation in institutional life.

– (1979): *Innamoramento e amore*. Milan: Garzanti.

– (1981): *Movimento e istituzione*. Bologna: Il Mulino (engl. trans. *Movement and Institution*. New York 1984: Columbia University Press.)

– The most important theoretical work by the author who pioneered the study of social movements in Italy. The book describes the »statu nascenti« situation in which social movements are formed and relates it to the process through which creative and innovative phases of social life are transformed into new institutions. A large amount of comparative material on both historical and contemporary movements is provided.

Altieri, L., Caselli, C., Faccioli, P. and Tarozzi, A. (1983): *Tempo di vivere. Nuove identità e paradigma giovanile dopo il '77*. Milan: Angeli.
This book analyzes the life experiences of ex-militants in the 1977 alternative movement in Bologna. It focuses on the relationship between anti-institutional political participation, the transformation of individual life-styles, and the emergence of new patterns of identity among young people.

Ardigò, A. (1980): *Crisi di bovernabilità e mondi vitali*. Bologna: Cappelli.

Barone, C. (1984): »Ecologia: quali conflitti per quali attori«, in: A. Melucci (ed.) *Altri codici*. Bologna: Il Mulino.

Bartolomei, G. and Fiore, C. (1981): *I nuovi monaci. Hare Krishna: ideologia e pratica di un movimento neo-orientale*. Milan: Feltrinelli.

Beccalli, B. (1977): »Protesta giovanile e opposizione politica«, *Quaderni Piacentini* 64.

– (1981): »Cultura e protesta giovanile in Europa e negli Stati Uniti«, *Inchiesta* 54: 63-70.

Biagi, A. (1982): *Sociologia dei processi nazionalitari*. Verona: Fiorini.

Bianchi, M. and Mormino, M. (1984): »Militanti di sé stesse. Il movimento delle donne a Milano«, in A. Melucci (ed.) *Altri codici*. Bologna: Il Mulino.

Biorcio, R. (1987): »Ecologia e politica nell'opinione pubblica italiana«, *Polis*, 1: 517-564.

Biorcio, R. and Lodi, G. (eds.) (1988): *La sfida verde. Il movimento ecologista in Italia*. Padua: Liviana.
Contributors analyze distinctive features of both activists and supporters of the Green Lists as well as activists and major organizations of the environmental movement. Some case-studies of local mobilizations are also included.

Bobbio, L. (1988): *Lotta Continua. Storia di un'organizzazione rivoluzionaria*. Milan: Feltrinelli.

Bongiovanni, G. and Bartolomei, P. (1984): »Lotte antinucleari e sistema politico: Alcuni interrogativi sul movimento ecologico«, in A. Tarozzi and G. Bongiovanni (eds.). *Le imperfette utopie*. Milan: Angeli.

Caioli, L.: Calabrò, A.R.; Fraboni, M.; Leccardi, C.; Tabboni, S.; Venturi, R. (1986): *Bande: un modo di dire*. Rockabillies, mods, punks. Milan: UNICOPLI.
Possibly the widest coverage of youth subcultures in a metropolitan area in Italy. Among other issues, special attention is paid to connections between social antagonism and symbolic antagonism.

Calabrò, A.R. and Grasso, L. (eds.) (1985): *Dal movimento femminista al femminismo diffuso. Ricerca e documentazione nell'area lombarda*. Milan: Angeli.
Several case-studies of women's mobilizations in Milan and in Lombardy are put together here. The reader provides an empirically detailed account of the development of the feminist movement throughout the seventies and the early eighties.

Canciani, D. (1980): »Minoranze etnico-linguistiche e ricerca sociologica in Italia«, *Città e Regione*, 6 (3): 114-134.

Catanzaro, R. (ed.) (1990a): *La politica della violenza*. Bologna: Il Mulino.

– (ed.) (1990b): *Ideologie, movimenti, terrorismi*. Bologna: Il Mulino.

Cattarinussi, B., Pelanda, C. and Moretti, A. (eds.) (1981): *Il disastro: effetti di lungo termine*. Udine: Editrice Grillo.

Cella, G.P. (ed.) (1979) *Il movimento degli scioperi nel XX secolo*. Bologna: Il Mulino.

Ceri, P. (1979): »Perché azioni unitarie sono precedute e poi seguite da azioni separate?«, *Rassegna Italiana di Sociologia* 20 (4).

Ceri, P. (1986): »Mobilitazione delle risorse o risorse della mobilitazione?«, in A. Melucci (ed.) *Movimenti sociali e sistema politico. Quaderni della Fondazione Feltrinelli 32*. Milan: Angeli.

Ceri, P. (1987a): »Le basi sociali e morali dell'ecologia politica«, in: P. Ceri (ed.) *Ecologia politica*. Milan: Feltrinelli.

Ceri, P. (1987b): »Dopo Chernobyl. Il ›nucleare‹ come nuova frattura nella politica e nella società italiana«, in: P. Corbetta and R. Leonardi (eds.), *Politica in Italia. 1987*. Bologna: Il Mulino.

Crespi, F. and Mucchi Faina, A. (eds.) (1988): *Le strategie delle minoranze attive. Una ricerca empirica sul movimento delle donne*. Naples: Liguori.
An original and creative expansion of Moscovici's approach. Contributors analyse pro-abortion campaigns run by women's groups in several Italian cities. Much use is made of sophisticated discourse analysis techniques.

Crespi, F.; Rositi, F.; Sciolla, L.; Pistoi, P.; Saraceno, C. (1983): »Studi sull'identità«, special issue, *Rassegna Italiana di Sociologia* 24 (1).

Cuminetti, M. (1983): *Il dissenso cattolico in Italia*. Milan: Rizzoli.

della Porta, D. (1982): »La crisi del movimento femminista in Francia«, *Il Mulino* 31 (6): 828-58.

della Porta, D. (1987): »Storie di vita e movimenti collettivi. Una tecnica per lo studio delle motivazioni alla militanza politica«, *Rassegna Italiana di Sociologia*, 28: 105-131.

della Porta, D. (1988): »Recruitment Process in Clandestine Political Organizations. Italian Leftwing Terrorism«, in: B. Klandermans, H. Kriesi and S. Tarrow (eds.), *From Structure to Action*. Greenwich, Conn: JAI Press.

– (1990): *Il terrorismo di sinistra*. Bologna: Il Mulino.
The book places the raise and fall of terrorist groups in the broader context of changing Italian politics of the Seventies. Systematic attention is paid both to the structural and political facilitators for the explosion of political violence, and to the role of social networks and micro mobilization contexts in fostering individual's commitment to leftwing terrorist groups.

– (ed.) (1984): *Terrorismi in Italia*. Bologna: Il Mulino.
This reader includes contributions about both leftwing and rightwing terrorism in Italy during the seventies. Different cultural traditions and political strategies are dealt with in a comparative effort.

della Porta, D. and Mattina, L. (1985): »I movimenti politici a base etnica: il caso basco«, *Rivista Italiana di Scienza Politica* 15(1): 35-69.

della Porta, D. and Pasquino, G. (1986): »Interpretations of Italian Leftwing Terrorism«, in: P.H.Merkl (ed.), *Political Violence in Contemporary Society*. New York: Free Press.

della Porta, D. and Pasquino, G. (eds.) (1983): *Terrorismo e violenza politica*. Bologna: Il Mulino.

della Porta, D. and Tarrow, S. (1986): »Unwanted children. Political Violence and the Cycle of Protest in Italy. 1966-1973«, *European Journal of Political Research*, XIV: 607-632.

De Marchi, B. (1986): »Italian Sociology and the Study of Social Movements«, *International Journal of Mass Emergencies and Disasters* 4(1).

Diani, M. (1984): »L'area della nuova coscienza tra ricerca individuale ed impegno civile«, in A. Melucci (ed.) *Altri codici*. Bologna: Il Mulino.

Diani, M. (1986): »Dimensione simbolica e dimensione sociale nelle esperienze di nuova coscienza. Il caso dell'area milanese«, *Rassegna Italiana di Sociologia* 27(1): 89-116.

– (1988a): Isole nell'arcipelago. *Il movimento ecologista in Italia*. Bologna: Il Mulino.
Environmental collective action in Italy is analyzed here from a social networks perspective. The main focus is on the changing structure of relationships between con-

ventional environmentalist organizations and political ecology groups. Special sections are devoted to the movement's activists and to the emergence of the Green Lists.

– (1988b): »Italy: The Liste Verdi«, in F. Muller-Rommel (ed.), *New Politics in Western Europe. The Rise and Success of Green Parties and Alternative Lists.* Boulder, Co./London: Westview Press.

Diani, M. (1990): »The network structure of the Italian ecology movement«, *Social Science Information* 29 (1): 5-31.

Diani, M. and Donati, P. (1984): »L'oscuro oggetto del desiderio. Leadership e potere nelle aree di movimento«, in: A. Melucci (ed.) *Altri codici.* Bologna: Il Mulino.

Diani, M. and Lodi, G. (1988): »Three in One: Currents in the Milan Ecology Movement«, in: B. Klandermans, H. Kriesi and S. Tarrow (eds.), *From Structure to Action.* Greenwich, Conn.: JAI Press.

Donati, P.R. (1984): »Organization between Movement and Institutions«, *Social Science Information* 23(4/5): 837-59.

– (1989): »Dalla politica al consumo. La questione ecologica e i movimenti degli anni settanta«, *Rassegna Italiana di Sociologia*, 30:

Donati, P.R. and Diani, M. (1985): *Movimenti sociali contemporanei. Bibliografia 1975-1984 / Contemporary Social Movements. A Bibliography 1975-1984.* Milan: UNICOPLI.

In spite of putting a heavier accent on Italian production, the volume provides readers with a world-wide perspective on the most impressive contributions to the field of social movements and collective action in the 1975-84 decade. A system of key words in English make it manageable even by an international readership.

Donati, P.R. and Mormino, M. (1984): »Il potere della definizione: le forme organizzative dell'antagonismo metropolitano«, in A. Melucci (ed.) *Altri codici.* Bologna: Il Mulino.

Dynes, R.; De Marchi, B. and Pelanda, C. (eds.) (1987): *Sociology of Disasters. Contributions of Sociology to Disaster Research.* Milan: Angeli.

Ergas, Y. (1981): »Politica sociale e governo della protesta«, in S. Belligni (ed.) *Governare la democrazia.* Milan: Angeli.

– (1982a): »Allargamento della cittadinanza e governo del conflitto: le politiche sociali negli anni settanta in Italia«, *Stato e Mercato* 6.

– (1982b): »1968-1979. Feminism and the Italian Party System«, *Comparative Politics* 14(3): 253-279.

– (1986a): *Nelle maglie delle politica. Femminismo, istituzioni e politiche sociali nell'Italia degli anni '70.* Milan: Angeli.

Mainly focussing on women's struggles, this book analyzes the difficult relationship between the political institutions and the social movements in Italy in the seventies. The basic concern of political authorities in developing new social policies was with the weakening of the antagonistic potential expressed by protest movements rather than with the starting of a new reformist phase in Italian politics.

– (1986b): »Politiche istituzionali, mobilitazioni collettive e domande di riconoscimento. Il caso delle conne«, in: A. Melucci (ed.), *Movimenti sociali e sistema politico. Quaderni della Fondazione Feltrinelli 32.* Milan: Angeli.

Evangelisti, V. (1984): »Punks. Nuove forme di antagonismo sociale«, *Il Mulino* 33(1): 77-110.

Fabbrini, S. (1986): *Neoconservatorismo e politica americana. Attori e processi politici in una societa in trasformazione.* Bologna: Il Mulino.
Fabbrini, S. (1988): *Politica e mutamenti sociali. Alternative a confronto sullo stato sociale.* Bologna: Il Mulino.
Topics covered in this book exceed by far the analysis of social movements. In fact, it takes up the wider theoretical question of how many politics change in front of recent modernization processes and in front of the crisis of the keynesian welfare state. It is worth mentioning here, however, as the role of social movements in such changes is also analyzed in full.
Farro, A. (1986): *Conflitti sociali e città. Napoli 1970-1980.* Milan: Angeli.
Urban conflicts and movements are analyzed in a metropolitan area (Naples) where new cleavages and actors interact with traditional sources of protest such as unemployment and public authorities' corruption.
– (1990): *La rottura e l'equilibrio. Cultura e politica ambientaliste.* Milan: Angeli.
Ferraresi, F. (ed.) (1984): *Le destra radicale.* Milan: Feltrinelli.
Ferrarotti, F. (1976): »Sulla psicologia dei movimenti sociali«, in: *Lineamenti di sociologia.* Naples: Liguori.
– (1979): *Alle radici della violenza.* Milan: Rizzoli.
– (1981): »Social Marginality and Violence in Neo-urban Societies«, *Social Research* 48 (1): 183-222.
– Ferrarotti, F.; De Lutiis, G.; Macioti, M.I. and Catucci, L. (1978): *Forme del sacro in un'epoca di crisi.* Naples: Liguori.
Garelli, F. (1979): »Processi di differenziazione nel campo religioso«, *Quaderni di Sociologia* 28(4).
Goio, F. (1981): »Movimenti collettivi e sistema politico«, *Rivista Italiana di Scienza Politica,* 11(1): 3-45.
Grazioli, M. and Lodi, G. (1984): »La mobilitazione collettiva negli anni ottanta: tra condizione e convinzione«, in: A. Melucci (ed.) *Altri codici.* Bologna: Il Mulino.
Isernia, P. (1983): »I movimenti per la pace: una realità in divenire«, *Il Mulino* 32(2).
Lanternari, V. (1974): *Movimenti religiosi di libertà e di salvezza dei populi oppressi.* Milan: Feltrinelli.
The volume analyzes in comparative and historical persepctive a wide spectrum of millennial religious movements which occurred in the Third World under the general assumption that they are an important vehicle for the rebellion of people oppressed by colonialism.
La Valle, D. (1982): »Comportamento sindacale e teoria dell'azione«, *Quaderni di Sociologia* 30(1): 1-21.
Lerner, G.; Manconi, L. and Sinibaldi, M. (1978): *Uno strano movimento di strani studenti.* Milan: Feltrielli.
Lodi, G. (1984): *Uniti e diversi. Le mobilitazioni per la pace nell'Italie degli anni ottanta.* Milan: UNICOPLI.
A detailed account of the Italian peace movement in its structure and action. Forms of mobilization, leadership, and organization are described and the double structure (latent networks, visible campaigns) is investigated.

– (1990): »The Italian Peace Movement between Politics and Society. The Campaign against Euromissiles«, in B. Klandermans (ed.) *Peace Movements in International Perspective*. Greenwich, Conn.: JAI Press (forthcoming).

Lodi, G. and Diani, M. (1986): »Regioni e movimenti: le mobilitazioni antinucleari«, in: M. Cammelli (ed.) *Energia e regioni. Politiche istituzionali e strumenti di governo*. Bologna: Il Mulino.

Lodi, G. and Grazioli, M. (1984): »Giovani sul territorio urbano: l'integrazione minimale«, in: A. Melucci (ed.) *Altri codici*. Bologna: Il Mulino.

Lumley, B. (1990): *Cultures of emergency*. London: Verso.

Macioti, M.I. (1980): *Teoria e tecnica della pace interiore. Saggio sulla Meditazione Trascendentale*. Naples: Liguori.

Manconi, L. (1983): »Movimenti e nuovi movimenti: identità e negoziazione«, *Quaderni Piacentini* 8: 75-113.

– (1988): »Il nemico assoluto. Antifascismo e contropotere nella fase aurorale del terrorismo di sinistra«, *Polis*, 3: 259-286.

Manconi, L. and Dini, V. (1981): *Il discorso delle armi. L'ideologia terrorista nel linguaggio delle Brigate Rosse e di Prima Linea*. Rome: Savelli.

Melucci, A. (1974): *Lotte sociali e mutamento*. Milan: CELUC.

– (1977): *Sistema politico, partiti e movimenti sociali*. Milan: Peltrinelli.

– (1980): »The New Social Movements: A Theoretical Approach«, *Social Science Information* 19(2): 199-226.

– (1981a): »Ten Hypotheses for the Analysis of New Movements«, in: D. Pinto (ed.), *Contemporary Italian Sociology*. Cambridge: University Press.

– (1981b): »New Movements, Terrorism and the Political System«, *Socialist Review* 56.

– (1982): *L'invenzione del presente. Movimenti, identità, bisogni individuali*. Bologna: Il Mulino.
A theory of identity is outlined and applied to contemporary movements. A detailed analysis of the relationship between new social movements and the political system in Italy is provided as well.

– (1984b): »An End to Social Movements?«, *Social Science Information* 23 (4/5): 819-36.

– (1985): »The Symbolic Challenge of Contemporary Movements«, *Social Research* 52.

– (1987): *Libertà che cambia. Un'ecologia del quotidiano*. Milan: UNICOPLI.

– (1988): »Getting Involved. Identity and Mobilzation in Social Movements«, in: B. Klandermans, H. Kriesi and S. Tarrow (eds.), *From Structure to Action*. Greenwich, Conn.: JAI Press.

– (1989): *Nomads of the Present*. London: Hutchinson Radius/Philadelphia: Temple.
The volume offers a systematic account of the theoretical work carried out in the last ten years by the author. Contemporary social movements are viewed as challenging the cultural and symbolic codes of today's complex information systems. New conflictual issues develop, therefore, including ones involving time, space, interpersonal relationships, and lifestyles.

– (ed.) (1976): *Movimenti di rivolta. Teorie e forme dell'azione collettiva*. Milan: Ets.

– (ed.) (1984a): *Altri codici*. Bologna: Il Mulino.
Account of a large research project on the Milan metropolitan area. Four types of new social movements are analyzed (youth, women, neo-religious, environmentalist). They

are compared in terms of mobilization processes, leadership, organization and ideology. An experimental research method based on group interaction is presented.
– (ed.) (1986): *Movimenti sociali e sistema politico. Quaderni della Fondazione Feltrinelli* 32, Milan: Angeli.
Melucci, A. and Diani, M. (1983): *Nazioni senza stato. I movimenti etnico-nazionali in Occidente*. Turin: Loescher.
An effort to reconsider the experience of contemporary ethnic and nationalist mobilizations in the western world is carried out in this volume. The analytical framework is provided by the latest contributions to the sociology of social movements, thus implying a shift away from traditional interpretations of such phenomena.
Mucchi Faina, a. (1983): *L'abbraccio della folla*. Bologna: Il Mulino.
A general discussion of psychosocial contributions to the analysis of crowd behavior. It provides both an excellent review of the traditional approaches and recent international literature and an original synthesis of psychological and sociological perspectives.
Olson, M. (1965): *The Logic of Collective Action*. Cambridge, MA.: Harvard University Press.
Pace, E. (1983): *Asceti e mistici in una società secolarizzata*. Padua: Marsilio.
Pasquinelli, Sergio (1989a): »Un territorio da inventare. Volontariato e politiche sociali in Italia«, *Il Mulino*, n. 4.
Pasquinelli, Sergio 81989b): »Voluntary Action and Welfare State. The Italian Case«, *Non-Profit and Voluntary Sector Quarterly*, n. 4.
Pasquino, G. (ed.) (1984): *La prova delle armi*. Bologna: Il Mulino.
Passerini, L. (1988): *Autoritratto di gruppo*. Giunti: Florence.
A creative application of oral history and life biography techniques to the analysis of political activists of the Sixties and Seventies. Bordering between social analysis and autobiography.
Pistoi, P. (1980): *Una comunità sotto controllo*. Milan: Angeli.
– (1983): »Identità e mobilitazione politica«, *Rassegna Italiana di Sociologia* 24(1): 79-104.
Pizzorno, A. (1966): »Introduzione allo studio della partecipazione politica«, *Quaderni di Sociologia* (15(3/4): 235-87.
– (1978a): »Political Exchange and Collective Identity in Industrial Conflict«, in: C. Crouch and A. Pizzorno (eds.) *The Resurgence of Class conflict in Western Europe since 1968*. London: MacMillan.
Although strictly focusing on worker's mobilizations, this essay provides a substantive contribution to a better understanding of collective action at large. In doing so, it puts the emphasis on the notion of collective identity as a precondition to overcome the logic of free-riding.
– (1978b): »Le due logiche dell'azione di classe«, in: A. Pizzorno, E. Reyneri, M. Regini and I. Regalia *Lotte operaie e sindacato: il ciclo 1968-1972 in Italia*. Bologna: Il Mulino.
– (1983a): »Identità ed interesse«, in L. Sciolla (ed.) *Identità*. Turin: Rosenberg e Sellier.
Collective identity may account for mobilization, as it provides a market where individuals can »spend« their rewards and can expect them to be adequately valued.
– (1983b): »Sulla razionalità della scelta democratica«, *Stato e Mercato* 7.

– (1986): »Sul confronto intertemporale delle utilità«, *Stato e Mercato* 16: 3.25.
– (1987): »Considerazioni sulle teorie dei movimenti sociali«, *Problemi del Socialismo*, NS, n. 12: 11-27.
The role of identity in mobilization processes is reconsidered in the light of recent developments in the »resource mobilization theory«.
Pizzorno, A.; E. Reyneri, M. Regini and I. Regalia (1978): *Lotte operaie e sindacato: il ciclo 1968-1972 in Italia*. Bologna: Il Mulino.
Ranci, C. (1985): *Volontariato, bisogni, servizi. Esperienze e modelli di intervento delle associazioni di volontariato a Milano*. Milan: Angeli.
Regalia, I. (1984): *Eletti e abbandonati. Modelli e stili di rappresentanza in fabbrica*. Bologna: Il Mulino.
Romagnoli, G. (1976): *Consigli di fabbrica e democrazia sindacale*. Milan: Mazzotta.
Rusconi, G.E. (1984): *Scambio, minaccia, decisione*. Bologna: Il Mulino.
Ruzza, C. (1989): »The Italian peace movement«, in L. Kriesberg (ed.), *Research in Social Movements. Conflict and Change. A Research Annual*. Greenwich, Conn: JAI Press.
Sassoon, J. (1984a): »Ideologia, azione simbolica ritualità: nuovi percorsi dei movimenti«, in A. Melucci (ed.) *Altri codici*. Bologna: Il Mulino.
Sasson, J. (1984b): »Ideology, Symbolic Action and Rituality in Social Movements«, *Social Science Information* 23(4/5): 861-72.
Sciolla, L. (ed.) (1983): *Identità*. Turin: Rosenberg e Sellier.
Statera, G. (1975): *Death of a Utopia*. New York: Oxford University Press.
– (1979): »Student Politics In Italy: From Utopia To Terrorism«, *Higher Education* 8(6): 657-67.
– (ed.) (1983): *Violenza sociale e violenza politica nell'Italia degli anni settanta*. Milan: Angeli.
Stefanizzi, S. (1988): »Alle origini dei nuovi movimenti sociali: gli ecologisti e le donne in Italia. 1966-1973«, *Quaderni di Sociologia*, 34, n. 11.
Stefanizzi, S. and Tarrow, S. (1989): »Protest and regulation: the interaction of state and society in the cycle 1965-1974«, in P. Lange and M. Regini (eds.), *State, Market and Social Regulation*. Cambridge: Cambridge University Press.
Tarozzi, A. (1982): *Inizative nel sociale*. Milan: Angeli.
Drawing upon printed materials as well as in-depth interviews, this work analyzes the Citizens' Initiatives in West Germany as examples of the vitality of »life worlds« threatened by the extension of systemic control.
Tarozzi, A. and Bongiovanni, G. (eds.) (1984): *Le imperfette utopie. I limiti dello sviluppo tra questione ecologica ed azione sociale*. Milan: Angeli.
Tarrow, S. (1982): »Movimenti e organizzazioni sociali: che cosa sono, quando hanno successo«, *Laboratorio Politico* 2(1): 121-53.
– (1984): »I movimenti degli anni '60 in Italia e Francia e la transizione al capitalismo maturo«, *Stato e Mercato* 12: 339-62.
– (1986): »Protesta e riforme istituzionali in Italia: movimenti, eventi e cicli politici«, in A. Melucci (ed.), *Movimenti sociali e sistema politico. Quaderni della Fondazione Feltrinelli 32*. Milan: Angeli.
– Tarrow, S. (1989a): »Mutamenti nella cultura di opposizione in Italia, 1965-1975«, *Polis*, 3; 41-63.

– (1989b): *Democracy and Disorder: society and politics in Italy. 1965-1975*. Oxford: Oxford University Press.

Vasale, C. (1980): *Terrorismo e ideologia in Italia*. Roma: Armando.

The Study of Social Movements in West Germany: Between Activism and Social Science[1]

Dieter Rucht

The existence and activities of social movements, on the one hand, and social-scientific study of them, on the other, are usually linked closely together. The flourishing of social movements is likely to promote, although with some delay, a corresponding boom in research on social movements. West Germany did not follow such a pattern, though, for a long period of its existence. In the post-war period at least, the general public had mixed feelings about discussing social movements. This term was by no means neutral as it had been heavily exploited by the Nazi-regime. For many people, social movements were discredited per se as a means for influencing the political process. For a number of reasons, certainly going beyond mere terminology, the Nazi-movement did not induce sociological social movement analysis. Until today, this movement has rather been an object of study of political scientists and historians.

The labor movement also did not become a central object for sociology. The conflict between labor and capital had already been moderated and mediated during the Weimar republic. This processes continued in the period after the Second World War. Mainly due to the effects of the Nazi regime, but also as a result of profound socio-economic changes, the labor movement could not re-establish its once vital counter-cultural networks. It very soon crystallized into the institutionalized forms of unions and parties, and

---

1 An earlier and shorter version of this essay was presented at the Annual Conference of the French Society of Sociology, September 29-30, 1989, in Paris and published – in German – under the title »Die Analyse der neuen sozialen Bewegungen in der Bundesrepublik – eine Zwischenbilanz« in Forschungsjournal Neue Soziale Bewegungen, Sonderheft 1989. I am grateful to Roland Roth for comments on earlier versions of this article.

was thus hardly perceived as a movement, although its representatives tried to maintain such an image. Major efforts at studying the labor movement were undertaken only by historians and tended to focus on the 19th century and the early decades of our century. The category of »social movement« was used only as a label in this research, but not as a conceptual key for analysis.

Surprisingly enough, the extra-parliamentary opposition (including the student revolt in the late 1960s) also did not lead to systematic sociological analysis. It was the object of many essays focusing on problems of democratic theory, Marxist thought, cultural critique, etc., of course. But it was hardly analyzed in terms of an empirically oriented social movement research (for one of the few exceptions, cf. Allerbeck et al., 1973). One reason for this lack of empirical investigation was the fact that, even in the 1970s, the study of social movements had not been institutionalized in the universities. There were no chairs devoted to social movements, never mind entire institutes.[2] The field of social movements was not treated as a subdiscipline of sociology; it was absent in most introductory volumes and textbooks in sociology. Another reason seems to be the fact that most of the theorists and activists who succeeded in getting positions at the universities retained a peculiar distance from their political past and preferred to study topics other than the movements of the 1960s. More significant attempts at analyzing the student movement, and its societal context in particular, have only recently been undertaken.

To be sure, social movements were an important object for the classical German sociology. But the great authors, such as Karl Marx, Georg Simmel, Ferdinand Tonnies and Max Weber, did not provide refined conceptual tools for the analysis of social movements. In addition, many of the social scientists of the Weimar era who had been close to social movement analysis, e.g. Karl Mannheim and Lewis Coser, or who, like Rudolf Heberle, devoted much work directly to the study of social movements, did not return from

2 It would be misleading to attempt to deduce the actual research interests from the names of institutes. For example, the unit »Institutions and Social Movements« in the social science faculty of the Frankfurt university is not actually engaged in social movement research.

emigration. From their positions abroad these scholars could hardly exert a strong impact on West German science.[3]

Given these conditions, the field of social movement analysis was largely abandoned. The old traditions had been broken off; the topic was not rooted in the academic sphere. Consequently, sociological journals in the postwar decades included only a few articles on social movements and most of them were not written with respect to current problems. This was also true for sociological work (Pankoke, 1970) focusing on the »social question« and social movements. A two volume reader on collective behavior (Heinz and Schöber, 1973), which was largely composed of translated essays by US scholars, did not gain much attention in the academic community. Even a book entitled »Soziale Bewegung« (social movement) by the Bielefeld-based sociologist Otthein Rammstedt, did not have much resonance in the first few years after publication – although it was published in the period when the so-called new social movements were flourishing. The reasons for this were, first, that it put a high emphasis on epistomologic questions. Second, the more systematic aspects of the essay, among them the ideal-typical model of a movement's life cycle, were not related to contemporary movements.[4]

It was not until the 1980s that an intense and increasingly professional reflection on social movements took place. This growing interest was clearly a reaction to the burgeoning of various movements which had developed after the student movement. Although this movement experienced a great decline after its spectacular peak in 1967 and 1968, in many respects it stimulated a variety of other groupings and movements. These ranged from the new women's movement (a direct offspring of the student revolt) up to the revitalized peace movement of the 1980s. Not surprisingly, many of these groups attracted the attention of social scientists who tried to document, analyze and interpret them. With respect to individual movements, a number of more or less scholarly books and articles were published in the mid-seventies (e.g. Krechel 1975, on the new women's movement, and Mayer-Tasch 1976, on the citizen initiatives). There was also a growing interest in their forerunners, particularly in the peace movement of the 1950s and 1960s (Otto,

---

3 It is worth mentioning, however, that Heberle's book on social movements (1951) was translated into German and published in 1967 under the title »Hauptprobleme der Politischen Soziologie« (Main Problems of Political Sociology).

4 Rammstedt first tried to apply his life-cycle model to a specific movement in a later publication. In this work he examined the new peace movement (Rammstedt, 1989).

1977), the broad range of counter-cultural groupings (Hollstein, 1979) and the so-called extra-parliamentary opposition including the student revolt of the late 1960s (Bauß, 1977). The authors of these publications were in many cases (former) movements' activists or at least they took a sympathetic stance.[5] In an overall view, these studies did not pursue ambitious theoretical and analytical goals, but rather aimed at describing, documenting, and promoting the movements. During this period movements were typically perceived as single phenomena. The authors tended to use the term »social movements« in the same way as the movements did in referring to themselves; it served simply as a label and did not raise any definitional and conceptual problems.

It was only in the late 1970s that the perception of these phenomena changed. Both the activists and the scientific observers began to interpret single movements as parts of a more encompassing ensemble that was initially referred to by various catchwords: »Zweite Kultur« (second culture, Peter Glotz), »Gegengesellschaft« (countersociety, Walter Hollstein), »neopopulism« (Jürgen Habermas, Bernd Marin), »alternative movement« (Wolfgang Kraushaar, Josef Huber, Joachim Raschke), »new social formations« (Adalbert Evers and Zoltan Szankay), etc. In this period the impression emerged that these movements would form a powerful force which would be willing and capable of challenging the overall social and political order.

Originating among social scientists, the concept of »new social movements« took hold and thus superceded the former catchwords.[6] This label encompasses, in particular, the new women's movement, citizen initiatives focused mainly on housing, urban planning and marginalized social groups, the movement against nuclear power, the broad spectrum of the ecology movement, the so-called »alternative movement« comprised of self-help groups, co-operatives, self-run youth centers, squatters, etc., and the new peace movement. It is difficult to trace whether the label new social movement was drawn from abroad, e.g., from France, or if it originated independently in Germany. Although this category occasionally came under heavy attack, it was not replaced – probably due to a lack of convincing alternatives. It also has been assimilated into the language of established politics in the meantime and, despite its vagueness, seems to hold its ground.

---

5 For a remarkable exception, see Langguth 1976. An updated and revised edition of this book was published in 1983.

6 It is clear that this term was not introduced as a well-reflected analytical category. Roth (1982, 79) and Nelles (1983, 83) admit that the term arose only for lack of a better one.

In the early 1980s the phenomenon of new social movements became a more or less central point of interest in various monographies (Hirsch, 1980; Raschke, 1980; Evers and Szankay, 1981; Brand, 1982; Rucht, 1982). It was political scientists, in particular, and not so much sociologists[7], who studied this phenomenon and its predecessors. It also became a topic of various conferences (see the readers edited by Grottian and Nelles, 1983; Hartwich, 1983; Falter, Fenner and Greven, 1984). An initial, basically descriptive, comprehensive study was soon published (Brand, Büsser and Rucht, 1983). It was followed by a series of writings focussed on specific conflicts, single movements, particular aspects of various movements and further comprehensive studies (e.g., Vester, 1983; Schmidt, 1984; Roth, 1985; v. Beyme, 1986; Rucht and Roth, 1987; Rolke, 1987; Rucht, 1989a; 1990; Roth, 1989; Wasmuht, 1989, Fuchs, 1990). There was also a growing interest in historical movements of the late 19th and the early 20th century which, in many respects, could be seen as forerunners of contemporary social movements (Conti, 1984; Linse, 1986).

Starting in 1983, a relatively intense cooperation between the respective social scientists took place. In the mid-eighties, this debate, which up until then had been centered only on West Germany, became broader. Systematic and more general aspects of the analysis of social movements were raised (Gerdes, 1984; Raschke, 1985; Neidhardt, 1985; Schneider, 1987; Nullmeier and Raschke, 1989; Huber, 1988); social movements and corresponding scientific analyses from other countries were discussed (Brand, 1985; Rucht, 1984; Japp, 1984; Mayer, 1985; Wasmuht, 1987, Rothgang, 1990).

Although the political impetus of the new social movement has gradually abated in the last few years, and most activitists have shifted toward more pragmatic political concepts, social movement research in West Germany continues to flourish. An impressive body of literature[8] has been produced to date which is, however, less than convincing in terms of quality.

After these introductory remarks including a first broad overview of the development of the study of social movements, I will deal more systematically with (1) theory and concepts, (2) methods, (3) empirical results, (4) in-

---

7 Probably the first genuine sociological essay on new social movements was that of Eder (1983) presented at the convention of the Sociological Association in 1982. In 1985, the section on »Sociological Theories» held a conference on »Social Movements and Social Evolution« in Munich.

8 See the recent bibliographies in Nullmeier and Raschke (1989), Wasmuth (1989), Roth and Rucht (1990, forthcoming).

stitutional aspects of research and (5) debates and open questions in this field of study.

I. Theories and Concepts

It has already become at least implicitely clear that theoretical and conceptual interests had remained underdeveloped for a long time in West Germany. Even for the present it can be observed that theorizing in this field is far from being very advanced. In general, only tentative propositions have been presented. Distinct theoretically oriented »schools« have not been established thus far. Sharp theoretical controversies have also not taken place, but are likely to occur in the near future.

As in many other European countries the category »social movement« is typically used in West Germany to refer to a collective effort at promoting a fundamental societal change. With this definitional element – in contrast, e.g., to the resource mobilization approach – a boundary is drawn between a social movement and pure group interest politics centered around single issues or a specific clientele. Unlike such approaches as that of Alain Touraine, in Germany the term social movement is not necessarily linked to the category of class. This relatively broad understanding, however, implies some difficulties in distinguishing between social movements, on the one hand, and political or cultural movements in the strict sense, youth religions, terrorist groups, short-lived political campaigns, more spontaneous collective actions and diffuse ideologic currents, on the other.

In general, *structural* concepts and theories are clearly dominant among the West German theoretical approaches to social movements. Several variations of these structural approaches can be found. For instance, Habermas (1981) interprets the emergence of new social movements as a reaction to the process of the »colonialization of life world« following the imperatives of the economic and the political systems. Raschke (1985), in his encompassing historical and systematic analysis of social movements, relates the *new* social movements to a post-industrial type of society and assumes that these movements focus on problems of the way of life (»Lebensweise«). Brand (1989) and Rucht (1988) refer to versions of modernization theory which still have not yet been well elaborated. These authors link (new) social movements to breakthroughs of modernization in the realms of economy, politics and culture. Eder (1982; 1986) relates the new social movements to a new societal stage of morality and collective consciousness, although he has recently raised some doubts about the »progressive« potential of these movements (Eder, 1989). Offe (1985; 1990). Other sociologists (e.g., Nedelmann, 1984; Halfmann, 1984) base their interpretation of new social movements on changes of interest mediation in contemporary welfare states. Still other authors (Hirsch and Roth, 1986; Roth, 1989a; Mayer, 1985), who adhere more closely to the marxist tradition, draw on the economically oriented »regulation« school and assume a crisis of the Fordist mode of capitalism. In this line of thought, the new social movements are seen both as results and catalysts of an emerging pattern of »post-Fordism«.

These structurally-oriented concepts are combined in part with such theorems as the shift to postmaterial values (drawing on Inglehart's work), a change of political generations (e.g., Fogt, 1982), or an overload of modern welfare states due to an »inflation of expectations« (Klages, 1980). It can be said for nearly all of these macrostructural concepts that they pay little attention to the constitution and mobilization processes of movements on a micro level.

Compared to the broad range of the structural concepts mentioned above, *actor-centered* theories are clearly marginal. There are, however, some proponents of a methodological individualism who, mainly drawing on theories of rational choice, are trying to explain individual engagement in the context of social movements (e.g., Opp 1984; 1988). Simply for systematic reasons, however, these concepts do not apply specifically to *new* social movements. One of the few actor-centered approaches which does not focus on the individual, but on collective actor, is that of Gerdes (1985). His study on regionalist movements in France was theoretically inspired by phenomenology and symbolic interactionism.

Worth mentioning also is a not yet further elaborated approach represented by Japp (1984). Influenced by the work of Touraine, he centers on the aspect of the self-constitution of social movements, and at the same time, aims at integrating some of the premises of Luhmann's functionalist theory.

(New) social movements have only quite recently been discussed in the light of a straightforward functionalist systems theory (Luhmann, 1986; Bergmann, 1987; Ahlemeier, 1989). Here, emphasis is given to aspects of societal self-monitoring and self-mobilization as key functions of social movements, whereas aspects of their genesis, organization and strategy have been largely neglected.

Partly in the context of some of the concepts mentioned above we also see a growing interest in the analysis of particular aspects of (new) social movements. This is true, for example, for questions related to their collective identity (Nelles, 1984), their internal communication and interorganizational relations, the institutionalization and professionalization of movements, and strategies (Leif 1985; 1990; Nullmeier, 1989; Roth, 1987; 1989; Rucht, 1984; 1990; Kretschmer and Rucht, 1987). Largely unconnected with these writings, a considerable body of literature has been produced in the framework of the still less institutionalized women's studies focusing on the feminist movement.[9] Only recently, some feminist writers have also taken a critical stance toward the new social movements literature (see section V). Finally, there are also approaches centered on more specific areas or issues such as subcultures (Schwendter, 1973), youth protests (Scherer, 1988), right wing groups (Dudek and Jaschke, 1984; Rau, 1985; Feit, 1987; Stöss, 1989), political extremism (Infratest, 1980; Backes and Jesse, 1989), political violence (Zimmermann, 1989) or terrorism (Bundesminister des Innern, 1981-84; Hess et al., 1988). In most cases, these studies dealt only indirectly with social movements.

II. Methodological Approaches

Given the relatively late start experienced by social movement research in West Germany, it is not surprising that the methodological discussion, as far as this field is concerned, is still underdeveloped. Only few writings deal more generally with methodological issues (Gerdes, 1984; Nullmeier and Raschke, 1989). In the period up to the early 1980s, most of the work was based only on an unsystematic use of methods and sources. Among these were reports from journalists, interviews with movement leaders, surveys, case studies, documents from social movement organizations and participant observation. These sources were used for analysis with very different pur-

9 See, for instance, Schenk (1980), Knafla and Kuhlke (1987); Clemens (1989) and Rubart (1987). Most of this literature deals only with specific aspects of the movement. Compared to several thorough historical studies of the German women's movement, there is still a surprising lack of information on the new womens' movement. There are no comprehensive and empirically detailed studies available on the new women's movement (Clemens, 1989, 255).

poses and points of attention. Various methods and sources were often combined without, however, really being applied in a sophisticated, exhaustive and well-documented manner. Moreover, this type of ad-hoc analysis was not always explicitly guided by theories and research hypotheses. As a rule, most of this work was carried out by a single person usually lacking in the resources to develop and implement research using more ambitious and costly methods. Partly due to this lack of resources, but also to the complexity of the new social movements, most of the encompassing studies are based on secondary analysis (Brand, Büsser and Rucht, 1983/1986; Raschke, 1985; Roth 1985; Rolke, 1987).

Studies relying on particular methods such as content analysis, personal interviews with activists, participant observation, etc. were usually narrow in their spatial, temporal and/or sectoral scope. The focus on particular questions, however, occasionally involved other methods, when a specific aspect was interpreted to be part of a broader phenomenon that could only be grasped by such specific methods. This was true for several case studies on specific conflicts within the context of broader movements. Similarly, most of German cross-national work and studies of movements in foreign countries were also based on primary analysis of interviews and documents together with a secondary analysis of already published studies (Gerdes, 1985; Mayer, 1985; Wasmuht, 1987; Rucht, 1989; 1990a; Rothgang, 1990; Liebert, 1986).

Survey research, as far as representative polls are concerned, dealt only marginally with social movements or suffered from pragmatic restrictions that could hardly allow for generalized findings. For example, empirical data from survey research focussed on party alignment and voting behavior with regard to the Green Party were used simply as data on the new social movements in general (e.g., Bürklin, 1984). In these cases, the fact was ignored that many participants in these movements took a skeptical stance towards political parties in general or were involved with other parties such as the Social Democrats or the Liberal Democrats.

One exception was the Eurobarometer-surveys which were implemented in various Western European countries including West Germany. Among other things, these surveys referred explicitly to various new social movements starting in 1982. In the meantime, the respective data have been used by several authors to discuss new social movements (Watts, 1987; ZEUS, 1989; Inglehart, 1989) without, however, taking into account various methodological deficits (Fuchs and Rucht, 1990). At least for West Germany, we have additional data which, up to now, has not been fully exploited for empirical analysis (Pappi, 1989; Fuchs, 1990; Schmitt, 1989). Another useful source, although generally based on surveys which are only indirectly related to social movements, would be the work focussed on political participation and unconventional/radical behavior (e.g., Barnes, Kaase et al., 1979; Kaase, 1982; Kaase and Neidhardt, 1990; Infratest, 1980).

Only very recently have several major research projects on new social movements been initiated which are expected to be more ambitious in terms of methodology and methods (see section IV). In part, these projects also put more emphasis on quantitative analysis largely neglected thus far.

III. Some Empirical Findings on New Social Movements

Despite their usually unsystematic use of empirical data, many of the early descriptions and analyses of the new social movements in West Germany exhibited a convergence in most of their empirical findings. By and large, these tentative results were confirmed by more recent and more ambitious empirical work. In the following I will briefly present some of these findings organized around key aspects without, however, referring to the respective literature in most cases.

(1) *The new social movement sector as a whole*: In the self-image of most of the followers of the new social movements there is a relatively clear dividing line between these and earlier movements, and in particular, the labor movements and its heirs, the labor unions and Social Democrats. These organizations are perceived to represent an »old« concept of progress, based on personal discipline, bureaucratic structures, representative forms of politics, high division of labor, economic growth, etc.

The New Left, and in particular the mobilized students of the 1960s, were the first significant force to challenge this concept – though they still shared many ideas of the Old Left. Despite the fact that some analysts of new social movements are divided over the question whether the New Left was really the first new social movement, rather than an intermediary between these and the previous progressive movements, there are hardly any doubts that the student revolt marked a breakthrough in West Germany's political culture, and thus, opened a breach which could be widened and filled by the ensuing movements.

While the student movement quickly lost momentum and soon broke apart, the following major movements proved to be relatively stable despite some periods of internal crisis and a temporary decline of their activities. Since the early 1970s, West Germany experienced the rise of several movements centered around social and urban problems, gender roles and feminism, nuclear power, environmental issues, youth protests, and military strategy and disarmament. Broadly speaking, these protest activities were based on two major ideological currents. While the first strand was an emancipatory, offensive current full of hopes and expectations, the second strand was more defensive and pessimistic, focusing on the negative side-effects of continuous modernization and economic growth. These currents merged together over the years and formed a highly active and politicized movement sector with considerable overlaps by the end of the 1970s without losing its political and organizational heterogeneity.

Today, this movement sector has lost its radicality and capacity to challenge the elites in power to a great extent. There is, however, hardly a sign that this sector has become weaker in terms of protest activities and organizational strength. On the contrary, indications from ongoing research suggest that protest activities have significantly increased in the 1980s.

(2) *Social structure*: According to most of the studies, younger, well educated people from the »new middle class« are strongly over-represented in the new social movements. Particularly high is the percentage of professionals and employees from the human service sector. This tendency seems to be weaker the more one moves from core activists to mere contributors or sympathizers. Although women are still under-represented among the social movement's activists, we have indicators that their percentage is higher in the movements compared to their percentage in parties and interest groups.

(3) *Political orientation*: Depending on the concerns of the various movements, people from a very broad political spectrum can be found as adherents of the new social movements. There are some issues, such as environmental pollution or low-flying military planes, where activists from all political positions joined movement organizations and protest activities. For the majority of the other movements, however, like those focusing on women's liberation, nuclear energy, alternative economy and peace, most of the adherents lean toward to the political Left, ranging from social democrats to radical communists and the so-called »autonomous groups«, whose ideas are

close to anarchism. Surveys have shown that left-postmaterialists are heavily over-represented among those who strongly approve the major new social movements (Müller-Rommel, 1985; Pappi, 1989, Fuchs and Rucht, 1990).

While the late 1970s were marked by relatively strong »antisystemic« attitudes and, in consequence, a sharp division between challengers and the establishment, this polarized constellation has become blurred during the 1980s. The mainstream of the new social movements has become more pragmatic; close interaction with, and even financial support from, public authorities is widely accepted. This trend, however, has also strengthened radical tendencies at the fringe of the movements. It is obvious that a small but highly active sector of »anti-imperialist« and »autonomous« groups has emerged. These groups are prepared for disruptive and militant protest whatever the occasion, be it the conference of the World Monetary Fund hosted in Berlin, be it a major meeting of the New Right which has recently, with the rise of the »Republican Party«, become relatively strong in the electoral area.

The overall tendency toward a more pragmatic political concept is also reflected within the West German Green Party. Both the so-called fundamentalists and the more traditional left-wing groups, who still have a marxist leaning, are losing ground within the party, whereas the »realists«, favoring a close cooperation or even an alliance with the Social Democrats, are steadily getting stronger.

(4) *Organization and infrastructure*: A characteristic of the overall organizational structure of the new social movement sector is its heterogeneous and decentralized nature. Bureaucratic organizational forms are usually rejected for ideological reasons. Despite this prevailing »anti-institutional attitude, it cannot be denied that more conventional structures, e.g. national associations based on individual membership, are becoming increasingly important. There is, however, no movement in which single organizations could attain hegemonic positions.[10] The women's movement and the alternative movement, based to a large extent on grassroots groups, appear to have the greatest degree of organizational decentralization whereas the environmental movement ranges on the other side the scale.

---

10 The new peace movement in the 1980s was a special case. Many of its activities were directed by a national coordinating comittee composed of a broad spectrum of various organizations and more diffuse networks (Leif, 1987; 1990). This comittee was heavily dependent on the support of grass-roots groups, however.

As already mentioned above, there are large overlaps between the adherents of various movements. According to surveys, a considerable share of those interviewed belonged to two or more movements. This tendency is also reflected in the willingness of different movement organizations to ally for common campaigns and protest activities. Support for these close links between various strands within and between movements can be also found on the local level where »alternative milieus« have been formed over the years. These milieus are based mainly on personal relations, similar lifestyles and cultural codes, and a common political background. Particularly in the late 1970s, some observers saw the rise of a »Zweite Kultur« (second culture) with regard to these alternative milieus whereas others discussed the danger of forming – willingly or not – a type of ghetto.

In addition to the existing organizational infrastructure of each specific movement a more general infrastructure has been formed. It ranges from local up to the national levels, including self-run restaurants, political clubs, youth centers, kindergardens, co-operatives, but also, more complex institutions such as publishing houses, research institutes, an »alternative« bank and a left-libertarian daily newspaper. Of course, many elements of the Green Party can also be considered as parts of this general infrastructure.

The establishment of movement milieus, and their corresponding infrastructural institutes including the »alternative« press (Stamm, 1988) may also explain their broad, and sometimes surprisingly successful mobilizations even in regard to issues and areas where no particular movement had previously existed. For example, the national census carried out in 1987 provoked considerable resistance among activists of the new social movements.

(5) *Strategies and forms of action*: Corresponding to the broad ideological spectrum of the new social movements, a reliance on very different strategies and forms of action can also be observed. Looking only at the media coverage one could be mislead because it often over-emphasizes large and/or radical actions which make good headlines in the mass media. Most of the activities are less spectacular, however, coming closer to the conventional action repertoire of interest group politics, e.g. collecting signatures, distributing leaflets, organizing hearings, contacting political representatives, etc.

In regard to the use of strategies and action forms over time, there were several periods in which the more radical forms of action peaked. Although we do not yet have thorough quantitative analyses, these periods of high conflict intensity appear to have been marked by the height of the student rebellion of 1967/68, the antinuclear protests of 1976-78 and 1985/86, and the youth protests and the squatter movements of 1980-83). It was primarily in such periods that elements of these respective movements clashed violently with the police. The new peace movement, which had its boom between 1982 and 1984, brought the country's largest mass mobilization, but – given the movement's central aim of peaceful co-existence – without violence. Many participants in this movement, however, sympathized with or even participated in various acts of civil disobedience which previously had been only used by small minorities. Among these were not only radical leftist but also Christian groupings.

In addition to the peace movement, which was able to mobilize up to one million people in the country's largest mass demonstrations and to collect five million signatures against the deployment of cruise missiles, various other movements also had a considerable mobilization capacity. This was not only true for the anti-nuclear power movement, but also, for movements focussing on less spectacular issues. For example, the local movement against the extension of the Frankfurt airport was able to attract more than 100,000 participants in a mass demonstration in 1981.

(6) *Impacts and outcomes*: Except for some case studies, the societal and political impacts of the new social movements have not yet been studied systematically. Once again, we end up with a very differentiated picture. In regard to specific conflicts, e.g. struggles against large-scale industrial projects or critical political decisions, there have been a few outstanding successes of protest groups, and certainly, a much larger share of defeats. In the great majority of cases, however, I believe we would find at least partial successes. Similarly, a closer look at the impact of the new social movements on various policies would probably reveal an uneven balance, ranging from partial successes to only marginal influence. With a few exceptions, no significant procedural gains could be made, e.g. extending the possibilities for citizen participation in government. The long-term effects of institutional bodies which have been created in public administration due to the pressure of protest groups (e.g., agencies for women's rights) cannot yet be adequately measured. These bodies may in part be purely symbolic, but they may also have considerable aggregate effects through a variety of minor changes.

Both established politics and protest movements have lost much of their mutual antipathy since the early 1980s. On the local level in particular, many groups and organizations now play mediating roles, thus weakening the prejudices on both sides and contributing to forms of cooperation which, at least in some areas, would have been impossible before the 1980s.

In trying to assess the impact of movement activities on policy styles, political conflict management, values and the political culture in general, one can only speculate as so many intervening variables come into play. I would argue, however, that the new social movements did have a tremendous effect in »opening« and »normalizing« a West German political culture hitherto characterized by a wishful desire for harmony and an antidemocratic authoritarian heritage.

IV. Institutional Aspects of Social Movement Research

Many of those who began the study of new social movements in West Germany already had practical experience in the movements. These observers were predominantly young and barely established in the social sciences. Usually they had no institutional backing and pursued their movement studies in addition to their primary duties at universities or elsewhere. Partly due to this weak institutional basis, partly also because of their proximity to the objects they were studying, these scientists organized themselves in fashions similar to these movements, forming loose, decentralized networks based on personal relationships and informal communication. This was, and still is, also true for the national study group on new social movements. It was established in the fall of 1983 as a discussion circle which developed a loose affiliation to the political sociology section of the German Society of Political Sciences (DVPW). Since its formation, the study group organized two or three meetings per year, each attended by 30 to 40 social scientists, who ranged from graduate students to more experienced researchers. A small newsletter initially served the purposes of internal communications. Early in 1988, due to the initiative of some members, this very provisional newsletter was transformed into a regular journal appearing quarterly (»Forschungsjournal Neue Soziale Bewegungen«). This journal focusses exclusively on the study of new social movements. In the meantime, it has become an attractive forum for students of social movements in the German-speaking countries. Although the journal's explicit aim is to mediate between movements' activists and researchers, it serves mainly the latter group and is becoming more and more professional.

In the early 1980s, the study of new social movements was dominated by political scientists although they were not very well equipped with the appropriate theories and analytical frameworks for this task. After some delay, sociologists also looked toward this new area. They usually had better conceptual tools and dealt with the phenomena in a more systematic manner, focussing also on concepts of social movements in general. After considerable progress in this field of study, the differences between these two disciplines no longer play a major role.

Contacts with researchers from other European countries and the USA were established starting in the middle of the 1980s. The international state of the art was gradually incorporated into the West German debate on social movements. International exchanges have also intensified. Indicators for this trend are several international workshops and publications in which German researchers took part (Klandermans, Kriesi and Tarrow, 1988; Klandermans, 1989; Dalton and Küchler, 1990).

Another sign of the growing professionalization and institutionalization of this field is the initiation of several ambitious research projects conducted by individuals or teams of social scientists. Worth mentioning are projects on the relationship between socio-structural changes and social movements (Oertzen, Vester et al. in Hannover – cf. Geiling and Vester, 1990), the development of local movement milieus since the mid-sixties (Roth et al., Berlin) and a historical and cross-national comparison of middle class radicalism (Brand, 1989). Another indicator of the growing institutionalization of social movement research is the establishment of a research unit on »The Public Sphere and the Social Movement«, headed by Friedhelm Neidhardt, at the Science Center Berlin for Social Research (WZB). Since its formation in 1988/89, this research team has initiated a series of projects. Among these are a study of the relationship between movement activities and public opinion, an analysis of protest events since the foundation of the Federal Republic (Rucht and Ohlemacher, 1990) and studies on social movements in a cross-national perspective.

V. Debates and Open Questions

As can be seen from the discussion above, the study of social movements is a vigorous but still very recent field of research in West Germany. Given this situation, it is no wonder that both the theory and the methodology in this field are not yet very sophisticated. Only in the last few years could social scientists from West Germany catch up with the state of the art in the international community.

Since most of the work done on various social movements was and still is mainly descriptive, and theories were only proposed in a tentative manner, few controversies have arisen among the students of social movements. Another consequence of the brief existence of this field is that social scientists have raised many more questions than they have been able to answer through systematic research.

The first significant criticism on the dominant approach to new social movements was made by Richard Stöss (1984), a researcher specializing in political parties. His criticism dealt mainly with the category »new social movements«. This concept appeared highly unclear to him as it was used in many ways and because various writers identified very different single movements which they attributed to the complex of new social movements. Stöss provocatively took the position that new social movements were more a myth than reality. This critique was, however, more epistemological than substantial. Nevertheless, it fueled the still ongoing discussion on the question of what is »new« in the new social movements, a debate which had already begun in the early 1980s (Eder, 1982). Surprisingly enough, Stöss appears to have reconciled himself with the concept in so far as he has started to use it without raising his former objections (Stöss, 1987).

Another critique of the mainstream of the new social movement approach came from certain feminist writers (e.g., Kontos, 1986; Clemens, 1989). They did not question the usefulness of this approach in general, but its tendency to subsume the women's movement – which they perceived to be a very special case – under this broad label. In particular, these critics attacked (male) proponents of the new social movement approach for ignoring the key category of partriarchy which was neglected in the prevailing explanations for the rise of new social movements. Other feminist writers (e.g., Metz-Göckel, 1987) admit that the women's movement shares at least some common features with movements such as the environmental and peace movements. Still other women researchers, outspoken feminists and more moderate social scientists, do not have any problems at all in interpreting the women's movement as a constitutive part of the broader sector of new social movements (e.g., Knafla and Kuhlke, 1987; Rubart, 1987).

A third challenge to the new social movement approach came from Michael Greven (1988), a left-wing political theorist. He, too, questioned the appropriateness of the category of new social movements, arguing that it is unclear, and that so little empirical evidence has been offered thus far to demonstrate the common features of the various movements under discussion or to distinguish between the old and new social movements. Moreover, he criticized the high degree of specialization shown by some social movement researchers, their sympathetic attitude toward their research objects, and their tendency to idealize the movement's internal structure which, according to Greven, was not as democratic as many would assume. This attack, published in the newly established »Forschungsjournal Neue Soziale Bewegungen«, provoked responses in the next issue of the journal (Brand, 1989a; Roth and Rucht, 1989). The respondents argued that only some of the points made by Greven were acceptable and that most of these had – ironically – already been explicitly discussed by those researchers who Greven intended to criticize. Other counter-arguments referred to Greven's highly selective reading and the inappropriateness of some of the criteria he used in his critique. After this first round of discussion, the debate was picked up by other social scientists in the subsequent issues of the journal. It seems that the focus of the debate is now shifting from methodological and conceptual questions of the new social movement approach to their role in West Germany's political culture and problems of the civil society in general.

Still another challenge to the new social movement approach is a more theoretical one. Some social scientists have begun to treat the topic of (new) social movements on the basis of functionalist systems theory, drawing in particular on the work of Niklas Luhmann (Bergmann, 1987; Ahlemeier, 1989). It is clear that social movements would by no means be conceived as social actors with a capacity to influence the course of history from such a perspective. Luhmann (1986) himself has a tendency to perceive contemporary social movements only as dysfunctional and anachronistic elements in a highly differentiated modern society. According to him, they mainly produce »noise« and, at least, have a certain capacity to indicate problems, but are far from understanding how society works. A closer reading of Luhmann's statements reveals that there may not only be theoretical arguments, but also personal sentiments, coming into play here. This is not the case for Ahlemeier (1989), who strongly adheres to Luhmann's general approach nevertheless. The theoretical debate advanced by this approach has been largely implicit up to now. Proponents of the new social movement approach, in particular those closer to an actor-centered perspective, have not yet reacted to the functionalist challenge. A reason for this silence is probably the fact that these first functionalist writings on social movements have been highly abstract, containing virtually no empirical evidence, whereas most of the other researchers are not so interested in a type of general theory which, as many would argue, is schematically applied to virtually all social phenomena without consequences for empirically oriented research.

Turning finally to open questions in the field of social movements, it is quite clear that the variety and richness of contemporary movements in West Germany could not adequately be grasped by observers of limited experience and poorly equipped both conceptually and institutionally. Therefore, much of the work which has been done in this field is closer to investigative journalism than social research.

Though we have some knowledge regarding the »surface« of the new social movements, i.e. their ideologies, their main organizations, the basic characteristics of their adherents, their major protest campaigns, etc., we still lack in-depth information on all these aspects (Nullmeier and Raschke, 1989, 250). For instance, little work has been done on processes of micro-mobilization. Moreover, our knowledge of both micro and macro aspects of various movements is very unbalanced. Little is known, e.g., about the organizional structure of the women's movement, the so-called autonomous groups and the more culturally oriented movements. This is, of course, partly a result of the fact that it is more difficult for researchers to get access to these groupings. In addition, the interaction within and between various movements, including the dynamics of movements and counter-movements, has rarely been studied in detail. Moreover, there is a significant lack of cross-sectional, cross-national and long-term comparisons of social movements. Such studies would be particularly helpful in clarifying the specific features of the new social movements and providing a broader empirical basis for general theories of social movements in modern societies. Finally, we have only scant knowledge of the political and societal impact of these movements on different levels.

It is likely that the study of (new) social movements in West Germany will continue to attract many researchers in the near future. First, many academics, among them also social scientists, participate in social movements. It is this group, in particular, which is sustaining a continuous process of self-monitoring within the movements. Second, former activists, now rooted in the academic field, are continuing to analyze the movements using both earlier insight and gradually improved conceptual tools. In part, these researchers have maintained their ambition of not only being close observers of the movements, but also, intervening in their discourse. Together, groups of both current and former movement members are forming the type of »reserve army« mentioned by Klandermans and Tarrow (1988, 16) which will keep the study of social movements alive. Third, a group of »pure« academics, originally closer to such fields of study as social change, party politics, interest mediation, political participation, etc., has become increasingly interested in the study of (new) social movements. This shift of attention also has to do with the continuing vitality of the movements themselves insofar as they were formerly considered to be only a short-lived transitory phenomenon. In addition, the recent outbreak of oppositional movements in Eastern Europe, including the GDR, has also led researchers in both German states to analyze these phenomena. First attempts at networking individuals engaged in ongoing and planned research have been already been initiated, and will probably intensified, in the near future.

Taking all these aspects into consideration, there is a high probability that the study of social movements in Germany, which was first neglected for many decades and became only relevant in the 1980s, will continue to flourish. Hence, the field of social movements, which was an important one in the heyday of classical sociology, is likely to regain its relevance and become a constitutive element of political sociology. At present, it seems that most analysts in this field are still more concerned with political activism at the expense of social science which, of course, does not exclude political engagement. There are indications, however, that social movement research in Germany will move toward a better balance between activism and professionalism.

Annotated Bibliography

Ahlemeier, H.W. (1989): »Was ist eine soziale Bewegung? Zur Distinktion und Einheit eines sozialen Phänomens«, *Zeitschrift für Soziologie* 18 (3): 175-191.

Theoretically oriented essay from a functionalist perspective influenced by Niklas Luhmann.

Allerbeck, K. (1973): *Soziologie radikaler Studentenbewegungen*. München/Wien: Juventa.

Backes, U.; Jesse, E. (1989): *Politischer Extremismus in der Bundesrepublik Deutschland*, 3 Vols., Köln: Wissenschaft und Politik.

A comprehensive work on both left and right extremism including a broad overview and discussion of the literature in this field (Vol. 1), an analysis (Vol. 2) and a colletcion of documents (Vol. 3).

Barnes, S.H.; Kaase, M. et al. (1979): *Political Action. Mass Participation in Five Nations.* Beverly Hills, Ca.: Sage Publications.

Bauß, G. (1977): *Die Studentenbewegung der sechziger Jahre in der Bundesrepublik und Westberlin.* Köln: Pahl-Rugenstein.

Bergmann, W. (1987): »Was bewegt die soziale Bewegung? Überlegungen zur Selbstkonstitution der ›neuen‹ sozialen Bewegungen«, in: D. Baecker (ed.), *Theorie als Passion.* Frankfurt: Suhrkamp, 262-393.

Beyme, K. von (1986): Neue soziale Bewegungen und politische Parteien. *Aus Politik und Zeitgeschichte,* (No. 44): 30-39.

Brand, K.-W. (1982): *Neue soziale Bewegungen, Entstehung, Funktion und Perspektive neuer Protestpotentiale. Eine Zwischenbilanz.* Opladen: Westdeutscher Verlag.

Discusses a broad range of approaches for the explanation and interpretation of the new social movements, among them linear and cyclical approaches. The latter are categorized in »need-defence« and »rising-demand« approaches.

– (1989): ›Neue soziale Bewegungen‹ – Katalysatoren der Postmoderne? Unpublished manuscript, München.

– (1989a): »›Bewegungswissenschaft‹ oder Bewegungsforschung? – Einige ›ganz unironische‹ Anmerkungen zu Michael Th. Grevens Beitrag«, in: *Forschungsjournal Neue Soziale Bewegungen* 2 (1):50-53.

– (ed.) (1985): *Neue Soziale Bewegungen in Westeuropa und den USA. Ein internationaler Vergleich.* Frankfurt: Campus.

Collection of essays on the development of the new social movements in various countries (West Germany, France, Great Britain, Sweden and the USA) and a comparative final chapter focusing on opportunity structures for social movements.

Brand, K.-W.; Büsser, D.; Rucht, D. (1983): *Aufbruch in eine andere Gesellschaft. Neue soziale Bewegungen in der Bundesrepublik.* (Third and revised edition 1986) Frankfurt: Campus.

The first comprehensive descriptive study on the new social movements and their predecessors in the 1950s and 1960s in West Germany.

Bundesminister des Innern (Hrsg.). (1981-84): *Analysen zum Terrorismus.* 4 Vols. Opladen: Westdeutscher Verlag.

Clemens, B. (1989): »Der ›männliche‹ Blick auf die Frauenbewegung«, *Neue Gesellschaft/Frankfurter Hefte* 36 (3): 249-258.

Conti, Ch. (1984): *Abschied vom Bürgertum. Alternative Bewegungen in Deutschland von 1980 bis heute.* Reinbek: Rowohlt.

Dalton, R.J.; Küchler, M. (eds.). (1990): *Challenging the Political Order.* Cambridge: Polity Press.

Dudek, P.; Jaschke, H.-G. (1984): *Entstehung und Entwicklung des Rechtsextremismus in der Bundesrepublik,* 3 Vols., Opladen: Westdeutscher Verlag.

Eder, K. (1982): »A New Social Movement?«, *Telos* 52 (Summer), 5-20.

– (1983): »Was ist neu in den neuen sozialen Bewegungen?«, in: Matthes, J. (ed.), *Krise der Arbeitsgesellschaft*? 21. Deutscher Soziologentag 1982, Frankfurt: Campus, 401-411.

– (1986): »Soziale Bewegungen und kulturelle Evolution«, in: Berger, J. (ed.), *Die Moderne. Kontinuitäten und Zäsuren*. (Soziale Welt, Sonderband 4), Göttingen: Schwartz, 335-357.

– (1989): »Die ›Neuen Sozialen Bewegungen‹; Moralische Kreuzzüge, politische Pressure Groups oder soziale Bewegung?« in: Wasmuht, U. (ed.), *Alternativen zur alten Politik? Neue soziale Bewegungen in der Diskussion*, Darmstadt: Wissenschaftliche Buchgesellschaft, 177-195.

Evers A.; Szankay, Z. (1981): »Das gerissene Band – Überlegungen zum neueren Verhältnis von sozialem Wissen und sozialen Bewegungen«, *Prokla* 11 (43):43-59.

Falter, J.W.; Fenner, C.; Greven, M.Th. (eds.), (1984): *Politische Willensbildung und Interessenvermittlung*. Opladen: Westdeutscher Verlag.

Feit, M. (1987): *Die ›Neue Rechte‹ in der Bundesrepublik, Organisation – Ideologie – Strategie*. Frankfurt: Campus.

Fogt, H. (1982): *Politische Generationen*. Opladen: Westdeutscher Verlag.

Fuchs, D. (1990): »The Normalization of the Unconventional. Forms of Political Action and New Social Movements«, Discussion Paper FS III 90-203. Wissenschaftszentrum Berlin.

Fuchs, D.; Rucht, D. (1990): *Support for New Social Movements in Five Western European Countries*. Paper presented for the ESF/ESCR-Conference on Political Participation in Europe. Manchester, January 5-8.

Geiling, H.; Vester, M. (1990): »Die Spitze eines gesellschaftlichen Eisbergs: Sozialstrukturwandel und neue soziale Milieus«, in: Roth, R.; Rucht, D. (eds.), *Neue Soziale Bewegungen in der Bundesrepublik Deutschland*. Enlarged and updated edition. Bonn, Bundeszentrale für politische Bildung (forthcoming).

Gerdes, D. (1984): »›Verhalten‹ oder ›Handeln‹? Thesen zur sozialwissenschaftlichen Analyse sozialer Bewegungen«, in: Falter, J.W.; Fenner, C.; Greven, M.Th. (eds.), *Politische Willensbildung und Interessenvermittlung*. Opladen: Westdeutscher Verlag, 645-654.

– (1985): *Regionalismus als soziale Bewegung. Westeuropa, Frankreich, Korsika: Vom Vergleich zur Kontextanalyse*. Frankfurt: Campus Verlag.
Study on regionalist movements from an phenomenologist viewpoint with special attention to the Corsican movement.

Greven, M.Th. (1988): »Zur Kritik der Bewegungswissenschaft«, *Forschungsjournal Neue Soziale Bewegungen* 1 (4):51-60.
A critique of the present state of research on new social movements in West Germany, focusing on the category of new social movements, the closeness of researchers to their objects, and the lack of empirical data, e.g., on the internal structure of these movements.

Grottian, P.; Nelles, W. (eds.) (1983): *Großstadt und neue soziale Bewegungen*. Basel: Birkhäuser.
A reader on new social movements in the urban context, mainly based on papers presented on a conference of political scientist held in 1981. This reader reflects the early discussion on new social movements in West Germany.

Habermas, J. (1981): *Theorie des kommunikativen Handelns.* 2 Vols. Frankfurt: Suhrkamp.
Major theoretical work with brief discussion of the emergence of new protest potentials as reactions to the »colonization of life world«.

Halfmann, J. (1984): »Soziale Bewegungen und Staat. Nichtintendierte Folgen neokorporatistischer Politik«, *Soziale Welt* 35 (3):294-312.

Hartwich, H.-H. (ed.) (1983): *Gesellschaftliche Probleme als Anstoß und Folge von Politik.* Opladen: Westdeutscher Verlag.

Heberle, R. (1951): *Social Movements. An Introduction to Political Sociology.* New York: Appleton-Century-Crofts.

Heinz, W.R.; Schöber, P. (1973): *Theorien des kollektiven Verhaltens.* 2 Vols., Darmstadt und Neuwied: Luchterhand.
Collection of essays on collective behavior based almost exclusively on Anglo-American contributions.

Hess, H. et al. (1988): *Angriff auf das Herz des Staates. Soziale Entwicklung und Terrorismus.* 2 Vols. Frankfurt: Suhrkamp.

Hirsch, J. (1980): *Der Sicherheitsstaat. Das ›Modell Deutschland‹, seine Kosten und die neuen sozialen Bewegungen.* Hamburg: VSA.

Hirsch, J.; Roth R. (1986): *Das neue Gesicht des Kapitalismus. Vom Fordismus zum Post-Fordismus.* Hamburg: VSA.
General discussion of the emergence of a new societal mode of production and regulation, the so-called »post-fordism«, which, among other things, is characterized by new types of social movements.

Hollstein, W. (1979): *Die Gegengesellschaft. Alternative Lebensformen.* Bonn: Neue Gesellschaft.

Huber, J. (1988): »Soziale Bewegungen«, *Zeitschrift für Soziologie* 17 (6): 424-435.

Infratest Wirtschaftsforschung GmbH (1989): *Politscher Protest in der Bundesrepublik Deutschland.* Stuttgart: Kohlhammer.

Inglehart, R. (1989): *Cultural Change.* Princeton, N.J.: Princeton University Press.

Japp, K.P. (1984): »Selbsterzeugung oder Fremdverschulden. Thesen zum Rationalismus in den Theorien sozialer Bewegungen«, *Soziale Welt* 35 (3): 313-329.

Kaase, M. (1982): »Partizipatorische Revolution – Ende der Parteien?« in: Raschke, J. (ed.), *Bürger und Parteien.* Opladen: Westdeutscher Verlag, 173-189.

Klages, H. (1980): *Überlasteter Staat – Verdrossene Bürger? Zu den Dissonanzen der Wohlfahrtsgesellschaft.* Frankfurt: Campus.
Interpretation of the growing dissatisfaction and protest of citizens as a result of an inherent tendency of modern welfare states to rise expectations without disposing on adequate means to fulfill these hopes.

Klandermans, B.; Tarrow, S. (1988): »Mobilization into Social Movements: Synthesizing European and American Approaches«, in: Klandermans, B.; Kriesi, H.; Tarrow, S. (ed.). *Organizing for Change. Social Movement Organizations Across Cultures.* Greenwich, Conn.: JAI Press, 1-40.

Klandermans, B.; Kriesi, H.; Tarrow, S. (ed.) (1988): *Organizing for Change: Social Movement Organizations Across Cultures.* Greenwich, Conn.: JAI Press.

Klandermans, B. (ed.): *Organizing for Change: Social Movement Organizations Across Cultures.* (International Social Movement Research 2). Greenwich, Conn.: JAI Press.

Krechel, U. (1975): *Selbsterfahrung und Fremdbestimmung. Bericht aus der neuen Frauenbewegung*. Darmstadt und Neuwied: Luchterhand.

Kretschmer, W.; Rucht, D. (1987): »Beispiel Wackersdorf: Die Protestbewegung gegen die Wiederaufarbeitungsanlage«, in: Roth, R.; Rucht, D. (eds.), *Neue soziale Bewegungen in der Bundesrepublik Deutschland*. Frankfurt: Campus, 134-163.

Kontos, S. (1986): »Modernisierung der Subsumtionspolitik. Die Frauenbewegung in den Theorien neuer sozialer Bewegungen«, *Feministische Studien* 5 (2):34-49.

A critique of male new social movement theorists which subsume the women's movement under a more general concept without acknowledging the specificities of the women's movement and the centrality of patriarchy as an analytical category.

Langguth, Gerd (1983): *Protestbewegung. Entwicklung, Niedergang. Renaissance. Die neue Linke seit 1968*. Köln: Verlag Wissenschaft und Politik.

Detailed documentation of protest organizations of the New Left after 1968 with special attention to radical communist groups. An earlier version of this book was published in 1976 under the title »Die Protestbewegung in der Bundesrepublik Deutschland 1968-1976« (Köln: Verlag Wissenschaft und Politik).

Leif, Th. (1985): *Die professionelle Bewegung. Friedensbewegung von innen*. Bonn: Forum Europa Verlag.

– (1990): *Die strategische (Ohn-)macht der Friedensbewegung. Kommunikations- und Entscheidungsstrukturen in den achtziger Jahren*. Opladen: Westdeutscher Verlag.

Detailed empirical study of the strategy and organizational background of the national steering committee of the West German peace movement between 1982-1985.

Liebert, U. (1986): *Neue Autonomiebewegung und Dezentralisierung in Spanien. Der Fall Andalusien*. Frankfurt: Campus.

Linse, U. (1986): *Ökopax und Anarchie. Die Geschichte der ökologischen Bewegung in Deutschland*. München: dtv.

Short history of the development of German environmental movements past the late 19th century.

Luhmann, N. (1986): *Ökologische Kommunikation*. Opladen: Westdeutscher Verlag.

Mayer, M. (1985): »Urban Social Movements and Beyond: New Linkages Between Movement Sectors and the State in West Germany and the United States«, Paper delivered at the Fifth International Conference of Europeanists, Washington, D.C., October 18-20, 1985.

Mayer-Tasch, P.C. (1976): *Die Bürgerinitiativbewegung. Der aktive Bürger als rechts- und politikwissenschaftliches Problem*. Reinbek: Rowohlt.

Wide-spread book on the phenomenon of the citizen initiatives which are considered to form a social movement. This category, however, is not discussed in terms of social movement research.

Metz-Göckel, S. (1987): »Die zwei (un)geliebten Schwestern. Zum Verhältnis von Frauenbewegung und Frauenforschung im Diskurs der neuen sozialen Bewegungen«, in: Beer, U. (ed.), *Klasse Geschlecht. Feministische Gesellschaftsanalyse und Wissenschaftskritik*. Bielefeld: AJZ, 25-57.

Müller-Rommel, F. (1985): »Social Movements and the Greens: New Internal Politics in Germany«, *European Journal of Political Research* 13 (1):53-67.

Nedelmann, B. (1984): »New Political Movements and Changes in Processes of Interest Mediation«, *Social Science Information* 23 (6):1029-1048.

Neidhardt, F. (1985): »Einige Ideen zu einer allgemeinen Theorie sozialer Bewegungen«, in: Hradil, S. (ed.), *Sozialstruktur im Umbruch*. Opladen: Leske + Budrich, 193-204.
Essay promoting the idea that social movements should be perceived as »mobilized networks of networks«.

Nelles, W. (1983): »Neue soziale Bewegungen und alte Politik«, in Grottian, P.; Nelles, W. (eds.), *Großstadt und neue soziale Bewegungen*. Basel: Birkhäuser, 83-100.

– (1984): »Kollektive Identität und politisches Handeln in Neuen Sozialen Bewegungen«, *Politische Vierteljahresschrift* 24 (4):425-440.

Nullmeier, F. (1989): »Institutionelle Innovationen und neue soziale Bewegungen«, *Aus Politik und Zeitgeschichte*, No. 29:3-16.

Nullmeier, F.; Raschke, J. (1989): »Soziale Bewegungen«, in Bandemer S. von; Wewer, G. (eds.), *Regierungssystem und Regierungslehre*. Opladen: Leske + Budrich, 249-272.
Condensed overview on the literature on social movements with special emphasis to political science.

Offe, C. (1985): »New Social Movements: Challenging the Boundaries of Institutional Politics«, *Social Research* 52 (4), 817-868.

– (1990): »Reflections on the Institutional Self-Transformation of Movement Politics: A Tentative Stage Model«, in Dalton, R. and Kückler, M. (eds.), *Challenging the Political Order. New Social and Political Movements in Western Democracies*. Cambridge: Polity Press, 232-250.

Opp, K.D. et al (1984): *Soziale Probleme und Protestverhalten*. Opladen: Westdeutscher Verlag.
Study based on a survey of supporters of the antinuclear power movement in two West German cities. According to the authors the data confirm a rational choice model of participation in social movements.

Opp, K.D. (1988): »Community integration and incentives for political protest«, in: Klandermans, B.; Kriesi, H.; Tarrow, S. (eds.), *From Structure to Action: Social movement Research Across Cultures*, Greenwich, Conn.: JAI Press, 83-101.

Otto, K.A. (1977): *Vom Ostermarsch zur APO. Geschichte der außerparlamentarischen Opposition in der Bundesrepublik 1960-1970*. Frankfurt: Campus.
A insightful history of the development of the extraparliamentary opposition in the 1960s focusing mainly on the peace movement and the leftist groupings which preceeded the student movement.

Pankoke, E. (1970): *Sociale Bewegung – Sociale Frage – Sociale Politik. Grundfragen der deutschen »Sozialwissenschaft« im 19. Jahrhundert*. Stuttgart: Ernst Klett.

Pappi, F.U. (1989): »Die Anhänger der neuen sozialen Bewegungen im Parteiensystem der Bundesrepublik«, *Aus Politik und Zeitgeschichte*, No. 26: 17-27.

Rammstedt, O. (1978): *Soziale Bewegung*. Frankfurt a.M., Suhrkamp.
Important essay on social movements in general, including an epistemologically oriented discussion of the category of social movements and the presentation of an idealtypical life-cycle model of social movements.

– (1989): »Zur Theorie der Friedensbewegung als sozialer Bewegung«, in: Wasmuht, U. (ed.), *Alternativen zur alten Politik? Neue soziale Bewegungen in der Diskussion.* Darmstadt: Wissenschaftliche Buchgesellschaft, 140-158.

Raschke, J. (1980): »Politik und Wertwandel in der westlichen Demokratie«, *Aus Politik und Zeitgeschichte*, No. 36: 23-45.

– (1985): *Soziale Bewegungen. Ein historisch-systematischer Grundriß*, Frankfurt: Campus.

A voluminous and authoritative study of social movements, dealing with a range of systematic aspects. This book also discusses various historical movements in Germany. In a historical perspective, a basic distinction is made between preindustrial, industrial and postindustrial (= new) social movements. In systematic terms, the author distinguishes between politically and culturally oriented movements.

Rau, W. (1985): *Konservativer Widerstand und soziale Bewegung.* Frankfurt: Peter Lang.

Roth, R. (1982): »Trendbericht Neue Soziale Bewegungen«, *Literatur Rundschau* 7 (7):79-94.

– (1983): »Gesellschaftstheoretische Konzepte zur Analyse neuer sozialer Bewegungen«, *Politische Viertejahresschrift* 24 (3):311-328.

– »Neue soziale Bewegungen in der politischen Kultur der Bundesrepublik – eine vorläufige Skizze«, in: Brand, K.-W. (ed.), *Neue soziale Bewegungen in Westeuropa und in den USA.* Frankfurt: Campus.

Comprehensive essay on new social movements in West Germany.

– (1987): »Kommunikationsstrukturen und Vernetzungen in neuen sozialen Bewegungen«, in: Roth, R.; Rucht, D. (eds.), *Neue soziale Bewegungen in der Bundesrepublik Deutschland*: Frankfurt: Campus, 68-88.

– (1989): »Neue Soziale Bewegungen als politische Institution: Anregungen für einen theoretischen Perspektivenwechsel«, *Forschungsjournal Neue soziale Bewegungen* 2 (special issue):33-51.

The thesis of this article is that the new social movements, though their policy impact may be modest, have been successful in so far as they have become a quasi-institution in West German political culture.

– »Fordismus und neue soziale Bewegungen«. in: Wasmuht, U. (ed.), *Alternativen zur alten Politik? Neue soziale Bewegungen in der Diskussion.* Darmstadt: Wissenschaftliche Buchgesellschaft, 13-37.

Roth, R.; Rucht, D. (1989): »Reaktionen aus dem Ghetto – Anmerkungen zu Michael Th. Grevens ›Kritik der Bewegungswissenschaft‹«, *Forschungsjournal Neue Soziale Bewegungen* 2 (1): 44-49.

– (1990): »Wohin treiben die neuen sozialen Bewegungen?« in: *Neue soziale Bewegungen in der Bundesrepublik Deutschland.* Bonn: Bundeszentrale für politische Bildung (forthcoming).

– (eds.) (1987): *Neue soziale Bewegungen in der Bundesrepublik Deutschland.* Frankfurt: Campus

Widespread collection of essays focussed on particular movements or conflicts and on more systematic aspects of new social movements in West Germany.

Rothgang, H. (1990): *Die Friedens- und Umweltbewegung in Großbritannien.* Leverkusen: Deutscher Universitätsverlag.

Rubart, F. (1987): Women in new social movements – Womens' Lib as a new social movement. Paper prepared for ECPR Joint Sessions of Workshops, Amsterdam 10-15 April 1987.

Rucht, D. (1982): »Neue soziale Bewegungen oder: Die Grenzen bürokratischer Modernisierung«, in: Hesse, J. J. (ed.), *Politikwissenschaft und Verwaltungswissenschaft* (Politische Vierteljahresschrift Sonderheft 13), Opladen: Westdeutscher Verlag, 272-292.

Rucht, D. (1984): »Zur Organisation der neuen sozialen Bewegungen«, in: Falter, J.W.; Fenner, C.; Greven, M.Th. (eds.), *Politische Willensbildung und Interessenvermittlung*. Opladen: Westdeutscher Verlag, 609-620.

– (1988): »Themes, Logics and Arenas of Social Movements: A Structural Approach«, in: Klandermans, B.; Kriesi, H.; Tarrow, S. (eds.), *From Structure to Action: Comparing Social Movement Research Across Cultures*. Greenwich, Conn.: JAI Press, 305-328.

– (1989): »Environmental Movement Organizations in West Germany and France: Structure and Interorganizational Relations«, in: Klandermans, B. (ed.), *Organizing for Change: Social Movement Organizations Across Cultures*. Greenwich, Conn.: JAI Press, pp. 61-94.

– (1989a): »Protestbewegungen«, in: Benz, W. (ed.), *Die Geschichte der Bundesrepublik Deutschland*. Vol. 3: Gesellschaft, Frankfurt: Fischer, 311-344.

– (1990): »The Strategies and Action Repertoire of New Movements«, in: Dalton, R.J.; Küchler, M. (eds.), *Challenging the Political Order*. Cambridge: Polity Press, 156-175.

– (1990a): »Campaigns, skirmishes and battles: antinuclear movements in the USA, France and West Germany«, *Industrial Crisis* Quarterly 4 (3): 193-222.

Rucht, D.; Ohlemacher, T. (1990): *Documentation and Analysis of Protest Events in the Federal Republic of Germany, 1949-90*. Paper presented at the European Consortium for Political Research, Joint Sessions of Workshops, Bochum 2-7 April.

Schenk, H. (1980): *Die feministische Herausforderung. 150 Jahre Frauenbewegung in Deutschland*. München: Beck.

Scherer, K.-J. (1988): *Jugend und soziale Bewegung. Zur Soziologie der bewegten Jugend in Deutschland*. Opladen: Leske + Budrich.

Schmidt, M.G. (1984): »Demokratie, Wohlfahrtsstaat und neue soziale Bewegungen«, *Aus Politik und Zeitgeschichte*, No. 11: 3-14.

Schmitt, R. (1989): Sicherheitspolitik und Friedensbewegung in der Bundesrepublik Deutschland. Unpublished manuscript, Mannheim.

Schneider, N.F. (1987): *Ewig ist nur die Veränderung. Entwurf eines analytischen Konzepts sozialer Bewegungen*. Frankfurt: Lang.

Schwendter, R. (1973): *Theorie der Subkultur*. Köln: Kiepenheuer & Witsch.

Stamm, K.-H. (1988): *Alternative Öffentlichkeit. Die Erfahrungsproduktion neuer sozialer Bewegungen*. Frankfurt/M.: Campus.

Stöss, R. (1984): »Vom Mythos der ›neuen sozialen Bewegungen‹. Neun Thesen und ein Exkurs zum Elend der NSB-Forschung«, in: Falter, J.W.; Fenner, C.; Greven, M.Th. (eds.). *Politische Willensbildung und Interessenvermittlung*. Opladen: Westdeutscher Verlag: 548-565.

Provocative essay on the debate on new social movements. The author criticizes the disparate use of the notion of new social movements.

Stöss, R. (1989): *Die extreme Rechte in der Bundesrepublik.* Opladen: Westdeutscher Verlag.

Vester, M. (1983): »Die ›Neuen Plebejer‹ – Thesen zur Klassen- und Schichtenstruktur und zu den Entwicklungsperspektiven der neuen sozialen Bewegungen«, in: Hartwich, H.-H. (ed.), *Gesellschaftliche Probleme als Anstoß und Folge von Politik.* Opladen: Westdeutscher Verlag, 213-224.

Wasmuht, U. (1987): *Friedensbewegungen der 80er Jahre. Zur Analyse ihrer strukturellen und aktuellen Entstehungsbedingungen in der Bundesrepublik Deutschland und den Vereinigten Staaten von Amerika nach 1945: Ein Vergleich.* Gießen: Focus.

– (ed.) (1989): *Alternativen zur alten Politik? Neue soziale Bewegungen in der Diskussion.* Darmstadt: Wissenschaftliche Buchgesellschaft.

Collection of theoretial and empirical essays on new social movements.

Watts, N.S.J. (1987): »Mobilisierungspotential und gesellschaftspolitsiche Bedeutung der neuen sozialen Bewegungen. Ein Vergleich der Länder der Europäischen Gemeinschaft«, in: Roth, R.; Rucht, D. (eds.), *Neue soziale Bewegungen in der Bundesrepublik Deutschland.* Frankfurt: Campus, 47-67.

ZEUS (1988): (Zentrum für Europäische Umfrageanalysen und Studien), Environment Attitude Evolution, ZEUS-Report No. 10, Universität Mannheim.

Zimmermann, E. (1989): »Political Unrest in Western Europe: Trends and Prospects«, *West European Politics* 12 (3):179-196.

Switzerland: A Marginal Field of Research in an Underdeveloped Social Science Community

Hanspeter Kriesi

I. Introduction

In Switzerland, there has been little research done on social movements in general, or on new social movements in particular. To some extent this apparent lack of research on social movements can be attributed to the specific institutions of the Swiss political system which have induced social scientists to study processes of political mobilization under somewhat different perspectives: I am referring to the *direct democratic* elements of the Swiss political system which allow for the institutionalized articulation of dissent on its different levels. The Swiss direct-democratic institutions include the (compulsory and optional) referendum and the popular initiative.[1] These imply quite different logics: while the referendum allows intervention at the end of a process of political decision-making, the initiative sets such a process in motion. While the referendum may serve as a popular veto of a decision taken by the elite, the initiative has an agenda-setting function. The referendum has become a major weapon in the hands of established interest groups. In his classic study, Neidhardt (1970) has shown how the institution of the referendum has changed and stabilized the political system of Switzerland in a rather unexpected way. It has led to the development of

1 On the national level, constitutional changes have to be submitted to a vote by the citizens (compulsory referendum). Changes in existing laws or new laws have to be submitted to such a vote if 50.000 citizens demand it (optional referendum). The initiatives provide the opportunity to propose a constitutional change via referendum. 100,000 signatures are required for an initiative. Similar provisions exist on the cantonal and local levels. For a review of the pertinent institutional arrangements on the cantonal level, see Auer (1978).

elaborate pre-parliamentary mechanisms of conflict resolution which allow for the integration of all major political forces into the system. In order to eliminate the risk of a referendum at the end of the process, the pre-parliamentary arrangements grant all political forces capable of launching successfully a referendum a voice as well as political concessions. The *popular initiative*, however, has turned out to be a favorite instrument of groups challenging from the outside of the political system as is shown by the analyses of Delley (1978), Gruner (1969), Sigg (1978), and Werder (1978). Reviewing the history of the initiatives on the national level, these authors are able to show that initiatives have served as major forums for the articulation of oppositional demands. Historically, initiatives have been launched primarily labor movement organizations to articulate their opposition. Since the early seventies, however, this instrument has increasingly been used by new social movements organizations. (NSMs) (Kriesi et al., 1981, App, 1987). Swiss social movements often develop so-called *»initiative movements«* (Epple, 1988), i.e. currents within broader movements which specialize in the use of the instrument of the initiative to articulate the demands of the broader movement. Thus, the study of initiatives can be considered as an indirect contribution to the research on Swiss social movements.

Related to the direct-democratic access to the Swiss political system are two other types of research with some relevance to the study of social movements. The first one concerns the *analysis of referenda on specific issues.* Such analyses are regularly done on the basis of representative surveys (Vox-Analysen), or by using aggregate data on the level of cantons (the Swiss provinces) and communities (Nef, 1980; Nef/Roesenmund, 1984). Although these analyses do not have any theoretical pretentions, they nevertheless provide important descriptive material concerning the development of the political cleavage-structure and the size and the kind of mobilization capacity of the different political forces (including social movements) in the country.

The other type of research at least indirectly related to the study of social movements is concerned with the determinants of *individual political participation and non-participation.* The level of individual participation in elections and referenda on specific issues has traditionally been rather low in Switzerland when compared to other European countries (Dittrich/Johansen, 1983). In the post-war period the level of participation has steadily decreased even more (Levy/Zwicky, 1984). While the initially low level of participation has at least in part been attributed to the extraordinarily high level of participation usually expected from a Swiss citizen – given the direct-democratic institutions – the steady decrease of the level of participation in elections and referenda began to pose a serious legitimacy problem for the authorities towards the end of the sixties. This triggered a considerable amount of research. As early as 1952, Girod had already analysed collective and individual causes of non-participation. A large number of studies followed in the seventies and early eighties: Ballmer-Cao (1980, 1988), Ganguillet/Kriesi (1983), Giger (1976, 1980), again Girod (1971), Girod/Ricq (1970), Schmidtchen (1980), Sidjanski et al. (1975), Tharakan (1983). The majority of these studies applied theoretical approaches from the classical American studies on political participation and used survey-type research to test their hypotheses. The aforementioned analysis of referenda also contributed to this branch of research. Although not dirctly related to the study of social movements, the question of why some people do not participate in elections and/or referenda also has some relevance for the question of why some people do not participate in mobilization processes initiated by social movements.

There are, however, studies more directly related to the mobilization of social movements. Given the comparatively small size of the Swiss social scientific community and its low degree of specialization such studies often have an isolated character. They have usually been done by social scientists who are not specialized in the field, but whose attention has been attracted to it for one reason or the other. Often, case-studies of social movements have been carried out by non-experts, such as (former) activists reflecting on their experiences, journalists or writers. Increasingly, social movements are also the subject of students' master's theses. Most of these studies are primarily descriptive; they document the movements in question without explicitly analyzing them in theoretical terms. At least five types of movements of the post-war period have been studied to some extent; the right-wing anti-foreigner's movement, the regional movements in the Jura, the so-called »youth-movements« of the end of the sixties and the beginning of the eighties, the ecology movement, and the peace movement. I will not deal here with historical studies of movements before the second world war nor with most of the work on the labor movement.[2]

2 The organizations of the labor movement have, of course, also been studied, but insofar as this has been the case, it was most often not their movement-character which was at issue. An exception is the documentation of the Arbeitsgruppe (1989), which gives an overview of the history of the Swiss labor movement up to the present. The last chapter

II. An Overview of the Studies of Different Movements

The *anti-foreigner's movement*, the most important Swiss movement in the sixties, has tried to restrict the number of foreigners in Switzerland: The research of Windisch (1978, 1978a, 1981) and his colleagues, using an approach reminiscent of that employed by ethnomethodologists, attempts to identify the basic dimensions and mechanisms of reasoning of those mobilized for or against this movement. More recently, Saint-Ouen (1986) has discussed the vicissitudes of the movement's Genevan branch. Given its importance, it comes as a surprise to the reviewer that very few studies have concerned this movement.[3]

A considerable amount of work has, however, been done on the *regional movements in the Jura*. The ethno-regional conflict in the Swiss Jura has been exceptional not only because of its long duration, but also because of the unusual level of violence it has caused: In the Jura, a separatist movement has clashed with an anti-separatist counter-movement. Among the more important recent contributions to this field of study, Harder (1978), Henecka (1972), Prongué et al. (1984), Rennwald (1978, 1984) and Schwander (1977) mainly give historical accounts of the development of the conflict. Windisch/Willner (1976) undertake a phenomenological analysis of the symbols and reasoning employed by the two sides involved. Bassand (1976) attempts to explain the conflict in terms of structural variables (class, language, religion) on the basis of an analysis of voting returns. A brief introduction to the conflict given by Höpflinger (1980) and Ganguillet (1985) provides a complete overview of its historical development as well as an interpretation in terms of an ethno-regional conflict using concepts of the resource mobilization approach as well as a review of those authors dealing

---

also contains annotated documents from the more recent past concerned, among other things, with the impact of the New Left on the labor movement. The concentration on the past-war period, in particular, excludes the monumental study by Gruner and his associates (1987-1988), which documents in four volumes the social situation, the organization and the struggle of the Swiss labor movement in the period 1880-1914.

3 Counter-movements have generally received very little attention by Swiss scholars. One exception is an article on the fundamentalist Catholic movement in the Valais (Raboud, 1983), which, however, is mainly concerned with the ideology and the socio-economic preconditions of the movement and has very little to say about its mobilization. A valuable overview of a very wide range of right-wing mobilization attempts has been assembled by a team of journalists (Frischknecht et al., 1984).

more specifically with ethnic and regional marginalization and subsequent mobilization.

The »cultural revolution« of the late sixties, which also had its repercussions in Switzerland, and the explosion of protest experienced in the urban centers of Switzerland during the early eighties have been dealt with under the label of *»youth protest«* in this country. Accordingly, their interpretation has primarily been the province of psycholoists, social workers, youth sociologists and all kinds of self-declared experts on questions concerning youth. Sociological attempts to approach the question of the rebellion in the sixties in more political terms typically reflected the general preoccupation of the time with matters of participation and non-participation: In the course of a survey on adolescents and young adults in the Canton of Zurich, Blancpain/Häuselmann (1974) asked, among other things, questions of political participation, political orientation, attitudes towards political violence, and general interest in politics.[4]

The debate on youth protest really erupted with *the urban movements of the early eighties*. The most influential interpretations of that time were probably the »Theses« of the Federal Youth Commission, which offered an unexpected amount of insight into the events, and the »Anti-theses« of a retired philosopher (Hersch, 1981), which tried to re-establish the traditional, common-sensical notion of what had happened.[5] Several authors heavily involved or concerned with the movement have contributed accounts documenting important aspects of the mobilization process without, however, analyzing them (Hänny, 1981; Howald et al., 1981; Lindt, 1981; Ménetrey, 1982; SP (1980); Züfle/Jürgmeier, 1982). We find more of an analytical approach with Béroud, (1982), Haller (1982), Kriesi (1984) and Willener (1984). The interpretations in Haller's reader are not limited to the Swiss events and psychoanalytical or sociopsychological aspects. Willener uses Touraine's sociology of action in a very personal and stimulating way to in-

4 An exception to this general scheme is a Swiss sociologist working in Berlin, Walter Hollstein (1970), who wrote a sociology of youth protest movements already at the end of the sixties.

5 Both »Theses« and »Anti-theses« sold tens of thousands of copies. In an insightful contribution, Steinauer-Cresson/Gros (1984) have analyzed the structure of the reasoning of the Anti-theses. Several additional papers in vol. 10 (1984) of the Swiss Journal of Sociology deal with the youth movements at the beginning of the eighties. A special issue of this Journal (vol. 11,2, 1985) on the sociology of youth, that appearing only one year later, has, however, virtually nothing to say on the topic.

terpret the Zurich movement's culture and that of its adversaries and sympathizers. Béroud's short overview argues in a similar vein. Kriesi, too, starts out with an analysis of the arguments of the different parties to the conflict. He goes on to reconstruct the events and to situate them in a more extended historical and structural context. More recently, these studies have been complemented by a description of the counter-culture in Geneva (Gros, 1987), and by a case study of two of its important action groups (Buchs et al., 1988).

The *ecological protest* in Switzerland, growing since the early seventies, has been documented in various ways. Studies of the use of initiatives have discovered that an increasing number of initiatives deal with ecological questions (App, 1987, Moser, 1987). In a systematic analysis of post-war period political mobilization addressing ecological issues, Levy (1981) has shown a general increase in protest events. Studies concerned with the implementation of national highway policies (Bassand, 1986) and of energy policies (Mironesco, 1986) have indicated how the ecological challenge has increasingly affected the implementation of such programs.

Aspects of the ecology movement have also been the object of a case study done by a journalist (Gasche, 1981), a comparative study of three local action groups against urban renewal projects (Auer and Levy, 1986), and a classical participation study (Giger, 1980), and of two studies on the most important environmental organizations (Giger, 1981; Meyer, 1987). From an Olsonian perspective, Meyer compares representative samples of two major automobile associations – the dominant traditional one (TCS), and the »alternative« one (VCS). In a remarkable analysis, she is able to show, among other things, that members of the traditional organization join mainly because of the selective incentive of the services provided while the members of the »alternative« association mainly join because of the collective incentive of transportation policy. Finally, the resistance against *nuclear power* plants, which has been particularly strong in Switzerland, has been documented in detail. A short overview of the development of the movement is given by Epple (1981) and by Kriesi (1982, chapter 2). Schroeren (1977) has written a case study on the occupation of the nuclear power plant site in Kaiseraugst that really sparked the movement and a journalist (Curdy, 1988) tells us how this project had finally been abandoned in the late eighties. Kriesi (1982) has studied the resistance against plans for another nuclear power plant from a resource mobilization perspective.

The *peace movement* has become the object of increasing attention during the eighties. In the post-war period, the peace movement has launched a considerable number of initiatives articulating national issues, including, the introduction of a civil service, a referendum on armament issues, and the banning of nuclear weapons in the Swiss army and Swiss arms exports. None of these initiatives has, however, had any impact at all on Swiss policy (Epple, 1988). In the early eighties, the movement has, first, been rejuvenated by the international resurgence of the peace movement, as described by Epple (1986) and by Bein and Epple (1987). Then, it was again a national issue which mobilized the movement to a considerable extent: the question of the abolishment of the Swiss army raised by a popular initiative launched by the Young Socialists. Several volumes document the mobilization of the people's initiative for a »Switzerland without an army«, describe its ideological background and analyze some sociopsychological mechanism of resistance against mobilization for this cause: Brodman et al. (1986), Gross et al. (1989), GSOA (1989), Pestalozzi (1982). Several historical studies complement these works. Gross (1989) discusses the history of the anti-militaristic tendency within the labor movement. Amherd (1983) presents the post-war history of the peace movement. The handbook edited by the »Forum für praxisbezogene Friedensforschung« (1986) contains an overview of the historical development of the Swiss peace movement in general, as well as a portrayal of all the organizations and groups constituting it at present. Finally, Finger (1989) presents an overview of the peace movement in Europe and the United States, its history and some future perspectives. It also briefly addresses the status of the Swiss peace movement.

Apart from the new social movements discussed in more detail below, I have uncovered a few studies on miscellaneous aspects of other NSMs. There is quite an elaborate »*alternative scene*« in Switzerland, first documented in Holweger/Mäder (1979) and also described in Mäder (1983). Vieli (1988) discusses the establishment of alternative enterprises. There are innovative *consumer's movements* documented in Pestalozzi et al. (1980) and, from another from a point of view akin to Castell's treatment of urban movements, by Weber-Jobé (1977).

Still another rather important movement in the Swiss context is the *solidarity movement* – solidarity with those discriminated against in the third world and with the foreign immigrants discriminated against here. But there are hardly any studies of this movement. Wicky (1985) describes the case of an important organization within this movement in the framework of a larger project (see below). De Rham and Martin (1976) critically analyze the discourse of one of this movement's SMOs. A special issue of the »Widerspruch« (1989) addresses some aspects of the solidarity movement in Switzerland. Finally, the absence of anlyses of the *women's movement* is striking. Ballmer-Cao (1988) has presented a first study of the women's avant-garde as part of a larger study of the conservatism of Swiss women.

In at least one respect Switzerland provides a very attractive setting for the study of social movements. The high degree of institutional, structural and cultural variation of contexts within a rather limited geographical area provides a unique opportunity for the comparative study of very diverse mobilization processes. A *large study of political mobilization*, which dealt extensively with mobilization through social movements, has attempted to make systematic use of this opportunity. In the first phase of this study, a systematic inventory of about 6,200 events of unconventional political mobilization in the post-war period (up to 1978) were collected, applying the ideas and the methodology developed by the Tilly's (1975) and by Gamson (1975). In a second phase, a sample of 10 more the less systematically chosen mobilization processes were studied in great detail using an approach inspired by the resource-mobilization school and concentrating especially on the structural and cultural determinants of *political potentials* forming the basis for political mobilization. Three types of potentials were distinguished: traditional ones (primarily situated in rural, peripheral contexts and based on identities having a territorial or ethnic referent), socialist ones (the potential of the classic labor movement) and new, subcultural ones (primarily located in the professional fraction of the new middle class in urban, central contexts and characterized by counter- or anti-cultural tendencies). Examples of the mobilization of each one of these potentials were studied and systematically compared. The results of the first phase are summarized in Kriesi et al. (1981), those of the second one in Kriesi (1985). A complete list of all the events collected in the first phase is provided by Tschopp (1981). The aforementioned studies of Ganguillet (1985), Kriesi (1982, 1984), Levy (1981) and Wicky (1985) were written during the course of this project. Several other contributions also grew out of it: popularizations of the results of the first phase (Levy/Duvanel, 1984; Duvanel/Levy, 1984), a detailed case study of a dissident farmer's organization (Härry/Ladner, 1983) and a study of the contextual determinants of citizen's protest (Zwicky, 1982).

III. Methodological Orientations

The methodological approach chosen by a specific author is heavily determined by the type of professional training he or she received and by the institutional context in which he or she is working. Given the low degree of development of the social sciences in Switzerland, many of the authors contributing to the study of social movements have had no research training at all (such as some of those documenting the urban youth movements) and accordingly, do not make any self-conscious methodological efforts. Many authors, moreover, have been trained in history or law (such as the ones writing on the initiatives) and use the methodologies of their own fields.

Among the social scientists in the narrower sense of the term who have been studying political mobilization in Switzerland, the political scientists have either relied on surveys – in the classical participation studies and the analysis of referenda – or they have analyzed data gathered from official sources – such as election and referendum returns. Political scientists, however, have had only a minor part in the analysis of collective political mobilization. The major studies were done by sociologists. Among them, very diverse methodological approaches have been used. On the one hand, there are a number of excellent *qualitative* studies done by sociologists from the French-speaking part of the country. The work of Windisch and his colleagues on the anti-foreigners movement is based on qualitative interpretations of some thousand letters sent to the editors of several newspapers and of French-speaking Swiss TV. Willener and Windisch's study of the Jura movements similarly makes use of a qualitative analysis of the discourse employed by representatives of the movement and of the symbolic content of their actions. The work of Willener and Béroud on the youth movements is also based on a critical phenomenology of the culture of the movement and the other parties involved.

The sociologists from Zurich working in this field have relied much more on *quantitative* approaches. Information on mobilization events collected in the first phase of their large project has been identified and documented on the basis of a very diverse pool of sources (newspaper archives, yearbooks, social-historical sources, specialized journals and magazines, official documentations). Due to country-specific circumstances (decentralization, the linguistic division of the country, and strong political orientations of the major newspapers) and the diversity of the events studied (not only violent events, but also, less conspicuous ones), Tilly's advice – to base the study on the systematic analysis of a single newspaper – has not been followed (Kriesi et al., 1981: Chapter 2). Several aspects of the events (location in time and space, issues and concerns articulated, forms of articulation, actors carrying out the process, anatagonists and their reactions, success) have been coded and analyzed systematically. Zwicky (1982) has analyzed information on these events together with other contextual data on the aggregate level in respect to communities and cantons. Levy/Zwicky (1984) have extended these analyses. The analysis of aggregate-level data has been very prominent in the research on referendum returns done by Nef and his associates at the Sociological Institute in Zurich.

In the second phase of the large study described above, the selected mobilization processes were analyzed on *three levels* and, correspondingly, three types of instruments were used: on the level of the development of the mobilization process, data collection proceeded on the basis of the analysis of documents and secondary analyses of the data on the events; on the level of the organizational infrastructure extensive interviews were held with representatives of the different groups; on the level of individual mobilization, finally, written questionaires were used to collect the appropriate information from the members and sympathizers of the different organizations and groups involved (Kriesi, 1985: Anhang I). An attempt was made to integrate qualitative and quantitative data in the comparative analysis of the different mobilization processes. In the summary account of the results (Kriesi, 1985), qualitative descriptions of the development of the different processes (based primarily on the information derived from the first two levels) are presented together with a systematic quantitative comparison of the different processes (based primarily on the information derived from the third one). Among the specific reports on different cases, only the one on the anti-nuclear movement also makes an analogous attempt (Kriesi, 1982).

In other cases, the reports are mainly based on qualitative information, partly due to the *resistance* of the concerned movements to the research done on them in general and to quantitative methods in particular. A detailed account of the critical relationship between the researcher and the urban youth movement of Zurich can be found in Kriesi (1984: 243-54), as well as in a similar account by Kriesi (1982: 274-87) regarding the anti-nuclear movement. In an interesting postscript to the study of Weber-Jobé (1977), the consumer's organization studied by her trenchantly criticizes the underlying theoretical assumptions of the author contributing to the reader's understanding of the issues involved.

IV. Some Empirical Findings

It is, of course, not possible to summarize even part of the diverse results that have been obtained in the different studies mentioned in section 1. I would like to highlight only some of their empirical findings. As has been pointed out above, the *initiative* has been *the* institutional channel for the articulation of political opposition in Switzerland. In the early years of its existence it has primarily been used by the organizations of the labor movement. Later on, with their incorporation into the political system, social democrats and labor unions have made considerably less use of this instrument without, however, completely dispensing with it. Small oppositional parties growing out of movements (such as the small rightest parties, the small parties of the New Left or the left-liberal Landesring) have increasingly submitted initiatives in the post-war period, together with ad hoc committees and SMOs coming from the new social movements. With respect to the latter, the institution of the initiative has functioned as an incentive to transform regionally-based movements into national ones (Kriesi, 1982; App, 1987).

On the national level, the initiatives have had a rather *limited direct impact* (only a very small number of initiatives have been adopted by referendum), but *indirectly* they have exerted considerable pressure on the decision-making of the political elite, generally, but not exclusively (e.g. the initiatives of the anti-foreigners movement in the post-war period and of fascist movements in the thirties) in a progressive direction. Werder (1978: 164) goes as far as to maintain that the pressure exerted by the initiatives has been functionally adaptive for the political system as a whole by providing a counterweight to the veto-power of the mighty economic interest groups. Delley (1978:168 ff.) argues in a similar vein. These evaluations stand in sharp contrast to those of the political elites, who have always viewed the initiatives with some suspicion and have been particularly concerned about the dangers implied by the »flood of initiatives«. They considered these to be the result of irresponsible behavior, rather than as the consequence of a profound social change which had not been accounted for by their own decisions (Delley, 1978).

Recent analyses allow us to differentiate these results somewhat. On the one hand, initiatives seemed to have been more successful on the cantonal level than on the national one (Kriesi et al., 1981; Moser, 1978). It is interesting to note that ecological concerns have not only been those most often articulated by cantonal initiatives in the eighties but, followed by concerns about fiscal matters, they have also been the most successful. On the other hand, the analysis of the success of national initiatives since the mid-seventies indicates that demands for fundamental reforms or demands implying substantial reorientations are not taken into consideration by the system at all (App, 1978). This latter result is in line with an earlier study which observed an increasing closure of the system especially in the Swiss German speaking part of the country (Kriesi et al., 1981). With many issues, the net effect seems to have been an increasing polarization, which is most clearly illustrated by the development in the area of energy policy, where the traditional »helvetian compromise« has no longer been attained (Linder, 1987). By its initiatives and related actions, the anti-nuclear movement has succeeded in slowing down and even stopping the nuclear program in Switzerland; but it has not been able to impose an alternative policy. For the time being, non-decision making predominates in this issue area. With other issues, however, such as the national roads issue studied by Bassand et al. (1986), more integrative solutions have been found: potential resistance has to some extent been absorbed by elaborate consultation procedures which have been institutionalized in reaction to the growth of the environmental protest.

The discussion of the policy effects of initiatives has to be amended by the *repercussions* of the availability of this institution *upon the movements* using it. In a very interesting study of the effects of initiatives on the peace movement, Epple (1988) argues that the movement has been primarily weakened by its frequent use of this direct-democratic institution. First of all, it has been forced to formulate limited demands in order to fulfill the criterion of »thematic unity« required for initiatives. It also had to make substantive concessions and formulate its demands in a rather moderate way. Second, it has incurred considerable opportunity costs because initiatives drained resources away from other activities.[6] Finally, the movement has become more centralized and developed bureaucratic tendencies as a result of these mobilizations. They are typically launched »from above«, and the grass-roots are more or less forced to follow suit in the campaigns. While persuasively arguing for the case of the peace movement, one should not overlook the possibility that a movement can also profit from having to mo-

---

6 An excellent example of an SMO that has completely exhausted its resources by launching an initiative is provided by Baumann's (1985) case study of the young Christian Democrats in the Valais.

bilize for a referendum campaign for an inititative it has launched some time ago. This has, for example, been observed in the case of the anti-nuclear movement which has re-emerged from a slump thanks to such a campaign (Kriesi, 1982).

As the analysis of the inventory of mobilization events has shown, not only did the number of initiatives increase markedly at the end of the sixties, but there was also an *enormous rise in the number of mobilization events* (initiatives, referenda, petitions, demonstrations, strikes, symbolic actions, etc.) in general. At the same time that the conventional participation in elections and referenda continued to decrease, an explosive growth took place in the mobilization of citizens along the institutionalized lines of protest-articulation and along non-conventional lines of direct action. This mobilization reached its peak in the mid-seventies and decreased again somewhat during the recession in the second half of the seventies without, however, falling back to the low level of the period before 1968. If one uses the distinction made between the three potentials, it can be shown that the mobilization of all three increased at that time. But it has, above all, been the mobilization of the new potentials which accounts for the staggering increase in the level of mobilization (Kriesi, 1985: 44). This rising level of unconventional involvement in »new politics« (Gruner, 1983), as well as the lower and increasingly selective (Nef, 1980) degree of conventional participation, has been interpreted in terms of a *fundamental structural change*.

As Levy/Zwicky (1984) argue, this structural change has led to the erosion of the relevance of traditional norms of citizen's participation. On the aggregate level of analysis they noted a *substitutive* relationship between conventional participation (measured by voter turnout) and unconventional mobilization (measured by number of mobilization events). At first sight, this result seems to contradict the well-known finding of a *cumulative* relationship between different forms of political activities (see e.g. Barnes/Kaase, 1979). It becomes less contradictory though, if we take into account that it pertains to an aggregate level of analysis. On this level, we find a concentration of mobilization events in the most developed urban regions, i.e. precisely where the voter turnout is particularly low. To deduce from this result an analogy for the level of individual participation would, however, be a mistake. As the analysis of the activists from different movements has shown, they are – in line with the argument of Barnes/Kaase – not only much more active in direct-action type activities than the average Swiss citizen, but also, considerably more active along conventional lines (Kriesi,

1985: Chapter 12). The activists responsible for the mobilization events form a rather small minority concentrated in precisely those urban contexts where the traditional norms of citizens' participation have eroded most and where the number of apathetic citizens is also particularly high.

The *traditional potentials* studied by Kriesi and his associates were all located in peripheral, rural contexts, but this is not to say that they cannot be found elsewhere, too: the adherents of the anti-foreign movement studied by Windisch or by Saint-Ouen have also been located in urban contexts. Moreover, even in a peripheral region, the potentials may have structurally quite diverse roots. They may consist of a particular segment (such as farmers) or the whole of the local population (such as the one in the North of the Jura) opposed to the dominant center of the political system. They may be made up of an emerging local counter-elite (such as the new technocrates in the Valais) opposing the traditionally conservative political elite within the context. Or they may be composed of a particular segment of the local population opposing another segment within the same region (such as in the South of the Jura). The criterion dividing the local population, in the lattter case, typically cuts across the class cleavage as the division of the local population is based on a constellation of structural, institutional and cultural factors which can be found in most ethno-regional conflicts and which is typically rooted in the historical background of the region (Ganguillet, 1985).

Traditional potentials tend to be *defensive*, fighting for the preservation of the traditional privileges, but this, too, is not necessarily so. They may also be *offensive*, voicing traditionally-held grievances or articulating certain regional demands which have long since been met in other parts of the country. In spite of this diversity of structural roots and orientations, traditional potentials all seem to be characterized by *a collective identity with an ethnic or territorial referent*. Thus, the ethnic identity is crucial to the understand of the conflict in the Jura (Ganguillet, 1985). Or, to name another example, the three types of supporters of the anti-foreigners movement distinguished by Windisch et al. (1978) are all characterized by their nationalism, although it is a nationalism of a specific kind; there are xenophobic nationalists, the populist nationalists and the technocratic nationalists.

The dynamic development of the mobilization of all potentials depends on specific structural and cultural characteristics and on the organizational resources and strategies of the different parties to the conflict in question. According to the Swiss experience, the mobilization of traditional potentials turns out to be particularly explosive if an offensive movement clashes with an antagonist within the same peripheral context (the case of the South of the Jura). In the case of the separatist movement in the Jura (North and South), it is interesting to note that it has been (partially) successful without having powerful allies within the political system – a lack which Ganguillet (1985) attributes to its inter-class character and to the exclusiveness of its focus. Because the established political organzations (parties, unions, interest organizations) are primarily organized along class-lines; they do not easily lend themselves to coalitions with such movements. The exclusive focus on the question of the Jura and the little interest in the issues raised by new social movements may also explain the indifference of the latter to the separatist movement. The separatist movement has, however, proved to be extraordinarily flexible in constantly adapting itself to changing situations, in developing an organizational differentiation allowing for optimum mobilizing efficency and in utilizing a rich repertoire of unconventional actions.

To explain the fluctuating patterns of success of the *anti-foreigners movement*, Saint-Ouen (1986) first notes that this movement is articulating a cleavage that runs across the traditional left-right dimension, and which, following Inglehart and Sidjanski (1975), he describes as »traditionalist-modernist«. Then he goes on to argue that the nationalist populists have repeatedly been able to pick up on themes which preoccupy the populace, such as the concern about the »false refugees«, and which are not articulated by the established political parties. He maintains that their success, however, has been only of a temporary nature because the bourgeois parties have generally tended to integrate elements of the populist demands into their policies, and thus undermined the electoral basis of the nationalist right.

With respect to the *new social movements* the Swiss finding generally correspond to those from other countries (Kriesi, 1985). The activists are predominantly young professionals in the social and cultural service sector, they are generally progressive and leftist in orientation, and they have a very high level of protest potential (in the sense of the term used be Barnes/Kaase). The organizational infrastructure of the NSMs is generally very loose. Membership criteria hardly exist and supporters are all rooted in a network of groups submerged in the everyday life of the counter-culture and its ramifications. In spite of the overall leftist orientation of their constituency, the Swiss NSM sector has two currents which may be distinguished. The first strongly identifies with the labor movement and approaches the NSMs from the point of view of the »old« movement. The second approaches the labor movement from the point of view of the NSMs. The latter approach the organizations of the former only insofar as they may be instrumentalized. The confrontation between these two currents has decisively shaped the history of the Swiss anti-nuclear movement (Kriesi, 1982).[7]

In his analysis of the Zurich movement Willener (1984: 170ff.) distinguishes between two basic forms of culture in addition to the dominant one: between *counter-cultures* trying to institutionalize their own counter-norms (often direct inversions of the established norms) and *»anti-cultures«* not trying to establish alternative norms at all and do so by rejecting any kind of norm expect for the one rule that all rules have to be abolished. As he points out, the notion of time is very different in the three types of culture: dominant cultures are of much longer duration than counter-cultures which, in turn, last longer than anti-cultures. The latter disappear very rapidly and often by being absorbed into the mass culture (»Kulturindustrie«). These distinctions between different types of cultures may be fruitfully applied to distinguish between different types of NSMs. The Swiss urban movements of the early eighties have been rather anti-cultural in character. These movements wanted everything here and now, in stark contrast to the veterans of the earlier NSMs who have (at least in part) been building their counter-cultural institutions for quite a number of years now (for examples see Holenweger/Mäder, 1979). Moreover, the movements of the early eighties were dissociative in the sense that they were no longer concerned with changing the more encompassing society (establishing counter-norms), rather, they were concerned only with their own well-being (on the island of the autonomous youth center in Switzerland). Willener advances the very general hypothesis of an acceleration of the development of cultures which, he argues, is to be attributed to the way mass media have developed. The implications of this general hypothesis for the analysis of the career of NSMs are quite intriguing: on the basis of this hypothesis one could, in a very speculative way, expect that movements may no longer have the chance to develop along the lines of the Weber-Michels model because of the general cultural trend preventing the long-term institutionalization of new projects.

---

7 For a general discussion of the relationship between new social movements and the Swiss party system, see Kriesi (1986).

V. Institutional Aspects of Social Movement Research

There is no institutionalized research on social movements in Switzerland. The promising start of the research group responsible for the larger project discussed above has led nowhere. This group had been created within the framework of the National research program on decision-making processes in the Swiss democracy,[8] which in turn had, among other reasons, been initiated because of the political elite's growing concern with the »participation crisis« (Zwicky, 1984). National research programs have a duration of only a limited number of years. Although one of their goals is the creation of qualified researchers, at least in the social sciences only very limited provisions have been made to stabilize those potentials developed in the course of such programs (Freiburghaus/Zimmermann, 1985). Follow-up programs do not exist and participation in new programs implies a change of orientation. Given the generally very limited resources of the social sciences in Switzerland – there are, for example, very few permanent positions at universities nor national research programs, research groups often disband after the termination of a project. Research on social movements will continue to be based mainly on semi-professional work or ad hoc research triggered by specific events.

A remarkable aspect of the social sciences in Switzerland is the fact that scholars from the two major language areas do not generally take note of each other. An analysis of the citation patterns of French-speaking and Swiss German-speaking Swiss sociologists (Geser/Höpflinger, 1980) has shown that the French-speaking sociologists usually cite their colleagues in the French-speaking part of the country and in France while the Swiss German-speaking sociologists usually cite Swiss German, German and Anglo-saxon work. Similar tendencies may also be noted in the field of the social movements. First of all, researchers have tended to conduct studies of mobilization process only in the language region of their origin. The case of the large comparative study is an exception in this respect, but even in this study, no systematic comparisons between corresponding movements from different language regions have been conducted. Second, contacts across the language barrier have generally depended on more or less incidental personal relationships. Professional meetings or workgroups focused on social movement research where scholars of both parts of the country could meet do not exist.

---

8 Nationales Forschungsprogramm Nr. 6.

VI. Debates, Controversies, Desiderata

There are few professional debates or controversies in the field. Although there was a considerable controversy over the urban youth movements of the early eighties, involving professional interpreters. With the suppression of these movements the debate on the subject has subsided. Typical for the Swiss intellectual climate is the refusal of Prof. Jeanne Hersch to participate in a debate on the »Theses« and her »Anti-theses« in the volume of the Swiss Journal of Sociology devoted to questions of youth movements in Switzerland (Vuille, 1984).

The main desideratum at present concerns the stabilization of research groups that would be able to take an active part in the international debates on the research on social movements and participate in internationally comparative research in order to put the Swiss movements into perspective. With respect to comparative research, a first start has recently been made with the inauguration of a research project by the present reviewer, which attempts to compare the development of the NSM sector in four Eropean countries during the eighties. In addition to the Netherlands, France and the Federal Republic of Germany, Switzerland is included as well.

With regard to the agenda for future research on social movements in Switzerland, I think there are three general points to be kept in mind: First, future research should attempt to clarify the effects the direct-democratic institutions have on the development of movement politics in this country. Direct-democratic institutions provide a unique opportunity structure for movement politics. The question of whether the movements profit from the direct-democratic institutions, or whether these institutions constitute a trap, remains largely unresolved: do these institutions allow social movements to have an exceptional impact on politics, or do they above all contribute to the moderation of their claims, the co-optation of their leaders, and to the demobilization of their supporters? Such a clarification presupposes international comparisons. Second, Switzerland is also unique for its great amount of structural and cultural heterogenity. For example, it seems that the differences which exist between France and the Federal Republic of Germany regarding the mobilization of new social movements are to a large extent replicated on the level of the Swiss cantons: the situation in the French-speaking cantons closely resembles the one in France whereas that of the Swiss German-speaking cantons is rather similar to the one in the Federal Republic. Social movement research should compare in a systematic way the variations in the development of particular movements between the different parts of the country. Third, Switzerland provides an interesting setting for the study of the backlash against new social movements. In the late eighties, the increasing impact of the strong Swiss environmental movement has been giving rise to a counter-movement of growing importance – the »Party of the automobile drivers«. Similarly, the Swiss solidarity movement has been confronted with a massive xenophobic counter-movement in the past which is reasserting itself as a result of the increasing number of political refugees seeking asylum in Switzerland. Future research on Swiss movements should focus not only on the interaction between authorities and new challengers, but also, on the interdependence of new challengers and populist movements from the right reacting against what they consider to be too many concessions benefitting the new challengers.

Annotated Bibliography

Amherd, L. (1983): *Geschichte der schweizerischen Friedensbewegung. 1945-1980.* Bern: Abteilung für neuere Geschichte der Universität Bern.

A detailed description of the history of the different SMOs of the peace movement in the post-war period.

App, R. (1987): »Initiative und ihre Wirkungen auf Bundesebene seit 1974«, *Schweiz. Jahrbuch für politische Wissenschaft* 27: 189-206.

A discussion of the success of the initiatives on the federal level since the mid-seventies. Indicates the difficulties associated with demands for fundamental reform.

Arbeitsgruppe für Geschichte der Arbeiterbewegung Zürich (1980): *Schweizerische Arbeiterbewegung. Dokumente zu Lage, Organisation und Kämpfen der Arbeiter von der Frühindustrialisierung bis zur Gegenwart*, 3. erw. Auflage, Zürich: Limmat Verlag.

Auer, A. (1978): *Les droits politiques dans les cantons suisses.* Genève: Georgi.

Auer, A. et R. Lévy (1986): »Les mouvements de quartiers face aux autorités et aux partis: expériences à Genève, Lausanne et Richterswil«, *Annuaire Suisse de Science Politique* 26: 171-191.

Compares the varying success of three local political mobilizations and explains it in terms of differences in the local political context as well as in terms of differences in the strategy and the cohesion of the mobilizing group.

Ballmer-Cao, T.-H. (1980): *Analyse des niveaux de participation et de non-participation politiques en Suisse.* Bern: Lang.

– (1988): *Le conservatisme politique féminin en Suisse: mythe ou régalité?* Genève: Georg.

An analysis of the relation of Swiss women to politics on three levels – the level of the women's political elite (members of the national parliament), the feminist avantgarde, and the female citizens. Unfortunately, the analysis of the avantgarde is quite limited; it is exclusively based on a re-analysis of the data of Kriesi et al. (1981) concerning events mobilizing women only.

Barnes, S.; M. Kaase et al. (eds.). (1979): *Political Action*. London: Sage.

Barrier, G. (1989): »Merkwürdigkeiten in der Solidaritätsbewegung«, *Widerspruch-Sondernummer*: 159-64.

Bassand, M. (1976): »Le séparatisme jurassien: un conflit de classe et/ou un conflit ethnique?« *Cahiers internat. de Sociologie*. 61: 221ff.

Bassand, M., T. Burnier, P. Meyer, R. Stüssi, L. Veuve. (1986): *Politique des routes nationales. Acteurs et mise en oeuvres*. Lausanne: Presses polytechniques Romandes.

An analysis of the formulation and implementation of the program for the construction of the Swiss national highways. Shows an increasing importance of »peripheral« actors in this originally purely technocratic process among whom action groups of new social movements play an important role.

Baumann, A. (1985): »Die Proporzinitiative der Jungen CVP im Wallis«, in: H. Kriesi (ed.). *Bewegung in der Schweizer Politik*. Frankfurt: Campus: 127-157.

Bein, T., Epple, R. (1987): »Zur Geschichte der »neuen« Friedensbewegung in der Schweiz«, in: *Friedensanalysen*. Frankfurt: Suhrkamp.

A history of the Swiss peace movement that emphasizes the relationship between »old« and »new«.

Béroud, G. (1982): »Valeur travail et mouvement de jeunes«, *Revue internationale d'action communautaire*, 8/48: 5-30.

A critical phenomenology of the culture of the Swiss youth movement of the early eighties.

Blancpain, R., Häuselmann, E. (1974): *Zur Unrast der Jugend*. Frauenfeld: Huber.

The classic study of the Swiss youth at the beginning of the seventies. Based on a survey among adolescents and young adults in the Canton of Zurich, with information, among other things, on political participation, political orientation, attitudes with respect to political violence, and general interest in politics.

Brodmann, R., Gross, A., Spescha, M. (eds.). (1986): *Unterwegs zur Schweiz ohne Armee. Der freie Gang aus der Festung*. Basel: Z-Verlag.

A reader with contributions from figureheads of the Swiss left discussing the purpose and the context of the initiative for a Switzerland without an army.

Buchs, V., Bonnet, N. Lagier, D. (1988): *Cultures en urgence. Mouvements contre-culturels: de l'alternative à l'intégration*. Genève: les editions I.E.S.

A case study of the local counter-culture at Geneva with special attention paid to two particular action groups, the »AMR« and »l'Etat d'urgence«.

Curdy, G. (1988): *Kaiseraugst: le défi. Vie et mort d'un projet de central nucléaire*. Lausanne: Editions d'en bas.

A journalist's account of the history of the nuclear power plant project at Kaiseraugst, from the occupation of the site in 1974 up to 1988 when the political elite gave it up.

Delley, J.D. (1978): *L'initiative populaire en Suisse. Mythe et réalité de la démocratie directe*. Lausanne: l'Age d'Homme.

An important study of the Swiss popular initiative. Discusses the historical origins of the inititative and political debates surrounding it, analyzes the initiatives of the post-war period in detail and presents a theoretical interpretation of this direct-democratic institution.

Dittrich, K., Johansen, L.N. (1983): »Voting turnout in Europe, 1945-1978: Myths and Realities«, in: H. Daalder and P. Mair (eds.). *Western European Party Systems. Continuity and Change.* London: Sage.

Duvanel, L.; Lévy, R. (1984): *Politique en rase-mottes. Mouvements et contestation suisse.* Lausanne: Réalités sociales.
A popularized version of Kriesi et al. (1981).

Epple, R. (1981): »Schweiz – Atomare Präzision«, in: L. Mez (ed.): *Der Atomkonflikt.* Reinbek: Rowohlt.

– (1986): »Die schweizerische Friedensbewegung – Alte Wurzeln – Neue Blüten«, *Schweiz. Jahrbuch für Politische Wissenschaft* 26: 193-210.
A history of the Swiss peace movement that emphasizes the relationship between »old« and »new« within the movement. Almost identical to Bein/Epple (1987).

– (1988): *Friedensbewegung und direkte Demokratie in der Schweiz.* Frankfurt: Haag + Herchen.
An important dissertation about, among other things, the direct and indirect impacts of seven national initiatives of the Swiss peace movement in the post-war period. Comes to very pessimistic conclusions about the possible impacts of such initiatives. Stresses above all the negative repercussions the initiatives have on the movement organizations that launch them.

Finger, M. (1989): *Les 10 bonnes raisons pour adhérer au nouveau mouvement de la paix:* Lausanne: editions L.E.P.
A rather popular overview of the state of the art of the peace movement in Western Europe and the U.S. and its future perspectives.

Forum für praxisbezogene Friedensforschung (ed.). (1986): *Handbuch Frieden Schweiz.* Basel: Z-Verlag.

Freiburghaus, D. und W. Zimmermann (1985): *Wie wird Forschung politisch relevant?* Bern: Haupt.

Frischknecht, J.; Haffner, P.; Haldimann, U.; Niggli, P. (1984): *Die unheimlichen Patrioten. Politische Reaktion in der Schweiz. Ein aktuelles Handbuch.* 2. Auflage. Zürich: Limmat Verlag.
A journalist's account of the extreme right in Swiss politics. Important source for someone who wants an introduction to the subject.

Gamson, W. A. (1975): *The Strategy of Social Protest.* Homewood, III.: Dorsey.

Ganguillet, G. (1985): »Le conflit jurassien: un cas de mobilisation ethno-régionale en Suisse«, *Rapport Nr. 2 du projet de recherche »Le citoyen actif«.* Institut de Sociologie de L'Université de Zurich.
A history and an analysis of the regional conflict in the Jura. Argues that the ethnic identity is crucial for understanding this conflict.

Ganguillet, G.; Kriesi, H. (1983): »Der heimatlose Bürger im Leistungsstaat«, *Schweiz. Jahrbuch für politische Wissenschaft.* 23: 141-60.

Gasche, U.P. (1981): *Bauern, Klosterfrauen, Alusuisse.* Bern: Zytglogge.
A case study of the mobilization against the industrial pollution caused by the major Swiss aluminum producer in the Valais.

Geser, H.; Höpflinger, F. (1980): »Professionelle Orientierungen in der schweizerischen Soziologie«, in: Hischier, G. et al. (Hrsg.): *Weltgesellschaft und Sozialstruktur. Festschrift für Peter Heintz*. Diessenhofen: Rüegger.

Giger, A. (1976): *Der politische Bürger*. Universität Zürich: Dissertation.
A classical political participation study.

– (1980): »Politisches Bewusstsein und Partizipation«, *Schweiz. Zeitschrift für Soziologie* 6: 447-62.
Presents the results of a survey among the members of the Swiss World Wildlife Fund.

– (1981): »Umweltorganisation und Umweltpolitik«, *Jahrbuch für Politische Wissenschaft* 21: 49-78.
Discusses the three major organizations of the Swiss ecological movement at the beginning of the eighties: WWF, SNB (a traditional environmental protection organization) and SGU (a new, elitist ecological interest group).

Giroud, R. (1952): »Facteurs de l'abstentionnisme en Suisse«, *Revue Française de Science Politique*: 349-76.

– (1971): *L'électeur Genevois*. Centre de Sociologie: Université de Genève.

Girod, R. et C. Ricq (1970): »Microsystèmes sociaux et abstentionnisme électoral à Genève«, *Annuaire Suisse de Science Politique*: 71-90.

Gross, A. (1989): »Die Bedeutung der ›Schweiz ohne Armee‹ in der Geschichte der schweiz. Arbeiterbewegung«, in: A. Gross et al. (ed.). *Denkanstösse zu einer anstössigen Initiative*. Zürich: Realotopia Verlagsgenossenschaft.
A history of anti-militarism in the Swiss labor movement which stresses the influence of several key personalities and distinguishes between a number of phases in the relationship between anti-militarism and the labor movement.

Gross, A., Crain, F.; Erne R. und Furrer, S. (eds.). (1989): *Denkanstösse zu einer anstössigen Initiative*. Zürich: Realotopia Verlagsgenossenschaft.
A reader discussing the relevance of the initiative for a Switzerland without an army for the social-democratic party.

Gruner, E. (1969): *Regierung und Opposition im schweizerischen Bundesstaat*. Bern: Haupt.

– (1987-1988): *Arbeiterschaft und Wirtschaft in der Schweiz*. 1880-1914, Vol. 1, 2a, 2b, 3. Zürich: Chronos.
A monumental study of the development of labor movement organizations and their struggles between 1880 and 1914.

Gruner, E.; Hertig, H.P. (1983): *Der Stimmbürger und die neue Politik*. Bern: Haupt.
An analysis of the political competence of Swiss citizens on the basis of the Vox-surveys, which are regularly held after each vote on initiatives and referenda, as well as a theoretical interpretation of recent trends towards »new politics«.

GSOA-Gruppe für die Schweiz ohne Armee (1989): *GSOA-Jahrbuch 88. Texte und Debatten zur Schweiz ohne Armee vom Jan. 88 bis Dez. 88*. Zürich.

Haller, M. (eds.) (1981): *Aussteigen oder Rebellieren, Jugendliche gegen Staat und Gesellschaft*. Rowohlt Spiegel-Buch.
An interpretation of the youth protest at the beginning of the eighties in Switzerland and elsewhere in Europe. Contains mostly psychoanalytical or sociopsychological contributions.

Hänny, R. (1981): *Zürich, Anfang September*. Frankfurt: Suhrkamp.

A writer's account of the events in Zurich in September, 1980. Gives a good impression of the atmosphere that surrounded the Zurich movement at that time.

Harder, H.-J. (1978): *Der Kanton Jura: Ursachen und Schritte zur Lösung eines Schweizer Minderheitenproblems*. Bern: Lang.

Härry, D.; Ladner, A. (1983): »Opposition in der Bauernschaft: Die Union des producteurs suisses (UPS)«, *Bericht Nr. 1 des Forschungsprojekts »Der aktive Bürger«*. Zürich: Soziologisches Institut der Universität.

Hennecka, H.P. (1972): *Die jurassischen Separatisten*. Meisenheim am Glan: Hain.

Hersch, J. (1981): *Antithesen zu den »Thesen zu den Jugendunruhen 1989«*. Schaffhausen: Verlag Peter Meili.

A very influential, reactionary interpretation of the »youth movements« in Switzerland at the beginning of the eighties.

Holenweger, T. und Mäder, W. (1979): *Inseln der Zukunft? Selbstverwaltung in der Schweiz*. Zürich: Limmat Verlag.

Gives an overview of the alternative sector in Switzerland at the time.

Hollstein, W. (1970): *Der Untergrund. Zur Soziologie jugendlicher Protestbewegungen*. 2. Auflage. Neuwied: Luchterhand.

An early, interesting analysis of counter-cultural protest.

Höpflinger, F. (1980): »Der Schweizer Jura – Erfolg und Folgen einer regionalistischen Autonomiebewegung«, in: D. Gerdes (Hrsg.): *Aufstand der Provinz*. Frankfurt: Campus.

Howald, R.; Jürgmeier, R.; Salmann, R.; Scheucher, P. (1981): *Die Angst der Mächtigen vor der Autonomie*. Horgen: Gegenverlag.

Inglehart, R.; Sidjanski, D. (1975): »Electeurs et dimension gauche-droite«, in: D. Sidjanski et al. (eds.). *Les Suisses et la politique*. Bern: Lang.

Kriesi, H. (1982): *AKW-Gegner in der Schweiz. Eine Fallstudie zum Aufbau des Widerstands gegen das geplante AKW in Graben*. Diesenhofen: Rüegger.

A case study of a particular regional branch of the Swiss anti-nuclear movement. Implicitly uses a resource mobilization perspective. Contains, among other things, survey results of the supporters of the movement.

– (1982a): »Soziologische Methodologie und die Rebellion der Betroffenen«, *Kölner Zeitschrift für Soziologie und Sozialpsychologie* 34 (4): 732-44.

Discusses the difficulties that arise in empirical studies of new social movements. Makes suggestions about how one could proceed to overcome these difficulties.

– (1984): *Die Zürcher Bewegung. Bilder, Interaktionen, Zusammenhänge*. Frankfurt: Campus.

A case study of the Zurich movement. Discusses the ideas of participants, antagonists, and third parties about the movement; presents a structured account of its development; and makes an attempt to interpret what has happened from a structuralist perspective.

– (1986): »Perspektiven neuer Politik: Parteien und neue soziale Bewegungen«, *Schweiz. Jahrbuch für politische Wissenschaft* 26: 333-350.

Discusses the relationship between new social movements and political parties in the context of the Swiss political opportunity structure. Speculates about the relevance of »old« and »new« cleavages for this relationship.

– (ed.) (1985): *Bewegungen in der Schweizer Politik. Fallstudien zu politischen Mobilisierungsprozessen in der Schweiz*. Frankfurt: Campus.

Presents the main results of a comparative analysis of eight political mobilization processes in the early eigthies in Switzerland. The cases studied include the mobilization of a union, of traditional movements and of new social movements.

Kriesi, H.; Lévy, R.; Ganguillet, G. and Zwicky, H. (eds.) (1981): *Politische Aktivierung in der Schweiz. 1945-1978*. Diessenhofen: Rüegger.

A study of the 6,200 political mobilization events featuring a systematic analysis of newspapers and other documents. The main result indicates the enormous increase in the number of such events since the end of the sixties.

Lévy, R. (1981): »Politische Basisaktivität im Bereich der Umweltproblematik«, *Schweiz. Jahrbuch für politische Wissenschaft* 21: 9-37.

A reanalysis of the data presented in Kriesi et al. (1981) that pertain to environmental issues.

Lévy, R.; Duvanel, L. (1984): *Politik von unten. Bürgerprotest in der Nachkriegsschweiz*. Basel: Lenos.

The German version of Duvanel/Lévy.

Lévy, R.; Zwicky, H. (1984): »Politische Partizipation und neuere Aktionsformen«, in: U. Klöti (ed.). *Handbuch Politisches System der Schweiz*. Bern: Haupt.

An extended analysis of the data presented in Kriesi et al. (1981). They argue that a fundamental structural change has led to the erosion of the relevance of traditional norms of citizens' participation. Indicates a substitutive relationship between conventional participation and unconventional mobilization.

Linder, W. (1987): *La décision politique en Suisse. Genèse et mise en oeuvre de la législation*. Lausanne: Réalité sociales.

A summary account of the results of the national research program Nr. 6 that dealt with political decision-making in Switzerland. Contains overviews of the results of several studies referred to in this review. Takes note of the increasing relevance of new social movements in Swiss politics.

Lindt, N. (1981): *»Nur tote Fische schwimmen mit dem Strom«. 12 bewegte Portraits aus Zürich*. Zürich: eco Verlag.

A writer's account of 12 biographies of militants in the Zurich movement. Interesting document for the analysis of individual mobilization processes.

Mäder, W. (1983): »The alternative movement in Switzerland«, in: A. Sicinski and M. Wemegah (eds.). *Alternative ways of life in contemporary Europe*. Tokyo: The United Nations.

Menétrey, A.C. et le »Collectif de défense« (1982): *La Vie ... vite. Lausanne bouge 1980-1981: une chronique*. Lausanne: Ed. d'En Bas.

Meyer, H. (1987): *Raumstrukturen und Entscheidungsprozesse*. Diplomarbeit am Geografischen Institut der Universität Zürich.

Contains a systematic comparison of two surveys among representative samples of members of the TCS, the major automobile association, and of the VCS, the »alternative« automobile association. Comes to interesting conclusions from an Olsonian perspective.

Moser, Ch. (1987): »Erfolge kantonaler Volksinitiativen nach formalen und inhaltlichen Gesichtspunkten«, *Schweiz. Jahrbuch für politische Wissenschaft* 27: 159-88.

Shows that initiatives on the cantonal level are generally more successful than on the national level. Indicates that initiatives dealing with ecological issues are not only the most numerous, but also, the most successful in the cantons.

Nef, R. (1980): »Struktur, Kultur und Abstimmungsverhalten«, *Schweiz. Zeitschrift für Soziologie* 6 (2): 155-90.

An ecological analysis of referenda in Switzerland relating voting behaviour to structural and cultural aspects of their contexts.

Nef, R. und M. Rosenmund (1984): »Das energiepolitische Plebiszit vom 23. September zwischen Entwicklungserwartung und Wachstumskritik«, *Schweiz. Zeitschrift für Soziologie* 10 (3): 689-722.

Neidhart, L. (1970): *Plebiszit und pluralitäre Demokratie. Eine Analyse der Funktionen des schweizerischen Gesetzesreferendums.* Bern: Francke.

The classic study of the Swiss referendum. Shows the latent functions of this direct-democratic institution which have implied a far-reaching transformation of the direct democracy into a negotiation democracy.

Neidhart, L. und Hoby, J.P. (1977): *Ursachen der gegenwärtigen Stimmabstinenz.* Zürich: Soziologisches Institut der Universität.

An influential study of the reasons for the low participation rate in Swiss referenda. Unfortunately, it is based on a very small sample.

Pestalozzi, H.A. (ed.). (1980): *M-Frühling.* Bern: Zytglogge.

A participant's account of the movement that tried to take over the Swiss chain store giant »Migros«, a cooperative which has, however, defended itself successfully against the rebels from within.

Prongué, B. et al. (1984): *Nouvelle Histoire du Jura.* Porrentruy: Société jurassienne d'Emulation.

Raboud, I. (1983): »MGR Lefèbvre et ses fidèles valaisans«, *Schweiz. Zeitschrift für Soziologie* 9 (3): 617-38.

Rennwald, J.-C. (1978): *Combat jurassien.* Lausanne: Institut de science politique.

– (1984): *La question jurassienne.* Paris: editions entente.

Rham, G. de; Martin, S. (1976): »L'initiative ›être solidaire‹, un pluralisme mystificateur?«, *Annuaire Suisse de Science Politique* 16: 139-50.

A critical analysis of the discourse of the initiative movement demanding more solidarity with the immigrant workers in Switzerland.

Riklin, A. und Kley, R. (1981): *Stimmabstinenz und direkte Demokratie.* Bern: Haupt.

Saint-Ouen, F. (1986): »Vers une remontée du national-populisme en Suisse? Le cas des vigilants genevois«, *Annuaire Suisse de Science Politique* 26: 211-24.

Schmidtchen, G. (1980): »Repräsentiert der Nationalrat die gesellschaftlichen Probleme der Schweiz?« *Zeitschrift für Parlamentsfragen* 3: 366-86.

Schroeren, M. (1977): *z.B. Kaiseraugst. Der gewaltfreie Widerstand gegen das Atomkraftwerk: Vom legalen Protest zum zivilen Ungehorsam.* Zürich: Schweiz. Friedensrat, Nr. 6 der Schriftenreihe.

A detailed account of the occupation of a nuclear power-plant site at Kaiseraugst. Provides especially useful insight into the preparation of the occupation by the regional action groups.

Schwander, M. (1977): *Jura – Konfliktstoff für Jahrzehnte.* Zürich: Benziger.

Sidjanski, D.; Roig, C.; Kern, H.; Inglehart, R.; Nicola, J. (1975): *Les Suisses et la Politique*. Bern: Lang.
Virtually the only existing study of the political behavior and political orientations of a representative sample of Swiss citizens.

Sigg, O. (1978): *Die eigenössischen Volksinitiativen 1892-1939*. Bern: Francke Verlag.

SP der Stadt Zürich (ed.) (1980): *Eine Stadt in Bewegung*. Zürich.

Steinauer-Cresson, G.; Gros, D. (1984): »L'hymne au »bon sens« ou la ritualisation du faux débat sur la jeunesse«, *Schweiz. Zeitschrift für Soziologie* 10 (1): 131-54.

Tharakan, J. (1983): *Political Attitude of the Non-Voters in Switzerland*. University of Zurich: Dissertation.

Thesen – Eidgenössische Kommission für Jugendfragten 1980 (1980): *Thesen zu den Jugendunruhen 1980*. Bern: EDMZ.
The very influential, »official« interpretation of the Swiss youth movements. It has surprised everyone by its openness and its moderation.

Tilly, Ch.; Tilly L. and Tilly, R. (1975): *The Rebellious Century. 1830-1930*. Cambridge: Harvard University Press.

Tschopp, A. (1981): »Datenhandbuch über politische Aktivierungsereignisse in der Schweiz. 1945-78«, *Bericht Nr. 7 aus der Interdisziplinären Konfliktforschungsstelle*. Universität Zurich.
A source-book that contains a brief description of each one of the 6,200 events studied in Kriesi et al. (1981), as well as detailed registers containing keywords which facilitate finding particular types of events.

Vieli, H.P. (1988): »Von der ›Gegengesellschaft‹ zur Selbstverwaltung«, *Widerspruch* 15: 85-93.

Vox-Analysen der eidgenössischen Volksabstimmungen 1977ff. Bern: Forschungszentrum für Schweizer Politik.
Short empirical accounts of the voting behavior of the Swiss citizens, based on representative surveys done immediately after referenda. Constitutes an important source for the analysis of direct democratic institutions.

Vuille, M. (1984): »Avant-propos«, *Schweiz. Zeitschrift für Soziologie* 10(1): 127-9.

Weber-Jobé (1977): *La Fédération romande des consommatrices. Mouvements de consommateurs et transformation sociale*. Lausanne: Institut de science politique.

Werder, H. (1978): *Die Bedeutung der Volksinitiative in der Nachkriegszeit*. Bern: Francke Verlag.
Analysis of the national popular initiatives of the post-war period. Concludes that initiatives have important indirect impacts even if they are hardly ever accepted by a popular vote.

Wicky, M. (1985): »Die Erklärung von Bern«, in: H. Kriesi (ed.): *Bewegung in der Schweizer Politik*. Frankfurt: Campus: 220-37.

Willener, A. (1984): *L'avenir instantané. Mouvement des jeunes à Zurich*. Lausanne: Editions P.-M. Favre.
Stimulating phenomenological analysis of the »anti-culture« of the movement of Zurich. In contrast to a »counter-culture«, an »anti-culture« does not try to establish alternative norms, but rather, rejects any kind of norm except for the one rule that all rules have to be abolished.

Willener, A.; Windisch, U. (1976): *Le Jura incompris: fédéralisme ou totalitarisme?* Vevey: Delta.

Phenomenological analysis of the symbols and reasoning employed by the separatists and the anti-separatists.

Windisch, U. (1981): »La structure profonde de la xénophobie. Analyse thématique ou socio-cognitive?« *Schweiz. Zeitschrift für Soziologie* 7 (2): 233-56.

– (1978): »Ideology: Key to Power«, in: P. Birnbaum et al. (eds.): *Democracy. Consensus and Social Contract.* London: Sage.

An interesting discussion of the »helvetian ideology« based on an analysis of the discourse of the anti-foreigners' movement.

Windisch, U.; Jaeggi, J.-M.; de Rham, G. (1978): *Xénophobie? Logique de la Pensée Populaire.* Lausanne: Ed. L'Age d'Homme.

A study of the fundamental structure of thought of the supporters and adversaries of the anti-foreigners' movement.

Züfle, M.; Jürgmeier (1982): *Paranoia City oder Zürich ist überall.* Reinbek: Rowohlt.

Zwicky, H. (1984): »Forschungstendenzen in der politischen Soziologie«, *Schweiz. Zeitschrift für Soziologie* 10 (1): 97-124.

– (1982): *Politische Aktivität. Illegitimität und Stabilisierung. Eine Untersuchung kontextueller Determination von Bürgeraktivitäten und Unzufriedenheit in der Schweiz.* Diessenhofen: Rüegger.

A dissertation based on Kriesi's et al. (1981) data which attempts to study the context-specific determinants of citizens' protest.

The Study of Social Movements in Austria

Anton Pelinka

I. The Special Political Framework

The Austrian political system may be characterized by a number of specific features creating special conditions for the development of social movements:

- An unusually high degree of centralization of the party system. The ability of the two major parties, the Socialist Party of Austria (Sozialistische Partei Österreichs, SPÖ) and the Austrian People's Party (Österreichische Volkspartei, ÖVP), to mobilize a large majority of voters is unusually high. Up to 1975, the percentage of the electorate which voted for either of the two major parties in the general elections had been increasing and peaked at above 90 percent. Since the late 1970's, however, a significant decline can be observed.[1]
- An unusually high degree of organization in the traditional parties. Almost one-third of the voters are organizationally linked, as official party members, to one of the major parties. Within some sectors of the Austrian society the degree of political organization has reached an absolute maximum – as is the case among farmers in Lower and Upper Austria.[2]
- An unusual continuity of the party system. The traditional Austrian parties are deeply rooted in the 19th century. Twice they have founded re-

---

1 Pelinka: Abstieg des Parteienstaates – Aufstieg des Parlamentarismus. Zum Wandel des österreichischen Parteiensystems. In: Anton Pelinka, Fritz Plasser (eds.): Das österreichische Parteiensystem. Wien 1988 (Böhlau).

2 Anton Kofler: Parteiengesellschaft im Umbruch. Partizipationsprobleme von Großparteien. Wien 1985 (Böhlau), especially pp. 46-69.

publics (1918, 1945)[3] and authored constitutions, while influencing the entire society in an especially intensive way. The political parties as recruiting institutions control not only the political system, but also, the society itself.

Behind those special conditions, the fragmentation of the Austrian society also has to be taken into consideration.[4] Austria, a minor country in Central Europe since 1918, is divided into subsocieties. Each subsociety consists of a camp (»Lager«, pillar). The two major camps are the Socialists and the Christian Conservatives. There is a smaller camp, the Pan-Germans. As it is typical for splintered societies loyalities beneath the national level have developed. As a result of an integration of the different camps the process of nation-building is being delayed or even halted.

For social movements, the fragmentation of the Austrian society creates restrictive preconditions. In the past, social movements not associated with the traditional camps did not have a chance to develop. The only social movements able to have a lasting impact were found within one of the traditional camps.

Historically, this dominance is especially reflected in the integration of the different economic and non-economic interest groups into the traditional camps. For instance, before the Austrian Federation of Trade Unions (Österreichischer Gewerkschaftsbund, ÖGB) was founded in 1945 there was not one trade union organization, but rather, several Socialist, Christian and Pan-German union movements.[5] Moreover, there was not a single, overlapping, national youth movement, but rather, various Socialistic, Christian and Pan-German oriented youth movements.[6]

---

3 Melanie A. Sully: Political Parties and Elections in Austria. The search for Stability. London 1981 (Hunt).

4 Gerhard Lehmbruch: Proporzdemokratie. Politisches System und politische Kultur in der Schweiz und in Österreich. Tübingen 1967 (Mohr).
G. Bingham Powell, Jr.: Social Fragmentation and Political Hostility. An Austrian Case Study. Stanford 1970 (Stanford University Press).
Arend Lijphart: Democracy in Plural Societies. A Comparative Exploration. New Haven 1977 (Yale University Press), especially pp. 25-52.

5 Fritz Klenner: Gewerkschaften in Österreich. 3 Vol. Wien 1951, 1953, 1979 (Verlag des ÖGB).

6 Gerhard Seewann: Österreichische Jugendbewegung 1900-1938. 2 Vol. Frankfurt am Main 1971 (Piper-Verlag).

The Austrian Nazi Party (NSDAP) was the first successfull social movement to cross the borders of the traditional camps. Rooted in the third camp, i.e. the Pan-German camp, the Austrian Nazi movement, the Austrian NSDAP, nevertheless succeeded in attracting different groups and traditions within the Socialist as well as Conservative-Christian camps.[7] The NSDAP's ability to use the generation gap to break into the two major camps contributed significantly to the success of the Austrian Nazi movement. The younger generation within the two major camps was especially susceptible to the appeal the Nazi movement was able to develop.

After 1945 and the catastrophe, for which the Nazi movement in Austria was also responsible, the Pan-German camp seemed to be discredited. The two other camps were completely restored to their traditional forms. The greater distance between the Catholic Church and the newly established party of the Christian-Conservative camp, the ÖVP (The Austrian People's Party), had to be considered as a new factor.[8] The two major traditional camps and their two dominant political parties, then reestablishing themselves, were able to control the Second Republic from the very beginning. But contrary to the period before 1934, it built upon the model of »consociational« democracy and dominated all social sectors as a political cartel.

The total restoration of the camps was completed in 1949 with the re-establishment of the, now weakened, Pan-German camp – represented between 1949 and 1956 by the League of Independents (Verband der Unabhängigen, VDU) and afterwards by the FPÖ, the Freedom (or Liberal) Party of Austria (Freiheitliche Partei Österreichs).[9] With this development, the Austrian society and social and political system, seemed to be dominated by a two-and-a-half (or »limping« two) party system and by a two-and-a-half camp system indicating a kind of perpetual rule – to a degree a specific Austrian pattern.

As early as the late 1970s, disintegrating tendencies could be observed in the all dominating two-and-a-half party system and camp systems. The first indication was a »de-alingment« of the party system: the result of more

---

7 Bruce F. Pauley: Hitler and the Forgotten Nazis. A History of Austrian National Socialism. Chapel Hill 1981 (The University of North Carolina Press).

8 Rainer Nick: Schwesterparteien. CDU/CSU und Österreichische Volkspartei. Ein Vergleich. Innsbruck 1984 (Inn-Verlag), especially pp. 65-67.

9 Max E. Riedelsperger: The Lingering Shadow of Nazism. The Austrian Independent Party Movement since 1945. New York 1978 (Columbia University Press).

flexible voting behavior.[10] The concentration of the party system weakened as smaller parties on the local and regional levels competed successfully for votes and seats in parliament. These newly established parties of the early 1980s were not merely offsprings or autonomous parts of the traditional camps and they were able to avoid integration into the traditional parties. Furthermore, they were clearly based on interests, on cleavages beyond those interests and on cleavages traditionally significant for the fragmentation of the Austrian society.

The new social movements were responsible for this development. And the social factor behind the new social movement was, once more, the generation conflict. All analyses clearly indicate that »youth«, besides »education«, is the main factor which bore on the new social movements of the late 1970s and the 1980s.[11]

The Austrian peculiarities have to be seen in the perfect institutionalization of social movements typical for an industrial society. Social movements in Austria, an impact of the »material« cleavages of 19th century industrial society, were organized as political parties and as interest groups linked to the party system. Beyond the camps, there was practically nothing left for creating the dynamism necessary for social movements.

The first significant trends of emancipation could not be seen until the late 1970s when an emancipation of social movements from the camps, traditional political parties and interest groups occured. The new social movements, no longer conditioned to integrate themselves easily into the already existing political structures, started a dynamic process of emancipation. For the first time in Austria we can really speak of social movements: political mobility that is not channeled, centralized, preshaped, or controlled.

10 Fritz Plasser: Parteien unter Streß. Zu Dynamik der Parteiensysteme in Österreich, der Bundesrepublik Deutschland und den Vereinigten Staaten. Wien 1987 (Böhlau), especially pp. 23-30.

11 For a general overview, see Joachim Giller: Soziale Bewegung und Wertwandel in Österreich. Von der »Studentenbewegung« zu den »Grünen« und »Alternativen«. Wien 1984 (Berichte und Informationen).

II. Theoretical Approaches

The different approaches social scientists employ to analyze and interpret new social movements in Austria can be categorized in a manner analogous to analyses and interpretations in Western Europe and North America:[12]

- Post-materialism. As is the case in other countries Ronald Inglehart's publications have significantly influenced the Austrian analysts. Based on the evidence that the materially-satisfied, younger, better-educated Austrians are more inclined to participate in new social movements, a »post-materialist« type is seen as mainly responsible for new social movements. New social movements are to be seen therefore as an indication or material satisfaction, for increased sensitivity to non-material values and with ecology as a central, new value. Post-materialism in Austria is contrary to the »philosophy« of economic growth represented by the corporatist »social partnership«. For this reason, the impact of the post-materialist approach is interpreted as an escape from the network of corporatist institutions especially well-developed in Austria. The new social movements, primarily analyzed as phenomena of post-materialism, are seen as the beginning of the end of the corporatist »economism« considered to be deeply rooted in Austria's Second Republic.[13]
- Decline of values. This approach does not explain new social movements as an exchange of one value system with another – as the post-materialist approach does. Decline of values means, at least tentatively, the total abolition of values. This culturally pessimistic approach is supported by evidence of the decline of all traditional links, including the decline of official church membership and church attendance as well as the decline of active participation in political parties and interest groups. »Distancing oneself from politics« is a syndrome describing those attitudes perhaps

12 For the integration into the international discussion, see Samuel H. Barnes, Max Kaase et al.: Political Action. Mass Participation in Five Western Democracies. Beverly Hills 1979 (Sage).
Joachim Raschke: Soziale Bewegungen. Ein historisch-systematischer Grundriß. Frankfurt am Main 1985 (Campus).
Carl Boggs: Social Movements and Political Power. Emerging Forms of Radicalism in the West. Philadelphia 1986 (Temple University).

13 The »postmaterialism« approach has been used rather early by Fritz Plasser, Peter A. Ulram: Unbehagen im Parteienstaat. Jugend und Politik in Österreich. Wien 1982 (Böhlau), especially pp. 131-145.

even better. Concerned with the fragmentation of Austrian society, this approach leads one to the conclusion that loyalties within the camps are withering away without being replaced – that the process of nation-building as a process of integrating the camps has not been successful in the long term.[14]

- New elites. This approach, which can be linked with the post-materialist approach without difficulty, emphasizes the explosive impact educational reform policies – though delayed in Austria – have on new social movements. During the last two decades high schools as well as universities have been opened on a large scale. Social barriers limiting access to different social elites have opened dramatically, too. As a result, positions in the social hierarchy have become more and more competitive. The tradition of inheriting social privileges has been challenged more and more. The new social movements, characterized by an educational level well above the average, represent a »counter-elite« facing the »traditional elite«. The specific Austrian aspect is that this new cleavage is not, as the traditional cleavages used to be, a horizontal one (right vs. left, christian-conservative camp vs. socialist camp), but a conflict between (by all means elitist) »outs« and (also elitist) »ins« – with the generation factor as an explicative, significant, and intervening variable.[15]
- Alienation. According to this approach, the fundamental oppositional attitude expressed by the new social movements indicates a deep social, and especially, economic crisis. The economic crisis, always seen in connection with the ecological crisis, cannot be down-played any longer by optimistic expectations in economic growth as was typical during the first decades after 1945. The new social movements have to be interpreted as a throughly rational response to social conditions and contradictions becoming more and more evident. In Austria, this explanation was backed by a conflict typical for the peace movement – the conflict with a specific Austrian military industrial complex which is primarily modelled on the pattern of a »mixed« economy with a strong dependance on government. The main actors of this complex (politicians, representatives of the public and state-owned industry, managers) are most often products of the socialist camp. The alienation-approach can be easily linked with the post-

14 Peter Gerlich: Nationalbewußtsein und nationale Identität in Österreich. In: Pelinka, Plasser, »Das österreichische Parteiensystem«, op.cit.

15 See the cluster-analysis by Plasser, »Parteien unter Streß«, op.cit., pp. 247-262.

materialist approach, too. Alienation tries to explain, more or less, the objective conditions of the creation and of the rise of new social movements, with post-materialism explaining the subjective conditions.[16]

III. Methodological and Institutional Aspects

Research on new social movements in Austria is typically not limited to specific methodologies. Rather, it uses the whole variety of traditional empirical social research: surveys, case studies, participatory observations, content analyses; a specific methodology has yet to be developed for research on new social movements in Austria.

To a certain extent, this is due to the lack of a special institution established exclusively or even mainly for the analysis of social movements. But significant numbers of researchers are located at institutions such as the following;

- University departments, especially the Departments of Sociology and Political Science at the Universities of Vienna, Graz, Innsbruck, Salzburg, Linz and Klagenfurt. The drawback of those institutes is their lack of faculty. Social science in Austria is still comparatively understaffed and underfinanced. University departments have to compete with one another for additional research funds as do the universities in general with extra-university institutes.[17]
- Extra-university institutes, which perform consultative social research primarily for various political bodies. In particular, the Institute for Empirical Research (Institut für empirische Sozialforschung, IFES), which traditionally is linked with the SPÖ, and the Fessel and GFK Institute (Fessel und Gesellschaft für Konsumforschung Institut), which cooperates

16 For a contribution from the viewpoint of theoretical sociology, see Max Prisching: Krisen. Eine soziologische Untersuchung. Wien 1986 (Böhlau).

17 The underdevelopment of social sciences at Austrian universities can be proved easily. For instance, within the three universities, having a fully developed masters and doctorate programs in political science (Vienna, Salzburg Innsbruck), on March 1, 1988, 25 permanent faculty positions existed (professors and assistant professors) – about the size of one of the better developed departments of a US university. The situation in sociology, on this quantitative level, is not much better at Austrian universities.

with the ÖVP. The disadvantage of those institutes is their lack of openness. The most important and interesting research produced by these two institutes, while funded by political parties, is not revealed to academia or the public at least for a certain period.[18]

- Extra-university institutes, which are connected to just one specific political party. There is, for instance, the Institute for Advanced Studies and Scientific Research (Institut für höhere Studien und wissenschaftliche Forschung), the Institute for Conflict Research (Institut für Konkfliktforschung) and the Social Science Studies Association (Sozialwissenschaftliche Studiengesellschaft). The last one was founded by the Austrian Trade Union Federation, but its results are in most cases completely open to other interested parties.[19]

Social research, related to new social movements, is mainly sponsored by three Austrian employers:

- The Federal government (especially the Federal Ministry for Science and Research and the Ministry of Labor and Social Affairs) as well as the state governments authorize or subsidize research projects dealing partly or exclusively with new social movements.[20]
- The Foundation for the Promotion of Scientific Research (Fonds zur Förderung der wissenschaftlichen Forschung) distributes Governement research funds. The universities are represented in this foundation, and their votes are decisive, especially concerning the direction of sponsored

18 Walter Fessel: Politik in Zahlen. Beginn und Wandlung der politischen Meinungsforschung in Österreich. In: Fritz Plasser, Peter A. Ulram, Manfred Welan (eds.): Demokratierituale. Zur politischen Kultur der Informationsgesellschaft. Wien 1985 (Böhlau).

19 One of the first empirical analysis of Austrian voting behavior was published by the Social Science Studies Association. Karl Blecha, Rupert Gmoser, Heinz Kienzl: Der durchleuchtete Wähler. Beiträge zur politischen Soziologie in Österreich. Wien 1964 (Europa).
The first general attempt to describe empirically election phenomena in Austria has been made by the Institute for Advanced Studies and Scientific Research. Rodney Stiefbold et al. (ed.): Wahlen und Parteien in Österreich. Österreichisches Wahlhandbuch. 3 Vol. Wien 1966 (Österreichischer Bundesverlag und Verlag Jugend und Volk).

20 Between 1984 and 1986 the Federal Ministry of Science and Research sponsored a rather large, interdisciplinary research project dealing with the general topic of »crisis«. A number of the final papers relate to new social movements. Rudolf Burger et al. (eds.): Verarbeitungsmechanismen der Krise. Wien 1988 (Braumüller).

research. During the last years, the share of social research within the foundation's framework has been increased significantly, but medicine and natural sciences nevertheless still dominate.

- The Jubilee Foundation of the Austrian National Bank (Jubiläumsfonds der Österreichischen Nationalbank) is able to react rather flexibly to new challenges. This foundation, financed by the National Bank, has sponsored social research including many projects in the field of new social movements. Within this foundation, reflecting the political structure of the Bank, the interests of the two major parties dominate.[21]

The results of research on new social movements is made public in different ways:

- Publication of books. The small Austrian market for social science publications dealing primarily with Austrian questions, requires subsidies. Nevertheless, especially during the first years of public awareness of new social movements, some of the most important publications were published as books. By emphasizing the difference between formal and informal political participation Deiser/Winkler[22] formulated an important criterion for the understanding of social movements in Austria. Plasser/Ulram have stressed, for the first time, the importance of the generation conflict for the interpretation of developments in political attitudes and in political behavior.[23]
- Publication of journals and yearbooks. Social science analyses and interpretations can be found especially in the following Austrian journals and yearbooks: Austrian Journal for Sociology (Österreichische Zeitschrift für Soziologie, published by the Austrian Association for Sociology); Austrian Journal for Political Science (Österreichische Zeitschrift für Politik-

---

21 That does not mean that party politics dominates the scientific analyses financed by the Jubilee Foundations. See, for instance: Max Haller, Kurt Holl (eds.): Werterhaltungen und Lebensformen in Österreich. Ergebnisse der sozialen Survey 1986. München und Wien 1987 (R. Oldenbourg und Verlag für Geschichte und Politik). This research and the publication were sponsored by the two foundations mentioned above, the Federal Ministry of Science and Research and by the State Government of Styria. This book includes indispensable interpretations of new social movements – for instance, related to the change of values, pp. 54-75.

22 Roland Deiser, Norbert Winkler: Das politische Handeln der Österreicher. Wien 1982 (Verlag für Gesellschaftskritik).

23 Plasser, Ulram, »Unbehagen im Parteienstaat«, op.cit.

wissenschaft, published by the Austrian Association for Political Science); Journal for Social Research (Journal für Sozialforschung, originally published by the aforementioned Social Studies Association, now internationally based and published by the International Studies Association for Interdisciplinary Social Science); and the Austrian Yearbook for Politics (Österreichisches Jahrbuch für Politik, published by Andreas Khol, Günther Ofner and Alfred Stirnemann).

- Research papers. Research projects, initiated and/or subsidized by the government or by the already mentioned funds, result more often than not in papers written exclusively for their employers. For this reason a rather high percentage of research is not available to the general or even academic public, and therefore, remains more or less unknown.
- Doctoral or Master's dissertations. Of dissertations dealing with new social movements, mainly from the fields of sociology or political science, only a relatively small number have been published (e.g., Platzer).[24] The majority of social science dissertations are available only through the restricted channels of the universities. Notably, a rather large number of case studies remain as unpublished dissertations.

IV. Summary of Results and Questions for further Research

The present results of social science represent a largely undisputed diagnosis of new social movements in Austria.[25]

- There is no doubt that new social movements are a phenomen of the »new middle classes«. This is indicated by voting behaviors characterized by a decline of predictability, an increase in flexibility and a growing tendency towards a preference for new parties.
- There is no doubt that the most important social factors for the »new middle classes« are youth and education. The younger and better edu-

---

24 Renate Platzer: Bürgerinitiativen in Salzburg. Eine vergleichende Untersuchung der Bürgerinitiative »Schützt Salzburgs Landschaft« mit der »Initiative für mehr Lebensqualität im Lehel«. München 1983 (Minerva).

25 Peter A. Ulram: Um die Mehrheit der Mehrheit. Die neuen, angestellten Mittelschichten 1975-1984. In: Plasser, Ulram, Welan, »Demokratierituale«, *op.cit.*

cated Austrians are, the higher is the probability of an »adequate« political and social behavior.

- There is no doubt that the »new middle classes« are affected by the economic crisis only to a lesser extent. New social movements can be seen as a phenomen of those segments of the society which, at least comparatively, are comfortably well off.

Of course, the explanations for these results are, in many cases, divergent. The most important divergence in interpreting the rise and the strengthening of new social movements derives from the question of how the evidence of a socio-economic crisis is considered. Are new social movements mainly the consequence of such a crisis?[26] Or are new social movements mainly the impact of a *delayed* modernization of Austria?[27]

With this contradiction probably the most important question for further research on new social movements in Austria is defined. The two general hypotheses are:

- New social movements in Austria are the result of a social and especially economic destabilization. Austria, for decades considered to be one of the most stabilized capitalist countries in the world, is now more and more affected by the gravity of the crisis and the depression that is typical for western, capitalist societies. Austria is losing its economic privilege.
- New social movements in Austria are the result of the defeudalization of the political system as well as that of the political culture, indicating an emancipation of a growing minority of citizens. The tradititonal camps are loosing their ability to integrate. Set free, these citizens are enjoying a kind of liberty. Owing to the significant lack of liberalism in Austria, this had been virtually unknown until now.

Lastly, both hypotheses mean that Austria is losing some of her peculiarities: Combinations of pessimistic and optimistic outlooks. New social movements in Austria appear in specific social, political and economic frameworks – but

26 Prisching, »Krisen«, op.cit., especially pp. 546-638.

27 »Modernization« as adaption to progressive, international trends – see Anton Pelinka, Fritz Plasser: Compared to What? Das österreichische Parteiensystem im internationalen Vergleich. In: Pelinka, Plasser, »Das österreichische Parteiensystem«, op.cit.; Melanie A. Sully, »Winds of Change in the Austrian Party System«. In: Pelinka, Plasser, »Das österreichische Parteiensystem«, op. cit.

their background and dynamism have to be seen in the context of the development of new social movements in other industrialized societies. Because they are confronted by an extremely traditional political environment, new social movements are indirectly working for the »Westernization« of Austria. The Austrian society will be »normalized« – especially with the effects of new social movements. The political structures typical for Austria are crumbling. The political loyalities also typical for Austria are dying. The new social movements are the wind of change, the wind of normalcy, reminding Austria that she is not the »island of the blessed«.

The social consequences, particularly for the political system, are summarized by Fritz Plasser in a diagram. He combines the traditional »right vs. left« pattern with the contradiction of materialist and postmaterialist attitudes. The result is an empirically-based diagram demonstrating the innovative effect of new social movements.

Plasser's results demonstrate that the new social movements are creating a new dimension for the Austrian party system. Plasser's explanation has to be seen as representative of the understanding social scientists have developed for new Austrian social movements:

- New social movements do not abolish the »right vs. left« pattern, but they broaden it significantly by adding a new dimension.
- New social movements in Austria are influencing all traditionally established groups; they are independent from any special background and they are not rooted in just one special camp.
- New social movements are responsible for a pluralism which did not exist before within the traditional, rather inflexible, extremely stabilized party system. The party system is becoming more pluralistic as well as more polarized.
- The effects new social movements have for a party system are typical for the whole society. The political system, strongly dominated by political parties, and the political attitudes of Austrians, heavily influenced by dominant political parties, are now being challenged and faced with change.
- New social movements in Austria thus represent social innovation and political change.

Diagram: The Position of Cluster-types and Party Preferences, according to Plasser.[28]

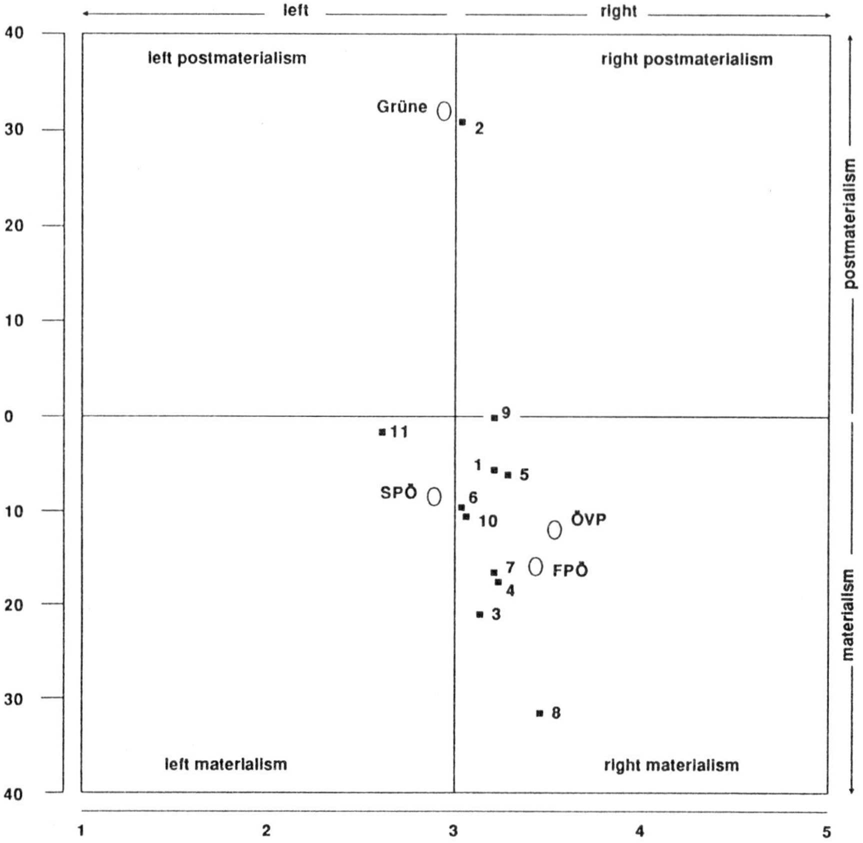

C 1 - social-conservative mainstream
C 2 - postmaterialist vanguard
C 3 - welfare state apathy
C 4 - career oriented conventionalists
C 5 - bourgeois-conservative traditionalists
C 6 - party-dissonant "children of nature"
C 7 - integrated system conformists
C 8 - potentially alienated materialists
C 9 - not yet activated green potential
C 10 - social reformist growth interests
C 11 - social democratic traditionalists

28 Plasser, »Parteien unter Streß«, op.cit., pp. 260. The different clusters are deducted and explained on pp. 247-262.

Beyond these interpretations there are still significant lacunae for further researchers to address. For instance, there is no scientific analysis on the style of new social movements in Austria and there is no analysis concerning the changes of conflict behavior of these movements. There are some attempts to explain specific Austrian conditions by describing the relative weakness of the Austrian students revolt around 1968.[29] What is still lacking, however, is a systematic »micro«-analysis of new social movements. An article about the cases of Zwentendorf and Hainburg could be seen as one step in that direction.[30]

By using different analyses, including unpublished dissertations, Herbert Gottweis has developed a useful typology for further research on new Austrian social movements.[31] Stressing the Austrian situation, Gottweis provides a brief overview of:

- the new women's movemet,
- the single-issue initiatives,
- the anti-nuclear movement,
- the new youth movement,
- the peace movement,
- the third-world movement.

This typology emphasizes the peculiarities of new social movements in Austria such as the predicament of a peace movement in a permanently neutral country. New social movements are interpreted as symptoms as well as factors for the overdue political mobilization of an extremely stabilized society.

As compared to other Western industrialized countries, the particular limits of the Austrian political system and the Austrian society explain Austria's retarded political, economical, social development. Austria's »model« has been characterized as an extremely stabilized system whose stability

---

29 Elisabeth Welzig: Die 68er. Karrieren einer rebellischen Generation. Wien 1985 (Böhlau). The work of a journalist, this book does not claim to be a scientific analysis.

30 Bernhard Natter: Die »Bürger« versus die »Mächtigen«. Populistischer Protest an den Beispielen Zwentendorf und Hainburg. In: Anton Pelinka (ed.): Populismus in Österreich. Wien 1987 (Junius).

31 Herbert Gottweis: Neue soziale Bewegungen in Österreich. Rahmenbedingungen, Verlaufsformen, Folgen für das politische System. In: Der Bürger im Staat, Stuttgart, 2/1988, pp. 139-144.

may appear as either social peace or social escapism.[32] It is this very nature which the new social movements criticize, and in this critizism develop their values.

The existence as well as the impact of new social movements can be interpreted as a trend toward »Deaustrification«. Through the new social movements, the Austrian political system and the Austrian society are losing some of their »typically Austrian« characteristics. In that sense, new social movements in Austria are a factor in the country's Internationalization.[33]

Annotated Bibliography

Burger, R. et al. (eds.). (1988): *Verarbeitungsmechanismen der Krise*. Wien: Braunmüller.
This book includes different studies focusing on »crisis« as the stimulus for changes in Austria.

Deiser, R.; Winkler, N. (1982): *Das politische Handeln der Österreicher*. Wien: Verlag für Gesellschaftskritik.
Based on a survey of 1980, different types of political participation in Austria are characterized and analyzed. The focus is on significant changes.

Giller, J. (1984): *Soziale Bewegung und Wertwandel in Österreich. Von der ›Studentenbewegung‹ zu den ›Grünen‹ und ›Alternativen‹*, Wien, Berichte und Informationen.
An historical explanation of the politically-articulated, new social movements in Austria.

Gottweis, H. (1988): »Neue soziale Bewegungen in Österreich. Rahmenbedingungen, Verlaufsformen, Folgen für das politische System.«, *Der Bürger im Staat* (2) 1988, 139-144.
The same article is also published in Siegfried Gerlach et al.: »*Österreich*«. Stuttgart: Kohlhammer, 129-147.
This article provides an overview of the consequences new social movements have had on the Austrian political system. It gives a good summary of different issues and trends.

Haller, M.; Holm, K. (eds.). (1987): *Werthaltungen und Lebensformen in Österreich. Ergebnisse des sozialen Survey 1986*. München: R. Oldenburg / Wien: Verlag für Geschichte und Politik.
Using broadly based surveys, the authors of the different articles demonstrate interdependencies among social developments, political beliefs and behavior. Many contextual relations are provided for new social movements, but they are mostly indirect.

---

32 Anton Pelinka: Windstille. Klagen über Österreich. Wien 1985 (Medusa).

33 For the comparative aspects, see Peter Gerlich: Consociationalism to Competition. The Austrian Party Sytem since 1945. In: Hans Daalder (ed.): Party Systems in Denmark, Austria, Switzerland, the Netherlands and Belgium. New York 1987 (St. Martin's Press). Anton Pelinka: Austria. In: Gerald A. Dorfman, Peter J. Duignan (eds.): Politics in Western Europe. Stanford 1988 (Hoover Institution).

Kofler, A. (1985): *Parteiengesellschaft im Umbruch. Partizipationsprobleme von Großparteien*. Wien: Böhlau.

The book concentrates on significant developments in the major Austrian parties with particular emphasis on internal structures and changing attitudes within the parties.

Österreichische Zeitschrift für Politikwissenschaft 2 (86) (1986): »Schwerpunktthema: Neue soziale Bewegungen.« Wien: Verlag für Gesellschaftskritik.

5 Articles; 4 of them concerning Austria are the result of a conference on new social movements organized by the Austrian Association of Political Science in December 1985.

Pelinka, A. (ed.): (1987): *Populismus in Österreich*. Wien: Junius.

Of the different articles, those written by Sieglinde Rosenberger on the feminist movement, Andreas Maislinger on an anti-army movement, Bernhard Natter on aspects of the ecological movement and Anton Pelinka on theoretical aspects of corporatism versus new social movements are directly related to the topic.

Pelinka, A; Plasser, F. (eds.). (1988): *Das österreichische Parteiensystem*, Wien: Böhlau.

In this rather extensive reader – dealing with virtually all aspects of the Austrian party system – a few articles are directly related to the new social movements: the general introductory articles by the two editors, Herbert Dachs' article on green parties and movements, and Peter Gerlich's article on the development of the Austrian identity.

Pelinka, A.; Plasser, F. (eds.). (1989): *The Austrian Party System*, Boulder: Westview.

The US edition of the reader includes all the articles mentioned above referring to new social movements in Austria.

Plasser, F.; Ulram, P.A. (1982): *Unbehagen im Parteienstaat. Jugend und Politik in Österreich*. Wien: Böhlau.

This book offers the first general description and analysis of the consequences of new social movements for the Austrian political system.

Plasser, F.; Ulram, P.A.; Welan, M. (eds.). (1985): *Demokratierituale. Zur politischen Kultur der Informationsgesellschaft*. Wien: Böhlau.

Articles written by Peter Gerlich on green-alternative tendencies, Peter A. Ulram on the new middle classes, Christian Haerpfer on long-term trends in voting behavior and Walter Fessel and Rudolf Bretschneider on electoral research are directly related to the topic.

Preglau, M. (1987): *Wachstumskrise und Gesellschaftstheorie. Krisenanalyse am Beispiel der Frankfurter Schule*. Frankfurt: Campus.

Written by an Austrian sociologist, this book is not related directly to Austria, but it is an Austrian contribution to a theory of social crisis and new social movements.

Prisching, N. (1986): *Krisen. Eine soziologische Untersuchung*. Wien: Böhlau.

This interdisciplinary work deals with the primarily economically-defined crises; many aspects are linked to new social movements.

Stock, W. (ed.). (1986): *Ziviler Ungehorsam in Österreich*. Wien: Böhlau.

Seven chapters discuss civil disobedience with particular emphasis on Austria's peace movement.

Ulram, P.A. (1990): *Hegemonie und Erosion. Politische Kultur und politischer Wandel in Österreich*. Wien: Böhlau.

Peter A. Ulram provides a broad overview of changes in Austrian political culture reflecting the impact of new social movements.

Umdenken (1984): *Umdenken. Analysen grüner Politik in Österreich.* Wien: Junius.

13 articles discussing ecological attitudes in Austria, especially those of political parties and interest groups and their relationships to new social movements.

Research on Social Movements in Sweden

Ron Eyerman and Andrew Jamison

I. Introduction

More than any other in Europe, Sweden's post-War political culture has been dominated by old social movements, those associated with the conflicts between capital and labor. The very term ›movement‹, when expressed in the Swedish word *rörelse*, carries associations to the Social Democratic party and the working class. Social democracy is known to its leaders, members and opponents as ›The Movement‹. In Swedish one speaks of the contract bargaining between capital and labor as a *rörelse*, and political speeches from the left side of the political spectrum are always spiced with reference to ›the movement‹, the meaning of which is clear to everyone.

This is all not so unusual when one reflects on the fact that there has been only one really significant social movement in Sweden since the 1930's, thus giving the concept its seemingly fixed meaning in the political culture. This political and cultural hegemony has also affected the scientific discourse, an effect that is reflected in sociological research. Older social movements, which come in two varieties if one includes the period before the first world war, have institutionalized research both in the universities and in their own research and education institutes. Working class research is carried out at the Arbetslivcentrum (The Center for the Study of Working Life) in Stockholm and in working groups at various universities around the country, while research on the earlier *folkrörelser* (people's movements), like the temperance movement and the evangelical movements, are institutionalized through a special research delegation.[1] The broader anglo-saxon term social move-

1 The agency in charge of research on ›popular movements‹. The Committee for Popular Movement Research (Delegationen för Folkrörelseforskning) has compiled an extensive bibliography, Solberg (1981).

ments meaning an area of sociology does not exist, or has not existed until very recently.[2]

The bias towards the old social movement has accompanied a tendency in Swedish sociology to focus on issues related to social welfare and the welfare state (Fridjonsdottir 1987). This has had the positive effect of generating interesting developments in the sociology of work, health and safety and in social welfare in general, but the negative effect of making it difficult for any ›new‹ social movements to establish either a scientific or, more importantly, a political identity.

Whether due to cracks in this hegemony or to influence from abroad there are now signs that research into the new social movements has begun in earnest. The first sign is the fact that the very concept of social movement in its anglo-saxon and continental meanings is now gaining acceptance in Swedish sociology (Olofsson 1986; Eyerman and Jamison 1989a). Since the Swedish term is so connected to a particular ›movement‹ and given the historical connotation of the other possible terms *ideella rörelser* or folkrörelser, the English term is the one that is most often used. This can also be understood in terms of the hegemony of English and of American sociology in general, a hegemony which goes back to the post-war period. The recent debates in such journals as *Telos* and *Social Research* and the books by Alain Touraine and his colleagues in France have also affected this development. However, by far the most important cause of these cracks in the scientific culture is the emergence of the new social movements themselves, as political phenomena to be taken with some seriousness.

While there is still disagreement among researchers in the field about how exactly to define a ›social movement‹, one thing seems to be clear: a movement is a form of popular, collective political action which is neither organized nor steered from above. A movement is a more or less spontaneous outburst which threatens the hegemony of the existing political culture through developing ideas and organizations which both reflect and condition more long-term shifts in values and social structures. What were called movements in other Western societies, the student movement, the women's movement, the peace movement and so on, never really achieved ›movement‹ status in Sweden (Rubart and Peterson 1986). That is, the conflicts around education and politics, the war in Vietnam, disarmament, gen-

2 Lundqvist (1977) offers a summary in Swedish of the international debate on the study of social movements, one of the first to appear.

der relations and so on, were, after early spontaneous outbursts, quickly re-organized within the established political frameworks.[3] The student movement was quickly captured by the VPK, a Eurocommunist party, and redefined as an alliance between academics and the working class, and the women's movement at first influenced by developments abroad soon divided along lines defined by the established left-right political and cultural traditions. In other words, these ›new movements‹ came soon to be redefined and captured by the old ones. It need only be recalled that one of the leading ideologists and activists in the anti-Vietnam and peace movement was the late leader of the Social Democratic party and Prime Minister Olof Palme, a fact which made it difficult to define these issues in opposition to the established political culture. They could too easily be incorporated.

The flexibility, not to say repressive tolerance, of the governing Social Democratic party and of the Swedish state in general has created other difficulties for the establishment of new social movements. It should be said, of course, that this flexibility can be interpreted in many ways depending upon ones own ideological position. Leaders of protest movements appear to have a relatively easy time finding careers in the established career structures. Examples are too easy to find; two of the more recent one involve the environmental movement. A former activist in the campaign against nuclear energy is now a leading spokesman for the Social Democratic party in the environmental ministry and a leading figure in Swedish Greenpeace is a former high level social democratic administrator (Jamison 1987). It seems ›the movement‹ swings both ways. However, as noted, it is the environmentalist movement which has opened the most cracks in the hegemony of this incorporationist political culture (Vedung 1988). This is perhaps because environmental issues, more than the issues of gender relations and world peace, have the potential for most threatening the productivist mentality which underlies Swedish political culture. As long as women's issues can be translated into questions of money and equality of opportunity, they can quite easily be accepted into the established frameworks of both left and right. The only crisis in this translation occurred when economic growth could no longer be assumed to continue at the rates of the 1950's and 60's. Environmental issues however, have the potential, as Alain Touraine has pointed

3 An example of a ›backward‹ looking study can be found in the follow-up study of student activists in Sweden in 1968 being carried out in Lund. The results of the earlier study can be found in Lundberg et al. (1970).

out, to challenge the very idea of economic growth and thus to call into question the values central to the current hegemonic political culture (Touraine 1981).

If we define ›social movement‹ in experiential terms as a break with the established political routines, then the period which culminated with the national referendum on nuclear energy in 1980 saw the development of a real new social movement in Swedish society. (Eriksson et al. 1982; Jamison 1987) The older parties for a time lost control of the nuclear issue: it could not be easily contained in the established frameworks and translated into issues of money and employment, i.e. old movement issues. Spontaneous demonstrations and organizations formed around environmentalist issues, and while the old parties attempted to keep pace and to reorient their ideologies, for a time they were the followers rather than the leaders of the »movement«.

Despite the apparent rapid incorporation and marginalization of political movements, the study of social movements is gaining ground. This has taken the form of backward looking, both nostalgic and more straightly sociological and historical, studies of the early days of »the movement«, when workers, farmers and others were really »in movement« and forward looking, highly ideological, books about »new« social movements. The middle ground – more distanced studies of contemporary social movements – is relatively vacant, as yet. This too is a result of the highly emotional connotation given the concept »movement« in the Swedish political culture. In this context (as Touraine shows), speaking about social movements involves taking a stand about the »old« ones, and for some, involves being propagandists for the »new« ones.

II. Theoretical and Methodological Approaches

This background is important to have in mind in considering Swedish research on social movements. Indeed, it helps explain why there is so little research on social movements compared to, say, Denmark or Holland. Most social movement research has been focused on the »old« movements on the working class and it has been highly descriptive. Until quite recently, it has, for the most part, fallen into the ethnographic, even folklorist tradition of social history that has been so strong in Sweden. This means that the theoretical, or historiographic approach is highly traditional, although, in recent years, a group of intellectual historians in Umeå has begun to develop a more sophisticated approach to labor movement history. Drawing on the conceptualizations of working class culture developed in Britain by E.P. Thompson and his followers/critics, Ronny Ambjörnsson and others have attempted to problematize the concept of class consciousness within the Swedish context (Qvarsell et al. 1986; Ambjörnsson 1988). They have examined working class institutions and organizations as well as early social democratic leaders and spokesmen from the perspective of a critical intellectual history. At several points, their work converges with research carried out by other intellectual historians who have been writing on the intellectual and ideological roots of the »Swedish model«.

Much of this intellectual historiography is part of an ongoing reassessment of Swedish social democracy. The descriptive and, at times, highly self-congratulatory historiography of the old social movements has been confronted with a more reflective and critical historical interest during the past ten years. It has also been confronted with theoretical approaches emanating from the new social movements themselves. But in much the same way that the new social movements have had difficulty establishing an independent identity for themselves within the Swedish political culture, new theoretical approaches to the study of social movements have also had difficulty establishing themselves within the Swedish academic culture.

The most explicit follower of the »new social movement« approach has been Gothenburg sociologist Mate Friberg, who has written a series of books and articles pointing to the new »post-material values« associated with the new movements of environmentalism and feminism. We will discuss Friberg's approach in more detail below. Our own perspective on social movements – what we refer to as a cognitive approach – seeks to link the study of social movements to the social study of science and technology. By identifying what we call the »knowledge interests« of the new social movements, we focus on the contribution that social movements play in the development of knowledge. We have also sought to problematize the relationship between social movements and intellectuals, particularly within the Swedish context.

Mention might also be made of the research on the women's movement that has been conducted by Abby Peterson. As with our own research on environmentalism, Peterson analyzes feminism as a challenge to the Swedish political culture. It is perhaps not accidental that much of the work on new social movements in Sweden has been carried out by emigre researchers from the United States. Even Friberg's research has been difficult to assimilate into mainstream Swedish sociology, which has preferred to ignore the new movements or to minimize their social and political significance. The quantitative methods of Swedish empirical sociology have been applied elsewhere than to the study of the new sociological movements. This can be expected to change, however, with the recent (September 1988) entrance into parliament of the Green party, which has inspired the beginnings of electoral and membership surveys of the Green party by political scientists (e.g. Vedung 1989).

III. Empirical Findings and Institutional Aspects

Since the mid-1970's, there has been a loosely-organized research group on social movements at the Department of Sociology at the University of Gothenburg (»rörelseforskningsgruppen«). Led by Mats Friberg, the group has conducted a number of studies of specific movements, which we will discuss in the following section. It has cooperated with several other university departments in Gothenburg, such as the Center for Interdisciplinary Studies, which has long been involved, both through research and education, in environmental activism; the Department for Peace Research, where Björn Hettne has written on developmental strategies in Third World, as well as on alternative developmental theories and »alternative movements« in developing countries; the Department of Music, where a number of studies have been carried out on the new »music movements« in Sweden; and with the Department of Architecture at Chalmers Technological University, where there has been research directed toward the »housing movements«. In addition, Friberg and Hettne have together been associated with the United Nations University project on Peace and Global Transformation. Also worth mentioning are the close ties that Friberg has established with the Norwegian peace researcher Johan Galtung; all of these conceptions, but escpecially the latter, have recently manifested themselves in a particularly visible way, through the publication of three anthologies jointly edited by Friberg and Galtung – *Crisis, Movements, and Alternatives* (*Krisen* [1983], *Rörelserna* [1984], *Alternativen* [1985]). The three volumes contain contributions by movement activists, as well as by researchers associated with Friberg's group and the other institutions mentioned above.

These books are the only substantial general studies of the new social movements in Swedish. They provide a wealth of empirical and theoretical material, but since they are written primarily for the general public – and for movement activists themselves – the material is perhaps more ideological and journalistic than sociological. Our discussion will mostly be drawn from the middle volume on movements, but it might be useful to consider briefly some of the arguments of the other two volumes, so that the reader might better be able to understand the intellectual context of the Gothenburg group.

The crisis afflicting modern society is, for Friberg and Galtung, deep and fundamental; it is modernization itself that is at issue, and not merely one or another variety. Both capitalism and socialism are considered equally bankrupt, since the crisis is seen not so much in economic, as in moral or ethical terms. There is almost a millenarian flavor to Friberg's position, and he cites, with approval, »new age« writers like Mark Satin and Fritiof Capra. It is the belief in materialist values that is seen as the main problem, or as Friberg sometimes calls it, the industrialization project. For Friberg and Galtung, the crisis is an international, or global one: the developing countries are just as much afflicted by it as the industrialized countries. Indeed, part of the potential that is seen for the new social movements is in linking up with groups in developing countries that are also in opposition to the industrialization project.

Friberg's account leaves room for a number of different – even conflicting – formulations of this central theme. One important influence has been Pitirim Sorokin's idealistic sociology, with its long cycles of historical change, based on different types of dominant value systems. The recent theorizing over business cycles, or Schumpeterian »long waves« of industrial development, has also been important. Friberg tries to indicate how social movements are both reactions to particular historical processes, as well as carriers or instruments of new historical processes. More popular works, such as Alvin Toffler's *The Third Wave* and, perhaps even more importantly, Charles Reich's *The Greening of America* (which Friberg refers to as a »classical analysis«) have also been sources of inspiration for Friberg's perspective. To reiterate, the main point is that industrialization is on the way out – even though Friberg is explicitly vague about when the new »post-industrial society will actually come into being. Civilization, however, is seen to be facing a transformation similar to the transition from agriculture to industry.

Unlike Alain Touraine or Daniel Bell, Friberg is not particularly concerned with providing material explanations, or even empirical evidence, of this transformation. He takes the transition as an established fact. He proposes a »subjective« emphasis rather than an objective one, a focus on values, mentalities, ideologies, rather than on material or objective »factors«. His main category, for analyzing both the crisis, the movements, as well as the alternative, is the category of »life-style«.

In the first essay of the volume on movements, Friberg writes that the new social movements »protest *against* the technocratic system and they are *for* a radical humanist alternative in all aspects of life from work to housing to social relations to culture. There is no doubt that *a new mentality* is on the rise throughout the western world. This new spirit liberates human energy and gives power to all the citizen initiatives which are now taking place throughout society.« (»Försörjarnas protester och levnadskonstnärernas alternativ« in *Rörelserna*, p. 19.)

Friberg posits a fundamental distinction between the new and the old movements, since the old movements were constitutive of industrial society. Friberg sees the new movements as the carriers of »post-materialist« values, and he is thus more interested in the movements as a whole – or, more accurately perhaps, as an idea – than in the actual movements as they have organized themselves. Friberg's approach is to attempt to show what the different movements have in common, rather than to analyze any conflicts or tensions among them. It is thus no accident that the particular movements that he and his colleagues have studied – and grouped together in the movements anthology – have primarily been studied in ideological terms, and that Friberg's own work has increasingly taken an ideological form. After the anthologies, he has been involved in a future study of an »Alternative Sweden« that has been part of an attempt to have various new and old social movements work together on a futures research project. The study is being conducted in connection with similar studies in Denmark and Norway, and represents a major effort to coordinate ideological discussions among »alternative« groups and researchers.

A second center for research on the new social movements in Sweden has been the Cooperative Institute in Stockholm (*Kooperative institutet*), which is an independent research body supported by the Cooperative Federation (*KF, Kooperativa förbundet*). The research carried out by the institute has primarily dealt with the new forms of cooperatives that had sprung up in Sweden, both amongst producers and consumers, and the institute has also sponsored conferences and seminars on the new ideas of cooperation that are being developed outside of Sweden.

A final center for research in the new social movements is the State Youth Council (*Statens ungdomsråd*), which conducts research of its own, as well as supporting and publicizing research at the universities. The Council also supports the »movements« themselves, in particular the various activities primarily within music and culture that have been characteristic of young people's socio-political behavior since the emergence of rock 'n roll. New cultural centers and music halls, organized and largely administered by young people themselves, have been encouraged and, in part, sponsored by the Youth Council.

The Friberg/Galtung volume on movements contains articles on the youth movement, the women's movement, the cooperative movement, housing movements, the communes movement, regional movements, the environmental movement, the peace movement, and even the new religious movements. They are written, or the most part, by people who have produced full-length studies on these movements in Sweden, although the peace and environmental movement chapters are written by activists. These movements have not yet received detailed academic scrutiny in Sweden.

The chapter on youth movements, by Erling Bjurström, who has previously been associated with Friberg's group and is now employed by the Youth Council, is a summary of a larger study that was published in 1980. Although Bjurström apparently shares many of Friberg's assumptions and concerns, his own research is more specifically influenced by the idea of a »generational consciousness« as formulated by Karl Mannheim and others. Bjurström is thus not terribly concerned to distinguish between cultural and political movements; the »youth movement«, is the general socio-cultural experience of youth, and thus includes both overtly political activity as well as more established cultural activity. Bjurström focuses on the shifts of generational attitude, locating and analyzing a fundamental discontinuity between the youth movements of the 1960's and those of the 1970's. His research takes the form of a sociologically-informed popular history of young people's ideological perspectives, and a goal deal of attention is thus directed toward popular music, and the attitudes that are expressed in music and other aspects of »life-style«.

Another contributor to the movements anthology, Britta Jonsson, has also been associated with Friberg's group, even though she did her graduate work in sociology at the University of Uppsala. Jonsson has also moved from the university to the Youth Council, where she now coordinates youth research. Her chapter is also a summary of a larger study – on the rural communes that were developed in Sweden during the 1970's. (Jonsson 1983) Jonsson's research is highly empirical, involving a large number of interviews with the communards; and her results are similarly empirical, analyzing the motivations and the specific personal events that led to the founding of the four rural communes that she studied.

The contribution on the women's movement in the Friberg-Galtung movements volume is called ›Women in Movement‹ (Kvinnor i rörelse) and written by Eva Björkander-Mannheimer. Following the ideological tone set by the editors, the treatment of the women's movement offered here is political-literary rather than empirical. Although some reference is made to historical events, such as the struggle over the right to vote and early connections between the student and the women's movement in the late 1960's, the two key concepts, »women« and »movement« are left unspecified. In the style of F. Alberoni's *Movement and Institution*, the author writes: ›a definition of the women's movement must include all forms of expressions for womanly energy-thoughts, gestures, actions – that in some way and with some measure or womanly self-respect directs itself to other women or to their lives and problems. Therefore: as soon as two women – women, who set for themselves a certain type of problems – find themselves in a public sphere, the women's movement is created ...‹ (p. 88) given such a broad phrasing, it is not surprising that the author's discussion of the women's movement lacks precision; for it is unclear as to when such a ›movement‹ really could be said to begin and to develop. Also, on the basis of such a definition any and all members of the female gender are participants in the ›movement‹ when they act publicly in concert, making it hard to separate either the issues at stake or the possibility of their successful fulfillment, not a very promising way to delineate an area of political action, let alone an area of sociological research.

In complete contrast to this ideological-literary approach to the women's movement is that of the sociologist Abby Peterson. In a series of articles this author presents a well grounded analysis of both the structural foundations and the action areas of the contemporary Swedish women's movement. Where Eva Björkander-Mannheimer sees the women's movement as romantic, cultural protest against modernity and modernization, Peterson finds its roots in a protest against the way contemporary Swedish politics is organized. In an article entitled ›The Gender-Sex Dimension in Swedish Politics‹ (1984), Peterson argues that the new women's movement is best understood as responding to the exclusion of women's problems and interests by a political culture which focuses on problems of production and distribution, rather than on reproduction and caring. Like other advanced industrial societies, Swedish political life centers around the conflict of interest between labor and capital, interests organized through political parties polarized along a left-right dimension. Where Sweden differs from many other industrial societies is in the fact that its farmers have maintained a strong political profile in the Center Party and thus have not, as in other countries been incorporated into one or another hegemonic political party. This fact has led Peterson, as well as many other commentators, to add a rural-urban dimension to an understanding of Swedish politics, in addition to the previously mentioned left-right dimensions. As Peterson sees it, the contemporary women's movement results from the exclusion of reproductive and gender-specific interests from politics as defined by these parties and this political culture. Her definition of the women's movement is thus broad, but empirical, and includes ›... all women's organizations, women's solidarity and action groups, and temporary protest actions of women, united by a political interest in one or more of the categories of the gender-sex dimensions‹ (p. 23). Thus, the woman's movement is both a reaction against this exclusion and an attempt to extend the area of politics to include specifically ›woman's issues‹. Here the viewpoints of Björkander-Mannheimer and Peterson begin to coincide. Both would argue that it is the specific tasks which women perform in society, the reproductive labor connected to home and family, as well as those occupations which are their public and paid extensions, which forms the basis of a common ›culture‹ and, in political terms, a common interest. This culture and these interests are just those which the old movements and the established political culture have not heeded; thus the emergence of a political women's movement on a broader basis than the older suffragette movement, which sought only the right to participate in politics and not to redefine the aim of politics itself.

A more traditional sociological study of the contemporary Swedish women's movement can be found in a doctoral thesis presented at the University of Gothenberg in 1983 (Streiffert 1983), which builds empirically on a survey and historical analysis of three women's organizations in Gothenburg, one dominated by middle-class and professional women, one connected to the Social Democratic Party and one further to the radical left. Theoretically the study draws on Robert Merton's notion of reference group and on role theory. Streiffert uses the latter as a way of defining the relation between the individual, the organization and the social movement. For the individual woman, the movement is both an organization and a frame of reference that gives the individual a sense of belonging and purpose to complement that provided by the concrete social group to which she belongs. Further, the movement is also a collective actor operating in a field with other collective actors in conflicts over power in society. The results of her empirical survey reveal the aging membership of the two socialist women's organizations and the younger, more dynamic character of the middle class organization. Data also concerns the various motivations offered by women for their participation in these organisations. Another recent doctoral thesis, *Kulturpedagogik i Tekniksamhälle* (Cultural Education in Technological Society) by Bosse Talerud, contains a chapter on ›the women's movement and culture critique‹ which summarizes much of the Swedish material on the ideological and pedagogical aspects of the new women's movement. The author builds on a theoretical framework adapted from A. Gramsci and other critical marxists such as Lukacs and Adorno.

The recent comparative study of the environmentalist movements in Sweden, Holland and Denmark carried out at the University of Lund by Ron Eyerman and Andrew Jamison, in collaboration with Jeppe Laessoe (Denmark) and Jacqueline Cramer (Holland), builds upon the theoretical framework provided by Frankfurt critical theory and the sociology of knowledge. This four year study entitled Environmentalism and Knowledge is designed to uncover the relationship between the ›knowledge interests‹ of the movement, defined in terms of the types of knowledge they presuppose and produce, and the concrete political strategies they adopt in their national contexts. The study aims at being both historical and analytical, offering a history of environmentalism and the environmentalist movements in the three countries and explaining differences in terms of national political cultures. In this study, the focus in on the cognitive as well as the organizational and tactical aspects of social movements. The focus on knowledge provides a way of studying the development of world views in social movements, how these congeal and fragment as basis for collective identity, and how such worldviews impact upon the wider social and political context, influencing, for example, the development of science and technology as well as the more specific national political culture.

IV. Conclusion

From the above examples of Swedish research into the new social movements it should be clear that the field is at present underdeveloped. This can in part be explained by a lack of vitality in the movement's themselves – they barely exist as living political forces. The hegemonic political culture in place since the end of World War 2 – dominated by a reformist and statist social democratic party – has managed through its skillfully applied flexibility to contain potential movements by absorbing both issues and individuals. The success in managing and developing the Swedish economy has played no small part in this successful adaptation. Even today, with the political scene dominated by issues related to the environment and especially to nuclear energy, the social democratic movement has sought to contain any threatening collective behavior by posing as the ›environmentalist party‹. With the coming into parlament of the Green party, however, in 1988, the political culture experienced a shock – and it will be interesting to see exactly what that shock brings with it, by way of studies on social movements in the years to come (see Vedung 1989 and Jamison 1989 for preliminary assessments).

Annotated Bibliography

Ambjörnsson, R. (1988): *Den skötsamma arbetaren (The conscientious worker)*. Stockholm: Carlssons.

Cramer, J.; Eyerman, R.; and Jamison, A. (1987): ›The Knowledge Interests of the Environmental Movement and Its Potential for Influencing the Development of Science‹, in: S. Blume et al. (eds.). *The Social Direction of the Public Science*. Dordrecht: Reidel.

Eriksson, B. et al. (1982): Det förlorade försprånget (The lost initiative). Gothenburg: Miljöförbundet.
The story of the national referendum on nuclear power as told from the inside by activists.

Eyerman, R.; Jamison, A. (1989a): ›Social Movements: Contemporary Debates,‹ Department of Sociology, University of Lund.

– (1989b): ›Environmental Knowledge as an Organizational Weapon: The Case of Greenpeace,‹ *Social Science Information* 2.
– (1990): *Social Movements: A Cognitive Approach*. Cambridge: Polity Press.
Friberg, M.; Galtung, J. (eds.). (1983): *Krisen (Crisis)*. Stockholm; Akademilitteratur.
– (1984): *Rörelserna (Movements)*. Stockholm; Akademilitteratur.
– (1986): *Alternativen (Alternatives)*. Stockholm; Akademilitteratur.
These books cover a wide range of new movements and ideas and offer a fairly broad overview of movement activity and research from the viewpoint of the activist-intellectual.
Frieberg, M.; Hettne, B. (1982): ›Processes of Penetration and Mobilization in Third World Countries‹ Institution for Peace and Conflict Research, University of Gothenberg.
– (1984): ›The Greening of the World: Towards a Non-Deterministic Model of Global Processes‹, in: A. Herb et al. (eds.). *Development as Social Transformation*. Tokyo: United Nations University.
Fridjonsdottir, K. (1987): ›Social Change, Trade Union Politics, and Sociology of Work,‹ in: S. Blume, et al. (eds.). *The Social Direction of the Public Sciences*. Dordrecht: Reidel.
Gidlund, J. (1978): *Aktionsgruper och lokala partier: Temporära politiska organisationer i Sverige 1965-1976 (Action groups and local parties: temporary organizations in Sweden)*. Umeå: Gleerup.
Gromark, S. (1984): ›Boendegemenskap som drivkraft‹ (Tenant's collective as motivating force) in: M. Friberg, J. Galtung (eds.). op. cit.
Hettne, B. (1983): ›Den västerländska utvecklingsmodellen ifrågasatt‹ (Questioning the Western model of development) in: M. Friberg , J. Galtung (eds.). op. cit.
Inglehart, R. (1977): *The Silent Revolution. Changing Values and Political Styles among Western Publics*. Princeton: Princeton University Press.
Jamison, A. (1987): ›The Making of the New Environmental Movement in Sweden‹, University of Lund, Department of Sociology.
– (1988) ›Social Movements and the Politicization of Science,‹ in: J. Annerstedt and A. Jamison (eds.). *From Research Policy to Social Intelligence*. London: Macmillan.
– (1989): ›The Greening of Swedish Politics,‹ paper presented at the annual meeting of the British Political Studies association, University of Warwick.
Jamison, A.; Eyermann, R.; Cramer, J. (1990): *The Making of the New Environmental Consciousness. A Comparative Study of the Environmental Movements in Sweden, Denmark and the Netherlands*. Edinburgh: Edinburgh University Press.
Jonsson, B. (1983): *Alternativa livsformer i 70-talets Sverige (Alternative forms of life in Sweden)*. Uppsala: Department of Sociology.
Lundberg, S.; Månsson, S.-Å., and Welander, H. (1970): *Demonstranter – En sociologisk studie (Demonstrators: a Sociological Study)*. Stockholm: Liber.
Lundqvist, S. (1977): *Fölkrörelserna i det svenska samhället 1850-1920 (Popular Movements in Swedish Society 1850-1920)*. Stockholm: Sober.
Olofsson, G. (1986): ›Efter arbetarrörelsen: om vad som är nytt och socialt i de nya sociala rörelserna‹, *Zenit* 93. (After the working class movement: on what is new and social in the new social movements).

Peterson, A. (1981): ›Kvinnofrågor, Kvinnomedvetande och klass‹, *Zenit* 2 (The women's question, women's consciousness and class).

– (1984): ›The Gender-Sex Dimension in Swedish Politics‹, *Acta Sociologica* 27, 1.

– (1985): ›The New Woman's Movement – Where Have All the Women Gone?‹ *Women's Studies International Forum* 8 (6).

Peterson, A.; Merchant, C. (1985): ›Fred med jorden: Kvinnor och miljörörelsen i Norden‹ (Peace with the Earth: Women and the Environmentalist Movement in the Nordic Countries), *Natur och Samhälle* 34.

Qvarsell, R. et al. (1986): *I framtidens tjänst (In the service of the future)*. Stockholm: Gidlunds.

Rubart, F.; Peterson, A. (1986): ›New Social Movements and Political Autonomy in Sweden: Political Protest Between Autonomy and Integration.‹ Umeå, Department of Sociology.

Ruin, O. (1960): *Kooperative förbundet 1899-1929*. Lund: Berlingska.

Solberg, G. (1981): *En bibliografi över folkrörelseforskning*. Stockholm: Liber.

Streijffert, H. (1983): *Studier i Den Svenska Kvinnorörelsen* (Studies in the Swedish Women's Movement). Gothenburg.

Thelander, A.-L. ›The Public as a Pressure Group‹ Department of Sociology, University of Lund.

Thörnberg, E.H. (1943): *Folkrörelser och samhällsliv i Sverige (Popular movements and social life in Sweden)*. Stockholm: Bonnier.
A classic text on social movements in Swedish society.

Touraine, A. (1981): *The Voice and the Eye*. Cambridge: Cambridge University Press.

Vedung, E. (1988): ›The Swedish Five-Party Syndrome and the Envrionmentalists,‹ in: K. Lawson, and P.H. Merkl, (eds.). *When Parties Fail: Emerging Alternative Organizations*. Princeton: Princeton University Press.

– (1989): ›Green Light for the Swedish Greens,‹ in: F. Muller-Rommel (ed.). *New Politics in Western Europe: The Rise and Success of Green parties and Alternative Lists*. Boulder: Westview.

Zetterberg, H. (1977): *Arbete, livsstil och motivation (Work, Lifestyle and Motivation)*. Stockholm: SAF (Swedish Employers Association).

Ås, B. (1975): ›On Female Culture: An Attempt to formulate a theory of women's Solidarity and Action‹, *Acta Sociologica* 18, 2-3.

Research on Social Movements in Denmark

Peter Gundelach

I. Denmark and Social Movements

The peasant's and the worker's movements represented the social forces which modernized Denmark from a feudal to a capitalist society. The peasant's movement began as a religious movement, but in the 1840s peasants created political organizations which, in alliance with the intellectual bourgeoisie, were the force behind changing the political system from a monarchy to a constitutional democracy. The alliance lasted only a few years. Later, the rural and urban bourgeoisie united and had a very strong influence in society. Among other things, they restricted the democratic constitution in their favour.

The emergence of the working class and its economic and political movement around 1870 did not change this immediately. Only after three decades did the united forces of peasants and workers succeed in transforming the constitutional government into a modern democracy.

Both peasants and workers formed economic institutions which played roles as makers of continuity, and the cultural organizations of the movements were important in socializing the members of the two classes. In contrast to most other European countries, both classes were important until around 1960 when the number of peasants rapidly diminished.

I give this brief historical sketch because I wish to stress that even after World War II two classes still greatly influenced the shaping of modern society, and mainly, through social movements. Thus, it is not surprising that the term »social movement« has always had positive connotations in the Danish language. Consider the term coined by a historian after World War II: »the people's movements«.

The old movements have always been associated with the modernization of society. They expressed progress. In Denmark, distinct from probably all other countries, there have never been important conservative movements. Of course, the influence of conservative forces was expressed in many ways in society, but almost never as a social movement. Even the fascist movement in the 1930s was pretty weak. The new social movements reflect the same general pattern. Denmark, for instance, has never experienced any strong anti-feminist or anti-environmental movements.

Thus, in Denmark, social movements as a concept expresses freedom and conjures up positive rather than negative associations. This probably also means that the suppression of the new social movements has taken place, and still does, is probably more subtle in Denmark than in many other countries. Through their corresponding political parties the old social movements succeeded in making laws which helped them, for instance create »free« schools to socialize children from the peasant or the working classes. These laws still function and have also been used by some new social movements. The basis for building new institutions is made easier by the fact that the arrangements are useful for the old movements as well.

In sum, the term social movements and the importance of the old movements have meant that in Denmark the new social movements have had a cultural background which favoured them, and especially, for making state-subsidized institutions such as schools for children and adults, etc. The new as well as the old social movements have been an expression of progress and change rather than of reaction.

II. Grass-Roots Movements in Denmark

The term »grass roots movements« is the popular Danish expression for new social and political movements. The more famous of the early grass roots movements in Denmark was the march against nuclear weapons on Easter in 1961. Thousands of marchers fought their way through snow on the road to Copenhagen. The march was important because it was a break with the political climate of the 1950s and with the attitude of »we can't do anything, anyhow«. Later during the sixties several other movements related to the youth revolt occurred. Significant was the squatter movement, especially in Copenhagen. The international protest movement against the Vietnam War was a very important mobilization of young persons and became the symbol of a fight against oppression. And the movement against Danish EEC-membership in 1972 was a symbol of national autonomy. These movements were rather broad and mobilized thousands of participants.

There were, however, many more movements. The women's liberation movement started in 1971 and soon became extremely influential. The environmental movements also began around 1970 and formed many local movements in all parts of the country. Part of the environmental movement was the fight against nuclear power plants. The parliament had passed a law which in principle favoured nuclear power plants and urged the government to build them if the problems of nuclear waste could be solved satisfactorily. Another part of the environmental movement concentrating on air, sea and food pollution and created many sophisticated actions.

The mushrooming of all the groups happened during the years when many other changes of a similar kind took place. The youth revolt had an important impact on culture. A bill was passed granting students considerable influence at the universities. In urban planning citizens were given influence as local authorities were obliged to discuss goals and concrete plans with them.

Finally, an area in Copenhagen, Christiania, was declared a free city. The area was occupied by some 1,000 mostly young persons who wanted to live their own lives outside the influence of other parts of society.

All this happened at the end of the sixties and at the beginning of the seventies. However, there were very few social science attempts to analyze these phenomena. Books and articles on the movements in this period were mostly pamphlets distributed by the movements themselves or journalistic material. It was as if social scientists did not discover these phenomena, or, if they did, they thought of the movements as scattered, short-term events with no broader impact on society. Thus, the literature on the social movements in their early days is very incomplete, difficult to get access to and in general only related to individual movements.

III. The First General Danish Studies

This rather grim picture changed in 1977 when several projects were initiated at the same time at the Institute of Political Science of the University of

Aarhus. Three projects emerged from different contexts which, up to now, are the only general projects on grass roots movements in Denmark. In this section I will discuss these projects plus another study, and in the following sections I will go on to analyze other projects which concentrate on specific segments of society, e.g. case studies of the women's movement, ecology movement etc. »General studies«, in this context, does not mean that the research uses a broad theoretical framework. As shall be demonstrated below, critics of the studies have emphasized the limitations of the political science approach, then a dominant perspective in the studies. Thus, they have argued that the focus on political activities, to a smaller or larger extent characterizing the three projects, was a limitation because the researchers overlooked the cultural expressions of movements and did not realize that they carried out important activities that were not political in the traditional sense of the word, i.e. related to the institutional political system.

It was probably by accident that the first studies of the new social movements originated in Aarhus. One explanation, however, could be that the institute had recruited many young researchers at the beginning of the seventies and they were now ready to begin major projects. Another explanation was that the institute had been influenced to a rather small extent by the strong conflict between the capital logic school of Marxism and other orientations within social science. Capital logic had a heavy influence on the Institutes of Sociology in Copenhagen. At the new universities, founded in 1966, 1972 and 1974, the intellectual climate had not yet reached a level where researchers could initiate major projects.

As mentioned, in 1977 three projects were under preparation. There was, however, little contact between the researchers. In 1977 a fourth small project was done. It was a part of an OECD study on Public Involvement in Decision-Making Related to Science and Technology. In just three and a half months, a young researcher, Poul Erik Mouritzen completed a study which resulted in a report to the OECD: *Public Involvement in Denmark,* 1977. The report concentrates on citizen participation in planning, environment, the Anti-EEC-Movement and the issue of nuclear power plants. Finally, the report discusses whether citizens are interested in having influence on research. Because of the very limited time available to do the report, of course, it could only give a very brief description of the issues and movements involved in what was analyzed as a new kind of public participation. The report did not explicitly use general social science theory, but the implicit argument of the book was to regard grass roots activity as an instrumental activity aiming at influencing public decision-makers. The report was published in Danish in a somewhat extended version (Mouritzen, 1978). During its preparation, the report was discussed by a group of researchers including, among others, representatives from the three projects under preparation. This report put grass roots movements on the agenda. It sold rather well and was widely discussed. Its critics found its theoretical position too narrow as it concentrated on political science. Some of this criticism and attempts to broaden the notion of grass roots movements were published in the journal *Politica* (vol. 10, No. 4). The journal is published at the Institute of Political Science, University of Aarhus. The theme of the mentioned issue was »grass roots«. It was edited by Peter Gundelach whose article explaining the emergence of grass roots movements was a first attempt to give a systematic survey of the literature (Gundelach, 1979).

The data for the institute's three projects were collected in 1979, but apart from this the projects were very different and, to be frank, uncoordinated except for some sharing of information and cooperation between the studies done by Gundelach, Svensson and Togeby.

The three projects were: the power project, the participation project, and the organization project.

The *power project* was a large project intended to study the power structure in Denmark. The study was strongly influenced by a similar study in Norway where the government had formed a committee to advance the understanding of participation, influence and power in the Norwegian society. There were strong links between Norwegian researchers and the Danish research group which consisted mainly of researchers from the Institute of Political Science. In Denmark, the project consisted of several parts: a study of civil servants, a study of governmental committees, a study of interest groups, and most important in this context, a general survey on the political activity of the adult Danish population. Rather late in the preparation of the project the researchers felt the need to encompass »unconventional« political activities and they included a few questions on grass roots activities. The general idea of the project was that the citizens may use different channels to gain influence. The press, voting, membership in organizations are some examples. Unconventional political activity is of particular interest to us here. As implicitly stated, these activities played a very minor part in the overall project. This is also reflected in the fact that the research team placed only a few questions on this topic in the questionnaire. The results are reported in

Goul Andersen's article (1980) in a book which gives the first results of all parts of the power project in relation to participation.

The book is called *Folkets veje i dansk politik*, which is roughly translated into *Citizen's inroads into the Danish political system*. This also gives a precise account of the theoretical assumptions of the study. Considering its institutional relation, the study is, as expected, rooted in political science literature. The idea of the project is to look upon various roads of influence as a substitute for each other. Grass roots activities may be one of these. Data are scarce on grass roots activities. The questions consider only instrumental activities and grass roots activities are regarded as individual activities along with, for instance, participation in an interest group. The women's movement activities, for example, are not explicitly discussed because they are not considered »political«, i.e. attempting to change political decision-making.

Later, the author of the part of the project on grass roots movements changed his perspective (Goul Andersen, 1981). In the latter article, he argues that it is necessary to distinguish between the event of grass roots action which was the core of the survey and the grass roots organizations as movements. The events often associated with grass roots activities may have been organized by other groups and some grass roots movements do not initiate actions/events. This differentiation is consistent with the differentiations between the organization of the movement and the event itself used by Dahlerup (1986) in her study of the Danish Women's movement, although this latter study was of course in no way related to Goul Andersen's article.

The second of the three studies, the *participation project*, was done by Svensson and Togeby and is most fully reported in their 1986 book, *Politisk opbrud (Political Remodelling)*. This study is also rooted in the political science tradition, but is quite different from the power project. The participation project focused on the role of participation in the political socialization of youth. The general interest of the study is whether grass roots participation among young persons results in a different kind of political socialization compared to the traditional political socialization processes via the parties. From this perspective the primary interest is, of course, young persons. Secondly, it is important to use a very broad concept of political activity. The project conducted a survey of 2,200 young persons aged 16-28 in order to obtain sufficient data for analyzing less frequent activities. The survey was carried out in one county, the county of Aarhus, and is therefore not representative of Denmark as such, even though the occupational make-up, etc. of the county of Aarhus is quite similar to that of Denmark. The research design is quite sophisticated. Before interviewing the researchers tried to map all kinds of grass roots activities in the area. The results were used to create specific questions on participation. The idea was to ask the interviewed persons whether they participated in this or that concrete demonstration, etc., instead of asking only if they had joined a demonstration as such within the last one or two years.

The design proved fruitful since the researchers did measure a very high proportion of grass roots activities. The researchers investigated instrumental as well as expressive activities. The argument was that to young people politics is part of a way of life in which political participation is an element of the culture of youth groups – that attending a rock concert (Rock against Nuclear Power), for instance, is also a political expression. Political participation is formed along networks.

The major weakness of the project was that the data concentrated on education as the independent variable. Later, however, the researchers found that the class relationship of the activists is probably more important than their education. The data on class are rather weak, and it will be an obvious task for a new project to test more specifically the grass roots participation as explained by the class relationship of the participants. The book by Svensson and Togeby (1986) is an extremely careful analysis of the political participation of young persons. The central argument is that grass roots activity is the political activity of the new middle classes and that young persons are mobilized into the political system through grass roots movements resulting in serious problems for the political parties. Methodologically, the important lessen of the project is not to pose general questions, but to begin by carefully mapping the research field and analyzing the possibilities for action. The disadvantage of this strategy is, of course, that this is impossible to do except in quite a small area.

Svensson and Togeby replicated the 1979 survey of grass roots activity in 1988, interviewing people in the 19-37 years of age range, and thus covering the age groups of the 1979 study, plus persons ten years older. This design allowed for both generational and age group comparisons. When the results of the project are published, Svensson and Togeby will be able to analyze whether grass roots activity is linked to certain age groups or whether it is a generational phenomenon.

The third of the initial projects did not take political science, but *organization* theory, as its point of departure. Gundelach's angle was to study the organizational structure of the new movements. The major source of inspiration was that of Gerlach and Hine (1970) and the research design was inspired by a Swedish project (Gidlund, 1978). Gundelach assumed that the segmented, flat structure of the new social movements was an expression of the values of the participants. In contact with political decision-makers this structure would tend to be suppressed because political decision-makers demanded a hierarchical organizational structure of the organizations with whom they would negotiate. Since the values of the participants depended on education and occupation, and the values of the decision-makers depended on, among other things, the local area, the design of the project was to investigate three local areas varying according to urbanization: a city, a small town, and a rural area. In each location the researchers mapped the grass roots organizations. Where the two other projects had the individual as the object, Gundelach's project had the organization as the object of study.

In each local area political decision-makers, politicians, and civil servants were interviewed about their attitudes towards the social movements. The leaders of the movements were asked about the organizational structure, functions and activities of the movements. The members of the movement were asked to fill out a questionnaire about their participation. The questionnaire was handed out at a meeting in the movement. Thus the data on individuals were not representative, and due to the varying irregular attendance at the meetings in various organizations, the data are difficult to compare. The data from the project were reported in the book *Græsrødder er seje (Grass-Roots are Tough!)* (Gundelach, 1980).

The city area investigated was the city of Aarhus, the second largest city of Denmark. With only 250,000 inhabitants it is still a small city compared to other European cities. Part of Gundelach's project, therefore, included a study of movements in Copenhagen, the only major city in Denmark by international standards. Gundelach's assistant, Leif Thomsen, did a study of two movements opposed to growth and development – one in the inner city and one in a suburb. He also did a study of the men's movement. Data from Thomsen's study are a part of the general study by Gundelach and are partly used in the book mentioned. However, the data on the urban movements have also formed the basis for a book by Thomsen (1981) which will be discussed below.

In conclusion, the three projects on grass roots, though loosely connected, placed the Institute of Political Science in the centre of the analysis of new social movements. The project by Goul Andersen et al. did not have a major impact on the discussion, but both Gundelach's and Svensson's and Togeby's projects have played an important role in providing more information on who participates and how the new movements are organized.

However, there was also some criticism of the projects. The major thrust of criticism of the projects by Mouritzen, Goul Andersen, and Svensson and Togeby was that they were much too concerned with the political system at the expense of seeing the relation of the movements to society at large. Another criticism also directed at Gundelach was that the projects were too general when what was needed were empirical projects analyzing specific conflicts, the actors, and the impacts of the actions. The argument is that one should use different theory for different movements. This criticism was most strongly voiced by Thomsen in his book on urban movements (1981).

IV. Results of the General Studies

At the time of the early theoretical works on grass roots movements, two hypotheses on political activity were generally advanced. Both were inspired by Norwegian social science. The first was the so-called resource hypothesis. It stated (Martinussen, 1977) that political action was a function of an actor's individual and collective resources. The hypothesis had been tested in a major Norwegian project around 1970. The argument was that political action, e.g., grass-roots activity, would be more frequent among persons with many resources (e.g. higher education, time, membership in interest organizations, motivation). The other hypothesis was the so-called grass roots hypothesis which was advanced in the mentioned Norwegian power study. It said that grass roots activity was a substitute for other kinds of political action. Thus persons with few resources would not have access to normal channels of political influence and would create their own: the new social movements.

In their book from the power project, Olsen and Sætren (1980) were able to show that the grass roots hypothesis was false. The Danish studies on individual activity have confirmed this result. However, this does not mean that the almost tautological resource hypothesis is correct in its very general formulation. It must be strongly qualified in order to describe the participation pattern in new social movements. As stated, the most thorough and comprehensive project is that of Svensson and Togeby and the following results are based on their book.

The results are much in line with other European research on new social movements. The participants in the new social movements are young persons belonging to the »new middle class«, i.e. civil servants with a relatively good education, with jobs in the health, education and social service sectors.

Svensson and Togeby's data are not sufficient for a precise testing of the relation between class and grass roots participation. However, they show that among civil servants with »matriculation certificates«[1] some 60 per cent were very active in new social movements. An even stronger confirmation of the hypothesis is that an estimate of other groups is impaired by the fact that other groups of employees with less education have such a smaller number of activities that computation is problematic.

A presumably less frequently reported result in the literature is that there is no difference in grass roots activity between men and women. In probably all political science research it has been concluded that the political activity of women is less than that of men. In this piece of research, however, we find for the first time almost identical rates of participation. One even finds that young women with the »matriculation certificates« make up the more active group. Even more interesting is the fact that the identical participation goes for all kinds of movements. In some cases women even have higher rates of participation. In movements regarding children (e.g., movements for smaller fees in kindergartens) and gender politics the women play a much more important role than men.

The explanation for these findings is suggested by Togeby (1984) in another report from the project. She argues that the rapid increase in the number of working women has created a new consciousness – especially among younger women. Among other things, this is expressed in attitudes which contain a general distrust of a political system, a leftist orientation and a negative attitude towards male dominance. The structure of the new social movements and the culture of the movements allow the women to be politically active in ways which do not exist to the same extent in most other political organizations.

In sum, participation in the new social movements in Denmark shows many of the same results as in other countries, but one gets the impression that the Danish scene is more biased than in many other countries. The Danish studies show that grass roots activity is to a large extent limited to certain groups in the population: the young members of the new middle layers.

---

1 A university entrance exam taken after 12 years of public school.

Data on the organizational structure are given by Gundelach (1980). He shows that the structure varies according to urbanization. In the countryside organizations normally are quite similar to traditional associations. In cities the movements are organized in the manner described by Gerlach and Hine (1970), the so-called SPIN-organizations: a loosely-organized, fragmented kind of organization in which there are many semi-autonomous groups and in which the coordination is secured by over-lapping memberships.

This is the general picture. However, the strategy of the movement has a great impact on the organizational structure. Movements whose primary goal was to influence decision-makers were more likely to have association-like organization structures, whereas movements that sought foremost to influence the norms and values in society had a very loose structure with no formal leaders. The strategy of the movement was a much stronger determinant of the structure than, for instance, the age of the movement. Several movements had existed for a much as a decade and maintained a decentralized structure.

Gundelach (1984) has argued that the explanation for the SPIN-organization can be found in the fact that the participants of the movement are the new middle layers, whose attitudes follow an alternative value paradigm compared to other parts of the population. The new middle layers have values such as decentralization, environment, protection, etc., and they express these values in the organizations in which they are active. A similar argument has been suggested by a professor of literature (Fjord Jensen, 1984), who argues that the culture of the middle layers is reflected in the movements. This theory can also explain the difference between movements in the country and the city. In the country the variations in the class relationship of the participants are greater than in the cities.

In an analysis of movements as organizations an important question is whether the movements had attained at least some of their goals. Gundelach's research (1980) showed that approx. 3/4 of the 104 organizations studied claimed to have had success. In contrast, the public decision-makers who were interviewed strongly disagreed. They said that the movements had had very limited success. The explanation of this difference is probably that the different answers reflect variations in interests and that the respondents have different understandings of the term success. For the decision-makers movement sucess meant that they should give concessions to the movements. In this respect the decision-makers were right. The movements generally have had little impact on public policy. The participants of the movements said that social learning processes were a criterion for success and it appears that participation in movements in fact has such educational and motivational effects.

From the viewpoint of the analyst it is difficult to ascertain which movements have had some degree of success. Probably there is a difference between the movements. The local, small one-issue movements trying to influence specific elements in public policy generally have had little success. However, the large, nation-wide, and internationally-inspired movements such as the ecology movement and the women's movement have had influence on both the decision-makers and the norms in society. This, however, is difficult to measure. There have been some changes in laws and other decisions, and in general the decision-makers are more in favour of the movements' views now than for instance ten years ago. The same goes for the public. One very important consequence of the activities of the environmental movement must be mentioned. The fact that there are no nuclear power plants and that the government has completely cancelled plans to build them are no doubt consequences of the activities of the movement.

Both on the organizational level and the individual level, the Danish research is quite clear. Participants in the movements were members of the new middle class and the organizational structure was loose and decentralized with much autonomy to local groups.

In the last two years Lise Togeby has conducted two major surveys of grass roots activity. Both are comparative. As mentioned, Togeby and Svensson have replicated their 1979 study with the additional ten year age group. Togeby has also carried out a Nordic comparative project (with the Norwegian Oddbjørn Knutsen) on grass roots activity and social values. Togeby's results are published in her book *Ens og forskellig. Græsrodsdeltagelse i Norden.* (»Alike and Different. Grass Roots Activity in the Nordic Countries«). Århus: Politica 1989.

This comparison shows marked differences among the Nordic countries. The activity is quite low in Finland and highest in Sweden whereas Norway and Denmark come in a little behind Sweden. The Danish grass roots activity of the late 1980s can be characterized by people arguing for their own (narrow) interests. It is to a much smaller extent an expression of a general political mobilization. The level of activity is explained by characteristics of the political system: for instance, Finland has many traditional associations connecting the citizens to the decision-makers. In Denmark Togeby claims that politicians have been very efficient in taking the wind out of the sails of the movements by entering into discussion with the movements and accepting several of their demands.

Quite another type of comparison is carried out by Gundelach (1988) in his comparison of old (19th century) and new social movements. This book uses secondary analysis of present and historical data. The argument is that new waves of social movements are associated with major shifts in the social structure. Gundelach states that the goals and organizational characteristics of the new social movements may be explained by the emergence of a new type of society: the programmed society. Compared to the industrial society, the programmed society is characterized by a continuation of capitalism, although this economic structure has been changed by globalization and the very large public sector.

Although very different, the projects by Togeby and Gundelach both attempt to give a fuller understanding of social movements and grass roots activity in Denmark. However, these general studies do not go into the many movements in detail. In contrast, other studies concentrate on only one movement. We will now turn to these publications.

V. Literature on Specific Issues and Case-Studies

The literature on specific movements is very varied indeed. Some of the literature is written by researchers not connected to the movement, some of it by researchers who are participants in the movement, and finally the largest part of the literature is produced by ordinary members of the movements. In the bibliography the latter category is only included in cases where there is little other material about the movement. The variations in the literature can also be seen in the fact that the authors seldom make comparisons to other movements or try to create more general theories. Much of the literature reflects specific movements and often as an element of the internal debates in the movement. The following paragraphs will give short accounts of the literature on the specific movements.

A. Women's Movement

The best analysis of the movement is given by Dahlerup (1986) in her historical account of the movement. The movement began in 1970 and for the first three to four years featured a period of direct action. In fact, a demonstration brought the very first public recognition of the movement. A small group of women marched down the main pedestrian street of Copenhagen dressed grotesquely in a way which caricatured the commercialized image of women as sex objects. Later at the Town Hall square they deposited the exaggerated feminine elements of their costumes in a dustbin marked »Keep Denmark Tidy«.

This was just the first of many actions. Even more important was that women in Copenhagen occupied a house where they established a women's centre. In other cities, the women's centres were rented for a small fee in an agreement with local authorities. Though, very loosely organized, the movement spread all over the country.

Summer holiday camps on the island of Femø were started in 1971. Admitting only women, the camp has continued every summer since then and new camps have been established in other parts of the country. Apart from these still on-going activities, the first stage of the movement was characterized by many ideological discussions, not only in the core of the movement, the consciousness-raising groups, but in all parts of society. The women tried to introduce a feminist perspective on almost all activities in society. For instance, the women's movement participated in the campaign against Danish EEC-membership up to the referendum in 1972. Of issues central to women were free abortion (the act was passed by the Parliament in 1973) and the demand for equal pay (which became a part of the general agreements of the labour market, also in 1973).

Since the mid-seventies direct actions by the movement have almost stopped. This second stage of the movement was characterized by proliferation and the established of a feminist counter-culture. The movement spread all over Denmark. Outside the big cities women's groups were less radical. Ideological discussions continued and influenced all parts of society, but the discussions were less passionate.

Gradually a feminist counterculture became established. The women organized counselling groups and various courses at the women's centres. A feminist magazine, a publishing firm and the publishing of books by female writers, together with women's theatre groups, film teams and music bands, composed a feminist culture. Finally, Women Studies was introduced at the universities. This second stage of the movement lasted until 1980.

In the third stage, many of the cultural activities have continued, but the activist core of the movement has disappeared. Instead of having only a few centralized meeting places the movement now has many specialized centres, for example, the crisis centres in some big cities. Local public authorities have cooperated with the women's movement to create special activities for unemployed women, etc. Culturally, the establishment of the world's first Museum of Women's History in the city of Aarhus is important.

Thus, the new women's movement has changed a lot in the less than two decades it has existed. It is still a movement but now it undertakes very few overt actions. Nevertheless, the movement still influences many elements in society and the cultural activities of the movement have been the most innovative cultural feature of society in the last ten years.

Women's studies have gradually become institutionalized, but, except for Dahlerup's analysis of the movement within a political science framework, studies of the women's movement are few. The consciousness-raising group as a core element of the movement has been studied by Agger (1977). She identified the typical group and described its qualities as a technique for changing the attitude of the participants. This is the best account of this extremely important element in the women's movement. Besides the abovementioned brief account by Dahlerup (1986), there is no general analysis of the structure of the movement and its changes except for very descriptive publications by the movement itself. Likewise, there are no systematic studies of the characteristics of the participants of the movement, though Flensted Jensen et al. (1977) mention that the core of the movement consists of highly educated young women.

In short, what we know about the movement is mostly about its ideology and cultural expression, less about its history and changing strategies and almost nothing systematically about its organization and membership. The social and cultural consequences of the movement, even though they seem to be very impressive, have only been superficially studied. The literature on the women's movement from sources outside the universities is enormous. Magazines, booklets, articles, etc., without a social science perspective, but which may give relevant information on the movement, number in the hundreds.

B. Environmental Movements

The environmental movements in Denmark have gone through phases which in many respects are similar to those of the Women's movement. The initial phase in the late 1960s was characterized by very provocative actions and the movements have gradually developed into professionalized, and in some ways, pressure-group organizations. Læssøe (forthcoming), who has described this trend, doubts whether environmentalism can still be considered a social movement. Within the general field of environmentalism two movements have been more important. The NOAH and the OOA, Oplysning om Atomkraft (Organization for Information on Nuclear Power). NOAH is an environmental movement which stresses anti-pollution. It has played a major role in public debate setting environmental issues on the societal agenda and creating many imaginative actions. The movement has also published numerous articles and books. It is decentralized and anti-hierarchical and has an imported network of local groups. The book by Meulengracht Olsen et al. (1980) offers the best information on the movement, but it is entirely written by activists in the movement. Besides stating and arguing about the goals of the movement, an interesting discussion concerns its strategy. This involves an analysis of the movement's relation to the state and the wisdom of founding a green party.

The NOAH is against formal relations with the state; they are afraid to »get their hands dirty«. They fear that the state will suppress the movement in such a subtle way that the movement's activists will never really be able to tell what has happened. Formal relations with the state will also mean that the movement's participants who would be negotiating with the state would gain a strong position in the movement, perhaps be considered as leaders, and thus come into conflict with the movement's decentralized structure.

These are also the arguments against a green party. The party would legitimate state measures not sufficiently radical and the influence of the party would be quite small. Influence is stronger, the movement argues, when the state is pressed from the outside.

The Danish Green Party, which had elected several members to the local administration in 1983, was founded by other minor environmental movements. NOAH still finds this strategy questionable.

The other movement, OOA, is a specialized environmental movement. The movement has been the major opposition to the government's plans for nuclear power plants. These plans were abandoned in 1985. Thus, OOA has succeeded, but the movement is now arguing for alternative energy sources, a topic that they also discussed before. This movement has been studied by Bjarne Herskin (n.d.), who, using a Pablo Freire inspired theory of learning processes, published a preliminary report on the characteristics of the activists. Unfortunately, the project has not been finished. The other material on the movement is written by activists. There is little information on the organization structure of the OOA, but its decision-making structure is probably quite centralized. There are many local groups. As with the other movements, there is no information on membership and the like.

Other environmental movements, such as Greenpeace, have not been studied in any detail. The general impression is that the environmental movements have been very important in creating public debate. Also, the fact that the government has given up nuclear power plants was no doubt heavily influenced by their activities. Environmental movements are especially interesting in that they have been strongly associated with many different experiments such as organic farming and alternative energy. This shows how the social movements may not only be considered in terms of political action, but also in relation to broader social changes.

C. Urban Movements

The late 1960s was a period of major change in Copenhagen. The inner city was deteriorating and several slum houses were left by the renters. During the same period many young persons came to stay and study in Copenhagen. The squatter's movement, which at a time occupied a considerable number of houses, succeeded in making the parliament pass a measure which legalized these occupations. The legalization eventually meant the death of the movement even though squatters occasionally occupied a few houses.

The movement has not been studied by social scientists apart from one small book on a part of the movement and its occupation of a house (Henriksen, 1972).

Even though the large squatter movement disappeared, other movements related to the urban structure appeared. They were against general slum-clearance and wanted to influence change in the inner city. One major goal was to prevent the building of apartments that would be too expensive for the working class, but the conflicts were also a struggle for autonomy.

Corresponding movements in the suburbs of Copenhagen and other large cities occurred in the large, newly built areas. They were fighting for as much control of the area as possible, but most importantly, against rent increases. In several places rent strikes were organized.

Changes in urban structures and corresponding social movements will be briefly discussed in this section. In the sections which follow the present youth movements, successors to the early squatters movements will be reviewed.

The literature on urban movements is scattered and varied. On the one hand, there are several studies which concentrate on the changes in urban structures and the resulting urban movements. On the other hand, there are action research studies in which the researcher takes an active part in the movement and/or sees himself/herself as a participant.

The first type of research is mainly Marxian and inspired especially by French and English urban sociologists (Castells, Harvey, Pickvance and others). The articles by Kirsten Simonsen (1982, 1985) are the best examples of this tradition. She regards the new social movements as responses to changes in the urban space and the increase in collective consumption which itself is a result of the rise of the modern welfare state. These articles are almost entirely theoretical.

An empirical study of urban movements was carried out by Thomsen (1981) in a book which was an independent part of Gundelach's general project mentioned above. Thomsen investigated two very different movements, one in the centre of Copenhagen and another in a western suburb. The book focuses on the social movement which responded to a planning proposal in Høje Tåstrup, west of Copenhagen, slated to become a second centre outside the city. It focuses on local community activities, the history of the movement and the interests of the various local actors. There is little analysis of the participants and the organization of the movement. Theoretically, the book is strongly inspired by works of Manuell Castells, but the attempt to implement this very general theory to the Danish study is not quite successful.

Another kind of social movement study is done mainly by urban planners (trained as architects or geographers). The more important studies, such as the one by Kiib (1984), were carried out in villages or small cities. As with other kinds of action research, the books and articles produced are few and of a different nature. They have less concrete description and more analysis of actions and what should be learned from them. Kiib has created a model for collective learning processes; see also Kiib and Marling in Simonsen et al., (eds.) (1982).

In conclusion, many social movements and local protests against city and regional planning, including citizen's groups and local houses established in several cities by the citizens in collaboration with the local authorities, have not been intensively studied. Knowledge of these movements is scarce and unsystematic. The action research approach is probably the more interesting because the researchers have tried out a new research concept. These studies, however, seldom appear in print. The local actions, demonstrations and perhaps slide shows or other kinds of communication are more important.

D. Youth Movements

BZ is the name of various groups of young urban squatters who occupied several houses in central Copenhagen and a few in the city of Aarhus. Eventually they were thrown out by the police, but in several instances they managed to occupations lasting 6 to 8 months. They adopted an organizational structure similar to that of a commune. This movement is reported only in one study apart from the documents published by members or sympathizers of the movement. The book by Madsen et al. (1982) is a series of interviews with members of the movement and a description of their activities. It focuses on the dreams and ideas of the youth and it attempts to analyze the counter-culture with which the squatters identify themselves. The core of the squatters' project is anti-elitist and anti-hierarchical which, among other things, is expressed in the group's total refusal of the association-like organization structures the authorities try to force upon them. The young squatters structure their daily life by the principles of free choice, free initiative and little organization.

The research design was a mix of interviewing, observation and partly action research. This method is discussed in an article by the senior member of the research team, Leif Thomsen (1983).

No doubt the BZ-movement was one of the more difficult movements to study. The youth reacted strongly against all kinds of theory and analysis by other parts of society. There are no data concerning the participants, except that one gets the impression that there are at least two groups: one who come from middle class families with many resources and to whom the political and social message of the movement is important, and the other consisting of those who have little contact with their parents, with few resources and whose primary motivation is to find a place to live where they can be by themselves.

A couple of books with short stories, poems and descriptions from the movement, together with a few films, are important supplements to the book by Madsen et al.

E. Peace Movements

There have been two important waves of peace movements after World War II and both were internationally inspired. The first occurred from approx. 1960-1968 and the second, begun a few years ago, is still going on.

The book by Jørgensen (1973) offers an interesting account of the first wave. He does not present any theoretical analysis, but gives a precise historical description. The movement's first major demonstration was a 61 km march from the city of Holbæk to Copenhagen. The march took place several years in a row, but it is best known for a photograph of the march from 1961 depicting several hundred demonstrators fighting their way through the snow. This picture has become a symbol of the emergence of new social movements out of the relative political indifference of the 1950s.

Like most other movements, most of the participants were young. Styrk (1963) has published a book including interviews of 17 participants. Membership lists did not exist, but the number of persons which subscribed to the journal of the movement reached its maximum in 1965 with 12,000. In 1967 the movement dissolved. The first peace movement shared the organizational characteristics of most of the new social movements. The loose organizational structure was held together by friendship ties, meetings and actions. Local groups (which reached a peak with some 60 groups) were autonomous.

The second wave of peace movements was not independent from the first. Many groups had existed off and on since the 1960s, among them several local women's peace groups. They are interesting because they seem to consist of women from all parts of the country and from many different social groups. The primary motivations of the women has been their role as mothers in a world threatened by a nuclear disaster.

The 1980 wave of the movement was triggered by NATO politics. The movement has many local groups and the mentioned groups of women are a very important part of the movement. There have been peace camps, peace rallies, and other kinds of actions with many hundreds of participants. A.-D. Christensen (1989) has written an interesting book on a women's peace camp outside a NATO control centre. From a feminist perspective the author describes the actions as well as the every-day life of the women in the camp. The motivation of the women and the consciousness-raising consequences are analyzed from in-depth interviews with a few activists. The book tries to relate the peace camp to non-violence and feminist theory.

From a political science perspective Michael Krasner (Queens College, CUNY), who has worked at the Institute of Political Science, University of Aarhus, made a telephone survey of the origins, activities and strategies of local peace groups. The Danish peace groups are to be compared to British groups. Results from the study have not yet been published, but with Nikolaj Petersen, Institute of Political Science, Krasner has published an article which focuses on the political impact of the movement (Krasner and Petersen, 1986).

Finally, Christensen (1989) shows that the peace movement has succeeded in democratizing the matters of security politics. The movement has challenged the traditional belief that discussions on security politics are relevant for experts only.

This widening of the public decision-making process and the public's demands for more influence is the same for all areas of social life.

VI. The Empirical Studies: A Conclusion

Even though the rate of participation in the new social movements in Denmark is very high, social science studies of them are rather limited. The general surveys have revealed that the members of the movements are highly educated, rather young and middle class. In general, their organizational structure is loose and decentralized, but there are important differences among the movements.

The empirical research on new social movements in Denmark can be classified into three groups:

1) Individual political activites. These so-called grass-roots activities have been investigated in several projects. The 1988 replication of the 1979 project by Svensson and Togeby means that it is possible to measure changes in

grass roots activity during the 1980s. The analysis of the 1988 study will reveal whether grass roots activity is related to certain age groups or if it is associated with a specific generation. The Nordic study can be used for international comparisons between relatively homogeneous countries. Compared to other countries Denmark has had a large number of related projects making quite comprehensive and advanced methods of analysis possible.

2) Studies of individual movements have been numerous and done mostly by researchers who have been more or less strongly connected to the movement. These studies have clearly indicated the importance of consciousness-raising and cultural activities. However, there are very few studies which combine hard data on the movement with historical accounts and a thorough analysis of the attitudes of the participants. One important exception is Christensen's study of the Ravnstrup peace camp, but this is only a minor albeit important and spectacular part of the peace movement.

3) Historical acounts of social movements in which old and new social movements are analyzed in a general theretical framework. Gundelach's (1988) comparison is based on secondary literature and research projects. Presently there are no projects in which empirical research of new and old social movements are combined.

The study by Leif Thomsen is also concerned with a comparison between old and new movements, but he focuses on the »identity formation process«. Thomsen's central analytic concepts are hegemony and civil society. He studies the old and new social movements in a very broad setting as reactions against the hegemony of the dominant class and as attempts to establish a civil society and areas of autonomy. Brief accounts of parts of the project are given in Thomsen (1985, 1986).

These two studies, together with an article by Jensen and von Nordheim Nielsen (1985) as well as several articles in a conference report (Christensen et al., 1986) represent a new wave of social science studies characterized by a more careful analysis of the new social movements. The virtues and advantages of the old movements were discussed as well. Out of a situation where the new movement, to put it crudely, was almost entirely considered in a black or white perspective depending on one's political orientation, the discussion has now reached a new stage with many shades.

The fact that approximately half of the members of the movements are women has not been fully analyzed. As Christensen (1986) argues, we need to ask why this is so by combining knowledge of the everyday activities of the women and their participation in the movement. For instance, what is the relation between women's values and the political and cultural expressions of the movement?

A similar »why« should be posed to the established research conclusion that most of the participants are members of the new middle class. The argument (Svensson and Togeby, 1986; Gundelach, 1982) was that the work experiences of the new middle layers – the relative autonomy in a job where they work with people – is vital to the understanding of the correlation.

A related discussion concerns the relations between values and grass roots activity. Gundelach (1988) suggests that grass roots activity is closely linked to new so-called green values. Togeby (1989), on the other hand, argues that the traditional left-right dimension is closely linked to traditional green values. Almost all persons voting for the left have green values. This means that it probably is not useful to distinguish between the two in an explanation of values which determine grass roots activity.

VII. Institutional Aspects in the Study of New Social Movements

There are no Danish centres for the study of new social movements or the like. The bulk of hard data research has been carried out at the Institute of Political Science, University of Aarhus. Some of the major movements, including the women's movement and the movement against nuclear power plants, have created their own information and training centres. Systematic research has not been done at those centres, but the movements themselves have produced many books and articles on their organization and ideas. Many of these publications have served the purpose of introducing the movement to new-comers. Some movements own houses, publish magazines or are associated with publishing companies. Such internal information networks play an important role and they are a vital source of information even though it is often biased.

Thus, the centres of the movements and the researchers associated with them are important institutional elements in the study of social movements.

As mentioned, studies at the universities are quite scattered. However, there have been some professional meetings on new social movements. Gundelach organized a Nordic course for researchers interested in new social movements in 1980. An autonomous work group on the study of new social movements under the European Group for Organizational Studies (EGOS), of which Gundelach was the facilitator, had a meeting in Denmark in 1984. In 1985 a conference on new social movements was organized by the »Centre for the Study of the Welfare State« – a group of researchers mainly from the universities. One sub-theme was the new and old social movements in relation to the welfare state. Papers from the conference have been published in Christensen et al. (1986). Finally, two attempts to create public debate which were not part of a social movement should be mentioned. Their ideas, however, do reflect the ideology of several activists in new movements.

The first was initiated in a book by a philosopher, a politician and a professor of physics (Meyer et al., 1978) entitled *Oprør fra midten (Revolt from the Centre).* Employing a theory of needs they argued for a decentralized »equilibrium« society. This book created a very strong political debate. The authors have commented on the debate in a book from 1982. Their first book was also published in German in 1979. One of the authors, Niels I. Meyer, was also active in an attempt to create a series of research projects on ecological, decentralized alternatives to the present society. The second attempts to create public debates on a number of projects related to ecology, decentralization and social experiments. This idea originated in Norway where the parliament had funded many projects. The principle of this so-called Nordic Alternatives Campaign was to create and study alternatives to the current societal development in each country and to establish cooperation between social alternatives in the Nordic countries. The campaign's application for funds was rejected by the Danish parliament.

In Denmark, Leif Thomsen is associated with the Norwegian project. He is presently preparing a book in which he proposes an alternative societal model based on general theories of social change and the analysis of the learning processes in the social movements and social experiments.

VIII. Debates

Many of the international debates on new social movements, e.g. for or against the resource-mobilization approach, have gone over the heads of Danish social scientists. Much of the discussion has centered on local reactions to Danish publications.

The first Danish book on new social movements by Mouritzen et al. (1978) was reviewed in an essay by Hans Kiib (1979), a renowned critic of the political science approach.

Kiib argued that the political science approach is too narrow. Political science only studies social movements in their relations to public decision-making and fails to see their wider norm-changing and consciousness-raising elements. This criticism has been accepted by several political scientists. In the book by Svensson and Togeby (1986) grass roots activities are defined as political activities directly or indirectly influencing political decision-making. Examples of indirect influence are the consciousness-raising groups of the women's movement which in the long run are aimed at »changing the distribution of values in society« (Svensson and Togeby, 1986:68).

The general approach to studying grass roots movements, which has been used in several studies, has been criticised by Thomsen (1981:307f). The core of his argument is that one should not study individual activities or a movement with general methods. Movements should be studied in their historical context and in the specific social space in which they function. His own book is an example of a much better research method, he says, because his work on urban movements has concrete descriptions of the urban structure, the political actors and the social conflicts in the area. He considers the movement's fight for cultural autonomy as the most important part of the analysis and he argues for varied research methods with broad descriptions of the movement. This attempt seems fruitful in the sense that it may allow us to gain a fuller grasp of the social space in which the social movements exist. So far this very complicated and demanding theoretical frame-work has been presented only in a very sketchy form (Thomsen, 1985, 1986).

The discussions mentioned thus far have taken place among social scientists. However, interesting discussions have also taken place in the new social movements themselves. In these discussions several social scientists have taken part.

One example is related to the ecology movement. Around 1980 the members of the ecology movement had lengthy debates on the issue of strategy. Should the movement enter into formal relations with the state and should it participate in the foundation of a green party? The more important parts of the movement were against these activities because they feared that they would be faced with more disadvantages than advantages from these relations. They argued that they would gain little influence while serving to legitimate state activities if they formally cooperated with the state. This discussion was also favored in the book by André Gorz (1979) on the authoritarian state. Translated into the perspective of the ecology movement, the problem can be posed as follows: since we are members of an anti-authoritarian movement we must discuss which strategy we can use as the state is the only actor able to force industry to make anti-pollution measures. This means that the more we push for ecological solutions the stronger we want the state to become. Thus the result of the movement's activities could be »eco-fascism«. The movement of course could not solve this dilemma, but as mentioned earlier, the movement is still against a green party. The central part of the movement has not participated in establishing the Danish Green Party which was founded partly by members of minor ecology movements.

The general impression is that during recent years there has been little discussion on the topic of new social movements in general. The publication of the book by Svensson and Togeby (1986) has caused some public debate on the relation between grass roots politics and »politics as usual« and especially on the role of the political parties.

Quite another discussion is reflected in the anthology of papers from a conference on the Welfare State (Christensen et al., 1986). In the section on social movements several researchers discuss the relation between the old and the new social movements, and especially, the role of the movements in society. The debate is partly influenced by the works of Alain Touraine (1977, 1981). Do the new social movements replace the old social movements, and especially, the labour movement? This is a question posed in several articles and the answer is generally negative. Some of the articles analyze the possible alliances between the two types of movements, and generally, the authors see the role of the worker's movement as strong and important. One exception is an article by Gundelach who argues that the new social movements should be studied in terms of a new social science paradigm since the old paradigm was established in the 19th century as a reaction to the problems of the modern society.

With regard to empirical data the projects by Svensson and Togeby allow for a comparison of the situation in 1979 and 1988. So far only preliminary results have been published. Togeby's Nordic study means that it is possible to compare the five Nordic countries in the late 1980s. Both studies concern grass roots activity and not the movements themselves. However, these projects are a strong foundation for comprehensive analyses of the character and change in this type of political activities.

The projects have raised such questions as the characteristics of the political system in relation to grass roots activity and the individual's motivation behind grass roots activity. As mentioned, Gundelach (1988) suggests that social movements are created from new green values whereas Togeby (1989) argues that the traditional left-right dimension is more important. This, in turn, has consequences for the evaluation of the role of the movements in relation to the political system.

This is probably where the debate presently stands, but it is not a heated one. The change in the new social movements, meaning that they have become more acceptable to the public and the decision-makers, and the changes in the appearance of the movements, meaning that there are much fewer overt actions, have gradually taken the grass roots movements off the agenda.

Thus in 1989, ten years after the first major projects in grass roots movements were conducted at the Institute of Political Science, University of Aarhus, the institute has become the unofficial centre for the study of new social movements in Denmark. Svensson and Togeby's comprehensive and careful data collection makes it possible to analyze empirically from survey data the development in the political activities of the decade. Gundelach's book places the new social movements in a larger historical perspective. With these projects the social science's study of new social movements in Denmark has proven to be cumulative as well as theoretically and empirically fruitful.

Annotated Bibliography

Agger, I. (1977): *Basisgruppe og kvindebevidsthed.* København; Danmarks pædagogiske Institut/Munksgaard.

A careful analysis of a consciousness-raising group using a special technique developed by the women's movement. The book compares the technique of the Danish movement to other women's movements and argues that the peculiar Danish structure is a reflection of the Danish movement's development. Includes a summary and Appendix in English with a description of models and topics for consciousness-raising groups.

Balle-Peterson, M. (1985): »Everyday Rainbows: On Social Movements and Cultural Identity«, *ARV Scandinavian Yearbook of Folklore.*

The argument in this ethnological analysis is that the defining characteristic of all social movements is its cultural force. The commitment to a new identity results in a questioning of the dominant culture. Social movements are cultural volcanoes. Examples from the commitment process in old as well as new social movements are given.

Christensen, A.-D. (1986): »Kønsperspektivets relevans og konsekvens for forskningen i de nye sociale bevægelser«, in: Hänninen-Salminen, E. et al. (eds.), *Kvinnor och makt: Kvinnoperspektiv på »välfärdsstaten«.*

– et al. (eds.). (1986): *Velfærdsstaen i krise – sociale og politiske bevægelser.* Aalborg Center for Velfærdsstatsstudier.

– (1989): *Ulydige kvinders magt*, Aalborg: Aalborg Universitetsvorlag.
This book is a careful analyis of the so-called Ravnstrup camp outside a NATO control centre. The camp existed from July 1984 to September 1985. In connection with the camp were various actions. This piece of feminist research describes the story of some of the participants and analyzes the feminist and non-violence ideology of the women in the camp.

Christensen, J. (1989): »Fredsbevægelsen og demokratiet«, in N. Petersen; C. Thune (eds.), *Dansk Udenrigspolitisk Årbog 1988*: København, Dansk Udenrigspolitisk Institut.
The article argues that the peace movement has been able to make security politics, because the movement has questioned the traditional belief that security matters were of concern only to experts. The movement has made opposition to the security policy more legitimate.

Dahlerup, D. (1975): »Den nye danske kvindebevægelse«, in: D. Dahlsgård (ed.): *Kvindebevægelsens hvem-hvad-hvor.* København: Politiken.
A short historical account of the new Danish women's movement in a handbook on women's movements in many countries.

– (1977): »Studiet af sociale bevægelser«, in: E. Damgaard; C. Jarlov; C. Sørensen (eds.). *Festskrift til professor, dr. phil. Erik Rasmussen, 2. april 1977.* Århus; Politica.
The article attempts to put social movements on the political science research agenda and argues for more empirical work on new social movements.

– (1986): »Is the new Women's Liberation Movement dead? Decline or change of the Danish feminist movement, 1970 still today«, in: D. Dahlerup (ed.). *The New Women's Movement. Feminism and Political Power in Europe and USA.* London: Sage.
A political science description of the women's movement, its history and its more important dilemmas. Three historical steps are identified and it is argued that the movement is transforming itself rather than dying even though many overt actions are no longer visible.

Fjord Jensen, J. (1984): »Frigørelsens dialektik«, *Kritik* 68: 129-146.

Flensted-Jensen, E.; Frastein, S.; Steen Pedersen, A. (1977): *Mellem opgør og tilpasning 1-2.* Århus: Modtryk.
These two books are a history of the women's movement and its relation to social development. The Marxist theoretical position explains the women's movement and women's living conditions from the standpoint of a materialistic theory. Typical of early studies of women's movements in the sense that the interest of the authors is to relate the women's revolt against socialism.

Gerlach, L.P.; Hine, V.H. (1970): *People, Power, Change. Movements of Social Transformation.* Indianapolis/New York: Bobbs-Merrill.

Gidlund, J. (1978): *Aktionsgruper och lokala partier. Temporära politiska organiationer i Sverige 1965-1976*. Umeå: CWK Gleerup.

Gorz, A. (1979): *Ølkologi og frihed*. København: Politisk Revy.

Goul Andersen, J. (1980): »Deltagelse i græsrodsaktioner«, in: D. Damgaard (ed.). *Folkets veje i dansk politik*. Københaven: Schultz.

Part of a major project on political participation based on a survey of a representative sample of the adult Danish population. 13 questions relating to »actions« are the basis of the article, but it is unclear how the interviewers understood the term »action«. Only instrumental activities were analysed.

– (1981): »*Græsrodsbevægelser, en indkredsning«*, *GRUS* 3: 7-37.

An attempt to classify new social movements from the social conflicts which cause them to arise. The classification is tested in an empirical study using the data in Goul Andersen (1980). The conclusion is that one should not overestimate the difference between the new social movements and other channels of political influence.

Gundelach, P. (1979): »Folklaringer på dannelsen af græsrodsorganisationer« *Politica* 10 (4): 21-71.

This article discusses various explanations of the emergence of new social movements and concludes that a mixture of structural and social explanations should be used together with so-called provoking factors.

– (1980): *Græsrødder er seje!* Århus: Politica.

A study of new social movements analysed as political organizations. Data include questionnaires to leaders and members of the movements and unstructured interviews with political decision-makers in three areas varying according to urbanization. Data on members are weak.

– (1982): *The New Middle Layers, Grass-Roots Organizations as Alternative Values*. Århus: Institute of Political Science.

– (1984): »Social transformation and new forms of voluntary associations«, *Social Science Information* 23 (6): 1049-1081.

A theoretical article discussing the relation between new and old social movements in Denmark. The argument is that the social basis and the organizational structure of the movements reflect a changing class structure and the values of the participants.

Gundelach, P.; Togeby, L. (1984): »Græsrødder og rutinepolitik«, in: J. Elklit, O. Tonsgaard (eds.), *Valg og vælgeradfærd*, Århus: Politica.

Explains the determinants of grass roots movements and suggests a classification. Illustrates the participation in the movements and shows the socio-economic characteristics of the participants.

Gundelach, P. (1983): »Gamle og nye bevægelser, gamle og nye teorier«, in: A.D. Christensen et al. (eds.), *Velfærdsstaten i krise – sociale og politiske bevægelser*, Aalborg, Center for Velfærdsstaatsstudier.

– (1986): »Græsrodsbevægelser og aktioner«, in: F. Mikkelsen (ed.), *Protest og oprør. Kollektive aktioner i Danmark 1700-1985*, Århus: Modtryk.

Describes the original preconditions for new social movements and the actions of the movements in a historical/social science reader on collective actions over last 300 years.

– (1988): *Sociale bevægelser og samfundsændringer*, Århus: Forlaget Politica.

This book contains a comparison between the movements of the 19th century, such as the labour and the peasant's movements, and the new social movements. The emergence of new waves of movements is explained by changes in the general social structure which creates new social groupings and new social values.

Herskin, B.K. (No date): *Aktivisten – på vej mod en ikke-ideologi*, København: Institut for Organisation og arbejdssociologi.
A preliminary report on the learning processes of the participants of social movements. Case-study of the ecology movement, but with broader explanations. Theoretically inspired by Paolo Freire. A final report has never been published.

Jemsen, J.; Søgaard, V.; Simonsen, K. (1981): »Byudvikling og sociale bevægelser«, *Politica* 13 (2): 103-118.
Movements attempting to change local areas are explained structurally by state intervention in collective consumption which politicizes the problems of the cities. A theoretical article which discusses the strategies of the mvoements: integration or mobilization.

Jensen, P.H.; von Nordheim Nielsen, F. (1985): »De nye sociale bevægelser, arbejderbevægelsen og velfærdsstaten«, *Kurasje*, 37: 47-67.
This theoretical article explains the growth of the new social movements in terms of the emergence of the social democratic welfare state. State bureaucracies are important structural principles for the goals of the movements. The authors are critical of the new movements because they, compared to the labor movement, are more diffuse and less stable and lack a general concept of the development of society.

Jørgensen, K. (1973): *Atomvåbnenes rolle i dansk politik med særligt henblik på Kampagnen mod Atomvåben 1960-68*. Odense: Odense University Press.
A historian's account of the early Danish peace movement. The best available description of the movement. No theory. English summary.

Karsbøl, H. (1985): »Vilkår for lokalpolitisk deltagelse og protest«, in: S. Villadsen (ed.). *Lokalpolitisk organisering*. Københaven: Jurist- og økonomforbundets Forlag.
In the light of the local government's implementation of welfare-state politics, the author analyzes local protest movements and their increasing importance. The administration of the municipalities from the central state conflicts with the citizen's articulations of need and interest in local politics.

Kiib, H. (1979): »Græsrodsbevægelser i Danmakr«, *Politica* 10 (4): 115-127.

– (1984): *Cirkus i byen – om landsbybevægelse og offentlig planlægning*. Århus: Modtryk.
A very unusual book on social movements on planning in villages. Concentrates on learning proceses in social movements and gives inspiration to movements. Part of the book is also available as a slide show.

Krasner, M. (1985): »Politisk udvikling i den nye danske fredsbevægelse«, in: *Sikkerhed og Nedrustning I*. København: Det sikkerheds- og nedrustningspolitiske Udvalg.
An analysis of the new peace movement, especially its organizational structure. The argument is that the structure impedes the movement's ability to gain influence in political decision-making.

Krasner, M.; Petersen, N. (1986): »Peace and Politics: The Danish Peace Movement and its Impact on National Security Policy«, *Journal of Peace Research* 23 (2): 155-174.

The article discusses the relationship between political parties and the peace movements. The argument is compared to political parties. The strategy and the organizational structure of the peace movement mean that the impact of the movement on national politics is small. Taken from a case study, the article argues that the peace movement should exert influence on the Social Democratic party in order to have an impact on national politics.

Læssøe, J. (forthcoming): »The Making of the New Environmentalism in Denmark«, in: D. Jamison; R. Eyerman; J. Cramer (eds.), *The Making of the New Environmental Consciousness*. Edinburgh: Edinburgh University press.
This article describes the development of the Danish Environmental movements from the early action-oriented period to the present where the movements have become more professionalized and oriented towards corporate decision-making. The article describes different parts of the environmental movement from the Nature Conservation Society to Greenpeace.

Madsen, T.R.; Mellergaard, C.; Thomsen, L. (1982): *Ungdom 80. Ungdom som social bevægelse*. København: Forlaget Politiske Studier.
A case study of a youth movement in Copenhagen 1981-82. The study explains the emergence of a youth squatter movement, its activities and structure in that the youths are economically marginalized and without political influence. Interesting data collected throughout observation and interview. Little theory.

Martinussen, W. (1977): *The Distant Democracy. Social Inequality, Political Resources and Political Influence*. London: John Wiley. First published in Norwegian in 1973.

Meulengracht Olsen, A. et al. (eds.). (1980): *Miljøkamp – erfaringer, kritik, visioner. En debatbog*. København: NOAH's forlag.
A book on the environmental movement and its relation to society some ten years after its foundation. Articles on the history of movement, the strategy especially in relation to the state and other questions. Most articles are written by members of the movement.

Meyer, N.I.; Petersen, K.H.; Sørensen, V. (1978): *Oprør fra midten*. København: Gyldendal.

– (1979): *Aufruhr der Mitte: Modell einer künftigen Gesellschaftsordnung*. Hamburg: Hoffmann & Campe.

– (1982): *Røret om oprøret*. København: Gyldendal.

Mouritzen, P.E. (1978): *Borgerdeltagelse og græsrodsbevægelser*. Århus: Politica.
A descriptive study of citizen participation in relation to public policy. Emphasizes participation and new social movements in relation to planning, the Danish EEC-membership and nuclear power. The theoretical frame is rooted in political science, but poorly developed. Part of an OECD project on Public Involvement in Decision-Making Related to Science and Technology.

OOA (1984a): *Atomkraft nr. 45*. OOA – ti år i bevægelse.
A special issue of the journal of the OOA-organization in honour of its 10th Anniversary. Popular articles.

– (1984b): *OOA – Særtryk 23*. Græsrodsseminaret »I bevægeöse«.
Papers from a conference with many movements represented organized by the OOA-organization.

Olsen, J.P.; Sætren, H. (1980): *Aksjoner og demokrati*. Oslo: Universitetsforlaget.

Richard, A.B. ((1978): *Kvindeoffentlighet 1968-1975*. København: Gyldendal.

A book by a researcher in Danish literature investigating the women's movement from its cultural expressions. Not much social science theory.

Simonsen, K.; Jensen, H.T.; Hansen, F. (eds.) (1982): *Lokalsamfund og lokale bevægelser – en nordisk antologi*. Roskilde: Roskilde Universitetsforlag GeoRuc.

This is a Nordic reader on local administration, community and local social movements. It contains five articles on Denmark: a general one as well as articles on local administration, cities, social movements, and local actions. The articles are either reprints or concern topics already mentioned in other articles and books in this list.

Simonsen, K. (1983): »Lokal politik og sociale bevægelser«, in S. Villadsen (ed.), *Lokalpolitisk organisering*. København: Jurist- og økonomforbundets Forlag.

Using the concept of collective consumption the author discusses local movements and argues that the local government is the central organizer of every-day life thus making local protest groups increasingly important.

Strande-Sørensen, G. (1971): »Movements eller sociale bevægelser«, *Sociologiske meddelelser* 15 (1): 35-53.

Probably the first Danish sociological article on social movements. Raises a lot of theoretical questions, but from a contemporary perspective the article is not of great use. No empirical data. English summary.

Styrk, M.N. (1963): *Aktiv Ungdom. Samtaler med 17 unge fra Atomkampagnen*. København: Gyldendal.

Interviews with 17 participants in the first Danish peace movement.

Svensson, P.; Togeby, L. (1986): *Politisk opbrud*. Århus: Politica.

This is the most comprehensive Danish project on individuals' participation in grass roots activities. Based on a 1979 survey of some 2,000 young persons, the book investigates the rate of grass roots participation and relates this to other kinds of political activity. The general explanation for grass roots participation is that young persons become socialized into this kind of participation in the schools for higher education they attend.

Svensson, P.; Togeby, L. (1989): »Græsrodsdeltagelse mellem politisk moblisering og interessevaretagelse«, in: J. Elklit and O. Tonsgaard (eds.), *To folketingsvalg. Vælgerholdninger og vælger adfærd 1987 og 1988*, Aarhus: Forlaget Politica.

Using data from 1979 and 1988 the changes in the pattern of grass roots activity is invstigated. Apparently there is a difference in grass roots activity between men and women. For men the grass roots activity has changed into interest group-like activities. For women the mobilization has continued, and especially, in relation to political areas related to reproduction.

Teglers, J. (1985): »Fredsbevægelserne«, in: *Veje til fred. Håndbog i sikkerhed og nedrustning*. København: Gyldendal/Det sikkerheds- og nedrustningspolitiske Udvalg.

A very general and superficial description of the new and old Danish and international peace movements, their activities and their relations with political decision-makers.

Thomsen, L. (1981): *Den autoritære by. Kultursociologiske skrifter nr. 14*. København: Institut for Kultursociologi.

Investigates the changes in the urban area of a Copenhagen suburb and the causes of social conflicts and mobilization. The theoretical frame-work is drawn from Manuel Castells work but the relation between theory and data (interviews and observation) is not quite successful.

– (1983): »Samfundsforskningens praksis og ungdom som social bevægelse«, *Politica* 15 (4): 417-434.
A discussion of action research methodology in relation to the study of youth movements with a criticism of the study by Madsen et al. (1982) in which the author was the senior researcher.
– (1985): »Hegemoni og rum. Det civile samfund og de sociale bevægelser«, in: J.C. Tonboe (ed.). *Farvel til byen. Danske bidrag til den by-teoretiske udvikling*, Aalborg: Aalborg Universitetsforlag.
Using concepts of civil society and hegemony, the author analyzes old and new social movements. The argument is that social movements should be studied as reactions to attempts to establish hegemonistic systems and create civil societies in the contexts they operate.
– (1986): »Sociale bevægelser og social forandring«, in: A.-D. Christensen et al. (eds.), *Velfærdsstaten i krise – sociale og politiske bevægelser*, Aalborg, Center for velfærdsstatsstudier.
Togeby, L. (1980): *Politik – også en kvindesag*. Århus: Politica.
– (1989): *Ens og forskellig. Græsrodsdeltagelse i Norden*. Aarhus: Forlaget Politica.
This book reports the results from a survey on grass roots activity and social values which was carried out in the five Nordic countries. The variations in the level of grass roots activity are explained by characteristics of the political system.

The Netherlands: Action and Protest in a Depillarized Society

Philip van Praag, Jr.

The wave of protest in the sixties had reached the Netherlands as early as 1966. In that year, the Provo movement, a protest movement of young people established in 1965, made international headlines by throwing smoke bombs during the Crown Princess Beatrix's wedding and winning a seat at the municipal council elections in Amsterdam. The movement, lasting two years, had anarchistic tendencies, rallying strongly against entrenched patterns of authority and the consumer mentality of the welfare state.

The old adage attributed to Heinrich Heine that ›the Netherlands is always 50 years behind‹, seemed, at least for a short period, no longer applicable. Nevertheless, for social scientists researching the Provo movement and the never ending wave of protest actions and movements since then, the Netherlands no longer seemed so far behind. For a long time, the study of collective behaviour and social movements – not an especially flourishing field in the sociology and political science faculties of Dutch universities – was of a predominantly descriptive nature. Only during the past five years has the area undergone some change: some research projects are now based on a clearly theoretical framework and researchers seem more inclined to seek links with the ongoing international debate and theoretical development on new social movements, movement-networks and cycles of protest. There is, however, some justification for this neglect of protest-behavior and social movements by the social sciences in the Netherlands. Until the sixties, Dutch society was characterized by a high degree of social and political segmentation. The subcultures of Catholics, Calvinists, Liberals and Socialists were seen as the pillars of a political system, combining a minimum of interaction and communication at the grass roots level and intensive contacts and interlocking directorates at the elite level.[1]

In this setting of pillarization, the crucial question for the social sciences has always been how, in spite of subcultural tensions and conflicts, it could persist as a relatively open and stable democratic system.

For a long time, the focus of social and political research involved organizational factors in a fragmented society and political stability, while there was no interest in political change, political protest and collective behavior. When, during the sixties, the Netherlands was confronted with massive political protest, social scientists were as much taken aback as the rest of the Dutch population.

This article reviews the more important studies undertaken since the end of the sixties. It focuses on those concerning protest, action groups and social movements in the Netherlands since the phenomenon of Provo, without attempting to define new social movements – since there is a marked lack of consensus in this field.

I. Theoretical approaches

Over the years, and in varying degrees of intensity, different studies have centred around varying theoretical approaches. Some authors clearly sought to affiliate themselves with a number of theoretical traditions or attempted to reach a synthesis.

The first studies on the spectacular growth of political protest behaviour in the sixties belong to the theoretical tradition of political pluralism and its critics.

Protest was regarded as an attempt to re-open clogged or blocked channels of communication and influence.[2] However, researchers soon turned to the social characteristics of the protest, while ignoring the political background and internal dynamics of the numerous actions. 1972 saw the appearance of the first publication on the question of who takes part in protest ac-

---

1 Lijphardt, A. (1968), *The Politics of Accommodation: Pluralism and Democracy in the Netherlands.* Berkeley, CA: University of California Press, (2nd revised edition, 1975).

2 Van den Berg, J.Th.J., Molleman, H.A.A. (1974): *Crisis in de Nederlandse Politiek*; Alphen aan de Rijn, Samsom. Jolles, H.M. (1974): *De poreuze demokratie; een sociologische onderzoek naar het inspraakverschijnsel*; Alphen aan de Rijn, Samsom.

tion. Based on the results of an electoral survey, this study characterized participants according to sex, age, education, income, etc.[3] From 1979 onwards, a considerable amount of research into political participation has been published, closely connected on the one hand with the »Political Action« research project in the Netherlands and aimed, on the other, at a continuation and extension of such research (Thomassen e.a. 1983, Van Deth 1984 and Elsinga 1985). The theoretical framework of these studies is closely linked to that of the international project.

Participation is defined as all those activities directed at influencing the preparation, realization and/or effectuation of government policies. Three different forms of participation are distinguished: electoral, conventional and unconventional participation. In the following, we shall deal with the two latter forms only.

Conventional participation includes such actions as taking part in the activities of political parties, approaching civil servants and politicians and discussing politics. Unconventional participation refers to such activities as collecting signatures, demonstrating, boycotting, squatting and engaging in violent action. The latter category, unconventional or protest behavior, is of special importance in the study of social movements. Such research has questioned not only aggregated support of and actually taking part in the various forms of participation, but also, the relationship between political behavior – at the level of the individual – and social structural variables such as sex, education and occupation. Other research concerns the extent to which value-orientation, the level of political knowledge and political contentment can explain the variations in individual participation. Research into the extent and development of (post-materialistic) value patterns is also of importance (Van Deth 1984, Elsinga 1985).

Some work on a limited scale has been done on the influence of macroeconomic developments on participation and the willingness to take part in various activities.

The first theoretical approach discussed above centers around participants, their attitudes and convictions. The second viewpoint, now under discussion, focuses emphatically on collective action and somewhat on the process of mobilisation. In this field we find research into the effects of action and protest against government policy. This subject has received relatively

---

3 Molleman, H.A.A. 81972), »Wie voeren aktie«, in: *Acta Politica*, jaargang VII, pp. 99-111.

more attention since the end of the sixties. Originally, incidental action groups at a local level were the main point of focus. However, recent studies concentrate on both local action and the impact of peace and environmental movements on the implementation of national policy.

The first study (Kok e.a. 1971) has a strong basis in political science literature on pressure groups and lobbies. The successful protest-manifestation against the establishment of a hydro-sulphite Progil factory in Amsterdam's harbor district was conceived of as a typically modern way of influencing government policy. The analysis concerns the activities of groups for or against the factory, their resources and the interaction between the different groups and the municipal officials and members of the city council of Amsterdam.

Bronner et al. (1971) also defined action groups as a species of pressure groups although their study on 27 action groups, which in the period 1967-1969 had tried to influence the implementation of policy by the City of Amsterdam, was also based on Easton's (political) system theory. The origins of the various action-groups, their structures and resources, the interaction with the authorities in the different stages of decision-making, the impact of their actions and the repercussions on the future existence of the groups themselves all came under scrutiny.

To a certain extent, these studies set a trend for many impact studies to follow. However, since then the underlying concepts have undergone considerable modification and placed more emphasis on the decision-making process of the authorities. Not only have the concepts »non-decision« and »agenda-building« been adopted[4], but also, the notion of the political agenda itself has been elaborated into a phase-model of government decision-making.[5]

The impact of collective actions on government decision-making came under investigation in a significant number of case studies. Some examples include the influence of the Women's Lib movement on abortion policy

---

4 Bachrach, P.; Baratz, M.S. (1970), *Power and Poverty. Theory and Practice*; New York, Oxford University Press.

5 Eijk, C. van der and W.J.P. Kok (1975), »Non-decisions reconsidered«, in: *Acta Politica*, jaargang 10, p. 277-301 and W.J.P. Kok (1981). *Signalering en Selectie-rapport over een onderzoek naar de agendavorming van de rijksdienst.* S'Gravenhage, Staatsuitgeverij.

(Outshoorn and Van Soest [1975] and Outshoorn [1986]), the importance of environmental groups during the struggle against total closure of the Oosterschelde[6], the influence of the peace movement on decision-making on the neutron bomb and the deployment of cruise missiles (Everts, 1985, Maessen, 1979) and the influence of the squatter's movement on housing policy (Van Noort, 1984).

During the seventies, the term action group was widely used; the term ›new social movement‹ only came to be used systematically around 1979, probably influenced by the discussions in Germany and France.

A significant theoretical extension of research into the effect of political action on government policy has been formulated by Van Noort and Huberts and Rademaker (1987). They combine the political agenda-building model with aspects of the Resource Mobilisation Approach (R.M.A.). Both decision-making in all its phases and the performance of action groups or movements form the object of their research. Social movements are seen as organisational networks, at times forming coalitions, competing fiercely for scarce resources, cooperating and quarelling, but eventually as entities directed towards influencing government policies. Their analysis covers the origin of the political actions (the political entrepreneurs and the recruitment of the followers), the internal structure of the movement (culture, ideology and purpose), the mobilisation of the various resources, their strategy (persuasion, argumentation, demonstration, litigation and contestation) and external relationships. Emphatically, the Social Movement Organisation as an influential political factor forms the central object. The internal dynamics of the movement are relevant as far as it effects the attempt to influence policy.

An effect-study not connected with the aforementioned agenda-building tradition was published by Braam e.a. (1976). In the first part of this book a number of actions at the local level were carefully analyzed in order to establish the extent to which successful actions create inequality among the people involved. The central concepts were »influence for own gain« and »channel of influence«, operationalized as a link between an activist and a

6 Leemans, A.; Geers., K. (1983), *Doorbraak in het Oosterschelde beleid.* Muiderberg, Coutinho.

decision-maker. Braam's concepts have been largely ignored in the study of collective action. The second, descriptive part of this work contains an analysis of the mobilization process and the course of the seven actions under study.

In contrast to the theoretical approaches described above, the following focuses on explaining the origins of new movements and, often at the same time, analyzing internal dynamics. Because many studies lack a theoretical foundation, it is difficult to pinpoint any dominating tradition in the seventies. However, since 1983 the influence of the Resource Mobilization Approach is clearly evident in many publications.

A number of studies in the seventies show that the authors have chosen a macro-perspective, comparable in many ways to the functional break-down perspective, whereby collective action is regarded as a reaction to tension and problems which have developed in society as the result of structural processes of change. In this light, social movements may be seen as attempts to restore the equilibrium, that is, to solve the problems of the citizens concerned. An appealing ideology which defines problems and offers solutions is a prerequisite for the development of any social movement.

Ellemers (1979) distinguishes three fundamental social developments at the root of the waves of protest in the sixties. In the first place depillarization, largely due to the internal tensions and crises within the Roman Catholic Church in the Netherlands; second, the rapid rise of television, which radically broke through the isolation and segregation of various population groups in relation to each other; and third, the emergence of a new secondary elite, who saw their career prospects thwarted, but managed via the pillarized media to successfully compete for the chance to present their case. Moreover, Ellemers concludes that, in 1979, these conditions no longer exist.

Different authors have explained the turbulent changes in the sixties and seventies as a result of the emergence of new social groups. Both the shift away from the secondary sector to the tertiary sector within the economy, and the rapid growth of the quarterly sector gave rise to a new and relatively well-educated professional group. In its struggle to gain recognition and to conquer positions of power in society it has come into frequent conflict with other groups. Its members, particularly active within political parties, social movements and action groups, are, according to many authors, the dominant exponents of neo-democratic ideology. Characteristic of this ideology is its emphasis on the ideal of equality and its opposition to the entrenchment of private enterprise and centralised and bureaucratic government action (Kroes 1975).[7]

Schreuder (1981) sees the emergence of these movements as a reaction to problematic situations in society which may be economic, social and/or cultural. The emergence of social movements means that a society is unable to cope with its basic economic problems, those of leadership and government as well of integration and transfer of values. In this respect social movements are clearly of a voluntary nature.

Schreuder, however, is unsympathetic towards such approaches as R.M.A. Its sober and realistic analysis is in his one-sided vision; it lacks romance and tragedy. He sees the basis of the movement as a group, class or mass which is enraged. The atmosphere is emotionally charged, the actions are to a large extent expressive, the symbol of general discontent and an outlet for suppressed anger. There is a prominent leader at hand, who has charismatic power and the natural gift of gathering people around him.[8] For the purpose of analysing the emergence and development of a movement, Schreuder shows a strong preference for the Weber-Michels model.

Another, more recent macro-sociological view is apparent in the works of Van der Loo, Snel and Steenbergen (1984). These authors have examined the question of the extent to which the various new social movements in the Netherlands can be traced to a comprehensive cultural pattern expressing a cultural undercurrent in society.

This hypothesis of profound cultural change is explicitly based on the work of such authors as Capra, Offe and Cotgrove. At a cultural level modern society is seen as the embodiment of two contradictions: that between self-sacrifice and self-development and that between modernism and critical modernism (especially as far as the appreciation of economic and technological progress is concerned). These two dimensions are shown in a matrix (fig. 1). The authors place new social movements in the transitional stage between hedonistic culture and modern culture.

---

7 Also Daalder, H. (1974), *Politisering en Lijdelijkheid in de Nederlandse Politiek.* Assen, Van Gorcum; and Berg, J.Th.J. van den Berg and H.A.A. Molleman (1974), *Crisis in de Nederlandse Politiek.* Alphen aan de Rijn, Samsom.

8 Schreuder, O. (red.) (1985), *Moderne Bewegingen, oude thema's in een nieuw klimaat.* Zeist, Kerckebosch, p. 9.

Fig. 1: Different kinds of cultural change

	Self sacrifice	*Self development*
Modernism	Bourgeois	Hedonistic
Critical modernism	Traditional Christian	Modern cultural Critique

This transition is regarded as the cultural undercurrent while the change from a bourgeois to a hedonistic culture is seen as the dominant culture pattern. The authors concentrate on three questions:

- What are the central values and the modes of action in the new social movements and who are their leading actors?
- To what extent does the similarity between the different movements at the level of values, modes of actions and actors point to a common cultural undercurrent?
- In which way can future government policy and especially cultural policy adapt to such a cultural substream?

Following the Marxist tradition – only moderately developed in the Netherlands – various authors have focused on new social movements. Jacobs and Roebroek (1983) developed a theoretical framework featuring three levels in order to gain some grasp on the phenomenon. In the first place they compare new social movements with traditional organizations according to a list of seven ideal typical characteristics: organizational forms, type of discourse, problem areas and issues, forms of action, strategy, target groups and social composition. Second, they distinguish three levels within the movement: cadres, militants, and masses to be mobilized. According to Jacobs and Roebroek, numerous generalizations about movements neglect the difference between these levels. Third, they point to contradictions and contradictory tendencies within movements, such as basic elements versus elitist elements, concrete utopia versus the development of power and freedom-ideology (autonomy) versus pressure towards conformity.

Their description of the problem areas with which social movements concern themselves shows that their vision of the origins of new social movements closely resembles that of J. Hirsch.[9] They note a tendency towards a profound restructuring of the production and qualification structures, the disappearance of traditional social structures, the destruction of the environment and the increasing disintegration of normal working and living conditions for many people. These processes result in still more government intervention.

The new social movements emerge as a result of this development. It is no coincidence that the government is their prime opponent in many conflicts. Furthermore, Jacobs and Roebroek see the failure of the traditional Labour movement as at least partly responsible for the emergence of new social movements. Indeed, for a long time, most issues of conflict formed an integral part of the programme and practice of the Labour movement. They conclude that new social movements occupy an important position in the struggle between waged labour and capital alongside of the traditional labor movement although the movements organize another part of the working class.

Social scientists, concerned with the question of how structural and cultural developments in society influence individual motives for action, often fall back on presuppositions derived from Relative Deprivation theory. In this theory, protest behavior is seen as a response to a perceived discrepancy between people's expectations and their chance of attaining positions and goods regarded as valuable.[10] In his study of protest in the sixties, Ellemers for example presumes that people with restricted career opportunities are more apt to participate in protest-actions. Publications on the emergence of the second wave of feminism in the Netherlands, at times also reveal a train of thought based on this theory. As early as 1967, Joke Smit (for a long time an influential spokeswoman for the Women's Lib movement) was writing that »the women's discontent« results from, among other things, the opportunities which have come within reach, but which could not be realized. Because a woman is confined to her home and family, she has fewer educational opportunities and – if she is working – she has to be content with poor pay and few prospects.[11]

---

9 Hirsch, J. (1980), *Der Sicherheitsstaat. Das »Modell Deutschland«, seine Krisen und die neuen sozialen Bewegungen.* Frankfurt, EVA.

10 Gurr, T.R. 1970, *Why men rebel*, Princeton, NJ. Princeton University Press.

11 Smit, J. (1984), *Er is een land waar vrouwen willen wonen, teksten 1967-1981*. Amsterdam; Feministische Uitgeverij Sara.

In many recent studies, this tension between rising expectations for women and limited opportunities for their realization is regarded as one of the reasons for the development of the Women's Liberation movement. This is expressed in an English-language publication by De Vries: »The postwar economic changes that created more job opportunities for women might have been important in creating the contradictions that women increasingly felt about their position in society ... it is best to describe the beginnings of feminism here in terms of consciousness rather than in terms of action and activities« (De Vries 1981, p. 390-391).

Inspired by Ellemers and Freeman, another scholar states that the second feminist wave in Holland can be explained with the help of the concept of Relative Deprivation. Awareness of the social restrictions of motherhood and of discrimination in the public domain urged women around 1968 to protest. The question of why the women's movement should have started so early in the Netherlands, where relatively few women work outside of the home, remains unanswered. However, in applying this theory, no operationalization occurs at an individual level; structural developments merely lead the author to the conclusion that this is a case of Relative Deprivation.[12]

Some authors have attempted to solve this problem by testing at the individual level. Kroes (1971) developed a model which postulates that radicalism emerges in a constellation of groups of individuals with unequal shares in various social values such as class, status and power. In this view, such inequality leads to thwarted aspirations. In her study on protests of action groups Van Vonderen van Staveren (1974) uses a model in which relative deprivation is very prominent. Her concern is with the extent to which the perception of deprivation is influenced by feelings of impotence, by reference-groups, by the legitimacy of the government and by available information. However, her research mainly focuses on the choice of means of action by groups of citizens who are already aware of their social problems.

A model of Relative Deprivation is also used within the Political Action tradition. Thomassen (Thomassen a.o. 1983) has made a detailed study of the extent to which the rather sudden economic setback between 1974 and 1979 resulted in perceptions of material relative deprivation and of the translation of this tension into political terms by the individuals concerned,

12 Ribberink, A. (1986), »Het onbehagen verklaard, oorzaken van de tweede feministische golf«, in: *Intermediair*, 22. jaargang, nr. 31, p. 39-43.

e.g. in demands on the government, waning support for parliamentary democracy or in political violence.

The Resource Mobilization Approach (RMA) was introduced in the Netherlands rather late. Klandermans (1983) was one of the first to adopt it in his thesis. He is concerned not so much with simply adopting this approach, but rather, with critically amending and applying it. Influenced by social psychology and symbolic interactionism, he attempts to give more substance to the social psychological elements of collective action by emphasizing the relevance of perceived rather than objectively measured costs and benefits of participation. He claims that the willingness to participate depends on the extent of the grievances, frustrations and value systems in general. In his own model Klandermans distinguishes between Consensus Mobilization and Action Mobilization. Consensus Mobilization is the process whereby organizations within a social movement attempt to recruit support from those collectively concerned, or at least to formulate a mutually accepted definition of the situation. Next, Action Mobilization deals with the willingness to participate in activities in order to reach certain goals. Insight into the course of both processes of mobilization may be gained with the aid of the Expectancy Value Theory. Expected outcomes (expectations) of a collective action and the value of these outcomes are important determinants of the willingness to participate in an action. Since the perceived costs and benefits can be manipulated they are often the object of a persuasion campaign by the leaders of a social movement organization and by their adversaries.

An individual's willingness to participate depends on the perceived and actual values of this collective good. The distinction between the expected reactions of significant others and expected material costs and benefits like money, time or entertainment is also important. In connection with these expectations there is a collective motive to participate (the expectation that participation will produce the collective good), a social motive (the expected reactions of others) and a reward motive (non-social costs and benefits). Participation is a rational choice by an individual in a certain situation. This theory is called »a theory of willingness to participate« (Klandermans 1984). The model has been applied by Klandermans and some of his fellow researchers investigating the trade unions, the Women's movement and the peace movement.[13]

---

13 Briët, M., F. Kroon, B. Klandermans (1985), *Vrouwen en de Vrouwenbeweging; een onderzoek naar de manier waarop vrouwen betrokken raken bij de vrouwenbeweging en*

H. Kriesi was also influenced by the RMA. The Political Action Tradition, and authors such as Offe, also had some influence on his vision on new social movements (Kriesi 1986, Kriesi 1988, Kriesi and Van Praag jr 1987, see also under Switzerland). He also worked four years at the University of Amsterdam.

A recent publication on the Dutch Peace movement's local mobilization for the People's Referendum underlines the importance of the RMA assumption that Social Movement Organizations are vital during mobilization attempts. At the same time it provides a more extensive theoretical framework by including informal networks in the research. In particular, the so-called counter-cultural networks, built around groups, communes, projects, media and communication centers are important for new social movements (Kriesi 1988).

II. Methodological Orientations

The various theoretical orientations described above each have their own research traditions. Together, they cover a wide array of research methods. Researchers, influenced by more than one theoretical school of thought, often appear to adopt various research methods. The following paragraphs examine the research tradition of each theoretical approach.

The »Political Action« tradition frequently makes use of quantitative, large-scale surveys at a national, and sometimes international, level. The first publications concern a survey of 1200 people in 1974. Part of this group of respondents, together with a number of new respondents, were questioned again in 1979. Some of the important publications mentioned above are indeed based on panel-data, on the entire survey results of 1974 and 1979 and partly on the Eurobarometer survey results. Likewise, the various National Election surveys provided additional information about political participation in the Netherlands. Investigations into the impact of action groups and social movements directed at decision-making on a local or national level are found, on the one hand, in case studies of a descriptive nature (Kok e.a.

---

het effect van wervingspogingen van de groepen. Den Haag, Ministerie van Sociale Zaken en Werkgelegenheid. Klandermans, B. and B. Oegema (1984), *Mobilizing for Peace: the 1983 peace demonstration in the Hague.* Paper prepared for the 79th annual meeting of the American Sociological Association.

1971, Kroes 1975, Outshoorn and Van Soest 1977, Maessen 1979, Outshoorn 1986 and Huberts 1988) and, on the other, in comparative research on several action groups and actions adopting both a qualitative and a quantitative approach (Bronner e.a. 1971, Braam, e.a. 1976, Van Noort 1984). They include interviews with the protesters, citizens, the government officials and politicial decision-makers to whom protests were directed as well as studies of written material and qualifications of the essential data on the action. In applying an Agenda Building Approach, researchers attempt to reconstruct the various stages of the decision-making process in order to identify attempts at influencing it and to measure the actual effect of such attempts. Research into the internal dynamics of an action group or movement, its ideology, strategy and culture, is usually based on interviews, the examination of written material (Dijst 1986), and at times on reports and evaluations by participants (Jacobs, Roebroek 1983, De Ruyter 1986). Those authors who attempt to explain the development of movements from a macro-sociological perspective generally adopt a descriptive approach and support their arguments with rather selective quantitative data. Research by Van der Loo et al. (1984) combines a number of research methods: an extensive study of literature on movements already analyzed, interviews with a number of key figures and observations during several important manifestations by the movements concerned.

Authors who have been influenced by RMA also make use of various forms of research although they tend to focus on interviewing local activists in order to get some insight into the aim and structure of action and movement as well as on questioning activists and others involved in the mobilization process either by telephone or in writing (Briët, Kroon, Klandermans, 1985, Kriesi and Van Praag jr., 1987).

Kriesi utilized national survey data for his study on political potential, i.e., that part of the population which is prepared in principle to support certain actions.

III. Empirical Findings

Over the years, Dutch research has shifted its focus from actions and action groups to new social movements and the new middle class. This development was influenced by such spectacular and mass action as the squatter's and peace movements, the development of theories about new social movements in Germany and the gradual adoption of the Resource Mobilization Approach. However, a constant factor over the past 15 years has been quantitative research by scientists from different universities into the background, attitudes and values of activists and participants. Moreover, the results of that research reveal a remarkable continuity. In 1971, Molleman had already come to the conclusion that people who regard themselves as members of higher social classes are relatively frequently involved in actions. Since then the profile of the activists has assumed increasingly sharper contours: he/she is usually well-educated, young (although more likely to be around 30 than around 20), with a leftish political preference, still in training or employed in the socio-cultural services or in education.[14]

According to Rochan (1982): »action groups attract people who can most readily be characterized as middle class. In addition, action group membership is complementary with union or party activism.« Kriesi and Van Praag Jr. (1987) confirm that activists in the peace movement are very frequently involved in political parties.

While action groups have disappeared, at least from scientific literature, and social movements now occupy the stage it is clear, however, that the socio-cultural characteristics of the individuals involved have not changed. In addition, there is evidence of a definite coherence between post-materialistic value-orientation and the willingness to engage in unconventional participation (Thomassen e.a. 1983). Compared to other Western European countries, the Netherlands has many post-materialists and few materialists. Inglehart already noted this in 1971. There is, however, no evidence of a »silent revolution«.

According to Van Deth (1984) proportions between 1970 und 1982 have been reasonably stable: approximately 17% of the population may be regarded as post-materialists, 31% are pure materialists and 52% have a mixed orientation. Participation in protest action has not led to significant changes during the seventies, either, although a decrease in potential protest participation can be traced (Elsinga 1985). Kriesi and Castenmiller (1986) have specified and actualized these findings further. In the first half of the eighties, protest potential continued to decrease, but protest participation did increase. More people translated their willingness to participate into actual

14 Molleman, H.A.A. (1971), »Wie voeren Aktie?«, in: *Acta Politica*, jaargang VII, p. 99-111.

protest behavior. This increase is primarily the result of increasing participation in demonstrations, particularly in the mass peace demonstrations in 1981 and 1983. Most remarkable is the increased level of participation by young people (between 18 and 33 years). Action groups and social movements enjoy considerable leeway within the Dutch political system. There is, however, no unequivocal evidence that actually influence decision-making by local and national authorities. Nor is there any degree of consensus on the way such influence could be measured. Several case studies indicate that action achieves an effect (Kok e.a. 1971, Braam 1976 and Abma[15]). A research team at the Free University of Amsterdam in 1971 concluded, however, that demonstrations have no effect on the decision-making by Parliament although the »Union of Conscripts« (VVDM) would appear to have achieved a number of spectacular successes between 1970 and 1975 such as freedom of hairstyle, abolition of compulsory saluting of superiors, higher pay, etc.[16]

Since 1973, the women's movement has noticeably influenced the formulation of an emancipation policy by national government (Van Praag jr. 1985) although it was unable to close the gap between woman-oriented policy intentions and actual hostile policies with regard to income and social security. Most researchers refrain from generalizations about the conditions which ensure success in action. Daalder states, however, that the rapid growth of the number of action groups must be explained by the fact that they turned out to be an unexpected means of obtaining success such that people resorted less and less to indirect, institutional channels. Actions were an effective means to exerting influence.[17] This picture no longer seems to apply.

Rochan (1982) points to the necessity of differentiating between actions at the local and national level. Action groups have little impact at a national level, but are often successful at a local level. One of the rare recent studies to conclude that actions do indeed have an effect deals with the squatter's

---

15 Abma, E. (1978), »Acties pro en contra«, in: *Flouridering, kiezen of trekken*. Cahiers Biowetenschappen en Maatschappij 4, nr. 3, febr. 1978.

16 Werkgroep Vrije Universiteit (1971), »Invloed van demonstranten op de standpunten van Tweede-Kamerleden«, in: *Acta Politica*, jaargang VI, p. 417-440; Kok, W.J.P. (1977), »Kritische bewegingen«, in: Brentjens, H.J.H. en Turpijn Ch.F. (red.), *Welzijn en Krijgsmacht*. Deventer: Van Loghum Slaterus, p. 336-351.

17 Daalder, H. (1981) »Parlement tussen politieke partijen en actiegroepen«, in: *Acta Politica*, jaargang XVI, p. 481-489.

action at a local level (Van Noort 1984). He concludes that the threat of violence often leads to a reversal of proposed measures. A strong emphasis on a combative strategy, however, can become counter-productive. One of the most radical groups, namely the Squatter's movement in Amsterdam, was not included in this study. A movement's success generally means the reversal of certain government measures; only rarely are the movement's own policy alternatives realized. The most evident failures to influence policy at a national level were suffered by the anti-nuclear movement and the peace movement. The anti-nuclear movement failed to force the closure of two operating nuclear power plants and it is not unthinkable that – when public opinion has forgotten disasters like Chernobyl – the decision to build two new nuclear power plants will be taken.

The Peace movement failed to prevent the deployment of 48 cruise missiles in the Netherlands despite the mass mobilization of the population in 1981, 1983 and 1985 (Everts 1985, Klandermans e.a. 1988).

Huberts (1988) and Van Noort (1988) are responsible for the most extensive research into the influence of social movements on government policy. In his thesis, Huberts examined the extent of the influence exerted by protest and pressure groups on road-building in the province of North Brabant between 1967 and 1986. His most important conclusion is that the influence of the national authority in charge of road building (Rijkswaterstaat) and local authorities is still by far the greatest although the environmental movement did manage to achieve some influence on road building policy after 1975.

In another thesis, Van Noort produced comparative research into the development and influence of the anti-nuclear, the squatter's and the environmental movements, respectively. He distinguishes several factions in each movement: in the environmental movements moderates often working in established and institutionalized organizations as well as social critics; in the squatter's and anti-nuclear movements social critics and an autonomous faction. In the squatter's movement, the autonomists have strengthened their position over the years.

Van Noort has compared the three movements with regard to ideology, aims, resources, strategy and tactics. His notable conclusion is that the development of these movements was strongly influenced by perceived political efficacy and political opportunity structures. He does not think it is likely that their decline, especially visible in the disappearance of more radical factions, is a temporary one, nor that the nineties will bring some sort of revival.

Van Noort's conclusions on the influence of the movements on policy are well-balanced. The anti-nuclear movement helped delay the building of new nuclear power stations between 1975 and 1982. According to Van Noort the squatter's movement was able to influence local government policy, but its effect on national legislation was much smaller. The environmental movement's influence was greatest at the beginning of the seventies when awareness of environmental problems also existed outside of the movement. The economic problems which have plagued the Netherlands since the end of the seventies have resulted in decreased priority for environmental policy. During this period the environmental organizations continued to receive substantial government subsidy. It should be noted that Van Noort's study appeared in 1988 and since then environmental problems have again been given high priority by both public opinion and political parties.

In contrast to the situation in other countries it is remarkable that many studies in the Netherlands focus on the effects of action-groups and social movements. The explanation for this must be sought in the relationship between (new) social movements and the government which differs strongly from countries such as the Federal Republic of Germany. In the Netherlands, this relationship must be seen against the background of the traditional bargaining model which has always governed labour relations and the political practice developed during the period of pillarization of subsidizing various social groups and, if necessary, involving them in policy preparation. After the initial shock of the various protest manifestations in the sixties, the government soon decided to modify its policies with the regard to the student's movement, the Women's Lib movement, environmental groups, the gay movement and even the squatter's movement. Cooperation and consultation, rather than repression, were the government's first priorities. Also, young Moluccans – not participating in a new social movement, but the only group of activists which (in 1975 and 1977) carried out violent actions comparable, for instance, to political violence in countries such as Italy, Belgium and the FRG – were not repressed violently. Up till now, this policy has been rather successful; the Netherlands is one of the least (politically) violent countries in Europe. The benevolent politics of local and national government with regard to new social movements provided a number of them with considerable resources in the form of project-subsidies, housing, paid jobs, training facilities etc., and a certain influence on policy. One could say that the Dutch political system is relatively open to new demands and social needs. If one seeks comparison with other nations, the similarity with countries such as Sweden and U.K. is more pronounced than with Germany.[18]

The macro-sociological approach has produced a number of useful descriptions of various movements. Van der Loo et al. (1984) draw a concise picture of the development of some six movements, namely the environmental movement, the squatter's movement, the women's movement, the peace movement, the alternative work movement, and the individual development movement (*Suchbewegungen*, according to Habermas).

Van der Loo et al. contend that the examplary new social movement, characterized by autonomy, dissociative behavior, self-help, basic democracy, spontaneity and a dislike of leadership cults, does not really exist. Only the squatter's movement fits the bill more or less as do the smaller, more radical wings of the environmental movement, the women's movement and the peace movement. Most movements, however, are decidedly heterogeneous. This frequently results in internal contradictions, and particularly, where practical matters of internal functioning and strategy towards the authorities are concerned. All movements contain important reformist factions, primarily concerned with influencing decision-making, which therefore attach great importance to a pragmatic bond with political parties, trade-unions and various ministries. Van der Loo et al. also indicate the influence of different ideological traditions on the six movements (Fig. 2).

Fig. 2: Ideological origins of the new social movements

	ecology	squatters	women	work	peace	pers. growth
romanticism	++	+-	+-	++	+	+
left libertarian	+	++	+	++	+-	-
socialism	+	-	+	+	+	-
oriental mystic.	-	-	+-	+	-	++

++	=	great influence	+-	=	some influence
+	=	influence	-	=	no influence

18 Cf. Brand, K.W. (ed.), (1985), *Neue Soziale Bewegungen in West-Europa und den USA. Ein internationaler Vergleich.* Frankfurt, Campus, p. 323ff.

The dominant role of romantic sources of inspiration is significant. For this reason Van Deth (1984) considers post-materialism as romantic-individualism.

There are also more specific studies on the peace movement (Everts, Walraven 1984), two quantitative studies on the participants of the peace demonstrations of 1981 in Amsterdam and 1983 in The Hague (Schennink a.o. 1982, Kruisraketten ongewenst 1983), an analysis of the people's referendum of the peace movement (Klandermans et al. 1988, Kriesi 1988) and two general outlines of the environmental movement (Tellegen 1983, Kramer 1989). The radical wing of these movements is dealt with in more detail by Van Noort (1984) and Huberts, Van Noort 1986). Moreover, these authors have also drawn attention to the differences and similarities within forms of action, personal ties and values which characterize different movements. The subculture of the squatter's movement has been profoundly analyzed by Dijst (1986).

The years 1978 to 1983 were the heyday of the squatter's movement, the anti-nuclear movement and the peace movement; several successes were achieved and large masses mobilized. Surveys showed very wide support for the movement's demands. After 1985, the future had become uncertain for many movements as the anti-nuclear-movement's infrastructure, for instance, had completely disappeared. The women's and squatter's movements were subjected to heavy pressure although their channels of communication (media) and meeting places were still functioning to some extent. There are still squatted houses in Amsterdam and other cities although the number is decreasing. There is, however, no longer really any squatter's movement. The radical squatter's weekly ›Bluf!‹ stopped publication in 1988.

The peace and environmental movements have managed to maintain their structures though the former has definitely seen better times. It is no coincidence that these two movements contain several well organized and highly active groups. However, the mobilisation capabilities of all movements have declined sharply. The government's 1985 announcement of its intention to build two new nuclear power plants (after a moratorium of 10 years) failed to incite much protest. The anti-nuclear movement and the squatter's movements have disappeared. The more radical wings remaining within the other movements have been decimated and are fighting for survival. Since 1987, radical elements from the different movements manifest themselves mainly in attacks on Dutch firms with interests in South Africa, especially Shell.

Moderate factions within the peace movement, namely the Christian I.K.V., are going through a phase of re-orientation, loosening the bond with the other groups within the Peace movement and refraining from mass action for the time being.[19] For years now the women's movement has not resorted to mass action and it appears to have started a long march through the institutions. A considerable number of women's organizations still operate together within the Broad Platform for Economic Independence. One of the more successful organisations in the second half of the eighties was Greenpeace. This pragmatic organisation received a lot of support from young people. These developments cannot be explained by any important political re-orientation among the Dutch population. Many of the issues for which the movements stand are still widely supported. Ideas about the position of women in society continue to shift in an emancipatory direction. The absence of spectacular successes appears to have caused a certain amount of action fatigue. And in the absence of short-term success, movements have been unable to develop a long-term strategy. The preference for more radical methods of action, found particularly in the Squatter's movement and anti-nuclear movements, has had a counter-productive effect. Many sympathizers have turned away from such action thereby creating marked divisions within the movements. Strong resistance to increasing violence by certain groups is particularly significant within the squatter's movement. De Ruyter (1986) presents a clear summary of the internal debate in Nijmegen and Amsterdam and concludes that a culture of violence has been primarily responsible for the movement's bankruptcy. Vehement internal debate, however, did prevent a further escalation of violence. In isolated cases, anonymous small groups still resort to violence.

However, Kriesi (1986) is of the opinion that all this represents only a temporary decline. In his view, the social changes since 1945 have led to the emergence of an ever-growing group, the so-called professionals who, with their specific pattern of post-materialist values, will continue to leave their mark on society. Van Noort (1988) considers a revival of the movement around the year 2000 not impossible. A dissenting view is held by Duyvendak en Koopmans. They argue that the ›decline of social movements‹ is a construction of the media and accuse social scientists of a systematic neglect

19 Van Putten, J. (1986), *Toekomst voor de vredesbeweging*. Amsterdam/Amersfoort, Jan Mets/ De Horstink.

of the ›solidarity movements‹. In their view, the time of spectacular mass mobilisation is over, but the number of protest actions is not decreasing.[20]

IV. Institutional Aspects of Social Movement Research

Academic interest in new social movements waned in the second half of the eighties. A number of research projects have been finished or are in the process of winding up and will not be extended. The project »Private Organization and Power« at the University of Leiden, which included research into the effect of action on decision-making, has been completed. Moreover, the future of the different departments of sociology is uncertain in view of the cutback in public spending affecting the Ministry of Education.

At the Catholic University of Nijmegen, Schreuder et al. changed their object of study. Over the last few years they have been occupied with finding an explanation for the processes of pillarization and de-pillarization using concepts adopted from theories on processes of mobilization.

After completing their book on new social movements in the Netherlands, the University of Utrecht researchers Van der Loo, Snel and Steenbergen have directed their efforts into other fields of research.

Three institutions will continue to conduct research into new social movements during the coming years: the Peace Research Centre of the Catholic University of Nijmegen (Schennink et al.), the Department of Social Psychology at the Free University of Amsterdam (Klandermans et al.), and the Department of Political Science at the University of Amsterdam.

The research activities will concentrate on the peace movement. Schennink will continue to follow and analyze developments within the peace movement as well as study his own survey-data concerning the People's Referendum. Since June 1985 Klandermans and Oegema have been working on a panel-survey with 250 citizens in 4 medium-sized towns. It is a survey by telephone which was repeated three times by the end of 1986. Assuming that the peace movement is on its way out after the final decision of the Dutch cabinet and parliament on the deployment of cruise missiles in

20 Duyvendak, J.W.; Koopmans, R. (1989), »Hebben de peilers van de tijdgeest dan geen ogen in hun hoofd? De stille revolutie van de jaren tachtig«, in: *De Groene Amsterdammer*, 15 november 1989.

November 1985, they are primarily interested in the development of opinion on the peace movement. They are also examining other activities now undertaken by the activists of yesteryear (sustained participation).

In September 1988, Kriesi accepted an appointment as professor at the University of Geneva. From Switzerland, he still heads a comparative research project on the development of social movements in France, Germany, Switzerland and the Netherlands. The other participants in this project work at the University of Amsterdam. This project focuses on explaining the development of different social movements in the four countries by the ›opportunity structures‹ inherent in different political systems.

Coordination and cooperation between different researchers and projects in the Netherlands are conducted mainly on an informal basis.

V. Debates and Controversies

Eminent theoretical debate is rare within a poorly developed field of research. This has certainly been the case in the Netherlands. Vehement polemics or controversies have been rare and primarily concerned with the (political) evaluation of certain phenomena. When Schreuder presented an analysis of the ideology of the German Squatter's movement, its organization strategy, background and impact (based on news items from the German press) a number of students from the University of Nijmegen published a spirited reaction accusing him of hiding behind science in order to throw suspicion upon the German Squatters. Their arguments consisted of an analysis of his language, his use of concepts and theories and his method of research.[21]

The difference of opinion between Van Deth and Kriesi may have been less vehement, but it was nevertheless rooted in an evaluation of the phenomenon of »post-materialism«. The former is convinced that he is dealing with a romantically individualistic ideology, which also must be regarded as the ideology of a »new class« bent on bettering its social position. The self-

21 Schreuder, O. (1981), »De Krookbeweging, Verkenningen in de Duitse Bondsrepublick« in *Sociale Wetenschappen* (24), 236-262; Linden, D. von der et al. (1982), »Schreuder gekraakl, een kritiek op het artikel von O. Schreuder over krakers in de Duitse Bondsrepublick«, *Soziale Wetenschappen* (25), 54-73.

interest of the new middle-classes is of paramount importance as far as the relevance of post-materialism is concerned (Van Deth 1984).

According to Kriesi, the initiators of new social movements wage primarily a universalistic battle based on the conviction that the way in which material needs are fulfilled under the present social circumstances could pose a long-term threat to the satisfaction of future human needs (Kriesi 1986).

The question whether new social movements primarily serve particularistic or universalistic vested interests, and whether the wave of protest of the eighties has come to an end, can only be answered in the distant future. Meanwhile, research in the Netherlands has distinguished itself from that in other countries mainly in its emphasis on the influence of action groups or movements on decision-making by the authorities.

Annotated Bibliography

Benschop, D.; Walraven, G.; Wiersma, E. (eds.). (1986): *Vredesbeweging. Strategie en effectiviteit.* Nijmegen, Studiecentrum voor Vredesvraagstukken, cahier 38.
Reader on the effectiveness of the peace movement written by researchers and peace activists.

Braam, G.P.A. et al. (1976): »*Collectieve Acties*«, Meppel/Amsterdam: Boom.
Analysis of a number of local actions in order to determine the extent to which successful action created inequality among those involved.

Bronner, F., et al. (1971): »Aktiekomitees in Amsterdam«, *Acta Politica*, 125-157.
Article about the origins and development of 27 small local pressure groups (action groups) in Amsterdam. The subject matter is treated within Easton's theoretical framework.

Castenmiller, P. (1988): *Participatie in beweging, ontwikkelingen in politieke participatie in Nederland.* Rijswijk, Sociaal en Cultureel Planbureau, cahier 5 (1989.
Outline of political participation in the Netherlands, also tracing participation in social movements.

Deth, J.W. van (1984): »*Politieke waarden, een onderzoek naar politieke waardeorientaties in Nederlands in de periode 1970 tot en met 1982*« Amsterdam: CT-Press.
Analysis of the changes in value orientation and social positions in the Netherlands, especially the development of post-materialist values.

Dijst, T. (1986): »*De bloem der natie in Amsterdam. Kraken, subcultuur en het probleem der orde*. Leiden: C.O.M.T., 22.
A study of the subculture of the squatter's movement in Amsterdam focusing on the problem of social order within the movement.

Ellemers, J.E. (1979): »Nederland in the jaren zestig en zeventig«, *Sociologische Gids*, 1979, (26): 429-541.

Analysis of the waves of protest in the sixties in the Netherlands.

Elsinga, E. (1985): *»Politieke Participatie in Nederland«* Amsterdam: CT-Press.

This investigation, part of the Political Action project, deals with the modes and the development of political participation in the Netherlands in the seventies.

Everts, Ph.P.; Walraven, G. (1984): *Vredesbeweging*. Utrecht/Antwerpen, Het Spectrum, Aula 744.

Brief history of the Dutch peace movement from 1870 to 1984.

Everts, Ph.P. (ed.). (1985): *Controversies at home: Domestic factors in the Foreign policy of the Netherlands*. Dordrecht: Nijhoff.

Case studies about Dutch foreign policy; one of the studies analyzes the decision-making regarding the cruise missiles and the influence of the peace movement.

Huberts, L. (1988): *De politieke invloed van protest en pressie, besluitvormingsprocessen over rijkswegen*. DSWO Press: Leiden.

Research into decision-making by the national government on road-building between 1967 and 1986 in the province of North Brabant. The environmental movement seems to have been able to exert some influence, especially after 1972.

Huberts, L.W.; Van Noort, W.J. (eds.). (1989): *Sociale bewegingen in de jaren negentig; Stand van zaken en vooruitblik*. Leiden: DSWO-Press.

Different authors attempt to chart the possibilities and opportunities for movements in the nineties from several different perspectives.

Jacobs, D., Roebroek, J. (1983): *Nieuwe Sociale Bewegingen in Vlaanderen en Nederland*. uitg. Leon Leson: Antwerpen.

Analysis of the new social movements in the Netherlands and Flanders, strongly influenced by the work of J. Hirsch.

Klandermans, P.G. (1983): *Participatie in een sociale beweging, een mobilisatie campagne onderzocht*. Amsterdam: VU Boekhandel/Uitgeverij.

One of the first studies in the Netherlands based on a modified RMA-model. In this book a mobilisation campaign of the trade union is analyzed.

– (1984): »Mobilization and Participation: social psychological expansions of resource mobilization theory«, *American Sociological Review*, 49, 583-600.

Klandermans, P.G.; Kriesi, H.; Oegema, D.; van Praag jr, Ph.; Schennink, B. (eds.). (1988): *Tekenen voor vrede, het volkspetitionnement tegen de kruisraketten*. Assen/Maastricht: Van Gorcum.

Research on the People's referendum of the Dutch Peace movement (1985) against the deployment of cruise missiles in the Netherlands.

Kok, W.; Meyer, C.; van Ruiten, G. (1971), *Protest tegen progil, een onderzoek naar de achtergrond en de uitwerking van een protest*. Groningen: Wolters-Nordhoff.

Study of a succesful protest action against the establishment of a hydro-sulphite factory in Amsterdam's harbor area.

Kramer, J. (1989): *De Groene Golf*. Utrecht: Jan van Arkel.

Outline of the development of the environmental movement in the Netherlands by a leading environmental activist.

Kriesi, H. (1986): *Nieuwe sociale bewegingen: op zoek naar hun gemeenschappelijke noemer*. Oratie, Universiteit van Amsterdam.
Essay on the common characteristics of new social movements with special emphasis on the role of the new middle class.

– (1988): Local mobilization for the people's social petition of the Dutch peace movement«, in: Klandermans, B.; Kriesi, H.; Tarrow, S. (eds.): *From Structure to Action: Social Movement Participation across Cultures*, Greenwich, Conn.; JAI Press Inc., 41-81.
Analysis of the mobilisation for the people's petition of the peace movement. Emphasis on the effect of counter-cultural networks.

Kriesi, H.; Praag jr. Ph. van (1987): »Old and New Politics: the Dutch Peace movement and the traditional political organizations«. *European Journal of Political Research 15*, 319-346.
This article shows that many peace movement activists are involved more or less in leftwing political parties.

Kroes, R. (1975): *New Left, Nieuw Links, New Left; verzet, beweging, verandering in Amerika, Nederland, Engeland*. Alphen aan de Rijn/Brussel: Samsom.
Comparative study of the New Left movements of the United States, the Netherlands and Great Britain from a perspective of influence and mobilization strategy.

Loo, H. van der; Snel, E.; Steenbergen, E. van (1984): *Een wenkend perspectief? Nieuwe sociale bewegingen en culturele veranderingen*. Amersfoort: De Horstink.
Comparative research into six new social movements in the Netherlands focussing on whether these movements offer a new cultural perspective.

Maessen, P. (1979): »Wie stopt de Neutronenbom? – de geschiedenis van een aktie«. Transaktie, nr 4, 423-457. History of the mass action against the neutronbomb in the Netherlands.

Noort, W. van (1984): *De effecten van de kraakbeweging op de besluitvorming van gemeentelijke overheden*. Leiden: C.O.M.T., uitgave 15.
Research on the influence of the squatters' movement in four cities, namely Dordrecht, Den Bosch, Utrecht and Nijmegen. The author notes that violent action is most likely successful where the reversal of (proposed) measures is concerned.

– (1988): *Bevlogen Beweging, Een vergelijking van de anti-kernenergie-, kraak en milieubeweging*. Amsterdam: Sua.
Research on the origins, development and influence of the anti-nuclear energy movement, the squatter's movement and the environmental movement. The author notes some evidence of influence, but is careful not to overrate it.

Noort, W.J. van; Huberts, L.W.; Rademaker, L. (1987): *Protest en Pressie, een systematische analyse van collectieve actie*. Assen/Maastricht: Van Gorcum.
Outline of the different theories on collective behavior, and the author's own theory; strongly influenced by the Resource Mobilization Approach.

Outshoorn, J.; Soest, M. van (1977): *Tien jaar abortusstrijd in Nederland (1967-1977)*. Den Haag: Stichting Uitgeverij Dolle Mina.
Outline of the struggle of the women's movement in the period 1967-1977 legalizing abortion.

Outshoorn, J. (1986): »The rules of the game: abortion politics in the Netherlands«, in: J. Lovenduski and J. Outshoorn (eds.). *The new politics of abortion*. London: Sage.

Analysis of the politics of abortion in the Netherlands and the influence of the women's movement.

Praag, Ph. van (1985): »Tien jaar Emancipatiebeleid«, *Beleid en Maatschappij*, (12): 3-12.
Outline of the way in which the women's movement has influenced the definition of ›emancipation policy‹ in the course of ten years.

Rochan, Thomas R. (1982): »Direct Democracy or organized futility? Action Groups in the Netherlands«, *Comparative Political Studies*, 15 (1): 3-28.
Study of action groups in the Netherlands and their function within the Dutch political system.

Ruyter, D. de (1986): *Een baksteen als bewustzijn, de geweldskultuur van de kraakbeweging*. Den Bosch: Margeteksten.
Clear summary of the internal debate in the squatter's movement in Amsterdam and Nijmegen on radical and violent methods of action.

Schennink, B.; Bertrand, T.; Fun, H. (1982): *De 21 november demonstranten, wie zijn ze en wat willen ze*. Studiecentrum voor Vredesvraagstukken, cahier 25, Soest: Jo Mets.
Research into the characteristics and motives of the participants in the mass peace demonstration of November 21, 1981.

Schreuder, O. (1981): *Sociale Bewegingen, een systematische inleiding*. Deventer: Van Loghum Slaterus.
Introductry outline of theories about the origins, development, leadership, ideology and organization of social movements.

– (ed.). (1985): *Moderne Bewegingen, Oude thema's in een nieuw klimaat*. Zeist: Kerkebosch.
Reader by authors from the Netherlands and Belgium containing both theoretical essays from different traditions and a number of case studies.

Tellegen, E. (1983): *Milieubeweging*. Utrecht/Antwerpen: Het Spectrum, aula 734.
Brief outline of environmental protest world-wide with somewhat more attention given to the development of the environmental movement in the Netherlands.

Thomassen, J.J.A. et al. (1983): *De verstomde revolutie, politieke opvattingen en gedragingen van Nederlandse burgers na de jaren zestig*. Alphen aan de Rijn: Samsom.
In this study, theories and notions about the social, cultural and political change in modern societies are examined by analyzing the opinions of citizens in the Netherlands after the 1960s. This research is strongly influenced by the ›Political Action‹ tradition.

Vonderen-van Staveren, M.L. van (1974): *Protesteren in Actiegroepen*. Utrecht: Bijleveld.
Research, based on relative deprivation theory, into why people participate in action groups.

Vries, P. de, (1981), »Feminism in the Netherlands« in: *Women's Studies Int. Quarterly*, 4: 398-407.
Outline of the development of the women's movement in the Netherlands.

Part III
Debates and Perspectives

Resource Mobilization Theory: A Critique

Herbert Kitschelt

I. Introduction

Over the last fifteen years »resource mobilization« approaches to understanding social movements have gradually displaced older collective behavior perspectives which built on the notion of relative deprivation as a cause of protest mobilization. This change has focused attention away from protests as irrational and often inarticulate, utopian responses to grievances to the concrete interests, resources, skills and strategies that rational, calculating actors bring to bear on their mobilization of collective protest. This, at least, is an extremely simplified summary of what many North American researchers consider to be the essential of this key paradigmatic shift in the sociology of social movements.

Sober reflection on the actual accomplishments of resource mobilization (RM) approaches clearly calls into question whether a wholesale rejection of relative deprivation arguments is justified[1]. Moreover, one must consider whether the contributions of »Weberian« and symbolic interactionist perspectives which focus on the construction of subjective meaning and the process by which the »stakes« of movements are negotiated can be ignored. Additionally, there are the insights of a recent wave of West-European publications on social movements. Methodologically, these works are situated in the tradition of Marxian and functionalist macro-sociological analysis and

1 Brief surveys of the major »schools« of social movement research, including resource mobilization, can be found in Marx and Wood (1975), Tilly (1978), and Jenkins (1981).

relate the emergence of specific types of movements to the basic institutions and lines of conflict in a society[2].

In my critique of RM approaches, I will show that the theoretical insights of their competitors are necessary complements to RM perspectives and at times demonstrate the limited range of phenomena to which RM theories are applicable. Thus, my critique is aimed not at repudiating RM approaches, for they represent a definite theoretical advance over older collective behavior views. But like their competitors, they run aground when they overestimate their arguments' theoretical and empirical power. Although thoughtful proponents of RM approaches have always emphasized that they can provide only a *partial* explanation of collective mobilization, most research gives RM perspectives a centrality and hegemony which is not warranted.

Social theories can compete with each other in at least two different ways. First, different theories offer explanations for one and the same phenomen. In this case, only one can be true or false. Second, theories explain different aspects of a complex social phenomenon, but disagree on the theoretical and empirical importance of what they explain. In practice, debates among theoreticians proceed in a grey area between both types of competition. Theories overlap in their explanatory claims, but also cover different explananda or often disagree on the conceptualization of the explananda (because there is no descriptive language free of theoretical premises in the social sciences). This is also the case in the study of social movements. Collective protest and mobilization for change are extremely complex phenomena. It is important to understand the nature of the competition between different theoretical approaches in this light and to evaluate their respective claims accordingly.

I will argue that, in one respect, RM perspectives are really compatible and complementary to other approaches. They explain aspects of social movements for which other theories do not provide good explanations. A more comprehensive analysis of social movements thus must build on a theoretical eclecticism. In another respect, however, RM approaches ignore how critically dependent they are on other theoretical perspectives even in their core propositions. In other words, RM approaches are *not theoretically*

2 The most prominent representatives of this theoretical approach are Marcuse (1964, 1972), Touraine (1973, 1978), Melucci (1980, 1982), Habermas (1973, 1981) and Offe (1984, 1985). Implicitly, these approaches presuppose either a logic of relative deprivation (as Marx did) or a logic of cognitive and normative change of social structures and world views (as Weber or Schumpeter did) at the actor level of collective mobilization.

»self-sufficient«. Their key concepts and propositions become only operative, once other thories have at least been tacitly presupposed and the meaning of key concepts in the RM perspective interpreted in this light. For instance, the notions of »interests« and »resources« remain, without a grounding in macro-sociological and Weberian perspectives, entirely empty in RM approaches.

I conclude from my critique that it is time to set aside the battle between »paradigms«, »approaches« and »theories« in the social movements literature in favor of establishing links between fragments and components of each theoretical tradition to construct more satisfactory self-sufficient and comprehensive explanations of social movements. In this vein some authors have always been hesitant to embrace a particular »school« of analysis exclisively. And some proponents of RM theories, for example, have already begun to include elements of the Marxian and Weberian heritage in their work (cf. Garner and Zald 1982; Zald 1985), while their colleagues coming from European macro-structural and cultural traditions are willing to consider insights of RM studies (cf. Rucht 1984 and Raschke 1985).

RM approaches and studies define only a loose family of concepts, propositions, and research projects. There is no firm agreement on the theoretical core of this strand of research among all the authors who are said to contribute to RM approaches. I will briefly illustrate the theoretical breath and variation among authors to whose work the RM label is often attached. The imprecision of the RM label must be kept in mind when, in my second step, I distill a set of basic arguments from this wide range of contributions. The third step, then, is the core of the paper in which I try to show why RM approaches are not self-sufficient and in which ways require theoretical extension by other approaches.

II. Varieties of RM Approaches

RM approaches draw on micro-ecomomic and sociological theories, developed in the 1960s, which are applicable to the analysis of collective mobilization. A cornerstone is Olson's (1965) theory of collective action, which asserts that rational individuals will join an effort to provide a collective good only if the individual cost of participation does not outweigh individual benefits. In many instances, collective action thus presupposes not only the objective to provide a collective good, but also »selective incentives« to potential contributors. Otherwise, inividuals will »free ride« and attempt to benefit from the production of a public good without own contributions. Olson's theory shows that wants and deprivations do not directly translate into collective mobilization. Thus, it is a direct critique of relative deprivation arguments. Although Olson designed his theory for economic interest organizations, others have extended its applicability to other types of organization and collective struggles (cf. Hardin 1982).

Not all contributors to RM theory build on rational actor assumptions. Those who do usually have modified Olson's framework to account for a broader range of motivations and incentives to participate in collective action. »Political entrepreneurs», for instance, do not need selective incentives, because they derive »psychic income« from the pursuit of the collective good itself (Froehlich, Oppenheimer and Young 1971).

Among socal movements theorists, a rigorous application of rational choice theory to collective mobilization is comparatively rare. McCarthy and Zald (1973,1977) have tried to apply rational actor models to both the behavior of individuals in movements as well as the strategies of movement organizations. But even here, the micro-logic of collective action is not spelled out in detail, because the authors are more interested in the interplay between social opportunity structures, resources for collective action, and the behavior of social movement organizations.

Other authors who work under the loose cover of resource approaches have built more exclusively on structural theories of social conflict (e.g. Oberschall 1973). The sociological root of such work is Dahrendorf's (1959) theory of conflict and domination. Emphasizing the ubiquity of asymmetric power relations in modern societies, the signifiance of repression in the maintance of social order, and the pattering of social conflict by hierarchical organizations, Dahrendorf and his followers criticize what they perceive as the bias of functionalist sociology towards consensus models of social order. From Dahrendorf, as well as some neo-marxist authors, the developers of RM approaches have learned that conflict is not an irrational outburst, but rooted in structural tensions within society.

Among the more »structuralist« analyses of collective mobilization, Charles Tilly's work on protest movements in European history stands out. It emphasizes opportunities to act collectively, repression, solidarity, and violence in a broad »political process« analysis of collective action (cf. Tilly 1973; 1978; Tilly; Tilly and Tilly 1975). More recently, McAdam (1982) developed a process model of mobilization in which the indigenous organizational strength and the political opportunities for the articulation of protest are key varables. Another author who only partially builds on rational actor assumptions, but generally emphasizes the structural conditions and consequences of collective actions is Gamson (1975). His work examines the link between various attributes of social movements, such as the scope of their goals and constituencies, their choice of strategies, and their organization, on the one hand, and the success of protest actions, on the other hand.

Although contributors to RM theory disagree on the precise micro-logic and individual rationality that is involved in collective action, they share certain assumptions that set them apart from relative deprivation approaches. Not impulsive »passions«, but calculated »interests« guide collective mobilization. Movement participants are not marginal and alienated members of society who have lost their belief in a shared system of norms and institutional mechanism of conflict resolution; rather, they are intellectually alive and socially competent individuals whose activities are based precisely on their deep enmeshment in social networks. All authors also assume that the social structure generates collective interests and conflicts. Furthermore, they are opponents of the pluralist view of politics which reconstructs political action as an open market place of groups and ideas without admitting structural rigidities against the representation of some groups and demands. Although differences of interests and asymmetries are endemic in societies, collective mobilization and protest is not. What RM analysts try to determine, are the specific situations, in which grievances can be translated into collective action. The approach therefore focuses on the facilitators of communication and the organization of collective action, but also the external networks of supporters, sympathizers, or movements' adversaries.

Despite these similarities, the RM approach harbors many different views on the development and strategies of social movements. Tilly, for instande, might feel very uncomfortable being labelled an »RM theorists», because his work also emphasizes the symbolic constitution of solidarity in groups and differences among the psychological dispositions of actors (zealots, misers...). Here, the Weberian legacy plays some role. And McAdams goes so far as to reject the RM-label for his own approach. In his view, the latter puts too much weight on the importance of leaders and societal elites as aspects of the opportunity structure to mobilize collective protest, while he would focus more on the indigenous organizational capabilities of movements. And it is needless to say that many of the structural »RM theorists« do not share

Olson's reconstruction of collective action (for a critique see e.g. Gamson 1975: 55-71), although they rarely develop an explicit alternative theory.

The number of rigorous empirical studies guided by RM perspectives remains limited. Whereas relative deprivation theories focus on quantitative and comparative analyses of civil strife, RM approaches prefer an in-depth process analysis of particular movements. They reconstruct the mobilization of movements in much greater detail than preceding students. The trade-off, however, is the more limited scope and generalizability of their findings. Most research in the RM perspective are case studies on individual movements or narratives on the developments in a particular setting. This weakness may be due to the nature of the research object which is a fluid, flexible and fleeting phenomen that cannot be »mapped« and »preserved« in the process of analysis. Nevertheless, some ingenious research by Tilly (1978: appendix) and Gamson (1975) has shown the way to »interview« written documents in order to develop more systemataic and semi-quantitive indicators and data banks on collective mobilization.

To provide an idea of the research that has been done within the range of RM approaches, I will simply enumerate a few important studies: Tilly's work on protests, riots, and social movements in Europe since the 18th century (cf. again Tilly, Tilly and Tilly 1975); research on strike activities and social protest in contemporary capitalism (Hibbs 1973; Korpi and Shalev 1978); studies on the development of contemporary movements, such as the women's or the civil rights movement (Freeman 1975; 1979; McAdam 1982); analyses of the relevance of organization in social movements (Gamson 1975; Piven and Cloward 1977; Goldstone 1980); work on the omportance of »conscience constituencies« and sympathetic elites (in politics and the mass media) for the career of social movements (e.g., Lipsky 1968; Jenkins and Perrow 1977; Molotch 1979; Gitlin 1980); studies on the relationship between political opportunity structures and social movements (Eisinger 1973; Jenson 1981; Tarrow 1983; Kitschelt 1986); analyses of counter-movements and repression (Marx 1979; Lo 1982; Useem and Zald 1983); and analyses of the composition and change of national movement sectors (Zald and McCarthy 1980; Garner and Zald 1982; Tarrow 1983 and, in some respects, Brand 1985).

III. Some Basic Propositions of Resource Mobilization Approaches

The range of theoretical concerns and of empirical research among authors who are loosely considered to contribute to RM approaches illustrates the difficulty of critique what is not a coherent, unified scientific enterprise. I will, therefore, extract six propostitons from the wealth of observations and arguments among RM theorists that seem to me to be important and unique enough to deserve further analysis. Although they do not adequately represent the work of any single author or do not necessarily appear together in all contributions to the RM approach, they define a theoretical core of arguments that distinguishes this approach from its competitors. And it is these propositions that I will examine in the critical part of my paper.

- Individuals know what they want to accomplish through collective action. Clarity about the objectives and consequences of collective action is a necessary premise for the rational reconstruction of contributions to social movements.
- Inividuals are able to calculate cost/benefit ratios of participation in collective action. Moreover, they compare the marginal expected yield of different strategies and tactics of collective action in a given opportunity structure (e.g., violent vs. non/violent protest, broad vs. narrow demands).
- Grievances in society are ubiquitous, but movement entrepreneurs and protest organizations are the catalysts which transform amorphous masses and their demands into concerted and purposive movements. Although social movements are not identical with movement organizations, the latter are the »backbone« of collective struggles.
- Knowledge money and hours of labor, but also solidarity and legitimacy are the resources that enable movements to build organizations and launch effective struggles to attain their objectives. The way and the extent to which movements aquire these resources from their constituencies shape their activities.
- Movements act in contingent »opportunity structures« that facilitate or dampen their efforts to mobilize, pattern their strategies, and influence their potential success. Because movement participants respond rationally to contingent opportunities, movements are not subject to a rigid international logic of development. Movements neither follow a prescribed »natural history« of rise and decline nor do they involve »iron laws« of

cooptation and institutionalization in the existing social order. A rational perspective on social movement is, therefore, decidedly anti-determinist and anti-evolutionist.

- RM theorists employ the notion of »social movement« in a very broad sense. It covers all activities, or even beliefs and preferences, to change society by collective mobilization. This broad notion of social movements also implies a broad applicability of all propositions that RM approaches develop concerning the behavior of social movements.

IV. A Critique of Resource Mobilization Approaches

The strength of RM approaches is clearly based on their ability to show that the competing approaches cannot develop self-sufficient theories. Macro-sociological, relative deprivation and Weberian approaches often have little to say about the actual *process* of collective moblization. At best, they identify necessary, but not sufficient conditions for the rise of social movements.

Conversely, however, RM approaches also face a number of intrinsic problems and limitations that show they, too, are unable to provide the fundamentals for a self-sufficient theory of social movements. Six problems deserve special attention in this context.

(1) RM studies say little about the emergence and definition of the stakes involved in the struggle of social movements.

(2) They often operate with overly simplistic models of rational behavior.

(3) They tend to overestimate and overgeneralize the importance of formal organization for collective mobilization.

(4) Their analysis of resources and institutional contexts in which movements are placed requires an elaboration which would have to rely on macro-structural and Weberian approaches.

(5) If RM approaches addresses problems (1) to (4), they probably would have to abandon their strategically vague and broad notion of social movements.

(6) Viewed from a broad comparative perspective, RM approaches primarily reconstruct the dynamic of social movements in particular societies. In this sense, the approach is itself part of the societal process it tries to represent.

A. The Stakes in the Struggle of Movements

RM studies tend to take movements' objectives as given. At most, they treat goals and claims as »resources« movement organization can tactically manipulate in order to attract supporters and conscience constituencies[3]. In this sense, they project a »monological« image of social movements. Their aims are not subject to internal and external communication and learning in which the actors (and their adversaries) bring facts, values, reasons, and experiences to bear on strategic choices and purposes. Objectives are a fixed »second nature« of social movements.

In more structralist contributions to the RM approach, it is assumed that the constitution of collective interests can somehow be inferred from the production system (cf. Tilly 1978: 61). Methodological and substantively, such efforts resemble some of the more dogmatic versions of Marxist historicism in which interests can be »attributed« (Lukas 1923) to actors. An explicit reconstruction of how social structures can create the moral claims that individual actors develop in the process of building a movement is missing here. Here, RM approaches cut off an extremely important dimension in the emergence of social movements (cf. critically Fireman and Gamson 1979: 9). RM approaches ignore that the concepts of »interests« and »purposes« are inherently problematic.

It is the virtue of modern Weberian and macro-sociological perspectives to reconstruct the meaning of collective action by examing the societal structures and world views that prevail in modern societies (cf. Habermas 1973; Melucci 1980; 1985; Offe 1985). Moreover, even a sophisticated analysis of social structures, by itself, may not yield a satisfactory interpretation of collective interests. As Offe and Wiesenthal (1980) have shown for working class movements, the collective interests of social movemennts may be structurally under-determined: the marketplace constrains the potential range of interests the working class may pursue through collective action. Within this context, however, we can understand the formation of labor movements only, if we analyze the symbolic interpretation and the actual process in which workers constitute their interests.

---

3 McCarthy and Zald (1980: 8-9), for instance, hypothesize that competing social movement organizations addressing the same constituencies will engage in »product differentiation» to attract participants. From a different theoretical perspective one might wonder whether, conversely, the heterogeneity of groups, practices, and demands has given rise to different organizations in the first place.

By taking movement objectives for granted, RM theorists present an overly rationalistic and theological image of social movements (Japp 1984; Melucci 1981: 178-9). In reality, however, movement goals are ambigious and open to challenges and disagreements among the participants. Often the practices of protest behavior and the internal organization of movements are more indicative of the motivations why people join and the potential impact of movements on society than their explicit discourses on objectives and strategies.

In this situation, not a rational reconstruction, but only a contextual interpretation of actors' practices, values, objectives, and aspirations helps to understand the patterns of collective behavior. Theoretically, RM approaches are therefore not self-sufficient. Movements are not macro-subjects who behave according to standards of instrumental, purposive rationality. And also individuals do not live up to the standards that would enable them to act rationally.

If the rationality premise must be dropped, we are compelled to return to theories RM approaches wished to displace. For instance, theories of relative deprivation have experienced a certain revival in recent years, because they make a compelling case that actual deprivations do indeed influence movement objectives and mobilization. It is difficult to deny that accidents in nuclear facilities have fuelled anti-nuclear movements (Walsh 1981). As Klandermans (1984) has shown, also cognitive theories about actors' perceptions of potential stakes and opportunities in collective action are valuable instruments with which to explain mobilization. The cognitive maps of the world may tell more about human action than the premise of rationally chosen objectives and calculations (cf. Simon 1985). RM approaches, on the other hand, cut off the emotive, cognitive, and normative bases of collective action. In their zeal to prove the »rationality« of social movements, they ignore the »reasons« that contribute to collective action.

B. Joining Movements and Selecting Rational Strategies

If we deny that individuals and collectivities can act intentionally rational in the instrumental sense, utilitarian logics of collective action cannot explain why individuals join or abstain from collective action. Actors who cannot calculate their individual costs and benefits of alternative social commitments, cannot decide rationally. Numerous auxiliary hypotheses have been introduced to account for collective behavior which – in Olson's view – is patently irrational. Most important are efforts to widen the range of motivations and incentives that induce individuals to join collective efforts[4]. Others have explained the loopholes in Olson's theory by the uncertainty about costs and benefits of collective action that actors initially face.

All these arguments extend, but also denude the rational theory of collective action of its empirical content. Whenever collective behavior succeeds, some incentives for individual actors will be identified that made it possible. Similary, uncertainty about the consequences of decisions is so common that it explains everything, but therefore nothing.

The same problems we encounter in individual cost/benefit calculations of course apply to the rational choice of collective movement strategies, too. When the movements' objectives are ambigious, it is impossible to determine how instrumentally »rational« a movement acts. Rationality refers to an efficient relation between means and ends. When the ends are ambigious, we cannot assess the rational choice of means. But even where movements have precise ends, limited knowledge and uncertainties may undercut the choice of »rational« practises. As modern decision theories have shown, rationality assumptions make little sense in the study of individual and collective behavior, because they misrepresent the clarity of preferences and the reliability of knowledge on which decisions are based.

The self-sufficiency of RM approaches is endangered from two sides. From »below« the level of rational action, the individual's experience and evaluation of social reality, the suffering of deprivations explains the stakes and propensities of actors to engage in collective action; from »above« the level of rational action, the structural allocation of life chances, the constraints on action, and the world views that are (re)produced in a society influence the nature and direction of collective mobilization. The individual rational actor cannot be a starting point for social theory, but is itself a product and element of more micro- and macroscopic process (cf. Giddens 1979).

Why, then, is it nevertheless true that organizations which offer strong material selective incentives have greater enrollment than those which do not, e.g., environmental protection associations (cf. Hardin 1982)? And why do movements choose strategies that apparently can be interpreted as being

---

4 As critical background readings on incentives theory compare Wilson (1973: Ch. 2), Oberschall (1978: 307), Mitchell (1979) and Marwell and Olivier (1984).

consistent with rationality assumptions? For instance, the use of violence is a rational strategy for movements that do not have any other recourse to political decision-makers. Rather than resorting to a rationality theory, I suggest to reconstruct the behavior of individuals and social movements in the framework of an evolutionary theory of action. In a process of trial and error experimentation, social actors »find« viable collective strategies. Institutional constrains and the actors' cognitive and normative interpretations of the situations are the boundary conditions which narrow down the repertoire of protest behavior. Ex post, we attribute »rationality« to the evolutionary process of choosing strategies of action. The evolutionary approach, on the other hand, pays relatively little attention to rationality, but emphasizes cognitive, emotive, and institutional conditions that pattern action. From this perspective, the insight of RM approaches that opportunity structures shape the behavior of social movements is more fruitful than the theory of rationality that often underlies it.

This view sheds light on another issue to which I will return later: The rational theory of collective resource mobilization emerges and appears to work best in societies in which the agencies of social control are relatively weak and/or willing to accept some change. Because movements have opportunities to experiment with strategies of protest in these societies and develop a »fit« between institutional and cognitive constraints on the one hand and their repertoire of action on the other, it is easier to reconstruct the behavior of these movements as »rational« than in societies where the process of experimentation is suppressed.

An interesting study to test the evolutionary theory of strategy formation in social movements would compare protest events in socialist countries. In most instances, protestors cannot gain experience with effective and efficient strategies. In Poland, on the other hand, successive waves of protest over the years induced learning processes which enabled protest movements to choose increasingly sophisticated strategies.

C. The Significance of Movement Organization

RM studies greatly emphasize the importance of movement organization and coordination for the success of collective protests. In the utilitarian spirit of the paradigm, organization facilitates the effective pursuit of predefined ends. In a sense, the stress on organization is a healthy corrective to behaviorists and functionalist theories which tend to view social movements as faceless unstructured masses of people, often under the spell of charismatic leaders. But there is a danger that RM approaches commit the opposite mistake and attribute too much centrality to building movement organizations.

Gamson (1975) argues that the level of formal organization and the pursuit of limited, instrumental goals increases the chances that movements will actually attain their objectives. But Goldstein (1980) shows that Gamson's conclusion may very much depend on the movements entered in the analysis. Moreover, Piven and Cloward (1977) and Swank and Hicks (1984) provide some evidence that at least in the case of black riots in American cities, formal movement organization is not a necessary prerequisite. Organization may perhaps be a stumbling block to movement success.

The debate between Gamson and his critics sheds light on a number of important issues. Are there *types* of movements and situations when organization does not play a role? The empirical disagreement between Gamson and his critics could be possibly resolved if one was willing to go beyond the RM perspective and include Weberian and macro-sociological arguments. There may be movements whose very practises and aspirations preclude the use of formal organization. In this sense, Gusfield (1981) has argued that RM approaches »over-politicize« the phenomen of social movements and are too concerned with movements that express instrumental goals, but neglect movements in contemporary societies which rely on a cultural »quickening« of social change rather than organized protest and which never enter formal political arenas. In the same vein, representatives of macro-sociological approaches claim that advanced capitalist democracies promote a mobilization of movements that explicitly reject formal organization and thrive outside the realm of political institutions and strategic battles (cf. Melucci 1980, 1985; Donati 1984; Offe 1985). A dynamic of »loosely coupled conflicts« (Oberschall 1978), beyond formal organization and instrumental political struggles, appears to be more typical in the societies than the competing expectation of some RM analysts that formal organization and professionalization represent the dominant trend in the development of social movements in post-industrial society (McCarthy/Zald 1973; Zald 1985).

Another puzzling observation is that movement organizations often do not explain strong mobilization and the capacity of movements to capture the hearts and minds of large constituencies. Organizations and resources may be available – but they lack mass support. This is a curious problem that befell the organizations of the European peace movements in the 1960s and

1970s before they revived at the turn to the 1980s (cf. Rochon, 1988). Apparently, structural transformations of society, new deprivations and cultural changes in the symbolic interpretations of society prepare the environment for social mobilization. RM studies have little to say about processes in which potential threats are defined and large constituencies develop a consensus on the need for social change.

RM theorists tend to discount the structural and cultural frameworks in which movement organization may or may not gain significance as a vehicle of social change. Organization is not simply an instrumental facilitator of collective action, but also an expression of the movement practices and aspirations themselves: the medium can be the message. In this sense, the relevance and shape of an organization may depend on the nature of the movement in which it occurs. But RM theorists, with the partial exception of Tilly, have not tried to differentiate among movements and treat the significance of organization as a contingent element based on the stakes and practices of a movement.

My argument shows that RM approaches are not theoretically self-sufficient. The significance of movement organization is dependent on broader societal and cultural contexts which are not specified in RM approaches. The validity of propositions about movements organization is therefore contingent upon boundary conditions RM approaches are not able to specify with their own theoretical concepts.

In a similar vein, RM studies have not specified the significance of resources that movements employ to further their claims. It is curious that an approach which carries the concept of resources in its own label has done so little to develop a *theory* of resource mobilization in movements. What resources are remains strategically vague. Hence, there is no debate about whether the significance of resources for the mobilization of collective action varies across societal contexts and movement types.

This creates a great danger for RM approaches. As long as theory of resources and of the movements' needs for resources is missing, arguments that the availibility of resources determines a movements' capacity to mobilize will be as tautological as equivalent claims that relative deprivation gives rise to movements. Whenever a movement occurs, one is able to identify some kind of resource (or respectively some kind of deprivation) that will be held responsible for a collective mobilization. The theories would lose their arbitrariness only if one could tell when which resources should make a difference for the career of a specific movement. Here, macro-sociological and Weberian insights clearly would be needed to fill the gaps in both the RM and the relative deprivation perspectives.

D. Societal Contexts and Social Movements

RM advocates rightly point out that the older collective behavior literature has done little to illuminate the circumstances under which movements develop. Smelser (19639, for instance, vaguely refers to »structural strains« and a society's »conduciveness« to the development of movements. Older empirical studies resort to economic variables to operationalize strain. Although RM approaches explictly emphasize institutional constraints and opportunity structures, their advances over the relative deprivation theories are not always clear-cut. The hypothesis that the probability of social movements is expected to increase, when the amount of »free resources« in a society increases (McCarthy/Zald 1977: 1224) is equally vague – and empirical disputed – as Smelser's proposition shows that more differentiated societies give rise to norm-oriented movements, while less differentiated societies promote value-oriented movements. Again, the type of societal organization and the prevailing world views are critical determinants on which the status of such hypotheses depends.

RM theorists' greatest advances towards clarifying the link between social contexts and protest movements has been made in more limited empirical studies of the interplay between opportunity structures for protest and collective mobilization. Theories of the »middle range« are the real strength of RM approaches. For instance, in a given setting, one movement comes rarely alone. Movements set examples and create openings that induce the mobilization of other claims in similar ways. A decline of some significant movements, in turn, triggers the reverse chain reaction. Movements are part of broader »movement industries« and »movement sectors« which, in turn, are influenced by the agencies of social control in a society (cf. McCarthy and Zald 1980 and Tarrow 1983). Other research has shown links between the repressiveness or flexibility of political regimes vis-a-vis new demands and the development and strategies of social movements (cf. Eisinger 1973; Gamson 1975; Kitschelt 1986).

In many ways, however, RM propositions about the interaction between movements and their contexts could benefit from links to other strands of research on social movements. Weberian studies about the construction of meaning in social movements, for instance, could show why some institutional contexts do or do not have cultural significance for the mobilization of a specific movement. Together with macro-sociological studies about transformation of social structure, power relations and life chances, Weberian analyses could help to solve the puzzle that organizations and material resources in some movements appear to enhance their capacities for mobilization, but are counter-productive in others. For movements oriented towards cultural innovation, for instance, political opportunity structures may be of marginal importance.

What these considerations may teach us is that a satisfactory and comprehensive theory of social movements encompasses three different levels of analysis, the actors and their definitions of the situation, the institutions and formal movement organizations in which they act and the overarching societal context. It is mistaken to belief that social movement theories can develop explanatory self-sufficiency by elaborating only one of these levels. In an actor level framework, we reconstruct individual cognitive and normative orientations. In an organizational framework, we focus on the coordination and conflict among actors in concrete institutional settings. In a societal framework, we reconstruct the interplay of institutions and actors against the backdrop of central technological, economic, political and cultural patterns in a social formation.

One needs a three step recursive explanation to reconstruct the dynamic of social movements in a self-sufficient theoretical framework. Social patterns constrain the range of movements that may occur and the range of organizations they develop and which they interact. Institutional conditions, in turn, limit the potential practices and orientations that actors develop when they engage in social movements. Conversely, actors change institutions and organizations. The composite effect of these efforts may eventually modify the societal formation and induce the rise of new types of social movements.

In most instances, RM studies confirm themselves to an isolated treatment of the organization level. Sometimes, they exemplify certain actor-level premises, although I have argued that the utilitarian rational actor paradigm is often too narrow to reconstruct behavior in social movements. More sophisticated views of actors' orientations that may rely on cognitive theories and symbolic interactionism are usually missing. What is also completely absent in RM approaches in an elaboration of the societal level. McCarthy and Zald (1977: 1236), for example, argue that their partial theory of social movements assumes the American societal context. But they do not examine which contextual variables are critical for their hypotheses. What makes the American context unique? Which societal variables shape the movement dynamics in the United States? How do other contextual conditions at the societal level influence the mobilization of social movements elsewhere? These questions probably cannot be answered within the confines of the RM approaches. Efforts to go beyond the organizational level consequently rely on broader macro-sociologcal characterizations of modern society (cf. Garner and Zald 1982; Zald 1980: 68-70; Zald 1985).

E. Constructing Social Movements as an Object of Sociological Analysis

The absence of a societal framework in which the organizational study of social movements could be placed has the consequence that the concept of social movements itself, the explanandum of RM approaches, remains vague. There is next to no elaboration of the *theoretical object* which approaches try to analyze. From the perspective of a macro-sociological perspective, however, the range of phenomena that qualify as movements needs closer specification for each societal context. Not all protest events may be movements, and not all movements express themselves in protest events. A macro-socioligical theory would first strive to define a coherent object of explanation that we may label »social movements«.

From this perspective, the use of the concept of social movement in RM approaches is simultaneously too narrow and too wide. It is too narrow, because in the practice of empirical research it is mostly limited to protest events and collective mobilization that challenge political institutions and public policies. As Meluccci (1985) has argued, this excludes the possibilitiy of movements which are not focused on politics, but address issues of cultural change. The narrow conception of movements seems bound to the era of industrial capitalism. It is of limited use for an analysis of »post-industrial« social movements.

On the other hand, RM studies tend to rely on an extremely broad formal definition of social movements as the total of all collective activities (or even sentiment) oriented towards social change. The concept of social movement becomes an omnibus category for all protest activities. This definition is so encompassing that it is not clear whether it constitutes a coherent theoretical object of analysis (Melucci 1981). All differences among collective articulations of social change have disappeared The class of phenomena covered by this definition is so heterogeneous that few precise and informative theoretical propositions can be developed, let alone empirically tested. Or RM perspectives propose hypothesis which, upon closer inspection, are contingent upon the contexts and the nature of specific movements. The debate about the merits of formal organization in social movements to which I referred above illustrates this point well.

For this reason, especially macro-sociological, but also some contributions to other approaches have attempted to specify the theoretical object based on the contexts, content, or practices of collective action. Authors in a Marxian tradition have primarily distinguished efforts to change society according to the intensity with which they challenge existing elites, institutions or basic principles of societal organization (cf. Touraine 1973 and Melucci 1980). Others have tried to develop typologies based on certain properties of the demands and practices articulated in collective mobilization and related to societal contexts in which they occur (e.g. Smelser 1962; Gusfield 1963; Tilly 1978; Kitschelt 1985).

The theoretical construction of types of practices to change society rejects a facile identification of movements – as objects of theoretical analysis – with the labels that their leaders, their adversaries, or the mass media attach to certain practices of societal protest. Concepts such as »the« women's movement, »the« student movement, »the« workers' movement or »the« environmental movement make little theoretical sense once one uncovers that under each of these umbrella concepts there are different segments of protest activities that develop according to different logics of mobilization. For instance, the great organizational, strategic, and ideological differences within »the« women's movement render the notion of a single movement questionable. There are analytically different phenomena which express a different dynamic and meaning in modern societies (cf. Yates 1975; Gelb and Palley 1982; and Kitschelt 1985).

Typological work involves its own difficulties and frustrations (cf. Marx and Wood 1975: 370-375). But even incomplete typologies, grounded in historical-descriptive categories may have more analytic power that thin generalizations. Macro-sociological approaches may even explain why certain theories are better explanations for specific types of movements than others. In this vein, Kerbo (1982) claims that movements in industrial society can be explained mostly in terms of relative deprivation, while collective protests in contemporary societies require resource mobilization approaches.

One might challenge the substance of Kerbo's hypothesis, but his methodology of theorizing is instructive: Do different »types« of movements require different analytical tools to reconstruct the logic of their mobilization? Do theories themselves express a specific societal practice of change rather than universal laws of collective behavior? This question leads me to a final critical issue, the inability of RM studies to place themselves in a historical and societal context.

F. Interdependence Between the Theory and the Practice of Societal Movements

To avoid misinterpretations, I believe that the validity of a theory does not depend on its genesis. Nevertheless, we may be plausibly able to show that a theory develops in a certain historical conjuncture and represents a theoretical rationalization and reflection of common practices to change society. This does not necessarily render a theory untrue. A historical »archeology« of social theory is not always a critique of (particularist) ideologies. Nevertheless, such an analysis places RM theories in a perspective that may reveal their limitations more sharply.

Zald (1980: 61), one of RM's leading proponents, traces the new conceptual framework to the wave of social movements of the 1960s. Student, antiwar, women's and ecology movements involved highly educated activists and enlisted the sympathies of many academic social scientists, who were no longer willing to accept the interpretation of movements by the politically more conservative perspectives on collective behavior. Movements were obviously not the outburst of people who lacked the capacity to think and reason or were pushed to the margins of modern society. The failure of liberal politics, then, provided the historical and political problematic that helped to reorient academic reflections on social movements in the 1960s (Gusfield 1978).

I would submit, however, that this reflection on the practice of social science provides only part of the explanation for the rise of RM perspectives in American sociology and political science. Why, for instance, have European social scientists, who live in countries that experienced a comparable rejuvenation of social movements in the 1960s and 1970s rarely turned to RM approaches, but rather built on the Marxian and Weberian traditions?

In addition to differences of the academic communities in North America and Europe, I see two factors that contribute to the theoretical disagreements in the study of social movements. First of all, the comparatively open, fluid and decentralized American political system prevented a polarization between movements and the political establishment which became typical of most West European societies. In this environment, it was natural for American movements to operate on the institutional level of pressure group politics. European movements, on the other hand, were much more inclined to attack the foundations of advanced capitalist democracies in general and respond to the intransigence of the political elite with militancy. On one level, RM approaches with their emphasis on resources, organization, and coalitions are thus an adequate reflection of the practices of American movements. On another level, they also explain the differences between U.S. and European movements: elite intransigence polarized the climate in which the movements and agencies of social control operated. In this situation, movement adherents have no incentive to accept the existing procedures of conflict resolution and to develop a stake in the status quo.

There is a second element explaining the predominance of RM theories in the U.S.. As Hartz (1955) has shown in his seminal study on political culture and political theory in the U.S., critical, innovative reform movements in America have always been reintegrated into the dominant American ideological world view, utilitarian liberalism which emphasizes individualism, instrumental rationality, and pragmatic muddling through. In a sense, RM approaches are an intellectual heir to this vision. They are firmly rooted within the cultural universe of the hegemonic utilitarian liberalism in the U.S.. Most recently, even Marxist contributions to the theory of collective action have succumbed to the tempations of liberal-utilitarian thinking, as Przeworski and Wallerstein's (1982) influential work shows. In Europe, on the other hand, collectivist-socialist and communitarian-anarchist political traditions were never marginalized by a liberal-capitalist world view. This continuity of anti-liberal thinking (and political practice) has supported a structuralized and historicist reflection on the significence of (new) social movements in advanced capitalist democracies.

Both American and European theoretical approaches to the study of social movements thus grow out of unique historical and cultural configurations. Analyzing cross-national differences will put each theory in perspective and yield more comprehensive and sophisticated theories that more adequately capture the complexities of social movements.

V. The Future of Research on Social Movements

RM approaches have made important contributions to the study of collective action. But it may no longer be useful to pit schools and »paradigms« in the study of collective mobilization against each other. RM approaches do not provide a self-sufficient, comprehensive set of propositions, yet none of their competitors do either. Fruitless and dogmatic debates about »correct« and »false« paradigms must be displaced by efforts to combine their insights in the analysis of substantive problematics (Gusfield 1978: 123). The relevance of Marxian, Weberian, relative deprivation or RM approaches *vary* depending on the objectives research and the movements which are studied. And in some respects they have different, but complementary explananda. Structural theories explain *why* certain movements emerge and develop a certain structure, but RM approaches show *how* they mobilize for their claims (Melucci 1985). Unfortunately, the trouble is that answers to the »why« and »how« questions may be interdependent. For this reason, neither structural nor RM theories are self-sufficient.

A better understanding of social movements and of the power of social movement theories is furthered by systematic comparative research on movements and movement sectors across time, societal contexts, and types of movements[5]. The relative absence of comparative research on social movements may have contributed to the lack of theoretical integration in this field of studies. Comparative research requires careful theoretical frameworks, sensitizes researchers to the multiplicity of factors that influence the dynamic of movements, but are ignored in each of the »pure« sociological paradigms employed in the study of collective mobilization, and contributes to a focus on research question that close in on the interaction between societal contexts, organized practices, and beliefs or ideologies that shape social movements.

Despite the well-known difficulties of typological work in the social sciences, the present state of theorizing and research about social movements may render it useful to develop typologies of movements and societal contexts in which types of movements occur. These specifications of research objects and research sites may facilitate links between structural, organiza-

5 Recent efforts to move toward a comparative study of movement sectors include Garner and Zald's (1985) research on American and Italian social movement sectors, Kitschelt's (1985) comparison of new social movements in the U.S. and West Germany, and the comparative country analyses in Brand (1985).

tional, and actor-orientated approaches to the study of social movements. Types are clusters of variables whose values are empirically linked to each other. Types can be expressed as sets of hypotheses about the interconnection of variables. In this sense, typological work searches for systematic co-variations of structural contexts, organizational and strategic practices and ideological belief systems in collective mobilization. Although the literature on social movements provides numeroues typologies, they have not been placed in a theoretical program to link actor oriented, organizational, and structural approaches. As Weber has shown in his work on world religions and the rise of capitalism, sophisticated typological analysis is intimately linked to comparative research. In this sense, comparative analysis and conceptual development could be sources to overcome the fruitless battle of »paradigms« in the study of social movements.

Bibliography

Brand, K. (ed.). (1985): *Neue Soziale Bewegungen in Westeuropa und den USA*. Frankfurt: Campus.

Dahrendorf, R. (1959): *Class and Class Conflict in Industrial Society*. Stanford: Stanford University Press.

Donati, R. (1984): »Organization Between Movement and Institution«. *Social Science Information*, 23, (4/5): 837-859.

Eisinger, K. (1973): »The Conditions of Protest Behavior in American Cities«, *American Political Science Review*, 67: 11-28.

Fireman, B.; Gamson, W.A. (1979): »Utilitarian Logic in the Resource Mobilization Perspective«, in: N. Zald, D. McCarthy (eds.). *The Dynamics of Social Movements*. Cambridge: Winthrop.

Freeman, Jø (1975): *The Politics of Women's Liberation*. New York: Longman.

Frohlich, N.; Oppenheimer, J.A.; Young, O.R. (1971): *Political Leadership and Collective Goods*. Princeton N.J.: Princeton University Press.

Gamson, A. (1975): *The Strategy of Protest*. Homewood, Ill.: Dorsey Press.

Garner, R.; Zald, M.N. (1982): *Social Movement Sectors and Systemic Constraints. Toward a Structural Analysis of Social Movements*, Center for Research on Social Organisation, University of Michigan, Paper #259.

Gelb, J.; Palley, M.L. (1982): *Women and Public Policies*. Princeton, N.J.: Princeton University Press.

Giddens, A. (1979): *Central Problems in Sociological Theory*. Berkeley: University of California Press.

Gitlin, T. (1980): *The Whole World Is Watching*. Berkeley: University of California Press.

Goldstone, J.A. (1980): »The Weakness of Organization. A New Look at Gamson's ›The Strategy of Social Conflict‹«, *American Journal of Sociology*, 85, (5): 1017-42.

Gusfield, J. (1963): *Symbolic Crusade. Status Politics and the American Temperance Movement*. Urbana: University of Illinois Press.

– (1978): »Historical Problematics and Sociological Movements«, *Research in the Sociology of Knowledge, Science, and Art*, 1: 121-148.

– (1981): »Social Movements and Social Change. Perspective of Linearity and Fluidity«, *Research in Social Movements, Conflicts and Change*, 3: 317-339.

Habermas, J. (1973): *Legitimationsprobleme des Spätkapitalismus*. Frankfurt: Suhrkamp.

– (1981): *Theorie des kommunikativen Handelns*. Frankfurt: Suhrkamp.

Hardin, R. (1982): *Collective Action*. Baltimore: Johns Hopkins University Press.

Hartz, L. (1955): *The Liberal Tradition in America*. New York: Harcourt, Brace, Janovitch.

Hibbs, D. (1973): *Mass Political Violence. A Cross-National Causal Analysis*, New York: Wiley.

Japp, K.P. (1984): »Selbsterzeugung oder Fremdverschulden. Thesen zum Rationalismus in den Theorien Sozialer Bewegungen. Soziale Welt, 35 (3): 313-329.

Jenkins, J. (1981): »Sociopolitical Movements«, in: Samuel Long (ed.). *Handbook of Political Behavior*, 4. New York: Plenum.

Jenkins, J.; Perrow, Ch. (1977): »Insurgency of the Powerless. Farm Workers Movements (1946-1972)«, *American Sociologies Review*, 42 (2): 249-268.

Jenson, J. (1982): »The Modern Women's Movement in Italy, France, and Great Britain. Differences in Life Cycles«, in: F. Thomasson (ed.). *Comparative Social Research*, 5,.Greenwich, Connecticut: JAI Press.

Kerbo, R. (1982): »Movements of ›Crisis‹ and Movements of ›Affluence‹. A Critique of Deprivation and Resource Mobilization Theories«, *Journal of Conflicts Resolution*, 26 (4): 645-663.

Kitschelt, H. (1985): »New Social Movements in West Germany and the United States«, *Political Power and Social Theory*, 5: 273-324.

– (1986): »Political Opportunity Structures and Political Protest: Anti-Nuclear Movements in Four Democracies«, *British Journal of Political Science*, 16 (1): 57-85.

Klandermans, B. (1984): »Mobilization and Participation. Social-Psychological Expansions of Resource Mobilization Theory«, *American Sociological Review* 49 (5): 583-600.

Lipsky, M. (1968): »Protest as a Political Resource«, *American Political Science Review*, 62 (4): 1144-1158.

Lo, C.H. 81982): »Countermovements and Conservative Movements in the Contemporary U.S.«, *Annual Review of Sociology*, 8: 107-134.

Lukacs, G. (1971): *Geschichte und Klassenbewußtsein*. Neuwied/Berlin: Luchterhand.

Marwell, G.; Olivier, P. (1984): »Collective Action Theory and Social Movements Research«, *Research in Social Movements, Conflict and Chance*, 7: 1-27.

Marcuse, H. (1964): *The One-Dimensional Man*. Boston: Beacon.

– (1972): *Counter-Revolution and Revolt*. Boston: Beacon Press.

Marx, G.T. (1979): »External Efforts to Damage or Facilitate Social Movements«, in: N. Zald, D. McCarthy (eds.). *The Dynamics of Social Movements*. Cambridge, Mass.: Winthrop.

Marx, T.; Wood, J.L. (1975): »Strands of Theory and Research in Collective Behavior«, *Annual Review of Sociology*, 1: 363-428.

McAdam, D. (1982): *Political Process and the Development of Black Insurgency 1930-1970*. Chicago: Chicago University Press.

McCarthy, D.; N. Zald, M.N. (1973): *The Trends of Social Movements in America: Professionalization and Resource Mobilization*. Morristown, N.J.: General Learning Press.

– (1977): *American Journal of Sociology*, 82 (6): 1212-1241.

Melucci, A. (1980): »The New Social Movements: A Theoretical Approach«, *Social Science Information*, 19 (2): 199-226.

– (1981): »Ten Hypotheses for the Analysis of New Movements«, in: Pinto (ed.). *Contemporary Italian Sociology*. Cambridge, Mass.; Cambridge University Press.

– (1985): »The Symbolic Challenge of Contemporary Movements«, *Social Research*, 52 (4).

Mitchell, R.C. (1979): »National Environmental Lobbies and the Apparent Illogic of Collective Action«, in: C.S. Russell (ed.). *Collective Decision Making: Applications from Public Choice Theory*. Baltimore: Johns Hopkins University Press.

Molotch, H. (1979): »Media and Movements«, in: N. Zald, D. McCarthy (eds.). *The Dynamics of Social Movements*. Cambridge, Mass.: Winthrop.

Oberschall, A. (1973): *Social Conflict and Social Movements*. Englewood Cliffs: Prentice Hall.

– (1978): »Theories of Social Conflict«, *Annual Review of Sociology*, 4: 291-315.

Offe, C. (1985): »New Social Movements: Challenging the Boundaries of Institutional Politics«, *Social Research*, 52 (4): 817-868.

Offe, C.; Wiesenthal, H. (1980): »Two Logics of Collective Action«, *Political Power and Social Theory*, 1: 67-115.

Olson, M. (1965): *The Logic of Collective Action*. Cambridge, Mass.: Harvard University Press.

Piven, F.; Cloward, R.A. (1977): *Poor People's Movements. Why They Succeed. How They Fail*. New York: Random House.

Przeworski, A.; Wallerstein, M. (1982): »The Structure of Class Conflicts in Democratic Capitalist Societies«, *American Political Science Review*, 76 (1): 215-238.

Raschke, J. (1985): *Soziale Bewegungen. Ein historisch-systematischer Grundriß*. Frankfurt: Campus.

Rochon, T. (1988): Mobilization For Peace. The Antinuclear Movements in Western Europe. Princeton, N.J.: Princeton University Press.

Simon, A. (1985): »Human Nature in Politics. The Dialogue of Psychology with Political Science«, *American Political Science Review*, 79 (2): 293-304.

Smelser, N.J. (1963): *The Theory of Collective Behavior*. New York: Free Press.

Swank, H.; Hicks, A. (1984): »Militancy, Need and Relief. The Piven And Cloward AFDC Caseload Thesis Revisited«, *Research in Social Movements, Conflict and Chance*, 6: 1-29.

Tarrow, S. (1983): *Struggling to Reform: Social Movements and Policy Change During Cycles of Protest*. Cornell Studies in Interanational Affairs. Western Societies Program. Occasional Papers, No. 15.

Touraine, Alain (1973): *Production de la Société*. Paris: Seuil.

– (1978): *La voix et le regard*. Paris: Seuil.

Tilly, C. (1973): »Does Modernization Breed Revolutoin? *Comparative Politics* 5 (3): 423-447.

(1978): *From Mobilization to Revolution*. Englewood Cliffs: Prentice Hall.

Tilly, C.; Tilly, L.; Tilly, R. (1975): *The Rebellious Century (1830-1930)*. Cambridge, Mass.: Harvard University Press.

Walsh, E.J. (1983): »Resource Mobilization and Citizen Protest in Communities Around Three Mile Island«, *Social Problems*, 29 (1): 1-21.

Wilson, J.O. (1973): *Political Organization*. New York: Basic Books.

Yates, G.G. (1975): *What Women Want. The Ideas of the Movement*. Cambridge, Mass.: Harvard University Press.

Zald, N. (1980): »Issues in the Theory of Social Movements«, *Current Perspectives in Social Theory*, 1: 62-72.

– (1985): *The Future of Social Movements in America: The Transformation of Ends and Means*. Center for Research on Social Organization. The Unviversity of Michigan, Ann Arbor. Working Paper Series No. 328.

Zald, N.; McCarthy, J.D. (1980): »Social Movement Industries: Competition and Cooperation Among Movement Organizations«, *Research on Social Movements, Conflicts, and Change*, 3: 1-20.

Zald, N.; Useem, B. (1983): *Movement and Countermovement: Loosely Coupled Conflict*. Center for Research on Social Organization. University of Michigan.

The Continuing Vitality of Resource Mobilization Theory: Response to Herbert Kitschelt's Critique

Mayer N. Zald

I. Introduction

Herbert Kitschelt has written a thoughtful critique of resource mobilization theory, focusing primarily on its limits. He is especially good in articulating how broader studies of meaning-interpretation and societal creation and transformation of issues and »interests« may complement, or indeed supplant resource mobilization approaches for particular problems. Since I agree with much of his critique, it is useful to emphasize my differences, sometimes just of emphasis, in order to highlight the continuing vitality of the resource mobilization approach.

There is a tendency in the Kitschelt critique to take a »let all the flowers bloom« approach to the study of social movements. Thus, to some extent, he avoids the hard question of articulating a criterion of paradigm choice. In his desire to move beyond competing paradigms, he may have forgotten the value of paradigms at all; they help focus research, provide a matrix of interlinked concepts and assumptions, and pose a research agenda.

A paradigm is supplanted, in the social sciences at least, when the questions posed from within it seem to have little interest to students of the phenomena that are addressed, when the research gets stale and repetitive, when the cumulative evidence both or research and societal change seems to indicate that the paradigm is wrong or irrelevant.

At some time in the future, I am sure that will happen to resource mobilization approaches. But I believe that for now they present a vital and viable research paradigm. I will use this opportunity not only to reply to Kitschelt, but to clarify misconceptions about RM theory.

II. Grievances, Deprivation, and Relative Deprivation

In our earliest writings about social movements, McCarthy and I, in an attempt to sharpen debate and to focus clearly on mobilization processes, took an extreme position on the role of grievances in social movements. Our point was not that grievances were irrelevant to social movements, but that the size, scope, duration and cycles of social movements could not be directly attributed to the amount of deprivation or relative deprivation of a population. We objected to a pure grievance approach on several grounds, but primarily because

- it assumes that people act on grievances, without any attention to the cost, the alternatives foregone, of acting.
- it treats deprivations and grievances as »existing out there« rather than as somehow created by a social process, a social process which includes the role of moral and movement entrepreneurs.

Kitschelt appears to argue that some grievances are strong enough to generate social movement action. Thus, an accident at a nuclear power plant (TMI) is seen as generating collective action responses. Yet, here too, a comparative and deeper social psychologist analysis would lead one to see the implications of social structure and social process in the definition of grievances and the definition of actionable issues.

It is probably the case that it is useful to make a distinction between hard and soft grievances. Hard grievances are those in which a large fraction of some population is exposed to a clear change or chance of change in their living conditions: TMI; a potato famine in a country dependent on potatoes as a main staple; an overnight doubling of the price of bread, where bread is a staple. On the other hand, soft grievances occur or develop overtime and are subtle in their impact, more prone to changing social definitions. It is now the case in the United States that a seven percent unemployment rate is considered »normal,« a rate 75 percent higher than earlier accepted. The change has had immense implications for the actual well-being of people, but occured over time and in such a way that little collective action has been associated with it. Hard grievances more rapidly and clearly lead to collective action.

But even hard grievances, such as TMI, are caught in a social process. Assigning responsibility for TMI was part of a collective process. Who was at fault? The company? State officials? Federal officials? An earthquake could be much more damaging than TMI, but generate less social movement activity. Moreover, the nuclear accident at Chernobyl generates more social movement mobilization in Stockholm than it does in Kiev or Warsaw. The high costs of mobilizing in Kiev and Warsaw are part of the routine grounds of everyday life.

III. Rationality and its Limits

Once one takes a position that the cost of social action must be surfaced in explaining the amount and direction of collective action, a model of actor rationality, however limited, is implied. One decides to go to a meeting, or stay at home watching television; one chooses to stand in front of an approaching tank, or run away fast. The reasons for going to the meeting may relate to social pressures and a complex choice situation as well as the desire to achieve social movement goals. Standing in front of a tank may be a response to role embedded leadership requirements as much as to a belief in its tactical efficacy.

The model of rationality that is implied admits that goal preferences are or may be ambiguous, that actors act on limited and bounded rationality; it is a weak assumption of rationality. Nevertheless, if one wants to explain why some people with similar values, differentially participate in movements, (McAdam, McCarty, and Zald, 1988) or why larger riots reduce detection and increase participation (Granovetter, 1978) a rationality-cost equation will be useful.

RM theories vary in their dependence upon the Olsonian conundrum. It is very clear that Olson sharpened our thinking about the mix of social conditions and incentives that brought forth collective action. For one, he alerted us to the wide disparity between the distribution of beliefs in favor of a given collective condition, and the number of people who actually acted on those beliefs. For another, he made us think more deeply about interests, group identification, and value preferences. Olson's model presumes a strong assumption about rationality. Even if that model is wrong in some instances, it has been an enormous benefit in clarifying our thinking about the underlying processes.

IV. Cognitive and Symbolic Framing of Issues

Resource mobilization approaches were developed partly in response to the collective behavior and deprivation linked approaches that were prevalent in American social science up until the period of high mobilization created by the Civil Rights and anti-war movements. Cognitive social psychologies – attribution theory, script, and frame theory, were in their infancy. Similarly, critical and hermeneutic approaches to cultures were in their infancy and were not usually seen as relevant to the ongoing political struggles which engaged the attention of socially concerned social scientists. Indeed, one might argue that the application of a Geertzian or Foucault type analysis to the Civil Rights movement or to the anti-war movement would be profoundly conservative in its assimilation of the movement to a timeless deep structure of cultural change. Kitschelt is right to fault RM theorists (of all persuasions I might add) at both levels – their ignoring of cognitive social psychology and their imperviousness to culturological symbolic analysis.

However, I would argue that RM theory can be usefully tied to both and that symbolic analysis and cognitive social psychology can be linked through the concrete action structures so usefully dissected by RM theory. David Snow and his colleagues (1986) have recently shown how Goffman's frame analysis can be tied to conversion and participation processes in social movements. They show how personal ideology and perception is linked to the transformation of social identities and situations. On the other hand, William Sewell, Jr., (1985) and Theda Skocpol (1985) have usefully discussed (debated?) how cultural change and cultural continuity pervades revolutions. In that discussion, Sewell takes the broader, more macroscopic approach to the influence of culture and the definition of revolutionary action, while Skocpol examines the interplay of specific groups and their own local ideological cultures in choosing options.

Let me make an even stronger claim. The application of cognitive social psychology to social movements without an explicit attention to the distinct types of actors (by-stander publics, sympathizers, adherents, cadre, etc.) and the phases of movement mobilization and opposition suggested by RM theory will lead to an oversimplified and overgeneralized social psychology of movement participation. Similarly, critical and hermeneutic analysis conducted without close attention to the links between societal and cultural change and specific movement mobilization will once more lead to reified assertions about the conditions of life and alienation, only loosely connected to the real life situations and real political consequences confronting actors.

V. Resource Mobilization and the New Social Movements

European analysts of the so-called new social movements have rarely entered the debates that have preoccupied American students. This is not the place to go into the strength and weaknesses of the analyses of »new« social movements (many of which have strong historical antecedents, if not direct historical continuity). But it is appropriate to note that resource mobilization analysis would add a strong, concrete descriptive base to studies which often seem to float on air. It is impossible to even cursorily examine Peace movements in many European countries without noting the strong infra-structure provided by groups tied to Protestant churches. And the peace movement takes a very different shape in countries without that infrastructure. Resource mobilization theory, especially the McCarthy-Zald variety, has been correctly faulted for its over-emphasis on formal SMOs. But resource mobilization theory is equally applicable to loose congeries of groups. Movements without strong and immediate political goals may not develop the formal organizations and parties, the explicit coordinating structures, that others do. But they still go through a mobilizing process. Moreover, variations in national political structure and associational repertoires condition the nature of the social movement scene (Garner and Zald, 1985).

VI. The Continuing Vitality of Resource Mobilization Theory

Theories of the middle range vary in their staying power. Some attract little attention. Or a small boomlet of studies may be initiated which either confirm or disconfirm central tenets, or prove useful or unuseful in suggesting directions for further research. They then peter out. Either the topic is not important enough (for whatever reason), or competing paradigms prove more useful – scholars shift their interests or explanatory modes. Or a paradigm may guide scholars for several decades. Where is RM today?

Some early proponents have left the field. William Gamson, an early contributor to resource mobilization theory, is now largely concerned with discourse analysis in understanding the transformation of political agendas and political issues. Charles Tilly continues work on protest and collective action, but he also examines the play of geography and industry in the emergence of democratic regimes. I am now studying complex organizations. Yet any perusal of the current literature in American political science and sociology would be hard-pressed to see a decline in research tied to the resource mobilization paradigm. A younger generation of scholars find aspects of the approach important for posing issues, and suggesting problems. Doug McAdam (1986), a critic of McCarthy and Zald in his early work, argues that social movements may differ in the amount of risk that activism entails. He then shows that movements with high risk recruit and hold members in a way different than others. The research could not be done without careful consideration of risk and cost.

McAdam (1982) helped articulate the political opportunity variant of resource mobilization theory, arguing that social movement adherents and SMOs responded to changing political opportunities. Not grievances, but chances for success effect the mobilization potential.

Herbert Kitschelt (1986) extends the political model even further in his comparative study of political input and output processes in four countries (France, Germany, Sweden, and the United States) dealing with nuclear power protests. The extent of mobilization, the rise of ecological parties, and governmental responses are tightly intertwined. Much research needs to be done on the intersection of political structure, political opportunity, and social movements.

What all this suggests is that the resource mobilization framework retains its ability to suggest new lines of research, to incorporate and integrate findings and problems at both the micro and macro levels of collective action generation. Kitschelt is quite right to point to some fundamental tautologies and ambiguities in the framework. He is quite right to note its weaknesses and lacunae. It is not and was never intended to be a comprehensive synthetic framework (although its limits may not have been fully apparent to its proponents). Nevertheless, it continues to serve as a valuable guide and framework for identifying research problems and for linking discrete pieces of work to each other. It provides a recipe book for description of movement, tactics, and dynamics and a dense set of inter-linked processes for analysis.

Bibliography

Garner, R.; Zald, M.N. (1985): in: G. Suttles, M.N. Zald (eds.). *The Challenge of Social Control: Citizenship and Institution Building in Modern Society, Essays in Honor of Morris Janowitz*, Norwood, NJ: ABLEX.

Granovetter, M. (1978): »Threshold Models of Collective Behavior.«, *American Journal of Sociology*, 83 (6): 1420-1443.

Kitschelt, H. (1986): »Political Opportunity Structures and Political Protest.« *British Journal of Political Science* 16 (1): 57-85.

McAdam, D. (1982): *Political Process and the Development of Black Insurgency, 1930-1970*. Chicago: University of Chicago Press.

McAdam, D. (1988): John McCarthy and Mayer N. Zald, »Social Movements and Collective Behavior: Building Macro-Micro Bridges«, in: N. Smelser, S. Burt (eds.). *Handbook of Sociology*, Beverly Hills, CA: Sage Publications.

– (1986): »Recruitment to High Risk Activism: The Case of Freedom Summer.«, *American Journal of Sociology* 92 (1): 64-90.

Sewell, W.H., Jr. (1985): »Ideologies and Social Revolutions: Reflections on the French Case,« *The Journal of Modern History* 57 (1): 57-85.

Skocpol, T. (1985): »Cultural Idioms and Political Ideologies in the Revolutionary Reconstruction of State Power: A Rejoinder to Sewell. *The Journal of Modern History*, 57 (1): 86-96.

Snow, A.; Rochford, B.E. Jr.; Worden, S.K.; Benford, R.D. (1986): Frame Alignment Processes, Micromobilization, and Movement Participation. *American Sociological Review* 514: 464-81.

Sociological Theory as a Theory of Social Movements? A Critique of Alain Touraine

Dieter Rucht

Introduction

Probably no social scientist in Europe has devoted more energy to analyzing social movements than the French sociologist Alain Touraine. And probably no contemporary researcher in this field has provoked such controversy both at home and abroad. Surveying the reviews of Touraine's publications, one is struck by the degree to which opinion is divided in the scientific community. Some praise his work as »a major contribution to political sociology« and extol his »powerful and sound methodology« (Freiberg 1973, 273). Many others harshly criticize his work arguing that the substance of the book in consideration is »obscure« (Nagel 1983, 923), »highly unsatisfactory in methodological terms« (Rüdig and Lowe 1984, 22), and that the author's »excursions into grand social theory force the reader into a marsh of confusing concepts« (Smith 1976, 981). Still others, confronted with one of Touraine's numerous books, apparently feel confused: »This is one of those books academic reviewers could despair of. It is a very intellectual book, yet its appeal is essentially emotional. You either like it or you don't.« (Lebas 1985, 329)

This article offers a critical assessment of Touraine's writings on social movements.[1] Such an effort may be warranted for at least two reasons. First,

1 This article was originally inspired by a six-month research stay in Paris in 1984, where I was loosely affiliated with Touraine's institute. I wish to thank Alain Touraine for his hospitality. For comments on earlier versions of this essay, I owe thanks to Hanspeter Kriesi, Alberto Melucci, Christopher Rootes and Roland Roth. I am also grateful to Richard Rogers, Bruce Spear and Jeffrey Butler for assistance with the English version.

Touraine's work has been unevenly and incompletely assimilated. Many authors, especially those engaged in quantitative empirical research on social movements in the Anglo-american community, ignore Touraine's work and borrow their theories and categories from other authors. Scholars dealing explicitly with general concepts on social movements tend to mention Touraine, but usually neither discuss his work in detail nor draw on his conceptual propositions. Still others pick up some catchwords or categories without attending carfully to their theoretical contexts and implications. Only a few researchers seem fairly familiar with Touraine's approach, and still fewer explicitly develop their own concepts in the light of his work.[2]

A second reason why it may be fruitful to discuss Touraine's approach is that it now appears ready for a critical examination; surveying the development of his thought over the last four decades, one may begin to discern the conclusion of a distinct working phase. This is not to say that Touraine's productivity has diminished but rather, that the ambitious research program on social movements based on a particular body of theories and methods, can now be assessed with respect to both its premises and its concrete results. It may now be appropriate to assess how Touraine, while developing and applying his research program, drew any practical conclusion in responding to those critics who particularly focused on theoretical and methodological questions. After presenting a short overview of Touraine's scientific biography and its relation to political events, in the second section I will deal with the theoretical content of this work and its implication for the concept of social movements. Special attention will be paid to the author's interpretation of the present stage of social development, the role of social movements in ushering in a new era, and his perception of the discipline of sociology as a whole. Third, I will focus on the author's empirically-oriented work on social movements, and in particular, on the method he has created and applied. Finally, after summing up these interpretations and criticisms, I will offer a few concise judgements on his work.

---

2 One of the few exceptions is Alberto Melucci in Italy, who has done his doctorate with Touraine, and, to a lesser degree, Klaus Eder in West Germany. Not surprisingly, both scholars do have close affiliations to French sociologists. Other social scientists, which have paid some attention to Touraine, are Klaus Japp (1984), Roland Roth (1984) and Ron Eyerman (1984).

I. Some Notes on Touraine's Scientific Biography

In the early phase of his career, in the 1950s and early 1960s, Touraine was engaged in the field of industrial sociology under the mentorship of Georges Friedman.[3] Through his studies on the conditions and the consciousness of the labor force Touraine became convinced that these features have to be considered as they are linked to the general system of power in a given society. Consequently, he began to widen his horizon of interest. His dissertation »Sociologie de l'action« (1965) proposed at least three areas of interest Touraine has continued to develop up to the present. These include the sociology of »industrial civilization,« the conceptualization of sociology as a »science of social action,« and the analysis of social movements regarded as the central actors in society.

Besides numerous articles, Touraine has also written, or co-authored as the principal researcher, some twenty books. Facing this impressive body of literature the scholar is struck by how persistently he has pursued a research program beginning 1951, worked out in a provisionary form by 1961, and continuing to this day. Touraine is not only a researcher, but also, a committed citizen who actively intervenes in the political and intellectual discourse.[4] Although distancing himself from the Marxism which appealed to many French intellectuals during the postwar era, his politics are clearly

---

3 Together with other young academics such as Michel Crozier, Jean-Daniel Reynaud, Viviane Isambert-Jamati, Serge Moscovici, Joffre Dumazdier and Edgar Morin, Touraine was associated with a circle of researchers around Georges Friedman (see Düll 1975; Rose, 1979). Most, including Touraine (who studied history at the Ecole Normale Supérieure), were not originally trained in sociology. In the mid-fifties, Touraine dissociated himself from Friedman's ideas, and in particular, his mentor's conception of industrial work (Düll 1975, 113). From 1958 onward, Touraine founded and headed a research institution (»Laboratoire de Sociologie Industrielle«) at the Paris-based Ecole Pratique des Hautes Etudes. He was also a co-founder and co-editor of the journal »Sociologie de Travail« launched in 1959. His analysis of the three distinct phases of work in contemporary societies became very influential in the field of industrial sociology.

4 Raymond Aron, telling in his memoires how Touraine defended his thesis, gives us an insight into Touraine's vital character. »A. Touraine presented his thesis with the élan of a conquistador, then concluded with a poem in Spanish. The president of the jury then gave me the floor and I began: ›Returning to the earth‹.« (cited according to Lembert 1986, 691).

those of the Left.[5] He has always felt an urgent need for change in the given social and political order; he was and remains in search of those actors who could bring it about. During the early stages of his professional work Touraine hoped the labor movement might play a vital role in creating the alternative society he was striving for. But his analysis of the conditions and consciousness of industrial workers revealed that the labor movement had become more or less compromised with the given social order (1965; 1966).[6] »This institutionalization of the labor conflicts which transform the worker's movement into a truly political force has made it lose its role as a central social movement...« (1981, 12). Moreover, Touraine was skeptical about »industrial democracy;« he criticized the mainstream concepts used in industrial sociology, the »technocratic illusion« of conflict settlement (1955, 178), the dominant role of functionalist theory in sociology,[7] and conventional methods of empirical investigation based on interviews and the interpretation of documents (1966, 346).

Teaching at the university of Nanterre, Touraine witnessed at first hand the birth of the movement of May '68. Since the department of sociology was an epicenter of the unrest he became directly involved in the conflicts and by and large defended the rebellious students.[8] The energy and creativity of this revolt deeply impressed the sociologist. In the same year, Touraine published a book on the movement where he put forward the idea that this

---

5 »Touraine considers himself as »belonging to the leftists who are hostile to doctrines ... and are fascinated by all revolts and all revolutions.« (1965, 15*) »Yes, I would like to see an expansion of a social democracy, of self-regulation, of rights of minorities, of the possibility to contest, and I do believe in the existence of grassroots movements which will never become institutionalized.« (1977, 256*)

6 All bibliographical references containing only the respective year of publication and not author's name refer to works by Alain Touraine. Citations marked with a »*«, for instance, (1973, 12*), are my own translations from French or German editions of Touraine's writings.

7 In 1952, during a stay at Harvard University, Touraine was confronted by Talcott Parsons. That encounter seems to have deeply impressed Touraine – in a negative sense. »I have difficulties in bearing this false liberal aristocracy. And still worse was accepting the teaching of Talcott Parsons, the key figure in American sociology, who I never ceased fighting against.« (1977, 64) In spite of his strong antiparsonian bias, however, the theory Touraine later developed resembles Parson's early theory to some extent. For instance, Touraine gives the concept of action systems a central role in his theory.

8 Some students, including Daniel Cohn-Bendit, who were accused by a type of tribunal initiated by university officials, were defended by Touraine and Henri Levebvre (cf. Touraine 1977, 200).

revolt, despite its obvious limits, heralded a new era in history – a thesis which he worked out in more detail in his subsequent collection of essays entitled »La société postindustrielle« (1969).

Inspired by the events of May '68, as well as disappointed by the fall of the popular movement in Chile,[9] Touraine turned to social movements both as a researcher and a political man. He wrote on the Chilean military coup (1973a) and developed his experiences during a stay in California into a book about the student movement and the American university system (1972). This shift of interest, from industrial sociology to the study of social movements, is also reflected by his departure from the »Laboratoire de Sociologie Industrielle«, which he had established in 1958, to create the »Laboratoire des Mouvements Sociaux«, the forerunner of the »Centre d'Etudes des Mouvements Sociaux.«

In 1973, Touraine published his major theoretical book »Production de la société« which he had started to work on in 1966. Here one finds the basic concepts, categories and positions informing his approach to this day. This book can be considered a key to Touraine's approach, the so-called »sociologie actionaliste.«[10]

In 1976, when tens of thousands of French students engaged in a major strike, Touraine had a chance to apply the experimental research method he had been reflecting on for a couple of years – a task which to him had absolute priority (1974a, 243*). The elaboration and application of this method, which he termed »intervention sociologique,« became his dominant interest. Partly because not all of the people in his environment shared his concerns, Touraine left this second institute. He established a new research unit devoted mainly to his approach,[11] and consequently has named after his method: »Centre d'analyse et d'intervention sociologique.« In the following ten years, Touraine and his collaborators applied the method to other movements including the French antinuclear movement (1980b), the regionalist movements in France (1981a), the Polish Solidarity Movement (1983a), and

---

9 Married to a women from Chile, Touraine was continually interested in the fate of popular movements in Latin America and especially in Chile (see Touraine 1973a; 1988). Occasionally he spent some time travelling or teaching in Latin America.

10 For the debate surrounding this concept see Reynaud and Bourdieu (1966) and Touraine's reply to them (1966a); see also Ackermann and Moscovici (1966).

11 The most comprehensive presentation of this method can be found in Touraine 1978 and Touraine et al. 1983. Moreover, there are chapters in the empirical studies in which the method is explained.

the French labor movement (1984).[12] The initial motive for these studies was »to increase the capacity of these movements for collective action, and with this, that of the society as a whole.« (1977, 271)

Today it seems that Touraine's ambitions, both in political and scientific terms, remained largely unfulfilled. His conceptual writings run the risk of becoming repetitive. The intense research period on social movements is gradually coming to an end. This impression is also supported by the fact that Touraine's recent book on society and politics in Latin America (1988) is not really centered around the study of social movements.

II. Social Movements, Sociology, and Society

Again and again Touraine posed the fundamental question, formulated as early as 1965, of conflicts and actors who will shape our future: »Though it is still too early to identify and name the new cleavages, to define and to discuss consciously and passionately the weapons of the new social struggles, it is already time to aim at defining a new social structure, the new conflicts and the new social movements.« (1969, 118*)

Only years later did Touraine find an answer to this question. The new promising actor appeared to be the student movement, even though he was uncertain whether this collective actor was likely to become a social movement or if it had already attained this elevated status.[13] Faced with the end of the student movement a few years later, Touraine is again in search of the agent of history. In his »Production de la société« he addresses the fundamental question: »Which type of social movement in the industrial civilization will assume the role that the labor movement had during the central period of capitalist economy and nationalism at the beginning of industrialization?« (1965, 469*) Now his hopes are directed towards those movements

12 For various reasons, studies on the feminist and peace movements, carried out in the first half of the 1980s, were not completed.

13 On the one hand he writes: »The unrest and the student revolt will become a social movement only at the moment when they will call not for a specific but for a general fight.« (1969, 105*) »It is not yet an autonomous and fully developed movement.« (1969, 135*) But on the other hand, Touraine states: »As a matter of fact, a social movement of the highest significance has entered the historical stage...« (1969, 135*) »The student movement is truly a social movement.« (1969, 97*)

which he interprets as the heirs of May '68. »The century of socialism is over, and likewise the decade of the counter-culture. Now we have to concentrate on the really important aspect, that is the formation of new social movements which attack technocracy... The grandeur of the May movement stems from the fact that for the first time it has recognized this new battle field and fired the initial salvoes in that direction even though the movement has also fought battles of retreat. The antinuclearists are the direct heirs of May 68, and the women's movement, the regional or national movements also are engaged in this anti-technocratic battle which defines the new social movement.« (1980, 262*)

A. The Approach and its Position in Sociology

Since Touraine's concept of social movements is intimately linked to the way he perceives society as a whole it is necessary to refer to his general theory. What is the status of his approach? Which elements constitute the basis of an »actionalist« sociology, and how does this approach relate to other theories? Even though it is not easy to give an adequate presentation of this concept – Touraine offers dozens of theorems, categories and schemas, some of them varying not only from publication to publication, but also, within the same one – an effort will be made to characterize the status of this approach and to outline some basic assumptions.[14]

Remarkably, it is difficult to detect direct references to other work in sociology and philosophy. Only in his earlier writings does he conceive of his »actionalist« approach as a complement to structuralist and functionalist theories (1965, 90). But in his later work, without discussing these rival concepts in detail, he simply puts them aside with a testy gesture. Polemically, he rejects not only structuralist and functionalist concepts, but also, symbolic interactionism, empiricism, evolutionary theories of society and social phi-

---

14 Admitted, some of the key categories were not very clear to me and thus will likely be less clear for the reader of this article. What Gamson noted in reviewing »The voice and the eye« is not out of the ordinary for Touraine's work: »Those who contend that sociology is a form of mystification will find ample evidence throughout this book. Neologism abound and existent words are given special meanings, confusingly different from their ordinary meaning. One wades through a bog of paragraph-long sentences, grateful for the occasional simple declarative. Complicated schematic diagrams abound in the theoretical chapters, but these rarely clarify.« (Gamson 1983, 813)

losophy, and thus, leaving the impression that he stood in a desert: »The field of sociology is no longer occupied by the battalions of functionalism – they have withdrawn in disarray. This field lies nearly deserted before us; there are only some riders crossing through at a gallop, raising dust while disappearing.« (1974, 242*)

But Touraine also offers a more dramatic picture of sociology, a picture of fights and struggles, and of »sociology in crisis«. Fortunately, as we know, where is danger there is also a chance for rescue. »In my view,« Touraine tells us, »never before has sociology been in a more favorable situation than now.« (1969, 312*) There is no doubt that actionalist sociology promoted by Touraine is the way out of this crisis.[15] Without being overly modest, Touraine characterizes his approach as the key concept of sociology: »Actionalist analysis does not define the entity of sociology, but rather, its foundation as an autonomous social science.« (1965, 92*) Surprisingly, he identifies his actionalist sociology with the study of social movements. Thus it is to be understood more in terms of its content than its method (1965, 112). In more recent publications he maintains his aim »to reorganize the entire body of sociological analysis around this new idea, that of social movement.« (1981, 78; see also 1985, 786)

B. Society as a Hierarchy of Action Systems

Touraine's central theoretical principle is that contemporary society is not a system of reproduction but is creating itself in conflictual processes. Society is basically perceived as a »hierarchized set of *systems of action*, i.e. of social relations between actors who may have conflicting interests but who belong to the same social sphere and therefore share certain cultural

15 Over many years Touraine has apparently maintained his self-image as the authoritative author who solves the crisis of sociology. A reviewer of Touraine's collection of essays »Le retour de l'acteur« (1984a) describes this attitude sarcastically: »... this books reads like a manifesto in which Touraine offers a remedy to what he perceives as a detrimental crisis in sociology. Of course, the solution is to be found in the research that he has directed for the last 20 years and that consists of the analysis of social movements. The circle is complete and Touraine becomes involved in a justificatory argument that seeks to legitimize his own approach to society. Thus, sociology becomes the study of social movements.« (Desan 1985, 438)

orientations. A society is not founded upon its economy, nor upon ideas; it is not a combination of sub-systems or sub-levels. It has only two fundamental components: historicity, i.e. its capacity to produce the models by which it functions, and the class relations through which these orientations become social practices, still marked by a form of social domination. A society has neither nature nor foundations; it is neither a machine nor an organization; it is action and social relations. This idea sets a sociology of action against all the variants of functionalism and structuralism.« (1981, 25) The aforementioned hierarchy consists of three levels. The highest and most imortant level is conceived of as the field of »*historicity*« (l'historicité), which is formed by two dialectically interwoven components: *Class system* and the *system of historical action*. It is at this level where Touraine situates the category of »dominance« and the realm of class conflict, and thus, of social movement activities. Historicity, undoubtedly the corner stone of Touraine's theoretical framework, defines what is at stake for society as a whole. Historicity relates to the fundamental mode of dominance and the actors involved in this struggle over the content and forms of dominance.

On the second level of the so-called *institutional system* Touraine places the political institutions, and in particular, the state. In functional terms, Touraine ascribes the making of legitimate decisions here, emphasizing the category of »influence«. At this level Touraine situates *political* actors and conflicts, not to be confused with social conflicts, which take place only at the upper level. By definition, political struggles and political movements are not decisive in the production of society. Thus, they should be strictly separated from social movements. Only the latter can be attributed to the crucial battle over historicity.

Finally, there is the »*organizational system*« at the third and lowest level and related to the category of »differentiation.«

According to Touraine, the relationship of these three action systems on different levels cannot be conceived of as a unidirectional dependency: »Each system possesses a certain autonomy, but is also controlled by higher systems, to which, in turn, it is a restrictive factor.« (1976, 117f*) Taking the example of the political system, this relationship means that the system »is autonomous insofar as it is defined by a political collectivity, a specific social unity, which does not directly correspond to a field of historicity ... However, it is subordinated to historicity, i.e., both to the restrictions of a historical action system and the modes of dominance exerted by the ruling class.« (1974, 118*) Despite their subordinate position, action systems on lower levels may deviate from the logics of higher systems. At the level of the institutional systems, these deviations take the form of oppositional or innovative actions, which, optimally, may even anticipate a new quality of historicity. At the level of the organizational system, the exertion of social control may provoke resistance or the refusal of achievement. Thus, the overall system composed of specific sub-systems does not absorb and control all forms of behavior it produces. It also creates behavior which is transformed into either deviance or social change. (cf. 1974, 120) Because, by definition, the decisive conflicts of a society take place at the level of historicity, and it is there that social movements act, these become the key objects for Touraine's sociological analysis.

C. What is a Social Movement?

In his early studies of the consciousness of workers, Touraine distinguished three elements which ideally constitute class consciousness: identity, opposition, and totality (cf. 1966, 17). To be sure, the empirically existing consciousness is not necessarily class consciousness insofar as it may reflect these principles only in a distorted and unbalanced way. In his later work, Touraine applies this categorical triad more strictly to social movements (cf. 1973, 369ff.; 1981, 80ff.).

Identity refers to the conscious self-definition of a social actor. This definition, however, is not created through contemplative reflection, but only through a conflict which constitutes and organizes the actor. In turn, organization happens only when a social actor realizes who his real opponent is and thus constitutes the principle of *opposition*. These principles can also be applied to particular and marginal conflicts. With respect to social movements, however, Touraine conceives of identity and opposition in a stronger sense. The actor has to be challenged by a fundamental social force in a conflict in which the general orientations of social lives are at stake. This condition leads to the third principle, that of *totality*, which is »nothing other than the *historical action system*, whose antagonists ... strive for domination.« (1973, 363*) Thus, a social movement is »a collective behavior which is not directed towards the values of a social organization or towards participation in decision-making systems, but towards the stake of class conflicts, i.e., the historical actions system.« (1973, 365*) It follows from this definition that in each type of society only two social movements can exist. »Corresponding to a system of historical action there is a main class relation and consequently a pair of antagonistic social movements.« (1981, 94)

Social movement has to be understood as an analytical category. Empirically, »a social movement is never ›pure‹, because, on the one hand, it merges with organizational and institutional behavior, and on the other, it also has to be taken as an organization and sometimes nearly as a state within the state.« (1973, 367f*) But in an analytical sense Touraine stresses the dividing line between social movements and related phenomena: »A party, a trade union, a voluntary association, regardless which type they may represent, can never be identified as a social movement because these forms can also represent the reaction to an organizational crisis or to tensions within the institutional system.« (1973, 368f*) Once collective actors lose the capacity to integrate and to balance the principles of identity, opposition and totality, the actors – measured by the idea of a social movement – manifest themselves only in various deficient forms which either do not reach the level of a social movement or manifest themselves as a product of decay of a once viable movement. But it has to be acknowledged that these forms situated below the level of the historical action system, and which are called struggles (»luttes«), »cultural«, or »political« movements, may well be the heralds of a coming social movement.

Since, according to Touraine, past as well as contemporary societies are marked by class conflicts, and social movements are situated at this level of conflict, most of the empirical phenomena, for instance the fascist movement, are excluded by definition. This is the case because only *one* singular movement refers to each social class. Consequently, the categories of class and social movements have to be equated: »Social movement and class struggle are synonymous expressions; only the former will be used here, because to speak of class struggle would seem to indicate that classes, objectively defined, enter the struggle to defend contradictory interests. To speak of social movements is to state, on the contrary, that *there exist no class relations separable from class action*, from its cultural orientations and from the social conflict in which the movement occurs.« (1981, 94) Once the society is defined as a class society, and classes are equated with or at least closely related to social movements, the latter have to be considered as »normal« phenomena which are not related to specific periods or specific areas. Rather than being dramatic and extraordinary phenomena, social movements have a permanent character in the heart of social life. Although social classes are involved in conflicts, they still refer positively to a common basis, i.e. the same cultural patterns. (cf. 1984b, 8) For instance, both capitalists and the working class, though fighting over the control of means of production, accepted industry as a tool for societal progress.

Interestingly, in his more recent publications, Touraine tends to differentiate social movements from class. The latter »can be defined as a situation, whereas a social movement is an action, the action of a subject, that is, of an actor who calls into question the social form of historicity.« (1984a, 68) In particular, for our contemporary society, Touraine seems to feel uneasy about his former statements on the central role of class: »We cannot analyze our societies with the concepts of cast or *Stand* and less and less of class.« (1985, 777)[16]

D. Towards a Programmed Society and a New Social Movement

Touraine is not the kind of researcher who limits himself to descriptive analysis and/or to high specialization. His basic motive is to understand how society as a whole works, and what type of society we should expect in the future.

In principle, Touraine's visions about the future follow a scheme he has used to interpret the past. In his view, »the functioning of a society is dominated by its historicity and by its class relations, and therefore, by its social movements. But its change, in particular its transition form one societal type to another, requires another order of analysis in which the *state* occupies central place. This separation ... between the analysis of functioning and that of change, between *synchronic* and *diachronic* analysis, entails the abandonment of the evolutionist conceptions which claim that the functioning of a society can be explained by that society's place in an evolution leading, for instance, from the simple to the complex, from the transmitted to the acquired, or from the symbolic to the rational.« (1981, 26)

Taking a diachronic perspective, Touraine distinguishes between four types of societies: the agrarian, merchant, industrial and post-industrial society. Drawing on his aforementioned threefold hierarchy of interactive sys-

16 In another essay, Touraine goes a step further still in dismissing the category of class. Because social classes are more and more defined through a relation of dominance on the cultural level, on the level of ideas and needs, it becomes impossible to separate class situation and class action, class in itself and class for itself. »Therefore the term class has to be replaced by that of *social movement*.« (1986, 26*)

tems, he presupposes that within the agrarian society these interaction systems are still integrated. In the merchant society it is the organizational system which becomes distinct and separated from the rest. In the industrial society there is an additional differentiation between the institutional system and system of class relations. Finally, a post-industrial society is characterized by a differentiation on the highest level, that is, the separation of class relations and the system of historical action. According to Touraine, these various steps of societal differentiation include a growing willingness and capacity within a society of self-control. Thus, it is the post-industrial society which, for the first time in history, will reach a total capacity of self-control and self-production. Unlike earlier societies, this full capacity will be based on information. Hence, it is the struggle over the access and distribution of knowledge – and not over the means of production as in industrial societies – which is the substance of the decisive conflict. As a consequence of this potential for total self-production, conflicts no longer focus on a specific societal subsystem but may emerge everywhere, including in institutions such as schools, universities, hospitals, or homes for elderly people, and that is, institutions which formerly have been considered as marginal. In his most recent statements, Touraine emphasizes particularly the role of »culture« as a field of growing social conflicts.[17]

The transitions from one type to another are salient breaks marked by powerful social movements – Touraine's *historical movements*.[18] Thus, it was the liberal bourgeois movement that led to the merchant society, the worker's movement to the industrial society, and – still in statu nascendi – the new social movement to the programmed society.[19]

---

17 According to Touraine, from the seventies until today there was a displacement of protest from the economic to the cultural field (cf. 1985, 784; see also 1980, 20). For the emphasis on culture, see also his presentation entitled »Trois types d'action collective«, delivered to the Annual Meeting of the French Society of Sociology, 29-30 September 1989 in Paris.

18 »*Historical movements* are organized actions to control a process of passage from one societal type to another one. Here actors are no longer defined in purely social terms but first of all by their relationship with the State, which is the central agent of such historical transformations.« (1985, 776)

19 Interestingly, Touraine has a clear idea – although he presents virtually no evidence – about seven different stages which mark the transition from the industrial society to the programmed society (Touraine 1981, 21). He confirms that our society has already experienced three steps (decline of the old social movement, cultural crisis, the great refusal)

Each of these societies has to be conceived of as a class society. These antagonisms represent precisely the productive element of society. Emphasizing this aspect, Touraine strictly rejects the idea of the »reproduction of society«. Only »interests and privileges, only the forms of social and cultural organizations, have a tendency to reproduce themselves. By contrast, forces of production and class conflicts permanently exist as principles of change and elements of social strife.« (1974, 221*)

E. Critical Remarks

1. To be sure, Touraine's concept is richer and more differentiated than that presented in this essay. But in its basic structure, far from being substantiated by a discussion of relevant work in social history and an analysis of contemporary society, it has a voluntaristic character.[20] Given the present state of social science and its high degree of division of labor and specialization, Touraine's ambition to see himself as a later day Marx, to define the central concern and the key approach of sociology as a whole, may be impressive and courageous, but it risks becoming excessive and overloaded. There are doubts if the study of social movements can and should be the core of sociological analysis (cf. Boudon 1980, 109) and whether »sociology can only be constructed from the study of social movements, which, alone, can save us from the vain search for the nature or essence of society ...« (1981, 39). Many problems which may be crucial for a society and its related scientific disciplines are not articulated by social movements, and consequently, would be neglected in a purely actor-centered sociology focusing on social movements.

On the whole, Touraine tends to downplay the variety and significance of other approaches, although he acknowledges, at least in his more recent writings, »the relative autonomy of other schools.« (1985), 786)[21] As in vir-

---

and will experience four other steps (critique of the state, communitarian retreat, populism, new social movements).

20 »... Touraine is hampered by vagueness and an occasionally uneven and superficial familiarity with relevant sociological traditions.« (Hall 1985, 145)

21 Touraine seems to regard these other schools being of minor importance in so far as, according to him, they are not encompassing. They only refer to specific forms of the decomposition of social movements whereas a sociology of action »deserves a central

tually all fields of theory building and research, every scholar depends heavily on the work others have already done or are currently doing. At least one should be aware of these efforts and results. What is missing in Touraine's work is not only an intense and explicit discussion of other theories and concepts, but also, how he relates his work to empirical analyses in the same field. He seems to consider his own approach strong and powerful enough to stand alone.[22] Hence, he is not overly concerned with a cumulative and integrative effort in the field of social movements and it is hard to detect who the scientific ancestors on whom he relies might be. Probably, he dislikes the idea of building upon others. But, as one may rightly argue, we can see much more if we take a stand on the shoulders of others, and preferably, of »giants.« (cf. Merton 1965)

2. Reviewing Touraine's theoretical effort over the last decades one is impressed by its remarkable continuity. But this quality also has its negative side in the sense that he was overly attached to and probably enraptured by his early ideas. Rather than examining and revising his concepts in the light of ongoing debates, criticisms and self-critique,[23] the author was more engaged in a process of confirming and stabilizing his earlier positions, be it by radicalization, further refinement, variation, or simply repetition.[24] To be fair, it has to be noted that during recent years he has made some gradual conceptual shifts. As already mentioned, he tends to differentiate more clearly the notions of class and social movements. Recently, he has also placed more emphasis on cultural orientations and he has been more careful in making predictions about the heralds of a new society. But on the whole, he shows an outstanding tendency to make strong judgements, to distinguish sharply between what is wrong and right, what is central or marginal, what is out of date and what will be the essence of social conflicts in the future – statements which raise doubts about the assertion that the actionalist ap-

---

place precisely because of its capacity to understand and reinterpret other approaches.« (1985, 770)

22 »Touraine is apparently uninterested in or unaware of recent American work on social movements.« (Gamson 1983, 814)

23 For one of the few examples of self-critique, which, however, remains largely symbolic, see Touraine 1980a, 429.

24 »The method of *sociological intervention*, already ten times presented and discussed, entails no surprise.« (Segrestin 1985, 731*)

proach »is not a doctrine but a theory.« (1965, 473*) Indications of this orthodox attitude are the frequent use of words such as »always« and »never,« the readiness to reconstruct society from the archimedian point-of-view, the pertinent search for the highest meaning of a phenomenon, or the classification of protest groups as social movements or anti-movements, etc.

Over the years and even decades Touraine has employed an inflationary use of a rhetoric of crises, be it that of society as a whole, political parties, the French Left, sociology, etc. And in many cases, the author seems to perceive himself as the man who has assumed the burden not only of crisis analysis, but also of therapy. Not accidentally some observers have characterized the »evangelistic« (D.S. Bell) or »missionary« (A. Melucci) leaning of Touraine, whose attraction stems more from his passion and his engagement than from his scrutiny. In his work there is a tendency to overestimate not only the role of sociology[25] and intellectuals[26] in general, but also, his own approach both with respect to social sciences and social conflicts.

3. Particularly with reference to social movements and related phenomena, Touraine presents a multitude of categories, concepts, and schemas. He seems to be undecided about the direction of his own effort. On the one hand, he declares that »we should not invest too much time clarifying our categories; the real task is to create sociological theory.« (1974, 53*) On the other, he emphasizes that the goal of sociology is to formulate »precise statements about social mechanisms.« (1974, 54*) Apart from the contradiction between both statements, one wonders, regarding the former, if there is such a trade-off between the search for clarification of categories and the creation of theory as Touraine assumes. If we take the second statement seriously, we find that Touraine's hypotheses are usually situated on a too ab-

25 »Sociology is an act of enlightenment (»connaissance«) in the service of liberty. The latter cannot exist without the former.« (1973, 527*) Sociology is »an instrument for innovation and liberation.« (1974, 60*) Sociology »holds a central place in the programmed society just as economics did in the industrial society or political philosophy in merchant societies.« (1974, 91*)

26 »The intellectuals play an important role when they uncover historicity and the conflicts which accrete around historicity, but they have no power unless their ideas are embodied in the apparatus of control and management.« (1981, 220)

stract level to be really verifiable,[27] and there are also too few significant efforts to substantiate fundamental theoretical assumptions.[28] As far as I can see, the approach ends up with more taxonomy than theory.[29]

Taking the example of his hierarchy of action systems, one could raise a number of pertinent questions. What do the various terms mean (dominance, system of organization, etc.) and how are they related? What is the relevance of this theoretical construct for research? How can one substantiate the assumption of an hierarchical order in which, for instance, political conflicts have to be considered inferior to social conflicts, but superior to institutional conflicts? Taking the problem of technocracy, why is it that struggles against technocratic domination cannot be located at the level of the political system and the organizational system? Is it, apart from the taxonomic interest, really enlightening to attribute empirical phenomena to a certain level? Are there clear criteria for such attributions? How can we classify a complex, heterogeneous collective actor if only parts of it can be located at a certain level, if at all?

Referring to Touraine's terminology of action systems, one could question the implications of the category of »system« in an approach which distances itself from system theory. Referring to the premises of the actionalist interpretation of history, one could challenge the idea that history is only the product of conflicts. Can one neglect the flow of uncoordinated and uncontrolled events, of routine, unspectacular, and partly unconscious change as forms of societal reproduction?

---

27 The fundamental question which oriented the research program, that is if we witness the emergence of a new social movement, has already been answered before the research was carried out, or it has lead to the conclusion that some of the empirical movements may have the potential to become real movements. Only in the case of the 1976 student movement was a very clear statement made, saying that by no means is this a social movement. In that case, however, sociological research started when the movement was already over and the main result was not very surprising.

28 Although Touraine argues that »the role of a sociologist is to prove sociological assertations« (1974, 242*), critics say that he does not follow this maxim. »The concepts are too vague, the terminology too obscure, and the thinking too unsystematic to form a convincing or testable theory.« (Smith 1982, 981) »We are confronted with more affirmations than demonstrations.« (Dumazedier 1975, 604*)

29 »Touraine's is indeed a general systematic theory, but I would not call it a very successful one in explanatory terms.« (Collins 1976, 1506)

Another question, for instance, is why one should introduce the category of social movements, which, according to Touraine's earlier writings, is synonymous to that of class? If the latter explicitly distinguishes between »class in itself« and »class for itself,« there is no difficulty in avoiding the objectivist bias which Touraine wants to compensate for by using the term social movement.

4. Touraine's interpretation of the societal stages in history and the respective roles of social movements is overly crude. It is not grounded in the rich work of social historians. Moreover, one wonders why there should necessarily be only one pair of movements in one type of society. Are there not many indications that contemporary societies will become more differentiated, more fragmented, and thus may include many social movements, which, »in a strict sense, represent conflicting efforts to control cultural patterns (knowledge, investment, ethics) in a given societal type« (1985, 776)? Even if we would assume that in past history there was only one pair of social movements in a given society, this may change in future societies.

Is there only *one* meaning within a social movement? And why it is so important to unveil the meaning of a movement, thus neglecting its organization, strategy, adherents, public resonance, outcome, etc.? Surprisingly, Touraine is not very interested in questions, as many other scholars in the field of social movements persuasively argue, which are related to a movement's ideologies and aims, i.e., features which certainly have to do with the »meaning« of a movement's struggle? And why should »technocracy« be the only point of reference for a promising social movement in our society? Are such concerns as those emphasized by other movements such as »peace« or »environmental protection« or »personal identity,« necessarily of relatively minor importance? Would an escape from technocratic control guarantee peace, ecological reproduction, and identity? Even if we would take for granted the idea Touraine shares with many other social scientists, that information is the key factor for future societies, there are few reasons to separate the problem of information from that of wealth, power, and the means of production.

More than two decades after Touraine proclaimed the coming of a post-industrial or »programmed« society, he has made hardly an attempt to clarify the contours of this type of society. It is not enough to say that »research and development, information processing, biomedical science and techniques, and mass media are the four main components of post-industrial society, while bureaucratic activities of production of electrical and electronic equipment are just growing sectors of an industrial society defined by production of goods more than by new channels of communications and the creation of artificial languages.« (1985, 781)

5. A further point of critique relates to the fact that some categories and statements have not only remained vague, but also, confusing. Without presenting a detailed list of references here I would maintain that Touraine is not only undecided, but explicitly contradictory: Is he aiming at creating a theory? Is sociology in a crisis, and if so, should it be guided by values[30] and aim at the study of social actors? Is the labor movement a historical movement (defined as an actor that initiates the passage from one type of society to another) or a genuine social movement (as social class within an already established type of society)? Were the movements of '68, and later the antinuclear movements, genuine new social movements having reached the level of historicity?

III. Sociology and/or Intervention?

During the mid-seventies Touraine began to dwell on some of his earlier ideas in order to develop the distinct method for the analysis of social movements which he later called »sociological intervention.« The aim of this new method, as well as the actionalist approach formulated in the 1960s, was to »discover the social movement which in a programmed society will occupy the central position held by the worker's movement in industrial society and the civil liberties movement in the market society by which it was preceded.« (1981, 24) But Touraine wants to go far beyond a mere scientific discovery. According to him, sociological intervention aims »to recompose social movements wherever possible, to raise the level of conflicts, and to revivify historical action. I should not have undertaken this research programme had I not believed it was necessary and possible to define the actors, the field of struggle and the new stakes and hence theoretically and practically to re-form the analysis of society.« (1981, 221)

---

30 For this point of critique, see Dumazedier (1975, 604) and Trimberger (1978).

A. What is Sociological Intervention?

The method of sociological intervention has been presented in a whole series of publications by Touraine and his collaborators. This is not the place to go into details, but rather, to present a rough idea of the method's status and basics.

Sociological intervention differs radically from the methods usually applied in the study of social movements. »The analysis bears neither on a situation nor on opinions, but on the *self-analysis* which militants perform upon their collective action.« (1981, 27) Such an analysis requires the assistance of the researcher, who – in contrast to perceptions in mainstream sociology – cannot watch a movement as an object, but rather, has to intervene into the field he is studying although he may be rejected and the results of his intervention may be neutralized. »The researcher is used to entering his field of investigation equipped with plans, questionnaires and comparative data. Today, however, we need much more to recognize that the researcher and the orientation of his work are largely a product of research.« (1974, 270*) Consequently, the researcher has to be at the same time analyst and actor, without, however, confusing these two roles. »He stimulates the *self-analysis* of the group and at the same time, is the *actor of the intervention* ... He urges the activists to analyze the conditions necessary to bring the struggle up to the level of a social movement. The researcher speaks from a position which the activists can attain only by undergoing their *conversion.* Hence, the researcher has to take both the position of the analyst and that of the social movement. He *elevates the group.*« (1980b, 356*) The role of the researcher is quite unique in this methodological approach. »Intervention requires that the researcher be an *intermediary* between the militant group and the social movement by which its action is conveyed. It is this new conception of the researcher as neither observer nor ideologist that most clearly distinguishes intervention from other methods.« (1981, 27)

Because it is captured by its ideology and visions of utopia, the group itself is apparently not able to reach the level of historicity by its own means. »This can be done only if one no longer adopts the outlook of the actor, but takes instead the point of view of social relations. Only the sociologist succeeds in doing so, though as yet only in his analysis. If he wishes to transform the ideology into directives, he becomes not better than a doctrinaire whose influence weakens the action.« (1981, 98) Thus the researcher has to dissociate himself from the actor to the extent that the actor unveils the meaning of his action (cf. 1974, 22).

During the self-analysis of the group the crucial passage is the *conversion* initiated by the intervening researcher. This conversion of the group, in turn, must be preceded by a conversion of the researcher. The conversion enables the group to understand its action (1980b, 21). This means that the group recognizes the central hypotheses of the researcher as it is directed towards the most elaborated meaning of action. By this process the group transcends its level of ideological restriction and adequately realizes, according to a given historical situation, the principles of identity, opposition, and totality. This state is a necessary, but not sufficient, condition for becoming a movement. The rise and success of a movement depend not only on the conversion of other combatants, but also, on the battles themselves. The actor's effort to transform their analysis into an action program is the concern of an ongoing process of reflection both on the part of the activists and the researchers. For this process Touraine has coined the term »permanent sociology« (cf. 1981, 148f).

In practical terms, sociological intervention focuses on groups that have been recruited according to the researcher's preferences. Usually, the number of groups initiated by Touraine and his collaborators is small and ranges from two (studies of the 1976 student protests and the anti-nuclear protest) to five (study of the *Solidarity Movement*). These groups, composed basically of activists engaged in protest movements, are occasionally confronted with other people, among them experts, representatives of the state apparatus and firms, including outspoken opponents of the protest groups. The groups meet from time to time within a period ranging, from four months to roughly one year and a half, depending on the studies. The interactions and debates within these groups form the central, albeit not exclusive, body of »data«, from which the analysis of the movements and its environment are based.

The team of researchers develops ideas about the »highest meaning« of the struggle in which the group's activists are involved. The team confronts the activists with these hypotheses, and finally, ends up with an acceptance – and thus the conversion of the groups – or a rejection of them.

Obviously, this method has some remarkable parallels to the psychoanalytical situation in which the self-analysis (read: conversion) of the therapist (read: researcher) is a precondition for a successful therapeutic treatment of the client (read: discovery of the highest meaning of the conflict). The success of the client, who has learned to analyze this personal situation and to cope with his problems, corresponds to the success of the collective actor, who, by recognizing what is at stake in a given society and what his historical mission is, has reached the level of historicity. There is yet another parallel to psychoanalysis in Touraine's methodology in that the author tells us that it should be the activist who calls for the researcher (1974, 22).[31]

B. Some Critical Remarks

The method of sociological intervention has already attracted heavy criticism (cf. Amiot 1980; Barkan 1984; Gamson 1983; Kivisto 1982; Law 1984; Nagel 1983; Melucci 1989; Nelissen 1981; Rüdig and Lowe 1984; Smith 1982). I only want to recall some of these arguments and to add some new elements of critique.

1. One can question if an analysis of a movement as a whole can be done by focusing on only two or more sub-groups within it. These groups were, moreover, not natural but created by the research team. Why not study already existing groups and organizations within a movement belonging to different ideological strands, coming from different social strata, generations, localities, etc.?

2. Because the composition and internal dynamics within these groups are induced mainly by the research team, it is hard to control the extent to which this dynamic depends on contingencies such as the researchers' personalities, number, intensity of intervention, etc. Is there not a high probability that the same method, employed by a different team at a different place with a different group, would lead to different results? As far as I can see, problems of data selection, of potential artefacts, etc., are not seriously reflected. Touraine is aware of the problem that the researcher may influence the be-

31 On the one hand, Touraine states that a precondition for his method is that the actor calls for *and* (my emphasis) accepts the need of intervention (1974, 22), on the other he writes that actor must accept *or* (my emphasis) demand the intervention (1981, 27). In general, without really discussing the problem, Touraine seems to be aware of the extent to which his method comes close to a therapeutic constellation. Assuming that a sociologist who wants to understand social relations must intervene directly, Touraine rhetorically asks: »Isn't that analogous to the practices of a psychoanalyst?« (1974a, 243) For the striking parallel of Touraine's approach to psychoanalysis, see also Amiot (1980) and Touraine's response on that point, which ends with the statement that »it is not forbidden to establish a convergence (»rapprochement«) between the intervention and psychoanalysis.« (1980a, 426*)

havior and the answers of the actors. In the methodological appendix of the original (and not the English!) edition of Touraine and his collaborators' study on the French anti-nuclear movement they claim that »the comparison of at least two actor groups allows for the control of that researcher's impact« (1980b, 348*). It could be asked, however, how such a design would allow for a control if one team of researchers focuses on the actor group A based in Y, whereas the other team, composed of different researchers, focuses on actor group B based in Z. In the aforementioned study, the problem of controlling various factors is even more aggravated, because the two groups differed in many respects. The Paris-based actor group consisted of intellectuals not directly engaged in a struggle against a specific nuclear reactor; the second group, much more heterogeneously composed, was faced with the fast breeder reactor project in the countryside.

3. One can ask if the search for the highest potential meaning is a fruitful task. Even assuming that this highest meaning can be found in one or all of the groups under investigation one may ask if this tells us much about the dynamics and the historical relevance of the movement as a whole or if it reflects only the ideas of a number of activists, which, in turn, may be influenced by researchers. Still more fundamental is the question of what »high« meaning really means and what the empirical consequences would be if this meaning could be found in groups or even in movement as a whole? And what are the conclusions if, as was the case in the study of the two anti-nuclear groups, one group realizes the »conversion« and thus reaches the highest level of meaning while the other fails to do so? And, related to that case, one may ask if this is not a result of the different compositions and settings of the two groups under investigation. As a matter of fact the intellectual anti-nuclearists in Paris, far more open to sociological reflection, achieved their conversion whereas the group which was deeply involved in a local struggle against the fast breeder in Creys-Malville failed to do so. Unfortunately, Touraine is not very clear whether such a rejection of the researcher's hypothesis means the hypothesis was wrong, the researchers were not able to adequately present their hypotheses, or the group under consideration simply failed to acknowledge the adequacy of the hypothesis.

4. Even though Touraine insists on the pure sociological character of his investigation, one can ask if this method is not closer to a therapeutic, if not psychoanalytic, constellation, although the author points out the difference between an individual pathology and an oppressed social group. However, he seems much more interested in revealing what is still unconscious to the

actors through a dialogue than in studying their actual behavior. Moreover, in order to detect the hidden meaning of the group's struggle, the researcher himself has first to realize a kind of conversion as a necessary, albeit insufficient, condition for inducing the conversion of the group under consideration. But does a social actor necessarily need this interpretive offer to know what is really at stake in his struggles? Is it not a doubtful »missionary role of the researcher« (Melucci 1989, 201) at work here especially in a situation where the sociologist has to assist and enlighten the actor? And if there were an unconscious meaning in the actor's struggle, would it not require – as in the case of a psychoanalyst – the researcher to accompany the »client« over a long period, and listen attentively to him in order to unveil such a meaning?

5. If the sociological intervention has to be taken as a necessary but not sufficient condition enabling existing groups to find out the highest meaning of their action, one wonders how such historical movements as the labor movement could have ever attained the status of a social movement as long as it were not assumed that people like Marx and Engels practised a type of sociological intervention. Moreover, does the necessity of intervention mean that those movements which are not in the fortuitous position of being the object of sociological intervention, or which deliberately refuse to become engaged in the process of »permanent sociology« (as was the case with a lesbian group in Paris[32]), will have no chance of reaching the level of historicity?

6. It seems that Touraine, as the principal investigator, already had a preconceived notion of the highest meaning of a social movement before he started empirical research. Since the late 1960s it has been quite clear, according to Touraine, that this is the struggle for control in a programmed society. This was the explicit criterion required of an empirical group under investigation either to reach or to miss the level of historicity, and thus by definition, to be or not to be considered a social movement. In a similar vein, it was not surprising to find out through sociological intervention in the early 1980s that the worker's movement has come to an end, particularly since Touraine has been articulating this thesis since the mid-sixties.

Given their fluid and dynamic character, the study of social movements is certainly fraught with difficulties, and particularly as one respects such

32 In 1983 and 1984, Touraine's collaborators, aiming to study the feminist movement, failed to carry out a sociological intervention with respect to specific groups.

conventional methodological standards as representativity, validity, and reliability. But the problem with »sociological intervention« is that it makes little effort to go in this direction[33] or to formulate different standards which are transparent for the scientific community. Taking the admittedly extreme case of the study on the Polish *Solidarnosc Movement*, where many group discussions were recorded and transcribed, one wonders how and according to what criteria these many thousands of pages were evaluated and how the book could be published only four months after the completion of the data collection.[34]

IV. Conclusion

At least in France, talking about the sociological analysis of social movements is almost synonymous with talking about Touraine. He is an important element in the French scientific and intellectual community, inspiring not only sociology, but also political actors.[35] His name, and to a lesser extent his work, is well-known in many other countries for his studies in industrial sociology, his ideas about the coming of a programmed society, and his writings on social movements. Several of his books have been translated into various languages, including English, Spanish, German and Italian. Above all, Touraine aims not only to define the central concerns and key concepts

33 With regard to the problem of representativity, as it has been put by Amiot (1980), Touraine acknowledges the limits of his research (Touraine 1980a, 427). But when he refers to this problem in the study of the anti-nuclear movement, his explanations are highly unsatisfactory (see the methodological appendix which has been omitted from the English edition of the study). Also, the article of Dubet (1983) claiming to treat the question of validity in sociological intervention is hardly convincing.

34 For this point, see Kitschelt (1984). The study on the *Solidarity Movement* is perhaps a special case. In a conversation with Chris Rootes, Touraine admitted that this was not really an intervention in the way that the others were. Touraine intended to support his Polish colleagues for political reasons. Hence, the study's aim was more to give publicity to the Solidarity Movement than to write a scientific work (Letter from Chris Rootes to the author).

35 To a certain degree, Touraine seems to have contributed to the socialist party's partial acceptance of the anti-nuclear movement. There are also indications that he has had some influence on the discourse of the anti-nuclear movement in the late 1970s (cf. Rüdig and Lowe 1984).

of sociology, but also, to answer crucial questions about the present and future states of our societies.

Even though many observers may disagree on whether Touraine may be counted among the key figures in contemporary soicology[36], there is no doubt that he should be classified as one of the most important scholars in the field of social movements. He has produced an impressive body of literature based on an ambitious, but also, highly debatable approach. Unlike most of his colleagues, he tries to relate grand theory and micro-sociological empirical analysis. Rarely do sociologists take such clear, uncompromising stances. Touraine does not hesitate to reject competing approaches and he is seemingly not afraid of coming under attack himself. Whatever may be said for or against Touraine, there is certainly a wide recognition of his ambition and courage to create grand theory, to challenge virtually all major theoretical strands, and to put forward questions that concern not only the fate of sociology but society in general. In this sense, he counter-balances the strong tendency of social sciences to become fragmented into a host of overly specialized, unrelated subdisciplines.

Since progress in science is induced more by critique than by acknowledgement and affirmation, my intention was to unveil the pitfalls and flaws of Touraine's approach both on the theoretical and methodological level.

Summarizing my critique of Touraine's general concept, the following points can be made: First, the approach aspires to a hegemonic position in respect to the very core of sociology; it is too self-centered and not really developed in the light of competing concepts and theories. Second, there is a highly problematic tendency to guide and enlighten collective actors about the »meaning« of their struggle. Third, many hypotheses and statements are too vague to be tested empirically by Touraine's own attempts or to be confronted with other empirical research in the field. Fourth, even if we take the approach as a heuristic instrument there is an abundance of concepts, dictums, tables and categories which raise many questions but remain largely unanswered in his writings. Finally, there is a series of explicit contradictions in Touraine's work including several which are related to the central elements of the approach.

---

36 For instance, a publishing house states that Touraine is »one of the most prominent and influential social scientists in Europe« (backcover of the German edition of Touraine's Production de la société). Also, some sociologists rank him similarly (see Beosjes-Hommes 1974).

As for the method of »sociological intervention,« one has to admit that it is an innovative contribution to social movement research. During the last 15 years its elaboration and application to various movements has been his main concern. The creation of this method can be perceived as a reaction to certain deficiencies of conventional research on social movements, and particularly, research which often pretends to take a »neutral« position vis-a-vis its object under investigation. I believe that Touraine rightly points out that the study of a social movement can hardly be done through arm-chair reflection. And he is certainly right to demonstrate that being a researcher close to the social actor does not necessarily mean to merge or confuse the role of the analyst and activist. The researcher has to be both close to and distant from his object.

Nevertheless, there are some fundamental flaws in Touraine's method which have already been listed above. In a nutshell, it seems to me that the method tends to tell us much more about the profile and idiosyncracies of its creator than about his research object. This is not to say that one cannot find valuable insights in these empirical studies. But there are serious doubts that this method is the central key in analyzing social movements, that the method can be controlled[37] and thus used as an empirical test, or at least as a viable basis for interpretation, or that the study of social movements unveils the dynamics of our society.

In conclusion, I want to stress the need for a more intense study of Touraine's work by scholars in the field of social movement research – and vice versa. Mutual ignorance, global rejection, but also mere rites of citation can hardly contribute to progress in science.

Bibliography

Ackermann, W.; Moscivici, S. (1966): »La sociologie existentielle d'Alain Touraine«, *Sociologie du travail*, 8 (2):205-209.

Amiot, M. (1980): »L'intervention sociologique, la science et la prophétie«, *Sociologie du travail*, 22 (4):415-424.

37 »The problem is that the researcher can never be sure whether or not the observed action is the product of his or her interventions. Touraine's research procedure is unable to control its own effects.« Melucci 1989, 201.

Aron, R. (1983): *Mémoires: 50 ans des réflexion politique*. Paris: Juillard, 2 volumes.

Barkan, S.E. (1984): Review of A. Touraine et al., Anti-nuclear Protest: The Opposition to Nuclear Energy (1983), *Contemporary Sociology*, 13 (3):287-288.

Boesjes-Hommes, R.W. (1974): »Alain Touraine«, in: Rademaker, L. and Petersma, L. (eds.), *Hoofdfiguren uit de sociologie*. Utrecht: Het Spectrum, 227-237.

Boudon, R. (1980): *Die Logik des gesellschaftlichen Handelns*. Neuwied, Darmstadt: Luchterhand.

Collins, R. (1967): Review of A. Touraine, Production de la société (1973), *American Journal of Sociology*, 81 (6):1503-1506.

Desan, P. (1985): Review of A. Touraine, Le retour de l'acteur (1984), *American Journal of Sociology*, 91 (2):437-439.

Dubet, F. (1983): »Les critères de validation dans l'intervention sociologique«, in: A. Touraine et al., *La méthode de l'intervention sociologique*. Paris: Atelier d'Intervention Sociologique, 53-69.

Dubost, J. (1980): »De la sociologie de l'action à l'action sociologique: La pratique d'intervention d'Alain Touraine«, *Connexion* (29):143-166.

Düll, K. (1975): *Industriesoziologie in Frankreich*. Frankfurt: Europäische Verlagsanstalt.

Dumazedier, J. (1975): Review of A. Touraine, Production de la société (1973), *Revue française de sociologie*, 15 (4):601-605.

Eder, K. (1982): »A New Social Movement?«, *Telos* 52 (Summer):5-20.

Eyerman, R. (1984): »Social movements and social theory«, *Sociology* 18 (1):71-82.

Freiberg, J.W. (1975): Review of A. Touraine, Production de la Société (1973), *Theory and Society*, 2 (2):370-373.

Gamson, W. (1983): Review of A. Touraine, ›The Voice and the Eye: An Analysis of Social Movements‹, *American Journal of Sociology*, 88 (4):812-814.

Hall, J.R. (1985): Review of A. Touraine, The Voice and the Eye (1981), *Journal of Political and Military Sociology*, 13 (1):145-146.

Hannigan, J.A. (1985): »Alain Touraine, Manuel Castells and Social Movement Theory: A Critical Appraisal«, *The Sociological Quarterly*, 26 (4):435-454.

Japp, K. (1984): »Selbsterzeugung oder Fremdverschulden. Thesen zum Rationalismus in den Theorien sozialer Bewegungen«, *Soziale Welt*, 35 (4):313-329.

Kitschelt, H. (1984): Review of A. Touraine, Solidarity. The Analysis of a Social-Movement, Poland, 1980-1981 (1983), *Organizational Studies*, 5 (4):363-365.

Kivisto, P. (1982): Review of A. Touraine, The Voice and the Eye (1981), *Contemporary Sociology*, 11 (2):181-183.

Law, D. (1984): Review of A. Touraine et al., Solidarity: The Analysis of a Social Movement (1983), *The Sociological Review*, 32 (2):429-431.

Lebas, E. (1985): Review of A. Touraine, The Return of the Actor (1984), *Sociology*, 19 (2):329-330.

Lembert, C. (1986): »French Sociology: After the *Patrons*, What? Review Essay«, *Contemporary Sociology*, 15 (5):689-692.

Melucci, A. (1975): »Sur le travail théorique d'Alain Touraine«, *Revue française de sociologie*, 16 (3):359-379.

– (1980): »The new social movements: A theoretical approach«, *Social Science Information*, 19 (2):199-226.

- (1984): »An end to social movements? Introductory paper to the sessions on ›new movements and change in organizational forms‹«, *Social Science Information*, 23 (4/5):819-835.
- (1989): *Nomads of the Present*. Philadelphia: Temple University Press.

Merton, R. (1965): *On the Shoulders of Giants*. London: The Free Press.

Minguet, G. (1980): »Les mouvements sociaux, la sociologie de l'action et l'intervention sociologique: A propos de deux ouvrages d'Alain Touraine«, *Revue française de sociologie*, 21 (1):415-524.

Nagel, J. (1983): Review of A. Touraine, The Voice and the Eye (1981), *Social Forces*, 61 (3):923-924.

Nelissen, N.J.M. (1981): »Touraine's sociologische interventie: Een nieuwe methode voor de bestudering van sociale bewegingen?«, *Sociologische Gids*, 28 (1):36-52.

Reynaud, J.D.; Bourdieu, P. (1966): »Une sociologie de l'action est-elle possible?«, *Revue française de sociologie*, 7 (4):508-517.

Rose, M. (1977): *French industrial studies. A Bibliography and Guide*. Westmead, Farnboraough: Saxon House.

- (1977): *Servants of the Post-industrial Power? Sociologie du travail in Modern France*. London: Macmillan.

Roth, R. (1983): »Gesellschaftstheoretische Konzepte zur Analyse neuer sozialer Bewegungen«, *Politische Vierteljahresschrift*, 24 (3):311-328.

Rüdig, W.; Lowe, P.D. (1984): »The Unfulfilled Prophecy: Touraine and the Anti-Nuclear Movement«, *Modern & Contemporary France*, 20 (December):19-23.

Segrestin, D. (1985): Review of A. Touraine et al., Le mouvement ouvrier (1984), *Revue française de sociologie*, 24 (4):731-736.

Touraine, A. (1955): *L'évolution du travail ouvrier aux usines Renault*. Paris: C.N.R.S.

- (1965): *Sociologie de l'action*. Paris: Editions du Seuil.
- (1966): *La conscience ouvrière*. Paris: Editions du Seuil.
- (1966): »La raison d'être d'une sociologie de l'action«, *Revue française de sociologie*, 7 (4):518-527.
- (1968): *Le mouvement de Mai ou le communisme utopique*. (Le communisme utopique. Le mouvement de mai 68, 1972). Paris: Editions du Seuil.
- (1969): *La société postindustrielle*. Paris: Denoel.
- (1972): *Université et société aux Etats-Unis*. Paris: Seuil.
- (1973): *Production de la société*. Paris: Editions du Seuil.
- (1973a): *Vie et mort du Chili populaire*. Paris: Editions du Seuil.
- (1973b): »L'historicité«, in: *Une nouvelle civilization? Hommage à Georges Friedmann*. Paris: Gallimard, 3-44.
- (1974): *Pour la sociologie*. Paris: Editions du Seuil.
- (1974a): *Lettres à une étudiante*. Paris: Editions du Seuil.
- (1975) »Les nouveaux conflits sociaux«, *Sociologie de travail*, 7 (1):1-17.
- (1976): »Krise oder Mutation«, in: Touraine, A. et al., *Jenseits der Krise. Wider das politische Defizit der Ökologie*. Frankfurt: Syndikat, 19-49.
- (1977): *Un désir d'histoire*. Paris: Stock.
- (1978): (co-authored by F. Dubet, Z. Hegedus, M. Wieviorka), *Lutte étudiante*. Paris: Seuil.

- (1980): *L'après-socialisme*. Paris: Grasset.
- (1980a): »Réponse à Michel Amiot«, *Sociologie du travail*, 22 (4):415-430.
- (1980b): (co-authored by Z. Hegedus, F. Dubet, M. Wieviorka), *La prophétie anti-nucléaire*. Paris: Seuil.
- (1981): *The Voice and the Eye: An Analysis of Social Movements*: Cambridge University Press (La voix et le regard. Paris: Seuil 1978).
- (1981a): (co-authored by F. Dubet, Z. Hegedus, M. Wieviorka), *Le Pays contre l'Etat*. Paris: Editions du Seuil.
- (1982): *Mouvements sociaux d'aujourd'hui. Acteurs et analystes*, Colloque de Ceresy-la-Salle 1979 (sous la direction d'Alain Touraine). Paris: Les éditions ouvrières.
- (1982a): (co-authored by F. Dubet, M. Wieviorka, J. Strzeclecki), *Solidarité. Analyse d'un mouvement social. Pologne 1979-1981*. Paris: Fayard.
- (1983): (with essays from F. Dubet et al.) *La méthode de l'intervention sociologique*. Paris: Atelier d'Intervention Sociologique.
- (1984): (co-authored by M. Wieviorka, F. Dubet), *Le mouvement ouvrier*. Paris: Fayard.
- (1984a): *Return to the Actor* (Le retour de l'acteur. Paris: Fayard 1984). Minneapolis: University of Minnesota Press.
- (1984b): »Les mouvements sociaux: objet particulier ou problème central de l'analyse sociologique?«, *Revue française de sociologie*, 25 (1):3-19.
- (1985): »An Introduction to the Study of Social Movements«, *Social Research*, 52 (4):749-787.
- (1985a): »Sociological Importance and Political Failure of the French Anti-Nuclear Movement«, *Modern & Contemporary France*, 22 (July):63-64.
- (1986): »Krise und Wandel des sozialen Denkens«, in: J. Berger (ed.), *Die Moderne. Kontinuitäten und Zäsuren* (Sonderband 4 Soziale Welt). Göttingen: Schwarz, 15-39.
- (1988): *La parole et le sang*. Paris: Odile Jacob.

Commentary on Dieter Rucht's Critique

Alain Touraine

1. Dieter Rucht's analysis of my studies on social movements and his reactions to their content and to their style is of great value for me, because it gives a well-informed and unprejudiced image of them; I can easily accept it as a reliable expression of the way my work is generally perceived, of the reason why it stirs up some interest and many resistances.
2. The first and maybe most central discussion deals with the »nature« of my writings. Dieter Rucht insists on their dual aspect. I am a sociologist who participates or at least is interested in participating in public life. My studies on the student movement in France and the United States, of the Chilean military coup in 1973 and of Solidarnosc in Poland in 1981 were not neutral. That comes from the fact that the social or political processes I generally study are more or less directly identifiable with historical events rather then with objects of value judgments and political choices. But here, I do not see any difference between myself and other sociologists. The theories of modernization are just as ideological as the theories which support revolutionary guerillas in Latin America and both can contribute to social science analysis. What is important is to be aware that there is no objective definition of social movements. Each one implies a general approach. We must be conscious of this plurality and explicit about our own initial choice. Most discussions and controverses are meaningless as each participant speaks about a different object under the same name.

I see three main approaches. The first one considers a social movement as the result of the limitation or crisis of the political system. When the political supply is insufficient, demands are expressed in a wild, non-institutionalized way. This approach presupposes that all demands can be answered by institutional processes except when they imply a total rejection of the values, norms and institutions which are prevalent in a given society.

The second one considers, on the contrary, that actors, like for example workers, try to defend collectively private interests when they participate in strikes or political campaigns to get better working conditions or better wages. This view is no longer centered on the system's capacity to process social demands but on the actor's goals and interests.

The third one analyses social organization as the end result of central conflicts between powerful and powerless categories which strive to give to cultural values which are accepted by both categories opposite social and political forms. The example of industrialists and wage earners who both accept industrialism but try to link it with their own class interests has been often analyzed both by Marxists and non-Marxists.

It is necessary to add to these three properly sociological approaches a purely political or military one which considers social movements as warriors who are involved in a civil war.

Nobody can reject *a priori* any of these ways of constructing and analyzing conflict-oriented collective behavior. On the contrary, I explicitly accept the validity of these various approaches. I even observed that, in different societies, one of these approaches can be predominant not for intellectual but for political or cultural reasons. European countries, especially when they have been influenced by a social-democratic or a socialist regime, tend to accept widely the idea of a central class conflict. On the contrary, when the market economy is recognized as a central element of social organization, as is the case in most Western countries in the 80s, the analysis of competing interest groups and of collective bargaining processes takes on a central importance. In the United States during the 60s and the 70s, interest in social movements was clearly linked to the discovery of the incapacity of the legal and political system to solve many social and political problems – civil rights, student unrest, the Vietnam war – and with efforts to introduce liberal reform and create new institutional devices to answer satisfactorily social demands.

At a more analytical level, I identify these three approaches with one I call the institutional, the organizational and the »historicity« levels of social life. I do not pretend that any of these approaches is superior to others, but I insist that sociologists like myself who give a methodological priority to the analysis of central social conflicts can and must analyze the impact of such conflicts at the institutional and organizational levels, that is at the level of the decision-making systems and of the economic and administrative organizations which express power relations. Sociologists who identify themselves with other viewpoints must and can do the same effort to integrate various levels of analysis. Do they always?

The reason why Dieter Rucht perceives some aggression and too much ambition in some of my statements stems from my perception – right or wrong – to be in a minority situation while other viewpoints are so much identified with predominant ideology that they consider themselves as »natural«, as so many functionalists naïvely did during the 50s.

Western societies, because they are democratic, tend to give a priority to legal and political processes, to consensus and compromise. On the contrary, »revolutionary« regimes, parties or intellectuals, tend to speak in terms of social war, of contradiction of the necessary destruction of capitalism or imperialism to defend the interest of the working class or of the colonized countries. At least twice in my life I have had the experience of being marginalized and excluded by an hegemonic ideology. The first was during the 60s when the Parsonian school gave an elaborate ideological expression to the hegemony of the United States. The second was during the 70s and even early 80s, in France and in Latin America, when structural Marxism was predominant in academic circles and used authoritarian methods to eliminate competitors.

Coming back to purely intellectual orientations, I want to make clear that the various approaches I have just defined are more complementary and contradictory and that each of them should try to reinterprete with its own categories different types of collective behavior. I am surprised to read Professor Gamson's judgment that I am not interested in American studies on social movements. It is easy to check that I refer much more often to American studies than Gamson to European authors and I should be at least credited with a lasting interest for non-French problems and ideas.

3. If I consider now the historical content of my analysis, I can even more easily make clear that, far from being dogmatic, I am aware of the difficulties of defending my interpretation against others. I try to defend the view that we are passing from an industrial society – in which level problems occupy the central place – to a new type of society in which it is possible to identify a new central social conflict. This hypothesis is similar to the assertion of the first socialists in the mid 19th century that the political struggles which had been examplified by the French revolution were being substituted by »the social question«, that is, by labor conflicts. The arguments against such a view today are numerous and strong and most of my work, between 1973 and 1982, has been devoted to the analysis of these new social move-

ments. The results from the series of studies on the student's movement, the anti-nuclear campaign, regionalist's unrest, labor unions, women's lib groups, etc. ... were to a large extent negative for two reasons. First, because some of these collective actions expressed more clearly the crisis either of an institution or of a political ideology than the formation of a new social movement and were rapidly destroyed by internal contradictions. Second, because the 70s were dominated by »gauchisme,« that is, by confusing attempts to express new social and cultural demands in traditional revolutionary marxist vocabulary. In Western European and North-American countries organized action, leaders and ideologies were lagging behind new grassroot protests and innovations. And it is difficult for sociologists to be very much ahead of observable collective action. Nevertheless, we were able to observe, like others, both the growing autonomy of social movements, freeing themselves from the control of political parties and ideologies, and the central role of cultural problems in societies where »cultural industries« play a rapidly growing role, especially in health, education and mass communication.

The method of the sociological intervention was very useful in demonstrating the weakness and confusion of gauchist social and political protest movements based on an unstable mixture of ideas borrowed from the labor and socialist movement with new social and cultural demands. Considering the rather negative conclusions of most of my studies, I cannot understand why I am sometimes accused of discovering social movements everywhere!

As the situation has become more mature in the 90s than in the 60s and 70s, in the future I hope to be able to reformulate hypotheses about new social movements and to identify more clearly new central conflicts.

I am fully aware that the present historical situation is highly unfavorable to the idea of social movements. The dramatic failure of communist and rationalist regimes, and their transformation into totalitarian or despotic regimes, gives much strength to an entire voluntaristic view of social change and to a new rationalist image of social life as a set off market in which individual and collective actors develop a »limited rationality« to adjust themselves in a relatively positive way to an unstable and complex environment. Such a view is very far from the idea of a »central« social conflict and nobody can deny not only that it helps in analyzing many observable processes, but it actually makes obsolete an integrated vision of all forms of social behavior as direct manifestations of pervading class struggle.

4. It is out of the question to pretend that all protest movements or conflicts can be reinterpreted in terms of »grand« social movements. Not only are po-

litical pressures and economic interests widely autonomous, but my friends and I have been more and more interested in the study of what we call anti-social movements, like terrorism, which is a perversion of a social and national movement, or like populist nationalism, which we observe in Poland within and against Solidarnosc, or like the Latin-American guerillas, which are based on the negation of all forms of mass mobilization. There is no reason to believe that all aspects of social life are dominated by a conflict opposing two social categories. No more than to believe that sex life is entirely dominated by romantic love!

It is necessary here to make clear what opposes the notions of class, in a Marxist sense, and social movement. The first one implies the correspondence of an objective category and of a collective actor, of an economic situation and a political action. This is most clearly demonstrated by Marx's or Lukács' theory of class-consciousness, which is not class objectivity but identification of a social actor with natural laws of history. The working class is a natural force whose action manifests the contradiction between production forces and social relations of production. On the contrary, a social movement, in my definition, is a collective action aiming at the implementation of central cultural values against the interest and influence of an enemy which is defined in terms of power relations. A social movement is a combination of social conflict and cultural participation. Between classes there are contradictions, according to authors who belong to this school, while I consider there is both conflict and consensus between social movements.

5. The method of sociological intervention must be fully aware that the possible discovery of a central social movement in a given collective action does not mean at all that this »highest« analytical meaning determines the most important effect of a collective action. In 1976, we reached the conclusion that, in the anti-nuclear movement, there existed an anti-technocratic component which was challenging nuclear power. But we observed that this »highest« meaning of the protest movement was less important, politically and practically, than the crisis of industrial culture which was finding many expressions during this period. It could very well be said that in most cases the highest possible meaning of a collective action does not coincide with its main political and social effects. Exactly like in social-democratic countries, like Sweden or Great Britain, a class-oriented political action did not lead to revolution but to market economy and redistribution by the State of a large part of the national income.

6. The study of social movements has been my main preoccupation during the post-68 period. But I consider this period as an intermediary one. During the first two decades of my activity I was more a social historian than a sociologist. I was fascinated by industrial production and industrial conflicts because I was eager to understand a world in which I was entering and that my own education and humanities had not prepared me to understand. And now, after two more decades devoted to the search for new social movements in Western industrial societies, to the study of social political populist and nationalist action in Latin America, and to anti-totalitarian movements in communist-dominated Eastern Europe, I am more and more interested in a more global reappraisal of our political culture. The historicist viewpoint which identified social movements with economic development and progress in general corresponded to the experience of Western societies whose modernization appeared to be triggered out by the triumph of reason, science, technology, education and mobility of the factors of production. The 20th century, on the contrary, has been dominated by voluntaristic and authoritarian States. In a more peaceful way, Western mass consumption and mass culture refer to cultural and social policies and no longer to natural forces. Social movements are conceived of no longer as allies of rational and natural forces against traditions and privileges, but as forces of resistance against power systems and policies of accelerated and centralized transformations of behavior and institutions. Social movements are less and less »progressive« and more and more critical. While, in backward and authoritarian countries, as we find today in Eastern Europe, social movements can hardly be isolated from a general movement of liberation, in contemporary Western societies and in others they become more tightly linked with moral protest. This transformation is reinforced when ecologist's campaigns demonstrate the absence of parallelism between economic growth and social progress. That leads us back to the idea of natural law. We speak of human rights, but not exactly like we did in the 18th century, because the American and French Declarations of Rights identified man and citizen while today we defend the rights of individuals even against citizen's duties, for example, when we defend the boat people or oppressed minorities. The study of contemporary social movements leads us to abandon a unified, rationalist or progressist view of modernity and to redefine this as a growing tension between the logic of integration of economic or political systems and the defence of personal freedom. Some, like myself, think it necessary to re-introduce the concept of the subject, not in a cartesian or religious sense, but as

the effort of the individual to act as a person, to select, organize and control his individual life against all kinds of pressures. Others, like Habermas, oppose to the instrumentalist view of modernity the idea of intersubjectivity, communicative action and, in more practical terms, democracy. Discussions about social movements are centered around these various ways of rejecting or limiting the old ideals of participation to the progress of reason and social integration. This is the reason why I entered, some years ago, into a new stage of my work which is devoted to a critical study of the idea of modernity and to the definition of social movements as a defence of the subject and his personal freedom against the logic of integration and power of social, political and cultural systems.

7. Passing from a progressivist to a critical, from a political to an ethical view of social movements means abandoning all kinds of social philosophies. The interest of societies is no longer the source of social norms as it was in the 17th and 18th century political philosophies and in more recent functionalist sociology. The study of social change as well as the analysis of processes of integration – or disintegration – are basically independent from the study of social movements. It seems advisable to reject philosophies of history as well as functionalist theories of the social system. The idea of social movement has been too long part of these global theories; it should be used today as an instrument to break their excessive ideological pretentions. The concept of social movement itself must not be defined as a global explanatory principle even if it introduces the ideas of a central social conflict in a given society.

My last remark is that this view, like all others, is both an instrument of analysis and part of a specific culture. In Latin America, social movements are subordinated to political action, while Western European and North American countries experience a growing separation between social movement and political action. In East-European countries, social movements, like Solidarnosc in Poland, tend to be »total movements,« national, social and democratic at the same time. Because I studied the three situations, I am aware of the limitation of theoretical debates which are generally based only on Western European and North American data. The conclusion is that we must recognize that even our most abstract formulations correspond to a low theoretical level because they still heavily depend on specific historical situations and political cultures. Therefore comparative studies remain the most useful instruments for freeing ourselves from ideologies and reaching higher levels of analysis.

Comparing Social Movement Participation in Western Europe and the United States: Problems, Uses, and a Proposal for Synthesis[1]

Sidney Tarrow

When in the late 1960's the institutionalized policies of the postwar decades were challenged by worker, student and generalized discontent, scholarly certitudes were also shattered. From the calm assurance that ideology and militancy were dead, some experts concluded that mass politics had gone too far and that democratic institutions were threatened by hyper-mobilization (Crozier, et. al., 1975). Students of social movements were more cautious, but on both sides of the Atlantic they questioned inherited schemas and proposed new ones, launching two new paradigms – what has been called »resource mobilization« in the United States and »new social movements« in Western Europe.

On the European side, the most obvious casualty was the notion that the working class was a radical social movement's necessary basis and economic benefits its goal (Touraine, 1971). On the American side, the old idea that movement activity was caused by personal rootlessness failed to survive the decade (Oberschall, 1973). For both groups of scholars, the more contentious politics of the late 1960's and early 1970's represented a breath of fresh air for a subject that, for too long, had hovered on the edge of scholarly and political legitimacy.

In this wake of those years, even as it was becoming clear that both the »end of ideology« paradigm and its »crisis of democracy« successor were exaggerated stereotypes, serious research on social movements continued to evolve. For example, despite the vogue of marxist studies in the 1970's in

---

1 This article was first published in 1986 in International Journal of Mass Emergencies and Distaters, 4 (2), Special Issue on Comparative Methods and Research on Collective Behavior and Social Movements, G.T. Marx (ed.).

Europe, simple class models of mobilization would never recover, while in the United States, the idea that social movement participants were rootless alienates never reappeared. The field of social movement research has been permanently – and positively – affected by the movements and conflicts that marked both Western Europe and the United States since the late 1960's.

Thus far, all to the good. However, despite the common origins of the new field of social movement studies in the politics of the 1960's, we find little consensus between European and American scholars on problems, methods or subjects of study. Nor is there clarity on what constitutes a »new« movement and on how it differs from »old« examples of the same phenomenon. Finally, the problem of participation in social movements has been dealt with in different ways on each side of the Atlantic, with a predominant emphasis on the individual in the United States and on movements as a whole in Western Europe. The result, I shall argue, has been a field of study that adds up to the considerably less than the sum of its parts and which – to a result – has not yet had an impact proportional to the remarkable changes it has documented in Western societies.

The first problem to be faced in the comparative analysis of social movements is to understand this disjunction between two research traditions that have emerged differently from similar experiences. In Part One of this paper, I will offer some general observations on the two traditions, and illustrate them with respect to the two major authors – Alain Touraine and Mayer Zald. My second task will be to establish some broad guidelines to facilitate comparison in so diffuse and heterogeneous a field. This I shall attempt to do in Part Two. And the third is to propose a level of analysis that might allow for synthesis between the two major traditions. Based on an interesting and growing convergence among a group of European and American scholars[2], I shall argue for a partial synthesis around an extension of Klandermans' concept of »consensus mobilization« (1986) as a potential way of linking the structural approach of the new social movements school with the more micro-analytical approach of American scholars and those Europeans influenced by them.

---

2 Only as examples, I cite the work of my colleagues on the Council of European Studies Research Planning Group on Social Movement Participation; see Klandermans 1984, 1985 and 1986; Klandermans and Oegema, 1984 and 1985; Kriesi, 1982, 1985a and b and Kriesi, et al., 1985; McAdam 1982, 1983, 1984 and 1985; Melucci, 1980, 1982, 1985a and b and Melucci, et al., 1984; and Snow, 1976 and 1985 and Snow, et al., 1980.

I. The Two Traditions: Social Movement Research in Western Europe and the United States

Alberto Melucci writes:

> In the field of social movements, sociology inherits a legacy of dualism, coming from philosophies of history. Collective action has always been treated (either) as an effect of structural crises or contradictions, or as an expression of shared beliefs and orientations. ... The stress is in the first case on social-economic context, in the second on the role of ideology and values. Either actors are dispossessed of the meanings of their action, or they produce meanings and goals apparently without any constraints (Melucci, 1985c: 2-3).

When we contrast the American »resource mobilization« approach with the European new social movement paradigm we soon see that the European tradition provides bold structural perspectives on the genesis and goals of new social movements while the American one focusses on the alignment of individuals into movements and on individual decisions to participate in their actions. The strength of the first lies in its capacity to detect new cultural contents and new political potential in social forms that are not conventionally political (Offe, 1985); while the contribution of the second is to have linked the motivations for social movement activity to more »normal« forms of social behavior, thereby explaining it in as a rational expression of individual or group interest (Tilly, 1978).

The weakness of each perspective follows from its respective strength. The new social movement tradition predicts action that is occasional and differential from structural trends that are long-term and general; it focusses more on broad historical movements that are difficult to study empirically than on movement organizations with observable boundaries and behaviors; it posits as analytically central concepts like »collective identity« and the »imperatives of everyday life« that are difficult to observe in reality; and it seldom deals with individual level data on either the motivations or activities of movement participants.

The »American« tradition predicts action on the basis of individual, group and contextual variables that ought to provide better explanations than they in fact do; it focusses on social movement organizations to the detriment of the broader historical movements of which they are a part; and it has thus far been unable to link the rich findings it has produced on individual motivations and decision-making to the structural changes that its proponents in principle agree are at the heart of the formation of social movements.

The gap between the two traditions is particularly wide when we turn to the key problem of mobilization. For not only do they start at different levels of analysis – movement and individual; they appear to conceive of individuals, respectively, as passive and active participants with respect to social movements. It has not been easy for scholars in either tradition to deal with the translation of objective structural factors into individual decisions to join in social movement activities. And in few works within either tradition is there a calculus of how particular movement strategies, structures and actions react upon and are influenced by individual decisions to affiliate with or participate in social movements.

Equally important, while in the new social movement tradition the emphasis is on the formation of movements as collective actors, American researchers are more likely to focus on the decisions of individuals to affiliate with already created movements. For the former, individual decisions are reduced to a function of group or ideological formation, while for the latter, group formation is either taken for granted or reduced to the sum of individual decisions. Few writers in either tradition have recognized, as Snow et al. (1984) and Klandermans (1984) have told us, that *both* individual mobilization and movement genesis are important, and cannot be reduced to one another or explained with the same causes.

If there were a typical »new social movement« study[3], it would begin with a movement's emergence or goals and trace them to structural causes either found in the movement's programs or as identified by the observers who, at best, uses empirical data to infer structural causation and, at worst, applies the preformed template of a deductive model to all and sundry movements (see the critique in Roth, 1985). This can provide a suggestive »plausible fit« hypothesis of why movements emerge and of the role of historical events in their emergence, but it fails to verify why individuals choose to affiliate with them when they do and it leaves untouched the *processes* surrounding individual affiliation. Moreover, the approach tends to draw attention to those movements whose emergence can most plausibly be explained by macrostructural models and away from those which seem to be only distantly related to them – which is the case for many recent move-

3 This is, of course, a gross generalization, to which many exceptions could immediately be opposed. It also ignores the work of those European scholars working with individual data, such as the several contributions of Kaase, Klingemann, Marsh and others to Barnes and Kase, 1979, the fine work on Britain by Marsh, 1977, and the recent comparative work of Muller-Rommel, 1985a and b.

ments. Of European scholars associated with the new social movement approach, only Alberto Melucci and his collaborators have tried to devise methodologies fitted to the task of studying collective identity formation between the overly structural European approach and the highly individualistic American one (see, in particular, Melucci, 1980; 1982; 1985a, b and c; and Melucci, et al., 1984).

If there were a typical »American«[4] study, it would focus on a social movement orgnization or survey a group of individuals regarding their orientations and motivations. The structural roots and program of the movements appear mainly as these are perceived by the respondents , but seldom as expressed by cultural changes or as constraints on the type of affiliation or activity available to individuals. As for events that may trigger or constrain activity, these appear only in the background; indeed, the semi-automatic use of survey methods make events and actions somewhat external to the research design, with very few exceptions (see Klandermans, 1984; McAdam, 1984).

To illustrate some of these points, let us take one example each from the American and European traditions – Alain Touraine and Mayer Zald – and briefly contrast them. Neither is entirely »typical,« but both are important theorists, and each represents quite well the differential impact of the 1960's on the two cultures of social movement studies.

In three major theoretical works and a number of case studies,[5] Touraine has focussed since 1968 on the level of broad historic movements, going from there to a structural level of explanation for their appearance, goals and future (1968). Movements are conceived of as action systems (1984), their strategies and ideological production carefully delineated (including their cultural contexts and determinants) but their organization and leadership are dealt with only in passing (1968, 1971), and the motivations of the individuals attracted to them are deduced from their ideological goals and cultural

---

4 Here too, I ignore the many cases of American scholars influenced by European research traditions, and in particular, the path-breaking work of Tilly, 1969, and 1978, Shorter and Tilly, 1974, Tilly, Tilly and Tilly, 1975, Oberschall, 1973, Piven and Cloward, 1977, and my own modest contributions, 1967, 1983.

5 My major sources for this brief review are Touraine, 1968, 1971, 1978 and 1984. I have not considered his collaborative works, for example, with Dubet, Hegedus and Wieviorka, 1978 and 1981, or with Hegedus, Dubet and Wieviorka, 1980. Touraine's most original interpreter and extender is Melucci, 1977, 1982, 1985a, b and c, and Melucci, et al., 1984. His work has been suefully criticized by Amiot, 1980, Minguet, 1980, and Rucht in this volume.

character. The emphasis is on movements as collective actors that are produced by structural change and its cultural context, and on the evolution of fully fledged social movements from lesser phenomena (1978: 21).

In characterizing movements, Touraine deduces three basic principles (1978) – identity, totality and opposition – which has three major implications for the study of social movements: first, it limits the range of »true« movements to relatively few, thus excluding a large number of phenomena that are at the heart of American (and other European) studies; second, it draws attention away from the individual, to the extent that all three of Touraine's principles are collective properties of the movement (Indeed, the individual appears in Touraine's work mainly as the repository of the values implied by the structural trends he has deduced); third, it implies a progression from lower forms of collective behavior to higher ones, with the highest forms of all *the* social movement that can be proven to embody all three principles in their entirety.

Mayer Zald's work (much of it co-authored with either Ash-Garner or McCarthy)[6] represents a highly original application of organization theory to the study of social movements. In fact, Zald's focus is self-consciuosly not movements as a whole – which he defines as »sentiment pools« – but »SMO's«, or social movement organizations. In his work, leaders employ personal and organizational resources to find support for goals that they perceive are likely to gain a popular following. Support is granted, not because prospective followers are opponents of the system, share a collective identity or possess a global ideology, but because they have something to gain and not too much to lose from their affiliation. This down-to-earth notion of movement leadership and affiliation contrasts vividly, not only with the new cultural content and structural causes seen by Touraine and his followers, but also with the previous tradition of American social movement studies.

Zald's resource mobilization approach gives him the possibility of looking pragmatically at leaders' strategic advantages and disadvantages and at the incentives they can offer to prospective followers, but gives him less purchase on the group's ideology or relation to social change. Indeed, where Touraine's model is collective and cultural, Zald's is individualistic and economic, for his predominant intellectual debt is to neo-liberal and economic

6 For the major contributions of Zald and his collaborators to the resource mobilization school, see Zald and Ash, 1966, McCarthy and Zald, 1973, 1977 and Zald and McCarthy, 1979. Attempts to extend Zald's approach are Klandermans, 1984 and Tarrow, 1983. Useful critiques are found in Jenkins, 1983 and McAdam, 1982.

theory, and especially to Mancur Olson (1965). There is little in the way of structural determinants in this work, except in the limited sense that individuals' dispositions to affiliate with movements are affected by the increased leisure time and greater personal resources offered by prosperity. And where Touraine's approach narrows attention to a small number of structurally radicalized groups, Zald's broadens the focus to admit many movements that others might consider far more institutionalized (Jenkins, 1983).

To the extent that these two authors reflect general trends on either side of the Atlantic, it should be obvious why comparison between European and American social movements has been modest until now. First, since the two traditions do not mesh either theoretically or methodologically, many American and European scholars are only dimly aware of one another's work; second, the European emphasis on structure and the American focus on motivations produce data that are difficult to compare, even for those with an ambition to synthesize and a passing knowledge of more than one country; third, neither tradition has been markedly successful in producing comparative *research*[7] – the former because its preferred structural parameters are global and do not predict variations between countries, and the latter because individual motivations and decisions are difficult and expensive subjects to study in more than one political system.

Although comparison is not a magic answer to the problem of any field – least of all one that is a dispersed and changing as the social movement field – given the current gap between the dominant paradigms in the Western European and American branches of this field, comparison may offer a number of aids to better definition, more consistent operationalization and greater synthesis than has been apparent until now. At the very least, I shall argue, comparison will help scholars on both sides of the Atlantic to know whether they are studying examples of the same phenomena, and, if so, to what they can attribute the differences they find.

---

7 For a review of one type of comparative research – on the macro-political correlates of political protest and violence – by a European, but using mainly American sources, see E. Zimmermann, 1980. Comparative work has begun to be produced in abundance in West Germany. In addition, to Muller-Rommel, 1985a and b, see Brand, et al., 1985, Kitschelt, 1984, and Rucht, 1984. From France, see Castells, 1983. From Italy, see Diani and Melucci, 1983 and Statera, 1975. From Great Britain, see Webb, et al. (1983). From the U.S., see Nelkin and Pollak, 1981, Tarrow, 1983 and Tilly, Tilly and Tilly, 1975. I am not familiar with scholars from Scandinavia or the smaller European democracies carrying out comparative social movement research.

II. Comparing Social Movements: Uses, Examples, Problems

A rapid survey of English language texts in comparative politics turns up a remarkable finding: in this field few of the authors surveyed give more than passing attention to either social or political movements. The indices of seven popular texts in comparative politics were scanned for the following entries: »anomic groups,« »civil strife,« »collective action,« »dissent,« »movements,« »protest,« »revolution,« »riots,« »social movements,« »terrorism,«, and »violence.« The least hospitable to treatment of social movements was S.E. Finer's *Comparative Government* (1970), with no index references to these concepts; and the most hospitable was Almond and Powell's *Comparative Politics: System, Process and Politics* (1978, with 21 pages.[8] The term »social movement« itself turned up in none of the seven indices, while the most frequent term – »revolution« – was found in six out seven of the texts.[8]

Considerations of space force me to pass over this remarkable omission in silence. In this section, I will briefly review some of the advantages of comparison for social movement studies; second, I will give some examples of areas in which comparative research could help to clarify problems of analysis or interpretation; and, third, I will outline some particularly thorny problems that students of comparative social movements should expect to encounter.

A. Uses

First, comparison can be a corrective to the theoretically sweeping but generally narrowly tested structural models that have dominated much of the field until now. Social movements, being unusual phenomena, produce actions that may be classified as rare events. As a result, unlike other fields of sociology or political science, they have encouraged one-variable explana-

8 Comparative sociology texts have not been scanned in detail. They give the impression of being more likely to deal with topics like comparative social stratification than social movements or political protest. For example, see Dogan and Pelassy, 1981, Marsh, 1967, and Vallier, 1971. The comparative politics texts scanned were Almond and Powell, 1978, Bertsch, Clark and Wood, 1978, Blondel, 1969, Finer, 1970, Hitchner and Levine, 1967, Irish and Frank, 1978, and Merkl, 1977.

tions and structural paradigms. Comparison can help to correct this weakness by revealing that similar outcomes are frequently accompanied by partially or wholly different conditions, thereby forcing the analyst to adopt a more complicated or better specified model.

Second, comparison can serve as a check upon premature closure on what seems to the observer as »obvious« causal patterns that have emerged from narrowly drawn observations on individuals and groups in the same political system. When analysis of the same movement or behavior in another system shows little relationship between familiarly-coupled variables, the analyst is forced to specify the posited relationship better or translate it into more general terms that will cover the variety of conditions with which it is associated in different countries.

Third, comparison can sensitize observers to theoretical possibilities of social movements even when these are not evident on their home ground. For example, it is almost the only way to delimit the potential range of participation in social movements among groups at different »distances« from the movement's epicenter. This is important because social movements – unlike formal organizations – frequently lack observable boundaries.[9] If movement M attracts support from social group G in country a, but not in country b, then the range of attraction of each can be related to features of social structure, movement strategy or political opportunity structure. If we only study the movement in country b but not in country a, we may never know that its non-appeal to group G in the former is a theoretically interesting issue.

Fourth, comparison can help us to overcome the dilemma that the countries that produce the most research on social movement organizations may not be the ones in which these movements are most important or most typical. A good example is the large number of studies on the American Communist party that were done from the 1930's on. An observer from Mars in the 21st century might be forgiven for thinking that the CP-USA was a major force in American society during this period.[10] Comparison at least forces us

---

9 This is a major constraint on the utility of organizational approaches to social movements: the formal organizations on which they concentrate are often only the visible summit of an often-hidden iceberg of participants or supporters.

10 Gabriel Almond's *The Appeals of Communism*, 1954, was one of the few to systematically compare the American party to others, thereby underscoring its peculiarity in relation to European communist parties with a mass base.

to look at other countries in which similar phenomena can be found and may take a different shape.

Fifth, comparing similar movements across national lines can sensitize us to the variety of outcomes that movements enjoy or suffer under different conditions, thereby cautioning us against gross generalizations about the Iron Law of Oligarchy or the »inevitable« cooptation of revolutionary movements. Take the question of repression; while it is a constant of state response to social movements, its forms, its degree and whether it is accompanied by reform and accomodation will vary greatly between different systems. Given the vagaries with which outcomes can be causally linked to events, comparison is probably the only method that can give us a sense of balance about how political systems respond to social movements.

Sixth, comparison brings out the major factor that sociologists and social psychologists normally ignore – political institutions and their effects on the opportunities, constraints and channelling or social movement organization, forms of action and outcomes (Tilly, 1978). When similar sectors of social movement activity are compared in political systems with different institutional arrangements, the arrangements themselves are frequently found to correspond to differences in style, strategy or outcomes that individual or group variables within systems frequently fail to explain. The comparison of similar organizations, movements or sectors across national boundaries is probably the most fruitful way of detecting the influence of politics on collective action.

Finally, especially comparison across time can provide a healthy does of realism – or add empirical backing – to claims that »new« social movements are fundamentally different than what has come before. Pizzorno (1978) has written sensibly about strike waves that unless we compare them to past peaks of collective action, we are in danger of concluding that the revolution is upon us each time there is an increase in the magnitude of collective action.

The same is true of the *forms* that collective action takes. Tilly (1978), who has done more than anyone to reconstruct past repertoires of collective action, finds that little has been added to our basic repertoire since the strike become widespread in the 19th century. The Tillys' (1975) work shows that only a systematic comparison between past and present behavior of social movements can put into balance the importance of the »new« and the »old« in the new social movements.

B. Examples

Structural models

In the past, many sweepingly structural explanations of social movements were based upon reductive notions of mass psychology, social dislocation, or the mode of production, with little systematic attempt to link actual movements to their structural presuppositions in more than a metaphorical way. The findings of the last 15 years of research into new social movements, show that there was for a time the same danger. Many of the sudies were either generic or case study in method, non-comparative in scope and merely illustrated in one case or another the structural theories of post-industrial society that inspired them. With only a few exceptions, the latter failed to even define in what the »newness« of new social movements consisted, making few explicit comparisons between the supposed new movements and others that were now presumably »old.«[11] As Roth writes, the theories that have inspired many studies »prove to be especially inadequate when faced by the question of the ›newness‹ of new social movements. On the assumption of a coming postindustrial society, societal analysis was often hastily squeezed into some spectacular features that were empirically inconclusive ... research on new social movements must be embedded in the context of macrosocietal analysis – but without reductionism« (1985).

The only way to demonstrate the newness of new social movements and its relation to structural change would be to compare similar movements to different societies, beginning with their structural development and contradictions and the empirical reflections of the latter in social movement organizations and behavior. Recently some students, like Brand, et al. (1985), Kitschelt (1984) and Rucht (1984), have been attempting to compare similar movements in different industrial countries, starting from general structural premises but adding comparative variables like economic modernization (Rucht) and features of the institutional structure (Kitschelt) to the fundamental changes posited in advanced capitalist societies. Others, like Kriesi (1985), trace structural trends to career prospects for different generations,

11 For exceptions, see Melucci, 1980, Nedelmann, 1984 and Offe, 1983. The latter, however, while by far the most detailed deliniation of »new« and »old«, presents so dichotomized a vision that one wonders how so much of the »old« has survived into the 1980's, given the intractable nature of the new politics he describes. He no doubt will present more detailed empirical support for this vision in forthcoming work.

and thence to differential motivations for participation in social movements. In looking at these recent studies, one has a positive impression of increasing concreteness, greater comparative consciousness (if not actual comparative research design) and a shift towards the central theoretical question of how movements translate structural potential into mobilization.

Individualistic and group models

Particularly in the United States, we have many studies in which individual motivation or group environment provide plausible explanations for movement outcomes. But few researchers in this tradition attempt to combine, or even compare, individual and structural explanations of the disposition to participate in social movements.

An important problem in doing so is the absence of sufficient variance within systems in structural variables to enable us to examine the data in ways that can plausibly relate structural to motivational explanations. Recall the debates in the 1970's about the correlates of American black riot behavior.[12] Individualistic explanations like deprivation and group explanations like the relative size of the black population explained very little in the variance in actual riot outcomes city by city. With the exception of umbrella-like variables like »region«, structural factors in the American system explained little variance either. An important reason why is that, for structural variables to explain outcomes, there has to be significant variance in their range, something that may not have been the case in the ghettos of the 1960's. Only cross-national analysis of mass rioting by suppressed minority populations in different cities would have produced an adequate test of the structural models of urban rioting that proved unconvincing when applied to the American system alone.

Steps are being taken to move towards more adequate structural explanations of social movement activity from the starting point of the individual. Klandermans (1984) has innovated with a panel study of workers' propensity to strike over time, tracking changes in willingness to participate according to changing risk/reward incentives and their perceptions of the likelihood of others' participating and of achieving success. Della Porta and Mattina (1985), though not employing individual data, have ingeniously linked the

---

12 Not at all an expert in this field, I am guided mainly by the Spilerman, 1970, 1972 and Mazur, 1972, debate.

motivations of those who join Basque extremist groups to the structure and popular culture of the region. McAdam (1984), using individual questionnaire data, has compared attitudinal and structural explanations of participation in a high risk activity in the American civil rights movement. Tarrow (1989) using protest events data in Italy, has related variations in participation to variations in both political and economic structure. Overall, one has the impression that some empirical researchers coming from the »American« tradition are moving cautiously towards the more structural perspectives of the »new social movement« school.

The range of attraction problem

In a recent statement (1984), Tilly regards social movements as virtually equivalent to the interaction between insurgent populations and authorities – albeit one which may continue over a long period. In contrast, many scholars regard movement involvement more narrowly – as something that is virtually coterminous with membership in movement organizations, which risks excluding many who participate from outside these organizations.

Herein lies a fundamental barrier to developing an integrated social movement field. Students of new social movements have shown that conventional membership in conventional organizations is not chracteristic of many of the movements they study (Melucci, 1985b). But organizations' activities frequently stimulate the activation of those outside of their boundaries (Klandermans, 1986). The only reasonable solution, it seems to me, is to focus attention on both organization members and external participants in social movement activity, leaving as an empirical question the relative magnitude, the importance, and the relationship between the two. Using comparative analysis, this would draw attention to the factors which may explain a greater or less great range of attraction of social movement organizations.

For example, although the events of May 1968 practically shut down the French economy, their solution in June of that year and in the following devaluation essentially ended the French cycle of protest (Salvati and Gigliobianco, 1981). In contrast, though it never reached such a peak of conflict as in France, the Italian Hot Autumn was a »creeping May«, that continued well into the 1970's. What explains the different range and length of attraction of the two movements? Only a comparison of movement organizational strategies, individual motivations and calculations, and the structural development of the two systems and their internal conflict structures can explain the longer attraction of the Italian movement or the sharper peak of the French one (Tarrow, 1985).

Accidents of birth

We do not always study movements as a direct function of their importance or frequency in a system. Government grants, the attractions or fears of a movement, or intellectual and ideological traditions appear to be equally important. When we look at the large body of research on new social movements, it appears that much of it comes from the more advanced countries of northern or central Europe. But does this mean that the F.R.G. has produced more new social movements than Italy, for example? Or that West Germans, with a narrower party system, produce more research on the subject than Italians, who are possessed with their party system to the exclusion of studying almost all other actors or institutions?

In examining the resource mobilization paradigm, we see one possible effect of such accidents of birth. Designed in a period of affluence and expanding political resources in the United States, the picture it drew of social movement activity was rather a docile and institutionalized one (Jenkins, 1983; McAdam, 1982). As a result, concepts like »entrepreneurship« – which Zald clearly intended to mean *moral*, and not profit-seeking entrepreneurship – tended to take on a merchandizing quality. The same theory might have taken on a different coloring.

Comparative work between similar movements in different countries could put to the test whether the »merchandizing« elements in American social movement organizations hold outside of the United States. Comparison could also put to the test one of Zald's most controversal findings – that the increase in social movement activity he saw was in part the result of a more generous governmental and Foundation grant environment, for this was not evident in Western Europe.

Recently, resource mobilization concepts have begun to be applied to European situations, for example by Klandermans (1984), and Tarrow (1983 and 1985). Of work in progress, perhaps the most promising is della Porta's attempt to study the organizational resources mobilized by Italy's leftwing terrorist organizations (1985a). The application of resource mobilization concepts to more aggressive, more ideological and more risk-taking forms of social movement activity will allow us to test the theory and either extend its boundaries or restrict them with greater confidence to the area of its birth.

Movements and Outcomes

The most recurrent model in the social movement field has been the »career« model which sees movements as progressing internally from mass movement to bureaucratic organization and externally from insurgency to incorporation. But both comparative and historical analysis suggest that movements tend to arise under certain *systemic* conditions, appearing in large numbers during cycles of protest or crises and dying out or becoming senescent during periods of quiescence (Tarrow, 1983).

The fact that large numbers of movements appear during periods of unrest suggest that it may be the conditions of national politics and not factors internal to social movement organizations that drive their evolution and outcomes (Tilly, 1984). Therefore, it seems to follow that only the comparative analysis of social movements within and between cycles of mobilization can provide clues as to the conditions in which bureaucratization and or incorporation will take place.

Tilly (described in 1978), in a major project on English social protest, is assembling data on over 6,000 contentious events. Tarrow (1989) in a partial replication of Tilly's method, has collected data on over 5,000 Italian protest events and strikes for the period 1966-73. Olzak (1985), using similar methods, is amassing a unique dataset on American ethnic conflicts. These projects, which emphasize the action phases of protest events and social conflicts, have yet to demonstrate that they can chart the rise and fall of social movement organizations across time and space. Their major advantage lies in providing access to the changing repertory of protest and catalogues of the developing demands of the actors involved and their relation to each other over time. Through time series and cross sectional analysis of these data, systematic understanding of the dynamic of protest movements within and between broad historic cycles may soon be possible.

Politics and Social Movements

I have argued elsewhere (1983) for the insertion of the political opportunity structure into social movement studies. What this has to do with the decision to participate should be fairly obvious. Not only cycles of mobilization but variables associated with the presence or absence of influential allies, with openness of access to political institutions, and with the divisions within or unity of elites appear to affect people's willingness to participate in social movement activity (Ibid., Part. 3).

Resource mobilization theorists have been more sympathetic to this idea than »new social movement« theorists. Once assuming that resources to be mobilized determine the shape and degree of participation, it is a short and logical step to the conclusion that the political system can provide such resources. But resource mobilization theorists have been slower to conceptualize exactly how politics can fit into their schemes. Comparison can provide a »handle« on this problem by showing the political institutional arrangements in which participation is stimulated as opposed to where they are not. Kitschelt (1984) appears to be following such a strategy implicitly in his comparative work on environmental movements in four countries.

New social movement theorists have been somewhat less interested in specifying to the influence of politics on participation decisions. Perhaps because many of the movements they study are explicit reactions against the »old« politics (Offe, 1983; Berger, 1971), they have rather emphasized the social structural and cultural sources of participation. Comparison between countries with strong and weak party systems or between populations with high and low partisan identification would better help to demonstrate the non-political nature of the new social phenomena they study than repeated reassertions of their non-political character.

»New« and »old« in social movements

Though I have from time to time expressed scepticism in this essay at some of the more far-reaching claims of the new social movement school, one accomplishment deserves emphasis and approval: the array of new methods and approaches that have entered the field from this direction. American work has relied too heavily on the survey instrument to capture the processes inherent in group formation and individual affiliation. Kriesi (1985a) found that this type of instrumental has a precise (and negative) ideological connotation to the subjects of social movement research and is most likely to be rejected by them. Some American researchers, such as Snow (1976), have enriched our knowledge of religious movements through participant-observations, but this is a rarity in the United States.

The collective focus and cultural change emphasis of the new social movement tradition has led to greater methodological innovation. Touraine (1978) and his school have developed a method of »sociological intervention« that goes far – some might say too far (Amiot, 1980; Minguet, 1980) – towards bridging the gap between researchers and their subjects. The work of Melucci and his group (1984), though intervening less in the group's existence, perhaps goes further towards tapping its internal processes and dynamic. Kriesi (1985a) argues persuasively for »direct access« methods. Finally, methods of »life history« analysis, originally created to study the lives of »little people«, are being adapted by researchers associated with the Carlo Cattaneo Institute of Bologna on former Italian terrorists (della Porta, 1985b), and by Luisa Passerini on former participants in the Italian student movement.

But there is this danger: that unless they can be applied systematically to both new *and* old movements, methods which bring collective identities in new social movements may be self-reifying. For if they demonstrate »newness« in one case, and fail to investigate it in the other, we will not understand in precisely what the »newness« of the new social movements consists and we may be destined to rediscover a »new« politics every time a new issue or a new way of packaging it appears on the agenda.

C. Problems

Many problems of studying social movements have been touched on in previous sections of this essay. Here I would simply like to outline three which seem to me potential dangers in inhibiting successful comparative research on participation in social movements between Western Europe and the United States: the problems of the dispersed nature of the field, that of the varying costs and risks of social movement activity, and that of relating information on groups and organizations to data on movement cycles.

The dispersed nature of the field

Analysts have always considered a tremendous variety of phenomena to be social movements. Comparative analysis increases this potential range, especially when students from different areas attempt to communicate using different definitions and parameters of social movement activity. In making comparisons, we quickly become aware that the sectoral goals of the movement can have a strong impact on its organization, its strategy, and its motivational structure. Thus we cannot simply compare movements across countries; we must first ask what the movement is for, and make sure we are not comparing movements whose sectoral goals make for an entirely different universe of motivations.

Different definitions of social movements make the problem still more complex. For Touraine, a social movement must involve a collective identity, a desire for rupture and a totalizing ideology (1978); for McCarthy and Zald, virtually all new organizations which challenge some aspect of public policy would fit into the category of SMO (1977); for Tilly, it is only challenging groups intent on entry into the polity that engage in social movement-like collective action (1978); while I have used a hybrid definition involving: 1) leaders seeking policy changes or institutional access; 2) who claim to represent groups outside the polity; 3) and employ disruptive direct action; 4) against authorities or power holders in public or private institutions (1983).

Each definition produces a different population of groups and a different set of behaviors that are relevant, all of which makes it tremendously difficult to translate findings from one research tradition or country to another. For example, American public interest groups which specialize in lobbing cannot easily be compared to German environmental groups using direct action. There is no *a priori* reason to exclude either type of group, but a major effort at classification and preliminary comparison will be necessary before a systematic comparative analysis is undertaken.

The costs and risks of insurgency

Most students would agree that social movements operate in some way outside the routine political institutions and boundaries which define the acceptable limits of legitimate political activity. But such institutions and boundaries differ broadly in ways that make it difficult to define *a priori* what will be a social movement activity and what will not. It follows that the decision to participate in social movement activities will vary according to these rules of the game, as perceived by potential participants.

The problems that this raises are obvious. A strike may be illegitimate in an authoritarian system; it may test the boundaries of legitimacy in a semi-authoritarian one and it may be wholly acceptable in a liberal democracy. While strikes can certainly be compared between these three types of systems, it is not at all clear that strikers make the same kind of decision when they agree to go out on strike in each one. Even within liberal democracies, small changes can be crucial in affecting the risks and costs of joining in collective action; for example, the costs and risks of striking were reduced tremendously in the United States after the passage of thew NLRB (Piven and Cloward, 1977). We must at least take care to understand the institutional environment of people's decision to participate before comparing them in different societies or periods.

Organizations, Groups and Movements

I observed earlier that the focus of much European research is the movement – considering the latter as all those individuals who are emotionally and behaviorally involved in disruptive direct action against institutions or elites – while the subject of much American research is the movement organization. These contrasting foci are probably inevitable as long as European and American scholars continue to begin with different precepts of what is important. But since this contributes heavily to the current non-cumulative and non-comparable nature of the field, we should at least be aware that the findings of each school are not so much contradictory as complementary, since their proponents may be trying to explain or explore different things.

It may however, be possible to go somewhat further in the direction of synthesis than these remarks would suggest. For between the structural approach of the European school and the individualistic approach of the American one there is an intermediate area of social movement research that some scholars are beginning to explore and which has the potential to link the two traditions. I refer to the social, cultural and ideological environment in which social movemens are formed. In the final section of this paper, I will argue that the most fruitful direction for research of a comparative and a comparable nature to be done in both Western Europe and the United States at the present time lies in this intermediate area between structure and action.

III. Transforming Structure into Action: Consensus Mobilization and Social Movements

A hypothetical chain of causation for social movement participation that can help us in ordering groups, organizations and movements in a theoretical coherent way has been offered by Klandermans (1986):

Participation in social movements is something that takes place in the context of the formation of mobilization potentials, the formation and activation of recruitment networks and the arousing of the motivation to participate. It is important to distinguish these processes because they require very different activities of social movement organizations and different theories are needed to analyze them.

I will pick up on an extend Klandermans' threefold phase model and propose it as the skeleton for a framework within which to compare social movement participation in different countries. The effort may also yield a possible linkage between the structural approach of the new social movement school and the motivational one of the »American« one. To begin with definitions:[13]

By the *formation of mobilization potentials* Klandermans means the structural factors which produce the groups and individuals with a predisposition towards social movement participation. These factors, »resulting from developments in postindustrial societies, deprivations and aspirations from among the societal groups who most immediately experience their unfavorable consequences and among groups which are extra-sensitive because of the development of post-material values,« (ibid.) are the same variables that students of new social movements have emphasized. I believe that they constitute the objective and necessary – but far from sufficient – starting point from which to begin to understand decisions to participate in social movement activity.

By *arousal of the motivation to participate*, I intend what Klandermans has called (1984) »action mobilization« – that is, the activation of structurally determined potentials into action, either in the form of joining social movement organizations or participation in their activities. This is what the American tradition has emphasized, »with a great deal of attention to the mobilization of resources ... to the costs and benefits of participation and to the factors that influence them, but no attention at all to the formation of mobilization potentials movements draw from in mobilization campaigns.« (ibid.) Action mobilization is the endpoint of decisions to participate, but it

13 In the section that follows, I have tried to interpret the discussions of the workshop of the CES Research Planning Group on participation in social movements, held at Cornell University in August, 1985. I am most in debt to P.G. Klandermans' contribution (1984 and 1986), but also try to draw upon the papers presented by Hanspeter Kriesi, 1985b, Doug McAdam, 1985, Alberto Melucci, 1985b and David Snow, 1985, and on the discussions at the workshop. I wish to emphasize that the inferences made in the remainder of this paper are mine alone, and do not commit the other members of the planning group.

is not possible to understand without analyzing prior processes that are missing in much of existing American research.

What is mainly missing between these two foci is *The formation and activation of recruitment networks* – the »how« of social movement participation. I will define this area provisionally as the creation of networks, arenas and mentalities in which predispositions favorable to action mobilization are formed – where what Klandermans (1984) has called »consensus mobilization occurs.« It is this as-yet badly-defined, shifting and unformed area that I believe has the greatest potential for linking the two main European and American traditions of social movement research. No one has pioneered in this area more than Melucci, whose work on Milanese social movement networks has shown how empirical research can find a just milieu between actors »dispossessed« of their meanings through too-structural an approach, and the pure goals and motivations found in a too-individualistic approach, in Melucci's words 1985c:3).

Consensus mobilization is intended by Klandermans to describe the creation of a reservoir of sentiment pools by a social movement organization to draw upon eventually when campaigns begin. But it actually is part of a set of processus which – while responsive to both structural preconditions and mobilization campaigns – cannot be reduced to either one or the other and obliges us to take account of cultural trends, community and social networks and ideological processus within individuals and groups in order to understand how structural potentials are translated into decisions to participate. Although no thorough inventory of research and concepts with possible relevance to this intermediate area has yet been accomplished, the following examples may make more concrete what its boundaries may be and some of the problems encountered in defining them:

– Among the cultural trends often cited as having relevance to consensus mobilization is the concept of the »formation of new collective identities« which Melucci (1982) has seen as the translation of new structural contradictions into new solidarities. As Melucci explains it, collective identity »is nothing else than the shared definitions of the field of opportunities and constraints offered to collective action« (1985c).

Scholars using the concept of collective identity have not always been crystal clear in showing how structural trends translate into new collective identities. Nor has the term been used univocally or unambiguously by all its proponents. A key question is whether the concept helps to understand collective action that would not otherwise be explicable with more conventional concepts (for example, interest). Another is whether the solidarities that unite people over a particular issue or campaign continue to unify them once that issue is past. A third is how collective identities are formed – objectively, as seems to be Pizzorno's conception (1978) or »negociated«, as Melucci feels. If these problems can be clarified or overcome, the concept of collective identity may prove to be a key component of consensus mobilization.

– Community and social group network processes with implications for action mobilization have been studied by McAdam (1984 and 1985) and Snow, et al. (1984). In different ways, each writer has shown how the formation of networks broader than, and prior to, social movement participation is highly relevant to the capacities of social movements to mobilize people into action. Recently, Brand (1985, cited in Roth, 1985) has developed the concept of »scenes« in the larger West German cities, in which a movement culture is sustained by social networks.

The creation and reproduction of such movement surroundings are themselves interesting for empirical analysis, beyond the extent to which they provide a recruitment reservoir for movement organizers (Melucci, 1985c: 10). But there is a danger if the concept of »movement networks« replaces the traditional concept of movement organizations altogether as our focus of attention, leaving us with an »area« of socialization, negotiation and convergence whose empirical status or implications for social action are not at all clear. We should not underestimate the capacity of movement organizations – however their tutelage may be rejected by the members of new movement networks – to stimulate the latter into existence and act as a point of reference, if only of a negative sort.

– Finally, the »frame alignment« has been identified as a key internal process by Snow (1985), in which individuals re-interpret facts and relationships in ways which prepare the groundwork for their subsequent action mobilization. This is close to what Piven and Cloward (1977) mean when they discuss the concept of »transvaluation« and to Melucci's notion of »alternative codes« (1984). Snow's innovation is to use the concept of frame alignment to link individual motivations to political and social situations in which inherited frames of reference may be transformed, adapted or simply appropriated by leaders of social movements.

At this stage, we still need to know more about how frame alignment processes relate causally to decisions to participate. There is at least some evidence that they may follow, rather then precede, the first stages of participation in collective action. This is not just a traditional chicken-and-egg dilemma, but a problem of the causal relation between action and its rationalization. For example, della Porta (1985) has observed that Italian terrorists frequently appear not to have explicitly »decided« to engage in clandestine violent activity, so much as to have been led to it imperceptably through the consequences of previous actions.

These examples are put forward with no pretence that may are either exhaustive or proven, but to suggest how the formation of networks and of individual ideological processes may contribute to action mobilization through the creation of areas of consensus for action that go well beyond the preconditions for social movements found in objective structural trends.

The advantages of conceiving of consensus mobilization as a distinct analytical stage in the process of decisions to participate in social movement activity should be fairly obvious. First, it links the impersonal and largely invisible structural factors that are said to produce the groups and cleavages that lie behind social and political conflict to observable collective action. Second, it posits a plausible (and observable) role for group processes between the formation of mobilization potentials and action mobilization. And third, it makes it possible to apply theoretical concepts to their most appropriate level of analysis: structural theories to the formation of mobilization potentials, group, organizational or cultural diffusion theories to consensus mobilization, and motivational theories to action mobilization.

At this early stage, several questions still need to be raised about the concept of consensus mobilization and its analytical status and implications for social movements studies:

First, can consensus mobilization occur in the absence of a particular SMO able to take advantage of it, or at least (and here Melucci's work has much to teach) in the absence of the kind of SMO that can practically »use« such mobilization? Klandermans rightly argues that movement organizations themselves engage in consensus mobilization; the questions is whether they must do so for the process to begin, or whether it can be triggered by less intentional processes.

For example, the »punk« phenomenon that swept Europe in the last few years revealed many of the attributes of collective identity, social networks and frame realignment described above. But in the absence of an SMO interested in it, Punk appears to have ended in the marketplace, even in those countries – like Britain – in which it had a radical potential. If consensus mobilization occurs in the absence of concrete organizations to stimulate it, then the need is for anthropological studies of groups, communities and age cohorts, rather than of organizations, issues and movements.

Second, can consensus mobilization be stimulated by groups or organizations that are not its ultimate beneficiaries but which have other purposes or natures? One thinks of the role of the Black churches in stimulating the Civil Rights movement in the American South (Morris, 1981), or of the role of European unions earlier in the century as transmission belts for leftwing parties or movements. If such a process occurs, we must look beyond the mobilization campaigns of particular SMO's at the entire political opportunity structure of a social movement in order to understand how consensus mobilization occurs.

Indeed, as soon as we add a temporal dimension, the process may become even more complicated, for action mobilization of a particular group during an earlier period may become the basis for consensus mobilization that benefits another at a later time. For example, the Italian Communist party has often bewailed the fact that the terrorists of the 1970's were its »unwanted children« – e.g., a generation stimulated into political action by the PCI or its affiliates but unable to find in the party a satisfying outlet for their energies or ideologies.

Third, the logic of dividing analysis of decisions to participate into separate analytical phases – the formation of mobilization potentials, consensus mobilization and action mobilization – cuts directly across the grain of the dominant mode of social movement studies: e.g. studies of individual movements, organizations and policy issues. For once we posit that consensus mobilization can occur in at least partial independence of the particular SMO or issue area that it will ultimately benefit, it becomes clear that the entire process may not be issue-or even group-specific. In this case, the future participants may not even be recognizable empirically as such unless we are prepared to follow them historically through their own socialization, recruitment and political action. This is not impossible to accomplish, but the inherited traditions and methodologies of social movements studies, which on the one hand are based largely on individual survey data, and on the other on organizational case studies, will need to be seriously modified in order to carry out this task.

IV. Conclusion

What is certainly clear is that, in order to understand how successful social movement organizations are in tapping the potential for mobilization in the structural trends and cleavages of advanced industrial society, we will have to analyze the processes which produce consensus mobilization within social networks, new cultural contexts and individuals' norms and values and link these to both the structural trends and the actions that they supposedly produce.

In this way, we may be able to build bridges between the two dominant traditions of social movement research in Western Europe and the United States, so as to better understand the relationship between »new« and »old« social movements and better connect the far-reaching structural changes underway in western societies to the broad waves of collective action that have marked these societies since the 1960's.

The time is now ripe for such a re-examination. Although the dust has long settled on the first wave of the cycle of protest that began in the 1960's, the success of the Greens and the partial success of the European disarmament movement, the continuation of pockets of terrorism and the reappearance of a mass student movement in Italy and of minority rioting in Britain in the 1980s all point to the fact that the advanced democracies of North America and Western Europe have not returned to the quiescent politics of the 1950's, nor are they likely to in the predictable future. The fact that they are still functioning democracies after twenty years of economic and social change, institutional instability and turbulent mass politics makes more compelling a concerted attempt to understand the translation of structure into action.

Bibliography

Almond, G. (1954): *The Appeals of Communism.* Princeton: Princeton U. Press.

Almond, G.; G. Bingham Powell (1978): *Comparative Politics: System, Process and Politics.* Boston: Little, Brown.

Amiot, M. (1980): »L'intervention sociologique, la science et la prophétie,« in: *Sociologie du Travail* (4): 415-424.

Barnes, S.; Kaase, H. (eds.). (1979): *Political Action: Mass Participation in Five Western Democracies*, Beverly Hills and London: Sage Publications.

Bertsch, G.; Clark, R.P.; Wood, D.M. (1978): *Comparative Political Systems: Power and Policy in Three Worlds.* New York: Wiley.

Blondel, J. (1969): *An Introduction to Comparative Government.* London: Weidenfeld and Nicholson.

Brand, K. (1982): *Neue soziale Bewegungen. Entstehung, Funktion und Perspektiven neuer Protestpotentiale.* Opladen: Westdeutscher Verlag.

– (ed.). (1985): *Neue Soziale Bewegungen in Westeuropa und den USA. Ein internationaler Vergleich.* Frankfurt, N.Y.: Campus.

Castells, M. (1983): *The City and the Grassroots.* Berkeley, Los Angeles: U. of California Press.

Crozier, M.; Huntington, S.; Watunaki, J. (eds.). (1975): *The Crisis of Democracy. Report on the Governability of Democracies.* New York: NYU Press.

Della Porta, D. (1981): Théories et méthodes dans la sociologie des mouvements collectifs (Mémoire à l'Ecole des Hautes Etudes en Sciences Sociales, Paris).

– (1985a): »Left-wing political violence in Italy during the 1970's: The formation of terrorist organizations«, delivered to the IPSA Congress, Paris, August.

– (1985b): »Life histories and collective movements: A technique for the analysis of collective movements,« paper delivered to the International Workshop on New Social Movements, Bonn, August.

Della Porta, D.; Mattina, L. (1985): »Political cycles and ethnic mobilization: The Basque Case,« paper delivered to the International Political Science Association meetings, Paris, August.

Dogan, M.; Pelassy, D. (1982): *Sociologie politique comparative: Problèmes et Perspectives.* Paris: Economica.

Donati, P. (1984): »Organization between movement and institutions,« in: *Social Science Information* (4/5): 837-859.

Finer, E. (1970): *Comparative Government.* London: Penguin.

Hitchner, D.; Levine, J. (1967): *Comparative Government and Polities.* New York: Harper and Row.

Inglehart, R. (1970): *The Silent Revolution.* Princeton: Princeton U. Press.

Irish, M.; Frank, E. (1978): *Introduction to Comparative Politics, 2nd ed.* Englewood Cliffs: Princeton Hall.

Jenkins, J. (1983): »Resource mobilization theory and the study of social movements,« in: *Annual Review of Sociology,* 9: 527-553.

Kitschelt, H. (1984): »Protest strategies and policy impacts of social movements,« unpublished paper.

Klandermans, P.G. (1984): »Mobilization and Participation: A social psychological expansion of resource mobilization theory,« *American Sociological Review* 49 (10): 583-60.

– (1985): »Unionists, Feminists, Pacifists: Comparisons of Organization, Mobilization and Participation, ASA paper, Washington, D.C., August.

– (1986): »New social movements and resource mobilization: The European and American Approach,« in: *Journal of Mass Emergencies and Disasters,* 4(2): 13-39.

Klandermans, P.G.; Oegema, D. (1984): »Mobilizing for peace; the 1983 peace demonstration in the Hague,« ASA paper, San Antonio, Texas, August.

– (1985): »Campaigning for a nuclear freeze and local government in the Netherlands, ASA paper, Washington DC, August.
Kriesi, H. (1982): *AKW-Gegner in der Schweiz*. Diessenhofen: Verlag Ruegger.
– (1985a): »The rebellion of the research objects of social research,« unpublished paper prepared for the workshop on the analysis of social movements, Bonn, August.
– (1985b): »Structural determinants of latent political potentials: Cycles of protest and cyles of protest generations,« paper presented to the CES Research Planning Group Workshop on Participation in: Social Movements, Ithaca, New York, August.
– (ed.) (1985): *Bewegungen in der Schweizer Politik*. Frankfurt: Campus.
Lange, P.; Ercole, E.; Tarrow, S. (1985): »Phases of Mobilization: Social movements, generational recruitment and attitudes to dissent in a sample of Italian Communist activists,« unpublished paper.
Marsh, A. (1977): *Protest and Political Consciousness*. Beverly Hills and London: Sage Publications.
Marsh, R. (1967): *Comparative Sociology: A codification of cross-societal analysis*. New York: Harcourt, Brace.
Marx, G.; Wood, J. (1975): »Strands of Theory and Research in Collective Behavior,« in: *Annual Review of Sociology*, 1: 363-428.
Mazur, A. (1972): »The causes of black riots«, *American Sociological Review* 37: 490-492.
McAdam, D. (1982): *The political process and the development of black isurgency*. Chicago: U. of Chicago Press.
– (1983): »Tactical innovation and the pace of insurgency«, *American Sociological Review* 48: 735-54.
– (1984): »Structural vs. Attitudinal Factors in Social Movement Recruitment,« presented to the annual meeting of the ASA, San Antonio, August.
– (1985): »Macropolitical political processes and individual activism: building micro-macro bridges,« paper presented to the CES Research Planning Group workshop on participation in social movements, Ithaca, N.Y., August.
McCarthy, J.; Zald, M. (1973): *The trend of social movements in America: Professionalization and resource mobilization*. Morristown N.J.: General Learning Press.
– (1977): »Resource mobilization and social movements: a partial theory,« in: *American Journal of Sociology* 82: 1212-1241.
Melucci, A. (1977): *Sistema politico, partiti e movimenti sociali*. Milan: Feltrinelli.
– (1980): »The new social movements; a theoretical approach,« *Social Science Information* 19: 199-226.
– (1982): *L'invenzione del presente*. Bologna: Mulino.
– (1985a): »Movimenti sociali negli anni'80: Alla ricerca di un oggetto perduto?« in: *Stato e mercato* 14: 3-25.
– (1985b): »Multipolar action systems: Systemic environment and individual involvement in contemporary movements,« paper presented to the CES Research Planning Group workshop on participation in social movements, Ithaca, N.Y., August.
– (1985c): »The symbolic challenge of contemporary movements,« *Social Research*, forthcoming, Winter, 1985.
Melucci, A.; Diani, M. (1983): *Nazioni senza stato: I movimenti etnico-nazionali in Occidente*. Torino: Loescher.

Melucci, A. et al. (1984): *Altri codici: Aree di movimenti nella metropoli*. Bologna: Mulino.
Merkl, P. (1977): *Modern Comparative Politics*. Hinsdale, Ill.: Dryden.
Minguet, G. (1980): »Les mouvements sociaux, la sociologie de l'action et l'intervention sociologique«, *Revue Française de Sociologie* 1: 121-133.
Morris, A. (1981): »The Black Sit-in Movement: An analysis of internal organization«, *American Sociological Review* 46: 744-767.
Muller, E. (1980): »The psychology of political protest and violence,« in T.R. Gurr, ed., *Handbook of Political Conflict*. NY: Free Press.
Muller-Rommel, F. (1985a): »New social movements and the smaller parties: A comparative perspective,« in: *West European Politics* (1): 41-54.
– (1985b): »Social movements and the Greens: New internal politics in Germany,« in: *European Journal of Political Research* 13: 53-67.
Nedelmann, B. (1984): »New social movements and changes in processes of intermediation, *Social Science Information* 6: 1029-1048.
Nelkin, D.; Pollak, M. (1981): *The Atom Besieged*. Cambridge: MIT Press.
Oberschall, A. (1973): *Social Conflict and Social Movements*. Englewood Cliffs: Prentice-Hall.
Offe, C. (1985): New social movements: Challenging the boundaries of institutional politics,« in: *Social Research* 52 (4): 817-868.
Olson, M. (1965): *The logic of collective action*. New York: Schoken.
Olzak, S.; Di Gregorio, A. (1985): *Ethnic collective action in American cities 1877-1914: Research design and coding procedures*. Cornell University Sociology Technical Report, 85-1.
Piven, F.; Cloward, R. (1977): *Poor People's Movements*. NY: Pantheon.
Pizzorno, A. (1978): »Political exchange and Collective Identity in Industrial Conflict«, in: C.Crouch and A. Pizzorno (eds.). *The Resurgence of Class Conflict in Western Europe since 1968*. (London: Macmillan) Vol. II.
Roth, R. (1985): »Fordism and new social movements: Phases of social development as a framework for the analysis of social movements,« paper presented to the Workshop of analysis of Social Movements, Bonn, August.
Rucht, D. (1984): »Comparative new social movements, organizations and strategies,« presented at the EGOS Conference, Aarhus, Denmark, August.
– (1985): »New social movements: The state of discussion and research in West Germany,« paper presented to the Workshop on analysis of social movements, Bonn, August.
Salvati, M.; Gigliobianco, A. (1981): »May 1968 and the Hot Autumn of 1969: The Responses of two ruling classes,« in: S.Berger (ed.). *Organizing interests in Western Europe*. Cambridge: Cambridge U. Press.
Shorter, E.; Tilly, C. (1974): *Strikes in France 1830-1968*. Cambridge, Mass.: Harvard U. Press.
Snow, D. (1976): *The Nichiren Shosha Buddhist movement in America*. Ann Arbor, Michigan.
– »Frame Alignment Processes, micromobilization, and movement recruitment,« paper presented at the CES Research Planning Group Workshop on participation in social movements, Ithaca, N.Y., August.

Snow, D.; Zurcher, L.; Eckland-Olson, S. (1980): »Social networks and social movements: A micro-structural application to differential recruitment,« *American Sociological Review* 45(10): 787-801.

Spilerman, S. (1970): »The causes of racial disturbances: A comparison of alternative explanations,« *American Sociological Review* 35: 627-649.

– (1972): »Strategic considerations in analyzing the distribution of racial disturbances,« *American Sociological Review* 37: 493-499.

Statera, G. (1975): *Death of a Utopia*. New York: Oxford.

Tarrow, S. (1967): *Peasant Communism in Southern Italy*. New Haven: Yale U. Press.

– (1983): Struggling to Reform (Ithaca NY: Western Societies Program Occasional Paper No. 15).

– (1985): »The crisis of the late 1960's and the transition to mature capitalism,« in G. Arrighi, (ed.). *The Political Economy of Southern Europe*. London and Beverly Hills: Sage Publications.

Tilly, C. (1969): »Collective violence in European Perspective,« in: H.D. Graham and T.R. Gurr (eds.). *Violence in America: Historical and Comparative Perspectives*. New York: Prager.

– (1978): *From Mobilization to Revolution*. Reading, Mass.: Addison-Wesley.

– (1984): »Social movements and national politics,« in: C. Bright, S. Harding (eds.). *Statemaking and social movements*. Ann Arbor: U. of Michigan Press.

– (1989): *Democracy and Disorder*. Oxford: Oxford U. Press.

Tilly, C.; Tilly, R.; Tilly, R. (1975): *The rebellious century*. Cambridge, Mass.: Harvard U. Press.

Touraine, A. (1968): *Le communisme utopique: Le mouvement de mai*. Paris: Seuil.

– (1971): *The Post Industrial Society: Tommorow's Social History*. New York: Random House.

– (1978): *La voix et le regard*. Paris: Seuil.

– (1984): *Le retour de l'acteur*. Paris: Fayard.

Touraine, A.; Dubet, F.; Hegedus, Z.; Wieviorka, M. (1978): *Lutte etudiante*. Paris: Seuil.

– (1987): *Le pays contre l'Etat*. Paris: Seuil.

Touraine, A.; Hegedus, Z.; Dubet, F. (1980): *La prophetie antinucleaire*. Paris: Seuil.

Vallier, I. (ed.). (1971): *Comparative Methods in Sociology* (Berkeley and Los Angeles: U. of California Press.

Webb, K. et al. (1983): »Etiology and outcomes of protest: New European Perspectives«, in: *American Behavioral Scientist* 26: 311-322.

Zald, M.; Ash, R. (1966): »Social movement organizations: Growth, Decay and Change,« *Social Forces* 44: 327-341.

Zald, M.; McCarthy, J. (1979): *The dynamics of social Movements*. Cambridge, Mass.: Winthrop.

Zimmermann, E. (1980): »Macro-comparative research on political protest,« in: T. Gurr, (ed.). *Handbook of Political Conflict*. New York: The Free Press.

The Analysis of Social Movements: The State of the Art and Some Perspectives for Further Research

Friedhelm Neidhardt and Dieter Rucht

This final contribution aims at a critical assessment of recent research on social movements. Our intention is not only to praise advances that have been made in the last years, but also, to indicate directions for further study. One basis of this assessment will be the reports on specific countries and the more general essays of this volume. However, before summarizing this work in the light of our own criteria and concepts which we hope can structure the field, we will first make a *tour d'horizon* through the work on collective behavior and social movement research starting in the late 1940s. Rather focusing only on the present, this »historical« perspective may allow for a better identification of both advances and deficiencies in the study of social movements.

I. Some Comments on the Social Movement Research Since the 1950s

The abundance of studies published in the last four decades in the field of collective behavior and social movements can hardly be grasped in a short essay. In order to get at least a rough picture of the focal points, achievements and weaknesses of this field, rather than looking directly at the original contributions, we will deal with those reviews and comprehensive articles which were designed to give an overview and orientation. To put it briefly, we first attempt to assess the assessments. Of course, such a procedure for reducing complexity must be highly selective. Our intention was not to cover as many publications as possible, but to include those we considered to be significant and influential.

In a first round of selecting reviews which could be relevant for our purposes, it first became obvious that all of these pieces had been published in the Anglo-American sphere. Second, their number is rapidly increasing over time. The first observation indicates the high relevance of the field in the USA compared to other countries. From the growing number of reviews we can make possible conclusions about the growing number of publications which the reviews summarize. In areas where much work has been done there is a need for reviews summarizing and structuring the field for the benefit of newcomers or those approaching the field from the perspective of interested outsiders; increasing productivity in the field both allows for and requires new and updated assessments.

The field of collective behavior, first given shape in the 1920s by the Chicago School of Robert E. Park and Ernest W. Burgess, was heavily influenced by the tradition of European mass psychology. That line of thought, represented by Gustave LeBon, Gabriel Tarde and Scipio Sighele, flourished in the Old World at the turn of the century. Within this framework, social movements, if not totally neglected, were seen as only one form of mass behavior among such others as panic, fad, cults, rumour, fashion, etc. These forms of collective behavior were perceived as the opposite to conventional, respectively institutionalized behavior.

Though the Chicago School's symbolic interaction perspective was more highly elaborated than that of mass psychology, it nonetheless retained the fundamental distinction between conventional and collective behavior. The latter was seen as an outcome of rapid change and some kind of social breakdown, disorder or anomy.

During the period between the early writings of Park and Burgess (1921) and the middle of century the field of collective behavior stagnated. In the postwar period, the first assessments of this field were very skeptical. Anselm L. Strauss, for example, concluded that despite the fact that the sociological study of collective behavior was among the oldest of conventional fields it was »one of the most unworked of our research areas. It has never been in the forefront of research preoccupations. In recent decades we have had a series of successively popular fields (race, ecology, industrial sociology), and a number of rather steady interests (family, crime); but collective behavior phenomena have been almost wholly neglected as objects for serious investigation.« In particular, Strauss criticized »the crude descriptive level of knowledge and the relative lack of theory in this area« (1947, 352). Nevertheless, he saw some advances in at least three of four areas: »public opinion, propaganda, revolutionary movements, and perhaps the ideology of social movements« (352).

Among those who contributed most to collective behavior research was certainly Herbert Blumer. He was still heavily influenced by the Chicago School. His 1939 article[1] was widely received and laid the groundwork for many of the successive debates. But this is not to say that collective behavior soon became a coherent field of research. Many years after his pionieering article Blumer stated: »Interest in the field of collective behavior is unquestionably increasing. Yet, although much has been added to our knowledge of separate topics within the last two decades, no significant contribution has been made to the general analysis of collective behavior.« (Blumer 1957, 127) The author felt a »need of systematic conceptual analysis – an analysis that will establish a basic rationale, lay out the separate areas of important interests, and show their generic relationship.« (128) In fact, though Blumer offers some interesting propositions, i.e. the interactionist wisdom that movements are socially constructed, his emphasis was not so much on theory but on classification and taxonomy. He suggested differentiating between five types of collective behavior: (1) crowdlike behavior such as panic and riots, (2) mass behavior which is collective but not organized, (3) public and public opinion, (4) propaganda, psychological warfare and communist tactics, and (5) social movements. Among the latter, Blumer identified various subtypes, arguing that, to his knowledge, »no one has ever sought to develop a systematic topology of social movements,« and »certainly nothing has been written on this topic in the least ten years.« (150)

Blumer's writings already indicate a shift from short-lived phenomena, examined priliminary by social psychologists, to a sociological approach devoted to the analysis of more stable and organized forms such as social movements. In this respect, he also differed from the psychological approach of Hadley Cantril (1941) who, unlike most of his colleagues, has focussed on social movements, but with an emphasis on individual motivation and participation. Blumer argued for a genuine sociological approach to social movements. »A consciously directed and organized movement cannot be explained merely in terms of a psychological disposition or motivation of people, or in terms of a diffusion of an ideology. Explanations of this sort ... overlook that fact that *a movement has to be constructed* and has to carve out a career in what is practically always an opposed, resistant, or at least indif-

---

1 This article on »Collective Behavior« was reprinted in 1946 and revised in 1951.

ferent world.« (1957, 147) Social movements were characterized as »one of the chief ways through which modern societies are remade.« (154) As a consequence, Blumer considered the study of social movements as one of the most important areas in the field of collective behavior. For this field including the area of social movements Blumer saw »the urgent need for a conceptual framework that will make possible a coherent scheme of analysis and provide leads to better directed study.« (151)

In the same year that Blumer argued in favor of more conceptual reflection Ralph H. Turner and Lewis M. Killian published their volume entitled »Collective Behavior« (1957; 1972) which Blumer classified as an »excellent treatment in the field« (1957, 127). Indeed, this was the most comprehensive approach at that time. In some sense the authors could be seen in the tradition of the Chicago School as they viewed collective behavior as being rooted in a breakdown of a well-structured situation. On the other hand, social movements as a specific form of collective behavior, were no longer perceived to be totally erratic, disorganized and irrational. Rather than assuming that collective behavior emerges by contagion and imitation, the authors stressed the key role of an emergent norm which orients individuals to act collectively, and thus, forming a movement. With the crystallization of this emergent norm the movement takes shape and gradually becomes more organized and institutionalized, thus loosing its actual movement character. In that sense, social movements were not seen as the opposite of organized behavior, but as an early state of collective organization. This concept of social movements covered many empirical phenomena which formerly could be classified neither as spontaneous and irrational forms of mass behavior nor as highly formalized interest aggregation. As a consequence, the study of social movements became more attractive and important.

The growing significance of social movements as a specific type of collective behavior is also reflected in the literature of the following years. The 1964 »Handbook of modern sociology« edited by Robert E.L. Faris contains, in addition to an article on collective behavior by Blumer, Killian's contribution on social movements. This essay addressed virtually all relevant aspects of social movements, e.g. their genesis, their values and norms, their structures, their internal interactions, their consequences and the impact they had on social change. In a similar vein as some of his predecessors, Killian not only described the field of collective behavior as »a neglected area of sociology,« but also, he stated that »social movements have received relatively little emphasis« (Killian 1964, 426). A remarkable aspect of the article was the author's relation of social movements to the broader society and the suggestion that social movements could be interpreted not so much as creatures, but as the »creators of social change.« (1964, 426) Given such a perspective it was quite plausible to suggest a more encompassing analysis focusing on a movement's relationship to its environment. »Whatever the influence of other variables, the influence of the nature of the opposition and of the public reaction to a movement cannot be overemphasized. The opposition includes established groups and counter-movements which actively oppose the movement. The public includes an unorganized, uncommitted collectivity of individuals who may look sympathetically on the movement but may also disagree with it or hold it up to scorn and ridicule.« (450) Moreover, in line with earlier writings of Blumer and Killian as well as of authors such as C. Wendell King (1957) and Kurt and Gladys Lang (1961), Killian conceived of a social movement as a collectivity with a »complex and relatively stable structure, a broad program of change, and an elaborate ideology.« (1964, 432) As he dwells on the organizational structure of a movement, its internal dynamics, the role and types of both the leaders and followers, Killian appears in some of these respects as a forerunner of the resource mobilization approach.

With his emphasis on a movement's social environment and its role as an agent of social change, Killian was very close to the European tradition. With the exception of the less sophisticated mass psychology, the European mainstream since Karl Marx and Lorenz von Stein tended to interpret social movements as organized and strategically-acting collectives which could heavily influence the course of history. In the USA this tradition was represented by authors such as Rudolf Heberle, a German emigrant who devoted much energy to the analysis of social movements.[2] It is probable that Heberle remained a marginal figure in the American academic debates because he situated social movements within a historically-oriented *Political Sociology* (1951) rather than embedding them in the study of collective behavior as was commonly done. Nevertheless, he and Robert Gusfield wrote the two articles on social movements in the *International Encyclopedia of the Social Sciences* (1968). Interestingly enough, Heberle developed some of the

2 Like the above mentioned authors, Heberle was not enthusiastic about the state of the art. In 1949 he wrote that the analysis of social movements »is a difficult field in which little systematic theoretical work has been done.« (Heberle 1949, 347)

emphases later seen in the resource mobilization approach as he stressed the role of various organizations within a movement (committees, clubs, labor unions, parties) and observed that »the relations between the various groups constituting a movement are not always free of tension.« (1968, 441)

In contrast to Heberle, who could not really challenge the Chicago School tradition, the authors drawing on Parsons' structural functionalism played a significant role. This is particularly true for Neil Smelser's *Theory of Collective Behavior* (1962). In some respects Smelser was close to writers like Herbert Blumer and Ralph Turner. He, too, lumped together a broad variety of phenomena ranging from panic to value-oriented movements under the label collective behavior, arguing that these were outcomes of an unstructured situation, thus stressing the classical difference between collective and conventional behavior (Smelser 1962, 8). In that sense he can be seen as representing a »breakdown theory.« In sharp contrast to other authors, however, Smelser argued that the same theoretical framework could be used to analyze both forms of behavior (1962, 23). Drawing mainly on Parsons, he argued that »structural strain« is the basic condition causing collective behavior. On this premise he developed his well-known »value-added« approach to explain the occurence of collective behavior. Among the factors facilitating the development of social movements Smelser emphasized the role of pre-existing or newly created organizations and the formation of a »generalized belief«. The status of this belief seems at least ambivalent in Smelser's writings. In general, a tendency to perceive this belief as an irrational response »akin to magical beliefs« (1962, 8) can be observed. Although pursuing a genuinely sociological approach, Smelser's vision of the nature of these beliefs seems to be influenced by the old mass psychology.

Only with the resurgence of US-protest movements in the 1960s could the idea of movements as amorphous and irrational forms of collective behavior be finally broken down. At the same time, the focus of interest shifted from taxonomy and conceptual reflection to empirically grounded research. In their comprehensive review, *Strands of theory and research in collective behavior*, Marx and Wood (1975) cited many advances and changes in this field, which they considered as »one of the more vigorous areas of sociology in the last 15 years« (1975, 363). Apart from the rapidly growing number of publications, the increased funding of research, and the attempts at institutionalized cooperation between scholars in the field, Marx and Wood also pointed out such conceptual shifts as a blurring of the »artifical intellectual boundary between collective and ›non-collective,‹ or conventional behavior,« the »reducing of the area's estrangement from general sociology,« (414) the »greater self-consciousness about the kinds of questions chosen for study and the possible uses of the scholar's work,« (413) the growing attention to rational motivations underlying collective behavior and the role of organization in collective behavior, particularly in social movements, and the formulation of testable propositions. In addition to these advances, the authors pinpointed a number of deficits and caveats. The latter comprise a list of 22 »categorial imperatives along the lines of the Ten Commandments for those who would study social movements and collective behavior.« (515) Even in light of further advances in this field of study, most of these recommendations remain valuable. For instance, the authors suggest studying social movements in their organizational and environmental contexts, grounding statements in careful empirical observations and tests, including the use of quantitative data, differentiating between leaders and followers, followers and sympathetic bystanders, moving from static cross-sectional to dynamic cross-interactive models, and encouraging researchers to »appreciate the interactive and emergent character of much collective behavior beyond the causal impact of history, of broad social structural conditions, and on the personality of participants.« (417) Interestingly, Gary T. Marx and James L. Wood, though referring to authors such as Anthony Oberschall, Mayer N. Zald, Roberta Ash, John McCarthy and Charles Tilly, still did not classify their work under the heading of the resource mobilization approach. This image of a relatively coherent approach was rather a self-serving construct promoted particularly by Zald.

Our short overview of the collective behavior approach has demonstrated that the perception of social movements as spontaneous mass behavior faded away relatively early and was explicitly dismissed by some of the leading proponents of the collective behavior approach. In spite of this, resource mobilization theory, as it later came to be called, set itself apart from a simplified picture of the collective behavior approach, probably for the sake of a clear self-presentation. Regardless of whether its perception of older debates was correct or not, resource mobilization theory was certainly on the right track in stressing the organizational needs of movements, and in particular, the need for collecting resources, emphasizing the role of pre-existing networks for the emergence of new movements, and pointing out the complex relations of organizations within and between social movements.

Since the resource mobilization approach is presented and/or discussed in several articles appearing in this volume, we can restrict ourselves to some more general observations drawing mainly on recent reviews of social movement literature.

The resource mobilization approach took shape in the 1970s. In one of the first critical reviews of this approach, Ralph Turner (1981), although supporting some of its assumptions, relativized the significance of this approach and its sharp break with the collective behavior tradition. He argued that the resource mobilization approach had a number of restrictions – e.g. its assumption of the rationality of movement decision-making, the stability of movement goals, and the lack of relevance attributed to changes in relative deprivation – features which apply only to some social movements. With his eye on the great variety of social movements, Turner re-emphasized those factors which were downplayed by resource mobilization theorists, e.g. the role of values in the construction of social reality by social movements, the interaction between the movement core and the mass of adherents in decision-making and influencing the movement's forms of action, the integration of the analysis of movement organizations into the broader study of social movements, and the role of movement strategies and tactics and the responses they provoked (Turner 1981, 20).

In a similar vein, Craig Jenkins (1983) also argued against a one-sided emphasis on organizational resources in his review of resource mobilization theory and the study of social movements. He claimed that grievances cannot be neglected as a source of mobilization and that forms of collective behavior based on expressive actions oriented toward personal and not so much structural change may not be adequately grasped by an approach mainly designed to analyze rational-instrumental actions with organizational control over resources (Jenkins 1981, 529). With respect to the further development of the resource mobilization approach Jenkins had two suggestions. In regard to the »polity model,« which links regime changes and opportunities of political access, he argued that a broader variety of regimes should be studied and attention should be paid not only to different degrees of neocorporatism, but also, to authoritarian and one-party regimes. As for the »mobilization model,« which links collective interests and the pooling of resources, Jenkins voted for a more sophisticated social psychology of collective action. Such an approach should take into account the fact that collective interests are socially constructed and created by the mobilization process (549).

In the 1980s, the debate between the proponents of the collective behavior school and those of the resource mobilization approach gradually lost its importance. The resource mobilization approach no longer had to prove its raison d'être and became a part of »normal science«, i.e., seen as one approach among others. This tendency is nicely reflected in Morris and Herring's article. (1987) It begins by stating that there has been »an explosion of theoretical and empirical writings on social movements and collective action within the last decade. These writings have triggered debates, a new school of thoughts, defenses of old schools of thought and theoretical advances. Moreover, important research on social movement is being conducted in various disciplines including sociology, political science, history, economics and communications. « (1987, 138) The authors identified five perspectives on social movements as »classic« approaches: Marx's view of social movements, Weber's view, the collective behavior view (subdivided into the Chicago School and the Structural School of collective behavior), the mass society perspective and the relative deprivation view. In contrast to many other social scientists, Morris and Herring, rather than subsuming a great number of authors under the resource mobilization label, differentiated three subcategories of that approach. These were centered around the catchwords of »rational action«, »organizational/entrepreneurial« and »political process«. In addition, the authors presented a comprehensive table listing the responses of all these approaches to nine central questions concerning the nature and various aspects of social movements. Two additional features of this article are also worth mentioning. First, it provided a quantitative analysis of the respective shares of articles devoted to the classical theory and resource mobilization approach, as they were covered in four major sociological journals in the period of 1949 to 1983. Not surprisingly, the authors found a rapid decline of classical theory in the 1970s and 1980s, and a corresponding increase of the resource mobilization which, in early 1980s made up roughly 70 percent of all articles on collective behavior and social movements. Interestingly enough, in the period under investigation other approaches were almost marginal. The second remarkable aspect of this article was that it was based not only on a review of the literature, but also, on interviews with leading representatives of the collective behavior and resource mobilization approaches. The authors also presented remarks from these theorists. Using this method, the positions of the authors interviewed and differences between them came up much more distinctively than in their writings. According to the interviews, the major positions of collective behavior and resource mobilization theory are not likely to be synthesized. Based on that impression, Morris and Herring's concluding remarks remain reluctant and tentative. Rather than promoting a specific theory or an integrative concept, the authors, on the basis of their interviews, simply point out some aspects which would deserve more attention in future analyses, e.g. the role of ideology in social movements, the relationship between charisma and pre-existing organization, the interests that fuel social movements, and the relationship between social movements and governmental structures (1987, 191-2).

The review of the study of social movements by McAdam, McCarthy and Zald (1988) was organized differently. Rather than identifying a number of schools and arranging them in a more or less chronological order, the authors organized their essay according to two systematic criteria. First, they distinguish between a macro- and a micro-perspective. Second, they differentiate between aspects involved in the emergence of social movements and those dealing with maintaining or changing them. The authors combine their two criteria to form four categories. Within each category they situate and discuss recent literature according to certain catch words. In reviewing their article it is striking to see that most of these categories refer to an impressive body of literature. Thus, the question is raised as to where the authors still see aspects that are more or less neglected. At the end of their article, they stress three points: first, the relatively under-developed state of knowledge about the dynamics of collective action beyond the emergence of a movement; second, the need to analyze the effect of movement participation on the individual so as to understand the dynamics of individual activism; and third, the need for more systematic, qualitative fieldwork into the dynamics of collective action at the intermediate level between the micro and the macro levels (1988, 728-9). Although this review can be seen as an excellent contribution to the literature on social movements, it has to be emphasized that it is almost exclusively focused on the Anglo-American literature.

In regard to the last aspect, there are at least two recent articles which avoid such an ethno-centristic perspective although this ethno-centrism did have some justification given the fact that by far most of the work on social movements has been done in the USA.

Klandermans and Tarrow (1988) had the advantage of being familiar with both American and European literature. The authors state that since the revitalization of contentious politics in the late 1960s and early 1970s »two major new paradigms emerged: in the United States, what has been called ›resource mobilization‹ and, in Western Europe, the ›new social movement‹ approach.« (1988, 2) In an overall view, European scholars tend to focus »on larger structural issues – the structural causes of social movements, their ideologies, and their relation to the culture of advanced capitalist society –

whereas Americans developed their research mainly at the group and the individual level, looking systematically at the groups that organized mass protest, at their forms of action, and at the motivations of individuals who joined them.« (1988, 2-3)[3] Both approaches have emerged independently from each other. Recently, however, representatives from both approaches took notice of each other. And, largely due to the efforts of Klandermans and Tarrow, a debate was initiated which was aimed at a complementary use of both approaches if not systematically linking them. It was Klandermans in particular who, drawing on the resource mobilization approach, extended it to develop a concept of micro-mobilization in order to explain how individuals become engaged in movement activities. On the other hand, it was mainly Tarrow who, situating social movement activities in their larger political context, promoted a concept of »political opportunity structure« which can also serve as a basis for cross-national research. In his 1988 review article, Tarrow argued »that although there is continuing reason to distinguish between the internal logic of social movements and that of conventional political groups, the dynamics of collective action – even in its most ›expressive‹ and anti-political forms – are best understood in relation to the political process.« (1988, 422)

Summarizing this »review of the reviews« spanning four decades, three general observations can be made. First, with the increase of social movement activities the study of social movements also has intensified and become a solid research area. An indication of its growth and diversification is the increasing number and the increasingly detailed content of reviews in this area. Second, despite the large body of social movement literature and intense conceptual debates, only a part of the work has been really cumulative. Early insights into the nature and dynamics of social movements have been forgotten and have had to be »rediscovered.« Since the 1950s, a number of aspects have remained underdeveloped and some important questions have been repeated over time (we will refer to these at the end of this chapter). Third, although there were good reasons for the reviewers to focus on US literature in terms of both quantity and quality, European work on social movements, until quite recently, was totally neglected in the Anglo-Ameri-

---

3 Similarly, Tarrow confronts »macrosociological and cultural paradigms developed by the Europeans and the attitudinal and organizational studies of Americans« (Tarrow 1988, 422).

can world. In this case, it makes sense to take a closer look at the specifics of the study of social movements in some European countries compared to the USA.

II. Social Movement Research in Selected Countries

Drawing on the reports dealing with social movement analysis in nine countries we have a fairly good basis from which we can comparatively assess some parallels and convergences. It will also be of great interest to see to what extent the scholary work on social movements within a country has been affected by specific features of a national political culture including the profile and dynamics of its movement sector.

Differences in theoretical and conceptual preferences often seem to be an effect of specific national and even continental situations (the latter are discussed in Section III). As several contributions in this volume demonstrate, their empirical objects of reference, i.e. single movements or an overall social movement sector in a given country, differ widely. Consequently, not only different theoretical traditions, but also, different realities have shaped the perspectives of social scientists.

In general it can be stated that with the probable exception of the USA research on social movements was only a marginal field of social science up to the early 1970s. Only with the upheavals of the 1960s, the rise of the New Left and the new social movements, did this field get more attention in several countries. Where these movements have remained relatively insignificant (e.g., Austria, Sweden, Great Britain), the study of social movements in general has also remained underdeveloped. By contrast, in some other countries (USA, West Germany, Italy, the Netherlands, Denmark), research was more diversified, and focused on various movements' features such as organizational forms, ideology, social composition, forms of action, etc. It was also in these countries that the interest in (new) social movements first developed among political scientists and less so among sociologists. This may be due to the fact that in these countries the movements could present themselves, at least temporarily, as challengers to the political elites if not the given political system per se. With the exception of the USA, however, it can be stated that political scientists were usually not very well equipped with concepts to analyze social movements. Thus, after some delay, it was primarily the sociologists who dealt more systematically with social movement phenomena. Meanwhile, however, it seems that the boundaries between the disciplines no longer play a major role.

Another remarkable feature is that the main approaches used to interpret these movements seemed to be strongly determined by the weight of older movements, the intellectual heritage and the structural conditions of the respective countries. Thus, apart from occasional references to US researchers, the debates over social movements in a given Western European country tended to develop largely independently from debates in other countries. Even the resource mobilization approach was introduced relatively late in Europe (among the first were Klandermans 1983 and Rucht 1984). In the last few years, however, debates in all the countries investigated here have become more institutionalized.

Still another interesting aspect is the fact that the degree to which co-existing movements are perceived as single phenomena or as an ensemble varies, not only between Europe and the USA, but also, within Western Europe. Extreme cases are Britain, on the one hand, where the debate on social movements is fragmented though rich empirical studies can be found, and on the other, there is a lively debate in West Germany over the new social movements, and more recently, over social movements in general. Such debates obviously largely depend on the degree of interaction, and organizational and ideological overlap, between various movements. These features, in turn, can to a large extent be explained by specific features of the political systems.

It seems that the degree of openness and responsiveness of the political system to social movements is a crucial variable. The more open the political system, the more the movements tend to act independently from each other, and the more they are viewed as single phenomena. For instance, as Margit Mayer argues in her contribution to this volume (see also Kitschelt's essay), the prevalence of the resource mobilization approach in the USA reflects the way in which the politics of interests works there. As far as we can see, groups on the grassroots level in the USA tend to remain informal and without strong ties to higher levels while movement organizations on the national level are usually powerful, well organized, and come closer to the model of conventional interest groups. These movement organizations are primarily based on the support of individuals who are isolated from each other, and large-scale fund raising techniques, without having strong organizations on the local level. Although these national organizations may sometimes form tactical alliances they do not consider themselves as part of an overall movement sector based on a common ideology.

In comparison, the stronger emphasis of social movement research on the »alternative culture« and on problems of collective identity in Italy and West Germany appears to mirror specific features of the major movements in these countries. Differences between these »alternative« movements and their »conventional« environment are more conspicuous, and thus become both matters of conflict and the basis for a broader collective identity which includes strong »antisystemic« attitudes. Thus in these countries we find closer links between these movements on the horizontal as well as the vertical levels than in the USA.

Such observations may demonstrate the need for cross-national comparison. Basing their work on the experience of only one single country researchers attempting to draw general conceptual conclusions from that restricted viewpoint assume a certain intellectual risk. These conclusions may, not accidentally, vary from country to country without really being contradictory as long as intervening variables have been specified.

Apart from specific concepts and hypotheses one notes the differences in disciplinary traditions in the study of social movements in various countries. In some respect, the USA and Great Britain are extreme cases. In the USA since the 1920s, there has been ongoing interest in the fields of collective behavior and social movements. Based on these categories many aspects were studied empirically, and the field given its contours as a special area with its own place in the social sciences. As a consequence, a professional network was formed in the mid-seventies. An outcome of this intensified coordination was the creation of a particular section within the *American Sociological Association* and the publication of a newsletter (»Critical Mass Bulletin«).

In contrast to the situation in the USA, and despite the common language and close intellectual bonds between both countries, British scholars did not create a coherent research field devoted to collective behavior and/or social movements. At a first glance, research on social movements seems to be virtually absent in Britain. Only at a closer look may one discover considerable work on social movements, but under various other labels and disciplines. As a consequence, one finds much empirical work on related questions, but appreciably less conceptual and theoretical development.

In a different sense, the West German situation is quite unique when compared to Great Britain and the USA. Research on social movements was virtually non-existent up to the end of the 1970s. Partly due to the break with traditional sociological lines caused by the Nazi-regime, the study of social movements was not institutionalized at all. Then, mainly because of increasing social movement activities, the publication of related academic literatures suddenly exploded. Most of this increase can be attributed to the new social movements approach even though it does not form a coherent entity. This approach was recently questioned for various reasons (see the chapter on West Germany). Right or wrong – the prominence of the new social movements approach and the broad adoption of the notion of »new« social movements in West Germany cannot be denied. To a lesser degree, the same can be said for Italy, Austria, Switzerland, Denmark and the Netherlands. This is in contrast to the situation in the USA and Great Britain.

As for the USA, because of both the absence of a strong »old« socialist movement and the continuity of left-libertarian movements, the term »new« social movement is hard to accept. In Great Britain, where the reference point of an *old* movement undoubtedly exists, the low profile of the new social movements and, in part, their close linkage to the labor movement, make it hard to assume the existence of separate new movements. A similar statement could also be made for Sweden. In addition, a particular feature of Sweden's political culture comes into play. Dissenting voices tend to become quickly co-opted and integrated into the system of established interest politics. Thus, they lose their capacity to challenge the established order and their ideological and organizational profile.

France (unfortunately not included in our series of country reports) is also a special case. It was probably in France, and in particular through the writings of Alain Touraine, that the idea and concept of new social movements took first shape. Moreover, Touraine, who has headed an institute centered around the study of social movements for many years, together with his collaborators, has invested much energy in this field. Although the discussion of social movements in France has been clearly dominated, if not monopolized, by this group, its influence in other European countries (not to mention the USA) has been modest (Italy, West Germany) or completely marginal (Austria, Switzerland, Sweden, Denmark, The Netherlands). In part, the lack of cross-national assimilation of Touraine's approach could be attributed to the peculiarities of its theory and methodology, and therefore, is not acceptable for many researchers – both in France and in other countries. Moreover, there is a tendency of »self-centrism« which seems to be more common in the French academic world than in other countries.[4]

As a whole, research on social movements has been less professional, and institutional support has been much weaker in Europe than the USA. European scholars, if not former activists or sympathizers of social movements, often seemed too fascinated by the object under investigation to be able to take a scientifically distant position, formulate clear hypotheses, and carry out careful – and mostly unspectacular – empirical analysis. Another hindrance to the institutionalization of this field is also the fact – stated explicitly in the articles on Denmark and West Germany in this volume – that European scholars interested in (new) social movements rarely hold tenured positions and thus have more difficulties in carrying out more ambitious research projects.

By and large, the analysis of social movements seems to be characterized by a remarkable discrepancy in many European countries. On the one hand, there is the approach »from above«, i.e., an inclination to promote all-encompassing, but hardly verifiable theories, to grasp a great variety of empirical phenomena with one single label, to promote monocausal explanations, to relate concrete conflicts directly to macrosociological conditions, etc. Other scholars, taking the perspective »from below«, conduct case studies on single conflicts and campaigns, collect and interpret rich empirical material, but often without theoretical guidelines and without having clear criteria for collecting and analyzing their data. A consequence of this situation is the disproportion between the sheer quantity of publications and their relevance for the cumulation of theoretical and analytical knowledge. More specifically, the lack of attention paid to the intermediate level as compared to the macro and micro levels has to be criticized.[5]

---

4 Not accidentally, French researchers are under-represented or completely absent in most international congresses in the social sciences, and particularly, in the field of social movements, whereas the opposite seems to be true for those from the Skandinavian and some other Western European countries.

5 This is a criticism which McAdam, McCarthy and Zald have already made with regard to the US literature (1988, 729).

III. Reference Schemes for Recent Social Movement Research

The study of social movements in the USA and Western Europe has received increasing interest in the 1970s and 1980s. As already stated above, however, it was not until the mid-eighties that scholars of both continents began to study each other's work more intensely. Attempts were then made to relate the dominant approaches to each other, elaborate perspectives, and introduce new questions and concepts into the study of social movements.

A. Resource Mobilization Approach and New Social Movements Approach

As we could learn from both the reports on selected countries and the short comparative discussion presented above, research in Western Europe and the USA is diversified and does not follow a common set of premises and guidelines. However, from a more detached point of view, it can be seen that research in Europe and in the USA, which is based on different concepts and research strategies has proceeded in different directions. At least up to the late 1980s, there were good reasons for contrasting a European »New Social Movements Approach« and a North American »Resource Mobilization Approach«. Klandermans and Tarrow (1988) are quite correct in concluding that the main concerns of social movement literature in the two continents differed systematically: Structural approaches, relating social movements to the encompassing societal and political order, were more prominent in Europe, whereas aspects of movement's organization were more salient in the USA. We illustrate the specifities of the two perspectives in *Figure 1*.

According to Melucci, the new social movements approach is oriented towards the causes, the »why« of social movements, whereas the resource mobilization approach focuses more on the process of mobilization, the »how« of social movement activities (Melucci 1984, 821). As a matter of fact, the main characteristic of the new social movement approach is its emphasis on the *macrosocial conditions for movements*. Its basic assumption is that, on the one hand, deeply rooted processes of societal change (A) produce structural contradictions and collective problems (e.g., environmental pollution) which lead to the deterioration of quality of life (*»need defence«*

Figure 1: Resource Mobilization and New Social Movement Approach

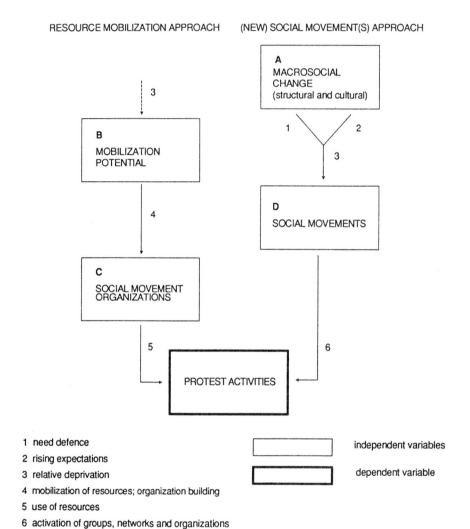

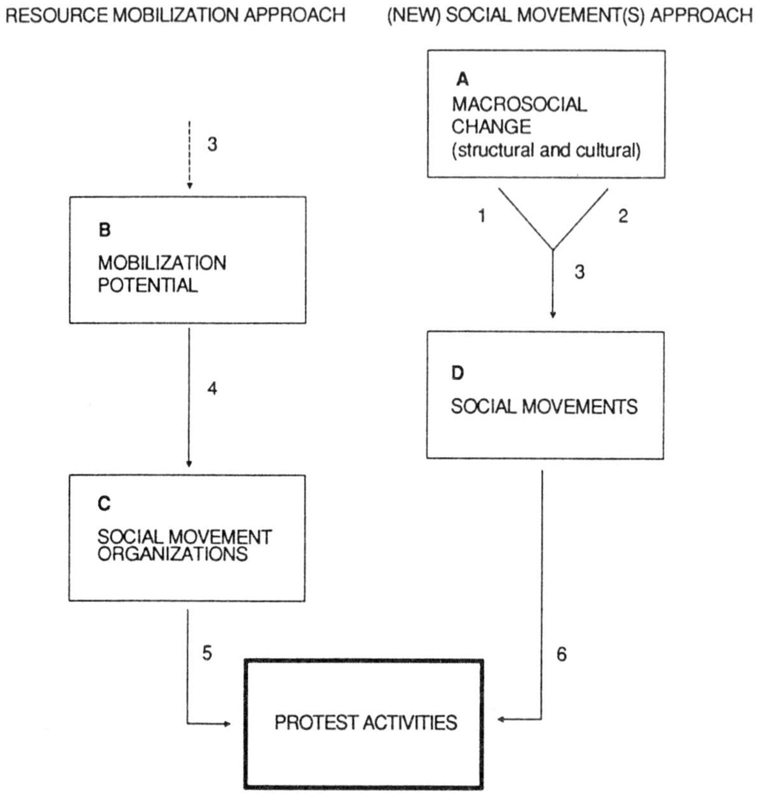

1 need defence
2 rising expectations
3 relative deprivation
4 mobilization of resources; organization building
5 use of resources
6 activation of groups, networks and organizations

independent variables (thin box)

dependent variable (thick box)

[1]). This process, on the other hand, is accompanied by a postmaterialist value change (B) which produces new aspirations and sensitivities among specific social groups, and in particular, the new middle class (*»rising demands«* [2]; Brand 1982). Both developments lead to *relative deprivation* (3) which, under certain conditions, fosters a *new kind of social movements* (D).

The resource mobilization approach tends to neglect the macrosocial causes of social movements. The potential for social movements and their underlying problems, whatever their nature may be, are simply presupposed (McCarthy and Zald, 1977). Emphasis however, is given to those factors largely ignored by the new social movements approach, i.e., factors that determine the activation of latent layers of interest into manifest *social movements* and *collective action*. Thus, the focus is on the actual process of mobilization. From that viewpoint, in respect to the specific case of the USA, resource mobilizationists stress – and perhaps over-emphasize – the role of *social movement organizations* (C). The crucial tasks of these organizations are to *mobilize resources* (2 and 4) such as money and people who devote time for the organizations, build coalitions, select leaders, etc.

It can easily be seen that both approaches deal with important aspects of social movements and thus could complement each other. A fundamental asymmetry of the two approaches should be noted, however. Whereas the resource mobilization approach claims, at least implicitly, to be applicable to all kinds of social movements, the new social movements approach by definition relates only to an historically-specific type of social movements.

Comparing the empirical bases of the two appproaches it is obvious that, as a whole, the new social movements approach is clearly less developed. This is not only a result of the lower continuity, professionalization and institutionalization of the study of social movements in Western Europe, but is also due to the fact that the new social movements approach tends to focus on a macrosociological level as it attempts to investigate the relation between social movements and broader phenomena of social change. Questions related to such a »big« issue are difficult to study empirically and scholars are tempted to advance heuristic and very general hypotheses which, by their very nature, are not directly verifiable.

The resource mobilization approach, on the other hand, implies a tendency to make careful empirical investigations of particular aspects of social movements, without, however, paying much attention to macrosociological aspects. For instance, questions of whether or to which extent contemporary movements can be seen as typical features of a given societal order, and how these movements affect that order, are virtually absent in resource mobilization literature.

As we have already suggested, however, a closer look at the contributions in this volume reveals that there is a much more complex reality behind this polarized picture.

First, in a synchronic perspective, one could argue that scholars on both sides of the Atlantic were first tempted to stress the differences instead of the common features of both approaches. In fact, however, a number of parallels can be found which have been largely ignored up to now. For instance, neither of these approaches accepted the assumptions of mass psychology that social movements were composed of alienated people driven by irrational motives. The attention paid by resource mobilization theorists to the role of movement organization, strategy and tactics was also widely shared in Europe. On the other hand, the concern with structural determinants usually attributed to the new social movement approach can also be found by scholars counted among resource mobilizationists (e.g. Tilly, Ash-Garner, Gamson, not to speak of authors relying on different concepts such as Paige, Moore, Piven and Cloward, McAdam, etc.). In particular, the political process model usually attributed to the resource mobilization approach[6] is close to one based on the new social movements approach. Finally, on both sides of the Atlantic we find some social scientists who, in their interests and preferred approaches, were always closer to the other side than to their own country or continent.[7] Though Klandermans and Tarrow were aware that »by no means were all Europeans advocates of the new social movements approach or all the Americans ›resource mobilizationists‹« (1988, 2), they tended to de-emphasize the large array of concepts that could be found on both continents.

6 As for Charles Tilly, there may be doubts if he can really be subsumed under the resource mobilization approach. Doug McAdam, another proponent of a political process model, clearly takes a critical stance toward this approach (1982).

7 This is true, e.g., for Jean Cohen in the USA who refers to writers such as Alain Touraine and Jürgen Habermas; this is also true for Karl-Dieter Opp and Ekkart Zimmermann in West Germany, who draw heavily on relative deprivation and Olsonian concepts in dealing with social movement activism. In general, we think it is fair to say that Europeans, at least since the early 1980s, paid more attention to the respective work of Americans than vice versa. Of course, this also has to do with the prominent role of the English language and the large number of social scientists in the USA.

Moreover, one should not overlook the internal differentiation within each of the two approaches.[8]

Second, in a diachronic perspective, a closer look at European and American approaches may reveal that differences between each of them and their respective forerunners are less prominent than it is usually perceived. Taking the American case, it seems that the dividing line between »classical« approaches of collective behavior and the resource mobilization approach has been over-emphasized by proponents of the latter, as Turner (1981) pointed out. For example, a movement's need for organization was already recognized by the »old« collective behavior approach, although not much energy has been invested in studying this aspect. Through this strong emphasis on their newness, differences between resource mobilization and

---

8 For the resource mobilization approach, Morris and Herring (1987) made the threefold distinction which we have already mentioned: »rational action«, »organizational/ entrepreneurial mobilization« and »political process«. A dual distinction has been suggested by Jenkins (1983) in referring to the »entrepreneurial model« and the »polity model«.

As for the new social movement approach, we will distinguish between three variations which could be labeled the cultural, the political and the integrative models.

First, there are approaches which emphasize the role of the new social movements in terms of fundamental conflict over cultural patterns. Far from forming a common school of thought, though, such various authors as Touraine (1981), Nelles (1984), Raschke (1985), Eder (1982) and Melucci (1988, 1989) assume that new social movements indicate a historically relevant struggle which is typically not centered on the control over economic and/or political power but focuses on the sphere of reproduction. In this perspective, problems of self-reflection, collective identity and collective learning processes would play an important role.

Second, there are approaches which place the new social movements closer to the realm of politics (e.g. Nedelmann, 1984), viewing them as the expression of a »new political paradigm« (Offe, 1985). Here, the emphasis lies on the distribution of power, state intervention and the side-effects of capitalist welfare states.

Third, various authors pursue a more integrative perspective and interpret new social movements in a broader structural framework which allows for both a historical and a systematic perspective. One variation of this line of thought, not yet well elaborated, is based on a theory of modernization which combines economic, political and cultural dimensions (Brand, 1989; Raschke, 1985; Rucht, 1988). Another strand, still closer to the Marxist heritage, interprets new social movements both as an outcome and a catalyst of the crisis of the »Fordist« mode of societal regulation (Mayer, 1985; Hirsch and Roth, 1986; Roth, 1989).

new social movement approaches also became overstated insofar as their respective references to classical theories were not the same.

There are additional reasons to relativize the juxtaposition of the resource mobilization and the new social movements approach. In the last few years, both have broadened their scope and more fully elaborated their use of categories and hypotheses. This lead to a blurring of conceptual dividing lines. On the one hand, it becomes clear that the resource mobilization approach, likewise any other concept, is shaped by its historical context, i.e., the situation in the USA since the mid-sixties (see Mayer and Kitschelt in this volume). Therefore, the question arises of to what extent this approach reflects a broader societal change and a new type of movement in the USA. Obviously, this question brings North American scholars closer to their European counterparts. On the other hand, the new social movements approach, confronted with its critics, is being forced to open itself up to a broader concept of social movements in order to answer the question of which aspects are or are not specific to new social movements. At this point, the question also arises of which elements of the resource mobilization approach could be adopted and integrated into such a broader concept of social movements.

In addition, direct exchange between students of social movements on both sides of the Atlantic contributes to weaken the dividing lines between both approaches since the last few years. Joint workshops have taken place or are being inaugurated; common publications have appeared (Klandermans, Kriesi and Tarrow, 1988; Klandermans 1989; Dalton and Küchler 1990). More and more students of social movements have transcended national and continental boundaries in their work, and thus, will contribute to the blurring of spatially-bound concepts. The increasing interest in cross-national and cross-issue research on social movements may also foster this tendency. This, however, is not to say that all approaches and research interests will merge together. On the contrary, with the attempt at formulating empirically verifiable theories and hypotheses, we would expect to see the emergence of more distinct concepts below the level of broad approaches.

In general, the different perspectives and areas of interest of the two approaches, rather than actually being contradictory, may well complement each other. This complementary perspective could be facilitated by the fact that, up to now, the theoretical substance of both approaches has been too weak to form a solid paradigm. Hence, although these two major approaches cannot simply be merged together, there are a few reasons to perceive them as contradictory (see Klanderman's and Tarrow's contributions in this volume). Efforts to establish a relation between the approaches may enable us to get a more complete idea of the social regularities behind the emergence, existence and impacts of social movements.

B. New Areas of Social Movement Research

Though we argue, along with other authors, for a closer linkage of the »New Social Movements Approach« and the »Resource Mobilization Approach,« the result of such a mutual enrichment would still be insufficient. An even better integration of the two research traditions of the 1970s and 1980s would still not cover all the major areas and aspects which are relevant for social movements. It is no accident that research has brought up new questions and new concepts. These, of course, in the light of the long tradition of the study field, are not as new as one might expect. In the following, we will refer only to two of these recent areas of interest: the concepts of the »political opportunity structure« and »framing processes«.

Political Opportunity Structure

The resource mobilization approach initially did not pay much attention to the broader societal context in which social movement organizations and »social movement industries« are embedded. But as soon as the mobilization capacities of movement organizations are compared in cross-temporal or cross-territorial perspectives, it becomes obvious that there are external conditions which may strongly hinder or facilitate efforts to mobilize (Garner and Zald, 1985). With respect to many movement activities, and in particular, to protest movements which deliberately enter the arena of public and political debates, political factors play a crucial role for successful mobilization. Several attempts were made to conceptualize these factors under the label of »political opportunity structure.« Drawing partly on the work of other authors, Sidney Tarrow (1983; 1989a) was the main proponent of this concept. In Tarrow's (1988, 429) view, political opportunities can be broken down into the following factors: the »degree of openness or of closure of the polity (Eisinger, 1973); the stability or instability of political alignments (Piven and Cloward, 1977); the presence or absence of allies and support groups (Gamson, 1975; Jenkins and Perrow, 1977); divisions within the elite or its tolerance for protest (Jenkins and Perrow, 1977); and the policy-making capacity of the government (Kitschelt, 1986).«

Given its affinity to macrostructural dimensions, and particularly, the embedding of social movements in society as a whole, this concept, though originally developed in the USA, was quickly adopted and in part elaborated or modified by European social scientists (Brand, 1985; Kriesi, 1989; Rucht, 1990). In respect to the new social movements approach, the concept of political opportunity structure can be seen as a tool for concretizing and differentiating environmental, and particularly, political conditions that may be favorable or unfavorable for social movements and their activities. In respect to the resource mobilization approach, the opportunity structure concept is a logical extension as soon as the emphasis is shifted from the micro- and meso-perspective of mobilization to the macro-level. Thus, there are good reasons not to perceive this concept as a third approach which competes with resource mobilization and new social movement approaches. With this in mind, we can enlarge the starting model as it was represented in Figure 1 by adding a further element, i.e., the political opportunity structure. Like the two initial approaches, this complementary concept also considers social movements and their collective actions as a dependent variable. *Figure 2* (see p. 447) illustrates the overall process of mobilization based on the accumulation of distinct resources through social movement organizations and on framing processes. (We will refer to the latter aspect later.) Both processes are fundamentally influenced by the characteristics of the political system. Depending on these conditions, mobilization will be either fostered or restricted – an aspect to which Tilly referred with his categories of »facilitation« and »repression«: the former lowering, the latter rising »the costs of collective action to the contender.« (1978, 55)[9] While Tilly's categories concern the strategies of the groups interacting with social movements, the concept of political opportunities relates to the environmental structures which may only partly be affected by strategic shifts in the movement's environment.

As Tarrow notes, the political opportunity structure is »less a variable than a cluster of variables.« (Tarrow 1988, 430) As long as we cannot refer to an elaborated theory, however, there are no clear criteria for the selection

---

9 In a similar vein, McAdam defines the »structure of political opportunities« as »the distribution of member support and opposition to the political aims of a given challenging group.«(1988, 128)

of distinct variables. Moreover, the variables suggested by several authors, including Tarrow (1983; 1988) and McAdam, McCarthy and Zald (1988), do not appear to have the same logical status, i.e., they form an incoherent set of variables. We believe that the notion of »structure« is still used too loosely (see Section IV. D below).

Framing Processes

Although the mobilization of resources is an important task of social movement organizations it is not the only one. Recent research was quite correct in stressing the significance of ideological processes directed at producing and maintaining the mobilization potential. Of course, the relevance of these processes related to motivations, perceptions and ideologies, was already acknowledged in earlier writings, i.e., in Blumer's notion of »agitation.« (Blumer, 1957, 148) In elaborating various steps towards participation in social movements, Klandermans (1984; 1988) distinguished »between consensus mobilization in the context of the formation of mobilization potential in a society and consensus mobilization in the context of action mobilization. The former refers to the generation of a set of individuals with a predisposition to participate in a social movement. The latter refers to the legitimation of concrete goals and means of action.« (1988, 178)

In general, it can be assumed that social movements pursue differential activities depending upon which groups they are adressing. Vis-à-vis their own adherents and the broader public social movements must initate a complex discourse aimed at pointing out problems, attributing causal factors producing them, and presenting and justifying solutions and strategies to realize them. Of course, these attempts at setting and structuring the agenda are far from being easy and non-controversal. Apart from the fact that various factions within a social movement usually compete with each other in framing processes, the movement's opponents, among them governments and the established political parties, control agencies and counter-movements, struggle to delegitimize the movement's frames and push forward their own versions. We think that the outcomes of these competitions are decisive for the impact of social movements on public opinion and, moreover, for their success in general (see Section IV. E).

Recently, several researchers in the US have begun to study these »framing processes« on both conceptual and empirical levels (Snow et al., 1986; Snow and Benford, 1988; Gamson, 1988; Gamson and Modigliani,

1989). Snow et al., for instance, present a relatively sophisticated concept. They differentiate between various framing strategies (frame bridging, frame amplification, frame extension and frame transformation) and phases within the framing process (diagnostic, prognostic and motivational framing). Also in Europe, the first attempts have been made to gain insights into some conditions, processes and forms of issues framed by protest groups (Gerhards, 1991; Gerhards and Rucht, 1990). As far as we can see, however, little emphasis has been devoted to the interactive nature of issue framing and, in particular, to the decisive role of mass media in this field. In addition, there is a deficit of reliable and manageable methods to analyze discoursive strategies and patterns of framing.

We will sum up this section by illustrating the two major recent advances of social movement research in *Figure* 2. It should give us an idea on how two recent concepts – political opportunity structure and issue framing – complemented earlier foci of interest. *Figure 2* should also demonstrate that, due to the recent exchanges, the initial contrast between the resource mobilization and the new social movements approach is fading away.

IV. Some Perspectives on Future Research

Section III of this essay aimed at presenting succinctly the analytically central topics which have been, and still are being, dealt with in recent social movement research. Figures 1 and 2 illustrate the main areas on which research has focussed in the last two decades. This formal presentation, however, tells little about the central questions and hypotheses under investigation. In that sense, the analytical framework of Section III leaves much open. In this final section we thus want to specify those questions and assumptions which, in our view, deserve special attention, but have only occasionally played a significant role up to now. Because we will be presenting our own ideas in another context (Neidhardt and Rucht, 1991), we shall limit ourselves here to some general notes and suggestions.

Figure 2: Recent Developments of Social Movement Research

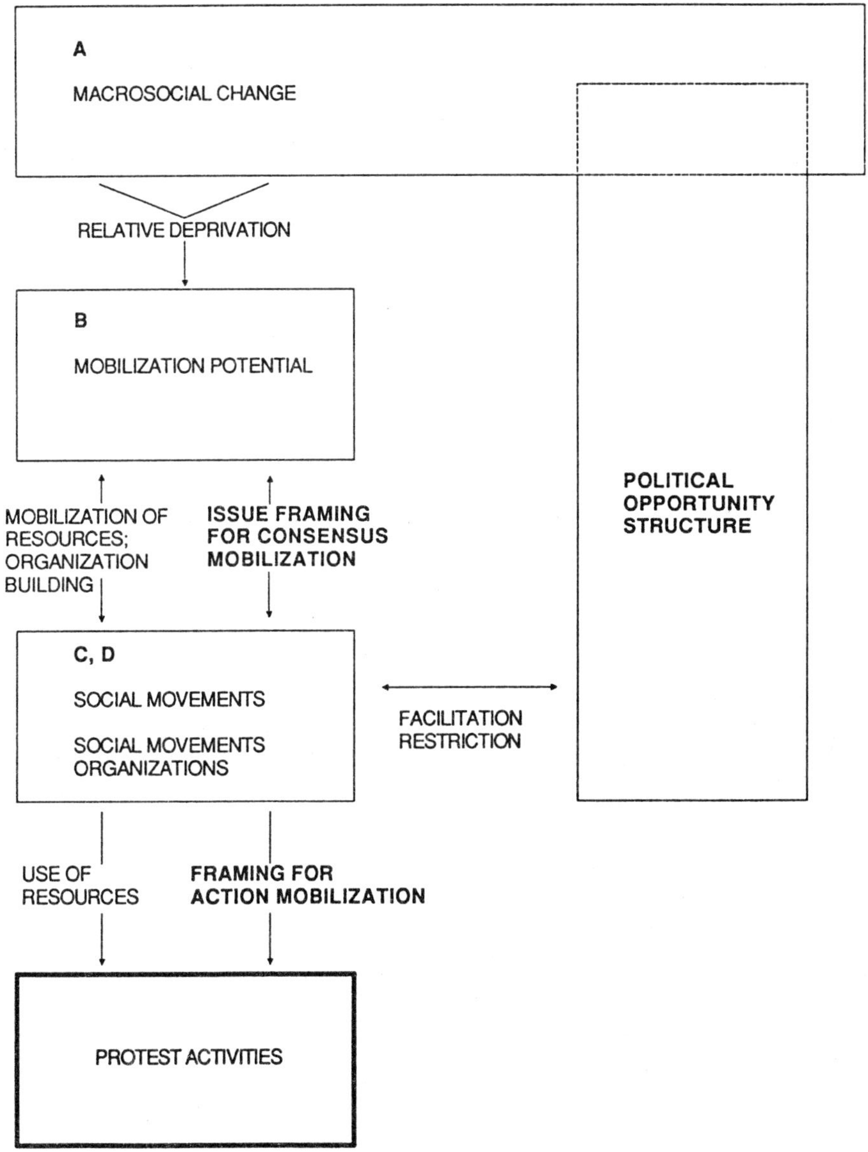

A. Social Movements and Modernization

Without a macro-sociological frame of reference social movement research risks missing relevant questions as well as the linkage to its parent disciplines, i.e., sociology and political science. Seeking a macro-sociological foundation for social movement research we could start with the fact that social movements are elements of modern societies and can thus be interpreted with respect to various features and problems of modernity. If we follow the system theory of modern societies as it was expounded, for example, by Parsons and Luhmann, the basic characteristic of modern societies is their composition of functionally differentiated sub-systems. During the long process of modernization, sub-systems such as religion, economy, politics and science gradually became separated from the integrated »life world« of the general populace. These sub-systems specialized according to their particular functions and became increasingly independent from each other. They created specific institutions of their own and were inter-related through a plethora of exchange processes, and thus, formed a highly complex and effective modern society.

As a result of modernization there is a growing need for structures designed to mediate on horizontal and vertical levels, i.e., between both functionally specialized systems and between these and the »life world« of the people in general. The latter aspect could also be perceived as the mediation of the macro and micro levels of society and between systemic functions and the needs and demands of individuals. On the macro level, the political-administrative system attained such a central position that, with the ongoing development of the welfare state, it was expected to respect certain common concerns and guarantee a set of collective goods. These are factors not sufficiently regarded by other sub-systems. From the perspective of the micro level, the role of parties and interest groups would be to pick up and aggregate individual needs in order to transfer these into the political-administrative system. From the view of the latter, parties and interest groups would also translate and legitimate the functional policy requirements for individuals.

We believe that the emergence of the dominant type of contemporary social movement, as well as its concerns and forms, is related to dysfunctions and deficits of interest mediation by means of parties and pressure groups. Social movements complement these institutions on the meso-level. Experience of the last few decades in several countries indicates that this complementary or compensatory role of social movements is not only sporadic and more or less accidental. On the contrary, it is directly connected with ongoing modernization and can thus be attributed to structural changes. Among these, for example, are changes in the system of political interest mediation as they have been discussed in political science under the label of neo-corporatism. Parties and interest groups change to a considerable degree when they are involved and institutionally incorporated into the polity in modern societies. The institutionalization of parties and interest groups within the governmental system increases their degree of organization, leads them to become less responsive toward specific issues and clientele groups, and reduces their potential for radical activities. These developments, in turn, create needs and opportunities for social movements. In respect to this trend, we think that social movements are non-random products of continuing modernization. One could argue that highly modernized societies have a tendency to become »movement societies«.

For several reasons, not all to be presented here, the likelihood of the emergence and stabilization of social movements is increasing with modernization. The more a society is perceived to be contingent, the more leverage points for social movements may come into play. One could go even further in arguing that social movements, at least in their most ambitious forms, are a feature of modern societies. The idea of conscious collective action having the capacity to change society as a whole came only with the era of enlightenment. Of course, collective action and popular movements also challenged authorities in earlier societies. In premodern periods, however, dissenters made claims and questioned authorities not to change society according to their own visions, but only to re-establish a traditional or divine order which had been violated.

B. Social Movements as a Special Type of Collective Action

Anchoring the concept of social movements in a theory of modern, functionally differentiated societies has consequences for further analysis insofar as it presumes both the idea of social movements and some basic questions related to it.

Up to now, research in the field of social movements usually suffered from a lack of clarity about its empirical points of reference. This situation led to continuous inconsistencies and contradictions both in empirical results and in theories. Elaboration is needed, at least, with regard to the following points: (a) presenting a general, but not ahistoric, definition of a social movement, (b) identifying – based on this broad definition – some fundamental types of social movements, (c) distinguishing variants within these types of social movements according to a phase model of social movements, (d) differentiating between various groups within or at the fringes of social movements.

As long as the existing taxonomies remain fundamentally vague on all these levels researchers will risk terminological confusion. This is not the place to trace all the problems resulting from the use of different and often foggy conceptions, to comment on a number of very useful and partly convincing attempts at clarification, or to present our own categorial and theoretical suggestions for the field of social movement as whole. We intend only to make some very brief comments on the four points mentioned above.

(a) In its broadest sense, we define a social movement as an organized and sustained effort of a collectivity of inter-related individuals, groups and organizations to promote or to resist social change with the use of public protest activities.

(b) For analytical purposes, two general types of social movements can be distinguished according to their overall orientation. On the one hand, there are movements which focus on the realm of politics. They try to change society by influencing the distribution and exertion of political power. On the other hand, there are movements which are oriented toward the realm of culture, i.e., belief systems, values, social roles, and cultural codes.[10] While the former, which we may consider a *sociopolitical* movement,[11] relies on instrumental action and challenges power elites and power structures directly, the latter, say, the *sociocultural* movement, relies on expressive action, seeks to change people's minds and their actual behavior, and to attain social change indirectly through the aggregated and long-term effects of individual behavior. Empirically, movements usually combine elements of both types. Those movements, however, which are closer to the sociopoliti-

---

10 To be sure, similar distinctions have been made in the earlier literature. Already at the turn of our century Sighele distinguished between outward and inward oriented forms of collective behavior. Other typologies distinguish between movements wishing to restructure society or individuals (Zald and Ash, 1966) or between politically oriented and culturally oriented movements (Raschke, 1985).

11 According to Jenkins, political movements »make changes in power arrangements, especially those structured through the state, a central part of their program.« (1981, 83)

cal type, tend to be more outwardly-oriented, and to focus on quantitative mobilization and the formation of broad alliances. Movements which correspond more closely to the sociocultural type tend to be more inwardly-oriented and focus mainly on qualitative mobilization (Rucht, 1988).
(c) It is a platitude that social movements change over time. Empirical research has shown that movements do not necessarily go through an inherent »natural« life cycle to end up in the status of institutionalization, but rather follow an unsteady course. Depending on the criteria used for observation and measurement, phases of expansion and contraction can be distinguished in looking on an movement as a whole over several years or decades. Although little systematic research has been done on movement cycles (with the exception of Tarrow's (1989) masterly study), we think that a movement's form of action, organizational composition, degree of radicality, language, etc. varies according to the phases which the movement passes through. Looking only at one of these specific phases an observer would be misled if he or she tried to present a general picture of a movement.[12]
(d) Another commonplace is that people involved in social movements play very different roles. The resource mobilization approach put more emphasis than most earlier approaches on distinguishing in functional terms among various subgroups within social movements (for an exception, see Lang and Lang 1961, 526). Taking into account the fact that movements do not have clear criteria of membership and that, consequently, the border between inside and outside is necessarily vague and broad, we suggest differentiating among the following categories with respect to the movement's adherents: *core activists* (which in turn could be subdivided into movement leaders, staff, transitory teams, etc.), *participants, contributors* and *sympathizers*. We are inclined not to consider contributors and sympathizers as part of a movement, but as part of a supportive environment. In regard to these categories, statements about a social movement and its surroundings would certainly need to be qualified.

---

12 Moreover, even when studying a single movement during one complete cycle or several cycles, an observer would be misled in interpreting this movement's dynamics if it is seen isolated from its broader context, i.e. the constellation and dynamics of a social movement sector, which, in turn, is influenced by macrostructural variables. This is not to say that every student of social movements has to end up with the gigantic task of studying cycles of social movement sectors within their overall societal context. But it should be clear that generalizations on the basis of case studies of specific conflicts or specific movements in very limited periods of time should be avoided.

Concentrating on the sociopolitical type of movement, some criteria have to be established in order to separate the concept of social movements from that of parties and interest organizations. If there were no significant differences between those collectivities – as some strands of the resource mobilization approach tend to assume – there would be no need for specific social movement research. A search for distinguishing criteria, however, can help us to understand more clearly the specific nature of social movements.

One way of distinguishing between social movements and such phenomena as parties is to acknowledge the decisive role of a particular kind of collective action. In order to attain their goals, social movements »produce« protest events which, in turn, can be part of broader campaigns and struggles. Hence, collective protest is the central »currency,« the medium of exchange between a movement and its environment. Protest activities require the commitment of people who are sufficiently motivated in order to participate and they are a social movement's primary resource. Social movements lack those means of power which parties and interest groups typically have at their disposal, e.g., direct political participation within the political decision-making system and pressure based on economic power and informational resources. Thus, social movements have to »march in the streets,« collect signatures, organize blockades, etc., in order to compensate for their lack of other resources. In that respect, social movements are also of particular theoretical interest.

Social movements are often considered as non-modern elements in modern society insofar as they do not follow the institutional pattern of functional differentiation. Rather than becoming part of the institutionalized system, they seek to influence it through disruptive actions taking place »outside« the system. For this reason, conflicts and turbulences arise when social movements break the rules of the game. Provocation creates reaction; police and courts come into play; counter-movements may flourish.

Apart from their tendency to use a non-institutionalized action repertoire, social movements have a second feature which seems anachronistic in modern societies, that is their organizational structure. Related to the dependence of social movements on the mobilization of many people is the fact that movements typically include and/or create organizations without, however, being identical with them. (Heberle 1968, 441; Jenkins 1981, 83) In contrast to bureaucracies, firms, parties or unions, hierarchical and highly specialized structures exist only in rudimentary forms in social movements. Moreover, membership and decision-making are not formalized. As a consequence, social movements could be more adequately conceptualized as »mobilized networks of networks.« (Neidhardt 1985, 197) Although these may include organizations and more or less formal commitees which coordinate and mediate between various components of the movement, these nuclei may have difficulties in guiding and controlling the movement as a whole. A lack of control is already caused by the fact that leaders and cadres of movements never really know who belongs to the movement and who does not.

We believe that a general concept of social movements and the operationalizations derived from such a concept should take into account the above mentioned characteristics, and, even more, should reflect these in the very definition. On that basis, the typical functional and structural problems of social movements would come into the focus of analysis. Two consequences result from such a strategy.

On the one hand, with regard to societal functions of movements, certain of their strengths and weaknesses can be theoretically postulated and empirically tested. Since social movements, unlike other more institutionalized groups, rely primarily on the commitment of many people, they are very sensitive to the moods and motives of both actual and potential participants. While mobilizing individuals and groups, social movements have few material incentives and thus try to convince their adherents that the individual motives and collective aims are very close to each other, if not identical. (Rammstedt, 1978) In this respect, mobilizing agents tend to be very responsive to the movement's »grass roots.« If so, the strength of social movements lies in a highly authentic expression of the interests of certain social groups which feel largely neglected by such institutions as parties and interest groups.

On the other hand, the weakness of social movements is caused by the fact that they usually lack the organizational capacity to transform their ideas into a well defined program and to implement it. Social movements are dependent on a broader public which may or may not perceive and appreciate their demands. In addition, social movements usually depend on parties and pressure groups which adopt the movement's demands and transfer these into the polity. Within the mediating sector of politics, social movements specifically serve to give the initial impulses for change. If this mediating sector were to be conceptualized as a system with a division of labor, one could assume that the societal function of movements within the realm of politics is mainly to keep parties and interests groups vital and to maintain their capacities for learning. From that perspective, social movements compensate for the inherent deficiencies of parties and interests groups as they tend to represent only »worthwhile« interests according to the logic of self-interest. If, however, parties and interest groups seem not to be responsive to movements demands, then there is a high probability that the movements will either radicalize their actions or transform themselves into parties and interest groups or split in regard to these strategies.

Related to this last aspect are certain structural problems of social movements. As collectivities which need organization without really being organizations, social movements constantly have to balance the organizational interests of core activists, such as leaders and staff members on the one hand, and diffuse expectations of »authentic« communication by participants and contributors on the other. Thus, in virtually every movement, a tension between such needs as effectivity and consensus, outward and inward orientation, pragmatism and fundamentalism can be observed. In this respect, social movements are hybrids following differing logics of action. This difficult task leads to typical contradictions and conflicts, and possibly to to factions and schisms. It would be instructive for the study of social movements to analyze such tensions in more detail. Often they manifest themselves in the internal confrontation of a movement and a party model of organization. An analysis of such developments could teach us more about the characteristics of social movements. An »ideal type« of a social movement is not only an object for abstract academic reflection but also, for practically-oriented theories which are be discussed and experimented on within the field itself.

C. Social Movement Milieus and the Fabrication of Protest

Empirical references to typical problems of social movements also reveal the precarious conditions for the development and stabilization of social movements. However, given the fact that social movements flourished in great numbers and in some cases over long periods in modern societies, the hypothesis seems plausible that favorable societal conditions must have existed for the development and maintenance of these movements. Investigating this aspect should be one of the central aims of social movement research. From such a perspective it would be necessary not only to explain the emergence of single movements, but also to answer the more general questions if, and in which sense, social movements can be perceived as an outcome of societal conditions. Hence, social movement industries may be an indicator for overall developments in modern societies that foster the »production« of social movements. Is it part of the dialectics of continuing modernization to generate structures and currents with premodern characteristics? Do functional differentiations in modern societies breed social movements which, in turn, can be seen as phenomena designed to counteract the trend toward the differentiation of societies?

Indeed, social movement milieus have developed and survived over the last decades in several countries. In Italy such milieus have been studied by Melucci et al. (1984); they have been also described in West Germany (Roth, 1987). Based on complex networks and »social relays« these milieus provide a social infrastructure which, together with subcultural forms of an »alternative« life style, not only imply the capacity, but also, the need for forging social movements.

The creation of specific roles for activists can be observed within these milieus. These activists, in contrast to the occasional participants in protest activities and contributors to social movement organizations, provide the organizational and ideological frameworks that are a precondition for sustained protest activity. As movement »managers« and »entrepreneurs« these activists run organizations; as »ideologists« they frame individual interests and motives in order to create a collective identity which includes the »we« and »they,« the definition of distinct problems, the identification of persons, groups and institutions responsible for these problems, the formulation of programs to overcome these problems, the propagation of utopian ideas which may serve as a long-term orientation, etc. All these points need further research. In this respect there are at least two aspects which seem to be particularly important.

First, assuming that modern societies tend to become »movement societies,« we could expect that alternative milieus which foster social movements can be stabilized and that the particular roles of activists and groups may become institutionalized. Can this be observed over longer periods of time? Which mechanisms guarantee the survival of such features? Which social groups play these particular roles? What are the incentives for, and vehicles of, movement activists? All these questions remain largely unanswered.

As to the second aspect of organizational components and infrastructure it is certainly the merit of the resource mobilization approach to have focussed on these factors. Proponents of this approach have rightly criticized the fiction of spontaneity underlying many former theories of social movements although, in same cases, resource mobilizationists went too far in emphazising the role of movement organizations (Killian, 1984). What was neglected, however, were some of the specific aspects of the organizational crystallization of social movements. If we are right in assuming that movements are not merely organizations, then the existing organizational elements and roles within social movements should involve specific features. Activists in social movements would be expected to differ systematically from functionaries in parties and managers in interest groups. The above mentioned structural problems of social movements should manifest themselves in typical role conflicts. Can this be found empirically?

D. Reference Groups and Opportunity Structures

The concept of »political opportunity structure,« which we already referred to in Section III, represents a major advance insofar as it explicitly deals with relevant factors of a social movement's environment. As already mentioned, however, the existing versions of this concept have not yet presented a very systematic account of such variables; political opportunity structure still tends to be a catch-all-category. Moreover, the notion of structure has not yet been clarified or always been taken seriously. The concept has also not led to general premises as to which structural constellations really provide opportunities for a social movement and which do not. We think that this concept can be clarified along the following lines.

First, structural analyses must identify elements between which the existence of relatively stable relationships is assumed. It would be fruitful to define the relevant reference groups of social movements as the key elements of opportunity structure (see *Figure 3*). Among these elements, we have to take into account (a) the political-administrative system, including its executive bodies, which appear to be the most important target groups of (sociopolitical) movements (Tilly, 1984). Given the fact that the collective actions through which social movements try to exert pressure on the political system often cause conflicts and juridical problems, (b) the agents of control, the courts in particular, should also be taken into account. Because the political system is likely not to be affected directly by movement activities, (c) intermediaries in the realm of politics such as parties and interest groups are also key factors in a movement's environment. Here, the crucial question is whether these bodies will or will not adopt the movement's demands so that

Figure 3: Reference Groups of Sociopolitical Movements

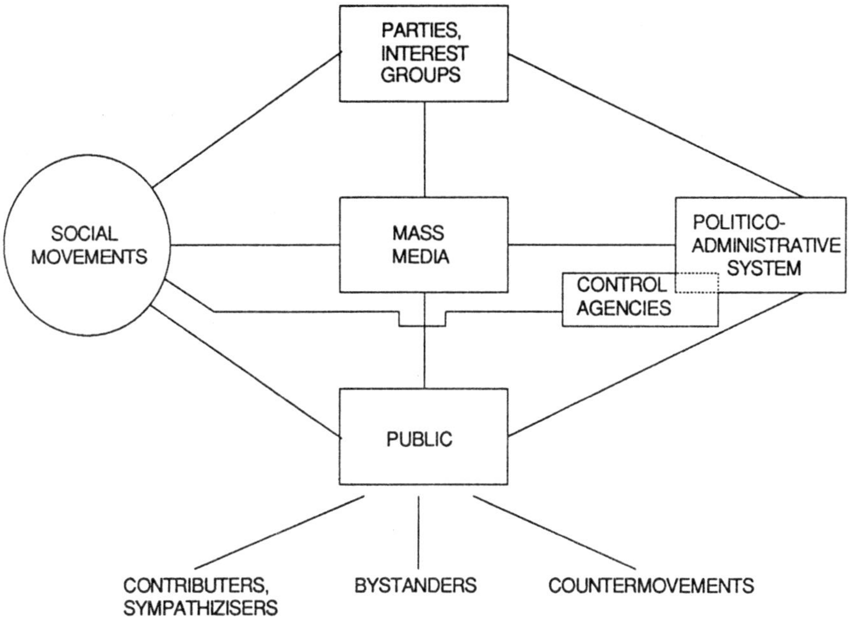

they can be brought into the decision-making system. This will depend heavily on (d) the reactions of the public. The question arises as to the extent to which the public will be divided into supporters or contributors, sympathizers, neutral bystanders and opponents or counter-movements. There are good reasons for assuming that the process and result of this differentiation of the public will be strongly influenced by the intensity and type of resonance which the movement's activities find in (e) the mass media.

In a second step, in which we regard social movements as a *dependent* variable within a framework of interaction composed of five key elements, we are assuming that a great deal of the variance in the opportunity structure which is found in time analyses and cross-national comparisons can be explained in terms and degrees of functional differentiation. In that respect, our thesis is that the possibilities of social movements to influence the political-administrative system correlate positively with the extent of differentiation in this field of interaction. (Of course, these possibilities will also depend on the relative strengths of the reference groups and their reactions to the social movement.) This thesis is based on two inter-related constellations.

On the one hand, differentiation means that the reference groups are separate and largely autonomous. In this respect, the chances of social movements for success increase to the extent that the public, mass media, parties/interest groups, and control agencies become both independent from the political-administrative system and from each other.

On the other hand, differentiation also applies to the internal structure of the reference groups. In this regard, the opportunities for social movements will depend not only on the differentiation of the political system into government and opposition, but also, on the degree of pluralism in, for example, the party system and the mass media.

The opportunities which exist for a social movement can be characterized, ceteris paribus, by the degree of differentiation within its external field of interaction. This limits the range of reactions of potential reference groups which social movements have to deal with. It does not, however, determine these reactions in a way that could be reliably calculated. The existing structures allow all players in the game to have various strategies or options. In a field which is only partly institutionalized, complex and surprising interactions have to be taken into account. This has not received the attention that it deserves for the study of social movements (Marx and Wood, 1975, 309-403).

Although recently there has been a growing interest in »political process models« (see, for instance, McAdam, 1982), we do not yet have differentiated models with an explanatory power at our disposal. Despite the uncertainties outlined above, we assume some regularities which could at least help us anticipate the kinds of interactions which can be expected under certain circumstances. We doubt, however, that it will be possible to identify stable positions of equilibrium. If it is asked which structural conditions and kinds of interaction are or are not favorable for social movements, we would rather expect curvilinear relationships with specific thresholds. (Granovetter, 1978) For instance, we can hypothesize that both a highly closed and a highly open political system are relatively unfavorable for the flourishing of social movements (Eisinger 1973, 28). There are instead medium degrees of opportunities and repression which seem to foster social movements and political protest (Gurr, 1969). Of course, it will be difficult for both the activists and the academic analysts of social movements to identify optimum points and crucial thresholds. Thus, there is a high risk for miscalculation by both groups.

E. Effects of Social Movements via Mass Communication and Public

The operational field of social movements makes it difficult for all interacting parties to optimize their actions. There is, therefore, a relatively high probability for conflicts and continuing conflict escalation. In this regard, we occasionally observe that the initial themes and lines of conflict change and shift. They are transformed into »metaconflicts« which no longer refer to the original aims of the movement, but to its actual »behavior« and to the society's reactions to it, and in particular, those of the mass media, countermovements and such agents of control as the police. The more unconventional the social movement activities, the greater the likelihood that the central issue emerging in the public arena will not be the genuine aims of the movement, but the movement itself, and its threat the social and political order.

From these observations we conclude that social movement research should concentrate more on the interactions of movements with other agents. Consequently, it would also be fruitful to shift to another perspective, i.e., to conceive of social movements not only as dependent, but also, as *independent* variables. Perceiving social movements as stimuli whose impact is to be investigated, the question of who or what is the object of their impact must be answered. For this question we suggest applying the model of reference groups, as it is illustrated in Figure 3, in order to observe the interaction between a social movement, on the one hand, and the political-administrative system, agents of control, parties and interest groups, mass media and the public on the other. We hypothesize that the impact of social movements on the political-administrative system – depending of the degree of differentiation in the overall field of reference groups – is only an indirect effect. Obviously, mass media and the public are highly relevant reference groups. These groups can, on the one hand, be directly reached by social movements. On the other, mass media and the public are able to transmit social movement concerns to parties and interest groups as well as to the legislative and executive bodies. If we are correct in this assumption, it would follow that mass media and the public deserve much more attention in social movement research than in the past.

Considering these relationships, it becomes obvious which conditions are most relevant for a movement's success. Movements must stimulate a positive resonance in the public. In order to determine how such a reaction can be realized, it may be useful to follow the early route which Ralph Turner (1969) laid out in his essay entitled »The Public Perception of Protest« (see also Jeffries and Turner, 1971; Altheide and Gilmore, 1972). Turner argues that »an optimal balance is needed between appeal and threat.« (1969, 815) They must provoke in order to be registered by mass media and heard by the public. At the same time, however, protest actions are designed to transmit a message perceived to be important and legitimate. Whether or not this is the case depends on competitive and antagonistic processes of definition and framing which take place in a complex public arena (Hilgartner and Bosk, 1988). Recent work of Gamson (1988) indicates the way in which such dynamic interactions could be studied. In the immediate future it will be crucial to work out both concepts as well as methods accordingly.

Summarizing our sketchy *tour d'horizon* of the field of social movements we would like to stress that advances have been made, particularly in the last two decades. Surprising, however, is the fact that precisely the most recent areas of interest – the embedding of social movement activities in a broader field of interaction, the emphasis on the social construction of issues, the role of mass media – have already been emphasized in the postwar period but were later largely forgotten. Today, therefore, we have to take up these early impulses, integrate them into more complex and systematic analytical frameworks, and to carry out more theoretically guided empirical research than we are accustomed.

Bibliography

Altheide, D.L.; Gilmore, R.P. (1972): »The Credibility of Protest«, *The American Sociological Review* 37 (1): 99-108.

Blumer, H. (1939): »Collective Behavior«, in: Park, R.E. (ed.). *An Outline of the Principles of Sociology*, New York: Barnes & Noble (revised 1951), 221-280.

– (1957): »Collective Behavior«, in: Gittler, J.B. (ed.). *Review of Sociology: Analysis of a Decade*. New York: John Wiley & Sons, 127-158.

Brand, K.-W. (1982): *Neue soziale Bewegungen. Entstehung, Funktion und Perspektive neuer Protestpotentiale. Eine Zwischenbilanz*. Opladen: Westdeutscher Verlag.

– (1985): »Vergleichendes Resümee«, in: Brand, K.-W. (ed.), *Neue soziale Bewegungen in Westeuropa und den USA*. Frankfurt: Campus, 306-334.

– (1989): Zyklen des »middle class radicalism«. Eine international historisch vergleichende Untersuchung der »neuen sozialen Bewegungen«. München (unpublished manuscript).

Cantril, H. (1941): *The Psychology of Social Movements*. New York: John Wiley and Sons.

Dalton, R.; Küchler, M. (eds.) (1990): *Challenging the Political Order: New Social and Political Movements in Western Democracies*. Cambridge: Polity Press.

Eder, K. (1982): »A New Social Movement?«, *Telos* 52 (Summer), 5-20.

Eisinger, P.K. (1973): »The Conditions of Protest Behavior in American Cities«, *American Political Science Review* 67 (1): 11-28.

Gamson, W.A. (1975): *The Strategy of Social Protest*. Homewood, Ill.: Dorsey.

– (1988): »Political Discourse and Collective Action«, in: Klandermans, B.; Kriesi, H.; Tarrow, S. (eds.), *From Structure to Action: Comparing Social Movement Research Across Cultures*, Greenwich, Conn.: JAI Press, 219-244.

Gamson, W.A.; Modigliani, A. (1989): »Media Discourse and Public Opinion on Nuclear Power: A Constructionist Approach«, *American Journal of Sociology* 95 (1): 1-37.

Garner, R.; Zald, M.N. (1985): »The Political Economy of Social Movement Sectors«, in: Suttles, G.D.; Zald, M.N. (eds.), *The Challenge of Social Control*. Norwood: Ablex, 119-145.

Gerhards, J. (1991): »Die Mobilisierung gegen die IWF- und Weltbanktagung in Berlin: Gruppen, Veranstaltungen, Diskurse«, in: Roth, R.; Rucht, D. (eds.), *Neue soziale Bewegungen in der Bundesrepublik Deutschland*. (Second, enlarged edition). Bonn: Bundeszentrale für politische Bildung (forthcoming).

Gerhards, J.; Rucht, D. (1990): »Unexpected Dissent: Two Case Studies on Conditions and Courses of Successful Protest Campaigns in West Germany«, paper prepared for the XIIth World Congress of Sociology, Madrid, 9-13 July.

Granovetter, M. (1978): »Threshold Models of Collective Behavior«, *American Journal of Sociology* 83 (6): 1420-1443.

Gurr, T. (1979): »A Comparative Study of Civil Strife«, in: Graham, H.D.; Gurr, T. (eds.), *Violence in America: Historical and Comparative Perspectives*. New York: Praeger, 572-632.

Heberle, R. (1951): *Social Movements: An Introduction to Political Sociology*. New York: Appleton-Century-Crofts.

– (1968): »Types and Functions of Social Movements«, in: *International Encyclopedia of the Social Sciences* 14: 438-444.

Hilgartner, S.; Bosk, C.L. (1988): »The Rise and Fall of Social Problems: A Public Arenas Model«, *American Journal of Sociology* 94 (1): 53-78.

Hirsch, J.; Roth, R. (1986): *Das neue Gesicht des Kapitalismus. Vom Fordismus zum Postfordismus*. Hamburg: VSA.

Jeffries, V.; Turner, R.H.; Morris, R.T. (1971): »The Public Perception of the Watts Riot as Social Protest«, *American Sociological Review* 36 (3): 443-451.

Jenkins, C.; Perrow, C. (1977): »Insurgency of the Powerless: Farm Workers Movement (1964-1972)«, *American Sociological Review* 42 (2): 249-268.

Jenkins, C.J. (1981): »Sociopolitical Movements,« in: Samuel, L.L. (ed.), *Handbook of Political Behavior*. Vol. 4. New York/London: Plenum, 81-153.

– (1983): »Resource Mobilization Theory and the Study of Social Movements«, *Annual Review of Sociology* 9: 527-553.

Killian, L.M. (1964): »Social Movements«, in: Faris, R. (ed.), *Handbook of Modern Sociology*. Chicago: Rand McNally, 426-455.

– (1984): »Organization, Rationality and Spontaneity in the Civil Rights Movement«, *American Sociology Review* 49 (6): 770-783.

Kitschelt, H. (1986): »Political Opportunity and Political Protest: Anti-Nuclear Movements in Four Democracies«, *British Journal of Political Science* 16 (1): 57-85.

Klandermans, P.B. (1983): *Participatie in een sociale beweging, een mobilisatie campagne oderzocht*. Amsterdam: Boekhandel/Uitgeverij.

– (1984): »Mobilization and Participation: Social Psychologicial Expansions of the Resource Mobilization Theory«, *American Sociological Review* 49 (5): 583-600.

– (1988): »The Formation and Mobilization of Consensus«, in: Klandermans, B.; Kriesi, H.; Tarrow, S. (eds.). *From Structure to Action: Comparing Social Movement Research Across Cultures*. (International Social Movement Research 1). Greenwich, Conn.: JAI Press, 137-196.

– (ed.), (1989): *Organizing for Change: Social Movement Organizations in Europe and United States*. (International Social Movement Research 2). Greenwich, Conn.: JAI Press.

Klandermans, P.B.; Tarrow, S. (1988): »Mobilization into Social Movements: Synthesizing European and American Approaches«, in: Klandermans, B.; Kriesi, H.; Tarrow, S. (eds.), *From Structure to Action: Comparing Social Movement Research Across Cultures*. (International Social Movement Research 1). Greenwich, Conn.: JAI Press, 1-38.

Klandermans, B.; Kriesi, H.; Tarrow, S. (eds.), (1988): *From Structure to Action: Comparing Social Movement Research Across Cultures*. (International Social Movement Research 1). Greenwich, Conn.: JAI Press.

Kriesi, H. (1989): »The Political Opportunity Structure of the Dutch Peace Movement«, *West European Politics* 12 (3): 295-312.

– (1989a): »Support, mobilization potentials for new social movements: Concepts, operationalizations, and illustrations from the Netherlands«, paper presented at the workshop »Vergleichende Analysen sozialer Bewegungen«, Berlin: WZB, 20-21 October.

Lang, K.; Gladys, E.L. (1961): *Collective Dynamics*. New York: Crowell.

Marx, G.T.; Wood, J.L. (1975): »Strands of Theory and Research in Collective Behavior«, *Annual Review of Sociology* 1: 363-428.

Mayer, M. (1985): »Urban Social Movements and Beyond: New Linkages between Movement Sectors and the State in West Germany and the United States«, paper presented at the Fifth International Conference of Europeanists, Washington, D.C., October 18-20.

McAdam, D. (1982): *Political Process and the Development of Black Insurgency, 1930-1970*. Chicago and London: The University of Chicago Press.

– (1988): »Micromobilization Contexts and Recruitment to Activism«, in: Klandermans, B.; Kriesi, H.; Tarrow, S. (eds.), *From Structure to Action: Comparing Social Movement Research Across Cultures*. (International Social Movements Research 1). Greenwich, Conn.: JAI Press, 125-154.

McAdam, D.; McCarthy, J.D.; Zald, M.N. (1988): »Social Movements«, in: Smelser, N.J. (ed.), *Handbook of Sociology*, Newbury Park: Sage, 695-737.

McCarthy, J.D.; Zald, M.N. (1977): »Resource Mobilization and Social Movements: A Partial Theory«, *American Journal of Sociology* 82 (6): 1212-1241.

Melucci, A. (1984): »An End to Social Movements? Introductory Paper to the Sessions on ›New Social Movements and Change in Organizational Forms‹«, *Social Science Information* 24 (4/5): 819-835.

– (1988): »Getting Involved: Identity and Mobilization in Social Movements«, in: Klandermans, B.; Kriesi, H.; Tarrow, S. (eds.), *From Structure to Action: Comparing Social Movement Research Across Cultures.* (International Social Movement Research 1). Greenwich, Conn.: JAI Press, 329-348.

– (1989): *Nomads of the Present. Social Movements and Individual Needs in Contemporary Society.* London: Century Hutchinson Ltd.

– et al. (1984): *Altri codici. Aree di movimento nella metropoli.* Bologna: Mulino.

Morris, A.; Herring, C. (1987): »Theory and Research in Social Movements: A Critical Review«, in: Long, S. (ed.), *Annual Review of Political Science* 2: 138-198.

Nedelmann, B. (1984): »New Political Movements and Changes in Processes of Interest Mediation«, *Social Science Information* 23 (6): 1029-1048.

Nelles, W. (1984): »Kollektive Identität und politisches Handeln in Neuen Sozialen Bewegungen«, *Politische Vierteljahresschrift* 25 (4): 425-440.

Neidhardt, F. (1985): »Einige Ideen zu einer allgemeinen Theorie sozialer Bewegungen«, in: Hradil, S. (ed.), *Sozialstruktur im Umbruch.* Opladen: Leske, 193-204.

Neidhardt, F.; Rucht, D. (1991): »Auf dem Weg in die ›Bewegungsgesellschaft‹? Über die Institutionalisierbarkeit von Protestbewegungen«, Discussion Paper FS III 91. Wissenschaftszentrum Berlin (forthcoming).

Nullmeier, F.; Raschke, J. (1989): »Soziale Bewegungen«, in: Bandemer, S.v.; Wewer, G. (eds.), *Regierungssystem und Regierungslehre.* Opladen: Leske und Budrich, 249-272.

Offe, C. (1985): »New Social Movements: Challenging the Boundaries of Institutional Politics«, *Social Research* 52 (4): 817-868.

Park, R.E.; Burgess, E.W. (1921): *Introduction to the Science of Sociology.* Chicago: University of Chicago Press.

Piven, F.F.; Cloward, R.A. (1977): *Poor People's Movements: Why They Succeed, How They Fail.* New York: Vintage.

Raschke, J. (1985): *Soziale Bewegungen. Ein historisch-systematischer Grundriß.* Frankfurt: Campus.

Rammstedt, O. (1978): *Soziale Bewegung.* Frankfurt: Suhrkamp.

Roth, R. (1987): »Kommunikationsstrukturen und Vernetzungen in den neuen sozialen Bewegungen«, in: Roth, R.; Rucht, D. (eds.), *Neue soziale Bewegungen in der Bundesrepublik Deutschland.* Frankfurt/M.: Campus, 68-88.

– (1989): »Fordismus und neue soziale Bewegungen«, in: Wasmuht, U. (ed.), *Alternativen zur alten Politik? Neue soziale Bewegungen in der Diskussion*, Darmstadt: Wissenschaftliche Buchgesellschaft, 13-37.

Rucht, D. (1984): »Zur Organisation der neuen sozialen Bewegungen«, in: Falter, J.W.; Fenner, C.; Greven, M.Th. (eds.). *Politische Willensbildung und Interessenvermittlung.* Opladen: Westdeutscher Verlag, 609-620.

- (1988): »Themes, Logics and Arenas of Social Movements: A Structural Approach«, in: Klandermans, B. (ed.), *From Structure to Action: Comparing Social Movement Research Across Cultures* (International Social Movement Research 1). Greenwich, Conn.: JAI Press, 305-328.
- (1990): »Campaigns, skirmishes and battles: anti-nuclear movements in the USA, France and West Germany«, *Industrial Crisis Quarterly* 4 (3): 193-222.

Smelser, N. (1962): *Theory of Collective Behavior.* New York: The Free Press.

Snow, D.; Rochford, E.B.; Worden, S.K.; Benford, R.D. (1986): »Frame Alignment Processes, Micromobilization, and Movement Participation«, *American Sociological Review* 51 (4): 464-481.

Snow, D.; Benford, R.D. (1988): »Ideology, Frame Resonance, and Participant Mobilization«, in: Klandermans, B.; Kriesi, H.; Tarrow, S. (eds.), *From Structure to Action: Comparing Social Movement Research Across Cultures.* (International Social Movement Research 1). Greenwich, Conn.: JAI Press, 137-196.

Strauss, A.L. (1947): »Research in Collective Behavior: Neglect and Need«, *American Sociological Review* 12: 352-354.

Tarrow, S. (1983): *Struggling to Reform: Social Movements and Policy Change During Cycles of Protest.* Western Societies Program. Occasional Paper No. 15. Cornell University.
- (1988): »National Politics and Collective Action: Recent Theory and Research in Western Europe and the United States«, *Annual Review of Sociology* 14: 421-440.
- (1989): *Democracy and Disorder. Protest and Politics in Italy 1965-1975.* Oxford: Clarendon Press.
- (1989a): *Struggle, Politics, and Reform: Collective Action, Social Movements, and Cycles of Protest.* Western Societies Programm. Occasional Paper No. 21. Cornell University.

Touraine, A. (1981): *The Voice and the Eye. An Analysis of Social Movements.* Cambridge: Cambridge University Press.

Tilly, C. (1978): *From Mobilization to Revolution.* New York: Random House.
- (1984): »Social Movements and National Politics«, in: Bright, C.; Harding, S. (eds.), *Statemaking and Social Movements. Essays in History and Theory.* Ann Arbor: University of Michigan Press, 297-317.

Turner, R.H. (1958): »Needed Research in Collected Behavior«, *Sociology and Social Research* 42 (July): 461-465.
- (1969): »The Public Perception of Protest«, *American Sociological Review* 34 (6): 815-831.
- (1981): »Collective Behavior and Resource Mobilization as Approaches to Social Movements: Issues and Continuities«, *Research in Social Movements, Conflict and Change* 4: 1-24.

Turner, R.H.; Killian, L.M. (1957): *Collective Behavior.* (Second and revised edition 1972). Englewood Cliffs: Prentice Hall.

Zald, M.N.; Ash, R. (1966): »Social Movement Organizations: Growth, Decay and Change«, *Social Forces* 44 (March): 327-341.